Totalitarianism and the Prospects for World Order

APPLICATIONS OF POLITICAL THEORY

**Series Editors: Harvey Mansfield, Harvard University, and
Daniel J. Mahoney, Assumption College**

This series encourages analysis of the applications of political theory to various domains of thought and action. Such analysis will include works on political thought and literature, statesmanship, American political thought, and contemporary political theory. The editors also anticipate and welcome examinations of the place of religion in public life and commentary on classic works of political philosophy.

Totalitarianism and the Prospects for World Order

Closing the Door on the Twentieth Century

By Aleksandras Shtromas

Edited by Robert Faulkner and
Daniel J. Mahoney

LEXINGTON BOOKS
Lanham • Boulder • New York • Oxford

LEXINGTON BOOKS

Published in the United States of America
by Lexington Books
A Member of the Rowman & Littlefield Publishing Group
4501 Forbes Boulevard, Suite 200, Lanham, Maryland 20706

PO Box 317
Oxford
OX2 9RU, UK

Copyright © 2003 by Lexington Books

British Library Cataloguing in Publication Information Available

Library of Congress Cataloging-in-Publication Data

Shtromas, Alexander, 1931–1999
  Totalitarianism and the prospects for world order : closing the door
on the twentieth century / by Aleksandras Shtromas; edited by Robert
Faulkner and Daniel J. Mahoney.
      p. cm. — (Applications of political theory)
Includes bibliographical references and index.
    ISBN 0-7391-0533-7 (alk. paper) — ISBN 0-7391-0534-5 (pbk. : alk.
paper)
  1. Totalitarianism. 2. Post-communism. 3. World politics—20th
century. I. Faulkner, Robert K., 1934– II. Mahoney, Daniel J., 1960–
III. Title. IV. Series.
 JC480.S48 2003
  320.53—dc21
                                 2003008162

Printed in the United States of America

∞™ The paper used in this publication meets the minimum requirements of
American National Standard for Information Sciences—Permanence of Paper
for Printed Library Materials, ANSI/NISO Z39.48-1992.

Contents

v

Preface: Shtromas's Tasks

Robert Faulkner and Daniel J. Mahoney

We were all "cursed to live in interesting times" during the twentieth century. Some, however, drank more deeply than others from its bitter cup. Alexandras Shtromas was one. He experienced more, and more deeply and intensely, than most of us who lived free and comfortable lives in America. A Lithuanian-born Jew, as a child he lived for more than two years in a ghetto. His parents and most of his family perished at the hands of the Nazis. With Hitler's defeat he—and his country—went from one totalitarian oppressor to another. He, however, did not immediately see that this was the case. He saw Stalin's Sovietization of his native land as its liberation, as setting it on the path to becoming "a truly humane and just socialist society." As a young man he had converted to Marxist-Leninism, and he was for a time an idealistic, ardent supporter of Stalin and the Soviet system. A true believer, he remained nonetheless open to reality and truth. From the outset he did not deny the brutality and corruption of most of the Communist cadres ruling his country. He progressively lost his ideological faith, first in Stalin and his system (the fateful day when the scales fell from his eyes was April 4, 1953), then in Marxism itself (by 1963). However, Shtromas did not become cynical, as did so many disabused Marxist-Leninists, and retreat into self-serving egoism or merely pragmatic accommodation with the regime. He became a dissident and in due time an émigré from the totalitarian world (1973). It was in the 1980s that we the editors came to know the man as he spent some time teaching in our respective institutions. The personal recollection of Shtromas by his former colleague David Marquand that follows this preface wonderfully captures the mixture of vast knowledge, warmheartedness, eccentricity, and dogged determination that characterized our now departed friend. It also describes his remarkable prescience about the distinctive vulnerability of the Soviet regime, long before that vulnerability became apparent to the world at large. We shall return to this important theme.

Formed by his firsthand experience of the two totalitarianisms of the age, and having awakened from the seduction of the Soviet dream-turned-nightmare, Shtromas set his lifelong focus and task: "to understand the totalitarian phenomenon and the processes of political change generally." The collection of Shtromas's writings here presented shows how faithful he was to his resolve, and how fruitful was his indefatigable reflection on the great realities—revolutions, wars, and tyrannies—that the turbulent twentieth century presented to all of us. In reading Shtromas the reader will encounter a passionate and expert tour guide, a man grand enough to attempt to comprehend a dramatic century marked by titanic struggles between liberal democratic regimes, and their "ideocratic" opponents, whether "atavistic" or "progressive."

To be sure, one does not have to agree with every claim made by Shtromas. A dissident from State orthodoxy, who found much disturbing conformity of thought in the free West, Shtromas did not intend to put in their place anything similar. He spoke his mind forcefully but calmly, and he would welcome spirited responses from his readers. The reader of the following pieces will meet not just an impressive scholar with great learning and a gift of clear analysis and exposition, but also a large soul who confronted monstrous evils without flinching. They will discover a lively mind and generous soul.

The reader will be able to retrace an intellectual itinerary that makes the perspective Shtromas finally attained even more credible and admirable. Shtromas's native "idealism" eventually deepened into an unshakeable commitment to humane ideals of truth, freedom, and justice. He fleshed out these liberal and Enlightenment ideals with an attachment to the idea and reality of the "nation," a turn not typical of contemporary liberals and one that makes for much of Shtromas's originality.

Shtromas was an ardent Lithuanian patriot, and he felt an especial fondness for national communities. Like Aleksandr Solzhenitsyn, he saw such communities as deeply spiritual formations, estimable natural-historical-cultural units that are essential parts of God's plan for humankind. As such they merit great respect. The reader will note, for instance, how many times Shtromas informs him that there are approximately 1800 nations in the world today! For him this was no mere number; it was a central aspect of his appreciation for the diversity inherent in human life. Likewise, in part for the sheer joy of it, Shtromas lists and describes people after people, nation or national grouping, apparently ad infinitum. He loved the reality of "peoples"; he loved saying their names and tracking their historical adventures.

Shtromas knew that true patriotism begins at home and then recognizes and respects the same in others. He may have been forced to leave his native Lithuania, but the pieces found in part IV, "The Baltic Pendulum," which deal with Lithuania, Estonia, and Latvia, indicate that he never ceased to ponder their fate. The reader will imagine Shtromas's pain as he recounts the mid-century history of the Balkan states when they were playthings between Hitler and Stalin. He will suspect Shtromas's quiet pride at recounting the Baltic resistance to Sovietization. He will feel Shtromas's analysis of an entire citizenry's passive dissent from their country's masters and ideological lie, as well as the more heroic activity of the so-called dissidents. Patriotism did not distort his study of his native land; it attuned him to the truth of suffering and virtue.

This was the case in part because his patriotism did not know the slightest trace of chauvinism or xenophobia. His was a patriotism whose feelings of national pride were informed and measured by reason and liberal principles. Thus he could appreciate that the twentieth-century history of the Baltic peoples was bound up with world-historical forces. Shtromas's patriotic concern was incorporated into a larger view of Hitler's and Stalin's ideological ambitions and their Machiavellian dealings with one another. These tiny countries could be but pawns in the larger conflict of nations and ideologies.

In time Shtromas attained a perspective that one could call "cosmopolitan nationalism." This perspective is especially on display in part VI, "Looking Toward the Challenges for the Next Century." There Shtromas imagines a humane, pluralistic post-totalitarian world. Peace among nations, nations fully themselves, recognized and established as such: this is his vision of humanity. The thinker who most helps him to articulate this vision is the eighteenth century Enlightenment philosopher, Immanuel Kant. Kant's cosmopolitanism combined a sturdy morality focused on individual dignity and conscience, with republican political principles and forms and a certain attachment to "peoples" or nations. Shtromas agrees with much of this, while magnifying Kant's nationalism with his own distinctive view of human nature. Man is not merely the bare individual of liberal political theory; he is co-equally a "collective" being who naturally pertains to his nation. In Shtromas's view, this collective marvel of human history both reveals and forms human nature. Shtromas almost becomes a "nationalist" poet in these latter pages. In reading them the reader might experience the poet's power and poetry's treble effect: elevation and inspiration; a call to wonder and reflect; and, in time, a need for a sobering comparison of the poet's vision with all-too-human reality. Tocqueville declared that democratic peoples need elevating visions and future goals to wrest them from their horizons. Shtromas helps us to raise our gaze to survey all of mankind, articulated as it is today in states and nations and tomorrow in what remains to be seen. It is for us to judge the sobriety of his vision.

Because of his generous loves, Shtromas was marked also by strong antipathies to what he considered injurious to mankind. Chief among these were the totalitarian ideologies and regimes. Then came, truth be told, "left-wing" ideas and policies: they approached, he thought, too close to the disastrous "socialist idea." Shtromas—the lover of freedom, who never disconnected liberty from conscience and responsibility—worried about the debilitating effects on individual souls and on the larger social fabric of the tutelary State. He was not uncaring, as some might think, but his care was for men's responsible souls and not only for their "security."

As one who had suffered Nazism and Communism, and who knew concretely the mortal threat that totalitarianisms posed to freedom as well as to peace, Shtromas was particularly concerned with those Western intellectuals professionally charged to comprehend the Soviet threat and to counsel the West's response to it. He was attuned to the problems in "Sovietology" in America and Europe, as well as to the attitudes and ideas of the governing political classes. He found much that dismayed him. The fight against "utopia in power" entailed that one had to battle at home against distorting ideas about the nature of the enemy. Two pieces in part II show him at his polemical best. In one he responds to a dovish apologist of the Soviet Union: the contest resembles a lion (Shtromas) being attacked by a hare (the estimable Sidney Hook weighs in, and firmly castigates the hare for his temerity). In another he engages a serious scholar, and the tone is quite different. There was ample room in Shtromas's world for informed men to debate and dispute. This attitude, however, was not always reciprocated by professional anti–anti-communists.

Shtromas was a proud and principled opponent of communist totalitarianism, but he did not exaggerate its strength or ignore the "contradictions" that plagued it. As early as 1981, he laid out the "endgame" of Soviet communism with remarkable perspicacity—and his analyses were largely ignored by the experts in the field. These experts, whether critical of or indulgent toward Soviet reality, had resigned themselves to its more or less permanent character. Because Shtromas knew that Soviet despotism could not survive the undermining of its ideological justification, he, in contrast, anticipated a period of "political change" culminating in the self-destruction of the regime. Only a few distinguished students of communism, such as Peter Reddaway and the Nobel Prize–winning poet and essayist Czeslaw Milosz, have adequately appreciated the nature of Shtromas's achievement. According to Milosz, Shtromas was one of the two or three serious voices in the West "who insisted that the Soviet Union was on the verge of collapse" at a time when nearly everyone else took its survival for granted.[1] The present book shows that Shtromas was no mere "prophet": his remarkably accurate predictions about the future of Communism were rooted in a deep familiarity with the ideological nature of the Soviet regime, in a thorough understanding of the dynamics of change in a despotism that had lost a sense of its animating purpose, and in a sober awareness of the requirements of true modernization.

The reader of this volume will confront a learned, decent, and pugnacious man who has much to teach us about the "age of ideology," and about the requirements of civilized order in any time or place. Alex Shtromas died prematurely in June of 1999, after a brief and heroic bout with cancer. He spent his last days designing and compiling this volume. Shtromas considered it his intellectual will and testament, and he asked us, the editors, to finish the job for him. It was our duty and privilege to do so. We edited what he had selected, leaving out an occasional duplicative text, and wrote the brief introductions to the six parts (except for part IV). In this task Alex's sister, Margaret Kagan, provided wise encouragement and constant support. We are also grateful to his widow, Violeta Shtromas, for her warm assistance. In turn, these family members so devoted to Alex wish to express their gratitude to all those involved. Special thanks are due Gerald Easter of Boston College's Political Science Department, who helped with the initial editing of the manuscript that Alex had left us and wrote the preface to part IV of the book. We also wish to thank David Bobb for the bibliography that concludes the volume, Danielle Granville for copyediting an earlier version of the text, Carmella Murphy for tirelessly typing and retyping this extensive manuscript, and Erik Dempsey for providing a comprehensive and detailed index.

We present these writings in Alex's memory with the confidence that they will provide salutary guidance for the next generation.

NOTE

1. Czeslaw Milosz, Milosz's *ABC*'s (New York: Farrar, Straus and Giroux, 2001), 24.

Foreword: On Shtromas

David Marquand

My friendship with Alex Shtromas lasted for more than twenty years, but for more than half that time my contact with him was sadly irregular and infrequent. We met in the autumn of 1978 at the University of Salford. I had just been appointed as Professor of Contemporary History and Politics, but had not yet taken up the post and was still working in the European Commission in Brussels. Alex was a candidate for a university lectureship in political theory. Though I was not yet an employee of the University I had the great good fortune to sit on the appointment board. I can't now remember much about it; but I do remember the extraordinary impression that Alex made on me. He was eloquent, persuasive, and amazingly well-read. Above all, he belonged to a species which has never been common in Britain, and which is now endangered. He was a true intellectual. He had a passion for ideas, and a rare ability to expound and understand them. What he would be like as a colleague I couldn't tell. How he would cope with the demands of teaching not particularly gifted undergraduate students in the alien surroundings of an overwhelmingly technological university was unclear. There was no way of knowing how well he would adapt to the rather insular norms of British academic life. Having started his career as a lawyer and criminologist, he was less well qualified on paper than at least one other candidate. But I had no doubt that we simply had to appoint him; indeed, that it would be a crime not to do so. With the help of an enlightened chairwoman, I won the day.

In the event, Alex turned out to be a marvellous colleague and a first-class teacher. We saw a lot of each other. The University's budget was savagely cut in the early years of the Thatcher Government, and for a while it looked as if our department might be abolished altogether. For me, by now departmental chairman, it was a stressful and taxing period; Alex was a tower of strength. But my fondest memories of him are not academic. They are of meals, sometimes *à deux*, sometimes with wives or colleagues, nearly always in Indian or Chinese restaurants, in the then still bleak and charmless surroundings of downtown Manchester. As befitted two loquacious foodies, we ate greedily and talked endlessly (his preference was for Chinese food, I seem to remember, mine for Indian, but I also remember that he introduced me to a superb Pekinese restaurant, which almost converted me). Our talks ranged widely—politics, the cinema, literature, and the personal gossip in which he unexpectedly delighted. He was a fierce, dogged, yet tactically adroit controversialist. Arguing with him was like arguing with a World War II Soviet tank sweeping and swerving across the steppes. In debate he gave (and expected) no quarter. For all that, he had great charm and warmth. Above all, he had a kind of blazing sincerity as well as an unusual blend of learning and wisdom.

To my initial surprise, he was fully capable of conveying these qualities to his students. For them, he was an exotic: it was as if a brightly colored parrot had suddenly appeared in an aviary full of drab and ordinary sparrows. But his exoticism was an asset; it meant that he had captured the imaginations of his students before he began to speak. His lectures were demanding, and his reading lists phenomenal; when he arrived in the department he almost caused a riot among the secretarial staff who had to type them out (this was in the days before word processors). But he soon won the secretaries over; and even weak students could see that he cared. I think he was probably the most popular lecturer in the department. A typical Salford memory is of tiptoeing along the corridor past his room in dank winter evenings (in those days my department's pedagogical flagship was a part-time degree, taught in the evenings to mature students), listening to his booming voice haranguing a class, which, I knew, would be eating out of his hand.

Apart from these personal qualities, what I remember most—particularly from the vantage point of the beginning of the twenty-first century—is his prescience. Two conversations, in particular, stand out. The first took place soon after the election of the present Pope. The election of a Polish Pope, Alex insisted, with his usual confident belligerence, would do more to shake the regime than anything that had happened since it was established. It might even prove to be a pebble which would eventually let loose an avalanche in which Polish communism would perish. I thought the prediction crazy then. It does not seem so now.

The second conversation took place at about the same time. This was long before Gorbachev and "perestroika." The second cold war was well under way. We began by talking about Spain, and the extraordinary path that Spain had followed since the still fairly recent death of Franco. Spain, said Alex, provided the most plausible model for political change in the Soviet Union. If the regime collapsed or was transformed, it would be at the hands of an insider—as yet unknown—trying to reform it from within. And, contrary to the conventional wisdom of most western sovietologists at that time, collapse or transformation was more probable than not. Despite its apparent imperviousness, the system was unstable; and it was unstable—a typical Alex point, this—because no one believed any longer in its foundational ideology. Curiously enough, my recollection is that when Gorbachev did come to power and began the Perestroika project, Alex doubted if he would turn out to be the grave-digger of the Soviet system. But that only shows that even Alex couldn't be prescient about everything. In the last resort, however, it is for others to judge his contributions to Soviet studies and political theory. What I remember is a big, powerful, warm, and curiously innocent human being. I miss him very much.

I

AUTOBIOGRAPHICAL INTRODUCTION

Alex Shtromas died before he could complete his own introduction to this volume, but he thought that the four little essays that follow would help serve the same purpose. They show him confronting the communist idea and regime that together supplied his "main formative experience." They show a morally serious man thinking out what posture to adopt toward the totalitarian oppressors. His disillusionment was typical of idealistic communists, which were not a large class, he writes. But what he made of that disillusionment was not at all typical. There are poignant vignettes here. Some ex-communists gave themselves over to despair. Others, trying to deny the "spiritual futility of their whole life," remained in a double-faced and soul-destroying official capacity. Shtromas himself supplies a brief credo addressed "to his students." Although he is cautious about all claims to political, religious, and partisan righteousness, his ultimate outlook goes beyond mere skepticism. "The purposeful thing is to put the wrong things right," he said to the Baltic Tribunal Against the Soviet Union. He cautions his Baltic friends against preoccupation with revenge. Aim to rebuild rather than to punish, and oppose only the evil system of which most of the oppressors are but "victims." But is such a generous and politic view compatible with Shtromas's own Kantian insistence upon personal moral responsibility? That is the thoughtful question raised, in the final piece, by an interviewer from "Moral Rearmament."

Statement to *Contemporary Authors*

ALEKSANDRAS SHTROMAS

Born in independent Lithuania, I experienced as a child two consecutive oc-cupations of my country: the Soviet (1940–1941) and the Nazi (1941–1944). Under the latter, our whole family was imprisoned in an extermination camp near Kaunas, Lithuania. Both my parents and most of our family perished at the hands of the Nazis. I survived only because, after more than two years of imprisonment, I managed to escape from the camp and, with the help of good Lithuanian people, to hide until the Soviet Red Army chased the Nazis out of my country and reoccupied Lithuania for the USSR.

My experience of Nazi and Soviet rule (until 1973) was the main formative experience that provided the motivation and driving force behind my edu-cational pursuits, research, and writing. Whatever I did or wrote was always dictated by my unending quest to understand the totalitarian phenomenon and the processes of political change generally. I will surely continue to pur-sue this quest until the last day of my life.

Reprinted from Susan Trosky, ed., *Contemporary Authors*, vol. 132 (London: Gale Research, 1991), 384.

The "Author's Testimony to the Baltic Tribunal Against the Soviet Union"

ALEKSANDRAS SHTROMAS

I belong to the very small minority of Lithuanians of my generation who, at a very young age, were converted to Marxism-Leninism and who therefore wholeheartedly accepted the forceful incorporation of Lithuania into the USSR, and zealously supported the Soviet communist regime thus imposed upon our country.

For people like myself the atrocities perpetrated by the regime—summary executions of resistance fighters, destruction of households harboring them, as deportations of "class-hostile elements" to Siberia—were an inevitable part of the ferocious "class struggle" that the regime had to win by whatever means in its power in order to transform Lithuania into a truly humane and just socialist society.

This is not to say that we were totally blind and did not notice the superfluous cruelties and blatant injustices that were at odds even with the most vigorous standards the Marxist-Leninist vision of class struggle could set. We were fully aware of them as well as of all other so-called excesses which, in our view, were only hindering a smooth passage of our country to socialism. But desperate about it all we were not. For we were convinced that everything that was wrong was due exclusively to the

Reprinted from Ingrid Kalnins, ed., *The Baltic Tribunal Against the Soviet Union* (Rockville, Md.: Baltic World Conference Publications, 1985), 140–43.

mistakes of the inept individual executioners of the Party's will—the "overdoers," the "deviationists," the "bureaucrats," the "careerists," and other "alien stock" that "attached themselves for the wrong reasons to the right socialist cause." We never hesitated in believing that Stalin and his closest companions in the leadership of the Party, as Bolshevik-revolutionaries and entirely dedicated Marxist-Communist idealists, shared both our convictions and concerns. And thus, as long as they were in charge, there was nothing for us seriously to fear. We knew that we worked for the best system, for the realization of the most noble human goals, and there was for us nothing overdramatic in the fact that in such a grandiose and novel enterprise as the communist construction certain mistakes and excesses were taking place. They had to.

But we were concerned. Concerned, first of all, about the opportunistic *apparatchiks* of the middle rank whom we knew only too well and who in their majority were either soulless bureaucrats or vengeful egotists, semi-literate people to whom Marxism, socialism, and any high ideals meant nothing at all, and who were simply happy to engage in high-handed and trigger-happy activities for their own sake or for the sake of an immediate personal gain. We feared that with the death of Stalin they could get out of control or, worst of all, even gain the upper hand and cause the degeneration of socialism into fascism. In a way, this meant that we already knew that Soviet Communism is actually indistinguishable from fascism, but by believing in the ability of Stalin's (and, in the Lithuanian context, in Snieckus's) leadership to preserve the Marxist-Communist identity of our state, and never to allow the fascist trends to prevail, we did not admit this knowledge even to ourselves.

It all changed with Stalin's death in 1953. The very people whom we suspected of being crypto-fascists, afraid of revealing their true ideological identity only because of Stalin's dominion, suddenly proved to be "less fascist" than Stalin himself. For, instead of fascist "frost" it was the "thaw" that came about with Stalin's death.

The rehabilitation of the "doctor-plotters" on April 4, 1953, a month after Stalin's death, was to me personally the straw that finally broke the camel's back. On that day the idea that the Soviet system was, in fact, fascist (moreover, super-fascist, since no other fascist system had such a total command over a reluctant society as the Soviet system had) suddenly struck me. I felt the sensation of having miraculously recovered full eyesight enabling me to see clearly things, which a moment before were blurred and indistinct. For if Stalin was at the source of the system's evils, all the blatant lies and deceptions on which it was based, then the system itself was perverse, irredeemable, and deserving only one fate—that of destruction.

From that date I became thoroughly and irreversibly anti-Soviet and as time passed, my anti-Soviet attitude only hardened. This did not mean, however, that I also became anti-Marxist. On the contrary, my Marxist convictions were very helpful in substantiating and making "scientifically waterproof" my newly-born anti-Sovietism. I even elaborated a whole Marxist theory of the Soviet society according to which it was the most reactionary and decaying form of capitalism, capitalism in its last, super-monopolistic and ultra-imperialist, stage of development. Now I expected the next stage to come about—the one of a true socialist revolution to do away with Soviet super-fascist totalitarianism. I remained a Marxist for about another decade. By 1963 my Marxist beliefs had evaporated too. This was due to my study of post-Marxist philosophy and also to the fact that the socialist revolution that I had expected to happen had not shown any signs of maturing even as an attitude of the "sound Marxist" sections of the Worker's Vanguard Party, let alone of the working class itself. On the contrary, bourgeois consumerism and capitalist attitudes started latently to prevail in the party, the working class, and society as a whole.

I think that my "ideological biography" is rather typical. To be sure, this eye-opening experience came to different people at different times—before or after April 4, 1953—but it was, no doubt, a universal experience for us all, an experience, however, to which again different people reacted in different ways. Some of the former idealists reverted to bitter cynicism and continued to soldier on with the regime in the pursuit of their careers. Some withdrew into the "neutral niches" of Soviet life (medicine, engineering, science, medieval history, etc.) where they could continue to work usefully without involving themselves in any public–political activities—in fact trying to insulate themselves as much as possible from everything official and public. A few chose to lead double lives, using their official positions as well as whatever public platform was available to them, to promote, at least on a small scale, the "progressive" and "nationally advantageous" causes. Only very few chose to state their new political views more or less explicitly by either word or deed. These people later became the first Lithuanian dissidents; all of them were former Marxist-Communists. The people of traditional–nationalist orientation joined the ranks of dissidents much later. But at least one friend of mine, the talented poet, Vladas Grybas, was unable to survive the shock of losing his blind faith in the Communist Party, the Soviet regime, and Stalin personally. In 1954, he committed suicide. With his death, I believe, went the last Lithuanian who was a true believer in the Soviet system and who was unable to exist otherwise—change his views or cynically adapt to whatever reality there was.

The saddest picture perhaps is presented by those former committed Marxists who, in their young days, had started to serve the regime out of enthusiastic idealism and who now still continue to do so albeit with all their high hopes and beliefs in it lost a long time ago. They went through two shocking disappointments. The first was that, counter to their expectations, after the class struggle was completed and socialism was proclaimed established, the quality and standard of life did not improve much, with the whole situation remaining as tense and oppressive as before. It appeared that the rivers of blood had been shed in vain and, moreover, for a blatant lie. It was, in other words, a shock of discovery that the high ideals they had entertained were fictitious and utterly unrealizable. The second was that they did not even acquire any real power. All power was concentrated in Moscow's hands, whereas they found themselves in the position of voiceless native servants of Moscow, whatever position they had locally occupied. In every move, they were dependent on instructions and permissions coming from Moscow and, on top, had to endure working under direct supervision of Moscow's envoys sent to each office to make sure that the natives strictly complied with Moscow's directives. All their dreams of being in charge of a new, socialist Lithuania (whatever the reality of socialism was) were thus completely shattered too.

Because of that these people hate the regime and the Russians even more intensely than the ordinary people, but, because of their exposed positions, they have to live double lives, hiding their true feelings and always making *"bonne mine a mauvais jeu."* This constant lying and hiding of one's true self is a psychological burden not very easy to bear. They try, however, to alleviate it by presenting themselves (also to themselves) as sober realists who make use of whatever positions they have acquired to advance, though in adverse conditions, Lithuania's long-term interests. They do not even pretend any more to be good Communists. They only claim that, in spite of serving an alien and oppressive regime, they remain good Lithuanians, caring for their country and people.

This is the sad story of the few former Lithuanian communist zealots who, in 1945, were youngsters of about 15–25, and who grew old only to realize the monstrosity of the cause they chose to serve and to try to reconcile themselves with the spiritual futility of their whole life's endeavor.

To My Students—Past, Present, and Future

ALEKSANDRAS SHTROMAS

I firmly believe in God and the act of Creation that He accomplished for purposes known only to Himself but do not adhere to any specific religious denomination. My belief in God is thus philosophical rather than religious. In terms of philosophy I am a self-confessed eclecticist who believes that there is some truth and wisdom in every philosophy and religion, but that none of them can claim to be in possession of absolute and/or finite truth and wisdom. Every philosophy or religion that makes such a claim is to me not simply wrong, but also extremely dangerous as it is a source of intolerance and, potentially, of spiritual and, consequently, also physical oppression. In ethics, likewise, I see every person and institution as containing elements of both good and evil. To me persons or institutions, however much evil there may be in them, are good if they have the inner potential to change for the better and seek improvement. Conversely, persons and institutions, however much good there may be in them, are in my view evil if they claim perfection and, consequently, do not lend themselves to change and improvement. In politics I

Reprinted from Ernest Kay, ed., *The International Dictionary of Profiles*, 9th ed. (Cambridge: U.K. International Biographical Centre, 1987), 722.

am a libertarian who believes in a minimal state and maximal individual freedom. In my view patience is the ultimate political virtue and therefore I reject violent politics in all its shapes and forms. Perhaps these attitudes account for the fact that I do not know of any extant political party I would be prepared to join.

Have Pity on the Hangman

ALEKSANDRAS SHTROMAS

Dr. Alex Shtromas gave the talk, on which this article is based, at an international conference in Caux, Switzerland organized by Moral Re-Armament, where he was chairman of a section on the Soviet Union and the Communist world. Some of the points made in the talk are then discussed with *New Tomorrow* editor, Michael Marshall.

What spiritual message could be given to the people of the Soviet Union from the standpoint of religion and universal religious principles? Because this country is in a state of totalitarian rule and because people are unable to do anything of significance, passions run high. People are frustrated and angry. They are angry at the government, but the government is very far away, so they become angry with each other. They are in a constant state of hatred. You try to compensate for the offences you have received from those chaps higher up, by taking it out on those who are more defenseless than you are.

This totalitarian system of rule boosts the immoral attitudes of anger and revenge. In such a situation you always look for a scapegoat to blame, and whom you can tackle. The government, as I said, is very distant from you, so people use scapegoats of different kinds—other nationalities, other social groups. They are trying to make comprehensible the object of their hatred.

Reprinted from Michael Marshall, ed., *New Tomorrow*, no. 3 (October 1977): 8–10.

This is the situation. How, as religious people, should we cope with it? What should our message to those unhappy people be?

Yevtushenko said it in political terms. He said that people became hangmen to each other, forgetting about the main hangman at the top. That is a very good image. We should fight against it and fight today by spreading a moral message, a spiritual message. As a person concerned with moral issues and having had all this experience of Soviet life, I would generalize my message to my fellows there about what they should do, or rather what they should not do in tackling their situation, in five main points.

The first would be: "Don't generalize the wrongs done by particular people, to whole nations, classes, races or groups to which those people belong." If you see somebody doing something which you hate, which is wrong, don't try to create a scapegoat out of the group to which the person belongs. In terms of Soviet society it is very simple. A Lithuanian sees that the KGB are mainly Russians, or that the Russians are in charge of the whole business, so they blame the whole Russian nation as the object that has to be blamed and hated and on whom they must take revenge, which is wrong.

The second message is: "Don't see the source of evil in the individuals who are its agents." Evil always has individuals as its agents. Don't take the individual as the source of the evil. Don't hate the person, don't blame him, since those individuals are as much the victims of the evil system they represent as you yourself are. They have either sick or weak souls which demand your compassion, your help and support, not your revenge or desire to exterminate them. As the great contemporary Russian poet, Alexander Galich, said: "The hangmen also have a terrible time. Have pity on the hangmen."

The third message is: "Don't search for the guilty outside your own personality. Do not try to find a scapegoat in anybody." It is purposeless to enquire who has done the wrong thing. The purposeful thing is to find the way to put the wrong things right. That is the constructive approach if we don't want to generalize, or to blame individuals who are as much victims as you yourself of the evil system, which they obey because of the weakness of their souls. So don't try to find who is the wrong-doer, who could be blamed or proclaimed guilty. It is unconstructive, because the next step will be to punish those people and to add to the suffering of everybody.

The approach should be a positive one, which means that when we encounter a situation that is wrong and unfair, we must think about the way to put it right, not how to blame the people or circumstances which are responsible for it. When we know what can be done to put the wrong right, the other thing we must do is ask people what their personal contribution to this could be.

Now the fourth message—this is all developing logically from one point to the next: "Confront evil for all people's sake, but never be in confrontation with any particular person, any particular group or any particular nation." We have to try to convert all people as far as we can to confront evil, and make clear where the evil is. The evil is always in systems, in some arrangements which make people robots serving this system of evil and never give a chance for the person's full and free expression. The system makes people prisoners. The higher up in the system they are, the more they are its prisoners.

The fifth point is: "Never reconcile with evil, but always reconcile with people even when they are agents of evil, for the sake of good and its triumph in you, as well as in your fellow man." If you confront anyone, and refuse to reconcile with him, be he a communist, a fascist, or your enemy with whom you are on vendetta terms, you will automatically be on the side of evil. So never reconcile with evil, always reconcile with people.

These are the five conclusions I reach in terms of moral issues and religious sermons that have to be delivered to people suffering from any kind of totalitarian rule, fascist or communist, because the frustration, anger, and sentiment of revenge is overwhelming and we must fight it before it is too late.

Marshall: Point three was, "Don't concentrate on finding out who is the guilty man." It seems to me that one of Solzhenitsyn's points in writing "The Gulag Archipelago" was that the people who ran this system under Stalin and are still holding comfortable positions—those guilty people should be exposed and accused of their crimes and without that there cannot be a real cleansing of the population.

Shtromas: We shouldn't lie. We should be honest and say everything. I don't deny the responsibility of anyone who has done something wrong. He must be responsible for his acts. But you shouldn't concentrate just on that. The problem is to detect the wrong in order to put it right. That is the first concern.

If you want to tackle people's responsibility, which is a very important cleansing issue I agree, that is a very different problem. What people tend to do is to confuse both those issues. They think that if they seek revenge, or settle the score with whoever was the wrong-doer, they will solve the problem, which isn't true. That's what Khruschev did really. That's what the Communists do. They try to find the guilty man—Stalin, and when Khruschev was removed it was him—and it seems to everybody, "Now we will be alright. Now we know who the guilty man is." But it doesn't solve problems.

One of the greatest Russian political thinkers was Saltykov Shchedrin, a writer of the nineteenth century. He predicted Stalin very well. He wrote a political novel which is the history of the "City of Fools," a type of historical fantasy. Once the city was in a big crisis and everyone was very annoyed because the level of the porridge in their plates kept going down every day. People were trying to find out what the cause of it all was.

Somebody said there were two very bad people in the town, Ivashka and Mikeshka, and it was all their fault. If they were to be killed, all the problems would be solved, because they were responsible for all the troubles. People were very enthusiastic about it. They caught Ivashka and Mikeshka. There was a big rock in the city and they threw them from the rock. But when they came back home after doing this splendid job, they found the level of porridge was even lower. So they thought, "Well, they probably were the wrong people. Who else could be responsible?"

Then they started to kill each other, until they realized in the end that there were very few people left in town, and no one was able to work in peace, and provide even the little amount of porridge they had had. So they thought things over and realized that killing someone was not the way to solve the situation. At that time the governor of the city dies and they have a new governor, who is a well-meaning chap, and there the story ends.

That is the attitude that comes straight away when you feel something is wrong. "Who is responsible? Let us punish him." And you substitute for the real solution of a problem, this kind of revenge against people you presume to be wrong. That is what is wrong. I don't take issue with Solzhenitsyn but his is a very different point. It is a problem of human responsibility.

Marshall: Can you explain then how you understand what he means about human responsibility?

Shtromas: His point is that if you want to have a healthy moral situation in a country, you have to proceed with the idea that people have to be responsible for their actions. One of the main problems of totalitarian rule is that people are deprived of responsibility by the totalitarian rulers. The same was true in Hitler's case. Everyone who was killing Jews said, "But we got our orders from the highest authority. We are not responsible for it."

The morally cleansing situation is when you maintain that under all circumstances you are still responsible for your actions. No one is going to take away your responsibility for what you do, no authority. God gave you freedom of choice for your action.

But that is another story. It is not revenge which we want to take on those people. What is important in cases like that is to show what people did. The greatest responsibility is to bring evil into the open. Read the Gospel of St. John. It says that the biggest weapon of the weak good against powerful evil, is that evil is unable to survive the light. Only good survives. So if you shed light you defeat evil, and that is what is good about it. You have to expose evil to light. People are still moral and responsible in their essence, and if they are just tackled in the proper way, that will be the right thing to do with them in order to remoralize them.

Marshall: In the next point, the fourth point, you said that evil exists in systems and the systems then make a person a robot, or prisoner, and unable to use their freedom. Is that not saying something contradictory to the idea of personal responsibility?

Shtromas: No, because those people who become robots are weak or sick souls. Not everybody is a hero, not everybody is a moral giant. People are people.

Marshall: What is your attitude to the concentration camp commandant who says I was only obeying my orders?

Shtromas: That is what I am saying when I say you should blame the system, you should blame the evil, not the person. You are giving respect to a person, for example to this concentration camp commandant, by putting him in the dock and saying, "Look, Johann or Ivan, you are responsible for your deeds. You are a person. You shouldn't see yourself just as a robot." His integrity and his standard will then become higher in the dock than it was in the concentration camp. There he was just a manipulable tool, a puppet. Very proud probably, indoctrinated, but still not a person. By putting him in the dock we increase him to the dimensions of a person, and say, "You are responsible."

Marshall: But some people will also argue, if you say that in his position as commandant he was not really a person, then how can you hold him responsible for what he did?

Shtromas: Well he was a person, but he behaved as a robot. He reduced himself through weakness of soul and conformed to a situation which was inhuman. He really deprived himself of his human personality, willingly, and that is why he is responsible for it. He had the choice. God has provided everybody with a choice and he made the wrong choice, and that is why he is responsible because he is still a human being, yet he reduced himself to the stance of a robot. He should not have done it. That is why he is responsible. We require from everybody that they be a personality.

Marshall: Why I asked the question was because many left-wing radicals in Western society say, "We must smash the system, the system is evil," and that becomes a substitute for looking at problems within themselves.

Shtromas: That is a very important point you raised and what I want to say is that I would seek to exclude the sentiment of revenge from dealing with people like the concentration camp commandant—the sentiment of anger against you because you did it. Instead I feel pity because you have behaved so inhumanly. You have degraded your soul. You are just dirty, and you have to undergo a procedure which will somehow, by exposing you into the light, cleanse you. That is what St. John says all the time.

We are fighting for every human soul and by exposing them and asking them to be responsible we are also cleansing their souls. That is why I am against revengeful measures like the death penalty. We have sick people who need to be cured or protected because they are not fully human—they are spiritually sick, and so have to be cured—or we have people who are reducing themselves willingly to the level of a villain, and they have to be responsible for that.

What I am fighting against is this slogan which is very popular among left-wingers, that people are the victims of circumstances. That is not so. People are people and we should see them as such under all circumstances. We are just making excuses, saying that people are defined or determined by circumstances, and we are reducing and degrading people by it. It is an antireligious statement. We are creations of God, not creations of circumstances. That is the high moral message that is contained in the idea of God and responsibility before God.

Now, coming back to the left-wingers. They try to say that the system is evil, and they have to smash the system. But they don't really talk in those terms entirely. They say that the system is just the tool of a group of people, the class of exploiters. That's the problem. If they said, "Smash the evil system, but don't touch people," then it would be an interesting point to discuss with them. You could say, "Well, what does it mean, to smash the system?"

What they say is that the system is innocent. It is the tool of those vicious people, the capitalists, who are just guided by their selfish interests. You see, the problem is that they are again degrading the human personality, because they say that probably everybody is selfish, but there is a minority who have got to a position where they can indulge their selfishness and make the selfishness of their group the attitude of the whole society, while all the others are deprived. So (they say) we have to exploit evil feelings like envy, because all those other selfish people haven't got the chance to be selfish in society. Everybody is a bourgeois, but if you have the rule of 100 million bourgeois, instead of four million, or ten million bourgeois (Marx says it will always be 10 percent) then it is a fair society because the selfish interests are shared.

What they are exploiting is the feeling, "I am unable to tolerate that someone is more successful than I am." So again they are taking revenge on people, on classes. That is the problem with the left, not that they want to destroy the system, but that they see the system as an innocent derivative from the selfish interests of a minority group of people which is trying to impose its own interests on the whole of society. So again they blame people, they take revenge on people, they are disrespectful to people.

What the Communists or left-wingers think about people is that the majority are governed by bourgeois, selfish, materialistic interests, which is the animal part and the dominant part of every human being, except for a committed elite, which is the Communist party. This is the minority, the minority which is selfless, which hasn't got any material interests, which is the spiritual part of every nation or group and which sacrifices everything for the sake of all people. Now this is another moral, personal argument for all power being in their hands—they deserve to be the absolute rulers because they are absolutely unselfish. They are the elite, the spiritual elite, in absolute power, distributing the wealth equally among everybody else—who is selfish—and eliminating this unfairness of one successful section of the population dominating the others. That is quite a simplistic picture, but it boils down to that inevitably.

So all my five points are really anti-leftist, and they deny the class approach or class analysis. They really seek to see the system as being a creation in its own right. A system is always the Devil's instrument. The individual is the instrument of God. That is my theory, my philosophy. It should be the main theological message today.

II

LOOKING BACK AT THE MAIN CHALLENGE OF THE TWENTIETH CENTURY: OVERCOMING TOTALITARIANISM

In part II, Shtromas takes us straight to the heart of twentieth century darkness, to meet its two prominent perpetuators of evil: Hitler and Stalin. They made life a living hell for millions upon millions of human beings. One aimed at a glorious, thousand-year "Third Reich," the other at "a socialist worker's paradise." What they produced was precisely the opposite. Hitler signed off on "the final solution," which annihilated six million European Jews; Stalin ordered "collectivization" (with millions of corpses as its bitter harvest), Show Trials, and purges, and constructed the totalitarian machine that was "the Soviet system." Both were men of clear-cut worldviews, adamantine wills, and ruthless cunning. Shtromas does not flinch before them and their works, because the responsibility of thinking in the twentieth century included confronting such evil. This is especially the case when evil's work was justified in the name of "ideology."

Hitler's was racialist, inveighing against the miscegenation of the races and blaming Jews, and their capitalist or liberal–bourgeois and communist dupes and lackeys, for the material and moral ills weighing upon "Aryan peoples." The German *Volk*, purified and honed to a razor's edge by Hitler and his Nazi cadres, would rid the world of the Jewish-bourgeois-socialist "*bacillus*" and would help to establish Nature's hierarchy of races. Stalin's Marxist-Leninist historical materialism located ultimate evil in capitalism and capitalists. The proletariat and its scientific spokesmen, the Bolshevik Party, were mankind's great hope. Much as we find these thoughts repulsive and their danger passed, these murderous ideologies have to be confronted even now by us. Otherwise we will fail in our responsibilities to comprehend the deeds based upon them and to do justice to those who perpetrated them, to those who suffered them, and to those who courageously resisted and vanquished them. Alexandras Shtromas did not shirk this duty. He often reflected upon both the general categories of "ideology" and "totalitarianism" and on their specific National Socialist and Marxist-Leninist incarnations. We do well to reflect upon these essential topics in his company (chapters 5 and 6 are particularly instructive on these important matters: "The Inevitable Collapse of Socialism," and "On Totalitarianism and the Prospects for Institutionalized Revolution in the USSR and China").

Shtromas did not fail to consider the real-world effects of these ideologies. On the one hand, he focused upon National Socialism's most characteristic deed: the annihilation of the Jews. On the other, he tirelessly analyzed "the Soviet system," at its core an amalgam of Marxist-Leninist ideology and a one-party totalitarian State. The reader will admire Shtromas's sure hand as he retraces the application of the two ideologies (see especially chapters 1, 2, 3, and 5: "The Jewish and Gentile Experience of the Holocaust: A Personal Perspective," "Making Sense of Stalin," "Marxism-Leninism in the USSR," and "The Inevitable Collapse of Socialism").

Four things distinguish Shtromas's consideration of "the holocaust" (a term he declined to capitalize), in addition to his firm grasp of the historical record and of the relevant statistics. First, Shtromas attributes a crucial role in Hitler's decision to pursue "the final solution" to Stalin's anti-Jewish actions, and to various ethnic groups' anti-Soviet (and anti-Semitic) violence against Jews during the first years of the German war effort in Eastern Europe and in Russia. While he acknowledges that his is a minority view, he believes that Stalin was Hitler's predecessor and instructor in the pursuit of "final solutions."

Second, Shtromas displays remarkable equanimity in attributing some responsibility and thus culpability to non-Nazis, both German and non-German, for the near annihilation of European Jewry (the reader cannot fail to wince at the account of Western leaders' shortsightedness and coldheartedness concerning Jews in the early days of Hitler's rule). Third, his equanimity rises to magnanimous levels with his refusal to absolve his fellow Jews of any misdeeds during this dark period (without in the least blaming the victims!). Finally, he was profoundly concerned that "the legacy" of this dark chapter in European history be based in truth, in a just assessment of agents and actions that avoids painting entire peoples with either a white or black brush. Shtromas, a Lithuanian-born secular Jew who escaped after two years' imprisonment in "a [Nazi] extermination camp near Kaunas, Lithuania," achieves something approaching a heroic perspective in these reflections upon the holocaust. It is difficult not to admire his search for truth and justice—which does not mean that everyone will agree with his controversial account of the causes of the Holocaust (the reader can turn to the opening pages of the book for Shtromas's own wrestling with "the moral issues" involved in judging and responding to these terrible "cases of conscience").

Given the "success" of Stalin's single-minded efforts in the Soviet Union and the resulting Cold War with the West, Shtromas devoted a good deal of his scholarly work to understanding the Soviet system. The pieces collected here provide a lucid sketch of Soviet realities from 1917 to the late 1980s and beyond. The major figures are deftly drawn: Lenin, Stalin, Khrushchev, Brezhnev, Chernenko, and Gorbachev. Each is presented in the context of the great overarching reality: "the Soviet system." This ideological regime was envisaged and set in place by Lenin, "realized" by Stalin, ceaselessly tinkered with by Khrushchev (the last true believer in Marxist-Leninism among the Soviet leaders), allowed to continue its slide into "feudal" oligarchic corruption by Brezhnev, and desperately "reformed" and finally dismantled by Gorbachev.

Shtromas rightly saw that to understand the Soviet leaders' domestic and foreign behavior, one had to place them in relation to Marxist-Leninism, which served as the glue of the system. Here he stands poles apart from mainstream academic "Sovietology," at least in its dominant contemporary forms. How one stood with respect to the regime's ideological rationale proved time and again to be the illuminating question for Shtromas.

The focus on "ideology" proves illuminating when turned upon itself. Shtromas, like Solzhenitsyn and Havel and many others, calls the ideology the great "Lie": socialist reality belied the socialist idea. Marxist-Leninism's historicist claim to total truth, absolute justice, and necessary and definitive progress, was refuted by communist reality as well as by the unchanging requirements of human nature.

These pieces are models of lucid political analysis. Shtromas, himself a dissident émigré, had a special fondness for dissent from established orthodoxies, including western academic ones. He certainly did not intend to offer one of his own.

1

The Jewish and Gentile Experience of the Holocaust: A Personal Perspective

ALEKSANDRAS SHTROMAS

I. "THEM" AND "US":
THE GIST OF HITLER'S NATIONAL SOCIALIST IDEOLOGY

In *Two Sources of Morality and Religion*, a book published in 1932, the great French philosopher Henri Bergson notes that human psychology is based on an instinctive division by each individual of the rest of humanity into two basic categories, those of "us" and "them." Throughout history, he maintains, the concept of "us" is permanently expanding as ever-larger groups of people are encompassed in it: family and clan consciousness have grown into the tribal one, and the tribal consciousness has extended into national consciousness; now various kinds of supranational consciousness are also starting to gain momentum.

To Bergson such a permanent expansion of the concept of "us" is the only measure of human progress. Bergson is, however, not sure whether this progress will ultimately lead to the total elimination of the concept of "them," to the "them" being dissolved altogether in the "us" embracing all mankind. He wonders whether we humans will be able to have enough spiritual resources to overcome our naturally divisive instincts and to reach the level of

Reprinted from the *Eleventh Annual Rabbi Joseph Klein Lecture* [April 10, 1989] (Worcester, Mass.: Assumption College Press, 1989), 3–26.

consciousness that could produce a world where there will really be "neither Greek nor Hebrew." If, against all odds, we humans will be able to reach that level of global consciousness and thus become one species under God, we will be saved, he believes; but if not, then we will fail our test before God who gave us the gift of free will and, most probably, by violently annihilating each other in various bloody confrontations and conflicts, will follow the way of the dinosaurs to extinction.

Bergson's book reflects, no doubt, the world in which it was written, a world increasingly dominated by militant ideologies, communist and fascist alike, which, by unashamedly exploiting the mass psychology of "us" vs. "them," saw the solution of mankind's problems in the elimination of the various vile and vicious "them" who, allegedly, block the way to a harmonious, decent, and happy existence, and who even threaten the very survival of the innocent and virtuous "us," be they (these "us") the working people or the racially pure and organically consolidated territorial folks of the world.

As the Spanish follower of Bergson Jose Ortega y Gasset remarks in his 1932 book, *The Revolt of the Masses*, only now in the twentieth century are we able fully to appreciate the truth of Nietzsche's *dictum* that mediocrity is death, for it is the mediocrities, people unable to produce any innovative and constructive ideas, who, in a desperate attempt at realizing their frustrated will to power, conceive and propel ideologies the only goal of which is to incite the alienated masses of modern urban societies to engage in a resolute struggle against their alleged exploiters and oppressors, a struggle which, without solving any of the authentic and, no doubt, grave problems of these masses, is ultimately only able to bring about total destruction and death.

Purely nationalist ideologies are, however, not so very deadly. They are of a limited or, at the most, of a regional scope and, therefore, their concept of "them" is also limited. Usually, the nationalists of one nation do not seek either the elimination or the enslavement of any other nation, but strive for what in the particular nationalists' view is justice in the relationship of their nation with other nations. Indeed, as long as the nationalists strive for their nation's acquisition of a decent place among and of an equal status with other nations, their goals are usually fully justifiable and commendable.

Hitler's national-socialist ideology was, however, not nationalistic at all; it was a global and universal ideology projecting a new, Aryan race-dominated world order and assigning Germany merely the role of the "self-sacrificial" vanguard in the struggle for that new world order. Because of this global dimension, Hitler's national socialism was a deadly ideology indeed. Hitler's "them" was the entire, globally spread "Jewish race" which in his view was about to take over the running of the world. Hitler believed that if the Jews were allowed to succeed in achieving their goal of becoming the world's rulers, they would ultimately bring about the demise of mankind, which thus had to be saved from them by all available means. Hitler's consistent and globally conceived anti-Semitism provided him with a kind of "internationalist" platform, allowing him to claim the role of the savior of all nations of the world, whatever their race might be, from annihilation at the hands of the Jews. Never mind that in the new world order the thus "saved" nations would have to be content with a place in the hierarchy of nations strictly determined by the "quality" of their race and, if not Aryan, accept the domination of the Aryans both from within and without their own realm. This arrangement, according to Hitler, would only benefit the racially "lower quality" nations as they would get in the Aryans' superior leadership and also the possibility of enjoying the fruits of the highest culture that only the Aryans were able to create.

Hitler, of course, admitted that the creation of such a new world order would not be an easy task. Only a multifaceted, intensive, and protracted "racial struggle" within and among nations, a struggle that might last an entire millennium, could bring it about. This millennium of acute "racial struggle," Hitler claimed, was opened by him and his National Socialist movement, and it would not stop till the Aryans finally and irreversibly defeated the Jews and whoever else had associated with them, thus becoming a faceless instrument of the Jewish cause. According to Hitler, the non-Jewish plutocrats and politicians of the Anglo-Saxon world, and the communists wherever they were active, had assumed the role of the pioneers of the Jewish cause. In Hitler's view, "plutocratic demo-liberalism" and Marxist communism were the two "murderous hands" of the world Jewry with which it was about to strangle mankind. Hence, to eliminate the Jews one had to eliminate first capitalism and communism, that is, to wage a war to conquer the world for National Socialism. Nietzche was right indeed: mediocrity is death; Hitler and his party have proved it beyond any doubt.

II. FROM A DEADLY IDEOLOGY TO THE PRACTICE OF THE HOLOCAUST

The way from the anti-Semitic National Socialist ideology's establishment of itself in power to the practice by the Nazi state of the Jewish holocaust was, however, not that straight. The ideology itself did not directly call for the mass physical extermination of the Jewish race. In *Mein Kampf* and in the twenty-five points of the "immutable" NSDAP (National-Socialist German Worker's Party) program, Hitler pledged himself only to exclude the Jews from the *Volksgemeinschaft* (the folk community), and thus to totally eliminate their distinctive influence on the way of life and attitudes of the German people, without specifying the means by which he intended to do so.

Initially, the policy into which this ideological attitude was translated found expression in the 1935 Nuremberg Laws, which deprived the Jews of German citizenship and reduced their status to that of mere subjects of the Third Reich.

According to these Laws, the Jews were not only disenfranchized and banned from holding positions in state offices and public bodies that dealt with or serviced the Aryans (for example, law firms and medical hospitals), they were also forbidden to engage in sexual, let alone marital, relations with non-Jews. A new crime, the *Rassenschande* (racial defilement), had been instituted by the Nuremberg Laws, carrying the punishment of imprisonment and, from 1939, of death. A segregationist law of unprecedented rigidity and ferocity ensured the total exclusion of the Jews from any meaningful participation in the nation's life, and at the same time made the Jews available to service the nation's needs in whatever way the government deemed necessary.

Segregation and deprivation of rights, however, were conceived by Hitler as only the first step in dealing with the Jews, a temporary measure which would allow him to start building the new *Judenrein* (Jew-clean) *Volksgemeinschaft* without much delay. His ultimate goal, and he never tried to hide it, was to rid Germany of the Jews altogether. In fact, the Nuremberg Laws were in the first place meant not to accommodate the Jews in Germany, but to provide a powerful incentive for them to leave Germany altogether. This goal the Nuremberg Laws did indeed achieve: most German Jews were ready to go and Hitler, on his part, was happy to assist their emigration by whatever means at his disposal. Already in 1934 he started to cooperate with Zionist organizations, trying to help them to take the Jews from Germany to Palestine, but the British authorities, anxious not to offend the Arabs, effectively blocked their way to the Promised Land. Most German Jews who nevertheless managed to get there and settle were smuggled in illegally by the Zionist underground.

Neither were the U.S. authorities too helpful in admitting German Jews to their land. They strictly observed the annual quotas for German immigrants and resolutely turned down all the "excessive" applications by German Jews to enter the United States. The famous story of the *St. Louis*, the ship which tried to get 930 German Jews to the United States via Havana (as immigrants from Cuba rather than Germany), but which, after having already reached Havana, was turned back to Germany, is one of many stories exemplifying the plight of the would-be German Jewish immigrants to the United States of that time.

Paradoxically, it was only Stalin who initially welcomed German Jews to the USSR. In 1934, he even created in the midst of South Siberia a Jewish Autonomous Province where the German Jews were allowed to settle. Some, especially those with pro-Soviet sympathies, made their home there, despite the inhospitable climate of Siberia, but unfortunately not for long. In 1937, the Soviet government sealed the borders altogether for ordinary foreign immigrants, which brought to an end German Jewish emigration to the USSR, and those German Jews who were already in Birobijan (the capital of the Jewish Autonomous Province in Siberia) were accused of being foreign spies and hired wreckers and were either executed or sent to the Gulag, from which they never returned. Stalin's mass execution of German Jews preceded Hitler's adoption of the policy of final solution by about five years.

Worried about the worsening situation of German Jews and, at the same time, unwilling radically to revise U.S. immigration policies, President Roosevelt called a representative international conference (only Mussolini's Italy and Stalin's USSR declined to attend), hoping that a collective effort of all democratic countries would allow German Jews to leave the Third Reich and settle elsewhere. Representatives of thirty-two nations met from July 6 to 14, 1938, in the French resort town of Evian, but only to state their collective unwillingness to do anything about helping the German Jews to enter their respective countries. The American delegate opened the conference by saying that the president had called it because the United States would "not modify its already liberal immigration policy" and thus was unable to solve the problem of German Jews on her own. The British delegate simply declined all propositions for accepting German Jews to his country, stating "the United Kingdom is not a country of immigration." He was followed by the Australian representative who said that Australia had no racial problem and was "not desirous of importing one." The delegates of the other twenty-nine nations, "following the leaders," expressed the equally unhelpful attitudes of their governments. Their views on this issue were so intransigent that they collectively declined even to give a hearing to the representatives of the Jewish organizations of the Third Reich (whom Hitler encouraged to go to Evian and to make there as strong a plea as possible). Nor did they agree to listen to the representatives of the Jewish World Congress and other Jewish organizations lobbying the Conference. The message of the free world to both the Nazis and the Jews was thus unequivocally clear: "We do not care." (Documents of and materials on the July 1938 International Conference on Refugees in Evian are available at the Ronald S. Lauder Foundation, F. D. R. Station, P.O. Box 5125, New York, N.Y. 10150).

One of the forerunners of the infamous *Kristallnacht*, the series of Nazi-inspired Jewish pogroms that swept Germany on November 9, 1938, was meant to shock the complacent free nations and force them to review once more their policy toward Jewish emigration from Germany, but, again, no one spoke out.

This is why in 1939, on the eve of World War II, Hitler was still left with three-fourths of Germany's Jewish population: of 550,000 German Jews, only about 140,000 had managed to get away (after the *Anschluss* in 1938, over 100,000 Austrian Jews were added to the number of Jews who remained in the by then enlarged Third Reich).

Being unable during the war to proceed any further with Jewish emigration, Hitler decided to get rid of the Jews in all countries that were coming under his control by deporting them to one of the remote isolated territories which he aspired to gain in war. This is how the Madagascar plan came to life. Even before having finally defeated France, Hitler repeatedly talked about wresting Madagascar from France and converting this remote and well-isolated island into a special territory for the resettlement of European Jewry. Madagascar indeed became one of the first territorial demands that Hitler presented to the Vichy government after France was finally defeated. Being in no position to argue with the victor, Pierre Laval, the premier of the

Vichy government, signed a treaty with Hitler conceding French sovereignty over Madagascar to Germany for the purpose of Jewish resettlement. Madagascar was, however, out of reach of the Vichy government, and Laval was unable to deliver what he had promised. Meanwhile in London, General de Gaulle denounced the treaty, declared the island inseparable from France, and rushed to establish his bases there. After a few months of administrative and military confusion, Churchill, with de Gaulle's consent, ordered the British Navy to take Madagascar and hold it under British occupation for and on behalf of free France. The Madagascar plan had thus flopped. Throughout the war the island was under British occupation.

Meanwhile, in 1940 and 1941, in Nazi-occupied Poland, Jewish ghettos had been established, turning the massive Jewish population of that country (2,500,000) into camp inmates and slave laborers. After the failure of the Madagascar plan, trainloads of Jews from Austria, Bohemia, and later also from other Nazi-occupied Western countries started arriving at Poland's Jewish ghettos, too. However cruel, this new Nazi policy toward Jews was not yet that of a straightforward holocaust or, to use official Nazi terminology, the final solution of the Jewish problem.

It seems to me, and here I may be at odds with some historians of the holocaust, that the idea of the final solution of the Jewish problem by means of total physical extermination of the Jewish population of Europe struck the Nazis only after they had attacked the Soviet Union in June 1941 and witnessed there mass killings of Jews initiated and perpetrated by local inhabitants themselves. Used to Stalin's ways of dealing with real or alleged enemies, and knowing that the Nazis considered Jews and communists their avowed foes, some Soviet citizens in the territories abandoned by the retreating Red Army did not waste time in waiting for instructions from the new authorities, but started exterminating Jews and communists on their own.

It must be said that, at the time, a great many gentile Ukrainians, Byelorussians, and Great Russians themselves perceived the hated Communist Soviet regime as a Jewish conspiracy against their nations, attributing, in an undifferentiated manner (and thus entirely falsely), the responsibility for the enormous atrocities of Communist rule to the Jews. For them, as well as for many Lithuanians, Latvians, and Estonians, communism was a Jewish cause, and a gentile communist was, though their own compatriot, no more than a mere Jewish groveler.

Indeed, the advancing German troops were greeted as their liberators from "communist-Jewish" oppression by great numbers of Soviet gentiles, with tears of joy in their eyes and with bread and salt, the most honorific symbol of welcome in these lands, in their hands. No wonder that these "liberated" people immediately started to settle scores with those whom they considered their former oppressors in the Stalinist way of mass executions. They knew no other way and perhaps did not want to know.

Alfred Rosenberg, the newly appointed *Reichsminister* for the occupied Eastern territories, faced with the mass killings of Jews, started sending urgent telegrams to Berlin asking the dispatch to him of police reinforcements without which, he claimed, it was impossible to stop the arbitrary killings and restore order. In response, Berlin relieved Rosenberg of responsibility for policing the area and endowed Heinrich Himmler, the *Reichsführer* of the S.S. and the Chief of the German Police, with sole and exclusive authority over all police operations in the occupied territories of the USSR.

Instead of stopping the killings, Himmler decided to properly organize and control them, creating for this purpose the notorious *Sonderkommandos*, special police units manned mainly by locals who had already distinguished themselves in "Jew-killings," but led and supervised by S.S. officers of the reinforced *Einsatzgruppen*, the special S.S. units that moved behind the German Army (*Wehrmacht*) troops and took responsibility for security in the newly occupied areas. The task Himmler assigned to the *Sonderkommandos* was to carefully conduct an experiment with the view of establishing the possibility of accomplishing a planned and systematic extermination of the Jewish people. Apparently the Nazi leadership deemed these experiments entirely successful, for on January 20, 1942, at the Wannsee Conference of the Nazi party leaders, the final solution was formally, though secretly, endorsed as the official policy of the Third Reich. Only then did the holocaust in all seriousness begin. A whole mass-extermination industry was built up to serve its purpose. In the following three and one-half years, this industry managed to devour the lives of about six million European Jews.

III. WHO SHOULD BE HELD RESPONSIBLE?

Although the above story is based not so much on personal experience as on research of available documents, it is nevertheless a part of my personal perspective. As a survivor of the holocaust, I have spent a substantial part of my life trying to learn about and understand the genesis of this most horrendous crime in human history. It is common consensual knowledge that Hitler and the Nazis conceived and perpetrated the holocaust, and that therefore they have to bear full responsibility for it. This view is to me, as to most people, naturally and indisputably true. What I have tried to find out in my study is whether this is the whole truth and whether, indeed, the full and undivided responsibility for the holocaust can be laid exclusively and solely on Hitler's and the Nazis' doorstep. The negative conclusion at which I have arrived is neither original nor new, but it is not widely known and does not form a natural and indelible part of our usual consciousness of the holocaust. That is why I decided to concentrate in this lecture on the problem of who else, beside Hitler and the Nazis, could be held to some extent responsible for the holocaust, and to stress more strongly the aspect of collective responsibility for this tragedy.

Indeed, to some extent, at least, the then political leaders of the United States, Britain, and France share that responsibility, too. Conscious of, but for expedient political reasons oblivious to, the Jewish plight, they did very little to help the Jews to leave Germany, obstructed the establishment of a Jewish settlement in Madagascar and, by doing so, were in fact pushing Hitler toward adopting the final solution. No one in the West could, however, successfully compete with Stalin for a share of responsibility for the Jewish holocaust. By having mercilessly exterminated from 1929 to 1933 all the industrious Russian peasants, some 10 to 15 million of them, Stalin was the first to introduce the practice of "final solutions" into twentieth-century politics, making such solutions conceivable and practicable also to others. The first to learn Stalin's lessons about final solutions were naturally his own subjects, some of whom, after being "liberated" by the Nazis, indeed quite naturally and spontaneously engaged in merciless terror against those whom they deemed to be the culprits for their immense sufferings under Soviet rule. I very much doubt whether the Nazis, without having witnessed how "Stalin's disciples" in German-occupied Soviet territories started to deal with the local Jews, would ever have contemplated attempting what they euphemistically called the "final solution of the Jewish problem."

Hitler and his followers were actively supported by certain groups of people all over Europe, which is to say that these groups of non-Germans also have to share with Hitler and the Nazis the responsibility for the implementation of Nazi policies. What attracted these people to Hitler was his uncompromising anti-Semitic ideology, which they wholeheartedly shared. They rallied around Hitler, genuinely believing that by joining forces with the *Führer* they would save their nations and the entire world from destruction by the Jews. Although, except for Leon Degrelle's Rexist movement in Belgium, the pro-Nazi political parties in Europe were relatively small, they existed everywhere and consisted of many thousands of extremely active, ambitious, and committed people, who later provided Hitler's occupational administration with a reliable core of indigenous collaborators. Many more people, previously uninvolved with the Nazis, also aspired to join the Nazi administration of their occupied lands and were eager to work for Hitler's projected New Order. Generally, the Nazis found in every country they occupied *many* more willing collaborators than they were able to use, a fact that greatly surprised Hitler himself, as he admitted more than once in his *Table Talks*.

The holocaust of European Jewry was a secret policy. The Nazis were especially keen to keep it secret from the Germans themselves. Therefore, Hitler's death camps were set up in eastern Europe and manned mainly by non-Germans. Only very few top positions in these death camps were occupied by Germans, members of a select group from among the most trusted functionaries of Himmler's S.S. The rest of the camps' personnel—executioners, guards, supervisors, managers—were either local nationals or other foreigners. In Poland's death camps, for example, the Ukrainians and Latvians provided the bulk of the guards and executioners. In the Kaunas ghetto (Lithuania), where, before escaping, I was an inmate for two-and-a-half years, detachments of Russian volunteers serving with the Germans were used from 1943 to 1944 to perpetrate several most atrocious extermination actions against Jews imprisoned there. We also saw on "camp duty" the legionaries of Jacques Doriot, members of French "volunteer" detachments fighting for the Germans on the Eastern front, and encountered quite a few Dutchmen in German uniforms, most of them members of the Dutch homegrown Nazi-type parties, who were charged with the task of making good use of us as slave laborers in German enterprises that they ran. But, of course, the "regular" majority of our guards and executioners were local Lithuanians. Only the commandant of the ghetto, three shift chiefs of the ghetto guards, and the chief of the ghetto workshops were Germans.

It follows from the above that, although in overall charge of its organization and execution, the Germans were only a small minority of those who participated in the practical accomplishment of the Jewish holocaust. Of course, the Germans who were the main organizers of and leading figures in the "holocaust enterprise" have to bear a higher degree of responsibility for its perpetration than their subordinate accomplices, whether Germans or not. This higher degree of responsibility no doubt applies, in the first place, to the Nazi rulers themselves who took the decision about the holocaust, the middle-rank S.S. and Gestapo officials (such as Adolf Eichmann) who were assigned to organize the implementation of this decision, and to the commandants and other top executives in the death camps who took charge of that decision's practical execution.

The fact that these main culprits were German does not, however, implicate in their crime the rest of the German nation, which in most cases not only remained uninvolved, but even had no precise knowledge of what was being done to the Jews "over there, in the East." One could question the morality of those Germans who preferred such comfortable ignorance to disturbing knowledge, but by no means could one accuse them of direct complicity in the Nazis' crimes. And even when questioning the morality of such an "ignorant" stance, one should not forget how insecure, insignificant, and impotent people living under totalitarian regimes usually feel. One should also remember, when discussing the German guilt problem, that Hitler took office with the support of only just over one-third of the German electorate (36.5 percent in the election of July 1932, that fell to 33.1 percent in the November 1932 election, the last fair election held in Germany before the end of World War II), and that even from those who had voted for him in 1932 he did not receive a mandate for introducing the Nuremberg Laws, to say nothing about a full-fledged Jewish holocaust. Hitler was fully aware of the total illegitimacy of his action against the Jews in the eyes of the German nation, and that is why he so carefully, in a truly conspiratorial manner, hid the holocaust from the German people, choosing other nations' territories and manpower to put it into practice (the mass-deportation of Jews from Germany "to the East," where, upon arrival, they were exterminated, began in 1943 and was presented to the public as mobilization of Jews for works supporting the German army's efforts on the Eastern front).

The holocaust was indeed a conspiracy secretly planned and executed by an ideologically zealous ruling clique behind the back not only of the German nation, but also of the directly uninvolved membership of the Nazi party itself. No particular nation can be held responsible for such a conspiracy, but the members of all nations, Germans and non-Germans alike, who participated in it should be pronounced guilty of the parts they personally played in the execution of that mass-murderous conspiracy.

IV. THE GENTILES FACING THE JEWISH HOLOCAUST

In every occupied nation, Hitler's active collaborators were of course only a small minority. The overwhelming majority of people tried not to get involved, hated the occupiers, and were mainly minding their own business. Resenting the Nazis on all other accounts, some of these people to one degree or another approved, however, of the Nazi policy toward the Jews.

There are many eyewitness accounts of how zealously some ordinary passers-by, when seeing a Jew trying to escape from an inmates' column, raised the alarm and even assisted the guards to catch the hapless would-be escapee, or of how readily people denounced their Jewish neighbors. The story about the ubiquitous Paris *concierges* willingly denouncing Jews is too well known to be told here once more, but it is worth mentioning that these same *concierges* created an effective network for hiding French prisoners of war who managed to escape from Nazi camps.

There was, however, in every nation, a small minority of extremely noble and courageous people who simply could not remain indifferent to the deadly plight that had befallen their Jewish fellow human beings. Risking their own lives and the lives of their families, such people did everything they could to save the Jews from extermination. They helped the Jews to escape from the death camps, hid them and generously shared with the hidden ones their meager wartime food rations. Their sacrifice was immense, but they felt that if they did not make it they would lose something much more important to them than even life—their integrity and self-respect.

I, for example, was saved by a Lithuanian lower-middle-class family, the Macenaviciuses, who for a period of time hid, sheltered, and fed, besides me, five more Jewish escapees from the Kaunas ghetto and the Ninth Fort. My sister with her husband and mother-in-law were hidden by a Lithuanian foundry foreman, Vytautas Rinkevicius, in a hideout specially built in the attic of the foundry. Before the war we were not acquainted with either the Macenaviciuses or the Rinkeviciuses; nor did they know us and our families. After having successfully escaped from the ghetto, I was brought by a mutual friend to the Macenaviciuses to spend only one night at their home. But for both Antanas and Marija Macenavicius, the idea that I would leave them the next morning without having anywhere else to go was so unbearable that they invited me to stay with them and their daughter as long as it would be necessary.

As for Rinkevicius, my brother-in-law met him in the foundry to which he was assigned as a slave laborer. A warm relationship developed between the two men, the foreman and his mate on death-row. Increasingly, the foreman Rinkevicius felt that he must do his utmost to save his new friend and his family from certain death. And so, together, the two men started to build the hideout where my sister with her husband and mother-in-law were kept by Rinkevicius for nine long months. Every day during that time Rinkevicius risked his life and the lives of his wife and children—the penalty for helping Jews in Nazi-occupied Lithuania was summary execution, not just for the guilty person, but for his whole family.

In Nazi-occupied Lithuania, as everywhere else under Nazi rule, the gentile population, in regard to the Jews and the Holocaust, had divided into three distinct groups: one minority actively engaged in collaboration with the Nazis, helping them to persecute and annihilate the Jews; another minority devoted themselves to saving the Jews; and the majority in between tried to live their lives, ignoring, as much as that was at all possible, both the Nazis and the Jews. Among this majority also, as everywhere else in Europe, there were people who were more or less sympathetic or more or less hostile to the Jews; there were even a few who thought that the Jews fully deserved their punishment. But on the whole these people tried to be indifferent to the fate of the Jews, saying that whatever they felt, there was nothing they could do about it.

Of these three groups, the behavior of the indifferent majority and of the self-sacrificial minority is the easiest to understand. In both cases it was, as Nietzsche would have said, "human, all too human." But how does one account for the behavior of the Jew-killers? How could man do to a fellow human being what the Jew-killers did?

An eminent Lithuanian poet, Marcelijus Martinaitis, in a recent statement published by a periodical in Vilnius (*Sajudzio zinios*, August 20, 1988) dismissed the Lithuanian Jew-killers as mere human trash present in every nation and belonging to no one. Indeed, criminal and perverted elements—murderers, robbers, thieves, sadists, psychomaniacs, and also, of course, pathological anti-Semites—are a part of every nation, and it is true that the Nazi mass-murder industry provided these elements with a perfect outlet to realize with impunity their murderous and rapacious instincts.

It would suffice to remember in this context the sadistic deeds of "Ivan the Terrible," which the surviving witnesses so eloquently and frighteningly described at Ivan Demjanyuk's trial in Jerusalem. I also know of a number of people who had no special political or ideological grievances against the Jews, but who gladly joined the murderous *Sonderkommandos* in Lithuania because of their innate anti-Semitism and/or the ample opportunities the membership in these death squads offered for plundering Jewish households and for stealing hidden valuables found on the corpses of Jews who had just been executed.

But I know of totally different people who joined the *Sonderkommandos*, too. A captured former squad leader of the *Sonderkommando*, which operated during the war in the region of a southern Lithuanian town, Prienai, when asked at his trial in 1952 whether he was guilty of murdering people, proudly answered: "I have never killed people, I was only killing communists and Jews." Here was an idealist, proud of having taken an active part in the cleansing of the face of the earth of what he deemed to be subhuman scum undermining his nation's and the rest of mankind's existence; he was even a hero, ready to die for his convictions rather than to degrade himself by a false repentance and pleas for mercy with the hated and despised communist enemy. There were too many such "idealists" among the Lithuanian Jew-killers for Martinaitis plausibly to dismiss all of them as simply human trash. The problem with the Jew-killers in Lithuania is indeed much more complex than Martinaitis would have it.

It is a fact that more than half of the membership of the tiny pre-Soviet Lithuanian Communist Party, about eight hundred people, were Jews. It is also a fact that these Jewish communists in 1940 and 1941 played prominent roles in the Soviet occupation administration of Lithuania. The most notorious interrogators of the Lithuanian branch of the Soviet security police, the People's Commissariat of Internal Affairs (NKVD), were Lithuanian Jewish communists, and many such Jewish communists manned the NKVD detachments, which randomly arrested and deported to Siberia the alleged class enemies and other so-called anti-Soviet elements of Lithuania. The visibility of a few Jews in the ranks of Soviet occupation administration of Lithuania led many Lithuanians in an undifferentiated manner falsely to believe that "Soviet power" was in fact "Jewish power" and that the Lithuanian Jews had betrayed their country, assuming in it the role of Moscow's "fifth column." No wonder then that as soon as the Lithuanians got rid of the Soviets (this they did in a national uprising on the first day of the Soviet-German war, taking control of the country long before the German troops were able to occupy it), a series of wild Jewish pogroms broke out in the country, the first Jewish pogroms on Lithuanian soil in the whole 600-year-old history of Lithuanian–Jewish cohabitation. It is believed that in Kaunas alone 3,800 Jews were killed during these pogroms. Along with these spontaneous acts of violence, the Lithuanian rebel troops started indiscriminately arresting Jews for their "collaboration with the Soviets" in a more organized but not less random fashion. In Kaunas, the thus-arrested alleged Jewish collaborators of the Soviets were assembled in a huge garage and cruelly massacred there the next day. My father was one of the victims of that Lietukis garage massacre. The German troops marched into Kaunas on the day of this massacre only to witness the last instants of that bloody orgy.

A very nice, timid, and well-educated Lithuanian lady once confessed to me that, although very much ashamed of that feeling, she was unable to suppress her hatred of Jews, however much she tried. This hatred, she told me, started in the spring of 1941 when an NKVD squad, consisting of three Jewish men and one Jewish woman, came to arrest her parents, whom she never saw again. The head of this NKVD squad was a Jew whom the family considered a friend.

The always-simmering, irrational hatred of Jews, fueled by such and similar events, called powerfully for revenge, and resulted in the massive violence directed against the Jews in wartime Lithuania. Another Jew-killer brought to trial in Soviet Lithuania in 1962 was asked in court: "Why did you shoot Jews?" His answer was: "Because in 1941 in Pravieniskis (a Soviet concentration camp in Lithuania) I was pulled out from under a mountain of corpses. In most cases the people who were shooting us were Jews."

Quoting such and similar facts, a contemporary Lithuanian samizdat author, A. Zuvintas, writes: "All this led the Lithuanians, who had lived peacefully for centuries together with the Jews, in the course of a single year literally to come to hate them . . . The Jews went too far . . . Within only a single year the innocent mockery of Jewish nature, speech and customs grew into a feeling of hatred. Can one really be surprised that with the beginning of the war there also began Jewish pogroms? . . . My letter is not an attempt to even the scores . . . I simply want to emphasize that the pogroms were only a response and that the first step was taken, in fact, by the Jews" (published in English, in *Cross Currents*, no. 8 [1989]: 65–66).

Indeed, the Lithuanians, as all the other people who were subjugated to Soviet rule and genuinely but mistakenly confused it with "Jewish rule," are entitled to put forward such motives in explanation of the behavior of their Jew-killers during World War II. Members of the nations that were not subject to Soviet rule, such as the Poles, the Croatians, the French, the Belgians and others, and who nevertheless produced proportionally no fewer Jew-killers than the Lithuanians, have no such explanations to offer. But are these explanations really valid? I am convinced that they are not.

These explanations are based on the false assumption that what some Jews have done wrongly makes the rest of the Jews automatically guilty for those wrongdoings. There were 240,000 Jews living in Lithuania before the war, 8 percent of Lithuania's total population. The overwhelming majority of these people were strictly orthodox Jews who had nothing in common with the communists and were as hostile to them as any true religious believer may be. Only a handful of assimilation-oriented Lithuanian Jews became communists or communist sympathizers, no more than two thousand or, at the most, three thousand of them, a tiny minority (about 1 percent) of the Jewish minority of Lithuania. What is most striking to me is that not only the Jew-killers and Jew-haters but even objective people like Zuvintas have entirely overlooked the fact that the Jews were persecuted by the Soviets on, proportionally, even a grander scale than were the gentile Lithuanians, which was only to be expected because the Soviets were fighting the bourgeoisie, and the bourgeois class in Lithuania was predominantly Jewish. Not less than 20 percent of the Lithuanians brutally deported in June 1941 to Siberia (altogether 34,200 people) were Jewish, that is two-and-a-half times more than their proportion in Lithuania's population; in the mountain of corpses in Pravieniskis concentration camp from under which Matiukas, the Jew-killer quoted above, emerged alive, there were, along with Lithuanian corpses, many Jewish corpses, too: Jewish and Lithuanian communists were shot indiscriminately by Lithuanian and Jewish anticommunists without making a difference between their nationalities or religions. How then, in the light of these facts, could an enlightened person like Zuvintas state that the Jews took the first step by oppressing and killing Lithuanians under the Soviets, and that thus the Jewish pogroms perpetrated by Lithuanians afterward were a mere response on their part to these Jewish acts? Is Zuvintas really unable to distinguish between the communist terror, directed at no one nation in particular and, at the same time, at all of them—be they Lithuanian, Russian, or Jewish—with the view of perverting and bastardizing their true national selves; and the Nazi terror aimed at the annihilation of one particular nation, the Jews? If this is so, if even people like Zuvintas fail to understand that it is preposterous to portray the communist terror in Lithuania in 1940 and 1941 as a joint Jewish–Russian enterprise for the annihilation of the Lithuanian people, and that, in fact, the communist terror of those days was jointly conducted by a few Russian, Jewish, and Lithuanian (yes, Lithuanian!) adherents of the Soviet regime against the majorities of all these and other nations impulsively resisting communist subversion of their authentic integrity, then what can one say about the others who are much less sophisticated and much more guided by their instincts?

The same indiscriminate accusations of entire nations of the murderous acts perpetrated by some members of those nations, either because of their ideological blindness or for the attainment of personal gain, are not alien to the Jews either. Don't we hear from some Jews that the entire German nation should be held responsible for the holocaust, although, as I pointed out above, most Germans, in contrast with the Lithuanians, Poles, Ukrainians, Russians, and other East Europeans in whose territories the holocaust was executed, did not even know much about the final solution, let alone the massive, industrial scale of its implementation? Are there not enough Jews convinced that the Poles, Lithuanians, Ukrainians, and other peoples in whose territories the mass exterminations of Jews took place are in their entirety the nations of Jew-killers and Jew-haters, despite the undisputable facts that so many Jews were saved by the members of these nations and that the majorities of these nations were uninvolved in the Jewish holocaust at all?

I sometimes wonder how the Jews would have behaved if they had changed places with the Lithuanians after the holocaust. Would there have been fewer Jewish Lithuanian-killers than there were Lithuanian Jew-killers? Would there have been as many Jews ready to risk their lives and the lives of their families in order to save Lithuanians as there were Lithuanians who did so for the Jews? I doubt it. What I am, however, sure about is that the majority of the Jews, as was the case with the majority of Lithuanians, would try to stay out of the whole bloody business of the holocaust. Not a very moral position but much better than involvement in vengeance and death.

V. OVERCOMING THE LEGACY OF THE HOLOCAUST AVERTING NEW HOLOCAUSTS

The holocaust affected very deeply indeed both the Jews and the gentiles who lived through it. Its traumatic experiences and subsequent complexes are very difficult for all sides to overcome. Perhaps the worst legacy of the holocaust is the increased tendency on all sides to ascribe collective guilt to entire nations and groups, and the enhanced unwillingness, also on all sides, to differentiate between the guilty, innocent and virtuous individuals who were present in all the nations involved, including the Germans and the Jews themselves, not to mention the Poles, Lithuanians, and other lesser protagonists of that awful bloody drama of European history.

After the demise of Nazism and the imminent disintegration of communism, this legacy could provide a fertile ground for the emergence of yet another global ideology or conflicting ideologies based on a new version of the confrontation between the virtuous "us" and vicious "them," whoever these new "us" and "them" may be. This could lead to another disaster. As the prominent Lithuanian poet and essayist Tomas Venclova has pointed out: "Whoever sets apart a particular group of people—national, religious, class, or any other group—and considers himself spiritually in no way related to this group, in essence is preparing a pogrom, concentration camp or totalitarian system. This is as basic and true as a–b–c" (T. Venclova, "Jews and Lithuanians," *Cross Currents*, no. 8 [1989]: 59).

Could such a new disaster be averted? I am sure it could, if all of us who either have gone through the experience of the holocaust or feel it to be a part of our own experience, would try as hard as we can to come at last to grips with that experience, lessen our partisanship and start looking at our own particular part and fate in the holocaust in more objective terms than before. There are hopeful signs that such a fruitful and calm reassessment of the holocaust is already taking place.

Poland is one nation in which this process has already acquired momentum. Two years ago, Jan Blonski, an eminent Polish literary critic, published in the Catholic weekly, *Tygodnik Powszechny*, an article that has reverberated throughout the country and set the tone for the now already ongoing process of bringing together the Jewish and Polish views of the holocaust. In that article Blonski said the following: "We admitted the Jews into our home, but we sent them to live in the cellar. At long last, we lost our home, and in that home the occupiers began to slay the Jews. How many of us concluded it was none of our business? Had we acted more wisely, more nobly, more like Christians, then the holocaust would probably have been "more inconceivable," more difficult to carry out, and would certainly have been opposed more boldly. Jewish blood remains on our walls and is soaked into our ground, whether we like it or not. It has soaked into our memory, into ourselves. We must honestly and boldly face the question of our responsibility. We should stop pointing out those things we could not possibly do . . . We should first say: 'Yes, we are guilty. . . . '" Commenting on that article, another Polish Catholic writer, Pawel Spiwak, himself half-Jewish, said in an interview: "At last, someone admitted that we are responsible, in a moral sense, for what happened. We have always been taught that Poles are victims. Now we find that we Poles could have made victims of others. It's healthy. It means we're normal" (*Wall Street Journal*, vol. 208, no. 2 [1989]).

Similar voices are heard also from Lithuania. The tone for the discussion there was set by Tomas Venclova in a 1976 *samizdat* article, "The Jews and Lithuanians," which in 1989 was reprinted in the official Soviet press, the organ of the Lithuanian SSR's Writers' Union, *Literatura ir Menas*. In this article Venclova wrote: "Nothing on earth will change the fact that at the end of June 1941 some Lithuanians, in front of the very eyes of a crowd of Lithuanians, annihilated defenseless people, even the fact that in the twentieth century many, almost all peoples, have done something similar. And I, a Lithuanian, am obliged to speak of Lithuanian guilt. Sadism and looting, hatred and shameful indifference to people cannot be justified; worse—they cannot be explained, they live in such dark corners of personal and national consciousness that to search for their rational origins is a fruitless labor. . . . One must not dump one's own guilt on other nations. They will figure out their own guilt. We must figure out our guilt and repent for ourselves. Properly speaking, this is what it means to belong to one nation or another. . . . We must understand forever that the destruction of the Jews is the destruction of ourselves, that the offense to the Jews is an offense to ourselves, that the liquidation of Jewish culture is an attempt on our own. . . . We lived together for six hundred years; perhaps this time is coming to an end; at such a time we cannot be hostile or indifferent. We do not have the right to claim that Jewish affairs do not concern us. Each and every outbreak of anti-Semitism concerns us" (*Cross-Currents*, 59).

Not knowing of any such words coming from a Jewish writer's pen, I feel it to be my duty to start filling this gap. Yes, we Jews lived together with our gentile hosts—Germans, Poles, Lithuanians, and others—for many centuries. We speak their languages, we are a part of their history and culture. There were some mutual grievances between us, but they cannot overshadow our commonality or change the fact that we are continuing to move together along the same path. Anti-Semitism is horrible, as anti-Germanism, anti-Polishness, anti-Lithuanianism, and all other "antis" are horrible. But it would be wrong on our part to pretend that all anti-Semitism is born merely in pure fantasy and prejudice of the gentiles, and does not at all, even in part, represent an exaggerated reaction to the real wrongs that some of us really did. As a Jew, I must reject the assumption that we Jews forever were just the faultless and powerless victims of other peoples' abuse and injustices, and must admit our own true faults, such as, for example: our certain insensitivity to some of the grave problems facing our gentile landsmen; our self-centeredness that only too often urged some of us to seek our particular goals without giving much consideration to how the achievement of these goals would affect the interests of others; the frivolousness that more than once led quite a number of us to assume that what is good for Jews must be even better for the gentiles. Too many of us, led by such considerations, were more than ready thoughtlessly to engage ourselves in all kinds of subversive and revolutionary activities threatening the integrity and even survival of our host countries. For this we have to confess our guilt. We must understand forever that the losses and defeats of our host nations are our own losses and defeats, and that their gains are also ours; that by the will of history we form with them, for better or worse, one people, and have to think and behave accordingly.

This lecture was meant to provide a Jewish contribution, however modest, to the nascent worldwide reassessment of the holocaust and its legacy initiated by my gentile counterparts, such as Blonski and Venclova. I tried to make my presentation as impartial and objective as it is at all possible for a Jewish survivor of the holocaust to do. Whether I succeeded or not is not for me to judge. I did what I could to avoid taking sides, either Jewish or gentile, and to side, as much as I could, with the truth which, I assume, none of the parties concerned is willing to reject.

2

Making Sense of Stalin

ALEKSANDRAS SHTROMAS

> Neither irrational nor ideologically incoherent, Stalin climbed to power in
> Russia in order to ensure the survival of Bolshevism.

Many traps await anyone bold enough to undertake a study of Stalin. One is
easily tempted to treat him as a paranoiac whose acts were both unnecessary
and irrational from any politically or ideologically coherent point of view.
One could accept uncritically the influential views on Stalin of his former associates, Trotsky, and Bukharin, as the prominent historians Isaac Deutscher
and E. H. Carr have done. Trotsky thought that Stalin was "the outstanding
mediocrity in the Party,"[1] and Bukharin claimed that Stalin was "not interested in anything except power."[2] He achieved that power, Trotsky argued,
through his domination "of an impersonal bureaucratic machine . . . which
had 'created him,'"[3] and used him as a champion of a thus newly created
privileged caste of bureaucrats.[4]

　　Alex de Jonge has happily avoided these temptations. His Stalin is a rational
and careful Bolshevik politician, who knew exactly what he wanted and who
pursued his goals with remarkable farsightedness and consistency. De Jonge

Reprinted from Aleksandras Shtromas, "Making Sense of Stalin," *The World and I*, vol. 1, no. 8
(August 1986): 432–44.

demonstrates that Marxism gave the Bolsheviks "a monopoly upon the truth," which meant that for them "everything was permitted." They saw themselves as an "enlightened minority acting on behalf of the majority ignorant of its best interests. . . . It behooved them, in the interests of humanity, never to relinquish their grasp. There could never be any question of 'consensus politics. . . .' [T]here could and can be no question of permitting a diversity of political opinion or seeking a popular mandate. . . . The party could never expect popular support, and it recognized that given the chance, an unenlightened populace would tear its leaders limb from limb; hence the need for the tightest of controls."[5] All this was supposed to be a temporary malaise, lasting only until the Bolshevik Party, in accordance with its scientific Marxist vision, could eventually build the "radiant future" for all the people to enjoy and, with hindsight, also to appreciate the party's once unpopular efforts to bring it about. "In the meantime," therefore, "for the party to relax its powers would be to betray a trust."[6] Within this frame of reference, de Jonge rightly notes, "readiness to kill for the cause was a sign that one was a good Bolshevik, free from bourgeois morality and ready to sacrifice the means to the end."[7] And in this sense, as in others, Stalin was indeed a perfect Bolshevik, in no way different from Lenin and Trotsky, both of whom "from the outset held terror to be a crucial instrument of government."[8] De Jonge approvingly notes Angelica Balabanoff's description of Stalin's later crimes as "links in a chain that had already been forged by 1920."[9] To that one could only add that Stalin's determination to pursue the Bolshevik cause by whatever means in his power was much more unbending and vigorous than either Lenin's or Trotsky's. Unlike these typical members of the Russian intelligentsia, Stalin was not an intellectual, but a practical "simple man" who would not allow any "abstract" moral scruples or humanistic considerations to interfere with his business. Stalin, therefore, was much more of an ideal Bolshevik than Lenin could ever have aspired to be. Ronald Hingley writes that "it is Lenin, rather, who emerges as a somewhat ineffectual Stalin-in-embryo."[10]

This observation provides an immediate glimpse of the rationale of Stalin's annihilation of the Old Bolsheviks who were predominantly members of that *myagkotelaya* (flabby) intelligentsia. According to de Jonge, "in terms of personal strategy Stalin was right to mount an attack upon the older generation of party members. It was there that a potential opposition might yet be found, and their removal would create vacancies for the Stalin generation to fill."[11] Stalin indeed was right in mounting that attack against the Old Bolsheviks, but not only in terms of personal strategy. There was much more to it. The justified fear that always haunted the Bolsheviks, de Jonge stresses, was "the fear of splitting the party and bringing it down, at which point no one's head would be safe."[12] Stalin realized better than anybody else that in this sea of popular hostility, nothing short of total subordination of the party's personnel to one sole leader, endowed with absolute authority, would be able to keep the party united, save Bolshevik rule, make it achieve its goals, and function properly. The Old Bolshevik intellectuals, quite good at subordination to one man's military-type command when launching risky attacks against entire sections of population entrenched in traditional social structures, would hardly agree to relinquish their role as policymakers and reduce themselves to the position of simple cogs in the party machine in the day-to-day running of the established socialist order that they felt was their collective creation. This is to say that after the collectivization of agriculture (and, with it, all the other active revolutionary tasks) was accomplished, the Old Bolshevik intellectuals had to go. There was simply no place for them in the ruling stratum of a routinely functioning socialist state—with the exception of those few on whose unswerving loyalty and submissiveness the sole ruler could entirely rely.

Simply to relieve these people from positions of power and authority was clearly not enough. Most of the Old Bolsheviks had established political names, hosts of supporters, friends, and sympathizers both within and outside the party—assets that they could use in self-defense even more effectively when out of office than within the self-disciplining apparatus of rule. Hence, they had to be eliminated from society altogether—to relieve them from their offices and leave them at large would create more problems than it would solve. It was the logic of the system, not the peculiar character of Stalin, that demanded the relegation of the Old Bolshevik intellectuals and their supporters to the gallows and labor camps. An entirely new flock of fully obedient administrators, handpicked by Stalin and owing their promotion "from rags to riches" solely to him, were readily available to replace them in the party and state establishment. This is what the Great Purges of 1935–1938 did indeed accomplish. "The system," as de Jonge rightly indicates, "created a form of natural selection, the survival of the most ruthless,"[13] and, one should add, of the most servile. In another place he concludes that "among Stalin's many achievements, by no means the least remarkable is his bringing on a generation of party men able enough still to be governing the Soviet Union nearly half a century later."[14]

When Stalin was so sternly and persistently promoting himself to the position of sole and supreme ruler of the USSR, his motives were not altogether selfish either. He knew only too well that no other member of the ruling Politburo was suitable for that role and that if any of them achieved supreme power, the whole Bolshevik enterprise would be fatally wrecked.

Indeed, under Trotsky, with his dogmatic reliance on the proletariat and his naive belief in inner-party democracy, the party would have degenerated into a semiparliamentary body not only lacking both the determination and will to implement his own radical policies, but inevitably becoming a vehicle for capitalist restoration; moreover, Trotsky's romantic commitment to world revolution would have forced the USSR into a major conflict with the leading capitalist powers before it was prepared to do so. This might have proven lethal to the Bolshevik cause. Bukharin, on the other hand, by tolerating private enterprise and making constant concessions to it, would most certainly have ensured the restoration of capitalism and the subsequent degeneration of the Soviet Party state into a bourgeois one. Unlike the theoretically "abstract-minded"

Bukharin—who genuinely, though unrealistically, believed that in conditions of free competition, socialism, as a system generating higher productivity, would naturally beat capitalism—Stalin concluded that in the Russia of that time the only way in which capitalism could be beaten by socialism was through political coercion and terror of mass proportions. As for the other potential contenders—Zinoviev, Kamenev, and Pyatakov—they so obviously lacked the qualities necessary for leadership that they were not even worthy of being seriously considered. Hence, it was not so much Stalin's personal ambitions as it was the best interest of the Bolshevik cause that demanded that he assume total power. As a true Bolshevik, in order to prevent his competitors from ruining the socialist experiment in the USSR, he had to do so, whether he really wanted to or not.

The supposition of de Jonge that Stalin was naturally defiant of any authority[15] and was bound by his character to seek unlimited power contradicts his own evidence. In fact, de Jonge had convincingly demonstrated that for many years Stalin unreservedly accepted the authority of Lenin and, in Lenin's absence, during the first few months after the February Revolution of 1917, the authority of Kamenev. He knew his place in the party hierarchy and had never broken the rules of subordination. It was only after a few years of close collaboration within the Soviet power establishment with the other Bolshevik leaders, none of whom he knew well before 1917, that he took their proper measure and gradually came to the conviction that none of these high-minded intellectuals, including Lenin himself, were sufficiently strong and realistic to provide the kind of leadership that could assure the victory of the Bolshevik cause. It was only then that he defied the authority of the party with his insubordination.

From de Jonge's detailed analysis of Stalin's conflict with Lenin over the Georgian question in 1922, we learn about the first instance of Stalin's drastically and openly challenging Lenin.[16] Stalin upheld his challenge until he was formally defeated by the majority of the party's Central Committee, who supported Lenin. Stalin's dismissive attitude toward Lenin was expressed in his spontaneous reaction to the late leader's *Testament*, in which Lenin refused to invest with sole authority any of the remaining members of the Politburo, including Stalin, and opted instead for a weak collective leadership that, in Stalin's view, threatened the very survival of the Soviet state: "Couldn't even die like a *real* leader," he was heard to mutter.[17]

From at least 1922 Stalin was firmly convinced that the cause of Bolshevism could be saved, and could triumph, only under his rule. It is difficult to deny that he was right. There was hardly another Bolshevik that could do the trick. Even Lenin could not. Ronald Hingley asks, "Was J. V. Stalin—were the 'phenomena' associated with his cult—really necessary?" He answers without hesitation: "Yes, if Leninism was to survive."[18]

Convincingly and in sufficient detail, de Jonge shows how skillfully Stalin eliminated all contenders for leadership and consolidated absolute power. With Zinoviev and Kamenev, he disposed of Trotsky. Then, by associating with Bukharin's moderate policies of gradually building "socialism in one country," he smashed Zinoviev and Kamenev, together with the whole "Left opposition" that at a later stage again included Trotsky. Having done that, "Stalin elegantly assumed their policies as he moved against Bukharin and the right."[19] By 1929 Stalin's victory over all his rivals was complete and needed only to be firmly consolidated by the Great Purges of the later 1930s.

Again de Jonge rightly concludes that such seemingly devious tactics do not mean that Stalin was seeking power for power's sake only. "Anything but a mere opportunist, he had a vision of the Soviet state, not only one which he would succeed in realizing but also one which endured long after his own death, serving to determine the shape of the country as we know it."[20] As a true Bolshevik, Stalin was indeed more than a mere megalomaniac; he was a firm and ardent believer in Marxism, in the bright socialist future of mankind. If he had a personal ambition, it was that he go down in history as the pioneer of that bright future, the man who first attained the radiant goal of socialism in one huge, continent-like country—setting the model for all the others. Maybe this personal ambition can explain the urgency with which he launched his "revolution from above" that enabled him, by 1936, to declare "the full victory of socialism in the USSR."

To sum up the arguments about Stalin's ideological convictions, de Jonge refers to a memo that he discovered in the British Foreign Office Archives. It was dictated by Gavrilovic, the Yugoslav ambassador to London: "Stalin has a fanatical belief in Marxist doctrine as resting on scientific laws which it is necessary to discover, elucidate, and follow carefully in order to succeed. He believes himself to be presiding over the vastest experiment in human history; he sees it as the birth of a child and dismisses the terrible birth throes as inevitable and certain to be forgotten after the child is born. . . . Stalinism . . . may be regarded as the pure and concentrated essence of a virtually infallible doctrine."[21]

This, I believe, provides the key to understanding all the otherwise rationally inexplicable policies that Stalin pursued both in domestic and foreign domains with such ardor and zeal—beginning with the super-industrialization and collectivization of the 1920s and early 1930s, and ending with the anticosmopolitan campaign of the late 1940s and the "Doctors' Plot" on the eve of his death in 1953.

COLONIAL INFERIORITY COMPLEX

Although the above picture of Stalin is based on arguments used by de Jonge, it reflects my own views to a much greater extent than it does his. His Bolshevist Marxism notwithstanding, de Jonge's Stalin is first and foremost one of those Georgians who assumed a Great Russian identity and, as is typical of colonials aspiring to assimilate with the imperial nation, became "more Russian than the Russians."[22] From 1917 onward, he steadfastly pursued policies "based on Great Russian dominance"[23] and, in time, even gave free rein to "blind Russian chauvinism."[24] Although de Jonge does not say so directly, it appears that in his view Stalin adopted Bolshevist Marxism only insofar as it provided him with an adequate ideological and political instrument for furthering the most ambitious Russian nationalist-imperial goals.

I, for one, find that to view Stalin as, at heart, a genuine Russian patriot is profoundly and dangerously erroneous. Stalin's colonial inferiority complex, from which de Jonge so heavily draws his arguments, in fact testifies against the author's thesis. Stalin was one of those colonials who, because of his "incurable" heavy accent and apparent "foreignness," could never have even aspired to become an organic part of the Great Russian ethnic milieu. Being unable to adjust to Russia, Stalin embarked on the course of adjusting Russia to himself, that is, to his globally conceived Bolshevik cause. And this is what he did with such staggering success and with total disregard for Russia and her best interests.

Similarly misleading in my view is de Jonge's claim that Stalin had by 1904 "[turned] his back upon Georgian culture" and identified himself "with the Muscovite heartland."[25] Indeed, de Jonge admits that "Stalin's admiration for Great Russian values never extended to the intelligentsia."[26] What then were those supposedly Great Russian values that commanded his admiration? Were they proletarian or peasant? At the time, Russia was industrially backward and contained few proletarian values worthy of admiration. Stalin himself prevented these values from ever developing. The Russian peasantry, whom Stalin destroyed, along with all their values, bestowed on him the nickname of *muzhikoborets*, the "murderer of peasants."[27] The great poet Osip Mandelstam attributed the name to him, and it will remain connected with his name as long as it is remembered. Perhaps the subject of Stalin's admiration was the czarist imperial state or the Russian aristocracy? But these were exactly the forces he wished to destroy. He also intended to destroy Orthodox Christianity, which he had so vehemently rejected in his seminary days.

Stalin felt nothing but hatred and contempt for Russia and all her national values. As an ardent Georgian nationalist,[28] he had learned to hate Russia and her imperial state in his early youth. He learned to despise Russia later, when as a Marxist revolutionary, he spent many years in the ethnic heartland of the country, mainly as an exile but also as a professional party worker. Here he acquired an intimate knowledge of the clumsiness and ineffectiveness of both the Russian people and the czarist state machine. Stalin's hateful and contemptuous attitude about Russia never changed. It only hardened. After all, Russia was the most difficult stumbling block in his endeavour to build "socialism in one country." It was the Russian nation with its imbued conservative outlook that he had to fight and defeat in order to achieve his great goal. In 1946, when Harold Wilson was a junior British trade minister, he recalls an exchange between Stalin and Mikoyan (an Armenian). Disturbed that something was not being properly handled, Stalin concluded by exclaiming, "To hell with the bloody Russians!" It was also typical of Stalin to say, when shaken in June 1941 by Hitler's sudden attack on the USSR and fearing his country's defeat in the war, "Now all Lenin's work will be undone forever,"[29] without even mentioning the likely fate of Russia and her people should Hitler succeed. Stalin expressed his profound contempt for the Russian people most derisively at the end of the war. He raised his glass in a mock toast to the "great Russian people" and thanked them for the enormous patience with which they had endured his government.[30]

Stalin recognized, however, the immense power that was inherent in the sheer size of Russia, the vast number of her people, and the enormous wealth of her natural resources. With his appreciation of these facts, Stalin acknowledged the futility of the Georgian nationalist struggle and sought an alternative revolutionary course powerful enough to subvert the Russian Empire as a whole. He found this course naturally enough in revolutionary Marxism, and wholeheartedly embraced its universal call for a socialist revolution. At that time all Marxists believed that Russia was on the eve of a revolution but only a few, among them Lenin and the Bolsheviks, thought her ready for a socialist transformation. Stalin was one of these few. He thought that Russia was uniquely suited not only for carrying out that coming revolution to its socialist conclusion, but also for sustaining socialism for as long as it would take to transform the rest of the world to socialism.

For Stalin, the possibility of building socialism in one country, if that country was as huge, as self-sufficient, and as socially lax as Russia, was the very substance of revolutionary Marxism and on that score—as far as the principle, not its implementation, was concerned—there was between him and Lenin no discrepancy whatsoever.

In this scheme Georgia, or for that matter any other small nation, did not have a separate role or place. All of them were destined to follow the same path and, if it was for Russia to lead the way to socialism, it was to Russia that these smaller nations had to look. In this sense one could say that Stalin indeed turned his back upon Georgia, although in his own view this was not so—the liberation of Georgia had now simply become a constituent part of a qualitatively larger liberation plan for all nations. It was the global cause of socialism that he embraced instead, not that of Russia's greatness and glory for which he could not care less.

This is not to deny the fact strongly stressed by de Jonge that Stalin, especially during and after World War II, gradually incorporated some elements of the Russian statist and xenophobic tradition into the official ideology and policies of the Soviet socialist state. There was, however, nothing in these moves that could have undermined or weakened the Bolshevik substance of Stalin's Soviet Party state. On the contrary, Stalin sought to strengthen the foundations of this sectarian state by luring the Russians into believing that it was their own national institution. By elevating anti-Semitism to official policy, he aimed at dispelling the conviction, common among the Russians, that the Soviet Party state was a Jewish imposition upon their country. At the same time, by associating the "Jewish wreckers" with the capitalist West, he sought to exploit the deeply in-grained anti-Semitism of the Russians in order to rally their support for his Bolshevik anti-Western policies. Stalin presented the policies as a defense against foreign enemies who were nurturing plans to attack Russia. Having been forced by the extreme circumstances of the war to rehabilitate a great part of the Russian state's historical legacy, after the war Stalin tried to use this legacy as best he could for reinforcing his own brand of sectarian, globally conceived Bolshevik policies that had nothing in common with authentic Russian national interests and goals.

Playing with the idea of Russian nationalism, Stalin induced many people, within the party as much as without, to proclaim their true national aspirations and to press the regime to incorporate them into its policies. These attempts, aimed in fact at transforming the Soviet Party state into an authentic govern-ment of Russia, were indeed extremely dangerous to the Bolshevik cause, and Stalin treated them accordingly. For this kind of nationalism Stalin had no con-cessions to offer, only swift and merciless repression. The mass arrests and ex-ecutions of 1949 aimed at destroying the Russian nationalist opposition in em-bryo are known in Soviet history as the "Leningrad Case," a term that is misleading: many of those arrested and shot in that case were leading figures of other provincial party organizations. Among these were not only N. Vozne-sensky (a Politburo member and Gosplan chairman formerly from Leningrad) but also the chairman of the RSFSR's Council of Ministers, M. Rodionov and many others who had no connections with Leningrad whatsoever. De Jonge mentions this new purge only in passing and fails to recognize its true nature. For him, as indeed for many other researchers, this purge was merely the re-sult of the feud between the Zhdanov and Malenkov factions in the party, in which the former, based in Leningrad, was thoroughly defeated.[31]

Even more disturbing than Stalin's branding as a Russian nationalist are, in my opinion, de Jonge's continuous assertions about the Russian nation's willing assent to Bolshevik rule in general and to Stalin's leadership in par-ticular. Defying the contrary evidence amply available in his own book, de Jonge boldly asserts that the Bolsheviks in Russia "enjoyed widespread sup-port from 1917 onwards."[32] The hard evidence shows that at the very high-est peak of their popularity, in November 1917, the Bolsheviks were able to get only somewhat less than 25 percent of the popular vote.[33] According to de Jonge, Stalin's atrocities did not affect Bolshevik popularity at all. In his view, the Soviet people easily assented to Stalin's terror from the late 1920s to the early 1930s,[34] as well as through the Great Purges of the second half of the 1930s[35] and all the other outbursts of Stalin's mass exterminations and repressions, seeing them as justified and necessary "as long as they were happening to someone else."[36] Apparently, to de Jonge's Western mind it is inconceivable that a government could operate freely and ruthlessly for sev-eral decades without enjoying or even caring for getting substantial popular support, so inconceivable that, whatever the evidence, he would regardless have come to the conclusions that "Stalin could never have succeeded had he gone "against the grain of his nation's culture,"[37] and that "he enjoyed a nationwide support at every level because he and his style of government were popular; he was truly a dictator of the people."[38]

What de Jonge apparently fails to realize is the fact that the Soviet Party state by its very nature is bound to be the state of a self-serving clique determined to assert itself and to promote its sectarian interests and goals at all costs and, if necessary, in direct confrontation with the whole nation under its imposed rule. This strikes me as especially strange because in many other places in his book de Jonge quite explicitly expresses that same idea.

In trying to explain this peculiar "assent" of the Russians to the indiscriminate terror waged against them, de Jonge rightly and convincingly invokes the extreme atomization of Russian society achieved by Stalin and the Bolsheviks during the years preceding the collectivization of agriculture. Had he stopped at that, there would be no need for him either to use the word "assent" or to look for any other explanations. But it is "assent" on which he insists and because of that he has to stretch his arguments in such a way that they could provide some substantiation for his indefensible thesis that Stalin won the Russians' "universal love through fear."[39] For example, he maintains that the Russians have, throughout their whole history, relished in reporting friends and neighbors to the authorities and that they therefore were delighted when Stalin elevated this activity to the level of a mass national sport.[40] Such passages as these, aimed at denigrating the Russians as a nation, permeate the whole book. The cumulative effect of all this is that the Russian people are depicted as belonging to a species different from that of normal human beings. All this leaves the reader somewhat bewildered, to say the least.

There is no need to debate this issue any further but one should perhaps stress that in fact the Russians under Stalin's regime behaved as any other nation in a socially-atomized state have behaved or would have behaved under the rule of sheer terror. No nation had, however, ever been exposed to terror on such a scale and for such a length of time as the Russians, and this in itself may be regarded as evidence of the real extent of the Russians' assent to Bolshevik rule. After all, in a number of places in his book partly referred to in the first part of this review, de Jonge himself stresses that Stalin and the Bolsheviks were ruling an almost entirely hostile population that, if opportunity had offered it a chance, would tear them "limb from limb."

In fact de Jonge renders a somewhat schizophrenic picture of both Stalin and his people. On the one hand, Stalin the Bolshevik, confronted by the wrath of the overwhelming majority of his people, squelches this wrath by means of mass terror. On the other, Stalin the Russian chauvinist enjoys the enthusiastic support of that same overwhelming majority. These two pictures of Stalin do not square. However much the author tries to present a consistent portrait, it remains confused, contradictory, and, ultimately, unconvincing. This is a situation to be applauded rather than deplored, for it will certainly help the readers of the book to reject de Jonge's utterly false message that the *true* monster, the *real* implacable enemy of the West lurking behind the villainy of the Stalinist system, might be the Russian nation itself.

CRUDE REDUCTIONS

Among de Jonge's explanations of the peculiar character of the Russians, his concept of "geoalcoholics"[41] is particularly crude. His explanation is that Russia's main problem was a "geoalcoholic" structure within which there was no place for a beer belt; as a result of this lack of a beer belt, the Protestant work ethic, allegedly evolved only by beer drinkers, failed to develop. Since only the use of compulsion, characteristic of the Soviet style of government, could "take the place of a nonexistent work ethic,"[42] de Jonge believes that the Soviet regime in Russia was indeed "necessary," though he disclaims any adherence to theories advocating historic necessities. Moreover, it would have evolved much along the same lines, with or without Stalin.[43] To be sure, "without Stalin the Soviet Union might have boasted fewer untimely deaths, but it is unlikely that it would have been less brutal. . . . Russia could never have become a superpower without a coercive regime."[44] This is being seriously contended in spite of the commonly known fact that Russia turned in its best economic performance (as did all other nations) during those relatively short periods of time when it possessed, at least in part, a liberal, market-based economy—that is, at the turn of this century (prior to the outbreak of World War I) and under the New Economic Policy (NEP).

I also find grossly inept the paradigm of a large Western corporation that de Jonge uses for explaining the substance of the Soviet regime. Operating as it does in a competitive market and coexisting in one political order with other similar bodies, such a corporation simply cannot be compared with the total Soviet state. Even a paradigm based on the *Cosa Nostra*, although much closer, would suffice only with the proviso that this body had assumed political power, had become the sole legal authority of the land, and had managed to eliminate all other groups and autonomous enterprises.

Besides such dubious concepts, de Jonge's work is also full of various inaccuracies.

Indeed, one would have to be completely ignorant of the true nature of Georgii Plekhanov, the founding father of the *European* moderate Marxist tradition that prevailed in the Socialist International until World War II, to accuse him of "intellectual brutality"[45] and brand him, together with Chernyshevsky and Lenin, as a typical Russian radical.[46] De Jonge seems to believe that the fact that Plekhanov was a *Russian* Marxist is enough to arrive at this conclusion, since he is very certain that no *Russian* Marxist could ever have been a figure which was considered moderate and enlightened.

De Jonge's description of Soviet Russia's intervention in Georgia in 1921 is totally inaccurate and flawed insofar as its comparison with Hitler's Anschluss of Austria is concerned.[47] He even fails to mention the local Bolshevik uprising in Borchalin, stage-managed in Moscow, that had set the scene and provided the justification for the invasion, which was launched in support of a socialist revolution allegedly started by the Georgian proletariat. Instead, the author alleges that Lenin tried to justify this invasion by claiming a need to stop the Georgian–Armenian war—something he never accomplished, for the simple reason that this war had taken place three years earlier (in 1918, when Lenin had, indeed, appealed for a cessation of hostilities, but had not even remotely suggested intervention) and was soon ended by the British.

Having missed the main point about the Soviet invasion of Georgia, de Jonge does the same when describing Soviet invasions into the three Baltic states in 1939. He compresses the description of developments in the three Baltic states over almost two years into a few sentences—completely distorting the reality by doing so, and also by referring to events such as, for example, the wholesale shipment to the *gulag* of the Baltic armies,[48] which had never taken place. Having wrongly dated the Soviet invasion of Finland as having started on November 3 (in fact it began November 30), 1939,[49] he then misjudges the role of the Allied Powers in preventing Soviet occupation and Sovietization of that country.[50] It is true that the Swedish government declined to let the British and French troops through, but there were plans to make Norway compliant with the British designs to that effect and thus making the possibility of Soviet confrontation with Allied troops real. Only after having realized this, did the Soviets agree to stop the war and sign the March 12, 1940 peace treaty with the same Finnish government they had pledged by their invasion to destroy.

One also wonders how de Jonge arrived at the conclusion that the collectivization of agriculture in the USSR claimed only "a little more than 5 million victims."[51] He refers to the Soviet official population figures, but I suspect that he used the analysis of these figures given by Sergei Maksudov. Maksudov, however, admits that the limited data used in his study (together with a number of interfering factors that are incalculable), did not allow him to arrive at any definite conclusions, and that the real death toll could easily be twice, or even more, as high as his calculations show. Indeed, most of the existing professional estimates suggest that the death toll exacted by the collectivization was between 10 and 15 million persons.

It is also rather strange to hear de Jonge say that Stalin was careful to spare the lives of the Russian artistic intelligentsia,[52] when only among the members of the Writers' Union more than 600, or about 50 percent, were exterminated in 1937–1938 alone. Not less strange are his arguments to prove this contention. Stalin, he says, erased from the death list the name of Mayakovski's widow, but this could not have been the case—Mayakovski died an unmarried man. If it was Lilya Brik, Mayakovski's mistress, whom de Jonge had in mind, there were many other reasons for keeping her out of the death list, not the least being the fact that her sister, Elsa Triolet, was the wife of Louis Aragon, and also a prominent French communist writer in her own right. As for Yevgenii Zamyatin, he was indeed allowed to leave the Soviet Union, but this happened in 1927, long before the purges, and at a time when cases of pushing dissidents out of the USSR were as yet not uncommon.

One could go on citing instances of de Jonge being out of his depth when dealing with certain aspects of his subject, but I would like to conclude with one that seems to me quite typical. It has to do with de Jonge's attempts at answering the question of why Stalin's interrogators so adamantly sought to secure confessions from accused people about crimes that they had never committed.[53] A few reasons are given, among them the preeminent role confessions have played in the judicial process of Russia throughout the ages, but the main and most obvious ones are not. Only a person with a rather shallow understanding of what was going on during the purges could have omitted to mention among reasons for extracting confessions, the need of procuring through them the names of alleged accomplices in order automatically to feed the machine of the purges and keep it going until further notice, and of putting some selected confessions on public display through show trials or otherwise, in order to convince the public at home and abroad that the purges were directed against real "enemies of the people" and traitors to the country.

The book abounds also in mistakes of which there are two main kinds: mistakes of fact and mistakes of spelling Russian and East European words and names. The latter perhaps would not be worthy of special mention had the author not tried sometimes to engage in some linguistic interpretations, as he did, for example, with the name of Colonel Pogrebny,[54] the man in charge of the Katyn operation. De Jonge wrongly associated that name's root with the roots of the words coffin (*grob*) and burial. *Pogreb* in Russian means "cellar" and this is the true root of Pogrebny's name; (for burial, *pogrebeniye*, the name would have had to be Pogrebel'ny).

Some of the factual mistakes are simply sad and some could be quite misleading. I shall list just a few of them in the sequence of their appearance in the book.

1. It was Stalin's legal father, Vissarion Djugashvili, not, as de Jonge says, his mother, who was an Osette;[55] the mother, Ekaterina Geladze, was of pure Georgian stock.
2. During NEP private enterprises were allowed to employ up to 20, not, as de Jonge states, 40 people.[56]
3. The Soviet Ukraine of 1935 is wrongly referred to as the Ukrainian People's Republic,[57] not as the Ukrainian SSR (the Ukrainian People's Republic was the Ukrainian independent "bourgeois" state finally destroyed by the Red Army in 1920).
4. According to the memoirs of Mikhail Yakubovich, the only survivor of the Menshevik show trial of March 1931, trial rehearsals were widely practiced already at that time; hence, they were not introduced as late as 1936 and "became common later,"[58] as de Jonge would have it.

5. The verse attributed to Yuz Aleshkovsky's satirical song about Comrade Stalin, the great scientist, comes in fact from Mikhail Isakovsky's official poetic apology of Stalin and is, in addition, misquoted—it should read:
"We believed you, Comrade Stalin,
More perhaps than we believed ourselves."[59]

6. It is untrue that "In a remarkable *volte-face*," Stalin "suddenly accepted the German interpretation of a Lithuanian boundary dispute."[60] Stalin had never disputed the German interpretation of the Lithuanian boundary, but simply ignored it by occupying, in June 1940, the whole of Lithuania. He also never denied that the USSR thus violated the German–Soviet Agreement of September 28, 1939, according to which a strip of Lithuanian territory was to be incorporated into Germany. After prolonged negotiations the whole issue was resolved in January 1941, whereby the Germans agreed to the USSR retaining the disputed strip of Lithuania in exchange for receiving in compensation "for territory loss," 7.5 million gold U.S. dollars (the exact price that the Tsar got for selling Alaska to the United States in 1868).

7. It is also untrue that Saltykov-Shchedrin's *Contemporary Idyll* was discovered and published in the early 1930s.[61] It was duly published during the author's lifetime in the late nineteenth century and had been freely available since. The few missing parts cut out by the tsarist censors were indeed discovered later and published for the first time only in 1941. However, the piece containing the famous demand of the governor to shut down *zakryt'* America (not "to abolish" it, as de Jonge had it translated),[62] was in the non-censored part of the story.

8. Continuing to stick to literary matters, the novel for which Ilya Ehrenburg received the Stalin Prize in 1948 was not *The Fall of Paris*, but *The Tempest (Burya)*.[63] For *The Fall of Paris*, Ehrenburg received the Stalin Prize in 1942.

9. Finally, the author is wrong when he suggests that in 1948 Tito broke with Stalin,[64] for it was Stalin who broke with Tito, and when he calls Gomulka a Jew,[65] which he was not—his wife was Jewish.

ATMOSPHERIC VIRTUES

De Jonge bases his research mainly on secondary sources, some of them not always sufficiently reliable. Sometimes one has a feeling that he is led by his source, which may account for many of the book's mistakes and inconsistencies. De Jonge's primary sources came from the archives of the British Foreign Office. Some of these sources have already been used by other researchers of Soviet history, most notably by Lord Nicholas Bethell, Count Nikolai Tolstoy, and Dr. David Kirby; some I have never encountered before. The information contained in these sources does not reveal anything new on Soviet matters, but it represents a uniquely valuable comment on the British misperceptions of Stalin and the USSR. In de Jonge's view, these misperceptions date from the 1940s. He contends that "The same cannot be said of British Embassy staff in the 1930s, when they displayed a remarkable grasp of [Soviet] political and social conditions."[66] But when one reads passages stating, for example, that "Stalin had become the prisoner of those young adherents he had recently brought into the party,"[67] one starts doubting whether this was so. I found even more astonishing the statements by Lord Chilston (the British ambassador) about Stalin's being not only "a great man,"[68] but also "a gentleman."[69]

On the whole, de Jonge's book, all its shortcomings and mistakes notwithstanding, is interesting and useful. It clearly belongs to the category of major Western biographies of Stalin, of which there are only a few and the latest of which appeared more than a decade ago.

To be sure, among all the existing Western biographies of Stalin, Adam Ulam's[70] stands out as the most fundamental, scholarly, solid, and consistent. It may be matched by Robert Tucker's when the concluding volume of his work will at last appear.[71] De Jonge's book is in the category of shorter and more popular biographies, to which also Hingley's[72] amd Deutscher's[73] belong. De Jonge's work does not match the latter two by its academic standards, but it has the advantage of appearing later and using some materials unavailable hitherto.

There is, however, one element that favorably distinguishes de Jonge's work from all of its predecessors. One could call that element "atmospheric." Indeed, de Jonge largely draws on the folklore of Stalin's time, which he learned of from conversations with many recent Soviet émigrés whom he befriended in London and elsewhere. His book is permeated by the episodes, jokes, and gossip of the period. I was most pleased, for example, to find in the book the quite convincing gossip about Stalin's in fact being the illegitimate son of N. M. Przhevalsky, the famous Russian explorer whose name has been given to the wild-horse species discovered by him in western Mongolia.[74] De Jonge also uses as his sources more of the literature produced by Soviet dissidents and émigrés that has not been translated into English. The introduction to the English-speaking readership of a number of facts previously unavailable is, no doubt, a significant contribution, unique to de Jonge. It is, for example, the first time that the most interesting story reported by A. Avtorkhanov in *Tekhnologiya vlasti*—the story about Stalin's seminary essay "Why Caesar Fell"—has appeared in English. According to that story, the sixteen-year-old Stalin developed in this essay an original theory on how, by supplementing and ultimately substituting all official institutions of the state by the personal power machine, a dictatorship can be effectively consolidated. Stalin maintained that if Julius Caesar had followed the rules of this theory, he would never have fallen. "The teacher asked him whether his plan smacked of an absolute monarchy. 'No,'" replied Stalin, "The power of an absolute monarch depends on the machinery of state power; in my plan state power is sustained by the machinery of personal power."[75] An attentive reader would not fail to recognize that about thirty years later Stalin was building his power base in full accordance with that theory, and, unlike Caesar, succeeded.

NOTES

1. See Leon Trotsky, *My Life* (Harmondsworth: Penguin, 1975), 534; also Leon Trotsky, *Stalin: An Appraisal of the Man and His Influence*, vol. 2 (London: Panther, 1969), 215.

2. Quoted in A. B. Ulam, *Stalin: The Man and His Era* (London: Allen Lane, 1974), 308.

3. Trotsky, *Stalin: An Appraisal*, vol. 1, 16.

4. Trotsky, *Stalin: An Appraisal*, vol. 2, 205–7.

5. Alex de Jonge, *Stalin and the Shaping of the Soviet Union* (New York: William Morrow, 1986), 127–28.

6. de Jonge, *Stalin*, 128.

7. de Jonge, *Stalin*, 129.

8. de Jonge, *Stalin*, 130.

9. de Jonge, *Stalin*, 132.

10. Trotsky, *Stalin: An Appraisal*. See Ronald Hingley, *Joseph Stalin: Man and Legend* (London: Hutchinson, 1974), 434.

11. de Jonge, *Stalin*, 315.

12. de Jonge, *Stalin*, 191.

13. de Jonge, *Stalin*, 280.

14. de Jonge, *Stalin*, 354.

15. de Jonge, *Stalin*, 30.

16. de Jonge, *Stalin*. Once before, during the revolution of 1905, he took a stance different from that of Lenin on the agrarian question; but immediately after having heard Lenin's view abandoned his own position and joined Lenin's. De Jonge has declined to mention this episode.

17. de Jonge, *Stalin*, 191. According to Antonov-Ovseenko's story, to whom de Jonge here refers, Stalin addressed this remark to Sokol'nikov who was sitting next to him when the *Testament* was read. The translation used by de Jonge is not precise either: Stalin said, in fact, "Ne mog umeret'kak *chestnyi* vozhd," which means, "Couldn't even die like an *honest* leader" (see Antonov-Ovseenko, *Portret tirana* [A Tyrant's Portrait] (New York: Khronika Press, 1980), 58, 385 n. 66.

18. Hingley, *Joseph Stalin*, 436.

19. de Jonge, *Stalin*, 218.

20. de Jonge, *Stalin*, 200–201.

21. de Jonge, *Stalin*, 397–98.

22. de Jonge, *Stalin*, 439.

23. de Jonge, *Stalin*, 109.

24. de Jonge, *Stalin*, 447.

25. de Jonge, *Stalin*, 57.

26. de Jonge, *Stalin*, 37–38.

27. The translation of *muzhikoborets*, literally "the peasant fighter," as the "murderer of peasants" is de Jonge's, 304).

28. Among the evidence of the boy-Stalin's Georgian nationalist zeal, his poetry published in 1895 by the Georgian-language magazine *Iveria* is peculiarly interesting since it reveals one of the least obvious facets of Stalin's character and ability. One of his typical Georgian nationalist poems is rendered by de Jonge in a free English translation, 30.

29. de Jonge, *Stalin,* 376 (with reference to Khrushchev).

30. de Jonge, *Stalin,* 439. The real meaning of this toast escapes de Jonge who is using it as an example of Stalin's Russian nationalist orientation.

31. de Jonge, *Stalin,* 460–61.

32. de Jonge, *Stalin,* 107.

33. de Jonge, *Stalin,* 110. While mentioning this figure here, he does not relate it, however, to the extent of popular support for the Bolsheviks at all.

34. de Jonge, *Stalin,* 274.

35. de Jonge, *Stalin,* 312.

36. de Jonge, *Stalin.*

37. de Jonge, *Stalin,* 13.

38. de Jonge, *Stalin,* 491.

39. de Jonge, *Stalin,* 462.

40. de Jonge, *Stalin,* 272–74.

41. de Jonge, *Stalin,* 19–20.

42. de Jonge, *Stalin,* 114.

43. de Jonge, *Stalin,* 490–91.

44. de Jonge, *Stalin.*

45. de Jonge, *Stalin,* 129.

46. de Jonge, *Stalin,* 40.

47. de Jonge, *Stalin,* 157.

48. de Jonge, *Stalin,* 365.

49. de Jonge, *Stalin.*

50. de Jonge, *Stalin,* 366.

51. de Jonge, *Stalin,* 287.

52. de Jonge, *Stalin,* 455.

53. de Jonge, *Stalin,* 336–40.

54. de Jonge, *Stalin,* 364.

55. de Jonge, *Stalin,* 24.

56. de Jonge, *Stalin,* 143.

57. de Jonge, *Stalin,* 317.

58. de Jonge, *Stalin,* 322.

59. de Jonge, *Stalin,* 338, where it says: "We believed *in you,* Comrade Stalin; More perhaps than *you* believed *in yourself*" (The original Russian test is misquoted accordingly).

60. de Jonge, *Stalin,* 372.

61. de Jonge, *Stalin,* 457.

62. de Jonge, *Stalin.*

63. de Jonge, *Stalin.*

64. de Jonge, *Stalin,* 466.

65. de Jonge, *Stalin,* 468.

66. de Jonge, *Stalin,* 235.

67. de Jonge, *Stalin,* 210.

68. de Jonge, *Stalin,* 313.

69. de Jonge, *Stalin,* 314.

70. Ulam, *Stalin: The Man and His Era.*

71. Robert C. Tucker, *Stalin as Revolutionary, 1879–1929: A Study in History and Personality* (London: Chatto & Windus, 1974).

72. Hingley, *Joseph Stalin.*

73. Isaac Deutscher, *Stalin: A Political Biography,* rev. ed. (Harmondsworth: Pelican, 1966).

74. de Jonge, *Stalin,* 24–25.

75. de Jonge, *Stalin,* 31–32.

3

Marxism-Leninism in the USSR

Aleksandras Shtromas

MARXISM-LENINISM AND SOVIET
SOCIETY IN THE CONTEXT OF HISTORY

When, after having seized power in Russia in November 1917, the Bolsheviks imposed upon that country the Leninist variety of Marxism as the sole foundation of Russia's new political myth, the great majority of that country's established and traditionally minded population had inevitably become politically alienated. This is not to say that Marxism was entirely alien to Russia. Indeed, from the beginning of the twentieth century Marxism had a significant influence on Russia's intellectual and political life but this influence was minor in the sense that it had never acquired a larger appeal among the masses, and only a certain part, by no means a predominant one, of the intellectual elite was affected by it. The Bolsheviks tried very hard to build upon that existing influence of Marxism in order to make it universal but their success in this respect was rather limited.

The new Marxist-Leninist political myth was internalized and fully accepted only by a certain, not large, proportion of idealistically minded

Reprinted from Aleksandras Shtromas and Morton A. Kaplan, eds., *The Soviet Union and the Challenge of the Future*. Vol. 3, *Ideology, Culture, and Nationality* (New York: Paragon House, 1989), 40–58.

young people from all sections of Russian society, as well as by some assimilatory-minded representatives of national minorities (the assimilationist Jews figured prominently among them) and some declassed people who in Russia were rather more numerous than in any other European country. All this amounted to a very strong zealot-type support for the revolutionary Bolshevik regime from a relatively small minority of committed people. Such support was enough for effectively ruling the country by dictatorial-terroristic means, but in no way was it sufficient for establishing rule by consensus.[1]

Under the circumstances, the majority of Russians had little choice but to adjust to the Marxist-Leninist political myth without ever having internalized or otherwise accepted it. People simply tried to survive in adverse conditions by pretending that they were converted to the regime's ideology and, then, to improve the conditions of their existence by positively responding to a variety of incentives that the Bolsheviks offered to "working people" in exchange for their outward loyalty to the regime and the values of Marxism-Leninism on which it was allegedly based. These opportunists, total strangers to the Marxist-Leninist ideology, were actually destined to form in time the largest bulk of good Soviet citizenry and even of the membership of the Soviet Communist party.

The opportunistic intake into the new Soviet elite became especially prominent in the late 1920s with the demise of the NEP. It had quickly overtaken the small regular idealistic intake and had reduced it, together with the politically committed Bolshevik Old Guard, to a small minority.[2] This minority was, however, to remain for some time in the top echelon of the party's hierarchy. Stalin was not yet powerful enough to replace it with his own promotees and devotees. Moreover, he still needed its commitment to the Bolshevik cause for the successful accomplishment of drastic revolutionary changes, such as the collectivization of agriculture, aimed at the "socialist transformation of Russia."

The situation changed drastically when this "socialist transformation" was accomplished and the country, in the 1930s, entered into the period of "socialist stability." Under these circumstances, Stalin needed only obedient and unscrupulous executioners of his will: the idealists became to him not only superfluous but, as potential challengers of his decisions, extremely dangerous too. Hence, they had to go and to be replaced by the opportunists in all significant offices of the country. By the mid-1930s Stalin had already enough power to realize such a replacement, but he was well aware that, if simply removed from office and left at large, the members of the Bolshevik Old Guard could be even more of a challenge than when in office where the inevitable bounds of collective discipline would have a restricting influence on their challenging activities.

The Bolshevik Old Guard were political figures with established names and reputations, large clienteles, and constituencies of support. But, most importantly, they had a lot of experience in revolutionary political and organizational work that, when left outside the disciplining framework of the office, they could easily and devastatingly turn against Stalin and his cronies in the newly staffed power hierarchy. Hence the only way for Stalin to get rid of them safely was to dispatch them directly from their offices to the gallows and the Gulag. This is what Stalin chose to do by skillfully using Kirov's assassination on December 1, 1934, for launching the Great Purge that was successfully accomplished by 1939.

MARXISM-LENINISM AND THE SOVIET OFFICIALDOM

The Great Purge signified the triumph of the opportunists and the almost total annihilation of the idealists.[3] The party's intellectuals, people like Nikolai Bukharin, David Ryazanov, Aleksandr Slepkov, Nikolai Krylenko, Evgeniy Pashukanis, and many thousands of their likes, were eliminated practically to a man by Stalin. Those left, mainly former Mensheviks and other professional "leftovers" of the old regime, being by then concerned much more about saving their skins than about ideals (people like Andrei Vyshinski and David Zaslavsky), were ready to follow every whim of Stalin's with extreme zeal.

Most of the few nonintellectual genuine believers in communism perished in the Great Purge, too, being thoroughly beaten in the ferocious struggle for survival by the cynical schemers swelling the party hierarchy in ever-increasing numbers. By the rules of natural selection, evolved during the Great Purge, the genuine believers were the "unfittest species," destined to be mercilessly swallowed by the Stalinist terror machine in the first place. Most of them were actually entirely devoted to Stalin, identifying communism exclusively with his leadership, but this did not help them. Under Stalin, for a functionary to be fit to survive, it was even not enough to renounce all personal convictions, all moral principles, replacing them with one single belief in Stalin's infallibility—as Mikhail Isakovsky declared in his poem on Stalin: "We so trusted you, Comrade Stalin, as, may be, we did not trust even ourselves"—it was necessary, in addition, to develop special intuitive skills and pliancy allowing one rightly to foretell, and to be in step with, Stalin's next move at the right time.

A few genuine believers in communism and even some true Marxist-Leninists did, however, survive Stalin's purges. Indeed, neither Stalin's nor any other rule by terror known to history has ever been able to annihilate totally all those against whom the terror was directed. Although the party and government machinery was perhaps the place most thoroughly cleansed from the presence of true believers, a few of them managed to remain in place even there. Among them was Nikita S. Khrushchev, Stalin's ultimate successor.

Khrushchev was of course a great survivor. He earned his right to stay alive by ably playing the role of the fool at Stalin's court and by ruthlessly executing Stalin's will in both Moscow and the Ukraine where, intermittently, he used to be placed as Stalin's all-powerful proconsul. Being semiliterate (he learned to read and write only at the age of twenty-three), Khrushchev was of course unable to grasp the intricacies of Marxist-Leninist theory, but in his own peasant way he religiously believed in the communist ideal and, when in power, seriously tried practically to implement it, assuming that the Soviet system over which he now presided was, for this purpose, the only suitable vehicle. As an avowed populist and experienced political practitioner, he no doubt knew only too well that the Soviet system in its rigid Stalinist shape did not work. But, as a believer, he was convinced that, if properly reorganized, that system could start working well enough to produce in the USSR an abundant communist society in a not-too-distant future—actually the party's program, reflecting Khrushchev's personal beliefs and officially endorsed by the 22nd congress of the Communist Party of the Soviet Union (CPSU) in 1961, scheduled the dawning of communism in the USSR for 1980.

With the view of finding the right formula under which the Soviet system would at last become functional with regard to this purpose, Khrushchev kept the country's apparatus of power and management in a state of constant reorganization as none of the newly introduced configurations and shapes of that apparatus made it work to his satisfaction. He acted like the monkey in Krylov's fable, who, being unable to play a musical quartet with three other animals, believed that the fault lay not with the musical skills of the players, but with their wrong sitting order, and constantly made them change their seats. This reorganizational urge only further paralyzed the system, endangering its overall operational capacity, and ultimately threatened its very survival.

Communist convictions practically turned the deeply frustrated and increasingly impatient Khrushchev into a *de facto* enemy of the Soviet system without him ever being able to realize that this was the case. His off-the-cuff speeches often matched, and sometimes even surpassed, the most radical dissident standards for the criticism of the system. Khrushchev's reorganizational drive had, by 1962, reached the critical point of undermining the basic foundation of the system—the monocentric domination of the party apparatus over all other power apparatuses and all walks of Soviet life—as exemplified by his abolition during 1962–1963 of most of the rural *raykoms* (party district committees) and, even more importantly, by his 1962 division of the provincial and territorial party committees (*obkoms* and *kraykoms*) into two such committees, one for industry and one for agriculture (that latter, major blow to the "party's leading role" had been preceded by the replacement in 1957 of the central industrial ministries by the local councils for national economy, the *sovnarkhozy*, which substantially undermined not only the power of the central authority but to some extent also that of the provincial and territorial party committees, as the territorial areas of the *sovnarkhozy* did not always coincide with the boundaries of the established administrative-territorial units over which these committees exercise their rule). Khrushchev's 1962–1963 moves went much too far to be tolerated by his purely system–preservation-*oriented*, cynically pragmatic colleagues. On

October 14, 1964, they staged a palace coup against Khrushchev, trying to save the system by removing him from office.

Khrushchev was indeed the sole member of the Soviet leadership that he himself had handpicked, and certainly the last Soviet leader, who was a believer in communism. His case demonstrates best the Soviet system's inability to accommodate and tolerate within the ranks of its functionaries the true believers who, trying to behave in accordance with their convictions, invariably break the rules of conformity with the system, thus endangering its continuous existence. Those who, instead of unquestioningly serving the system's needs, try to make the system serve their own communist or any other ideals can either break the system or, if the system survives their tinkering, will inevitably be rejected by it and, consequently, thrown out into the wilderness of "extra-structural" existence to which in the USSR all identified dissidents are automatically relegated. Only those who could convincingly pledge themselves once and for all to fully submit their entire personalities to obediently serving the system, may be allowed back into its fold. This is how Boris Yeltsin, after having undergone the humiliating ritual of public repentance, was readmitted into the ranks of the ruling elite, although on a much lower scale in the hierarchy than before, one that explicitly excluded personal decision making (he was appointed *Deputy* Chairman of the State Committee for Construction). Yeltsin is indeed a curiosity among the post-Khrushchev Soviet leaders whose only concern always was and is the preservation, whatever the costs, of the system that comfortably keeps them in power but that, as they are fully aware, is totally unfit for achieving communist affluence or any other ideal goals. Their policies may change but not the preservationist substance of these policies. They realize that the defensive immobility practiced by Brezhnev and Chernenko had served its course and become counterproductive. They branded it as stagnant and as "fostering" "brake-putting mechanisms" (*mekhanizmy tormozheniya*). They revert under Gorbachev to perestroika and glasnost, but they practice these policies, however, only insofar as they sustain the system as it stands, without interfering with its basic structure.

Whatever policies the post-Khrushchev Soviet leaders opportunistically applied, they always claimed them to be based on Marxist-Leninist ideology and aimed at the construction of a communist society. Like the notorious medical orderlies in Chekhov's famous short story who, though convinced that no such thing as a pulse exists, have to keep themselves in business by pretending to measure it, the Soviet leaders, in order to defend their rule, have to uphold their Marxist-Leninist identity and enhance the official status of communist ideology, without believing in the values, ideals, and goals enunciated by that ideology. Indeed, Marxism-Leninism and the communist ideal are their sole claims to, and legitimation of, power. Moreover, only as the "high priesthood" of this supposedly ultimate scientific creed, are they invested with a primordial and inalienable right to rule without being responsible in exercising it to anyone but themselves and the future. Without believing in communism, the Soviet leaders are thus bound to stick to their communist credentials and, in order to warrant these credentials, have to set themselves communist political goals both nationally and globally. To renounce communist ideology, or even substantially to side-step from communist politics, would be for them tantamount to relinquishing power, and to some of them such abdication may mean not merely the loss of status and position but also liability for crimes they committed on their way up the social ladder. The Soviet leaders are indeed trapped by their ideology and have no way of escaping from that ideological trap. And so they have to soldier on along the route laid down by that ideology as no alternative route is available to them.

This is, however, only one part of the story. The other part of it is that Marxism-Leninism provides an ideal instrument for an unrepresentative political clique to exercise absolute and unlimited power in an unchallengeable way. The idea of socialism, translated into the party-state's ownership and direct management of all the means of production and also into what is known as the concept of the leading role of the party, entitling the party-state to be in direct charge of all socially-relevant activities of the people, reduces every member of society into a mere servant of the ruling clique, which alone is entitled to set him or her tasks and to assess his or her performance in fulfilling these tasks either by reward or punishment. Any decentralization that would entail true autonomy for economic units and public bodies (and thus responsibility of people running these units and bodies not to the party-state's officialdom but to themselves and their workers and customers) would immediately alter that relationship between the rulers and the ruled. Not only would such autonomous social units stop being servants of the ruling political clique, but that ruling clique itself would either have to start providing these units with qualified political services or quit and give way to a government that the autonomous actors on the social stage could trust and consider qualified to render them such services. As the present ruling clique has no qualifications or experience in rendering political services, and as it knows no other way of ruling than through complete mastership over the totality of people's activities, for it to allow such decentralization would be equal to committing political suicide (if the top leadership even were to try, in a volte-face, to transform itself into a normal, political–service-rendering government of the country, that would amount to nothing less than a revolution from above, deviously perpetrated by the top leadership against the Soviet system and the rest of the ruling clique, which it is supposed to represent and lead. The checks and balances characteristic of the present Soviet oligarchic system would hardly allow the top part of the oligarchy successfully to perpetrate such an about-face. For a revolution from above to become possible, an autocratic regime must replace the oligarchic system first, and this the oligarchs, who learned the lessons of Stalin's purges very well indeed, will resist it as much as a revolution against the system itself).

Marxism-Leninism, by declaring the natural and ever-growing social demands for authentic decentralization anti-socialist and rejecting them outright on ideological grounds, effectively performs today the most important pragmatic task of sustaining the present Soviet ruling clique in power. Furthermore, Marxism-Leninism provides that ruling clique with a most powerful device for thoroughly controlling the political behavior of each individual. All Soviet people, including school children and pensioners, are on a daily basis requested to manifest in one form or another their adherence to the Marxist-Leninist ideology and the Soviet system of rule based on this ideology. Attending celebratory demonstrations, speaking or at least clapping at self-congratulatory meetings, voting several times a year for party-selected candidates to various positions, attending political-education classes, performing various "voluntary social duties" (e.g., the propagandistic ones), observing regular ideological rites and participating in all sorts of public performances, is the usual routine of every Soviet citizen's daily life. Roman Redlikh, when trying to distinguish totalitarian systems from all other systems of dictatorial rule, referred to these practices as a regime of "active unfreedom." According to him, the regime of "active unfreedom," forcing people constantly to show their enthusiastic approval of, and admiration for, their oppressors, is a distinguishing trait of a totalitarian dictatorship. The nontotalitarian dictatorships are satisfied with establishing a regime of "passive unfreedom" that demands of their subjects only to refrain from actively opposing or criticizing the established dictatorial rule.[4]

Any attempt of a Soviet citizen to escape from the duties that the regime of "active unfreedom" imposes upon him or her is noticed and recorded by the authorities who, when such attempts reach beyond the level of "pardonable laziness," single out the "guilty person" for punishment. In the beginning that punishment is relatively mild: exclusion from the regular line for promotions or, in a graver case, demotion; prohibition to travel abroad or official ignorance of legitimate pleas for improvement of housing conditions. In most cases such relatively mild pressures, amplified by an increasingly tense atmosphere of official suspicion and disapproval, are sufficient to change the person's ways and bring him back to the conformist fold. If that does not work, heavier measures of punishment are applied. People are thus forced into either active participation in the official lie or dissent.

It was the late Leonard Schapiro who said that the Soviet official ideology and the lie come "to the same thing, since in view of the fact that the ideology does not correspond to the reality which people see around them, its dogmas have to be reiterated with increasing persistence in spite, or because of, their falsity. . . ."[5] It was also Schapiro who observed that this ideology, or the lie, "acts as a binding force on those who might be ready to reject the Party and the system which it represents."[6] Indeed, in the USSR a person's continuous, though purely formal, public acknowledgment of adherence to the official ideology has become the standard way of proving that person's political loyalty to the Soviet Party–state. A person's readiness publicly to repeat the official lie is accepted by the party-state as this person's solemn pledge to seek the advancement of his or her personal interests and goals exclusively within the extant sociopolitical framework and be totally bound by its constraints. Only those people who are prepared to lie in order to avoid trouble and live as obedient members of the Soviet Party–state, satisfied with the rewards that thus may come their way, are treated by that state as its good and reliable subjects. All others are rejected and suppressed. Ideology in the Soviet Union has thus lost its traditional meaning of a set of people's genuine values, ideas, and goals. Instead of being "internalized," the communist ideology in the Soviet Union has thus been entirely "externalized" and transformed into a mere instrument of political rule and control. As Milovan Djilas succinctly summed it up: "Ideology in the Soviet Union is both *dead*—and very much *alive*! Dead at the level of faith, alive as an indispensable (tool and) rationale of policy."[7]

THE MARXIST-LENINISTS WHO SURVIVED STALIN

Among the few Marxist-Leninists who survived Stalin and his purges, many were Stalin's victims themselves. Having been rehabilitated by Khrushchev, they returned to their places of residence and gradually got reintegrated into the current pattern of Soviet life. There were also some believers among the members of the younger generation, those who in Stalin's time were mainly at school and who, because of young age, largely escaped the axe of Stalin's terror. Almost all of these younger people lost to Stalin's terror some members of their families and friends, but this sometimes only hardened their resolve to be good Marxists and Communists. These surviving Marxist-Leninist idealists were typically either students or people in the beginning of their careers; and some were already reaching the end of their active life as were most of the rehabilitated returnees from the Gulag. Almost none of them were established members of the current political or managerial elite.

The "idealistic communist remnants" in Soviet society divided into two broad categories based on their different attitudes toward Stalin:

First were the "idealistic leftovers" of Stalin's purges and other people affected by them in one or another way, who came to the conclusion that Stalin was a traitor to the lofty Marxist-Leninist cause and that his grip on power was the main obstacle on the way to the triumph of that cause. These people nurtured a dream about such a time when Stalin would be finally removed from the USSR's political stage, and the country would become able to revert to its genuine Marxist-Leninist and socialist origins, a process in which they aspired to participate actively and enthusiastically.

Second were those, mainly younger people, who accepted the official version of the purges and who continued to identify totally and unequivocally their belief in Marxism-Leninism with the personality of Stalin, seeing in his leadership the ultimate (and, perhaps, the sole remaining) guarantee of the country's, and the world's at large, following the right course toward the victory of communism.

It is important to note at this stage that these people, i.e., the remaining genuine Marxist-Leninists, were the ones who originated Soviet dissent as we know it today.

Many of the remaining Marxist-Leninist idealists of the first "anti-Stalinist" category were people who either have themselves been victims of Stalin's purges (for example, among the well-known later-day dissidents, the Medvedev brothers, Pyotr Yakir, Elena Bonner, Raisa Lert, et al.) or who were old enough consciously to witness the purges and develop grave doubts about Stalin's consistency with genuine Leninism (among the well-known later-day dissidents, for example, Naum Korzhavin and Alexander Solzhenitsyn, who were themselves imprisoned for expressing such doubts; Alexander Zinoviev, et al.). They were the enthusiasts of the de-Stalinization process initiated by the party under Nikita Khrushchev after Stalin's death and entertained high hopes for the country and for themselves in relation with it. Many of them who at the time of Stalin's death were not in the party joined its ranks during this period—the most notable example is that of Elena Bonner, the present wife of Academician Andrei Sakharov; the best explained one (in a most penetrative autobiography) is Dora Shturman[8]—and those who already were members but had kept a distinctively low profile became publicly visible, boldly outspoken, and even "pushy." These people very soon discovered, however, that their hopes about the party's intentions were misplaced, and that, like in Stalin's days, the party was not prepared to tolerate any independent initiatives or views, let alone attempts at pushing it into doing anything it did not itself plan to do beforehand. The rebuke by the party of these enthusiasts of de-Stalinization was swift, clear-cut and strong. However, not all the rebuked complied with the party and some intransigently continued to stick to their critical points in spite of severe repercussions (among the many victims of this rebuke were the chess grandmaster Mikhail Botvinnik who complied and Professor Yuriy Orlov who did not and who became later one of the leading Soviet dissenters). That is how, in 1956, dissent for the first time appeared on the visible surface of Soviet politics. It has continued unabated ever since, mainly along the same lines of defending the principles of Soviet legality, of enlarging the extent of human rights (individual and collective), as well as of some other issues related to the liberalization and democratization of the Soviet society.

One should stress once more that up to this point all these newly emerged dissenters were firm believers in Marxism-Leninism and in the very principle of the Soviet system of rule which, in their view, needed only to rid itself radically of Stalinist perversions and deviations in order to become perfect again. Soviet dissenters of the early and mid-1950s were typical products of the minority participatory political culture and therefore dared to challenge the powers that be on the consistency of their actual performance with the principles of Marxism-Leninism, which the frightened conformist majority would never have dreamed of doing.

The Marxist-Leninist idealists of the second category ("the believers in Stalin"), in the aftermath of Stalin's death, underwent a much more drastic change of mind. Some of them realized on April 4, 1953, that Stalin was, to a large extent, personally responsible for the evils of the Soviet system when the "killer-doctors" were rehabilitated and it became clear that Stalin personally was responsible for the false accusations against them. For some, however, that realization came about only in 1956, after the 20th Congress of the CPSU, where Khrushchev officially revealed the horrible crimes of Stalin. These revelations meant the collapse of their whole belief in the Soviet system of rule as such; but one should stress—not in the ideals of Marxism-Leninism, which remained for the time being their unshaken symbol of creed.

To these people who saw the ills of the Soviet regime only too well, Stalin had represented the last hope for the system's progressive improvement and for its staying on the right course to communism. The shocking discovery that Stalin himself was an initiator of the system's gross violations of justice and of its virtual degeneration into a fascist-type dictatorship convinced them that the system was totally irredeemable. Accordingly, these people started to develop their own radical Marxist-Leninist programs for the revolutionary change of the existing "fascist-type" Soviet system into a genuinely socialist one. They counted on massive support from the working class and the honest Marxist-Leninists in the party itself. In other words, they were advocating a new socialist revolution and were prepared to take a lead in it.

No wonder that these people preferred to remain anonymous and to conduct their activities clandestinely. The first such dissenters who became publicly known were the members of the Krasnopevtsev-Rendel group at the History Faculty of the University of Moscow. Their activities were disclosed by the KGB and in 1956 (in the very aftermath of the 20th Congress of the party) they were sentenced to long terms of imprisonment. This was actually the first recorded political trial that took place in the USSR after the 20th Party Congress.[9]

Perhaps the most outspoken summary of the views of this category of Marxist-Leninist idealists was given by a person who wrote in Soviet *samizdat* under the pseudonym of F. Znakov and whose identity has remained undisclosed.[10] In Znakov's view, in the USSR, under the name of socialism, super-monopolistic capitalism was, in fact, coercively and voluntarily established. As the result of Stalin's "great leap forward," by the mid-1920s the ownership of all the means of production in the USSR was concentrated in the hands of one super-monopolistic body (organized as the self-coopting and self-perpetuating leadership of the party), which combined its total economic domination with direct and unlimited exercise of political power. A fascist-type totalitarian dictatorship is the natural superstructure over the basis of super-monopolistic capitalism and this is into what the USSR's political system had in fact developed. F. Znakov claimed that from the Marxist-Leninist point of view the USSR had thus reached (though by coercive and artificial means) the last and the most reactionary stage of capitalist development—the one that Karl Kautsky used to call ultra-imperialism—and was therefore fully ripe for a genuinely socialist change. In other words, according to him, the general Marxist rule about the inevitability of a socialist revolution in a capitalist society had acquired in the present-day Soviet Union (and, as yet, nowhere else) its really concrete and practical expression. The author, by addressing his 1956 work to the Italian Communist leader, Palmiro Togliatti, wanted to enlist the understanding and support of the international communist movement for that "imminent, and this time real, leap from the realm of necessity into the realm of freedom." In his second essay, written ten years later, F. Znakov gives essentially the same analysis of the Soviet system and predicts its imminent collapse. This time, however, he does not make any references to either Marxism-Leninism or socialism and, instead of addressing himself to foreign Communists, appeals for understanding and support to the public opinion at large, both at home and abroad.

It follows from the above that Soviet dissent which has emerged during the mid-1950s–early 1960s was in all its varieties entirely Marxist-Leninist. It is perhaps natural that in a Soviet-type system people with a participatory political culture are the first to react to indications of change from above by entering the dissident arena, whereas the real dissidents, those who remained alien to official Marxism throughout all the years of Soviet rule, were skeptical about any changes within the same Marxist-Leninist framework and continued to live their lives in the way that was shaped in the preceding Stalinist period, that is, mainly as conformists—people keeping their genuine oppositionist views and values to themselves or expressing them publicly in an inoffensive manner such as, for example, participation in religious life.

MARXIST-LENINIST CONVICTIONS FADE AWAY

With the passage of time the Marxist-Leninist ideological framework within which the early Soviet dissenters used to express their views has gradually faded away. Those belonging to the first category of the Marxist-Leninist idealists (i.e., the "anti-Stalinists"), after having realized that the Soviet system is neither willing nor able to change in accordance with their views and values (it took them quite some time to realize this fact; the turning point here being the Soviet invasion of Czechoslovakia in August 1968), were forced by the sheer logic of life to reexamine their Marxist-Leninist convictions. The process of such reexamination was prompted also by their concentration on the issues of legality and human rights. Slowly but irreversibly they came to the conclusion that these are best catered to in conditions of a pluralist Western-type liberal democracy which, as they knew only too well, was incompatible with the very idea of the socialist state as conceived by Marxism-Leninism. In the end these people had to make their choice between the two and most of them made this choice by rejecting their original Marxism-Leninism and wholeheartedly embracing Western-type liberal-democratic views (the personal stories of Andrei Sakharov and especially of his wife, Elena Bonner, are here the most typical and eloquent cases in point).

Today the only people in this category who still claim to be Marxists are the twin brothers Roy and Zhores Medvedev. Their Marxist convictions, however, are highly questionable since their assessment of the Soviet society is not based on either class analysis or on the analysis of the relationship between that society's economic base and its superstructure. Neither do the Medvedev brothers reason about the USSR from the clear-cut standpoint of the interests of the working class. They talk rather about the abstract rights and freedoms of the people in typical bourgeois-democratic way. In fact, therefore, their self-proclaimed allegiance to Marxism seems to be nothing else but a politically motivated explicit declaration of total loyalty to the Soviet system, loyalty not only to its political formula but also to its entire political myth. Proclaiming this loyalty under the "code name" of their adherence to Marxism-Leninism, the Medvedev brothers believe that they are the only dissidents realistically contributing to the liberal-democratic change of the Soviet system. For they are convinced that such a change could be introduced only from above, i.e., by the Soviet leadership itself. It therefore seems to them that the most important task of the dissidents consists not in confronting and opposing the Soviet leaders (an activity that will only provide the "reactionaries" within the leadership with arguments against liberalization), but in persuading those of them who are in the "progressive camp" (of course, in their own Marxist-Leninist language) to opt for such a change and in assisting them in introducing changes. But the only way in which any Soviet leaders could be thus persuaded is, according to the Medvedev brothers, the way of convincingly showing them that the proposed liberal changes are entirely compatible with the Soviet political myth, do not entail any dangers for the system's continuity, and should even increase the system's stability and strength.[11]

It should be clear from the above that the controversy between the Medvedev brothers and the rest of the Soviet liberal-democratic dissidents is not so much about ideas as about political tactics. Marxism as a philosophy or ideology has nothing to do with it.

The most drastic change of mind took place among those people in both categories of the surviving Marxist-Leninist idealists who were unable to reconcile themselves with the ideological vacuum that was left by their disillusionment with and/or their rejection of Marxism-Leninism. The urge to fill this vacuum with a different creed turned some of them to older traditional ideologies, such as religion and/or nationalism. The ideological biographies of such people as Alexander Solzhenitsyn, Igor Shafarevich, Vladimir Maksimov, and Vladimir Osipov, to name but a few, are here the relevant cases in point. So is the revival of Zionism among the formerly Marxist-Leninist-oriented Soviet Jews.

Znakov tells us that by 1963 he "overgrew" his Marxism, too, and in philosophical terms became a "self-conscious eclectic." A few years before this happened, he, a professional scholar, was constantly mocked by his numerous academic friends and colleagues as "the last Marxist of the Soviet Union."[12] These friends and colleagues of Znakov apparently became "marxist agnostics," and many of them "militant Marxist atheists," much earlier than Znakov himself. The autobiography of the former Soviet general, Petro Grigorenko,[13] confirms that this process of "evaporation" of Marxist beliefs, however firmly they were held in the past, is not limited to the Soviet scholarly community but is rather typical for former "Marxist believers" in all sections of Soviet society. As N. Korzhavin, himself formerly an ardent Marxist-Leninist, pointed out, in the Soviet Union today only the unashamed cynics are still pretending to be Marxists; in fact, they are not; even the present Soviet rulers abandoned Marxism a long time ago, and for good, but they have to continue to use its phraseology for entirely pragmatic reasons.[14]

It follows from the above that Marxism, which was in the beginning the sole ideology of Soviet dissent, had by the mid-1960s almost entirely disappeared from the dissident ideological spectrum. Instead, Soviet dissent gradually developed a variety of ideologies, most of which were based on a modern reinterpretation of the pre-Soviet non-Marxist ideological creeds, such as democratic liberalism, religious idealism, different shades of nationalism, and combinations of all these.[15]

In personal terms the former Marxist-Leninists, as people with a participatory political culture, still dominated the dissident stage but now their views were in most cases virulently anti-Marxist. This provided the possibility for the "silent majority" of the traditional non- and anti-Marxists to abandon their long-standing position of silent and inconspicuous loners and to join the ranks of Soviet dissent. Some of them eventually did so. In the first place the Soviet dissidents were joined by the members of such national and religious minorities who had their special acute grievances. Their presence in the all-Union dissident movement became especially apparent after the "rights-defending" wing of Soviet dissent, in particular Andrei Sakharov himself, had actively involved themselves in the protection of their specific rights (the Crimean Tatars, Pentecostalists, Adventists, Evangelical Baptists, Zionists, and many other similar minorities provide the illustration of this point). But not only such specific minorities represented the traditionalist intake into the originally Marxist Soviet dissent. A number of mainstream religious individuals (such as Anatoly Krasnov-Levitin, Gleb Yakunin, et al.) as well as nationalists, none with any Marxist background in their past, both the Russian and the non-Russian ones, started to make their presence in its ranks felt too.

It would, however, be untrue to say that Marxism as an ideology of Soviet dissent is already entirely dead. In his *samizdat* works the late historian Alexandr Zimin continued to discuss the acute problems of Soviet society in purely Marxist terms.[16] Marxist methodology was manifestly present in the proposals for an integral reform of the Soviet system on which the scholars Len Karpinsky and Otto Latsis were working in the early 1970s and which were seized by the KGB in 1975.[17] A group of young scholars (mainly from the Institute of World Economics and International Affairs of the Academy of Sciences of the USSR) who were trying to revise Soviet communism from a Euro-Communist perspective and whose activities were disclosed by the

KGB in 1982 is in this context of special significance because it shows that there are signs of a Marxist revival among the younger, yet very little known, generation of Soviet dissidents. This fact is partly substantiated by the arrest in October 1984 of four young members of Moscow's Engineering-Physical Institute who, as the *samizdat* report indicated, were trying to "reassess Soviet reality from a Marxist postion."[18]

In spite of the above, Marxism as a dissident ideology is of marginal importance today in the USSR. During the 1960s and most of the 1970s Marxism, although already rejected by the mainsteam of Soviet dissent, still played an important role at least as an ideology the dissidents had to overcome and to combat. As Marxism before, anti-Marxism during this period of time was increasingly becoming the common ideological denominator for the dissidents who by now already greatly varied in their respective values and views.

This is no longer the case. For the dissidents of the 1980s Marxism becomes increasingly irrelevant, a subject not even worth discussing seriously. As a young Russian poet Yuriy Kublanovskiy pointed out, Russians of his generation (he is in his late twenties) are completely indifferent to Marx although they have to study him in schools and colleges: "Marx now," he continued, "is in the USSR of no interest to anyone and only a few individuals still continue to hate him."[19]

IS THERE A COMMON DENOMINATOR FOR PEOPLE'S AUTHENTIC SOCIOPOLITICAL ORIENTATION IN THE USSR?

It is in my view significant that Soviet dissent has not developed or acquired a radical political ideology calling for a revolutionary destruction of the Soviet system of rule and the establishment of another utopia, whatever its name. As was pointed out above, such an ideology was, in fact, offered by some Soviet dissidents in the mid-1950s–early 1960s in the form of a Marxist reinterpretation of the nature of the Soviet society and state (by F. Znakov, et al.), but it did not attract any significant following and was soon almost completely forgotten. It seems that the Soviet experience of an ideologically based revolution and its repercussions made both the intelligentsia and the people immune, indeed idiosyncratic, to any repetition of such an experience.[20]

The Soviet dissident movement as a whole, a few marginal exceptions, such as the All-Russian Social Christian Union for the Unification of the People (VSKhSON),[21] notwithstanding, is based on political moderation. It totally rejects political violence, unequivocally condemns terrorism wherever it takes place and by whomever, and for whatever purpose it is exercised, vehemently opposes the very idea of having any definitive blueprints for an alternative organization of society, and does not even believe in political struggle or any kind of activities that have to be conducted by conspiratorial or insurrectionist means. It considers patience to be the greatest and most important political value, is unequivocally committed to the rule of law and, accordingly, relies on making a feasible impact on the ongoing processes of social and political development, which should by themselves, in a natural and spontaneous way, decide the fate of the Soviet system of rule.

This is why the Soviet dissidents, many of whom were released by the Gorbachev administration from prison camps and places of exile during 1986–1987, on the whole support that administration's policies of *perestroika* and *glasnost'*, constructively criticizing the inconsistencies, limitations, and contradictions that mark the practical implementation of these policies. These dissidents participate in the activities of scores of newly formed informal pressure groups (the so-called *neformaly*), openly (though without explicit official approval) publish new periodicals, such as *The Express Chronicle*, which operatively reports the developments in the country's human rights situation; *glasnost'* in which a wide range of issues related to the present situation in the country are freely discussed, and scores of others. They are also ready to cooperate fully with the official media and do so whenever this is possible. The qualified support that Sakharov, without conceding any of his principles or views, lends to Gorbachev's policies is a classical illustration of the dissidents' constructive attitudes to Soviet political reality. The dissidents fully recognize the tremendous positive potential that *glasnost'*—the demand for which marked the beginning of the dissident movement in the USSR in the late 1950s—if it is to develop and acquire an unstoppable momentum, may have for the USSR's transformation into a truly pluralistic and tolerant society, and do whatever they can to enhance its chances to take proper root in Soviet social life, e.g., by using as much as possible the opportunities opened by it, to express publicly their views.

There is in the Soviet Union simply no room any more for utopian ideologies and movements of whatever kind. In this respect, one could say that the politically backward Russia pioneers a new sociopolitical mentality which, if mankind is to survive, has to conquer the world.

NOTES

1. For a more detailed substantiation of this thesis see Alexander Shtromas, *Political Change and Social Development: The Case of the Soviet Union* (Frankfurt: Verlag Peter Lang, 1981), especially 23–66.

2. This started with the so-called Lenin levy of 1924 when 200,000, mainly young career-minded workers were recruited to join the party "to compensate for the Party's loss of Lenin"; this one year's intake comprised about a third of the then total membership of the party of 472,000 (see Thomas H. Rigby, *Communist Party Membership in the USSR, 1917–1968* [Princeton, N.J.: Princeton University Press, 1968]) By 1928 the total membership of the party was already 1,304,471 (see *Bol'shaya Sovetskaya Entsiklopediya,* vol. 11 [The Large Soviet Encyclopedia] 1st ed., p. 533), which means that in three years after the "Lenin levy" had been completed, the membership of the party had almost doubled, making the career-minded opportunistic element in the party's ranks overwhelmingly dominant.

3. According to Robert Conquest's carefully analyzed data, among the 6 to 8 million people repressed during the Great Purge at least 1.5 million were members of the party. Of them only 50,000 were released alive from the Gulag by Khrushchev: the rest had perished. *The Great Terror*, 2d ed. (London: Macmillan, 1970), appendix A. This shows that the number of eliminated party members greatly exceeded the total membership of the party as it stood in 1928 (see previous note), which means that, along with the idealists, many "unfortunate" opportunistic recruits to the party also fell victims to the Great Purge.

4. See Roman Redlikh, *Stalinshchina kak dukhovnyi fenomen* [Stalinism as a Spiritual Phenomenon], 2d ed. (Frankfurt: Possev, 1971).

5. Leonard Schapiro, "Epilogue: Some Reflections on Lenin, Stalin, and Russia," in George Urban, ed., *Stalinism: Its Impact on Russia and the World* (Aldershot: Wildwood House, 1985), 416.

6. Schapiro, "Epilogue: Some Reflections," 424.

7. Milovan Djilas, "Christ and the Commissar," in George Urban, ed., *Stalinism: Its Impact on Russia and the World* (Aldershot: Wildwood House, 1985), 197.

8. See Dora Shturman, "Tetrad' na stole," in *Vremya I my* [Time and We] 53 (1981): 152–81. This is the most relevant part of a bigger *memoir* serialized in that magazine.

9. For a more detailed account on the Krasnopevtsev-Rendel case see Cornelia Gerstenmaier, *The Voice of the Silent* (New York: Hert, 1972).

10. There were two documents signed by F. Znakov that circulated in Moscow's samizdat at the time: *Otkrytoe pis'mo Pal'miro Tolyatti* [Open Letter to Palmiro Togliatti], dated 1956, was one, and *Pamyatnaya zapiska*, dated 1966, was the other. Only the latter has reached the West and is available in its original Russian version, in Radio Liberty, *Arkhiv samizdata* 374 (1966): 1–31. For a rather detailed summary of F. Znakov's views in English, see Shtromas, *Political Change*. There were more similar critical-programmatic documents circulating in Moscow's samizdat at the same time; one of the most prominent among them was the so-called testament of Academician Evgeniy Varga (for its English translation see *New Left Review* 62 [1966]: 134–53).

11. The political views of the Medvedev brothers are elaborately presented in Roy Medvedev, *On Socialist Democracy* (New York: A. Knopf, 1975). For their polemics with fellow dissidents see Roy Medvedev, "The Problem of Democratization and the Problem of Détente," in *Radio Liberty's Special Report* 359 (1973); Roy A. Medvedev, *Political Essays* (Nottingham: Spokesman Books, 1976); and Roy Medvedev, *On Soviet Dissent: Interviews with Piero Ostellino* (New York: Columbia University Press, 1980). In the latter work Medvedev already concedes that he is a socialist rather than a Marxist. For a very well substantiated scholarly account on the progression of Soviet dissenters from Marxism-Leninism to Western-type liberal democracy see Ferdinand J. M. Feldbrugge, *Samizdat and Political Dissent in the Soviet Union* (Leiden: Sijthof, 1975).

12. See Znakov, *Pamyatnaya zapiska*, 28–30.

13. See Petro Grigorenko, *V podpol'e mozhno vstretit tol'ko krys* [One Can Meet Only Rats in the Underground] (New York: Detinec, 1981). An abridged English version is *Memoirs* published in New York in 1982.

14. Naum Korzhavin, "Psikhologiya sovremennogo entuziazma" [The Psychology of Contemporary Enthusiasm] *Kontinent* 9 (1976): 123–33. It seems that by now the fact that Marxism-Leninism is in the Soviet Union in terms of faith a dead ideology has

ceased to be a subject for controversy and is admitted by everyone who touches upon this subject. All the authors of Urban's *Stalinism* agree on it and so do all Soviet dissidents from Solzhenitsyn to Sakharov. See Alexander Solzhenitsyn, *Letter to Soviet Leaders* (London: Fontana, 1974), 28, 46–49; Andrei Sakharov, "On Aleksandr Solzhenitsyn's *Letter to Soviet Leaders*," in Michael Meerson-Aksenov and Boris Shragin, eds., *The Political, Social, and Religious Thought of Russian Samizdat—An Anthology* (Belmont, Mass.: Nordland, 1977), 291–301.

15. There were also a few manifestations of outright fascist ideology. One of the most outspoken examples of it is an anonymous document *Slovo Natsii* that widely circulated in Soviet *samizdat* (for its English text, see "The Nation Speaks," *Survey* 17, no. 3 [1971]). For interesting attempts at classifying the ideologies existing in the USSR, see Andrei Amal'rik, "Ideologies in Soviet Society," *Survey* 21, no. 2 (1976); and Carl A. Linden, *The Soviet Party State: The Politics of Ideocratic Despotism* (New York: Praeger, 1983), chapter 4. A short survey of fascist ideological tendencies is given in Mikhail Agursky, "The Intensification of Neo-Nazi Danger in the Soviet Union," in Michael Meerson-Aksenov and Boris Shragin, eds., *The Political, Social, and Religious Thought of Russian Samizdat—An Anthology* (Belmont, Mass.: Nordland, 1977), 414.

16. Aleksandr Zimin, *Sotsializm I neostalinizm* [Socialism and Neo-Stalinism] (New York: Chalidze Publications, 1981).

17. The original text of Karpinsky and Latsis is not available. Its content is known only from brief summaries in *samizdat* reports concerning the event.

18. Published in *Russkaya Mysl'* [Russian Thought] 3568 (1984): 2.

19. Yuriy Kublanovsky, "Marks i SSSR" [Marx and the USSR] *Russkaya Mysl'* [Russian Thought] 3456 (1983): 5.

20. F. Znakov in *Pamyatnaya zapiska* (1966) himself recognized that facts have not borne out his predictions made in 1956. He complains that all sections of Soviet society, including the working class and the party's rank and file, instead of developing a revolutionary socialist orientation, are getting increasingly permeated by bourgeois consumerism and, gradually, also by the spirit of capitalist entrepreneurship, which manifests itself in the rapid growth of the "second economy," and wonders whether socialism is not merely the longest way for transition from feudalism to capitalism.

21. For a detailed account of VSKhSON, see John B. Dunlop, *The New Russian Revolutionaries* (Belmont, Mass.: Nordland, 1976).

4

To Fight Communism:
Why and How?

ALEKSANDRAS SHTROMAS

The communist Soviet regime is inherently expansionist and cannot come to rest until it either submits the whole world to a communist system of rule or perishes in the process of achieving this goal. The existence of such a regime in control of a superpower is in itself a constant threat to world peace—a fact that is not adequately realized in the West by either the policy-makers or the public. In this article the delusions about the nature and the policies of the communist Soviet regime are dispelled and a proposal for an adequate Western strategy toward the Soviet Union is elaborated. It is shown that the West can pursue this strategy by entirely peaceful and nonviolent means.

I. WHY? THE WESTERN MISCONCEPTIONS OF THE USSR

One of the most prominent experts on the Soviet Union, the French political scientist and historian Alain Besançon, succinctly suggested that "failure to understand the Soviet regime is the principal cause of its successes."[1] In his view, there are in any one Western country at any one time "rarely more than

Reprinted from *Making Sense of Stalin* [pamphlet] (New York: PWPA Press, 1985), 1–32, with a comment by Lloyd Motz, a rejoinder by the author, and a comment on a comment by Sidney Hook.

a dozen minds capable of understanding the Soviet phenomenon and of translating what they know into politically useable terms."[2] Unfortunately, such people are mainly confined to academic or émigré communities and usually do not exercise enough influence on the policy-making process of their respective countries.

The result is best exemplified by former U.S. President Jimmy Carter who, after being in office for three years, exclaimed *in surprise and indignation* that now (i.e., after the Soviet invasion of Afghanistan) he had finally realized that the Soviets are devious and cannot be trusted! To that one must add that the Soviets themselves willingly admit that they would hardly be able to survive, let alone succeed, if not for the assistance of the "useful idiots" in influential positions across the whole "bourgeois-decadent" world.

The Western misconceptions of the Soviet Union are many. The one that I consider to be most responsible for the naiveté, indeed innocence, with which the Soviet Union is treated by the West and from which, accordingly, the Soviets gain most of their strength, consists in the view that the USSR is not much more than a mere continuation of the pre-revolutionary (i.e., pre-1917) Russian Empire and that, therefore, the communist ideology upon which it claims to rest is, in fact, of no real political substance. To be sure, this ideology is used by the Russian Soviet state as an effective and succinct device of pursuing on a worldwide scale its national-imperial goals, but that is about all there is to it.

Nothing can be further removed from the truth than that assertion. For the Soviet Union is first and foremost an ideological state whose very substance is communism and whose rulers have at heart only one single interest, that of communist domination, not only over Russia and its vicinities, but over the entire world.

In the pursuit of this interest, they, of course, need Russia as the main source of their might, but no more than that, as Russia to them is only the means to their globally conceived ends, but by no means an end in itself. The Soviet rulers are indeed entirely indifferent to Russia and even more so to her genuine national interests. There is little doubt that, if they had to sacrifice Russia to ensure the triumph of communism on a larger scale and on a more secure basis than at present, they would do so without much hesitation (they are already now conducting their global policy at the expense of the vital interests of the Russian nation).

The Western refusal to see in communist ideology the prime mover of Soviet behavior, both at home and abroad, is a very dangerous delusion. The substance of that danger was clearly demonstrated to the West in the 1930s when it was dealing under the same "nonideological" assumptions with Hitler. Alas, the lesson was taught but not properly learned. It seems that the West simply lacks the imagination and will to take its ideological adversaries for what they really are. Instead, it prefers to project onto them an "isomorphic" image of rationally minded (though somewhat overrapacious) nation-states and then to treat them in accordance with this false image. The West would not even listen to what its adversaries have themselves to say about their policies and goals, dismissing it all out of hand as mere propaganda, simply because what they say interferes with the West's self-construed, self-comforting, and parochially self-contained image of the world.

Because of this self-inflicted blindness, the West still lives with the illusion that, if it were to concede to the USSR whatever the Soviets deem necessary for assuring their national security, it could in principle settle with them on a reliable and long-term basis all the outstanding issues making for the East–West conflict. It bluntly and obstinately refuses to realize that what would indeed be easily possible to settle with a truly national Russia is in principle unresolvable with the communist USSR.

In exactly the same way, the West was thoroughly convinced that by conceding the Sudetenland to Germany it had met Hitler's ultimate demand about uniting the whole German nation within one German state and thus brought about "peace in our time." As we know, it did not. The result of the West's 1938 Munich deal with Hitler was not peace but World War II. Nevertheless, today the West conducts business with the Soviet Union as if it never had the opportunity to realize how wrong was the assumption that in politics only national interests really matter and that therefore the global ideological visions of one's adversaries could be easily dismissed.

The simple and obvious truth is that with ideologically motivated powers, be it Nazi Germany or communist Soviet Union, no reliable or long-term compromise or coexistence is ever possible. For these powers will never come to rest until they either conquer the world, bringing it to uniformity in concordance with their ideological perceptions or perish in that process. *Tertium non datur*—a third choice for them is not available.

The Soviet Rulership: Ideological or Pragmatic?

Most Western politicians who have dealt with the Soviets, the former German Chancellor Willy Brandt perhaps the most typical among them, try to tell us that the present Soviet rulers are no ideologues, that in fact they are very realistic people who do not care much about communism and are exclusively concerned with pragmatic issues and goals. One has to agree that, differently from their predecessors, the founding fathers of the Soviet regime, the present Soviet rulers do not give a damn about communism or, for that matter, about any ideals at all. In this respect they are indeed very pragmatic, even cynical, people. What they, however, care about most strongly is sheer power. And the power they have inherited, and are bound to cling to, is the absolute dictatorial power of a communist ideological clique whose abstract global-mindedness prevented it from acquiring any large-scale genuine support among the nations (e.g., the Russians) under their rule (hence, the ruthlessness of their dictatorship). The communist ideology, by according to the present Soviet rulers as its "high priests" the inalienable and absolute right to total power, is, therefore, in sheer pragmatic terms indispensable to them. They could not do without it, since they are not representative of anybody or anything except this "ultimate" ideology. Hence, willy-nilly, they are stuck with it and have no choice but to pursue policies that are based on its premises.

There is also no way the present Soviet rulers could do away with the system of power based on the communist ideological assumptions and thus try to become genuine national leaders in their own right. Solzhenitsyn found that out when he addressed them with such a proposition[3] and, in response, was expelled from the country. The problem is that the present Soviet rulers cannot discard the communist ideology without at the same time finishing themselves off, not only politically but, most probably, also physically. Suffice it to remember that almost all of them made their way to the top by actively participating in the terrorist practices of Stalin's rule, exercised in the name of the "noble goals of communism." And there is nothing else, except these goals, which would justify the crimes they have committed and qualify them to the continuous tenure of the enormous power and privileges that alone can protect them from being treated as mere criminal murderers.

This reason alone, not to mention many others, explains why the present Soviet rulers have to remain unswervingly committed to communism and to the pursuit of the goals of global communist domination. This commitment has nothing to do with beliefs and ideals—it has everything to do with pragmatic power politics only. Without communism the Soviet rulers would be as good as dead, and whatever they are, they are not suicidal. This is as straightforward and simple as that. Hence, the apparent cynical pragmatism of present Soviet rulers should not mislead anyone. The more pragmatically self-interested they are, the more ideologically intransigent communists they are bound to be.

Why the USSR Is an Inherently Expansionist State

There is probably even more real substance in the Soviet rulership's commitment to communist world domination at present than there was at any other time. For now it is not any more only abstract ideals but the plain survival of a ruthless and cynical power clique that is at stake, depending on the success or failure of communism worldwide. In order to keep its people in submission, the Soviet state has to impress them constantly and convincingly with its irresistible might. Expansion serves this purpose best. It shows the peoples ruled by the Soviets that resistance is pointless. Indeed, how could their resistance stand any chance of success if even the most powerful countries of the world can do nothing about stopping Soviet expansion and choose to comply with Soviet constant infringements upon their best interests? This attitude could, however, drastically change if the Soviet expansion failed to succeed and proceed. Such a failure would convey to the people the message that Soviet power is becoming weaker and that, after all, resistance to Soviet rule may be meaningful. That in itself could have fateful repercussions for the survival of the unpopular Soviet regime. Hence, without successfully expanding to the outside world, the Soviet rulers would by now hardly be able to sustain themselves firmly enough in power at home. No other credibility is left to them except that of their unfailing ability to exercise repressive power effectively, and this very last credibility the Soviets cannot afford to lose.

But even more importantly, the Soviets have to do everything they can to eliminate the noncommunist "hostile environment" because its unsuppressed and flourishing existence just outside the borders of the Soviet bloc is in itself a lethal challenge to their regime. Even now the Soviets are unable to suppress the admiration of their young people for everything Western and the insistence with which they follow the lifestyles of their counterparts in the West, despite the conditions of life in the Soviet Union being extremely unconducive to their doing so.[4] Therefore, the Soviets know only too well that the West will take them over, if not from without, then from within, and this prospect frightens them to death. Knowing that they do not stand a chance in a peaceful competition with the West, they are left with only one option, to eliminate the Western system, and the best means to that end at their disposal is communist ideology with its powerful subversive and expansionist potential.

The Soviet ruling clique because of this is indeed in a situation like Dracula's. As Dracula would probably not have sucked other people's blood if he could have survived without doing so, the Soviet rulers would probably not have insisted on conducting their policy of global expansion of communism if they could have secured their power in a different and less risky way. But there is no different way for them, and this is what the problem is all about.

How Should the West Respond to the Soviet Challenge?

Faced with such a political reality, the West should start without delay a thorough revision of its policies toward the Soviet Union and define in a more consistent fashion what they should be. The policy of seeking a lasting accommodation with the Soviets by making concessions to their demands is illusory. There will never be a real accommodation between the Soviet Union and the West, and Western concessions to the Soviets will only encourage them to pursue their global plans more actively and energetically.

The policy of accommodation by deterrence and containment can have only a temporary and relative effect. It is a good policy insofar as it makes Soviet moves less provocative and drastic, but as a policy aimed at stopping Soviet expansion altogether, it is doomed to failure. No open Western-type society could ever effectively contain a closed, ideology-based one for the simple reason that the latter can always penetrate and subvert the former from the inside without it being able to reciprocate in kind. It is like trying to contain a cancer cell from metastasizing, which up to now humanity has been unable to do. This means that the policy of deterrence and containment is not a self-sufficient policy. It is valid only insofar as it assumes a subordinate, military security providing role within the wider framework of policies aimed at the total defeat of communism. To this policy whose strategic goal is the elimination of communist powers from the face of the earth and the restoration to their proper national selves of all nations captured by communism, inclusive of Russia herself, there is realistically speaking only one alternative—that of surrender to communism.

This alternative is advocated by those who have coined the catch phrase "better red than dead" or agree to subscribe to it. This alternative, however provocative and mindful of peace, is hardly valid. The problem with it is that unfortunately one cannot become red on a global scale and also remain alive. To be red, in the end, is as good as to be dead, and one should make no bones about it. This is so because the new communist world will by no means become a monocentric system.

Even now the Soviet Union is already unable to control all the communist powers that were in the first place established and controlled by it. Moreover, after having split away from their founding "Soviet mother," these powers either became extremely hostile to the Soviet Union—China and Albania are cases in point—or, as in the case of Yugoslavia, became the targets of Soviet hostility. If not for the powerful presence and containing influence of the West, the Soviet Union would have certainly attacked Yugoslavia in 1948 and China in 1969 with bloody wars ensuing as the result of these attacks. We have already witnessed a Vietnamese communist invasion and subsequent occupation of an equally communist Kampuchea, as well as a Chinese communist attack against an equally communist Vietnam. Just imagine what the situation would be if the whole world became communist and no restraining influence could be exercised on it from outside. The Orwellian scenario of *1984*, according to which the three totalitarian communist superpowers are in a constant state of war with one another, would have been beyond any doubt not mere fiction but historic reality.

It is unlikely that wars between or among communist powers would be as sloppy as Orwell has envisaged them to be in his novel and that they would proceed along the lines of the present war between Iran and Iraq. It is much more likely that these wars would be fought on a full nuclear scale, thus exposing mankind to a much more real threat of extinction than now. That is why to be red is tantamount to being dead, not in any figurative sense, but literally. That is why there is no real choice between being red and dead, whatever some myopic pacifists think about it. Communist world domination spells not peace but war, and one should never allow oneself to forget that when discussing Western policies toward the Soviet Union.

This practically leaves the West with no realistic policy option other than fighting communism resolutely and to the very end—that is, until its final defeat everywhere it is in power—and with no other strategic goal than that of a world without communism. No more, but no less either. This policy is much more than the policy of defending freedom and our own way of life. It is even more than the policy of liberating all individuals and nations from communist oppression. It is the only real policy assuring peace and physical survival of mankind and thus a policy to which any thoughtful pacifist should subscribe. Sooner or later the West as a whole, including its pacifists (but, of course, not its communists), will have to realize this fact and, however reluctantly, accept it. It had better happen sooner than later, since later can be too late.

II. HOW? NEITHER WAR NOR VIOLENCE

The second question, "How to fight communism?," could be quite easily answered if one would turn it around and ask, "How not to fight communism?" The answer would be clear-cut and simple—one shall not fight communism by waging war or employing any other military or violent means. On the contrary, one has to deter communism from waging a war against the West. This could be achieved only by the West making itself unassailable to a Soviet attack. After having secured that, one can assuredly begin to fight communism by using exclusively nonviolent, peaceful means.

The victory over communism should and will be decisively won by the determined engagement of the West in the battle of ideas, not of arms. The greatest asset in that battle is that communism as an ideology is already entirely and irreversibly dead within the hearts and minds of the people ruled by the communists.

The Soviet Society: Total Dissent and Total Obedience

My experience of life in the Soviet Union for about forty years, as well as my many years of thorough research of the Soviet political system, led me to the conclusion that Soviet society, not to mention societies of other communist countries, is one of total dissent. In 1974, for the first time after more than a decade, I met a convinced communist. This happened, however, after I came to Britain, and the convinced communist I met was, of course, British, not Russian. In Russia I met only convinced anticommunists or people who were not convinced about anything except their personal well-being, which insofar as official communist values are concerned, is one of the obvious forms of dissent.

Communist societies are, however, not only those of total dissent; they are also societies of almost total obedience to the powers that be. This apparent paradox becomes not paradoxical at all if one remembers the indiscriminate terror the communist authorities have for a great many years relentlessly waged against every nation they took over to rule.

Apart from its lasting intimidating effect, this terror was instrumental in shaping the new communist order. Under this order, national societies became so effectively atomized that people in them were left with little choice but to bow to the government that took effective charge of all socially relevant activities of every single individual and group. In addition, the government, by fully controlling all material resources and their allocation, made people totally dependent on it for their sheer survival.

Even under these circumstances, communists did not bring their rule by terror to an end. To be sure, by the mid-1950s, the Soviet authorities stopped using indiscriminate active mass terror, but they replaced it with the passive mass terror of total supervision, enabling them to repress, now in a truly selective but nevertheless determined and ruthless manner, every noncompliant individual or act. The terror changed its form and became more institutionalized and orderly, but it is still there. It is just its "spectacular" part that has gone, not the essence. No wonder that under such circumstances people are still forced to keep a low profile and avoid doing anything that the authorities would consider controversial, almost as much as during the time of "active terror."

This is how total dissent in the Soviet Union goes hand in hand with almost total outward obedience to the regime. That obedience is, however, a thin façade beneath which total dissent is simmering and getting ready to burst out into the open at the first convenient opportunity. In Hungary in 1956 and in Czechoslovakia in 1968, the whole world was witness to the abrupt end of that total obedience and the eruption of total dissent onto the surface of these societies. After the Soviet invasion of these two countries, the world also witnessed how fast total obedience was restored, with dissent again becoming almost invisible. It was fear and nothing else that made dissent disappear so quickly from the surface, but fear does not change people's hearts and minds, where dissent remains intact, grows ever stronger with every such experience, and awaits the next realistic opportunity to achieve victory before bursting out into the open again.

These two events provided the most convincing demonstration of how dissent and obedience in communist countries are intertwined with one another and what in certain circumstances makes the one prevail over the other. In addition, the Poles, who have provided such demonstrations on so many previous occasions—in 1956, 1968, 1970, 1976, not to speak of 1980—are now showing to the world something very different and new. Calmly but effectively, they refuse to become obedient to the communist authorities again as fully and unequivocally as they were before August 1980. This is how the deterioration of communist authority proceeds before the eyes of the world, making the latter for some strange reason worried rather than joyful about it.

The Role of the West in Assuring the Victory of Dissent

Total dissent in communist countries is indeed a tremendous potential force. What it needs most to transform itself into an actual one is Western support and full nonhesitant solidarity. If this support were forthcoming (and as yet it never has been, since the West has always been more afraid of undermining the status quo than of the communist threat), the collapse of Soviet rule from Berlin to Vladivostok would be a matter not of years but of weeks and months.

There are as yet no signs that the West is ready to review its political priorities and become bold enough to challenge and change the status quo, in spite of a realistic possibility of doing so. The West is still even willing to go out of its way to rescue faltering socialist economies of the Soviet bloc countries whenever such a need arises. With the Council for Mutual Economic Cooperation's (COMECON) overall debt to the West now reaching the 100 billion U.S.-dollar mark and projected to rise in 1984–1985 by another $25–50 billion,[5] there is no way one can pretend that these generous credits make any economic sense. With no political or even managerial strings attached, they are obviously irretrievable and spell a huge financial loss that, in the end, the Western taxpayer will have to bear. Nevertheless, the West insistently continues to pour huge sums of good money after bad, and the reason for its doing so can only be political. Indeed, by bailing out the almost bankrupt economies of the Soviet bloc, the West secures political stability in the countries of that bloc and thus tries to maintain intact the status quo in the world at large. The question is whether this goal is worth the effort and the expenditure. In my view, it is not. It is indeed time for the West to abandon such policies altogether and, instead of siding with communist governments, to come resolutely to the side of the dissident nations of communist lands striving for political change.

There is not so much that the West has to do to achieve this change of attitude. In addition to bringing an end to economic aid to communist countries, it has to start a policy of full support to, and close cooperation with, the peoples who are already engaged in an active struggle against communism. The forefront of this struggle is today in Afghanistan, which means that the West has to help the Afghans to achieve political unity under a legitimate coalition government, and then to assist that friendly government in its legitimate struggle for the country's freedom from foreign occupation. To make this struggle fully successful, it would be of ultimate importance for that Afghan government to appeal to the Soviet soldiers and officers to join the Afghan liberation forces and fight communism together under the old slogan "for your and our freedom." There is little doubt that this appeal would be effective enough to force the Soviets to withdraw their troops from Afghanistan fairly quickly.

The victory over the Soviets in Afghanistan could by no means remain an isolated event of mere national significance. If the Afghans were to prove— and that would be the first such proof since 1920—that the Soviets may be rolled back, other nations suffering under Soviet communist oppression would regain their hope of freedom and try to follow the Afghan example. The West should be ready for such a development and without hesitation extend its active support to these nations' efforts to get themselves engaged in an active struggle against communism, too.

In the first place, however, it is necessary for the West, already in the initial stage, not to limit its active support to Afghanistan only. To make itself truly credible as an ally of the peoples of communist-ruled lands, the West would have to extend its help simultaneously, and on a basically equal level with Afghanistan, to Jonas Savimbi's UNITA forces in Angola, as well as to the less visible forces of armed resistance to communism in Mozambique and Ethiopia.

Secondly, the West would have to declare publicly its full solidarity with the Polish nation. It should be made clear in this declaration that in case of Soviet or any other communist country's military invasion into Poland, the West will act exactly in the same way as the one suggested above for Afghanistan. Moreover, such a Western commitment must be given not only and exclusively to Poland. It has to be extended also to nations in the rest of Eastern Europe and elsewhere, thus becoming equally applicable to all cases in which Soviet invasion, in reaction to a nation's attempt to regain its freedom from communism, could be expected.

One should not be scared of the Soviet reaction to such declarations and actions. The Soviet Union is not going to go to war with the West because of them. As was already pointed out, the Soviet rulers are not suicidal, and it is not in their interests or traditions to start a war in which the survival of their system could be put at risk. All the wars that the Soviet Union in its whole history since 1917 has started were "safe wars." They were always waged against small nations (such as Finland or Poland) and only in a situation where no major power was prepared to provide the nation under Soviet attack with any substantial backing. There was never a case of the Soviet Union on its own volition openly engaging in military conflict with any major power. Even Japan was attacked by the Soviets only at the very end of the war when no real resistance on the part of the Japanese was possible. There are no indications that the present Soviet rulers are likely to change this constant "hyena-like" pattern of their international behavior. On the contrary, the indications are that they will not.

No doubt, the Soviet reaction to such Western declarations and actions will be even more hysterical than usual. The Soviet abuses directed against the West and the amount and tone of their anti-Western propaganda will certainly increase to an unprecedented level. But the limit of it all will be intimidation aimed at making the West retreat from its "intransigent" stance. On the other hand, the Soviets, as "peacemakers," will not spare any effort to get the West to agree with them on a new arrangement, which would basically mean the restoration of the previous situation. They would do no more. Therefore, there would be no real reason for the West to concede under Soviet pressure anything that would amount to reducing Western commitment to supporting the captive nations of Eastern Europe and elsewhere against Soviet aggression, potential or even actual.

The West's main problem in this process is not to lose its nerve, not to "blink first," so to speak.

If the West were able to come to grips with this problem, the process of "rolling back" communism would be effectively started without the Soviet Union being able to do much to stop it. And even if the Soviets did do something, events would probably get out of their control quite quickly anyway, primarily because the Russians under such circumstances would themselves be likely to join the anticommunist resistance forces. In that case there would be no need for any direct Western involvement in this "rolling back" process at all. The nations in communist captivity would be perfectly able to take care of it themselves.

To Fight Communism in the Noncommunist World

There is yet another aspect of fighting communism that is almost as significant as the previous one. Communism must be fought as an ideological and political force in the free world itself.

Communists in every country outside the Soviet realm are a natural constituency of the Soviet Union. Through them the Soviet Union learns about the world and optimizes its influence upon it. Trying to destroy the system under which they live, the communists become, consciously or not, the instruments of Soviet policy of inner subversion of each country not yet under communist control. Moreover, it is mainly by enabling the local communists to get to power that the Soviet rulers conduct their policy of global communist expansion. In this respect, foreign communists are indispensable to their Soviet counterparts since, as was demonstrated above, without that expansion they would hardly be able to sustain themselves in power within the present realm of their rule.

It would not, however, be fair to say that the Soviet Union uses foreign communists for its own purposes as some sort of agents or mere stooges. The communists outside the communist world sometimes need the Soviet Union even more than the Soviet Union needs them. For, in most cases, they are power-greedy political minorities that, without Soviet assistance and support, would never have been able to get even near to power, let alone to grab it exclusively for themselves and then use it without restraint for the implementation of their communist ideological goals.

It is thus that an unholy alliance between the Soviet Union and the communist parties outside the realm of its rule is formed to advance the expansion of communist totalitarianism throughout the world, the goal that is equally in the interests of all parties involved in this alliance, not just of the Soviet Union. This alliance is the main device that keeps communism afloat and allows it to succeed both in the Soviet domain and in the world at large. Therefore, by effectively fighting communism in the free world, one reduces at the same time the Soviet Union's capacity to expand, and, by that, also to survive. That is why this fight is so crucially important. On the other hand, the intensification of the fight against communism in the free world should produce more public awareness of communism and the USSR, which could be helpful in the West's switching its policies from supporting the status quo to the support of change in the USSR and its dependencies.

One should, however, stress over and over again that one has to fight communism in the free world solely by ideological means. Political repressions tend to strengthen communism, making its cause morally more plausible. A party that, in order to enhance its sectarian goals, uses the posture of a champion of the poor could be made more influential and dangerous by conferring upon it an aura of martyrdom. Many anticommunist dictators have had the opportunity to find this out but, alas, not as many have drawn from that experience the necessary conclusions.

CONCLUSION

As one may have noticed, I tried to briefly outline here a fourfold Western strategy for the victory over communism, which is my answer to the question, "How to fight and defeat communism?" without ever resorting to war or any other violent methods. To summarize briefly, one could say that in order to fight and defeat communism, it is necessary:

1. To deter communist powers from direct aggression against the noncommunist world, preferably by means of equitable multilateral disarmament, but if this proves to be impossible because of communist opposition, by a determined engagement to win the communist-imposed arms race.
2. To help dissent in communist countries to assert itself by means of effective use of Soviet-endorsed international instruments concerning the protection and enhancement of human rights and of the freedom of obtaining and exchanging information (broadcasting and sending literature to the communist countries being in that context the most important activities), and also by effectively stopping Soviet-supported or simply Soviet-sponsored expansion of communism around the world.
3. To stop helping, economically and otherwise, the rulers of the Soviet Union and its dependencies to maintain themselves in control over their countries and, instead, to start supporting and encouraging the forces engaged, or about to be engaged, in fighting communism for the national and social liberation of their respective nations.
4. To concentrate more actively on fighting communism ideologically in the noncommunist world, particularly by using to the fullest extent the potential of those few people who properly and adequately understand the real essence of communism and the Soviet Union.

COMMENT

Lloyd Motz
Astronomy Department
Columbia University
New York, New York

Dr. Alex Shtromas's article, from its very title, which envisions and, indeed, invites an endless epoch of conflict between the USSR and the rest of the world, is a recital of unverified accusations against a society with which we must live in peace and with which we must share the fruits of our planet, if this planet is to survive. True, Dr. Shtromas states that "one shall not fight communism by waging war or employing any other violent means," but he immediately contradicts this statement by outlining a plan "to start a policy of full support to, and close cooperation with, the peoples who are already engaged in an active struggle against communism." It is clear from what follows this sentence that Dr. Shtromas includes war, that is, "military action," in his call for "full support." But even if we accept Dr. Shtromas's thesis that "fighting communism" is the only path to universal peace (a contradiction in terms, at best), we must reject his solution owing to his bias and unsupported assumptions.

Some examples taken directly from the article indicate how weak Shtromas's arguments are. He reveals the quality of his thinking and the tenor of his thesis in his first paragraph by accepting Alain Besancon's statement that "failure to understand the Soviet regime is the principal reason for its success." To argue seriously that a regime or social system succeeded because it was not understood implies that, it if had been understood, it would have collapsed, which is illogical. It is even more illogical to accept, as Shtromas does, Besançon's assertion "that there are rarely more than a dozen minds in any one Western country at any one time capable of understanding the Soviet Phenomenon." Is this a serious evaluation of the intelligence of social and political scientists throughout the world? How presumptuous and arrogant of Shtromas to suggest that only he and a few others understand the "Soviet phenomenon," as though it were some kind of complex, subtle intellectual concept beyond the grasp of ordinary mortals.

How can one take seriously Shtromas's statement that, if the West fully supported the "dissent in communist countries . . . the collapse of Soviet rule from Berlin to Vladivostok would be a matter of not years but of weeks and months"? From its very inception, the Soviet Union overcame every possible obstacle to its peaceful development (including invasion by American and other troops) placed in its way by the rest of the world; and yet, weak as it was, it survived, expanded, and went on to bear the full brunt of, and to defeat, the Nazi war machine. In view of this, which Shtromas knows full well, it is unconvincing for him to argue that the Soviet regime would have collapsed if it had been understood and that it will collapse in a few weeks if we encourage and support its dissenters.

To go on with my evaluation, where is Shtromas's evidence for his assertion that the "Soviets themselves willingly admit that they would hardly be able to survive, let alone succeed, if not for the assistance of the 'useful idiots' in influential positions across the whole 'bourgeois-decadent' world"; or for his statement that the "Soviet rulers are indeed entirely indifferent to Russia and even more so to her genuine national interest"? The article contains many such unsupported assertions, as I point out below. But he violates logic as well, as when he states that the "substance of that danger [the supposed 'danger' assumed to stem from the Soviet Union] was clearly demonstrated to the West in the 1930s when it was dealing under the same 'nonideological assumptions' with Hitler." To argue, as Shtromas does here, that the ideological differences between the West and the Soviet Union, if not recognized as the source of the East–West conflict, must lead to a global catastrophe because that is what happened with Hitler makes no sense and leads him to a falsification of the present state of affairs. This falsification is seen when he implies that the Soviet Union is making territorial demands of the West with the threat of the use of force, just as Hitler did before invading Austria, Czechoslovakia, and Poland.

These are the most glaring examples of Dr. Shtromas's categorical statements and unwarranted conclusions; but almost every page contains others. For instance: "The simple and obvious truth is that with ideologically motivated powers, be it Nazi Germany or communist Soviet Union, no reliable or long-term compromise on coexistence is ever possible." Is not the United States government based on the ideology of total democracy? And if so, is the United States also included in Dr. Shtromas's assertion? Since he does not define the phrase "ideologically motivated" precisely, his statement is meaningless. We must also reject, as pure invention, his assertion that "these powers will never come to rest [whatever that means] until they conquer the world . . . or perish in the process." Such unsupported statements indicate a biased approach to the problems that the West and the USSR must solve together if they are to coexist peacefully and free of the constant threat of war.

I conclude my commentary by citing other examples of biased assertions:

1. "The present Soviet rulers do not give a damn about communism or about any ideals at all." This contradicts his previous statement that the Soviet rulers care only about communism and not at all about Russia or its people. In any case, how does Dr. Shtromas know so positively, without expressing any doubt at all, what goes on in the minds of the Soviet rulers?

2. "This commitment [to communism] has nothing to do with beliefs and ideals . . . it has everything to do with pragmatic power politics only.

Without communism, the Soviet rulers would be as good as dead." Does Dr. Shtromas ask us to accept such peremptory statements without proof because he has direct contact with some divine intelligence that gives him such information?

3. "There will never be a real accommodation between the Soviet Union and the West." "Never" is a very long time.

4. "To this policy . . . the total defeat of communism and the elimination of communist powers from the face of the earth . . . inclusive of Russia herself, there is . . . only one alternative . . . the surrender of communism." This is a direct call for war, at worst; at best, it is an appeal to aggravate the antagonisms between the West and the Soviet bloc, hardly a recipe for peace.

5. "That is why to be red is tantamount to being dead, not figuratively, but literally. That is why there is no real choice between being red and dead, whatever some myopic pacifists think about it." One wonders, in the light of this statement, why the 1.5 billion people (this includes the Chinese) now living under communism have not seen the light, as Shtromas sees it, and committed suicide. Indeed, it is very curious that Shtromas is still alive, for, according to his own confession, he "experienced [that is, lived under] communism for forty years" and survived his own dictum, "better red than dead."

6. "This . . . leaves the West with no option other than fighting communism resolutely and to the very end—until its final defeat everywhere— with no other goal than a world without communism." Again, a call for war, or, at best, unending conflict instead of peace.

There is no need to continue with this recital of Dr. Shtromas's aggregate of unwarranted conclusions to show the desolate quality of his ideas. Finally, however, one more feature tht characterizes this essay is its unrealism. For example, it is the height of fantasy and self-delusion to believe, as Shtromas does, that communism can be "rolled back" and, ultimately, eliminated globally by "helping the Afghans to achieve political unity under a legitimate coalition government . . . and simultaneously . . . extend help . . . to Jonas Savimbi's UNITA forces in Angola, as well as to the . . . armed resistance to communism in Mozambique and Ethiopia." How can anyone accept this? Measure this suggestion against the following facts: The full impact of MacArthur's armies failed to roll back communism in Korea; the Bay of Pigs assault against Cuba and the economic boycott against it have had very little effect on Cuba's communist regime; the many years of military action by the French and Americans against the communists in Vietnam led to a strengthening of the communist forces and a defeat of the French and American forces; and, finally, our actions in Central America have not deterred the revolutionary forces there.

REJOINDER

Alexander Shtromas

There is nothing much I can say about Professor Lloyd Motz's virulent attack on my article. I believe that the article itself contains a sufficient defense against this attack and that, therefore, there is no new case for me to answer. It could have been different, however, if Motz would have revealed his own positive views on what the Western strategy toward the Soviet Union should be and thus provided an alternative to my proposal. But this is exactly what he has failed to do, which to me is tantamount to the failure of his whole endeavor. For without having developed one's own concept of right strategy, there is no way one is able to prove in any convincing manner that any other strategy is wrong.

I think I understand why my article has provoked such an angry outburst by Motz. I have offended, indeed violated, all his firmly held beliefs about the nature of the USSR, the substance of the communist ideology, and the origins and directions of the danger to peace in the contemporary world. For Motz it goes without saying that in Russia the communist Soviet regime is totally legitimate, but I maintain that it is not. For him it is self-evident that Communists everywhere are exclusively concerned with bringing justice and prosperity to the backward national societies over which they rule, that therefore they enjoy in these societies the wholehearted support of the masses of ordinary people to whom justice in the precommunist times was denied (this belief is most eloquently expressed by Motz in the end of his comment), whereas I am bluntly stating that exactly the opposite is true and that communism is by definition global (i.e., a national and antinational) and extremely oppressive of all the peoples it rules. Finally, he is in no doubt that communism and the USSR are entirely benign and peaceful political forces and that, if it were not for the aggressive, selfishly motivated anticommunist posture of the developed countries of the West (the United States in the first place), the world would become a real haven of peace in which the developed West and the developing East could live side by side in perfect harmony. I, however, have dared to deny this and accuse, not the West, but the Soviet Union and the communists of aggressive expansionism aimed at world domination. No wonder that Motz was outraged by my article and in sincere indignation had passionately rejected all my "disturbing" views. Disturbing, indeed, they are, and I wish I were wrong and Motz right. Unfortunately, this is not the case and I have to stick to everything I said, however unpleasant it may be.

I could have finished my rejoinder on this rather sad note, but a couple of points need clarification. The first refers to the nature of the Soviet as well as any other communist state. It is probably not enough simply to say that—to quote from my article—"the Soviet Union is, first and foremost, an ideological state whose very substance is communism and whose rulers have at heart only one single interest, that of communist domination, not only over Russia and its vicinities, but over the entire world." To be sure, the Soviet Union is indeed a communist–ideocratic and teleocratic (i.e., a future goal-achievement oriented) state whose commitments and goals are not simply alien but contrary to the self-perceived interests and genuinely held views of the overwhelming majority of the people under its rule; but it should have been stressed much stronger that as such this state is also bound to be a *clique state*—a state whose only purpose is to enhance and promote at all costs the interests and goals of the small, ideologically zealous ruling clique against those of the people at large. In this respect it is of secondary importance whether, as in the beginning, this ruling clique consists of idealistic believers in a higher and better order of things, which they are determined to bring about against all odds by a revolutionary (e.g., terrorist) action, or of cynical opportunists who do not believe in any ideals at all but who, in order to survive, do everything they can to perpetuate the single ideology and teleology of the power they have inherited. The clique nature of this state remains exactly the same at all times and so remain also its basic policies and activities.

Motz has accused me of drawing unwarranted conclusions, based on bias and prejudice rather than on evidence and fact, but he has failed to produce any evidence himself. This is no surprise, since beliefs forming a person's holistic world view are of an axiomatic nature and everything that runs contrary to them is usually rejected without any substantiation. Motz, however, is wrong in assuming that my views on communism and the Soviet Union are as unwarranted as his beliefs. To satisfy, at least partially, his appetite for my evidence, I shall very briefly quote just a few elementary and undisputed facts:

1. No communist regime has been established by means of free elections or even as a *direct* result of a revolution that has done away with the old regime; all such regimes were created conspiratorially, by the communist political minority successfully staging a coup d'etat in the postrevolutionary era. None of them has ever dared to test its legitimacy through a free election, no matter how well consolidated its actual grip on power has been.

2. Every communist regime has initially (this initial period lasted in the USSR, for example, from 1918 till 1953) exercised its rule—aimed at the "socialist transformation" of the society it has taken over—by the means of relentless and indiscriminate mass terror directed against all sections of the country's population (for example, in Lithuania alone, about one third of the population was exterminated by the communists for the sake of "socialism" during the years 1940–1953).

3. Every communist regime is permanently founded on the principle of the "leading role of the party" which invests total political, social, and economic power in the hands of an a priori defined political apparatus to the exclusion of everybody else in society; terror, even after the prolonged initial period, remains the sole and constant response of the

regime to any challenge directed at this principle, even if such challenge comes from an unassuming single individual who happened to express, however mildly, and even privately, his dissatisfaction with the existing order of things.

4. Social sabotage and economic delinquency amplified by ubiquitous corruption are the way in which every society under communist rule defies the communist regime and its basic values on a perpetual and massive, indeed total and constant, scale.[6]

5. The society under communist rule, when given a choice, has always refused to support its communist regime and, as soon as the latter lost, albeit temporarily, its ability to exercise effective repression, spontaneously consolidated itself into a force opposed to the regime; this was manifested, not only in Hungary in 1956, in Czechoslovakia in 1968, and in Poland in 1956 and 1980–1981, but also in the USSR in 1941 (only a Hitler with his murderous anti-Russian policies was able to induce the reluctant Russians—but not before the war was in its second year—to heed Stalin's patriotic, *not communist*, appeals and to fight and win a war against Nazi Germany under his command).[7]

It was Motz's blunt refusal to recognize that the USSR always was and remains a clique state that has led him to that entirely wrong conclusion that if we were to adopt a policy of fighting communism, we would, by the same token, engage ourselves in "an endless epoch of conflict . . . against a society with which we must live in peace and with which we must share the fruits of our planet, if this planet is to survive." The second point I wish to clarify is that we would *not*. On the contrary, by decisively engaging itself in a fight against communism without using violence or waging war, the West would, in fact, enter into a real and genuine alliance with that society, helping it to assert its freedom from an oppressive totalitarian state. Only such an alliance can in the long run assure for us a firm peace and a lasting friendship with that society which will, no doubt, also entail the sharing of the fruits of our planet.

I do not see any logic in Motz's repetitive statements that the West's engagement in such a fight against communism equals war against the USSR. What does Motz have in mind when he continuously stresses this point? Does he suggest that, in retaliation to such Western policy, the Soviet Union, out of desperation, will launch a direct military attack against the West? But is it not clear that if the Soviets would consider themselves able to destroy the West without being destroyed themselves, they would have launched such an attack without waiting for any Western "provocations"? Their policy is directed toward making the West weak, divided, and complacent exactly because this would enable them to finish the West off without incurring any risks of destruction themselves. But as long as the West is remaining sufficiently united and strong to repel decisively any Soviet attack, the Soviets will certainly prefer to stick to the policy of "peaceful coexistence," whatever challenges and "provocations" short of war the West may present them with. Whatever the Soviets are, suicidal they are not.

And why should they not stick to this policy? After all, it is their view that the present international situation is nothing else but an antagonistic class confrontation between the "forces of socialism headed by the USSR" and the "capitalistic-imperialist bloc led by the U.S." All Soviet leaders, from Lenin to Chernenko, have consistently stated that the ultimate and supreme goal of the Soviet state is the destruction and elimination of capitalism and, as a result, the promotion of communism on a global scale; and also that, equally, the goal of the capitalist West cannot be other than the destruction of communism and of the Soviet regime in the USSR.[8] Hence, one of the major tasks of Soviet foreign policy (as Chernenko also stressed at the same meeting) is to deter the capitalist West, particularly the United States, from waging a war against the USSR and thus to keep the ongoing communist–capitalist confrontation within the framework of "peaceful coexistence of states with different social systems" (it is significant in this respect that Article 28 of the USSR's Constitution officially declares that Soviet foreign policy is "aimed at . . . strengthening the positions of world socialism" and, at the same time, proclaims the USSR's full commitment to the "principle of peaceful coexistence of states with different social systems." In their view, peaceful coexistence can perfectly assure communist world control). In other words, the Soviets view their struggle against capitalism, as a political behavior totally consistent with the policy of peace. Why shouldn't we follow their example and realize too that an ideological and political confrontation with communism is fully compatible with the policy of peaceful coexistence with the USSR and even with a fair degree of consultation and cooperation in interstate and international affairs?

There is really no need for us to be afraid of trying to match our policies toward the Soviet Union with the Soviet policy toward us. The Soviets expect it from us anyway and, in anticipation of our more decisive move in this direction, have already launched a hysterical propaganda campaign accusing us of shameless subversion and even of surreptitious preparation for nuclear attack. There is really nothing more we could do in this respect than we already stand accused by the Soviet Union of doing. It is therefore high time for us to try to live up to at least a few of the more innocuous of their accusations and invectives. There is nothing in it for us to lose and everything to gain.

No one can doubt that prevention of war is today the first and most vital political priority. It should also be clear that the more balanced the forces of the East and the West, the better the chances to keep the precarious peace intact. Military hardware is by no means the only element making for this balance. Equally important, and perhaps more, is the force of the policies each side is conducting toward its opponent. In this sense, the West is far behind the Soviets and I see the strategy suggested in my article as one possible way for us to catch up with them. In fact, all I have suggested in my article boils down to one simple thing: to extend the principles of equality and reciprocity in East–West relations from the narrow area of military strength to the entire field of policy-making.

I happen to agree with the late Mr. Brezhnev, who in his Report to the 25th Congress of the Communist Party of the Soviet Union (CPSU) (February 1976) stated that "détente does not in the slightest abolish or alter the laws of the class struggle." One could also say that "class struggle" does not abolish or alter "the rules of détente." The convulsive ups and downs in the East–West relationship notwithstanding, détente was and remains a commanding necessity for both sides of this relationship. As strange as it may sound, the assumption by the West of an active role in the "class struggle," if it is to come about, would certainly become a decisive factor for the resurrection of détente. It will of course be a different kind of détente than that of the 1970s—less ambiguous, more symmetrical. Being founded on realistic premises and on an equal understanding of its meaning, it will this time leave no room for illusory expectations or damaging disappointments. And it will be much more than simply détente. For détente between the governments would then be reinforced by a growing genuine *entente* between the peoples of the East and the West gradually uniting themselves in a common commitment to national freedom, individual human rights, and a world where the ideal of peace could be transformed into political reality.

COMMENT ON A COMMENT

Sidney Hook
Hoover Institution
Stanford University
Stanford, California

If there is such a thing as the will to misunderstand, Dr. Lloyd Motz's comments on Dr. Shtromas's article illustrates it. Dr. Shtromas explicitly states that the free world "shall not fight communism by waging war or employing any other violent means" of aggression. Indeed, his article could have been entitled more accurately "How to Defeat Communism Without War." Nonetheless, by crass disregard of context, Dr. Motz accuses him of contradicting himself when Dr. Shtromas writes—not immediately as Motz alleges but pages later—that the free world should "start a policy of full support to, and close cooperation with, the peoples who are already engaged in an active struggle against communism."

This is a scandalous abuse on Motz's part of the ethics of controversy. What immediately follows the first sentence quoted by Motz is the statement by Shtromas that once communism has been deterred from waging a war against the West, "one can assuredly begin to fight communism by using exclusively nonviolent, peaceful means." The second sentence of Shtromas cited by Motz as evidence of contradiction appears where Shtromas is discussing areas *outside* the Soviet Union, where other peoples are struggling to defend their freedom against communist aggression sometimes with the help of communist fifth columnists and of those whom Lenin called "useful idiots"—useful to communists.

At every point where Dr. Motz accuses Dr. Shtromas of calling for war between the United States and USSR, the context shows that Shtromas is talking about ideological conflict, of resisting communist subversion by better ideas, by more realistic policies based on knowledge of the realities of communist theory and practice.

Disagree with Dr. Shtromas's position as one will! But let us be fair to his argument. His main emphasis is on ideological conflict, that is, an intelligent response to the ideological attacks and crusades that the Kremlin perpetually wages against the free world. Indeed, Dr. Shtromas's position is not far removed from the policy of containment first formulated by George Kennan, who in a recent failure of nerve has abandoned it. If I understand Dr. Shtromas correctly, he is pleading for a resumption of the policy of containment but urges that it be pursued much more vigorously. For example, when the Soviet Union uses proxy Cuban troops to take over Angola or Mozambique, we must help those fighting for national independence; when Soviet armies invade Afghanistan and engage in genocidal practices, we must help the victims and organize world public opinion in protest; and when Solidarity is destroyed in Poland at the behest of the Kremlin, we must cease lending billions of dollars to communist countries or engage in any trade that enhances communist war-making capacity. Does Dr. Motz believe that the free world should do nothing to contain communist aggression? I assume that he is committed to the values of freedom and, therefore, as opposed to the extension of communist totalitarianism as he was to fascist totalitarianism.

Although I am sympathetic to the main thrust of Dr. Shtromas's argument, I am not prepared to underwrite all of his formulations. Some of them are unguarded and easily misunderstood by persons of goodwill and defective knowledge. Here is not the place to develop my own views on détente, the theory of deterrence, and how to preserve both our freedom and peace. I refer interested readers to my recent book *Marxism and Beyond* (Rowman & Littlefield, 1983), especially the chapter, "In Defense of the Cold War: Neither Red nor Dead." I do, however, want to clarify some points that Dr. Motz misunderstands.

To begin with, I find it extraordinary that Dr. Motz should challenge Dr. Shtromas's competence to explore the themes of the nature of communist theory and practice and the history of the Soviet Union. These are subjects he has studied all his life. He is a recognized authority in this area. This does not command assent to his view on our part, but they deserve a respect Dr. Motz does not accord them.

On the other hand, Dr. Motz's remarks do not at all inspire confidence in his qualifications for making informed judgments on the issues he discusses.

For example, he pictures the Soviet Union as if it were always and only a victim of aggression by the rest of the world. He seems unaware that from the moment of its birth the Soviet Union organized the Communist International to overthrow the freely elected governments of the West. He might learn something if he read "Lenin's Twenty-one Conditions" for affiliation of parties to the Third International whose consequence was the splitting of the working class in Italy and Germany, and the uncontested rise of Mussolini and Hitler to power. He speaks of this "invasion" of the Soviet Union by American troops not knowing that the stationing of a contingent of American troops at Archangel was to prevent war supplies from falling into the hands of the Imperial German army when Soviet Russia withdrew from the war. He does not know that the American troops at Vladivostok were there to prevent the Japanese from grabbing Siberia (when the United States legally recognized the USSR in 1933, Litvinoff withdrew the Soviet counterclaims for damages after President Roosevelt showed him the relevant diplomatic documents).

Dr. Motz also seems unaware of the tremendous service rendered to the Soviet Union when the Hoover Famine Relief saved millions of Russians from the consequences of the Kremlin's policies. Today in the Soviet Union this philanthropic endeavor is either ignored or described as a cloak for espionage! The Soviet Union is truly remarkable for its exploits in the field of propaganda! Here it has overtaken and surpassed the West. But few scholars will dispute Shtromas's contention that, to a very considerable extent, this economy of the Soviets depends upon technology bought, borrowed, or stolen from the West.

Some of Dr. Shtromas's contentions may indeed be challenged, but not by the literal-minded misconstructions of Dr. Motz buttressed by word inferences. For example, Shtromas quotes Besancon's statement that "failure to understand the Soviet regime is the principal reason for its success." This elicits from Dr. Motz the retort: "To argue seriously that a regime or social system succeeded because it was not understood implies that, if it had been understood, it would have collapsed. . . ." But it implies nothing of the sort! Besancon and Shtromas, too, are here not talking about a social system but of the success of the Soviet Union in its foreign policy. And they are saying—what many deem obvious—that if Western statesmen had better understood the Soviet regime, they would not have consented to Yalta, Teheran, and Potsdam; just as if Western statesmen of an earlier decade had understood the Nazi regime, they would not have stood idly by when Hitler marched into the Rhineland or hailed Munich as assuring peace in our time.

Dr. Motz is not the only American astronomer who has a Christian Science conception of the nature of Soviet policy. One thinks of Harlow Shapley in this connection. Regardless of the merit of Dr. Shtromas's particular assertions, on the basis of Dr. Motz's comment, Shtromas would be justified in asking the question Max Nomad put to Albert Einstein when the latter was preaching universal pacifism while Hitler was rearming: "I don't write on physics or astronomy; why do you write on politics?"

NOTES

1. See Alain Besancon, *Encounter*, July 1981, 90.

2. Besançon, *Encounter*.

3. Solzhenitsyn, *Letter to Soviet Leaders* (London: Fontana, 1974).

4. Abundant evidence for that is provided in Richard Tempest, "The Soviet Youth Culture," a paper presented at the AAASS annual conference in Kansas City in October 1983.

5. For these figures, see Walter Laquer, *America, Europe and the Soviet Union* (London: Transaction, 1983), 122.

6. For an impressive account of how this phenomenon expressed itself in the USSR, see Konstantin M. Simis, *USSR—The Corrupt Society: The Secret World of Soviet Capitalism,* trans. by Jacqueline Edwards and Mitchell Schneider (New York: Simon & Schuster, 1982).

7. For well-documented studies of Russian mass defiance of the Soviet regime in the beginning of the war and of the readiness throughout the war of a great many Russians to side with Hitler, see Alexander Dallin, *German Rule in Russia, 1941–1945: A Study of Occupation Policies* (Boulder, Colo.: Westview Press, 1981); George Fischer, *Soviet Opposition to Stalin: A Case Study in World War II* (Cambridge, Mass.: Harvard University Press, 1952).

8. The latest such statement by a Soviet leader was made by Chernenko on May 28, 1984, when he addressed in the Kremlin the meeting of the Communist Youth League leaders of the Soviet armed forces; see *Pravda*, May 29, 1984, and all major Western newspapers of the same date.

5

The Inevitable Collapse of Socialism

ALEKSANDRAS SHTROMAS

WHAT IS SOCIALISM?

Socialism was first and foremost conceived as a theoretical vision of a just society. This is to say that it is a moral rather than an economic or social concept. The noneconomic character of the concept of socialism is highlighted by the fact that no socialist has ever suggested that it could evolve as a result of natural and gradual economic development. On the contrary, socialists never tire of stressing that natural economic development inevitably leads to unjust and exploitative concentration of wealth—and by that also of economic power—in the hands of a tiny minority consisting of the most grasping and morally unscrupulous individuals. In their view, socialism can be introduced only by drastic political means that forcefully expropriate that evil minority and equitably distribute its wealth among all members of society.

Convinced of their moral superiority over the rest of the people who out of conformity or weakness of character comply with the rules of the unjust societies in which they happen to live, the socialists treat their opponents as selfish, antisocial, and basically immoral human beings who keep their fellow

Reprinted from Richard M. Ebeling, ed., *The Global Failure of Socialism* (Hillsdale, Mich.: Hillsdale College Press, 1992), 71–91.

men at bay by coercion and conscious deceit. The socialists believe that the use of any means at their disposal to eliminate such evil people from society is not only justified but mandatory. This belief alone makes the socialist a self-righteously arrogant and condescendingly intolerant person—a typical authoritarian personality in the sense in which Theodor W. Adorno, himself a socialist, defined this concept. And, of course, it also means that by such intolerance and self-righteousness, any consistent socialist movement or party inevitably becomes totalitarian.

There are many definitions of socialism—of what a socialist society should mean or embody. But in substance all these definitions boil down to the institution of public ownership of the means of production and, consequently, to central planning. What it means in practice the Soviet people, who have suffered from real socialism longest, have expressed in a joke comparing socialism to capitalism: "What is the difference between capitalism and socialism?"

The answer is: "Capitalist society is based on the exploitation of man by man, and socialism on just the reverse." They were not suggesting a moral equivalence between socialism and capitalism. They knew very well indeed that socialism is much worse than capitalism. In another joke, an Armenian lady asks Armenian Radio Erevan whether it is possible to build socialism in Armenia. The answer is: "Yes, madam, it is certainly possible, but it would be better to do it to Turkey," (i.e., the mortal enemy of Armenia). Or, in another variation of the same joke: "Is it possible to build socialism in Switzerland?" "Yes, it is possible, but what a great pity it would be," the answer goes.

The socialists preach public ownership because they deeply mistrust people, sincerely believing that all individuals are at heart corrupt and if left to their own devices will abuse the public interest. In other words, as soon as you place a public service in an individual's hands, this service will be performed not for the sake of the public but for the benefit and profit of that individual alone. So, in order to avoid that sort of perversion, you have to institute public ownership of the means of production. And then you have to direct the economy in the interest of the public as a whole by the method and means of economic central planning. That cuts waste, prices, artificial demand and supply, and serves the real needs of the real people. True, public services are still in the hands of individuals, but those are individuals who are performing a public duty, not those who are acting as profiteers—individuals who have no vested selfish interest in the things they manage. As servants of the public, they have no choice but to regard the interest of the public as their main commitment and interest. Their success and authority depends in these circumstances exclusively on how well they do their job and on nothing else, especially because profiteering, self-serving behavior, and corruption are treated as severely punishable offences.

Even a social-democratic welfare state is a variety of socialism, as it is nothing more than a watered-down concept of public ownership of the means of production or, more exactly, the primary stage of that ownership, when the state, on behalf of the public, confiscates the "excessive" wealth of those who are better off and distributes it to those who are less well off.

Socialists have never really analyzed the economic repercussions or results of the changes they advocate. They simply assume that if only people will work for the society as a whole—for the public at large, and in that sense also for themselves—they will do a better job. The selfless and altruistic individuals who genuinely believe in socialist ideals will deserve to occupy commanding positions in a socialist society, and the ordinary working people will enthusiastically support them in their noble efforts of leadership into a better and more rewarding life. This was one assumption, and it was undergirded by another: the belief that science, when applied to central planning, will allegedly render it faultless in all economic and social respects.

Ludwig von Mises was one of the first economic analysts in the world to prove with almost mathematical precision that these assumptions were wrong and that socialism was an unworkable and unrealizable concept. He did it in his famous essay, "Economic Calculation in a Socialist Commonwealth," published in 1920 when socialism was the prevailing political, moral, and social creed among Austrian and German intellectuals. These were Mises's compatriots and colleagues, but unlike him they saw in socialism a panacea for all social ills and ardently aspired to its implementation in their respective countries. These progressives of the Western world praised with unbridled admiration the socialist experiment mounted by Russian Bolsheviks and equated that experiment with Karl Marx's promised breakthrough from the realm of necessity into the realm of freedom. Though the practice of implementing socialism in Soviet Russia very soon proved that Mises was right and that his opponents were wrong, the latter firmly stuck to their beliefs, despite irrefutable evidence, and continued to reject Mises's analysis out of hand.

"WAR COMMUNISM"

When in October (by Western calendar, in November) of 1917, the Bolsheviks took power in Russia, they did so under three slogans that were not socialist at all. The first such slogan was immediate withdrawal from war and conclusion, even unilaterally, of peace with Germany; the second was giving land to the peasants; and the third pledged submission of factories to workers' control. In the beginning, they did indeed make good on those slogans. One of the first decrees they passed was the decree on land reform elaborated not by the Bolsheviks themselves but by the Socialist Revolutionary Party of Russia (the Escrs), whose program on land the Bolsheviks at the time of their takeover openly proclaimed as their own. And in the industrial plants they instituted workers' control committees to supervise the fair performance of managerial duties by the capitalist owners and thus to improve the conditions of their own work and pay. The Bolsheviks also immediately ceased hostilities with Germany and, in the short space of three months or so, negotiated with her and her allies a unilateral peace treaty. All thee initial measures were, of course, quite popular.

But as soon as the Bolsheviks consolidated their grip on power not only in the capital city of Petrograd but also in the provinces—and that took them about two to three weeks to do—they immediately changed their tune and began to introduce full-fledged socialism. The first socialist acts were undertaken already in December 1917 when the All-Russian Council on the Economy (VSNKh) was created and pushed aside workers' control, replacing it with control by the state's bureaucracy. By that time the Bolsheviks knew that they had badly lost the election to the Constituent Assembly, and they stopped caring about gaining and retaining popularity. Now they could use their consolidated state power for the sake of transforming the society they took over to rule into a truly socialist one without asking or seeking that society's consent. And this was what they began doing relentlessly since December 1917.

First of all, the Bolsheviks nationalized all banks (December 27, 1917). Then they introduced state monopoly on foreign trade (April 22, 1918) and gradually instituted direct state control over all economic activities in the country. By February 1918, they all but crushed the free-trade unions, which were quite well-developed in Russia, and transformed them into arms of the party and thus of the state. This process was formally completed during the first All-Russian Trade Union Congress that took place on January 20–27, 1918.

Also in February 1918, the Bolsheviks issued a new decree on land that abolished the first decree giving peasants private possession and instituted, on an exclusive basis, communal usage of land. The party was still too weak, however, to impose such an unpopular decree by force. They could hardly take on the whole countryside; so they introduced other more easily implementable extraordinary measures submitting the peasants to the state and giving the state full control over food supplies and distribution. Thus, step by step, during the spring and summer of 1918 the Bolsheviks established the system that entered history by the name of *prodrazverstka* (food requisitioning). By autumn, these and other similar measures amounted to the institution in Russia of full-blooded socialism and the total domination of the party-state not simply over people's economic activities but over all walks of their life generally.

When the Bolsheviks were forced to refute this policy in 1921 and to institute the New Economic Policy (NEP), they began referring to their socialist experiment of 1918–1921 as "war communism." It was a misnomer. All those measures that I sketchily described above were introduced at the time when Russia was in fact at peace. In December 1917 the cease-fire with Germany was signed, and by March 1918 the Brest-Litovsk Treaty was concluded and ratified. There was no war. Russia's civil war started much later in the late summer of 1918, and by then its economy and society had already become fully socialist.

Here is a brief chronology of the forceful socialist measures, called by Lenin "the Red Guard kind attacking offensive against capital," which were introduced by the Bolsheviks during December 1917–November 1918:

1. December 6, 1917—nationalization of large houses (housing more than one family);
2. December 15, 1917—the institution of the VSNKh and subordination of all economic activities to this new super-ministry and its over forty branches (*glavki*);
3. December 27, 1917—nationalization of private banks and their fusion with the state bank, confiscation of all private holdings in the banks' safes, confiscation of gold and other precious metals in private possession, confiscation of enterprises' profits in excess of wage payments and maintenance costs;
4. January 5, 1918—all payments of dividends and dealings in shares abolished;
5. February 9, 1918—socialization of land;
6. April 22, 1918—introduction of the state's monopoly on foreign trade;
7. May 1, 1918—abolition of inheritance rights;
8. June 28, 1918—nationalization of all industrial enterprises and workshops (this was the final act of nationalization that on an enterprise-to-enterprise and, later [beginning in March 1918] on a branch-to-branch basis, proceeded relentlessly beginning in December 1917);
9. May 9–August 4, 1918—a set of several decrees resulting in the establishment of food requisitioning and food distribution (*prodrazverstka*);
10. November 21, 1918—trade in consumer goods abolished altogether and replaced by their distribution under the auspices of the Commissariat of Food.

The initial Bolshevik experiment with full-blooded socialism was meant to last but, because the whole population of Russia rose in rebellion against it in 1921, the Bolsheviks were forced to retreat from that experiment in order to be able to retain power. By labeling their early policies as "war communism," they attempted to pretend that these policies were only temporary and extraordinary war-induced measures, and that the party did not intend to impose upon the people anything that the people were not ready to accept. "War communism" was for the Bolsheviks no more than an excuse meant to serve as a life-saving device.

The main signal for the Bolshevik retreat from socialism came in the form of the March 1921 uprising of the sailors at the sea-fortress of Kronstadt situated just outside Petrograd. This event was very significant, for the sailors of Kronstadt had always been the core of Bolshevik support and the main armed force the party could rely upon. As long as the Bolsheviks effectively controlled political power, they didn't care much about the support of the masses. As early as April 1918, Lenin said, for example, that he was not perturbed about the fact that his socialist policies were clearly putting the party on a collision course with Russia's working class: As long as we are able to enforce socialism, he maintained at the time, we should go ahead with it, whether the workers like it or not. When the fruits of socialist production will be made available to them, he further explained, the workers will rally around us and thank us for the enormous benefits that, because of our steadfast socialist policies, they will be enjoying.

Lenin could easily afford neglecting the "backward" opinion of the working class and all the "toiling masses" as long as he was able to suppress them effectively by force. But when this force itself, of which the Kronstadt sailors were the core indeed, started turning against him and the party, he had no choice but to back down and search for more popular—actually capitalist—policies. And this is what he did in the form of NEP.

Even before the Kronstadt uprising, huge areas of Russian peasant lands were in full revolt. Former Red Army fighters and commanders who struggled in the civil war on the side of the Bolsheviks were now the leaders of the anti-Bolshevik uprisings. The most well-known of these was the 1921 Tambov peasant uprising led by a former Red Army commander named Antonov. That same year, the workers in the cities were on strike (*volynki*) most of the time. They demanded free trade in food stuffs and freely negotiated wages. Kronstadt, in this context, was simply the straw that could finally break the camel's back. The Bolsheviks faced a dilemma: They could fall from power or institute the NEP, which was in reality a retreat, although only to small-scale capitalism.

Already in 1921 socialism proved to be an unworkable and ineffective economic system. In the words of W. H. Chamberlin, the author of perhaps the best history of the Russian revolution written in the West, "War communism may fairly be considered one of the greatest and most overwhelming failures in history." And a Soviet author, L. Kritzman, writing on "war communism" in 1925, added: "Such a decline in the productive forces not of a little community but of an enormous society of more than a hundred million people . . . is unprecedented in the history of humanity."

Mises and his 1920 analysis were vindicated by history in 1921. A year later, Mises developed his analysis into a powerful book called *Socialism: An Economic and Sociological Analysis* in which he could base his conclusions about the effective bankruptcy of socialism on what had *already been experienced* in Russia. The collapse of the Russian socialist experiment did not, however, change the mind of those in the socialist camp. Their message was still the same: "Socialism is the best of all economic systems. It failed to work in Russia because the Russian people were not ready for socialism and because it was a backward peasant, petty-bourgeois country." They steadfastly maintained that if socialism had started in Germany—and that was the great dream—then it would have succeeded (We saw how it really did "succeed" with Hitler after 1933).

THE NEP AND ITS AFTERMATH

The NEP was regarded by Lenin and the Bolsheviks as a temporary retreat. They called it the "peasant Brest" (at Brest in March 1918 they had temporarily surrendered to the Germans; now, they said, they had temporarily surrendered to the peasants). As at Brest, it was a retreat in order to advance.

But first, the details of the retreat: The NEP was launched in March 1921, during the suppression of the Kronstadt uprising when the 10th Congress of the party suddenly decided to abolish the food requisitioning system and replace it by a "tax in kind." (After having paid the tax, the peasant was free to sell the remainder to anyone he wanted on the free market.) The Bolsheviks also conveniently forgot their decree on land socialization and proceeded with the distribution of private peasant holdings as was foreseen in their Eser-inspired first decree on land (November 8, 1917). On May 17, 1921, the decree on wholesale nationalization (June 28, 1918), specifically the part concerning small-scale industrial enterprises and workshops, was also revoked. Thousands of small-scale state enterprises, most of which were by that time either closed or did not operate properly, were leased to private entrepreneurs. On July 7, 1921, individual citizens were granted the right to establish new private enterprises employing up to twenty people. In 1922, financial reforms cut down inflation, introduced a convertible currency (*chervonets*), and fully restored money as the universal legal tender in the country. Taxes in kind were replaced by monetary taxation, and private retail trade was authorized, becoming the major factor in the restoration of the country's economic health. All of Russia's heavy industry and the large factories in her light industry remained, however, state-owned and were run by the VSNKh and its appointees. The state also kept its holds on all banks and jealously guarded its monopoly on foreign trade.

That is what the Bolsheviks called retaining the "commanding heights" of the economy. Their strategy had a dual effect. First, all private businesses were kept totally dependent on the state and its assets and especially on the availability of supplies of state-produced or state-purchased commodities. In fact, the state put itself into the position of the supreme master of private enterprises without directly owning them. Second, the state competed with private enterprise in all fields of economic activity where the latter was allowed to operate. In agriculture, there were state farms (*sovkhozy*) running huge estates of former landowners; in trade, the state owned and ran wholesale and retail shops selling all items that were also on sale in private shops. There was no item produced by the private sector that the state would not produce, too (including repairs and other services).

Most Bolsheviks, Lenin among them, were convinced that socialism was by definition a system that guaranteed a higher level of productivity than the private sector could ever aspire to provide. For example, in a situation where a private factory and a state factory were both producing shoes, the state factory would inevitably win out. How? By applying modern technology and using the division of labor and other advanced means, the state factory would be able to afford to sell higher quality shoes for a cheaper price. In time, the private factory would be driven from the market. Lenin's vision was the vision of socialism defeating capitalism in a free market-style competition. It was an illusion, but he never realized it; he died in 1924, quite soon after the introduction of the ill-fated NEP.

Stalin probably never shared Lenin's illusions. He knew pretty well that if one continued merely to rely on market forces to do their job, socialism would be soon and irreversibly defeated by capitalism. Stalin was not an intellectual. He was a man of the real world and he knew exactly how economic forces in Russia actually operated. This is not to say that Stalin was not a convinced and committed socialist. He was simply sure that in backward Russia, with its population's "despicably petty-bourgeois" mentality, socialism would never be able to outcompete capitalism by peaceful means. He opted for the imposition of socialism by sheer force. In Stalin's view, once all alternatives were effectively suppressed, the people would accustom themselves to working in socialist conditions and eventually provide the higher level of productivity that only socialism was capable of realizing.

It was necessary to move to "war communism" once again, but to do it under conditions in which any scale of opposition would be rendered ineffective. In 1927, Stalin swiftly moved to suppress private enterprise, abolish free trade, and introduce price controls. By means of indiscriminate terror, he crushed peasants who refused to sell their products at artificially low prices set by the authorities also in 1927, and, by 1929, he moved to the wholesale collectivization of agriculture, an enterprise that finally realized, in a much better elaborated form, Lenin's 1918 decree on land socialization. The effort cost about 15 million peasant lives. I use the word, "about," because there are varying estimates on the number of lives Stalin sacrificed in his brutal determination to push the USSR once again to full-blooded socialism. The then KGB chairman, Vladimir Kryuchkov, claimed in March 1991 that 40 million people were executed or otherwise eliminated by Stalin's regime. Aleksandr Solzhenitsyn would take issue with that figure and put it at over 60 million, together with the victims of Lenin's regime. Whatever the truth may be, there is no doubt that scores of millions of Soviet people—Russians, Ukrainians, Kazakhs, and others—were sacrificed on the altar of the socialist Moloch.

In the twisted view of Stalin and most Bolsheviks worldwide, that sacrifice was more than worthwhile, for it opened for new generations of mankind the vista of a bright socialist future. This was indeed the substance of the Stalinist plan: First force people, mainly by a combination of indiscriminate terror and corrupting rewards for voluntary submission, to enter into a socialist structure. In the beginning it will be unacceptable to them, but they will eventually get used to it. After having properly appreciated all the advantages of socialism, the people will start to perform even much better than before. Then the terrorist grip could be relaxed, and the party could rest assured that people would support socialism out of voluntary commitment ever afterward.

SOCIALISM AFTER STALIN

Stalin, however, never relaxed the grip. Until his death in March 1953, he relentlessly ruled by the means peculiar to him—terror and corruption. In so doing, he brought the USSR to the verge of economic collapse. Facing this awkward situation, his successor, Nikita Khrushchev, decided that the time had come to reactivate the "creative spirit" of socialism: In 1956, he denounced Stalinist excesses and promised a life free of indiscriminate terror and of toleration of "socialist initiatives" by citizens. Khrushchev's liberalization proved, however, to be counterproductive. Instead of consolidating, socialism continued to deteriorate. In a more liberal climate, the rising forces of political dissent, black market activities, and mushrooming networks of graft evolving within the state-managed socialist economic structure accelerated. The people's reaction to the relaxation of socialism's grip on society proved to be purely capitalist.

Khrushchev did not relent or give up. He was probably the last member of the Soviet leadership who genuinely believed in the communist idea. The qualitative superiority of socialism over capitalism was to him an immutably axiomatic truth. He had been convinced that the reason why the Soviet system did not work was not any inherent weaknesses of socialism but the somehow incorrect or insufficient means and ways of its practical implementation. Hence he started an active search for a new magic formula—a different constellation of the socialist state's structures and functions—that would finally make socialism as productive and effective as it was supposed to be according to Marxist-Leninist theory.

After defeating the "anti-party" group in 1957, Khrushchev finally concentrated all political power in his own hands, and he started actively tinkering with the system. Since none of his initial changes brought about the expected improvements, he tried new changes again and again, reshuffling the system on an almost daily basis. Because practically everyone was an employee of the state, the whole nation was kept in a state of constant and permanent reorganization. Routine was completely destroyed; nobody did any serious work since they were anxiously awaiting the next day's new orders from the top. The USSR plunged into a chaotic standstill.

All Khrushchev's reforms were purely administrative. He never tried privatization or any other measures that wold liberate enterprises from the state's planning, management, or control. The foundations of socialism were never directly threatened, but they were systematically undermined by Khrushchev's "voluntarism" ("voluntarism" was the official charge leveled against Khrushchev by the party when he was ousted from power). Nevertheless, as long as the party apparatus remained in effective overall control, it was able to withstand the ruinous effects of Khrushchev's reforms and keep the system's integrity, on the whole, intact. Having finally realized that it was the party apparatus that brought all his reforms to naught and kept the old system going, Khrushchev decided to deprive it of real power by splitting it into two parallel and unconnected branches—one dealing exclusively with industry and another with agriculture. This attempted mortal blow to the system's integrity and to its dominant position was intolerable. The party *apparatchiks* finally rebelled against Khrushchev in an effectively organized conspiracy that culminated in the palace coup of October 14, 1964.

The new Soviet leader, Leonid Brezhnev, did not foster any illusions or ambitions about making socialism work in concordance with Marxist-Leninist ideological forecasts. He simply wanted to reconsolidate the system, repair it after the damage inflicted by Khrushchev, and keep it in the traditional Stalinist guise for as long as possible. Khrushchev's reforms were revoked and the Stalinist socialist structures comfortably restored. To accomplish this, Brezhnev did not need to resort to any large-scale changes. Nor did he need to employ indiscriminate terror as an instrument of his rule. He firmly suppressed and repressed real dissent as well as any challenge to the status quo generally, but anyone who at least outwardly complied with the system and its rules of social behavior was allowed to pursue his or her career and life plans without much hindrance. But, most of all, Brezhnev relied on the inertia of fear induced under Stalin and on the inertia of the system itself, also skillfully engineered by Stalin.

Trying to avoid Khrushchev's fate, Brezhnev granted his underlings in the party and state apparatus secure lifetime tenure of office and, as long as they were outwardly entirely loyal to the system and to him personally, he turned a blind eye to their self-seeking and corrupt activities. Taking advantage of such a benevolent attitude, the chiefs of local (republican and provincial) party committees and the heads of departments and ministries in charge of specific branches of national economy started forming their own mafia-type clans and treating their respective domains of authority as private fiefdoms. It was under Brezhnev's sixteen years of "stagnating" rule that feudal rot crept into the Soviet socialist monolith and gradually began to destroy it from within.

After a while, this gradual destruction manifested itself in declining growth rate of the Soviet GNP. From the mid-1970s on, the decline was registered even by the official statistics. These have always been fraudulent, reflecting not so much the economic reality as the boastfully fictitious reports of Soviet enterprises about their constant overfulfillment of the state's economic plans. But by then even the permanently cheating and lying Soviet enterprises were unable to sustain the fraud of Soviet economic growth. For the last Brezhnev year, 1982, the official statistical report of the USSR showed only a 2.5 percent growth of the GNP—the lowest figure in the whole history of Soviet statistical reporting. In real terms this translated into a zero or negative growth rate.

By 1980–1981 (the Polish Solidarity years), even the Soviet leadership understood that socialism was on the verge of collapse. They still did not budge, however, realizing that any drastic move aimed at reforming the system could actually precipitate total collapse. When Brezhnev died, Yuri Andropov tried to introduce certain reforms aimed at the elimination of the feudal rot and at invigoration of discipline, but even these were perceived as too risky. After Andropov's death, the Politburo called for Brezhnevism and appointed its living incarnation, Konstantin Chernenko, to supervise the reversal.

Only America's definite victory in the arms race—especially President Ronald Reagan's introduction of the Strategic Defense Initiative, which the Soviets were unable to match or effectively to respond to—put the Politburo reluctantly back on the path to reform that would at least enable the Soviets to catch up militarily. This is why the same Politburo men who opted for Chernenko and a return to Brezhnevism in 1984, after Chernenko died, made Gorbachev their chief officer on March 11, 1985, giving him a mandate to implement what was then called the program of *uskorenie* (acceleration) and perestroika (restructuring).

PERESTROIKA—SOCIALISM'S FUNERAL MARCH

Initially this program was rather modest. It consisted of a campaign for fast and drastic technological modernization of the Soviet economy and for introducing a stricter labor discipline in Soviet enterprises (hence the notorious antialcohol drive). In practical terms, after a year of grand talking, nothing positive had been achieved—the rate of the GNP's growth continued to decline. The inertia of the system was apparently too strong to be easily overcome by a few new decrees and urgings accompanied by some rather superficial administrative and disciplinary measures. In the Politburo's eyes, the inertia of the system translated itself into what they called the "human factor," i.e., the noncooperative, sabotaging attitude to perestroika of the local and branch *nomenklaturas* that the Politburo by mid-1986 finally decided to attack. In the next stage of reform, Gorbachev and the Politburo put before themselves as their main and most urgent task the elimination of the feudal rot from within, and firm recentralization of the system, so that functionaries on all levels would become reliable and active agents of reforms ordered from above.

In mid-1986, the policy of glasnost was introduced, and in January 1987 it was followed by the policy of *demokratizatsiya* (democratization). A year later, the latter was overcome and absorbed by the unplanned outgrowths of the *glasnost* policy. *Glasnost* allowed the official media to criticize any member of the local or branch *nomenklaturas* for sabotaging reform, corruption, or other illicit activities inconsistent with the Politburo's "new thinking." It was supposed to provide the foundation for a large-scale purge of the old

Brezhnevite power apparatus. But to undertake such a purge was not a safe task at all. The lessons of Khrushchev's demise were not lost on Gorbachev and the Politburo. They knew only too well that standing on their own in such a formidable confrontation they had practically no chance of prevailing over the lesser *nomenklatura's* opposition.

Gorbachev had no choice, therefore, but to try to harness support for his new policies from the strata outside the power apparatus, and to use this support as a protective shield against a possible onslaught of his own *apparatchiks*. First and foremost, he had to get such support from the Russian intelligentsia who traditionally wielded a great influence on the grassroots population and, therefore, possessed the potential of becoming a formidable political force. Glasnost was supposed to serve this purpose, too. Gorbachev extended glasnost to a significant relaxation of ideological censorship that, among other things, lifted the ban on some seminal elements of Russia's religious and cultural heritage as well as on a host of contemporary creative endeavors in arts and sciences.

This policy worked quite well at first. The intelligentsia and the public at large enthusiastically rallied around Gorbachev and effectively blocked the attempts on the part of the *nomenklatura* to oust him from power. But, introduced on such a large scale, *glasnost* inevitably acquired its own momentum, got out of hand, and spontaneously expanded, breaking in the process all the taboos that Gorbachev and the Politburo were still very keen to preserve. Ironically, glasnost and the people who took advantage of it—not anymore the subdued *apparatchiks*—became now the most formidable challengers to the party's leadership, to its ability to continue with the pursuit of socialist policies, and with its obstinate attempts to rejuvenate the socialist system; and in view of the strong nationalist/secessionist tendencies that the benefactors of glasnost have so intensively inflamed—they directly started challenging the continued existence of the USSR itself.

Faced with this new pluralist political reality, Gorbachev, after some characteristic hesitation, decided to join ranks with the conservative *nomenklatura* to limit glasnost and to resume control over the disintegrative social and political processes unwittingly unleashed by it. This is why by the fall of 1990 he started drastically swinging to the right. But it was already too late. The process of glasnost had effectively killed people's fear of the powers that be and had made them self-confident and aware of their real power. The popular opposition had formed itself into more or less coherent organized bodies (initially called the *neformaly*, meaning outsiders to the formal Soviet structures) and had acquired formidable and trusted leaders, among whom the figure of Boris Yeltsin powerfully stood out, as he was getting ready, if directly challenged, for a showdown with Gorbachev's leadership.

It was the Politburo's attempts to reshape socialism and make it viable again that unintentionally brought about the final collapse of Soviet socialism in 1991. By engaging into sporadic and vacillating reforms of the socialist system, Gorbachev and the Politburo demonstrated for all to see that socialism is irreformable, irredeemable, and that it spells not only economic but total bankruptcy. One could say that Gorbachev finally proved to the world that Ludwig von Mises's early analysis of socialism was entirely correct.

THE FATE OF WORLD SOCIALISM

As we have seen, socialism collapsed in Russia many times, and each time the Bolsheviks were forced to make certain concessions to capitalism—to the free market, to the free spirit living in each human being—in order to survive in power. Then, after having reestablished their power and having capitalized on the achievements of the conceded "capitalist spell," they managed to reimpose full-blooded socialism, which after some years would collapse again. In 1991, socialism collapsed for the last time, taking down with it the Bolsheviks themselves. Socialism is now beyond the capacity of resuscitation.

My remarks thus far have offered a brief analytical sketch of the life and death of the monstrosity called socialism as it existed in Russia. Without Russia's socialist presence and her support for socialist change worldwide, socialism, I am sure, will sooner or later collapse in every country in which it has previously triumphed. It has collapsed in Europe, Mongolia, and most of Africa. It is already collapsing in Cambodia and Afghanistan. The next candidates are Laos and Vietnam. Under the influence of changes in both Indochina and Russia, socialism in China will hardly be able to survive Deng Xiao Ping and his other octogenarian cronies in the Chinese communist leadership. The same applies to North Korea and its near-octogenarian, Kim Il Sung. And I am certain that with the severance of the economic aid previously so generously provided by the former Soviet Union, socialism, together with Fidel Castro, will fall in Cuba as an overripened fruit from a tree, sometime in 1992–1993. By 1993, with God's help, we will be living in a world free of socialism and the threat to human life and liberty that it has so formidably represented for the last seventy-five years.

That the Soviet collapse spells the end of totalitarian socialism in the usual Marxist-Leninist shape is today an indisputable fact even for those who disagree with my timetable. But what about socialism's social-democratic variety? As long as they participate in democratic politics and obey its rules, social-democrats, in my view, will never be able on a practical basis to implement their socialist programs to any significant extent. The socialists may win elections and form and lead governments, but if they wish to retain popular support and win elections again, they will have to conduct pragmatic, non-revolutionary, and thus basically nonsocialist policies. In this respect, Lenin was probably right on the mark when he called such socialists "the labor lieutenants of the capitalist class."

Indeed, the British Labor Party has never dared to put into its electoral manifesto the pledge of nationalization of the means of production that otherwise is an inextricable part of that party's program (clause 4 of the party's Statute). The Labor Party has lost every general election since 1979, because the British public does not trust that it would do a better job in implementing conservative policies than the Conservative Party itself. The socialist governments of France and Spain, in order to gain the reputation of good managers of their respective national economies and thus retain a chance to remain in power after the next general election, conduct economic policies that are almost identical with those of Mr. Reagan or Mrs. Thatcher. And the Swedish Social Democrats lost the last election to their conservative opponents because they stuck too rigidly to some of their more extreme welfarist and immigration policies.

The democratic socialists have only two options: They may turn to totalitarian socialism. When the USSR existed and strongly encouraged and supported such trends, this was a possibility to be reckoned with, especially in the Third World, but now it is a very unlikely one. Or they may reconcile themselves with the idea of being a party permanently incapable of implementing its ideals in the real world. This is all to say that the collapse of the Soviet Union is tantamount to the collapse of *all* varieties of socialism—totalitarian and social-democratic alike—on a global scale.

6

Dissent, Nationalism, and the Soviet Future

ALEKSANDRAS SHTROMAS

LOOKING AT THE NATIONALIST
ALTERNATIVE WITHOUT PREJUDICE

The recent historical experience of the civilized world's fateful struggle against Nazism and Fascism has psychologically conditioned us to be extremely suspicious of the growth of nationalistic ideology in any country, and especially so when that country happens to be powerful enough to cause substantial international trouble. We are also to some extent psychologically conditioned by the fact that in the confrontation with Nazism and Fascism the communist Soviet Union valiantly fought on the side of the civilized world, and it seems to us that this was largely due to the internationalistic content of the communist ideology to which the Soviet leaders, however nationalistic they may have been in their genuine outlook, were bound to pay allegiance.

These underlying psychological attitudes shape to a very large degree our present discussion of the Soviet Union's future: When facing the possibility of an openly nationalistic alternative, we instinctively tend to prefer the communist status quo. Even those of us who believe (erroneously in my view) that the Soviet Union is no more than a modernized continuation of the traditional Russian national-imperial state, somehow assume that the communist disguise exercises a taming influence on Soviet behavior and, therefore, are afraid that, when this disguise is lost, Russia will become a kind of neofascist state that is much rougher, less containable and, hence, more dangerous and difficult to deal with than the Soviet Union we know.

Reprinted from "Dissent, Nationalism, and the Soviet Future," *Studies in Comparative Communism* 20, nos. 3–4 (autumn/winter 1987): 277–86.

The great significance of the papers presented at the panel on Alternative Visions of the Soviet Future consists in their putting such and similar assumptions to the test of evidence on the actual state of Russian nationalist ideologies and movements from which an alternative Soviet future may spring. Each of these papers in its own specific way effectively demystifies the so-called Russian nationalist threat and, by doing so, allows us to allay the many fears related to it. Professor Darrell Hammer sums up the gist of these papers, suggesting in the beginning of his own contribution that "we ought at least to consider the prospect that the [Soviet Union] could evolve into a more traditional kind of authoritarian society which would be quite different from our own institutions, and yet would be more congenial and less dangerous for us than the Soviet system."

Hammer is doubtlessly right when he eliminates as unrealistic the possibility of a democratic and constitutional Russian state emerging in immediate succession to the present regime. Indeed, insofar as the prospects for political change in Russia are concerned, the real problem is not at all about the transition from dictatorship to democracy but about the transformation of the USSR's globally-oriented, ideocratic and teleocratic communist clique-state into a national system of government that may for some time yet remain authoritarian but that will gear its policies to the defense and promotion of largely pragmatically-defined national interests. As these interests and the policies springing from them are tentatively outlined in the current Russian nationalist and religious alternative visions, we are able, by studying them, to acquire now a sense of what they may be like.

RUSSIAN NATIONALISM AND EAST–WEST RELATIONS

It is most certain, for example, that if instead of the Soviet communist regime an authoritarian Russian national government were to emerge, one of the most urgent tasks of such a government would be to put an end to the seventy-years-old confrontation with the West relentlessly conducted by the Soviet state under the code name of international class struggle. Indeed, there are no such true Russian national interests that would be in conflict with those of either the United States or Western Europe and thus could justify on any pragmatically-conceived grounds a continuation of the present East–West confrontation. Russia has no territorial disputes with any of the Western powers, is not involved with the West in trade wars or other competitive economic pursuits, and as far as "influence zones" are concerned, these were delineated by the postwar settlement to Russia's more-than-full satisfaction and have never been seriously challenged by the West since.

The present East–West confrontation is therefore purely ideological and thus artificial. It is based on the Soviet ideological commitment to spread communism around the globe as widely as possible, which in terms of Russia's proper national interests themselves is not simply wasteful and sense-less but damaging and counterproductive; and the more successful the So-viet Union is in realizing this commitment the more contrary to Russia's true national interests it turns out to be.

Socialist expansionism gives Russia no economic advantages. On the con-trary, it imposes upon her an increasingly unsustainable burden of expenditure that never stops growing since, in addition to the costs of expansion itself, Rus-sia also has to bear the cost of maintaining in solvent condition the dwindling socialist economies of the ever-expanding number of her client-states. The strategic advantages that socialist expansionism is supposed to provide are also more than problematic. Even if assuming that Russia sees her national goal in world domination and for this purpose needs to get a strategic advantage over the West, such an advantage bought at a price that high is bound, in the long run, to turn into a major strategic disadvantage. The problem here is that the na-tions of Soviet client-states are far from being thankful for Russia's care. On the contrary, in the course of getting the experience of the socialist way of life, even those of them that previously bore no prejudice against Russia are becoming her most implacable potential enemies, ready to join forces with the West against the Soviet Union at the first available opportunity. Since with every ex-pansionist success Soviet policing capacity wears thinner, while Western re-solve to contain the Soviet Union grows stronger, such an opportunity may eventually present itself in the not too distant future, spelling the demise of the Soviet Union and, in the long run, the breakdown of the Soviet Empire alto-gether. The Soviet Union stands no chance of winning a prolonged confronta-tion with the West on any grounds—political, economic, or military—but by pursuing an active anti-Western policy of communist expansionism, it risks to lose even those gains that in a different situation the West would never even have thought of challenging.

Hence, in order to ensure the long-term security of her borders and ren-der her position of a dominant regional power immutably stable, Russia badly needs to establish and foster most carefully a truly cooperative and harmonious relationship with the West. For that sake, Russia would have to stop sponsoring communist movements and regimes around the world and, ultimately, to renounce communism as the foundation of her policies alto-gether. As has been shown above, there is nothing for Russia to lose from such a radical move, and everything to gain. This move, in other words, would be in the interests of the West as much as it would be in Russia's own national interests.

In the climate created by Russia's renunciation of communism and the en-suing East–West reconciliation, the fact that the presently Soviet-ruled non-Russian nations will regain the right of freely choosing and shaping their sociopolitical and economic systems, thus becoming either entirely sover-eign or genuinely autonomous, will by no means impair any true Russian na-tional interests. Under the new peaceful circumstances, where there will be no more Western anti-Russian or Soviet-led anti-Western camps left, Russia's closest neighbors will remain naturally bound to Russia, as Latin America is naturally bound to the United States, with the remaining mutual tensions and suspicions gradually receding and being superseded by mutual interests in economic exchanges and regional cooperation. Furthermore, only in cooperation with the West can Russia ever aspire effectively and promptly to overcome her economic backwardness and thus reliably sustain her status as a world power. Large-scale Western technological assistance is only one necessary condition for Russia's fulfillment of that goal. Another one is Western provision of generous credits enabling Russia to import on a massive scale the widest range of Western high-quality consumer goods, which have to be immediately made available to the Russians in order to induce them to work conscientiously and try hard to earn good money. There are simply not enough locally-produced goods to go around and their quality and assortment are insufficient to create the necessary incentives.

All these arguments are at the core of the debate between the Russian nationalist dissenters and the regime. One could say even more, namely that the above ideas are the ones around which modern Russian national consciousness is being effectively formed. This being so, there is no need any more for the West to fear the consequences of political change in Russia. The West may now boldly transform its present commitment to the preservation of the status quo into an even stronger commitment to the promotion and active support of change. Hammer warns that the assumption according to which "any possible alternative to the existing regime will be less desirable (and perhaps more dangerous) from the point of view of western interests" is a dangerous one to make, and in the context of what has been said above, we can fully appreciate how timely and significant this warning is.

RUSSIAN NATIONALISM AND "WESTERNISM": THE TAXONOMIC PROBLEM AND ITS IMPLICATIONS

Having limited himself to the discussion of a number of those alternative visions that in his view stand a realistic chance of providing the basis for a post-Soviet regime, and also by subsuming these visions under his chosen heading of religious and nationalist alternatives, Hammer did not need to address himself to the problem of whether it is at all possible clearly to distinguish in the wide spectrum of Soviet dissidence between Russian nationalism and "westernism." For Hammer's purposes it entirely sufficed, without going into taxonomic details, to exclude from consideration such alternative visions that advocate what he deems to be the accomplishment of the unaccomplishable, namely a direct transition from the present order in the Soviet Union to a Western-style liberal democracy (Hammer names Andrei Sakharov, Elena Bonner, and Iurii Orlov as proponents of such visions, although one could argue that this misrepresents their position, which in fact centers on guaranteeing to the people their basic human rights rather than on introducing a full-fledged democratic system of government.) This taxonomic problem, however, inescapably arises in relation to Professor Vladislav Krasnov's and Dr. Nicolai Petro's claims (in Petro's case this claim is even declared in the title of the paper) that the subjects of their respective case studies are exponents of Russian national dissent.

This is one of the points on which I have to take issue with regard to both authors. In my view, neither Lev Timofeev, the subject of Krasnov's inquiry, nor the opponents of the project to divert the great Siberian rivers southward, with whom Petro's research is dealing, could be put into the category of Russian nationalists as opposed to that of the "westernists." Their dubbing as Russian nationalists could be justified as much as such dubbing of any other Russian dissident or nonconformist who, if and when he decides to act, does so for the sake of what he sees as the betterment of his nation's lot. In this sense all Russian dissidents or nonconformists, without exception, including the most ardent "westernists," could be classified as Russian nationalists.

Lev Timofeev's work is purely analytical and by its very tenor entirely non-ideological. Timofeev's analysis brings him to the conclusion that doctrinaire communism, together with the Soviet system found on its premises, has dismally failed to carry with them the country's population; Soviet people in their day-to-day activities continue to be guided by common sense, cultural heritage, and natural human drives, thus consistently defying the authorities but wisely managing to do so without challenging them openly. One could agree or disagree with this conclusion on either the strength of Timofeev's evidence or even temperamentally, but by no means on grounds of one's commitment to either Russian nationalist or westernist ideological perceptions. I for one feel a particular affinity with Timofeev's analysis of Soviet society because this analysis, independently and from within the country, confirms my own previously-reached conclusion that in the Soviet Union, underneath the surface of almost total obedience of the people to the-powers-that-be, functions a society of almost total dissent (I am grateful for Krasnov's acknowledgment of this fact in one of the footnotes of his paper). Quite a few Russian dissidents, whatever their orientation, would wholeheartedly subscribe to this conclusion, too, and some would reject it for one reason or another, but not because of its incompatibility with their ideological stance. To put it briefly, Timofeev does not lend himself for classification along ideological lines as either a Russian nationalist or a westernist—he is both and neither at one and the same time.

As for Petro's campaigners against the "project of the century," they do not fit under one nationalistic umbrella either. The partial issue of the protection of the environment and of preservation of the nation's historical heritage has managed to unite in action people of all persuasions—nationalists, "westernists," and those who are neither or a bit of both—simply because they felt for their country, its past, and future. Within this relatively large group one could perhaps identify some people as predominantly nationalist and some as predominantly westernist, but the group as a whole could not be defined by either of these terms.

What are then the ideological affiliations and divisions among the various sectors of Russian dissidence? I have already suggested that, as all of them care about the welfare of their nation, on the most general level all of them also could equally be defined as Russian nationalists. But there is much more to their unity than just that. One of the pillars common to all mainstreams of Russian dissidence is the concept of human rights. The "nationalist" Solzhenitsyn may argue with the "westernist" Sakharov about what kind of priority should be attached to the people's right to leave their country and return to it, but basically they will be at one as far as the whole issue of human rights' preponderance and the necessity for their being granted to the peoples of the Soviet Union is concerned.

Almost the same could be said also about the dissident perception of national rights. In the whole spectrum of Russian dissidence there are only two people directly advocating the retention of the present USSR's multinational state unity under all circumstances. One of them is the "nationalist," Igor Shafarevich, and the other, the "westernist" Roy Medvedev. Most of the others, "nationalists" and "westernists" alike—Sakharov, Solzhenitsyn, Orlov, Vladimir Bukovsky, Vladimir Maksimov, Kronid Liubarsky, Aleksandr Zinoviev, VSKhSON, and even the authors of the notoriously chauvinistic underground document *Slovo Natsii* (The Nation Speaks)—are in favor of allowing, or even forcing, the non-Slavic nations of the present-day Soviet Union to abolish their state links with Russia. There is less unanimity and more ambiguity with regard to the lasting retention of state unity among the three Slavic nations of the Soviet Union, but here again the "pros" and "cons" are almost equally divided among the "nationalists" and "westernists."

One may conclude from the above that on these most fundamental issues there is no way one could draw a precise dividing line between the "westernists" and the "nationalists." But if this is so, is any attempt at classifying Russian dissidents into "nationalists" and "westernists" at all justified?

Krasnov tries to answer this question by suggesting that the "westernists" "believe in the continuity of Soviet totalitarianism from the despotic tradition of the tsars," whereas the "nationalists" attribute Soviet totalitarianism "primarily and fundamentally, to the Communist idea itself." This distinction is, however, impractical, not to say spurious, since among the Russian dissidents no one to my knowledge has ever equated the Soviet regime with that of the czars or treated the former as a mere continuation of the latter. Some dissidents have indeed argued that the absence in Russia of a strong democratic tradition served as a factor conducive to the Bolshevik success in imposing on Russia their unprecedented coercive totalitarian system, but this is an entirely different proposition to which many nationalists themselves would at least in part subscribe. This proposition, however, has curiously enough never been directly made either by Sakharov or by Orlov, who are by reputation the leading "westernists," and could be attributed partly to Andrei Amalrik, partly to Grigorii Pomerants (in his case heavily counterweighted by profound admiration for Russia's traditional spiritual and cultural values opposing all forms of oppression and glorifying the freedom of man), and partly to Valerii Chalidze who in one of his works suggested that the meaning of Stalinism consisted in the abolition of communism and restoration of the Russian imperial tradition. One may justifiably disagree with all or some of these views, but it would be too far-fetched to contend that in them no distinction between the czars and the Bolsheviks is made or that by their nature such views could be qualified as "Russophobic."

In the whole Russian dissident literature I have never come across a view disputing the fact that Marxism-Leninism is a sectarian creed alien to the mainstream Russian tradition. Only some see in it a direct and crude Western imposition on Russia, whereas others stress that Marxism-Leninism in Russia, as everywhere else (irrespective of the fact that Marxism was born in Germany and its Leninist variety emerged in Russia), having attracted a certain section of the indigenous intelligentsia has become in that way a genuine, though marginal, element in the structure of Russian public opinion. I think this latter view is on the whole fairer and more balanced as is also the one that, without denying that the sectarian Bolsheviks, after having managed to grab and retain power in Russia, tried by all means in their power (e.g., by those of mass terror) to adjust the Russian nation to themselves, also maintains that in this process the Bolsheviks were forced to adjust in some ways to the Russians, too, the result of all that being a partial bastardization of both. (This is actually the view explicitly stated by Timofeev who, according to Krasnov, is a Russian nationalist.) Hence, here again, we are faced with a broad consensus within which there are many shades of different opinions concerning the Russian tradition and the degree of its affinity with Bolshevism. Some of these tend to exaggerate Russia's "innocence" and the role foreign (e.g., Jewish and other non-Russian) elements played in submitting Russia to Bolshevik rule, and some, on the contrary, tend to overstress the specifically Russian nature of Bolshevism, accordingly diminishing its original marginality in the Russian political spectrum and thus slightly smoothing over the fact that Bolshevik rule was brutally imposed on a largely unwilling and on the whole unsuspecting Russian population.

Hence, the bone of contention in this dissident debate is the role of Russia and of the Russian tradition in the establishment and consolidation of a Bolshevik-Party state. It is largely a historical debate whose main purpose, however, consists in properly assessing Russia's potential for initiating from within a change of its present political system and of evolving instead a truly decent and humane alternative. In this debate one could distinguish between skeptical pessimists and cautious or more enthusiastic optimists much easier than between "nationalists" and "westernists."

This is not to say that there is no real animosity in this debate. This animosity, however, springs from the extremely sensitive nature of interethnic and interreligious relations in Russia, and is practically unrelated to the differences in outlook between "nationalists" and "westernists." Some of the participants to the debate easily take offence when detecting hints about the

Jews or other non-Russians being the main culprits of Russia's debacle, whereas some others react likewise when similar things are said about the Russians.

Parallel and interwoven with this debate, another one goes on, concentrating on the issue of modernization. Here one could distinguish the "progressists," advocating for Russia a practically unfettered industrial and technological development (among these "progressists" are Sakharov, Orlov, Valentin Turchin, et al.) and "conservationists" who are opposed to such a development and would be content to settle for a zero-growth rate (e.g., Solzhenitsyn, members of the "rural prose" school in Russian literature, et al.). The "progressists" are usually dubbed "westernists" and the "conservationists" "nationalists," which is again imprecise because the issue at stake in this debate is not the fate of Russian national heritage or tradition (all parties involved claim their allegiance to that), but what policy would be best for Russia's all-around prosperity. Debates on the pace and level of industrial and technological development have always been and will continue to be for a long period of time a part of the national debate in all countries, and so it is and should be in Russia.

Finally, for the lack of anything better, one may try to distinguish between "nationalists" and "westernists" according to the differences in their respective attitudes to Western liberal democracy. But even this will not do. Among Russian nationalists perhaps only the marginal "neo-Fascists"—Shimanov, Skurlatov, the authors of *Slovo Natsii*, and a few semiofficial nationalist authors (e.g., Aleksandr Prokhanov)—are the ones who unequivocally denounce Western democracy as harmful and rotten, rejecting it altogether as a valid model for Russia's future. But even a program as nationalistic as that of the VSKhSON already assesses Western democracy on the whole positively, suggesting that a partial and appropriately revised and amended version of it should be introduced in Russia after the collapse of the present regime. Other nationalists, including Solzhenitsyn, while, like Hammer and myself, dismissing the possibility of Russia's immediate transition to Western-style democracy, consider it as a model that Russia with the passage of time may and should evolve and adopt though in a substantially adjusted and corrected form.

On the whole the problem of the relevance of the Western democratic experience to Russia's future greatly exercises the minds of all Russian dissidents, "westernists" as much as "nationalists." Almost all of them (with the few exceptions mentioned above) fully recognize the qualitative superiority of Western democracy not only over the totalitarian Soviet regime but also over all other tyrannic and despotic forms of government. On the other hand, there is hardly even one Russian dissident who would not see certain weaknesses in the Western system and would not be concerned about avoiding their importation to Russia and uncritical introduction into her post-Soviet order. Solzhenitsyn's criticisms of the spiritual flabbiness and other defects of the democratic West are the most outspoken and best known. But Sakharov also, while highly praising Western pluralism and democratic institutions, is not entirely uncritical of certain elements in the Western system, suggesting that they could be reformed by the way of convergence with some elements taken from socialism. For some others what they see as faults in the Western system could be compensated by according more influence to the churches, by restoring certain traditional Russian institutions (e.g., the monarchy, *zemstvos*, and some other institutions of *sobornost'*), or by introducing certain novel provisions that would be able to deal with crime, destitution, and other social ills more effectively than is the case in the West.

From what has been said above, I draw the conclusion that it is practically impossible to divide Russian dissidents into two totally separable (and implicitly mutually hostile) categories of "nationalists" and "westernists." Any thoroughly devised dissident taxonomy would require different and more detailed criteria under which these two rather crudely-defined classes may even disappear altogether. The significance of this conclusion reaches far beyond the problems of pure taxonomy. It fundamentally changes the whole established frame of reference within which Russian dissidence has been traditionally perceived and discussed. In the thus changed frame of reference one could not any more dismiss the "nationalists" as practically "non-dissenters" and the "westernists" as a tiny, isolated from the rest of Russia's population, and thus politically irrelevant, bunch of nice and brave people "with whom we fully sympathize." Russian dissidence, despite the complex variety of opinions that it combines, will appear in that new frame of reference as a coherent body of tremendous oppositional potential, which is to be seriously reckoned with by anyone concerned and always to be taken into account whatever aspect of Soviet politics, society, economy, or culture one considers. Unfortunately, both Krasnov and Petro by asking us to dismiss as hardly relevant the "westernists" and to accept that the "nationalists" are the truly potent dissident force, unnecessarily perpetuate the old frame of reference with its divisive and thus dangerously misleading implications. I very much hope that both authors will rethink their position on this crucially important issue and correct it accordingly. I am sure that from such a revision the revelatory value of their pioneering and perceptive studies will significantly increase.

COMMON SENSE AND POLITICAL CHANGE: THE TIMOFEEV PERSPECTIVE

The basic cohesion of Russian dissidence, as well as the spuriousness of the attempts at dividing it into squabbling factions of "westernists" and "nationalists," is, as a matter of fact, very convincingly substantiated by Timofeev. Krasnov duly points it out in discussing Timofeev's powerful idea about the formation in Russia of a "united front of common sense." I am not sure, however, whether Krasnov fully does it justice.

Rightly stressing Timofeev's intransigent opposition to any artificial models of Russia's future and very well explaining the reasons for his taking this stance, Krasnov nevertheless sees as paradoxical Timofeev's outright rejection of the very need of having a proper (not artificial) model of the future, one which could adequately equip and consolidate the common-sense-based popular opposition to the regime. What it seems to me Krasnov expects Timofeev to do is to present a kind of Ghandian program cum-organizational-outfit for passive resistance, and is astonished to find that in Timofeev's work such a program is missing. But Timofeev's gradualist approach to political change is much more Burkean than Ghandian and, therefore, for him common sense is by itself a sufficient device for providing people with all the programs and organizations they may need. Krasnov, I think, failed to notice that in Timofeev's conception common sense serves not only as the guide for people's way of survival under the inhuman Soviet totalitarian rule, but also as a shaper of the way for people to overcome and replace that rule altogether. For Timofeev, people's common sense is thus itself the source of the positive model of Russia's future and it is the model derived from common sense that Timofeev offers to accept as a guide for the future without any hesitation whatsoever.

As long as people manage to conduct their lives regardless of the official rules and in accordance with the dictates of their common sense, they create for themselves a small sovereign realm where the state can neither enter nor dictate. In this realm spontaneous relations, springing from activities induced by people's common sense, prevail, providing also the beginnings of a positive model of the future. By the force of the nature of people's behavior this initially small realm is bound gradually to expand, with the state reluctantly but inevitably retreating even further and conceding to the common sense ever more of its prerogatives in an ever-widening area. Timofeev believes that at a certain stage of that process there will come a time when the regime would have no better choice than to concede to people the full rights of conducting their lives in accordance with common sense, ultimately legalizing the social relations that were thus created. This is how, in Timofeev's view, political change in the Soviet Union, propelled and shaped by common sense, will come about.

It seems that Krasnov agrees with Timofeev's projected gradual way of political change in the Soviet Union. At the end of his paper Krasnov even suggests that this "Timofeevan" gradual process of change may one day result in the formation of a Solidarity-type movement in Russia. But is that the sole possible form in which change in the Soviet Union may materialize? We know from historical experience that all the main political changes have taken place when, to quote Plato, the polity's elite became a seat of disunion. Could a Solidarity-type movement alone—without a split in the elite, a part of which would be ready to join such a movement—be sufficient for bringing about political change? This question Krasnov did not either pose or answer. Also the possibility of political change in the Soviet Union being precipitated by elite confrontation and introduced by a counter-elite that has emerged victorious from that confrontation—without the involvement of any mass movements at all—has been entirely ignored by Timofeev, and neither was it brought into the discussion by Krasnov.

PUBLIC OPINION, DISSENT, AND POLICY-MAKING IN THE SOVIET UNION: THE SIGNIFICANCE OF THE CAMPAIGN AGAINST DIVERTING SIBERIAN RIVERS

Timofeev perceptively sees in public opinion and its maturation the main vehicle for enlarging the domain where common sense rules supreme and, ultimately, for bringing about political change itself. The study of the opposition to the river-diversion project undertaken by Petro is the most eloquent illustration of this point. Indeed, here we have a unique event when a major project initiated and approved by the Soviet government was effectively opposed and ultimately defeated by a powerful body of public opinion that had managed invisibly to form itself within the highly-atomized Soviet society and then burst out into the open to force the unsuspecting government into retreat.

It would be wrong, however, to equate this exercise focused on killing one particular government project with an oppositional dissident venture and, even more so, to draw from it conclusions about the apportionment of popular support for various dissident ventures in the country. And this is exactly what Petro is trying to do.

First of all, the campaign against diverting the Siberian rivers was aimed at preventing the government from doing something that it had not yet done but only was planning to do. This plan, as Petro meticulously shows in his paper, was open for discussion, and although it was meant to be discussed by scientists and officials directly or professionally involved in the project, prominent literary and cultural figures could "break into" that discussion without much risk to their official reputation and career. Secondly, to make their interference in that discussion entirely safe, these prominent literati and cultural figures were opposing the "project of the century" by appealing to such Russian national values, which the regime could not afford publicly to admit that it does not share (although in fact, these values were contrary to the "progressist" and heritage-neglecting attitudes of the regime).

All this has made the venture in question qualitatively different from any oppositional dissident venture that, usually, demands abolition or revision of an established political course or of already adopted and pursued policies, or criticizes in an unauthorized way the regime's historical record, trying thus to induce it to admit and correct the committed errors or crimes, or exposes the illegal practices of the regime, asking it to observe its own laws and to restore justice in particular cases of unlawfully convicted prisoners or dismissed employees, of people refused permission to join their relatives abroad, and many others. There is no such thing as a safe oppositional dissident venture. Everyone, however prominent and officially respected he or she may be, when getting involved in an oppositional dissident venture, does not simply take a risk but is certain that some unpleasant repercussions will follow, and those may range from being forced to sign a public repentance (an option available to the best publicly known figures only) to relegation, practically for life, to the Gulag or psychiatric asylums.

For the explanation of why the opposition against the "project of the century" has been able to rally much more public support than oppositional dissident ventures usually do, Petro should have looked first into these circumstances, which he, unfortunately, did not do. The facts tell us, however, that in the second half of the sixties, when people were still under the illusion that dissident ventures were relatively safe, such ventures also used to attract wide-scale support, equal to, and sometimes even surpassing, that received by the opposition to the rivers diversion project. But after that time, that is when it was established that an oppositional dissident venture is inevitably followed by state repression, no such venture, be its content "nationalist," "westernist," or of any other kind, ever managed to attract very many participants or open supporters. This fall in support for dissidence had nothing to do with the ideology on which one or another dissident venture was based. And many of them had a nationalist tenor par excellence.

I find, therefore, entirely misconceived, moreover, offensive, the following statement by Petro: "The dissident movement" (by which term Petro defines the "westernists") "in the Soviet Union failed to gain broad support behind it because of its limited and legalistic approach of human rights, and its appeals to western supporters. By contrast, patriotic sentiment appeals to strong visceral attachments of people, and in the case of the Volga diversion plan, gives them not only a cause but a specific agenda to act upon. . . . By its very orientation Russian nationalism displays a belief in the people which many dissidents lack—a crucial distinction to understanding the demise of the dissident movement and the much greater potential of a Russian nationalist movement."

As long as such and similar statements proliferate and are taken for granted, our understanding of the crucially important phenomenon of Soviet dissidence and, consequently, of the whole sociopolitical situation in the Soviet Union, will remain confused and misguided. It does not matter which part of the integral Soviet dissident movement we choose to belittle, castigate, or dismiss. What Petro has said about the "westernist" dissidents, many more people would probably say about the Russian nationalists, and vice versa. Whatever the particular difference in emphasis and preference, the basic divisive attitude will remain equally wrong. What I therefore see as most urgently necessary, is for our profession to take a fresh look at the whole problem of Soviet dissent, and form on that basis a new prejudice-free and truly-informed opinion. I am sure that such an opinion will be bound to appreciate the basically cohesive and coherent nature of Soviet dissidence and thus measure up to the real challenge it represents to both the Soviet regime and Western scholarship on the Soviet Union.

Maybe one could start this vital process of revision of our views on Soviet dissidence by undertaking a serious study of Timofeev's works so ably discussed in Krasnov's paper. Such a study would certainly help us to make much better sense of the very interesting and rich analysis by Petro of the significance of the controversy surrounding the rivers diversion project. It would also help us to put the alternative visions so perceptively investigated by Hammer into the right perspective of assessing without bias and prejudice the imminence and the nature of political change in the Soviet Union.

7

On Totalitarianism and the Prospects for Institutionalized Revolution in the USSR and China

ALEKSANDRAS SHTROMAS

Professor Michael Voslensky defines totalitarianism as "total control by an undemocratic power over all spheres of life in society" and calls its opposite pluralism.[1] One could accept this definition but not without certain qualifications. For as long as control, however total it may be, is exercised by human beings over human beings, it can never become perfect either in scope or in effectiveness. There will always remain some flaws and loopholes that people will use, acting individually and in groups, to their own advantage and in surreptitious defiance of the exigencies of the controlling power. Even the very agents of that power on all its levels, while ostensibly acting on that power's behalf, will be in fact pursuing, in the first place, their particular individual or group interests in preference to any other such interests. To be sure, sometimes these individual and group interests may more or less fully coincide with those of the power in whose name they are pursued (sometimes certain individuals and groups may even persuade the power to take up their interests as its own), but more often they will not. This is to say that no totalitarian system can ever reach the ideal of an absolute "ant-hill type" uniformity and that it thus will always remain to a certain extent pluralistic,

Reprinted from Aleksandras Shtromas and Morton A. Kaplan, eds., *The Soviet Union and the Challenge of the Future*, vol. 1, *The Soviet System: Stasis and Change* (New York: Paragon House, 1988), 46–69, with a rejoinder by Richard Löwenthal.

or, which is one and the same thing, that no totalitarian power is, or ever has been, truly totalitarian.

Totalitarianism is, however, a reality. In real life, as Voslensky rightly suggests, it has been embodied at least in the Soviet, Nazi, and Fascist systems. What these systems have in common is indeed a certain mode of social organization under which all outwardly extant and functioning groups or institutional bodies—be they political, economic, cultural, social, or any other—are incorporated as mere structural elements into a fully monolithic and all-encompassing political system headed either by a sole leader or by an oligarchic clique acting as a single institution of leadership. The basic task of any kind of such totalitarian headship is to ensure the preservation and reproduction of the monolithic and all-encompassing nature of the system over which it presides. The actual performance of the bodies of which that system consists, as well as the real behavior of groups and individuals operating within those bodies, is for the totalitarian headship a task of secondary significance, as long, of course, as the quality of performance of these particular bodies or the character of actual behavior of people do not represent a real threat to the totalitarian monolith itself, i.e., as long as political control over the whole of the system remains intact.[2] This implies the necessity of distinguishing, within the overall concept of totalitarian power, between two of its basic aspects—political control and actual rule. Totalitarian systems, in order to survive, have to be fully effective in exercising political control, while they may remain rather inept in actual rule.

Analyzing social relations inside Soviet industry during 1928–1941, Moshe Lewin succinctly observed that even in Stalin's time the Soviet political center found industrial enterprises "difficult to rule—but easy to control."[3] The difficulties of ruling Soviet society have since been greatly exacerbated, while the effectiveness of exercising political control over it has remained on the whole almost as effective as it has ever been. In Michael Urban's words, the contemporary Soviet Union represents a "spectacle of omnipotent impotence in the total power state."[4] Although this may be a somewhat exaggerated characteristic, there is no doubt that the basic substance of totalitarian power in contemporary USSR is described in it quite accurately. "Intrastructural dissent,"[5] which is a negative reflection of the Soviet system's capacity to rule, has by now become ubiquitous indeed and is not significantly receding under the attack launched against it by Gorbachev's Politburo.

The totalitarian system's capacity to rule is, however, not entirely unrelated to its ability to exercise political control. The reduction of the capacity to rule proportionately advances "intrastructural dissent," which, in its turn, gradually forms an alternative society in the USSR. While operating within the limits of the official system and thus not having as yet overcome the overall framework of totalitarian political control exercised by that system, this alternative society itself is by no means subject to the official system's control.

Hence, the growth and consolidation of the alternative society, being the direct result of the reduction of the totalitarian power's capacity to rule, inevitably limits also that power's ability to exercise political control. This process has the potential of undermining in due course the totalitarian power's ability to exercise total political control altogether. The realization of this potential that would have to be expressed in the alternative society's overcoming of the limits of the official system would mark the end of both Soviet totalitarianism and "intrastructural dissent."

Voslensky's definition of totalitarianism, however, even if modified and elaborated upon in the above way, is incomplete. It subsumes not only the modern totalitarian systems under Voslensky's own scrutiny, but also the traditional despotic societies that were the subject of Karl Wittfogel's *Oriental Despotism* and that do not belong to the totalitarian category, despite Wittfogel's conviction that they do. In order to define totalitarianism fully and adequately, it is necessary to identify certain specific traits that would thoroughly distinguish it from mere despotism. In this respect, Professor Richard Löwenthal's concept of totalitarianism seems to be very helpful indeed. According to Löwenthal, totalitarianism is "a new type of dictatorship aiming at an ideological-model-based total transformation of society."[6] Differently from all other dictatorships (e.g., despots), the totalitarian ones have seriously and persistently been committed "not only to keeping power, but also to using power for ever new attempts to achieve utopian goals, leading to recurrent revolutions from above."[7] Indeed, whereas mere despotism is a conservative and routine-oriented system, totalitarianism is a revolutionary and supreme-goal-achievement oriented one. While both these systems may be equally ideocratic, with only their ideologies being polarly different in substance (the despotic ideology will glorify the eternal yesterday whereas a totalitarian, the perfect tomorrow), only the totalitarian system is also teleocratic.

Voslensky's and Löwenthal's definitions of totalitarianism stress different aspects of this system and are therefore mutually complementary. One without the other would remain incomplete. It is true, however, that while being all revolutionary and future-oriented, some totalitarian systems have not managed to reach the level of mature despotism. As Professor Morton Kaplan rightly remarked, according to the above criterium, "there has been only one system that can be called totalitarian—the Soviet system."[8] The fact of the matter is that systems that are merely despotic are naturally so formed at the outset, whereas those that are totalitarian, after having been brought into existence by revolutionary action, inherit an old non-despotic society that it is the totalitarian system's task to transform into one that would possess all the traits of mature despotism. It took the Soviets about twenty years to get to the level of "despotic totality," and without Stalin it would have taken them most probably much longer to get there. Neither Mussolini nor Hitler had at their disposal the amount of time necessary for achieving their ultimate goals.

Again, Löwenthal's reference to totalitarian movements[9] that precede the totalitarian régimes and that create them by superimposing themselves upon society as supreme political authority, helps us to identify a totalitarian system even before it has acquired its really full despotic scale. In those terms one may define as totalitarian a system in which a totalitarian movement managed to establish itself as the supreme political authority of the land, and to consolidate this position to the extent of full subordination to itself of the state machinery, thus acquiring the capability of using this machinery unrestrictedly for the successful advancement of its rule over the rest of society. This implies the necessity of distinguishing between the maturing and mature, or developing and developed, totalitarianisms. In these terms the Nazi and Fascist systems were maturing or developing totalitarianisms, whereas the Soviet system, from the mid-1930s until the present day, is a mature or developed totalitarianism.

II

My recognition of the present-day Soviet society as totalitarian puts me at odds with Löwenthal who maintains that since the end of Khrushchev's era it is not totalitarian anymore.[10]

According to Löwenthal, in the first half of the 1960s the USSR entered into the post-utopian, postrevolutionary and, consequently, post-totalitarian stage of its development. Among the Soviet rulers "Khrushchev was the last believer in the utopian goals of Marxism-Leninism. . . . The end of his leadership also marked the end of their relevance."[11] For Russia the age of institutionalized revolutions from above had thus come to a definitive close.[12] In Löwenthal's view, the post-Khrushchevian Soviet rulers continue to cling to their dictatorial power not "in order to achieve utopia, in which they no longer believe, but in order to advance the economic modernity and political greatness of the nations they govern."[13]

Assessing this state of affairs against the background of his definition of totalitarianism, Löwenthal logically concludes that the USSR has not simply outgrown its former totalitarianism (that it had already done by the mid-1960s), but also is now fully transformed into an ordinary nontotalitarian dictatorship.

While fully agreeing with Löwenthal's definition of totalitarianism and sharing many (but by far not all) of his above arguments, I nevertheless find his conclusion concerning the nontotalitarian nature of the present Soviet regime wrong, not only by my standards but also his own. First of all, it seems to me that neither the present Soviet rulers' disbelief in Marxism-Leninism or in any communist ideals at all—a fact strongly stressed by Löwenthal and undoubtedly true—nor the analysis of actual policies the Soviet regime pursues, points to Soviet abandonment of utopian goals, let alone to their exclusive concentration on pragmatic tasks related to the execution of the functions of a national government.

One cannot simply dismiss the official claim about the whole Soviet domestic policy being centered around the utopian task of building a communist society in the USSR or explain it away as a mere code phrase for furthering the country's economic and social development. This will not do for the simple reason that communist construction in the USSR continues to be conducted in the same old ideological manner as before, that is, by putting conceptual considerations above economic dictates. Nor is communist construction neutral with regard to achieving economic and social results. By giving priority to central planning and state economic management, communist construction tends to stagnate society and impedes rather than induces the country's economic, technological, and cultural progress.

Löwenthal would no doubt try to account for that by referring to the absence in Russia of "a political tradition of democracy or a strong cultural tradition of human rights,"[14] which enables the Soviet rulers to seek economic progress without altering their dictatorial system of rule. But this particular system of rule encompassing control over all walks of life is as unprecedented in Russia as elsewhere. However much Russia lacked the democratic and human rights traditions, she had a highly developed tradition of small private enterprise and autonomous economic activity that the Soviet regime, instead of putting to rational use, continues vigorously to suppress—yet another instance of the pragmatic national interest being sacrificed by the Soviet regime to its ideologically-conceived utopian goal.

Even more obviously ideological is Soviet foreign policy. Its antagonistic attitude toward the "capitalist West" has no foundation in Russia's national interests whatsoever. There are no clashes between authentic Russian national interests and those of the United States or any other Western country over any substantive issue or in any territorial area. The actual East–West conflicts are all artificially construed by the Soviets on purely ideological grounds and to the detriment of authentic Russian national interests. For it is not confrontation but cooperation with the West that would benefit Russia most. Even Russia's imperial interests, let alone the political, economic, and military ones, would be best served by ending the confrontation between the two superpowers and substituting for it genuine cooperation. This is not to be, however, for the Soviet rulers, again, will never allow pragmatic national interests to prevail over the ideologically-conceived communist utopian ones. Hence, the East–West confrontation continues unabated, also the relentless Soviet foreign expansion, which, far from strengthening the power of the Soviet state and contributing to its assets, is an ever-increasing factor of political destabilization and a huge drain on Russia's national resources.

It follows from the brief analysis given above that the present Soviet regime is not as post-utopian as Löwenthal would have it, and also that its policies are determined largely by motives superseding those that derive from the tasks of simply advancing economic modernity and political greatness of the area under the Soviet regime's control.

What then are the true interests motivating Soviet policy-making if both genuinely ideological and purely pragmatic national commitments have to be excluded? Dealing with this problem elsewhere, I have arrived at the conclusion that these are the self-serving interests of the Soviet rulers themselves.[15] The Soviet Party–state established itself as an ideocratic and teleocratic entity whose utopian commitments and goals were not simply alien but contrary to the self-perceived interests and genuinely held views of the overwhelming majority of the people that it had undertaken to rule. As such it was bound to be a clique-state whose only purpose was to enhance and promote at all costs the interests and goals of the small ideologically zealous ruling clique against those of the people at large. Hence, Löwenthal's recurrent "institutionalized revolutions" from above.

The present Soviet rulers may not care about ideals, but they care most strongly about the preservation of their power. And the power that they have inherited, and are bound to cling to, is representative of no one, except the "infallible ideology of Marxism-Leninism" of which they are the ex-officio "high priests." Since it is only that ideology, and nothing else besides, that invests the present Soviet rulers with the exclusive and inalienable right to absolute power, they have to stick to it whether they believe in it or not. For these purely pragmatic reasons the present Soviet rulers must remain unswervingly committed to Marxism-Leninism and to the pursuit, domestically and worldwide, of the utopian goals of communism inherent in it. This is to say that the more cynically pragmatic the Soviet rulers become, the more ideologically intransigent communists they are bound to be.

To sum it up, the present Soviet rulers are not essentially different from their predecessors. They are in charge of a communist-ideocratic and teleocratic clique-state and have to act accordingly. From this perspective it is indeed "of secondary importance whether, as in the beginning, this ruling clique consists of idealistic believers in a higher and better order of things, which they are determined to bring about against all odds by a revolutionary (e.g., terrorist) action, or of cynical opportunists who do not believe in any ideals at all, but who, in order to survive, do everything they can to perpetuate the single ideology and teleology of the power they have inherited. The clique nature of this state remains the same at all times and so remain also its basic policies and activities."[16]

This, I believe, fully explains why I insist on defining the present Soviet system as totalitarian. To me it is largely irrelevant whether communist revolutionary utopian goals are pursued out of conviction or sheer opportunism. What matters is the fact that they continue to be pursued today as much as they were yesterday. And if this is so, the Soviet Union remains totalitarian according to Löwenthal's own standards.

Löwenthal may, however, disagree. He would most probably point out that the main feature of totalitarianism—the recurrent "institutionalized revolutions" from above—have gone from the Soviet scene forever. The Soviet society, he would most probably say, has acquired today a constant and stable sociopolitical shape, and this is the real background against which all talk about further pursuits of any utopian revolutionary goals amounts to nothing more than sheer phraseology that may have only one practical purpose, that of embellishing the boring conservative routine into which the Soviet society has in fact grown. I could not agree more. Indeed, in the Soviet Union today there is no room left for any more of the recurrent "institutionalized revolutions" from above that were so typical of Stalin's time and, though to a lesser extent, also of Khrushchev's. Khrushchevian-type erratic upheavals could not be repeated because of the danger to the system's stability this would inevitably involve, and all the conceivable measures aimed at further enhancement of the totality of the Soviet Party–state's control over all walks of Soviet life have already been taken, with nothing else left to accomplish.

In the USSR today the only "institutionalized revolution" from above that may still be envisaged is the one that would be aimed at restoring the civil society as an entity autonomous from the state and subordinated only to the rule of law. This would be, however, already an antitotalitarian revolution. In the series of "institutionalized revolutions" from above this one would surely be the last since it would be launched by a totalitarian power with the view of self-destruction.

The Soviet system—one in which totalitarianism, through all the recurrent "institutionalized revolutions," has acquired a fully developed despotic dimension (thus exhausting the potential for and putting a limit on further such revolutions)—is, however, in itself a remarkable revolutionary-type phenomenon. Never before has a nationwide social-political structure been created by the conscious revolutionary effort of a committed minority following a certain ideological blueprint and forcing, when needed by the means of indiscriminate mass terror, the unwilling majority to adapt to its constraints. This unprecedented revolutionary achievement is, however, cast into the shade by the permanent revolutionary action the Soviet Party–state has conducted for more than half a century in order to keep the Soviet society in its artificially created shape. When looking at the Soviet Union from that perspective, it is not so much the conservative routine that is emerging, but rather a ceaseless "institutionalized revolution" aimed at preventing the artificially created Soviet totality from falling to pieces.

On the other hand, Soviet international politics can also be seen as the Soviet Party–state's permanent engagement into what one could call an "institutionalized revolution" on a global scale. One may be skeptical about the extent of the Soviet commitment to world revolution, but one cannot deny that many a recent victorious communist revolution in Asia and Africa never would have materialized were it not for the Soviet Party–state's active "institutionalized" involvement in their making.

Hence, I believe that even by what is in Löwenthal's terms the decisive criterion, the Soviet Union remains today a fully fledged, mature, and developed totalitarian system. I hope that Löwenthal agrees.

III

In Löwenthal's view[17] the post-totalitarian era began in China with the death of Mao and the arrest of the so-called Gang of Four, being "definitely established with the 1981 reorganization of the party leadership and its document on party history."[18] However, not every student of contemporary China would agree with this view.

As Miriam London pointed out in a letter to me, that school of thought in Western sinology to which she herself belongs "sees something quite different, complicated and unstable. Basically," she continues, "we see the economic reform as a sort of Chinese NEP, originally undertaken as measures of expedience and crisis-management." This seems to me to be exactly the situation that at a certain point in time the Chinese communist authorities might be tempted to solve by yet another "institutionalized revolution" from above. Hence, Löwenthal's conclusion that "the period of institutionalized revolution had ended in China with a disorganization of the regime's institutional structure and a profound discredit of the idea of further revolutions" (i.e., with the Great Cultural Revolution) may be somewhat premature.[19]

Let us, however, begin where Löwenthal does—namely with the Maoist collectivization of Chinese agriculture.

According to Miriam London:

Collectivization began almost immediately, albeit in stages, after the land reform of 1950–1953, during which at least 5 million—one recent report alludes to 9 million—"landlords" (landowners) and "rich" peasants were cruelly executed. A new "kulak" element, formed of the more enterprising "middle" peasants, had barely a chance to assert itself.

The entire families and descendants of the landowners and better-off peasants were, along with any survivors, permanently stigmatized as members of "black classes." However poor they now were, peasants belonging to these newly defined hereditary classes were essentially outcasts, denied even the meager rights of other peasants, systematically persecuted, and made the perennial targets of brutal "struggle" during the incessant political campaigns (*yundong*) of the following two decades.[20]

Whatever caused Mao Zedong later to launch the "Three Red Flags" campaign, of which the Great Leap Forward and the establishment of communes were part, the result was the worst disaster of the century, and particularly for rural China, where 80 percent of the population lives. The official P.R.C. press has most recently admitted to 20 million people dead of hunger in the years 1959–1962—twice the figure first acknowledged in an earlier publication.[21] The more probable conservative figure is 25 million to 30 million dead.[22] In Jürgen Domes's estimation, the Great Leap set the country *back* "five years in industry and at least twelve years in agriculture."[23]

Mao Zedong not only failed to solve the old economic, political, and cultural problems that impeded China's modernization in the past, but he created new and more insoluble problems. For example, in agriculture, his policies not only reduced the peasantry to grinding poverty, but, because of amateur interference in the agricultural process, they resulted in a huge loss, through soil erosion and salinization, of already scarce arable land. The failure of his utopian venture of 1958 did not prevent Mao from trying partial experiments with the commune system again during the cultural revolutionary decade of 1966–1976. The resultant crisis in agriculture, the foundation of the Chinese economy, left the Dengist coalition no choice but to undertake reform. China could not afford any other solution. A recent editorial in a Peking newspaper, *Nongmin Ribao*, inadvertently explains why:

> At present, 80 percent of the Chinese people's means of subsistence . . . comes from agricultural products directly or indirectly. Would it do for such a great country like ours to rely on imported grain to solve its food problems? No. With a population of 1 billion, we shall need 500 million tons of grain annually to get along but there are only 200 million tons of commodity grain on the world market. The Soviet Union and Japan purchase about 80 million tons of grain annually. If 20 percent of our population were to rely on imported grain for food, we would need 100 million tons of grain. This is unmanageable. We do not have that much foreign exchange and, even if we managed to buy the grain, it would be impossible to transport it.[24]

In industry, Mao initially achieved much more, within the limits of the Soviet model. But scarcely had industry recovered from the setbacks of the Great Leap when the worse disruption of the Cultural Revolution took over. In many parts of the country factories closed down altogether, while opposing worker-factions battled each other. (When foreign reporters were first allowed into previously closed areas in 1977, they discovered several major factories still closed.) Thus, in addition to the usual ills of a socialist state-run industry—operation at a loss, overstaffing, inefficiency, sloth—the final decade of Maoism introduced the divisiveness of factionalism, which survives in submerged form to this day.

Stagnation in industry, population growth, and Mao's virtual dismantling after 1968 of the educational system all exacerbated another problem—unemployment. When Deng assumed power he was faced with two generations of "unemployables." The Red Guard generation of students had merely been handed diplomas for schooling never completed, and the next generation entered schools with newly revised curricula that deliberately discouraged academic learning. But even had these students acquired the requisite knowledge and skills for modern technology (they did not), they would have found scarcely any opportunity to apply them. Mao "solved" the problem by dumping millions of young people on the countryside. Many, however, slipped back illegally into the cities, where some found odd jobs in the "black" economy and others turned to crime.

As though this were not enough, the new leadership also faced the psychological consequences of the preceding Cultural Revolution, especially among the young. These consequences were, in brief, a widespread disillusionment, not only in Maoism, but in the communist *system*, and a loss of faith in the party and its ability to lead. A saying echoed among young people all over China and even found its way into the official press: "[(We, I)] have seen through everything." What this meant was that they could no longer be taken in by party propaganda or the Communist myth. In fact, many young people came to view the Cultural Revolution in retrospect paradoxically as "a good thing" because it irrevocably demolished false illusions. (I have heard such a view repeated lately by mainland students in the United States.)

The members of the coalition that formed around Deng Xiaoping were well aware of all this and more—a veritable Pandora's box of revelations had opened in the late seventies. Extraordinary measures were necessary not only to restore the economy but to counter the "crisis of confidence" in the party and its ideology. Deng Xiaoping had already become the symbol of revisionism, which in the popular mind signified a turn to a more tolerable, normal way of life. Moreover, he had clear seniority and controlled an old-power network with strong military ties. He was the only living leader who could possibly salvage the country and the party. (In the late seventies many educated Chinese expressed the view that if Deng were suddenly to die at this time, the situation in China could rapidly disintegrate into regional factional warfare—in effect, warlordism.)

All these factors combined to secure Deng the leverage he needed to initiate NEP, Chinese-style.[25]

In Soviet communist perception, NEP, it should be remembered, was not a policy of continuous, stable development but only a temporary retreat from the steadfast pursuit of socialist goals—a retreat necessitated by critical circumstances and aimed at preserving in these circumstances the monopoly of power in the hands of the Communist Party. After NEP had played its role by having cured the country's most disastrous social and economic ills, an outright communist attack on NEP followed, resulting in the total destruction of the social system shaped by NEP and the reintroduction of full-fledged socialism or, what in Soviet communist perception is one and the same thing, total state control over all walks of life in society. The Communist Party had no choice but to launch such an attack, for if it failed to do so and allowed capitalist elements and market forces to develop unabated, the party's power over the state and society sooner or later would be inevitably and irreversibly undermined.

The Soviet Communists were perfectly aware of this and from the very outset of their embarkation on NEP started preparations for reversing and abolishing it. In the Soviet Union during the 1920s, economic liberalization related to NEP was, with that view in mind, accompanied by simultaneous measures drastically suppressing all remnants of opposition to Communist rule and eradicating the slightest potential for the reemergence of such opposition within both the society at large and the Communist Party itself.[26] At the same time, Soviet rulers started to prepare their future attack on NEP by building up the machinery of the party and the state with the view toward increasing its repressive power to unprecedented proportions. One of the most telling examples of this preliminary buildup for a future attack was the 1922 reorganization of the security police (the Cheka) into the (GPU) with special military detachments put at its disposal.[27] Only after the completion of all these preparations, in the end of the 1920s, did the Soviet rulers feel secure about being able to win a decisive battle against the thus disarmed society, and only then did they dare launch their "institutionalized revolution" from above that abolished NEP and established the Stalinist variety of socialism.

The present situation in China in this respect (i.e., of securing Communist power in an NEP-type situation and asserting it when necessary against the revived "capitalist elements") is not entirely different. Wild Western hopes about Marxism being made obsolete in China, based on one leading article in the party's central organ, *Renmin Ribao* (The People's Daily), did not materialize. On the contrary, the Marxist ideological grip on the country has been significantly tightened as of late. Even the resolution of October 20, 1984, which officially launched the latest and most radical reforms, reiterated with strong words the Four Basic Principles, particularly the one concerning the leadership by the party.[28] As the prominent sinologist L. Ladany has observed, "the party schools in Peking and elsewhere still teach the old Stalinist Marxism. Also several manuals on Marxism have been published recently by official publishing houses. They, too, teach the old theory, a rigid form of Stalinist Marxism." Ladany also noted that "a disturbing nostalgia for things Russian is noticeable in China today. It was recently announced that 20,000 Russian book titles . . . are being imported into China this year. Some books written recently in China present the Soviet economic system in bright colors—and this is new."[29]

In a recent article Miriam London pointed out that

Peking is also calling for more subtle and effective political indoctrination programs in the schools in order to instill patriotism—which is flatly equated with loyalty to the Communist Party—and to demonstrate the superiority of so-called scientific Marxism over capitalism and discredit Western "bourgeois notions" of freedom and democracy. In a notorious speech in February 1985, [then] Party General Secretary Hu Yaobang, regarded as one of the most "advanced" reformists, explicitly stated that the role of the press in China was to serve as the "Party's mouthpiece." And a *Renmin Ribao* article last September warned the populace to beware of foreign spies, even among travelers, visiting relatives, trade representatives, and participants in scientific, technological and cultural exchanges.[30]

All this was further corroborated by the September 1985 National Conference of the Communist Party, which made it clear that the party would *not* countenance any attempts at introducing "bourgeois liberalism" in the name of Marxism and would seek to strengthen the party's ideological and propagandistic work.

The ideological limits have been set accordingly and were vigorously reit-erated by the 1987 campaign against "bourgeois liberalism" launched in re-sponse to the students' demonstrations of December 1986. There was not much new in this campaign. A decisive crackdown on open dissent took place in China in 1979 and culminated in the campaign against "spiritual pollution" of 1983. What in China is called "the changes of weather" have brought about a period of expanding relaxation in 1984–1986, but even then, political re-pression of "counterrevolutionary elements" was not abandoned. No one knows how many or how few political arrests had been made during that pe-riod, since such data are not available; but the New China News Agency re-ported, for example, that in 1984–1985 armed police squads patrolling large and medium-sized cities arrested about 170 "counterrevolutionaries."[31]

Neither has "relaxation" been extended to political prisoners, all of whom continued to serve their sentences through these years. International pleas for the release of China's most famous dissident, Wei Jingsheng, serving a fifteen-year sentence for advocating a "fifth modernization—democracy" were ignored by Chinese authorities. When a participant in a conference of about sixty over-seas scholars, sponsored by the United Front Department in June 1985 in Peking, asked Deng to free Wei, the latter snapped back angrily that as soon as Wei got out, he would only start creating chaos.[32] But the real precursor of the 1986 events and the resulting unleashing of the campaign against "bourgeois liberalism" in 1987 was the paranoid reaction of the central leaders to the anti-Japanese student movement that suddenly took off in Peking in September 1985 and spread to universities across the country. It was suppressed, although its slogans and demands, from the official point of view, were not as contro-versial as those under which the students mounted their protests in 1986.

The overriding message of the central leaders was unmistakable: no stu-dent movement must be initiated outside the party, which alone has the right to lead. The rationale—betraying shrill notes of defensiveness and anxiety this time around—was that only unity under the Communist Party can assure China's bright future and prevent chaos.[33]

Also, as it was the case in the USSR during the NEP, the central authorities were rapidly beefing up the security police during the period of "relaxation."

Enrollment in three major higher institutions for the police is reported by a well-informed Hong Kong journal to have increased more than 210 percent in 1985 over the previous year, and new professional security schools have recently been established.[34]

All that and other similar data did not at all indicate, as Löwenthal sug-gested, that China has passed the stage of "institutionalized revolution" and firmly entered into a postrevolutionary and thus post-totalitarian stage of its development. On the contrary, it rather pointed to the fact that, unless Com-munist rule in China is for some reason going to disintegrate, China would soon face the possibility of yet another "institutionalized revolution," bring-ing down the present reforms and establishing a "Soviet-type system of en-lightened Stalinist control."[35]

Already the Dengist reforms experience serious problems and lack of control. It is true, as Miriam London suggested before the student demonstrations of 1986, that the new economic policies brought fast, dramatic improvement in agricultural production and living standards, especially in good farming areas near large cities, with resultant benefit to urban dwellers. But improvement was extremely uneven and, along with the more complicated reform efforts in industry, gave rise to new situations and unexpected difficulties, which in turn led to periodic retrenchments or "pauses for breath." (The leaders admitted being taken by surprise by some of these developments and the extent of difficulty. Ideologists with a central-blueprint mentality never realize that the unexpected is to be expected.) However, there is evidence . . . that the reform faction does not see any road back, at least for the foreseeable future. Despite the seemingly intractable problems and complications that have arisen, often amounting to economic chaos, the reformists argue that there is no alternative to going ahead, even if this means "feeling one's way across the river by stepping stones." At the same time, they have had to defend this position repeatedly before the ideologically orthodox members of the top coalition, whose instinctive reaction to chaotic conditions is always to pull back and tighten controls. Such action, the reformists maintain, would mean a vicious circle dooming all hope of modernizing China by the middle of the twenty-first century. A recent article in the *Renmin Ribao* presents this argument in a nutshell: "If you tighten control whenever confusion occurs, this leads to rigidity, which leads to loosening of control, which leads to confusion, which leads to tightening control again."[36]

A fundamental cause of this "confusion" is that the loosening of central control takes place in the absence of any internal regulatory mechanism or accurate information feedback, which are essential to the operation of a freer economy. Articles in the press call for more economic laws and regulations, but also disclose that the qualified personnel needed to formulate and implement such laws are lacking.

The trouble is that the party cadres want to remain the law—and generally manage to do so. China has many little kingdoms within the larger kingdom. The central authorities periodically berate the middle-level cadres for merely going through the motions of reform, but, in fact, doing much as they please.[37] The wild policy swings and insecurity that have marked Chinese Communist rule have, indeed, affected these cadres but not as Löwenthal imagines. Many are digging in their heels, waiting for a new tide, after Deng's death, to sweep the reforms away. Uncertainty about central policy has also increased these cadres' dependence on local networks of "relationships," especially on tried and trusted friends of the same faction during the Cultural Revolution.[38] Since such networks operate for the exclusive benefit of the clique, they have wreaked havoc with many reform measures in practice, contributing to economic chaos and corruption.

It should also be held in mind that the great majority of the 40 million party cadres have an extremely low educational level and lack the competence to deal with the complex changes involved in "modernization." They perceive an ultimate threat to their power in the new emphasis on learning and expertise, against which many of them also retain an old Maoist prejudice.

The dissension within the top circles of power in Peking provides the middle-level cadres with good reason for continued uncertainty. The revisionists, centrists, and more orthodox Stalinists who basically constitute the top coalition have thus far managed to practice "compromise politics." As official statements sufficiently reveal, the present leaders understand that, after three and a half decades of extremely fickle policy, consensus and a public image of stability and unity have become a "life-and-death" matter for the party. Nevertheless, dissension at the top is an open secret and has caused continual, perceptible wavering of the policy line to the present. The more orthodox Stalinists at the power center blame the reforms, including the "open door" policy, for the rampant economic corruption and "spiritual pollution"—that is, the spread of "decadent bourgeois" and "capitalist" ideas, which they regard as alarmingly out of control. The entire leadership appeared greatly disturbed by elite university student demonstrations in the autumn of 1985 [let alone those of winter 1986], which blew the cover on popular resentment about perceived consequences of the reforms, notably rising prices, growing income disparity, and the self-enrichment of many party cadres and some of the leaders' "princeling heirs," through privileged business connections. Party Central's measures to deal with this worrisome popular mood have included defensive articles in the press "explaining" the "transitional" problems of the reforms, sometimes quite sensibly; exhortations to the party cadres to "obey the law" (meaning little more in practice than to "be good"); and the executions of several criminal playboy-sons of influential fathers, in order to cleanse the party image by demonstrating that everyone is "equal before the law." The last two measures hardly reassure the many Chinese who know well the fruitlessness of hortatory politics and economics and the arbitrary justice of party crackdowns.

The reporter-analyst Mary Lee recently noted: "Even sanguine observers say that until the back of [China's] economic and social problems is broken, Deng's organizational guarantee (of policy continuity through picked younger successors) will only last as long as he does."[39] It is in the nature of these problems to intensify, especially if the regime continues, at the same time, to pursue the inherently conflicting course of consolidating Soviet-type political and ideological controls. Quite a solid "phalanx" of more orthodox Stalinist cadres, backed by entrenched middle-level cadres with Maoist leanings, waits in the wings for the right moment to gain ascendance.[40]

I would like to conclude with the following thoughts, which were formulated by one of the leading Western authorities on China, Jürgen Domes. "If the policies of a socialist market economy should be continued until the end of this century, the forces they are bound to unleash in the urban society will sooner or later demand first a revision and then possibly even an abolition of the Four Basic Principles,[41] which, for all practical purposes, would mean the abolition of the totalistic single-party system." Since, in that case, the Chinese Communist Party would commit political suicide, and that can hardly be expected, "the possibility of a return to a Soviet-type system of centralized planning and a reduction of private initiatives has not significantly decreased during 1984 . . . all economic reforms and theoretical revisionism notwithstanding.[42]

"It is exactly in this projection that China's most severe developmental problem can be found. For following is the historical experience the world has witnessed since the Russian October Revolution of 1917 and the system that it created. Between socialism on the one hand and modernity and social progress on the other there exists—to put it into Marxist-Leninist terms—an antagonistic contradiction. They are incompatible."[43]

Contrary to what Löwenthal suggests, the situation in China is far from settled. Communist China is at the crossroads. The reforms introduced by Deng represent a lethal challenge to the embattled communist totalitarian system of rule. This system can be saved only by its launching of yet another "institutionalized revolution" from above. Nobody can say with assurance that this is what will inevitably happen. But it very well may happen, which Löwenthal either fails to realize or refuses to admit. If, however, it does not, then the still-totalitarian (not yet post-totalitarian, as Löwenthal would have it) communist regime in China will eventually crumble. Only at this stage will one be able to speak about China's transition from totalitarianism to post-totalitarianism.

NOTES

1. Michael Voslensky, "The Soviet System: An Historical and Theoretical Evaluation," in Alexander Shtromas and Morton A. Kaplan, eds., *The Soviet Union and the Challenge of the Future*, vol. 1, *The Soviet System: Stasis and Change* (New York: Paragon House, 1988), 5.

2. This particular feature of totalitarian systems is elaborated in more detail, but under a different angle, in F. Feher, A. Heller, and G. Markus, *Dictatorship Over Needs* (Oxford: Basil Blackwell, 1983), 110–16; and A. Arato, "Critical Sociology and Authoritarian State Socialism," in J. B. Thompson and D. Held, eds., *Habermas: A Critical Debate* (Cambridge, Mass.: MIT Press, 1982), 200–206.

3. M. Lewin, *The Making of the Soviet System* (London: Methuen, 1985), 257.

4. M. E. Urban, "Conceptualizing Political Power in the USSR: Patterns of Binding and Bonding," *Studies in Comparative Communism* 18, no. 4 (winter 1985): 209.

5. For my more extensive treatment of Soviet "intrastructural dissent" and its ubiquity, see: A. Shtromas, *Political Change and Social Development: The Case of the Soviet Union* (Frankfurt: Verlag Peter Lang, 1981), 67–82.

6. Richard Löwenthal, "A Theoretical Evaluation Without Historical Contents—A Commentary on Section 1," in Alexander Shtromas and Morton A. Kaplan, eds., *The Soviet Union and the Challenge of the Future*, vol. 1, *The Soviet System: Stasis and*

Change (New York: Paragon House, 1988), 36, hereafter referred as Löwenthal, "Comments."

7. Richard Löwenthal, "Beyond the 'Institutionalized Revolution' in Russia and China," in Alexander Shtromas and Morton A. Kaplan, eds., *The Soviet Union and the Challenge of the Future*, vol. 1, *The Soviet System: Stasis and Change* (New York: Paragon House, 1988), 14, hereafter referred as Löwenthal, "Paper."

8. Morton A. Kaplan, "The Necessary Conditions for Characterizing a State as Totalitarian—Commentary on Section 1," in Alexander Shtromas and Morton A. Kaplan, eds., *The Soviet Union and the Challenge of the Future*, vol. 1, *The Soviet System: Stasis and Change* (New York: Paragon House, 1988), 44.

9. Löwenthal, "Comments," 37.

10. Löwenthal, "Paper," 24.

11. Löwenthal, "Paper," 24.

12. Löwenthal, "Paper," 24.

13. Löwenthal, "Paper," 24.

14. Löwenthal, "Paper," 24.

15. See Alexander Shtromas, "To Fight Communism: Why and How?," in *International Journal on World Peace* 1, no. 1 (autumn 1984): 20–44.

16. Shtromas, "To Fight Communism," 37.

17. This last part of my comment will be devoted to Löwenthal's treatment of China. Not being a sinologist myself, I asked my sinologist friend, Miriam London, to present her own comment on Löwenthal's paper with the view of publishing it in this volume under a separate title. Although she turned down this request, Miriam London nevertheless most kindly supplied me with many written remarks on Löwenthal's text, permitting me to use them in my comment.

18. Löwenthal, "Paper."

19. Löwenthal, "Paper."

20. Miriam London elaborates: "In a 1972 interview, a peasant refugee told us: 'I don't know whether you understand this, but on the China mainland human beings are not all the same anymore. We (who belong to the black classes) are like earthworms on chicken farms. We can die at any time.'" (Remarks on Löwenthal's paper attached to a letter to Shtromas [March 25, 1986], hereafter referred to as "Remarks.") For a detailed analysis by the Londons of refugee accounts on hunger in China, see: M. London and I. D. London, "The Other China," *Worldview* 19, no. 5: 4–11, and no. 6: 43–48.

21. *Jingji Guanli* [Economic Management], no. 3 (March 1981): 3.

22. Roderick MacFarquhar has calculated a range of 16.5 to 29.4 million deaths. See his *The Origins of the Cultural Revolution*, vol. 2, *The Great Leap Forward, 1958–1960* (London: Oxford Univesity Press, 1983), 335. According to John S. Aird's analysis done for the U.S. Bureau of Census, "the net population loss during the famine years of 1959–1961 reached perhaps as much as 25 million people" (as quoted from V. Smil, "China's Food," in *Food Policy* [May 1981]: 76). As Jürgen Domes noted, even the minimal figure of 20 million is more than the number of people who died from famine in India in the thirty years from 1950 to 1980 (see his *The Government and Politics of the PRC: A Time of Transition* [Boulder, Colo.: Westview Press, 1985], 38).

23. Domes, *The Government and Politics of the PRC*.

24. *Nongmin Ribao*, September 28, 1985, as published by Foreign Broadcast Information Service, October 15, 1985. Miriam London remarks: "When China exports grain, this does not mean, therefore, that all hinterland areas have sufficient food, but

only that export from rich coastal areas is more feasible and earns foreign exchange." ("Remarks," as in note 20.)

25. This large extract is from Miriam London, "Remarks" (see note 20).

26. Simultaneously with the introduction of NEP, drastic measures were taken by central authorities in Soviet Russia to suppress and liquidate entirely the remnants of other socialist parties, to reduce dramatically the influence and undermine the organizational strength of the Russian Orthodox Church and other churches, and to destroy all other public bodies that were in any measure autonomous from the Bolshevik party. At the same time the 10th Congress of the Party that in 1921 introduced NEP adopted the notorious resolution, "On the Unity of the Party," which prohibited within it any factional activity and, in fact, all discord with the party leadership's views. For accurate reviews of these measures with the notable exception of those taken against the churches, see E. H. Carr, *The Bolshevik Revolution, 1917–1923*, vol. 1 (London: Macmillan, 1950), chapters 8 and 9; C. Bettelheim, *Class Struggles in the USSR First Period: 1917–1923* (Hassocks: Harvester Press, 1976). For a brief account of the early (1921) assault on the Russian Orthodox Church, see W. C. Fletcher, *A Study in Survival: The Church in Russia 1927–1943* (London: S.P.C.K., 1965), chapter 1; for a more detailed one, see D. Pospielovsky, *The Russian Church Under the Soviet Régime*, vol. 1 (Crestwood, N.Y.: St. Vladimir's Seminary Press, 1984), 93–112.

27. 129. For details on the GPU and its comparison with the Cheka, see E. H. Carr, *Bolshevik Revolution*, 179–83; C. Bettelheim, *Class Struggles*, 287–88.

28. Besides the leading role of the party, these are: socialism, proletarian dictatorship, Marxism-Leninism, and Mao Zedong thought.

29. *The Wall Street Journal*, September 30, 1985, p. 21.

30. M. London, "China Mirages," in *Freedom at Issue*, no. 89 (March–April 1986): 18.

31. London, "China Mirages," 17.

32. London, "China Mirages," 17.

33. London, "China Mirages," 18.

34. London, "China Mirages," 18.

35. The expression is J. Domes's; see *The Government and Politics of the PRC*, 238, 253, et al.

36. *Renmin Ribao*, October 17, 1985.

37. The saying in China is: "The top has policies and the bottom has countermeasures." The fact that such a saying is making the rounds and has been mentioned several times in the press (for example, in *Renmin Ribao* of January 17, 1986) indicates that this phenomenon is indeed widespread and cannot be ignored.

38. For more details of this particular form of factionalism in the party, see M. London and Ta-ling Lee, "China's Party Cadres Hedge their Bets," *The Asian Wall Street Journal*, July 16, 1985.

39. *Far Eastern Economic Review*, March 20, 1986.

40. This is another large extract from Miriam London's "Remarks" (see note 20).

41. For them, see Domes, *The Government and Politics of the PRC*.

42. Domes, *The Government and Politics of the PRC*, 257–58.

43. Domes, *The Government and Politics of the PRC*, 253.

8

Ideology and Conflict: Does Warfare Between "Isms" Belong to Past History?

ALEKSANDRAS SHTROMAS

Since the end of World War I ideology was the main source of conflict. This stopped after the collapse of the Soviet Union in 1991. Can the ideological conflicts resume their course in the foreseeable future? Theoretically such a possibility is not excluded, although fascism, national socialism, and Marxist communism have seen their day. Among other ideological tendencies, environmentalism seems to be the most promising candidate. It is more likely that the battle of ideologies will be gradually replaced by the ever intensifying struggle for ideals, such as individual and national freedom, human rights, and equality of condition.

I. PROBLEMS OF DEFINITION

Professor Kenneth Minogue defines ideology as "the project of creating social perfection by managing society."[1] One could infer from this that for Minogue an ideology is what it is only if it claims universality, that is, the capacity to serve as a valid blueprint for bringing perfection through management to any society on Earth, whatever particular—national, religious, cultural, economic, or geopolitical—characteristics that society may bear. It logically follows from this, as Minogue unambiguously himself states, that Marxism is truly paradigmatic of ideology or, in his own words, "the archetypal ideology."[2] Minogue also explicitly attacks those scholars who regard any political doctrine as ideology and include into the definition of ideology

Reprinted from Aleksandras Shtromas, "Ideology and Conflict: Does Warefare Between 'Isms' Belong to Past History?," *International Journal on World Peace* 14, no. 2 (June 1997): 31–76.

even "some bodies of ideas, like democracy, which were not political doctrines . . . at all."[3] I fully agree with Minogue that the term ideology as defined by Sargent, Vincent, and scores of other scholars exploring the subject, is practically unusable in any meaningful discussion because its literally limitless broadness and blurs the distinctions between ideology and a number of related concepts, such as, for example, religion, philosophy, ideal, value, policy, prejudice, etc. This is to say that Minogue's attempt at defining ideology in a narrower and more precise sense seems to me both necessary and highly commendable.

I think, however, that for the purpose of a proper definition of the concept of ideology the most appropriate way is to go back to the original definition given to that concept by Antoine Louis Claude, Comte Destutt de Tracy (1754–1836), the man who first introduced the concept of ideology to the world. In Destutt de Tracy's terms, *idéologie* is a science of ideas. Any ideas, if analyzed by Destutt de Tracy's methodology, could be either validated as based on experience and thus true or, if they are not lending themselves to such verification, should be discarded. In his four-volume work *Elements d'idéologie*, published between 1801–1813, Destutt de Tracy arrives at a system of such, in his opinion, true ideas (very liberal ones, by the way) and then focuses his attention on how to translate these "true" ideas into sociopolitical reality by conceiving appropriate programs of political action. Hence, according to Destutt de Tracy, an ideology: (1) is based on a verified cognitive general theory of universal and comprehensive nature explaining human beings and their relationship with the external world, including also other human beings; (2) expresses itself in a program of social and political organization of human beings; (3) entails the necessity of struggle for the realization of this program; (4) demands proselytizing and commitment; (5) addresses the public at large but confers a special role of leadership to properly qualified groups of intellectuals (*les idéologues* or, one could say, the enlightened "vanguard" of society).[4]

Destutt de Tracy excludes religion from ideology altogether, because he considers religion to be irrational and fictitious; and thus to him any sets of religious ideas are the ones destined to be discarded in the first place. For those, however, who do not share Destutt de Tracy's belief in the possibility of evolving a scientifically true ideology (and I am one of those myself, taking on this issue, unlike many others, a truly Popperian view), religion is as good a basis for formulating an ideology (in the sense of Destutt de Tracy's point [1] above), as is any secular theory claiming to be scientifically or otherwise true. In order to serve as a viable foundation for an ideology, a theory, it seems to me, should be able to present a claim to universal validity and comprehensive scope, sufficiently credible at least to some group (in addition, of course, to claiming to be the expression of ultimate truth); and religion-based theories are on the whole even more effective at presenting such claims than the secular ones.

The inclusion of religion into the category of possible foundations for elaborating an ideology brings into the concept of ideology yet another element that Destutt de Tracy was naturally unable even to consider—that of ethical values—which entails an ardent belief of that ideology's adherents not merely in the correctness of the ideology they profess but also in its absolute moral goodness. This, in turn, dictates the necessity for these adherents to subscribe to a specific hierarchical structure of ethical values corresponding to the ideology and usually based on the conviction that any means advancing the ideology's proclaimed ultimate political goal (which also constitutes the ultimate good) are perfectly ethical, however much at variance with the commonly accepted moral standards these means may be. Lenin's formula about the advancement of the goals of proletarian class struggle forming the sole criterion of morality[5] expresses this attitude in a nutshell.

With these revisions and amendments added, Destutt de Tracy's original concept of ideology provides for my purposes a perfectly valid definition. To sum it up, ideology should be understood as an action-oriented theoretical creed that: (1) has its foundation in a universal and comprehensive philosophy and/or religion; (2) establishes a specific hierarchical structure of ethical values, usually subordinated to what is believed to be the ultimate political goal; (3) sets out a program for the creation and operation of such a sociopolitical system that is uniquely suitable for implementing this goal; (4) entails the necessity of founding and running a closely-knit political organization devoted to the struggle for the practical realization of this program; (5) demands this organization's engagement in a proselytizing effort addressed to the public at large and a full commitment to its work on the part of the converted proselytes who have joined that political organization as members; and (6) confers a special role of political and theoretical leadership to the intellectually and morally advanced "vanguard" endowed, among other leadership functions, with the most important one—the authority for authentic interpretation in given practical-political circumstances of the ideology itself.

II. IDEOLOGY VS. PHILOSOPHY AND RELIGION

What is in my view important to stress first is the difference between ideology, on the one hand, and philosophy and religion, on the other. To me at least, philosophy is in the business of explaining the world and the man in it, as they are. It is using for this purpose the available knowledge on both the man and the world and tries to sum it up in a theoretically sensible and methodologically viable way. The modern philosopher who first sought to transcend the epistemological confines of philosophical inquiry and conceive a philosophical theory of practical action was, perhaps, Johann Gottlieb Fichte, whom Marx, in *The German Ideology*, not without reason, admiringly called the Napoleon of philosophy. When Marx, in his eleventh thesis on Feuerbach, said that "up till now the philosophers have only interpreted the world in various ways; the point, however, is to change it,"[6] he was in fact quoting Fichte and, at the same time, accomplished the great leap by which his own philosophy was to be transformed into an ideology *par excellence*. (Not, of course, into an ideology in Marx's own terms, that is, into "false consciousness," but into what Marx thought was a truly scientific social theory capable of properly informing practical sociopolitical action [i.e., a scientific ideology, as what, by the way, ideology was supposed to be in its original conception envisaged by Destutt de Tracy]).

Ideology is more akin to religion than to philosophy, as religions are also total and universal belief systems combining the questions of truth with those of human conduct by projecting for governing the latter a strict hierarchical structure of ethical values. Ideologies are, however, entirely "this-worldly," while religions are usually concerned about "things not of this world" and concentrate on personal virtues and modes of individual behavior capable of winning for a particular human being favor with God and thus ensuring peace and harmony for the eternal life of his or her immortal soul.

Professor Bhikhu Parekh made a succinct distinction between religious fundamentalism, as a device by which religion is translated into "this worldly" ideology, and religious revivalism or ultraorthodoxy, which represents different ways of expressing the faithful's concern about protecting the purity of religious faith and traditions from the severe challenges of modernity. According to Parekh, "Fundamentalism . . . arises in a society widely believed to be degenerate and devoid of a sense of direction, identity and the means of its self-regeneration . . . [and] represents an attempt to regenerate [society] by comprehensively reconstituting it on a religious foundation." In order to achieve this goal, fundamentalism "rejects the tradition, offers a 'dynamic' and activist reading of the scriptures . . . weaves a moral and political program around them, and uses the institution of the state to enforce the program." Parekh to me is absolutely right when he says that "[s]ince fundamentalism"—and, I would add, every religion-based political ideology in general—"reduces religion to ideology and charters it to an alien purpose, it inevitably distorts and destroys it."[7]

Indeed, an ideology may be based on an interpretation of a certain religious tradition, but by its very nature it is alien to, and works across the purposes with, a God-centered religion. Differently from Parekh, I do not think, however, that religious ideology of the fundamentalist kind is typical exclusively of modernity. As religion in premodern times was the dominant form of human consciousness, all premodern ideologies were inevitably based on religion. In my view, Thomas Münzer and Jean Calvin were typical religious ideologists, and so were also the puritans, both those who initiated the English revolution of 1640–1660 and those who sailed to North America to found a New England and with it to start from scratch a new way of life *in this world*, to found a new social and political system that would accord with their vision of religious virtue. One could say that they were the religious fundamentalists *avant la lettre*. The roots of religiously-based ideologies conceived in the Christian tradition go, in my view, as far back as to St. Augustines's *De Civitatis Dei*, and only since the thirteenth century Western Christianity, with and through St. Thomas Aquinas, learned thoroughly to distinguish between temporal matters and matters spiritual and eternal or, in other words, between the concerns of life in this world and the life with God *sub specie aeternitatis.*

Ideology should thus be treated as a concept distinct from the concepts of philosophy and religion. Using philosophies and/or religions as their basic source, ideologies *per se* represent, in fact, a bridge between them and practical political action. It is the program and methods of such action that form the ideology's main core. And it is because of such an overwhelmingly practical–political orientation, that an ideology is bound to distort and, ultimately, to destroy, the very philosophy and/or religion on which it claims to be built.

One could argue that this latter conclusion does not apply to Marxism, for Marxism is supposed to be a consistent and complex system of philosophical and economic thought from which a program for practical political action or, which is one and the same thing, an ideology, logically and coherently follows. But is Marxism really a philosophy? It is doubtful, because Marx used a quite skillful amalgamation of philosophical systems propounded by others— first and foremost by Georg Wilhelm Friedrich Hegel, but also by Lüdwig Feuerbach, Henri de Saint Simon, Johann Gottlieb Fichte, Adam Smith, David Ricardo, and a few others—in order to draw from it his own purely ideological conclusions expressed in the body of thought known as Marx's historical materialism. Marx's own claim to his role in the development of social thought is, by the way, not much different. In the letter to his friend Joseph Weydemeyer of March 5, 1852, Marx wrote, for example, that all he "did that was new was to prove: (1) that the existence of classes is only bound up with *particular historical phases in the development of production;* (2) that the class struggle necessarily leads to the *dictatorship of the proletariat;* (3) that this dictatorship itself only constitutes the transition to the *abolition of all classes and to a classless society.*"[8]

In other words, according to Marx himself, the novelty of his thought consisted in projecting a vision of class struggle resulting in the future institution of a workers' state (the dictatorship of the proletariat) that is going to work toward the creation of a classless, i.e., communist, society. The fact that he claimed this process to be objectively inevitable and unavoidable does not change the purely ideological nature of his self-defined original contribution to social thought, as such claims are usual for most ideologies trying to dress themselves up as the expressions of the ultimate truth. In the science-worshiping nineteenth century such a dress-up required one to claim for the ideology in question the status of an objective, moreover, scientific social theory; and this was what Marx actually did claim. It is by so doing that Marx had virtually distorted and, ultimately, destroyed, the classical Hegelian–Fichtean philosophical premises on which he founded his ideology. It is exactly this distortion and destruction by Marx of the original philosophical foundations of his ideology that leads so many of us to believe that Marx has indeed created a novel philosophical system that is entirely consistent with his ideology. My point is that Marx has created a mere ideology but, by carefully trying to present it as a consistent scientific and philosophical theory, fooled himself and so many of us into believing that this was indeed the case.

III. WHAT SYSTEMS OF IDEAS AND VALUES QUALIFY AS IDEOLOGIES?

So far we have identified two systems of thought and action that, in my analysis, qualify as full-fledged ideologies: religious fundamentalisms of any variety (and ancient or medieval as much as the modern ones; not to be confused, however, with what, following Parekh's classification, qualifies as religious revivalism or ultraorthodoxy) and Marxism. What are the others?

A. Socialism, Communism, Jacobinism

Pre- and non-Marxist varieties of socialism and communism qualify as ideologies, in my view, too. These include, in the first place, anarchism, as conceived in the works of William Godwin, Pierre-Joseph Proudhon, Mikhail Bakunin, and Petr Kropotkin, by now an over two-centuries old ideological tradition on the basis of which a number of international political movements were established in the nineteenth century, with some such movements continuing to function at the present time, too. Early communist ideologies were conceived in the seventeenth century by Gerard Winstanley who also created what one could call the first English communist party, the Diggers; and in the eighteenth century by Francois-Noël (called Gracchus) Babeuf who, in addition to having projected in his theoretical works a consistent communist world view, had also formed a clandestine political organization that plotted to establish the "Babeuvists" (the party of the followers of Gracchus Babeuf) as a communist government in an already republican France, but was found out and destroyed even before having started to stage their *coup d' état,* known under the name of the Conspiracy of Equals.

In the revolutionary situations of seventeenth-century England and eighteenth-century France, the civil wars and interventions taking place then were dominated by opposing ideologies not only on the radical fringes represented by the extremists, such as the Diggers or John Lillburne's Levellers in England and the Babeuvists in France, but also in the mainstream forces that actually played the revolutionary process out. The Parliamentarian Party (both the Presbyterians and the Independents) in seventeenth-century England was, no doubt, inspired by its ideological (to a large extent religiously fundamentalist) vision of a good and just society, and so were the leaders of the Third Estate in eighteenth-century France, although their ideological vision was purely secular and antithetical to any established religion. Faced with such an ideologically motivated challenge, the defenders of the old regimes in both countries had to respond by projecting their own traditionalist ideologies, based on such concepts as the divine right of kings and the sanctity of the "natural" hierarchical structures based on feudal rights and privileges. The radical Independents in England, who came to the fore with Pride's Purge—the ejection of the Presbyterian dominated Long Parliament and its replacement by the radical Rump executed by Colonel Thomas Pride—were as ideologically motivated in their actions as, over a century later, were the French Jacobins. If the former derived their ideology from religion, the latter, having rejected Christianity and the Church altogether, used as the foundation for their ideology the secular philosophies of the eighteenth century's French Enlightenment, mainly Jean-Jacque Rousseau's theory of the general will, which the Jacobin leaders (especially Maximilien Robespierre) managed to translate into a consistent program of revolutionary political action meant not only for France but for the world at large. All the pragmatically motivated and "feudalizing" adjustments notwithstanding, Napoleon's rule was in essence nothing else but a consistent continuation of the effort to entrench the Jacobin ideology in the politics of France and, at the same time, to propel the Napoleonic version of Jacobinism onto the rest of Europe, which at that time was tantamount to the entire world.

B. Fascism and National Socialism

Mussolini's fascism and Hitler's national-socialism were full-blooded universal ideologies, too. They were bound to be that, as they sought to provide an adequate counter-ideology to Marxist communism on a global scale.

It is true that both these ideologies were to a large extent preoccupied with their own nations, the Italians and the Germans, respectively. For Mussolini, the task of Italy was to recreate and embody the former greatness of the Roman Empire and to provide for the rest of the world what *Pax Romana* had provided for the ancient universe. Italy, according to him, earned the right to be in the forefront of contemporary political developments, as it was the first nation to establish for itself the total and absolute fascist state, one that in the twentieth century is uniquely able to propel a nation to a secure and bright future. The future will thus belong, according to the Fascist creed, to those nations that are going to establish for themselves in good time a fascist ideology-based totalitarian state; the nations whose decay went so far as to making them unable to create a totalitarian system of government, will have to subordinate themselves to the morally, culturally, and politically superior totalitarian powers. Hence, Italy is to become in the future a prominent, if not (because of its initiating role and rich historical tradition) the leading, partner in a world alliance consisting of a few totalitarian empires dominating the rest of the world. In Mussolini's own words, "[I]n the doctrine of Fascism, Empire is not only a territorial, military or mercantile expression, but spiritual or moral. One can think of an empire, that is to say a nation that directly or indirectly leads other nations, without needing to conquer a single square kilometer of territory. For Fascism the tendency to Empire, that is to say, to the expansion of nations, is a manifestation of vitality; its opposite, staying at home, is a sign of decadence: peoples who rise or re-rise are imperialist, peoples who die are renunciatory."[9] Thus much about the Italian fascist vision of the future world order and Italy's role and place in it.

Not less explicit was Mussolini about the universal nature of the Fascist doctrine itself. He squarely bases it on Hegel's philosophy of right and, more specifically, on his view about the state being the reality into which the absolute idea finally materializes itself. "The keystone of Fascist doctrine," he writes, "is the conception of the State. . . . For Fascism the state is the absolute before which individuals and groups are relative."[10] "Therefore," he states in another passage of the essay, "for the Fascist, everything is in the State, and nothing human or spiritual exists, much less has value, outside the State. In this sense Fascism is totalitarian, and the Fascist State, the synthesis and unity of all values, interprets, develops and gives a strength to the whole life of the people."[11] To Mussolini, "Fascism is a religious conception . . . besides being a system of government, [it] is also, and above all, a system of thought."[12] "If it is admitted," he continues, "that the nineteenth century has been the century of Socialism, Liberalism and Democracy, it does not follow that the twentieth must also be the century of Liberalism, Socialism and Democracy. . . . It is to be expected that this century may be that of authority, a century of the 'Right,' a Fascist century. If the nineteenth was the century of the individual (Liberalism means individualism), it may be expected that this one may be the century of "collectivism . . . and therefore of the State."[13] And he concludes: "If every age has its own doctrine, it is apparent from a thousand signs that the doctrine of the present age is Fascism . . . Fascism henceforward has in the world the universality of all those doctrines which, by fulfilling themselves, have significance in the history of the human spirit."[14]

Fascism is commonly regarded as an extremist nationalist ideology. This is a profound misunderstanding of the very essence of fascism. In fact, fascism is a universal and globally conceived ideology, based on Hegelian philosophical premises and setting conditions for all nation-states to meet the challenge of the twentieth century and either grow into fascist-totalitarian states or, alternatively, sink into subordination to those nations who have become such states, and, ultimately, into historical oblivion. The only truly nationalistic element in this doctrine is the praise of Italy for her being the first to initiate fascist-totalitarian statehood and for "rising again after many centuries of abandonment or slavery to foreigners."[15]

If Mussolini based his doctrine on the universal theory of the state, Hitler chose as a foundation for his ideological *Weltanschauung* the not less universal and global in scope, theory of the race. For Hitler, the paramount political institution is not the state but the Volk, or a nation as such, bound into an integral entity and a naturally organized body politic by racial ties of common blood of people sharing also a common soil (*Blut und Boden*). The state is just one of the institutions the Volk may use to serve its political purposes and interests, but the state is also prone to fall into the hands of the

Volk's enemies, as do liberal or communist states, which pervert the nation and contribute to its gradual disintegration and demise.

Like Mussolini, Hitler also envisages a new European and, ultimately, world order, but to him it was bound to emerge from the millennia-long racial struggle which, in his view, shaped the course of human history. The German nation is to Hitler not an end in itself, but rather a means to achieving that European and world order through the "thousand years' Reich" that Hitler instituted in Germany. The latter is to be in the position to continue with the struggle for achieving the end of the "new Europe" and the "new world order" after Hitler had passed away. This is to say that the German Volk, in Hitler's view, is designated to become a sort of a "fighting vanguard" of the Aryan race in its ceaseless (though, at most times, unconscious) struggle for becoming the globally dominant force. The Germans were destined to take upon themselves that vanguard role, because, being in Hitler's view, more than any other Aryan Volk exposed to miscegenation and racial degradation, they were the first among the Aryans to become conscious of the threat to their identity and continuous existence. That is why, under Hitler's leadership, they rose to the defense of their racial integrity, thus willy-nilly also taking upon themselves the championship of the Aryan cause generally and on the global scale. Hitler never excluded the possibility of Germany perishing, virtually becoming nationally extinct, in this long-lasting struggle, but Germany's sacrifice was supposed to ensure victory in the battle of Aryan supremacy on this planet and for establishing the New Europe and the New World based on this supremacy—a cause, in Hitler's view, worth perishing for. If, however, the Germans survived all the battles they would have to fight for the Aryan cause, Germany will, no doubt, occupy in the New World that will emerge as result of these battles an honorable place. Nevertheless, the purer national brands of the Aryans, those farther removed to the North and thus less spoiled by miscegenation (for example, the Scandinavian nations), will most certainly acquire in the established hierarchy of "racially pure Volks" a position superior to that of the Germans.

The first and most important task of the twentieth century's racial struggle is, according to Hitler, the elimination from the life and the social fabrics of all Volks, to whatever race—Aryan or sub-Aryan—these Volks happen to belong, of the Jews, the alien inclusion into each Volk which undermines its integrity from within and thus tries to subordinate the Volk to itself. The enormity of this task is made clear by Hitler's defintion of both the "Demo-Plutocratic Liberalism" and Communism as special Jewish devices invented for the purpose of subverting each nation and putting it under the alien Jewish control. This is to say that, in Hitler's view, the task of eliminating the Jewish menace to the world implies the necessity of destroying liberal democratic states as well as the states ruled by the communist parties, restoring all of them, bit by bit, to their original national-socialist integrity of organically structured and racially pure *Volkstums*. The alternative to the undertaking of this enormous task is, according to Hitler, the extinction of human species, including the Jews themselves, for this will be the inevitable result of Jewish rule over nations through the means of liberalism and communism. As he himself says, "[t]he end is not only the end of . . . the peoples oppressed by the Jew, but also the end of this parasite upon the nations. After the death of his victim, the vampire sooner or later dies too."[16] Hence, national-socialism is also a globally conceived universal ideology, a holistic world view aimed at remodeling the entire world in accordance with its own image. In this sense, national-socialism cannot be classified as a nationalistic ideology, despite the fact that it confers to the German nation a very special role in the process of the world's remodeling in accordance with Hitler's scriptures.

This is not to say that a national idea cannot in principle become a foundation for a universal ideology. But for a national idea to serve this purpose it has to posit a particular nation's superiority over all other nations and, by so doing, justify that particular nation's claim to rule the world. I, for one, am not aware of such an ideology having ever been in existence and, because of its sheer impracticality in preaching nothing positive but a war against the rest of the world, doubt whether it could have ever even been attempted to be formulated. There were of course warriors trying to conquer the world and put their own kin in charge of it, but even the most ferocious of them, Attila the Hun, apparently tried to do so not for the sake of establishing a Hun-dominated world empire, but in order to realize his universal ideological commitment to relieving humanity from the bondage of a settled civilization, every vestige of which he set himself the task of destroying. As shown above, neither Mussolini and Hitler nor Lenin and Stalin sought their respective nation's undivided domination over the world. They were all pursuing the institution of a much more complex "new world" based on a universal, not on a narrowly conceived, purely national, ideology.

One could, perhaps, say that the practice and legacy of colonial rule created in Great Britain and other colony-possessing European nations an attitude of national superiority with regard to the nations of the colonies they used to rule. This phenomenon is impressively discussed by, again, Bhikhu Parekh in "Decolonizing Liberalism,"[17] and there is nothing much I have to add to his brilliant analysis. What I would like to stress, however, is the fact that no colonial European nation ever made an ideological claim about its inherently constant superiority entitling it to a permanent rule over these "second-class" colonized nations, let alone over the entire world. Britain and other colonial masters claimed to exercise, with regard to their colonies, a civilizing mission that, after having been successfully accomplished, would allow them to release their colonies into, first, autonomous and, later, independent existence. And this, as we know, had indeed become the case.

C. Millian (Militant) Liberalism

The above by no means challenges Parekh's extremely well-presented and logically impeccable arguments about Western liberalism's colonial arrogance, its spurious anti-traditionalism, its extremely narrow definition of, and accordance of exaggerated importance to, "such values as autonomy, choice, individuality, liberty, rationality and progress;"[18] as well as liberalism's unwarranted denial of communitarian and other collectivist institutions of the non-European nations under his discussion. But these arguments represent a critique of Western liberalism as a universal ideology rather than as a foundation of the actually nonexistent Western claims to rule the Third World, let alone the entire world. Actually, Parekh's critique of the Millian variation of Western liberalism is valid in regard to all nations without exception, not only the ones that were colonized by Western powers and now form the Third World. A typical Millian liberal has no patience for communitarian collectivist beliefs and traditions wherever they continue to exist, be it distant India or nearby rural England. The Millian liberals had no understanding of or sympathy for the Irish national struggle and continue to wonder about the passionate attachment of some Welshmen to their "antiquated and useless language," treating the struggle for its preservation as incomprehensible, irrational, and thus reprehensible. According to Mill, nationalism of the backward rural nations is doomed to dissipate within the identity of the advanced urban nations, those that by virtue of their accomplished cosmopolitan modernization overcame the predominance over their way of life of any narrowly conceived collective identity and thus stopped being nationalistic in the traditional sense of the word. "Nobody can suppose," asserted Mill, "that it is not more beneficial to a Breton, or a Basque of French Novarre, to be brought into the current of the ideas and feelings of a highly civilized and cultivated people—to be a member of the French nationality, admitted on equal terms to all the privileges of French citizenship, sharing the advantages of French protection, and the dignity and prestige of French power—than to sulk on his own rocks, the half-savage relic of past times, revolving in his little mental orbit, without participation or interest in the general movement of the world. The same remark applies to Welshman or the Scottish Highlander as members of the British nation."[19] Being liberals, however, the Millians do not advocate direct suppression or forceful elimination of these "remnants of the past." What they see as their practical task is the initiation and enhancement of such "progressive" societal developments, which, they believe, are bound to bring about, as a result, the extinction of these remnants in a "natural way."

Meanwhile, by absolutizing individualism and, accordingly, treating every form of collectivism as a reactionary leftover of the "dark ages," a relic of the feudal past and a symbol of rural backwardness, Millian liberals in their day-to-day activities and propaganda militantly oppose collectivist tendencies and traditions, engage in an active combat for their elimination from the life of contemporary society altogether, and do so wherever such tendencies and traditions are to be found (and they are to be found everywhere, indeed). Although, as mentioned above, Millian liberalism treats all varieties of traditional collectivism, designating the differences among various national, cultural, or religious groups, as phenomena that, with the further progress of modernity, are due to vanish into the records of the historic past, every true Millian liberal nevertheless sees his task in pushing by all means in his power this process of progressive modernization forward and thus hastening its happy conclusion— the universal triumph of the liberal-individualist uniformity, accomplished on the ruins of all the finally vanquished traditional group identities. By all that, Millian Liberalism is indeed militant liberalism.

D. The Problem of Conservative Ideology

So far we talked about ideologies that are pretty obviously universal and conceived for global application. Furthermore, these already evoked ideologies are militantly revolutionary ones, as they set the goal of remodeling and reshuffling the established sociopolitical order and demand of their adherents to do their utmost in the struggle for, and realization of, the new order the respective ideology envisions. What then about the counterrevolutionary, conservative ideas? Do they not have a potential of developing into full-blooded ideologies? It was actually these ideas to the sets of which Karl Mannheim exclusively accorded the term ideology, while calling the revolutionary ones utopian—utopian, as long as they were inspired and driven by the vested interest in achieving change rather than by objectivity and "realistic thought" of which, Mannheim believed, only the relatively uncommitted intellectual class of society, the "intelligentsia," is capable. The revolutionary theories conceived by the intelligentsia could therefore qualify, in Mannheim's view, as nonutopian and situationally correct—*situationsgerecht*.[20]

To me, however, conservatism is, as a rule, not ideological. It expresses itself mainly in the not necessarily uncritical acceptance of, and accommodation to, the given social-political reality, usually accompanied by a certain nostalgia for that reality's original or past purity and a resentment of "bastardizing changes" introduced into that reality by recent modernizing currents and trends. Traditionalism, the instinctive attachment to familiar rituals and a routine way of life, that is, to what Max Weber so aptly called "the eternal yesterday," is no ideology but a natural result of a successful process of socialization. It is only when this reality is disintegrating and becomes increasingly unable to secure a successful socialization into it of substantial numbers of oppressed and/or alienated people that the normally nonideological conservative orientation may start growing into a set of ideas deserving the name "conservative ideology." This usually happens when there is an urgent need for the conservatives to present an adequate response to the spread and menacingly increasing impact of revolutionary ideologies.[21]

Comte Joseph de Maistre (1753–1821) could be seen as, perhaps, a typical founder and exponent of such a full-blooded conservative ideology. Basing his ultramontanist doctrine on medieval Catholic theology, de Maistre indeed sought to destroy the republican political doctrines of the French Enlightenment and to build upon "their ruins" a consistently all-round and universal ideology extolling royal absolutism. Paradoxically, one could define de Maistre's ideology as also a revolutionary one: his *Considerations sur la France*, the first attempt at its systematic presentation, was written in 1796 and called, in fact, for a revolution against the already-established republican regime in France.

On the other hand, the fascist and national-socialist ideologies of the twentieth century, though, no doubt, revolutionary, could also be defined as conservative, for they preached a revolution against the capitalist system, which, in their view, had itself in a revolutionary manner devastated the natural foundations and organic structures of traditional national societies that they now sought to restore on a new, modernized foundation. In other words, their revolutionary anticapitalist stance was presented as being actually a counterrevolutionary one, since, in their conception, capitalism itself was a perverse revolutionary imposition upon a naturally organic society threatening that society's very existence. Being born in response to the socialist-communist challenge, these ideologies thus positioned themselves to defend the conservative continuity of nations by combating not only the "divisive and leveling" Marxist ideology, but also—and in the first place—the whole tradition of "splintering individualism," including the established bourgeois-liberal order based upon, and centered around, this tradition. For them, the bourgeois liberal order has been, in fact, the primary cause of both the conservative continuity's destruction and the appearance of Marxism, as a device to accomplish that destruction in a definitive manner.

Indeed, as these few examples show only too clearly, it is very difficult to tell a conservative ideology from a revolutionary one, which is to say that the cognitive value of Mannheim's attempted distinction between ideology and utopia is extremely relative and makes sense only insofar as we are prepared (and I have already admitted that I am not)—together with Destutt de Tracy, Marx and Mannheim himself—to recognize that systems of sociopolitical ideas could be fully objective, realistic, and scientifically true. (This does not mean, however, that in my view all such systems of sociopolitical ideas are necessarily bound to be mere reflections of false consciousness [ideologies], rationalized wishful thinking [utopias], or a combination of both [the conservative ideas]; these systems of ideas usually represent honest and firm, though usually rushed and not properly substantiated, convictions about the nature of society and politics, the possibility of an effective solution for all sociopolitical problems and, above all, about the proper realization of the ideal of absolute justice.)

Ideologies we have so far defined as such, in addition to being universal, conceived for global application, and militant, are also holistic. They usually identify an enemy and believe that the defeat and elimination of that enemy (it may be a certain class, race, or nation, but also a set of prejudices and irrational attitudes from which their human carriers should be freed) is the key to universal salvation and the prerequisite to the creation of the ideal society, a "holistic" blueprint for which every such ideology has elaborated in advance. Although, as W. H. Dray by quoting May Brodbeck rightly stresses, the common opinion holds that "[c]ulturally, holism is intimately connected with hostility toward the liberal political individualism of the Western tradition,"[22] militant Millian liberalism is, doubtlessly, a holistic creed, too. Liberals of this denomination know exactly what in society is backward and thus rejectable, and what is progressive and thus deserving support and enhancement; they scorn national bonds and patriotic attachments, traditional loyalties, and "irrational prejudices" (e.g., religion) that are still a part and parcel of social fabric in all nations, and dream of a time when religions, national, cultural, linguistic, and other spurious differences dividing mankind will disappear and all men will become just human beings, equally rational and equally sharing the same individualistic liberal values. Believing that this "higher unity of men" will inevitably, sooner or later, come about, such liberals nevertheless do not shy away from social engineering and gladly resort to imposition of their "correct" ideas almost in the same way (though, maybe, not exactly as cruelly) in which non- and antiliberal ideologues do. It is this propensity that creates a remarkable affinity between Millian liberalism and socialism/communism, a propensity that had been quite clearly expressed in the later works of John Stuart Mill himself and that had inspired Herbert Spencer to oppose the Millian variety of liberalism and present his own, much more libertarian version of it.

IV. THE PROBLEM OF NATIONALISM

Alongside the universal and globally concerned ideologies, there exist hosts of specific sets of action-oriented ideas conceived for limited application—limited to a specific group of people, a nation, a country, or a certain ethnogeographic area of the world. The question is whether these latter sets of ideas—and especially nationalism as the most prominent of them all—also qualify as ideologies in terms of the definition given above.

It is in the nature of man to try to prove to himself and others that his practical claims are based on natural right and, consequently, the policies aimed at realizing these claims are those of attaining true justice. That is why in politics interests are always backed up by ideas presenting these interests as possessing absolute moral and legal value and thus indisputably reflecting the absolute standards of justice. And that is also why every set of even the most practical-pragmatic interest driven policies appear on the political surface as ideological. This is actually what is causing so much confusion between mere policy and ideology. Such an immutable relationship between pragmatic group interest-based policies and the ideas of absolute justice has been already noticed by Aristotle who formulated it as the basic rule of political struggle and disputes. According to Aristotle, groups of people engage in factional conflict mainly in order to aggrandize themselves, but they always portray their case in that conflict as that of true justice. In most cases, he notes, this is, however, a perverse notion of justice, one that justifies the self-serving goals of a particular group, for "while there is agreement that justice in an unqualified sense is according to merit, there are differences: . . . some [the socially inferior ones—A. S.] consider themselves to be equal generally if they are equal in some respect, while others [the socially privileged ones, usually the rich—A. S.] claim to merit all things unequally if they are unequal [superior—A. S.] in some respect."[23]

Of course, not all claims and policies aimed at realization of these claims are based exclusively on self-interest or self-promotion. In modernizing societies, for example, the need for an adequate response to the demands and challenges of modernity often creates opposite reactions roughly definable as traditionalist and progressive. Both of them are based not so much on any particular group interest (although these certainly also play an important role in determining a group's position toward modernizing changes) as on more general ideas of the "common good" or the national interest. The Slavophiles and westernizers in Russia's nineteenth-century politics are here a typical case in point, but their ideas were also strictly policy-bound and concerned about the future development of Russia only, not of the world at large. What these ideas were also lacking in order to qualify as full-blooded ideologies was a comprehensive and universal program for the creation of a new just society even in Russia, let alone on a global scale.

In the above sense, both the Slavophiles and westernizers were Russian nationalists, as their main, mutually shared concern was the well-being of the Russian nation. They only differed in their concepts of what is to constitute this well-being and how (by what sets of policies) it is to be achieved. These concepts were obviously mutually exclusive, but, at the same time, both were equally in dire opposition to the policies and practice of the actual Russian czarist state. This opposition was so acute that I would not even dare to call either of these tendencies patriotic. The commitment in both of them was to the Russian nation alone, despite, and in opposition to, the *patria*—the territorial expanse ruled by the autocratic regime, which, in their view, was illegitimately usurping the Russian national statehood. It is in that sense that the Slavophiles and Westernizers of Russia were nationalists *par exellence*, but hardly true patriots.

Even the extension of Russian nationalism into the supranational idea of Pan-Slavism, undertaken under the pressure of the Slavophiles by the Russian officialdom, did not change its basically policy formulation-directed nature. Conceived in Russia by the official historian Mikhail Pogodin (1800–1875) but passionately supported by significant forces among the southern Slavs, Czechs and, later, even by some groups of Poles (especially, Roman Dmowski and his Endeks, the People's Democrats), it was endowing the Russian czar with the function of the protector of all the Slavs and, more specifically, of their liberator from the alien Ottoman and Habsburg imperial yoke. In its Pan-Slavic shape, the official national policy of Russia was thus proclaiming Russia's duty to other kindred Slavic nations in facilitating their unification into one "brotherly" political entity under the Russian czar's tutelage. However imperialist, this policy (as well as the ideas behind its formulation) was limited by a precise boundary of the lands inhabited by Slavic nations in the Balkans and Central Europe and pursued a limited goal of their liberation from alien rule and incorporation into a "natural union" with each other and under the auspices of the most powerful member, Russia. Furthermore, not only did the Pan-Slavic idea not envisage any changes of the indigenous sociopolitical systems or of the traditional ways of life of the nations involved, but, on the contrary, it aimed at preserving and enhancing their true, conservatively defined identities and "selfhood."

In a way, Pan Slavism, as well as many similar creeds—such as Pan Germanism, Pan Turkism, Pan Iranism, Pan Arabism, *negritude* (even in its Haitian Duvalierist shape), and also South African apartheid—were no more than specific expressions or extensions of corresponding nationalist ideas that by their very nature are not universal, but particularistic, and either entirely self-centered or, if even expansionist, envisioning that expansion on a strictly limited, regionally-bounded scale defined by some kind of a common identity of the people who inhabit the region in question. All these "extended nationalisms" belong, however, to past history. Today's nationalism is predominantly uni-national, and we should therefore mainly consider its particular relationship to ideology.

The agenda of contemporary nationalism consists mainly of the stateless nations' attempts at dismantling the remnants of the old empires and the formally non-imperial multi-national states in order to gain for themselves autonomy and, eventually, equal sovereignty. This tendency is, of course, not entirely a one-way street, as the old imperial reflexes are still noticeable in the behavior of some governments of the former "masters of the world" and linger on in the mass psychology of the nations used to ruling other nations and instinctively still treating this "prerogative" as the way of their natural existence in the world. This sort of a "countertendency" is exemplified by Turkey's long and embittered struggle against Kurdish separatists or by Spain's reluctance to allow the Basques and the Catalans freely, by the way of a referendum, to decide whether they wish to continue to be a part of the Spanish state or, which is one and the same, to live under Castillian rule, which many of them consider alien. It is also demonstrated by the Zhirinovsky phenomenon in Russia, which reflects the nostalgia some, though not very numerous, sections of the Russian population still feel for the former Soviet Union; or by the remnants of the "Yugoslav syndrome" in Serbia, although the leading national idea there today is not anymore aimed at the restoration of old Yugoslavia but rather at the creation of a "mono-national" Great Serbia at the expense of Croatia and Bosnia-Herzogovina, both of which in a substantially diminished size the thus conceived Great Serbia would perhaps be prepared to tolerate as separate nation-states. These are, however, rearguard battles that the carriers of the imperial consciousness in the age of advancing democracy and human rights are bound gradually to lose. (The Dayton agreements is a rather typical indication of this process.)

The globally-wide process of national differentiation is leading, however, not, as one could surmise, to the fragmentation of the world's political structure—it is, in fact, accompanied by a strong, though substantially modified, enhancement of global integration. This worldwide integrative process is powerfully stimulated not only by the demands of the global economy and other objective factors driving the world toward ever greater aggregation but also by the will of the new political nations, which, in order to secure for themselves real independence from their previous masters and an equal position with other nations in the world at large, try to get themselves incorporated into wider regional and global institutions much more actively and in a significantly closer fashion than do any firmly established, traditional political nations. The active lobbying for their acceptance to NATO and the European Union by the newly independent states of Central and Eastern Europe is just one example of this integrative orientation of the nationalisms of the new political nations; another one is the much stronger commitment to integration into the structures of the European Union by the Scottish and Welsh peoples, as compared to the Englishmen, in the UK; by the Flemmings, as compared to the Walloons, in Belgium; by the Catalans and Basques, as compared to the Castillian Spaniards, in Spain. One could therefore say that the process of political change in the contemporary world follows quite accurately the Spencerian pattern of differentiation that precedes and becomes the prerequisite for a new and higher stage of integration. Indeed, the emerging new world order is likely gradually to limit state sovereignty in favor of regional and global political institutions expressing, respectively, supranational sovereignty or the sovereignty of mankind as a whole, but in a way that would make these institutions effective protectors of equal sovereign rights of all nations. It is in this ever more apparent process of national differentiation accompanied by global and regional integration that contemporary nationalisms acquire such a major, indeed central, significance in contemporary world politics.

Insofar as a nation tries to establish itself in the world as an entity independent from another nation's rule and recognizable as a separate and equal partner by other nations and the world at large, that nation's nationalism is akin to the demand of the individual for the recognition and guarantee of his right not only to equal liberty but to life itself; for a nation is a kind of collective personality which, differently from an individual human being, cannot survive without liberty even in sheer physical terms; it will, in the end, either get assimilated by the main nation of the state or is going to be otherwise annihilated by that state's ruling nation. In today's world of nation-states such nationalism inevitably translates itself into a demand by many a stateless nation for its equal right to self-determination and sovereign statehood. Therefore, as long as nationalism is understood as "primarily a political principle which holds that the political and the national unit should be congruent,"[24] as long as it demands for one's nation the equality of political condition, it is a natural and entirely healthy expression of the collective self-consciousness of the people who by free self-identification constitute that nation's membership and who by putting forward such demands present their bidding for sheer survival, for their historical continuity along with other nations.

It is wrong, in my view, to try to counter-oppose, as many scholars do, the rights of nations to individual rights, claiming that the latter take precedence over the former. The rights of nations in principle do not contradict the rights of the individuals, for no nation is willingly submitting itself to rule by a regime oppressive of the individuals who make up the body of that nation. Repressive authoritarian or totalitarian regimes by violating human rights of their subjects violate at the same time the right of the nation freely to choose the form of rule under which it wishes to live and thus become abusive and oppressive of the nation they falsely claim to rule in that very nation's best interests. It seems to me that the scholars who consider the rights of nations antithetical to the rights of individuals are actually confusing the nation with the nation-state, which indeed may submit itself either to an unpopular ideology or to a group pursuing through the state its vested interest at the expense of the interests of the nation and thus becoming oppressive of both the individual and the nation at large. On the other hand, the right of nations to self-determination and sovereignty on a par with other nations can become a real right only if it is rooted in individual human rights and is projected onto the political surface as a natural extension of these rights either exercised or claimed by a multitude of people as individuals in a simultaneous manner. For if the nation is an organic entity with which a great number of people freely identify themselves, no individual belonging to that nation can enjoy any rights accorded to him in an abstract and limited fashion ignoring or even suppressing his collective identity as member of a certain nation. As long as the individual has no right to be what he really is or wants to become—and this, in the first place, means being/becoming a member of what one considers to be one's own nation—he is not free and is thus deprived of his primary right to liberty. This is especially true of individuals who consider themselves members of one nation but are forced by another nation's state to assume that other nation's identity (Like the Kurds in Turkey).

Nationalism can, however, acquire different shapes and forms in any of its many varieties. It can be defensive and aggressive; friendly to, or at least tolerant of, other nations and chauvinist or xenophobic; democratic and authoritarian. All these shapes and forms can be found within the context of the whole benign nationalisms of stateless nations as much as within that of nations possessing their own nation-states and more often than not unjustifiably opposing the former kind of nationalism. I think that Aristotelian ethical theory provides perhaps the best available guide for determining the moral quality of every variety and aspect of nationalism and also for defining which elements in any nationalism are evil and reprehensible and which ones are benign and commendable.

According to Aristotle, good and evil are quantitative rather than qualitative categories. This is to say that excess or deficiency of a certain orientation or attitude are what makes it evil, but if this orientation or attitude expresses itself as the mean between these two extremes, then it is good. In this sense courage is the good and virtuous mean between the two bad extremes of foolhardiness and cowardice, the virtue of generosity is the commendable mean between the two blamable extremes of extravagance and stinginess, etc. Nationalism *per se* should be then also understood as the virtuous mean between the two evil extremes of chauvinism and abstract (national or even anti-national) catholicity, the former being the excessive and the latter the deficient expression of an individual's or a group's sense of collective national identity. Xenophobia, though less excessive than chauvinism, will find its place in the quantitative continuum between good and evil in a space much closer to the excessive extreme than to the virtuous mean. Hence, chauvinism and xenophobia, as two different degrees of excessive expressions of nationalism, are to be ethically evaluated as evil, but so is also catholicity, which fully ignores or even actively negates national identity and usually tries to substitute for it a universal ideology-based and artificially construed collective identity, such as, for example, a certain world religion, a certain worldwide social class or, ultimately, mankind as a whole.

Racism would lend itself to the same quantitative distinctions with regard to one's own race, but insofar as it proclaims the inferiority of other races, and this is what it usually is all about, it falls into the category of racist excesses, equal to those that in the case of nationalism, we have defined as chauvinism and/or xenophobia.

The deficient nationalism is, on the whole, a passing phenomenon, although the Millian liberals are still trying to stick to it. Other universal creeds, in order to survive, had to arrive at a compromise with the national idea and sometimes even concede some priority ground to it. The Roman Catholic Church, for example, successfully survived throughout the two millennia of its quite turbulent history only because it learned how to adjust to the national idea and work in the form of multiplicity of national churches much before Vatican II, although it was only Vatican II that, finally, had fully recognized the nation as a collective personality and, alongside the family, a natural form for the realization of the universal brotherhood of men—in fact, a further extension of the family onto the next step at which comes already the unity of all men under God. The Communists, who desperately tried but did not know how organically to square their catholic internationalism with the national idea, have badly failed in this endeavor and, accordingly, went by the board. I have no doubt that if the Millian liberals do not revise soon enough their uncompromisingly antinationalist and indiscriminately universalistic stance (and thus stop being Millians), they are going to go the same way, too.

As for excessive nationalism, even in its ugliest xenophobic forms, it is basically nonideological, too, although some sentiments that in the more extreme cases it usually evokes, may be used by an ideology to capitalize upon and draw its support from. For example, the sentiments of xenophobic anti-Semitism present to a certain degree in every nation were used by Hitler for spreading and popularizing his racist ideological message in which anti-Semitism played a pivotal role. On its own, however, xenophobia (e.g., anti-Semitism) does not have the capacity to develop into an ideology, as it is an orientation exclusively concerned with the alleged threat or danger an alien nation or national minority is supposedly able to represent to one's own nation. Xenophobes, in fact, are not at all concerned about any alien nation or national minority or, for that matter, about anything else outside their own nation's realm. The "aliens" are bothering them only insofar as they, in the xenophobes' view, interfere in some ways with their nation's life. As soon as the presumed threats or dangers these alien people presumably pose are evacuated from the xenophobes' own realm or are otherwise dissipated, they almost entirely disappear from the xenophobic frame of reference, too. Xenophobia is a nervously, or even hysterically, defensive attitude toward the "mysterious aliens," usually based on its bearers' profound national inferiority complex and on irrational suspicions fed by that complex. Usually it operates under the slogans: "Britain for the Brits," "France for the French," "Germany for the Germans," or "Russia for the Russians," without giving even the slightest consideration to the fate of the non-Brits, non-French, non-Germans, or non-Russians outside the realms of, respectively, Britain, France, Germany, or Russia.

Just to reiterate what has been already said above, an ideology, like that of Hitler's national-socialism, can benefit and draw a lot of its strength from the spontaneous xenophobic sentiments in every nation but, on their own, these sentiments could only inspire certain policies, not ideologies. In this sense neither the British nor Jean-Marie Le Pen's French National Fronts nor the German Republican and Vladimir Zhirinovsky's Russian Liberal Democratic Parties are ideological entities. Their exclusive concern is with policies which, in their view, would be able to preserve the integrity of their respective nations from what they perceive to be destructive "alien inclusions" into them. It seems to me that the most typical extreme and entirely open proponent of such xenophobic policies is the leader of the Bulgarian Renewal Party (*Vazrazhdane*) Father Gelemenov who proclaimed to have abandoned traditional nationalism as toothless and ineffective, embracing instead the combative Nazi ideology of Adolf Hitler. Following the prescriptions of this ideology, Father Gelemenov stated that he and his party are going to fight for the adoption of a law, according to which Bulgarian Turks and Roma Gypsies will be deprived of the rights of Bulgarian citizenship, made into Bulgarian subjects, and thus "subordinated to the Bulgarian nation." This, he said, is necessary because the policies of forceful assimilation and expulsion of the non-assimilable ones practiced by the Communist regime proved ineffective and would not yield the desirable results of building up Bulgaria as one nation's state, even if the current or a future regime would consider recurring to the application of these policies. This, despite Gelemenov's claims to the contrary, is by no means, however, an exact rendition of the Nazi ideology either in full or even in its substantial parts (Father Gelemenov, by the way, has never even mentioned the Jews), but a direct reference to the infamous 1935 Nazi Germany's Nuremberg Laws, which at the time were indeed designed for the purpose of implementing the "transitional policy" of "squeezing out" the Jews from Germany—not yet, however, for the ideological purpose of accomplishing "the final solution" of the Jewish problem.

As mentioned above, chauvinism in the extreme form of the belief that one's nation is superior to all others is, perhaps, the only variety of nationalism that has the potential of developing into an ideology, that is into a view about instituting a world order system in which this particular nation will rule the rest of mankind. But, as also noticed above, this is an impractical ideology that, at best, could be professed as a sort of a mere pipe dream. Much better suited for this purpose, as Hitler had proved quite convincingly, are racist, not nationalist, ideas, and in the discussion of ideology the former are the ones that are much more relevant than the latter, although the latter in its excessively xenophobic forms provide a fertile breeding ground for the former.

To summarize the above, no form of extant nationalism or nationalism *per se*—excessive or deficient, uni-national or imperial—could qualify as an ideology in terms defined above. As an expression of people's ultimate collective self-identification in the world, nationalism basically represents an orientation that inspires people's attitudes and behavior toward "the other" within their own realm and forms the major source for projecting and/or justifying such sets of policies and programs that are purportedly supposed to be the optimal ones for the nation in questions of well-being, security, and prestige. In that nationalism is no different from any other group-orientations—such as those of family (familism?), community (communitarianism?), corporation (corporatism?), or subculture (an "ism" in this case would be conceived in accordance with the given subculture's specific identity). It is, however, different from all the other group orientations in that it is the orientation of the ultimate group, that of the nation, whose identity either subordinates to itself or cuts across all other group identities.

V. ANY "ISMS" FOR THE FUTURE?

A. Marxist or Non-Marxist Socialism?

I am of the opinion that with the collapse of communist rule in the USSR and East and Central Europe, the Marxist ideology had definitely seen its day. This is, in my view, the case not only because the bitter experience of these countries proved it to be unworkable in both the theoretical and practical senses. Marxism was also proved obsolete as a viable critique of capitalism. First, the capitalism that was the subject of Marx's critique no longer exists. But, even more importantly, the substantive critique of modern capitalism's defects stopped being an exclusive prerogative of the contemporary adherents of Marxism a long time ago. The liberal-democratic theory, the ideas of individual and national liberty, the practice of defense of human rights and pursuits of justice in conditions of political freedom, proved in respect of such a critique to be a much more effective and powerful tool than Marxism in every variety of its interpretation; and, in combating injustice and social disasters in whatever sociopolitical system these phenomena took place (and each such system, including capitalism, produced more than its fair share of them), they—the liberal-democratic ideals—achieved much better practical results than had Marxism at any time and in any of its varieties or forms.

To a large extent the irreversible demise of Marxism is also the result of the general decline of scientism, of the by now almost universal healthy skepticism with regard to the absoluteness of scientific knowledge and the omnipotence of science as method of inquiry into man and society. As professor Noël O'Sullivan has convincingly shown,[25] ideologies claiming infallibility on the basis of their allegedly scientific veracity do not cut ground anymore today in what is fashionable to call the postmodern era, even with the most rationally minded people. Therefore, if socialism can at all survive in our post-scientistic and post-holistic times, it can do so only as an ethical idea, as a specific variety of the idea of justice or as a part of a religiously based morality. Marxist socialism obviously does not enter into any of these categories.

Ethical, non-Marxist socialism can, however, also develop into an ideology. Professor David Marquand, for example, argues that out of the five dimensions of socialism that have made it a powerful ideology, the pivotal four ones—namely, the socialist economic theory, a general social science, a platform for the advancement of social interests of the working class and the secular substitute for a religion (the basic ideological dimension)—have been eliminated by the demise of Marxism and its impact on the socialist idea generally. What in his view will remain of socialism for the future is its ethic extolling the values of community and fellowship. On that basis Marquand comes to the conclusion that socialism—maybe under a different name—is going to survive the test of time and will be prominently figuring in the battles of ideas in the future.[26] It seems to me, however, that ideas promoting community and fellowship are not specifically socialist and that they on their own could never make socialism survive as full-blooded ideology. The difference between Marquand and me on this score consists, I believe, in our different assessments of the potential of the free market system to provide for, and coexist with, adequate social justice and effective work of charitable institutions. Marquand's skeptical view of the free market, his disbelief in its humanistic potential, indeed imply the necessity of the resurrection of socialism as an economic and social theory and even as religious creed—that is, as a full-blooded ideology—because the present rise to dominant prominence of the liberal free market ideas and policies may, in his view, undermine "[r]eformed, welfare capitalism" which, according to Marquand, "is a gift of history, as fragile as it is precious."[27] In other words, capitalism, in Marquand's opinion, may now revert to its unbridled, unreformed, pre-Keynesian shape—the shape that made socialist critique of it valid and viable—and, subsequently, revive socialism as an ideology on its original scale and intensity.

I do not think that this logic of Marquand is correct. First, nothing can be resurrected in an identical form, especially phenomena that were tried in historical practice and did not prove to be a success. Second, policies in a democratic state depend on decisions made by the majority of that state's electorate. As long as this is the case—and today it is true for Russia and East and Central Europe as much as to the proper West—tensions between liberty and justice, which inevitably exist in every society, will each time be resolved in a fluctuating flexible manner—more restrictions of liberty for the sake of increasing justice at one stage, followed by relative liberalization on another stage, and then, by the introduction of some corrections and adjustments of liberal policies, inspired by the sense of justice and charity, on yet the next stage, etc. These fluctuating policies will for the foreseeable future most probably continue unabated, but they will hardly acquire an explicit ideological dimension. In a democratic polity explicitly ideological policies are the ones no political party, however ideologically inspired and committed it may be, can afford to put in an undiluted form to the electorate without losing the support of its mainstream sections. That is why even Margaret Thatcher, to say nothing about John Major, had to stress every so often that the National Health Service is safe with the Tories, and the Labor Party had never dared to include clause 4 of its constitution (on nationalization of the means of production), now already altogether abandoned by Blair's "new Labor," in any of its pre-election manifestos even in the headiest days of "old Labor's" socialist dogmatism.

It follows from the above, thirdly, that as long as the old- or new-style ideologically committed socialists are going to subordinate themselves to the democratic political process, their policies will willy-nilly drastically differ from their overall ideology. Only the revolutionary socialists of the Marxist-Leninist variety—those who defy parliamentarism and, in my view rightly, believe, as did Lenin, that socialists who value democracy above socialism betray the latter and by abdicating from ever implementing it into reality by revolutionary action become in fact labor lieutenants of the capitalist class—are the ones who remain and will continue to be in the future truly ideological socialists. But this is exactly that kind of socialism that has been thoroughly and irreversibly defeated with the demise of state-Marxism that had been established by "revolutionary action." Marxist or any other kind of revolutionary socialism cannot be resurrected in the foreseeable future due largely to the fact that its collapse in the former USSR and East and Central Europe has immensely fortified the foundations of the liberal-democratic order,

which could be reversed to an authoritarian one not by the pursuit of socialist or other abstract ideological goals anymore, but only by national emer-
gencies and nationalistically (that is by definition nonideologically) inspired
extraordinary tasks.

Finally, the values of community and fellowship are much better served
and strengthened by religious, local, corporate, and other similar voluntary
bodies than by socialist measures, whatever shape they take. For, in contrast
with these public sentiments and bonds, which draw on natural instincts of
fellowship in men, socialism is inevitably trying to involve into everything it
deems just and charitable the coercive machinery of the state and law, thus
expressing its profound disbelief in the natural goodness and cooperative,
charitable spirit of man. I believe, with Durkheim, that social history consists
of the unending search for such a sociopolitical system that could best accommodate the dual—individualist and collectivist—nature of man, which
implies the necessity of sociopolitical promotion of organic human partnerships based on communalism and fellowship. But also, together with
Durkheim, I believe that socialism is the least suitable, in fact a fake form for
such promotion. Only in Durkheim's era this was not yet a socially proven
fact which, I believe, at this juncture in time it already certainly is.

All this is to say that, in my view, not only Marxism but every other variety
of socialist or communist ideology is by now fully bankrupt and thus must
be excluded from consideration as candidates for an "'ism" for the future.

Thus, socialism and communism, as viable and powerful ideological
creeds, followed after the Soviet collapse in 1991 the way to oblivion fascism
and national socialism went in 1945, after having been not only militarily but
also morally thoroughly defeated in World War II. This does not mean that
there will be no socialist or communist ideologues left in the world at all; one
glance at the academic communities of the West would obviously belie such
a conclusion. But, as the neo-Fascists and neo-Nazis, the neo-Marxists and
other neo-socialist or neo-communist revolutionaries have been doubtlessly
relegated now to the position of eccentric political groupings acting on the
marginal fringes of national and world politics and will have to reconcile
themselves to remaining in that position at least for the foreseeable future.

B. Religious Fundamentalism?

I am convinced that no different destiny awaits religious fundamentalism, despite its recent expansion and prominence. To me the enhanced role religious
fundamentalism started to play in the last few decades of the twentieth century
is the natural result of rapid proliferation of the processes of modernization (or,
which is one and the same, of westernization) to, and subsequent seculariza-
tion of, all, even the remotest parts of our globe. Strongly affected by these
sweeping processes, traditional societies and communities reacted to them by
partly joyfully and thoughtlessly embracing them (mainly the Millian liberals,
but also the socialists and communists), partly by trying to adjust to them with-

out losing their traditional identity (the liberal nationalists) and, partly, by totally rejecting, and trying to mount a vigorous defense against, them. The very appearance in traditional societies and communities of the former two groups was by itself a strong incentive for the latter one to actively start combating modernization and considering to take extraordinary measures barring it from deeper penetration into their realm, and otherwise enforcing the traditional, premodern way of life in their respective societies and/or communities. As Professor Fouad Ajami has put it, "traditions are often most insistent and loud when they rupture, when people no longer really believe and when age-old customs lose their ability to keep men and women at home."[28]

On the whole, the vigorous resistance of conservative traditionalism to the extremes of modernization and the moral relativism that it tends, especially during the transition, to encourage, is a healthy phenomenon. Being by no means able to stop this process, such resistance makes it more moderate, more steady, and thus also compatible with the continuity of people's specific religious, cultural and ethnic identities, with the moral principles and spiritual values that, having been established long before the modern times, remain nevertheless a reliable guiding light for the people to take a lead from in the both modern and postmodern times.

Religious fundamentalism, in its more extreme and radical forms, is, however, capable of strongly overreacting to the challenges of modernity and, as it was shown above, turning into entirely modern and "this-worldly" political ideology capitalizing on people's modernization-related anxieties and strong conservative instincts. Founded on a universal religion, such an ideology also tends to preach not to one particular nation or religious community but to the world at large, trying to convert it to that ideology's particular eschatological vision. In all this, religious fundamentalism is but an inverse expression of revolutionary socialism/communism; and, vice versa, because revolutionary socialism/communism espouses the ideal of a rigidly organized, strictly regimented, closed—and by that supposedly also harmonious—society, it is itself nothing more than a specific form of fundamentalism professing to confront and prevail over the unstable, overflexible and thus, in their assessment, decadent society of the Western type—or, in other words, the open society.[29]

In my view, these fundamentalist ideologies—as well as the socialist/communist ones—are fighting hopeless rearguard battles against the unstoppable advancement of modernity which, by taking ever deeper root on a global scale, is rendering them increasingly marginal and, finally, is going to make them almost totally irrelevant. I fully agree with professor Mark Juergensmeyer's analysis according to which religious fundamentalism, after having grudgingly developed a tolerant attitude to secular nationalism, will have to merge in the end with the overall nationalist movement of the nation within which it operates, occupying in that movement a section which, however distinct, is going to form an organic constituent part of that movement.[30] Such an evolution of religious fundamentalism will substantively cut its ideological edge. The fundamentalists' universalistic claims within the framework of a nonideological nationalist movement will inevitably have to take the back seat and get subordinated to current, mainly pragmatically determined national–religious concerns and actions.

In his recent study, Professor Bernard Lewis has very convincingly revealed how, in fact, weak and divided Islamic fundamentalism is.[31] According to him, only two Muslim countries—Iran and Sudan—fell victim to the fundamentalists' revolutionary endeavors, and only in Iran have the fundamentalists realized some of their ideological prescriptions, while in Sudan the Islamic fundamentalists' ideological plan was fully consumed by the ceaseless civil war Sudanese fundamentalist rulers chose to wage against the non-Islamic and non-Arabic population of the country's Southern provinces, in a murderous but vain endeavor to forcefully Islamicize, too. In all the other Islamic states Muslim fundamentalism is kept under strict, though uneasy, restraint and, when daring to raise its head, is ruthlessly suppressed. The so-called Great Green Peril of Islamic fundamentalism is, therefore, in fact, not so much a reflection of political reality as the product of Western imagination anxiously looking after the defeat of Communism for yet another global ideological enemy and falsely identifying as such an enemy what Leon T. Hadar succinctly calls the "imaginary Muslim monsters."[32] Even people who believe that Islamic fundamentalism is the great new threat for the West to cope with, recognize that "militant Islam is as diverse as the Arabs themselves and the countries in which it is taking hold . . . that Islam is not inherently at odds with modernity" and that there are no serious grounds to believe that a "new 'Khomeintern'—a vast conspiracy led by Iran and Sudan"—is about to emerge.[33]

All this is to say that in my opinion religious fundamentalism generally and Islamic fundamentalism, in particular, are not the glimmers of the future, as so many believe them to be, but rather the last desperate and therefore remarkably intransigent defense lines of the passing premodern past; the fundamentalist ideological proponents of that past are determined to oppose the invincible challenges of modernity and, by so doing, turn them, as much as it is at all possible, to their own political advantage. What they really seek is to put themselves in charge of the traditional societies and/or communities in which they function and use the thus acquired political power for controlling the processes of modernization to their particular ideological preferences and the enhancement of their power and influence within their respective countries and the world at large (the ongoing Iranian experience with "Khomeinism" is the best proof that this is indeed the case).

The struggle of nations for equal sovereignty, allowing them to get integrated into the global (Western-dominated) system on their own nondiscriminatory terms, is willy-nilly going, in the end, to absorb and subordinate to its tasks the various extant religious fundamentalisms. These will have to mute their universalistic or "civilizationist" ideological claims and be driven to enhance those elements in their respective doctrines, which pertain to the strengthening of their particular nation's separate identity and the definition of that nation's place and role in the world.

C. Millian Liberalism?

The dominance in present-day world politics of the nonideological nationalist issues is, as mentioned above, equally undermining the strength and influence of the Millian kind of liberal ideology. Liberalism is today becoming increasingly inconceivable without due and proper recognition of collective human rights, which include not only the rights of nations, religious denominations, and minorities, but also the rights of various other communities forming themselves in concordance with their freely chosen specific moral and cultural traditions and values, to be what they are or wish to become. The ubiquitous and irreversible progress of modernization leading to global westernization is thus proceeding not in the way of creating a uniform liberal world society the Millian liberals always predicted and never ceased promoting, but by opposing the leveling liberal uniformity and protecting tradition and variety that are being thus incorporated into, and accommodated within, the pattern of the modern (and even postmodern) world. And this is exactly what makes Millian liberalism, with its intolerance of even the most natural and organic forms of collectivism, as well as to variety in general, as obsolete and unqualified for the role of an "'ism" for the future, as the other ideologies discussed above are.

D. Feminism? Environmentalism?

Are there any other candidates for an "'ism" for the future? In his chapter Minogue says: "Marxism and syndicalism have fallen on evil days, while feminism and environmental forms of salvation have in recent decades flourished mightily."[34] Feminism, in my frame of reference, does not by itself qualify as an ideology. It could only serve, within a broader anticapitalist ideological context, as an argument for stating that the capitalist system is inherently unable to provide for women a decent place and role in society and thus needs to be replaced by an alternative, ideologically conceived system that would, among other things, bring patriarchate to an end and ensure true equality of women with men. Without such a context, feminism turns into yet another policy item on the agenda of affirmative action, which could be handled in either a more or a less radical way.

"Environmental forms of salvation" are, however, different from all the other items encompassed by Minogue under the umbrella of "the morality of egalitarian humanism," as they are equally applicable to all categories of human beings and deal with the problem of sheer physical survival of the

human race as a whole. Nevertheless, Minogue does not pay to environmentalism any special attention. O'Sullivan also simply lists ecological issues, along with sexual and racial ones, as those that were "hitherto excluded" and that "the 'new politics' . . . postmodernism represents" seeks
to "include."[35] I think, however, that if one looks for a truly potent candidate to fill the ideological void the demise of Marxism produced in the contemporary world, environmentalism is the one to be singled out and identified as fully qualified to be such a candidate.

Apart from being an issue equally affecting all mankind and claiming to
represent the only reliable remedy for its assured survival on this planet, environmentalism has solid philosophical roots going all the way back to Jean
Jacques Rousseau and his call, "back to nature." The Rousseauist philosophical tradition of reasoning about the relationship between nature and man,
by having been extended to Edmund Husserl's phenomenology outlining
the periodical conflicts between man's intentionality and the constants
(and/or constraints) of the natural world, has firmly established itself in the
academe as a methodological discipline covering both natural and social sciences. Husserl's disciple, the greatest German existentialist philosopher Martin Heidegger, introduced phenomenological ideas on the relationship of
man and nature into every variety of modern existentialist philosophy; and
Heidegger's disciple, Jean Paul Sartre, by having constructed the "Practico-
Inert" concept of the world, provided quite a solid philosophical foundation
for practically every environmentalist movement or organization under the
sun. On the other hand, a special academic discipline, ecology, was created
in order to investigate the natural environment and the damage man is inflicting on it. The best known and most influential offshoot of this rapidly expanding discipline is the Club of Rome. Created in the 1960s, it still manages
to coordinate the efforts of the ecologists and other academics concerned
with the environment, which are directed at promoting zero economic
growth and other similarly radical measures and which, they claim, are the
only ones able to save mankind from self-destruction. As we see, the philosophical and academic foundations and credentials of environmentalism are
as, if not more, solid as those of Marxism.

Environmentalism has the potential of becoming a full-fledged ideology
not only because of this, but also because it appeals to the highest ethical
value: human survival—a value, that is, to which all other values should
be naturally subordinated—and is also capable of elaborating a comprehensive program for the creation of such a new sociopolitical system that
will be uniquely suitable effectively to protect the environment and
through it mankind itself. It goes without saying that environmentalism
also entails the necessity of building-up a closely-knit political organization struggling for its goals and actively engaging in propaganda and other
forms of proselytism; environmentalism naturally confers a special role of
leadership to its "vanguard," represented by the professional experts on
ecology, too.

Environmentalist ideology is incompatible not only with capitalism, but also with every other sociopolitical system promoting economic growth and technological progress. In this respect it is much more radical than socialism which, as Friedrich Nietzsche had aptly observed, differs from capitalism only insofar as it wants more of it. Turning all the way back from its modern philosophical foundations in phenomenology and existentialism to the classical primary source in Rousseau, environmentalist ideology would indeed acquire the potential to force all of us to go "back to nature" in the very literal sense of this phrase, branding those who are likely to resist, dissent, or simply manifest reluctance to follow that road not simply enemies but killers of mankind.

One should not underestimate the appeal of this ideology or its potential popularity either. Some religious groups may lend it their support and some underdeveloped countries may see in it their only chance to catch up with the more developed ones. I do not infer by so saying that this ideology will indeed become the next big menace threatening the survival of the free world. I hope it never does. But in a time of social crisis and dire stress, when people will start hungrily looking again for simplistic, ideological-type solutions to their complex and difficult problems, the environmentalist ideology will surely be standing ready for some desperate people to jump on its bandwagon and, paraphrasing Francis Fukuyama, bring us back to history again.

VI. IDEOLOGIES AND IDEALS

All ideologies, as was briefly shown above, have elaborated ready-made recipes to achieve a humane and politically viable new world order. But, alongside the ideological (quasi) solutions, the philosophical ones, which were formulating certain desirable ideals and then elaborating conditions for practical realizations of these ideals, were gaining throughout human history ever-increasing prominence and application, too. To clarify this point, I would suggest that Plato's ideal state, contrary to what Karl Popper had to say about it, was not an ideological projection of a totalitarian order he liked or preferred to other kinds of order, but an objective philosophical analysis of the conditions necessary for preservation of the original "best state," which to him was kingship and which he posited as the common political ideal agreeable to everyone. What Plato tells us is that, in order to arrest the natural and otherwise unstoppable process of the state's decay and deterioration from the original "best state" of kingship through timocracy, oligarchy, and democracy into tyranny and then nothingness, one must institute in that "best" or "ideal" state such a kind of sociopolitical organization that involves the suppression, especially among the political elite, of some basic instincts inherent in human nature and thus amounts to what we could call totalitarianism, but which, nevertheless, is the only one available to live up to this task and has to be recognized as such, whether one likes it or not. In effect, Plato leaves to us the choice for deciding whether the ideal he projects is worth the price we would have to pay for its secure institution and preservation, implicitly emphasizing that the refusal to pay that price would be tantamount to our acceptance of, and reconciliation with, the inescapable process of political decay and deterioration.

Similarly, there is nothing ideological in Kant's vision of perpetual peace. The six preliminary and three definitive articles of the Treaty on Perpetual Peace he envisaged, simply point out the prerequisites and mutual obligations that the parties involved in that treaty have to take upon themselves in order to avoid ever slipping back into a war against each other. In other words, Kant takes the ideal of a peaceful world as, at a certain stage in humanity's evolution, a commonly agreeable one and shows what it takes to secure its implementation and preservation.

Kant is impeccably consistent in according the pivotal role in the world to the nations of which it consists. According to his Preliminary Article 2, peace could not be achieved as long as there remains in the world a nation ruled by another nation without that former (ruled) nation's explicit consent. Nor should there ever be instituted a world government—an institution superior in its sovereign rights to the national governments. The federation of free states forming the League of Peace (*foedus pacificum*), the creation of which is foreseen by Kant's Definitive Article 2, "would be a federation of *nations*, but it must not be a nation consisting of nations." "The latter," he explains, "would be contradictory, for in every nation there exists the relation of *ruler* (legislator) to *subject* (those who obey, the people); however, many nations in a single nation would constitute only a single nation, which contradicts our assumption (since we are . . . weighing the rights of *nations* in relation to one another, rather than fusing them into a single nation)."[36] What Kant really projects in his *foedus pacificum* is a multitude of fully sovereign nation-states voluntarily submitting themselves to a single body of laws in accordance with which conflicts and disputes between them could be properly adjudicated and authoritatively resolved. For such an agreement on subordination to the same single body of law to become possible, all nations entering his projected *foedus pacificum* should, according to Kant, undertake the obligation under the Definitive Article 1 to be and remain republics, that is, to live under a constitution that, "first, . . . accords with the principles of the *freedom* of the members of society (as men), second, . . . accords with the principles of the *dependence* of everyone on a single, common . . . legislation (as subjects), and third, . . . accords with the law of the equality of them all (as citizens)."[37] In other words, equal freedom of nations under the law in the *foedus pacificum* should, to Kant, be based on equal freedom of individuals under the law within the nation joining the *foedus pacificum*.

This plan is to me typical of one projecting an ideal and totally antithetical to one basing itself on, or embracing, an ideology. Unlike the ideologues, Kant does not even try to establish a single set of universal principles to which people's existence would have, first, to be uniformly adjusted and, then, firmly subordinated. On the contrary, his whole endeavor is aimed at maximizing people's freedom to be what they are or want to become as individuals and nations, which is inevitably enhancing variety rather than uniformity. Kant's main task is to find a formula for such a pluralist world's political system that would allow for an optimal accommodation of that liberty-enhanced variety of different, and sometimes clashing, identities, interests, ideals, values, and goals, as well as for a peaceful handling and solution of contradictions and conflicts that are bound to flare up among their proponents.

James Madison, when writing the American Constitution and defending its principles in *Federalist Papers*, also sought not to eliminate factions and factional conflicts, as that would be tantamount to the elimination of liberty, but to create institutional arrangements able to control their effects. Neither Kant nor Madison had any illusions about human nature. They knew pretty well how "strong is this propensity of mankind to fall into mutual animosities"— so strong, as Madison says, "that where no substantial occasion presents itself, the most frivolous and fanciful distinctions have been sufficient to kindle their unfriendly passions, and excite their most violent conflicts."[38] But they also knew that this propensity is not limitless and that it can be organically subordinated to the commonly agreed concept of right. "Given the depravity of human nature," Kant wrote, . . . "one must wonder why the word *right* has not been completely discarded . . . as pedantic, or why no nation has openly ventured to declare that it should be. . . . The homage that every nation pays (at least in words) to the concept of rights proves, nonetheless, that there is in man a still greater, though presently dormant, moral aptitude to master the evil principle in himself (a principle he cannot deny) and to hope that others will also overcome it. For otherwise the word *right* would never leave the mouths of those nations that want to make war on one another. . . ."[39]

I think, here we have finally touched upon the basic difference between an ideology and an ideal. Ideology strives for the elimination of factional conflicts and, accordingly, projects formulae under which this goal can be achieved and universal harmony in human society established. An ideal, recognizing the "basic depravity of human nature," seeks to accommodate the freedom of engaging into factional conflict within a pluralist political system based on a commonly agreed concept of right. An ideal always seeks a balance between maximum liberty and preservation of order under the law, while an ideology seeks order by eliminating in one way or another those forms of liberty that sustain social diversity and foster factional (national, class, or other) conflicts. In this sense, Millian liberalism remains an ideology, while Kantian or Madisonian—and, by that same token, also Spencerian— liberalism is absolutely nonideological, as it concentrates on the elaboration of certain social techniques, of specific legal and political instruments and procedures allowing for simultaneous side-by-side existence and free competition of various ideologies and political doctrines, distinct material, and ideal interests, different and even alternative values and goals. In contrast to Millian liberalism, Kantian, Madisonian, or Spencerian liberalism allows for, and encourages, not only the expression of a person's individual nature and preferences, but also equally caters to that person's ability freely to express and foster his collective identity. In other words, it treats man not simply as an individual but, quoting Emile Durkheim's famous formula, as *homo duplex* or man possessing a dual, individualist, and collectivist, nature. And, together with Emile Durkheim, such a liberal assesses the quality of a society by that society's ability to accommodate and protect both the individualist and the collectivist natures of man.

Of course, one could say that Kantian, Madisonian, or Spencerian liberalism is also an ideology, and some people, indeed, do say so. It all depends, no doubt, on the usage of the term ideology, on how one agrees to interpret it. For example, the great Russian dissident human rights' campaigner, Nobel Laureate Andrei Sakharov, proclaimed himself and his associates and counterparts in the country and around the world "right defenders," or partisans and advocates of what he defined as "the ideology of human rights," which he sharply counter-opposed to "ideologies based on dogmas and various metaphysical beliefs aimed at the reconstruction of the world."[40] "The ideology of human rights," Sakharov explains, "is by nature pluralistic, it is the one and sole ideology allowing for the liberty of various forms of social associations and for the co-existence of these various forms, which endows man with the maximum liberty of personal choice."[41] In Sakharov's portrayal, this "ideology" is actually nonideological almost by definition. As he himself has put it, "the ideology of . . . human rights is perhaps the only one which has the potential to accommodate within itself such otherwise incompatible ideologies as the communist, the social-democratic, the religious, the technocratic, the nationalistic; it can also serve as the foundation for [sociopolitical] positioning of those men who do not want to tie themselves to any theoretical finesses and dogma and who are sick and tired of the multitude of ideologies none of which has brought people any, even the most elementary human happiness."[42]

I do not mind Andrei Sakharov and those who phrase their ideas likewise to call Kantian or Madisonian liberalism a "human rights' ideology." I am only sure that this kind of ideology is not the one which we defined as such above.

NOTES

1. See Kenneth Minogue, "Ideology After the Collapse of Communism," in Aleksandras Shtromas, ed. *The End of "Isms"? Reflections on the Fate of Ideological Politics After Communism's Collapse* (Oxford: Blackwell, 1994), 20.

2. Minogue, "Ideology After the Collapse of Communism," 7.

3. He cites Lyman Tower Sargent, an American, and Andrew Vincent, a Briton, as representative exponents of such views. For these scholars, and they are the great majority in the field, any value or belief system accepted by some group as fact or truth qualifies, without any further discrimination, as ideology (Minogue, "Ideology After the Collapse of Communism," 6).

4. For Destutt de Tracy's relevant and relatively easily accessible text in English, see Count Destutt de Tracy, "A Treatise on Political Economy to Which is Prefixed a Supplement to a Preceding Work on the Understanding, or Elements of Ideology; with an Analytical Table and an Introduction on the Faculty of the Will," in John M. Dorsey, ed., *Psychology of Political Science*, trans. Thomas Jefferson (Detroit, Mich.: Center for Health Education, 1973).

5. In his speech to the 3rd Congress of the Russian Communist Youth Organization on October 2, 1920, Lenin said: "We say that our morality is entirely subordinated to the interests of the proletariat's class struggle. . . . Moral is what serves to destroy the old exploiting society and to unite all the working people around the proletariat, which is building up a new communist society. . . . We do not believe in an eternal morality, and we expose the falseness of all the fables about morality." ("On the Tasks of the Youth Unions," in *V. I. Lenin, Collected Works*, vol. 31 [London: Lawrence & Wishart, 1960–1970], 291–94).

6. Karl Marx, "Theses on Feuerbach," in Robert C. Tucker, ed., *The Marx-Engels Reader*, 2d ed. (New York: Norton, 1978), 145.

7. See Bhikhu Parekh, "The Concept of Fundamentalism," in Aleksandras Shtromas, ed., *The End of "Isms"? Reflections on the Fate of Ideological Politics After Communism's Collapse* (Oxford: Blackwell, 1994), 107.

8. See in Robert C. Tucker, ed., *The Marx-Engels Reader*, 2d ed. (New York: Norton, 1978), 220.

9. Quoted from Mussolini's fascist ideology foundation-laying article, "The Doctrine of Fascism," which he published in 1932 in the Italian Encyclopedia; See its abridged rendition in: Terence Ball and Richard Dagger, eds., *Ideals and Ideologies: A Reader* (New York: HarperCollins, 1991). The citation quoted is on p. 297.

10. Mussolini, "The Doctrine of Fascism," 295.

11. Mussolini, "The Doctrine of Fascism," 290.

12. Mussolini, "The Doctrine of Fascism," 289–90.

13. Mussolini, "The Doctrine of Fascism," 295.

14. Mussolini, "The Doctrine of Fascism," 297.

15. Mussolini, "The Doctrine of Fascism," 297.

16. Adolf Hitler, *Mein Kampf*, trans. Ralph Manheim, (Boston: Houghton Mifflin, 1971), 327.

17. See in Aleksandras Shtromas, ed. *The End of "Isms"? Reflections on the Fate of Ideological Politics After Communism's Collapse* (Oxford: Blackwell, 1994), 85–103.

18. Shtromas, *The End of "Isms"?*, 93.

19. J. S. Mill, *Utilitarianism, Liberty and Representative Government* (London: Dent, 1912), 363.

20. "The concept 'ideology,'" Mannheim writes, "reflects the one discovery . . . that ruling groups can in their thinking become so intensely interest-bound to a situation that they are simply no longer able to see certain facts which would undermine their sense of domination. . . . [I]n certain situations the collective unconscious of certain groups obscures the real conditions of society both to itself and to others and thereby stabilizes it. The concept of utopian thinking reflects the opposite discovery that certain oppressed groups are intellectually so strongly interested in the destruction and transformation of a given condition of society that they unwittingly see only elements in the situation which tend to negate it." (Karl Mannheim, *Ideology and Utopia: An Introduction to the Sociology of Knowledge*, trans. Louis Wirth and Edward Shils [London: Routledge & Kegan Paul, 1936], 36 [reprint 1972]).

21. This is what Mannheim actually also believed to be the case. In his brilliant analysis of the conservative idea (see Mannheim, *Ideology and Utopia*, 206–15) he even attributes to it in this "accomplished form" a utopian quality, thus blurring his own distinction between ideology and utopia to the point of unrecognizability. Where I differ with Mannheim is in his reduction of ideology to the instinctive, subconsciously defensive attitude toward the sociopolitical status quo. Apparently, what to me is ideology, for Mannheim is either utopia or an entirely realistic, *situationsgerecht* social theory.

22. W. H. Dray, "Holism and Individualism in History and Social Science," in Paul Edwards, ed., *The Encyclopedia of Philosophy*, vol. 4 (New York: Macmillan, 1967), 53.

23. Aristotle, *Politics*, book 5, ch. 1, p. 13, trans. Carnes Lord (Chicago: University of Chicago Press, 1984), 148.

24. Ernest Gellner, *Nations and Nationalism* (Oxford: Blackwell, 1983), 1.

25. See Noël O'Sullivan, "Political Integration, the Limited State, and the Philosophy of Postmodernism," in Aleksandras Shtromas, ed. *The End of "Isms"? Reflections on the Fate of Ideological Politics After Communism's Collapse* (Oxford: Blackwell, 1994), 23–44.

26. See David Marquand, "After Socialism," in Aleksandras Shtromas, ed. *The End of "Isms"? Reflections on the Fate of Ideological Politics After Communism's Collapse* (Oxford: Blackwell, 1994), 45–58.

27. Marquand, "After Socialism," 51.

28. Fouad Adjami, "The Summoning," in *Foreign Affairs* collection of articles, Agenda 1994: *Critical Issues in Foreign Policy* (New York: Foreign Affairs, 1994), 150; the article originally appeared in the September/October 1993 issue of *Foreign Affairs* as a response to Samuel P. Huntington's provocative piece on the presumably forthcoming clash of various civilizations which, after the end of the Cold War, the world, according to Huntington, is facing as a new major challenge.

29. I share this idea with the contemporary leading Russian philosopher, Grigory Pomerants; see, for example, his "Fundamentalizm I XX vek" [Fundamentalism and the 20th Century], in *Literaturnaya Gazeta* [The Literary Gazette, Moscow], no. 7 (5487) of February 16, 1994, 11.

30. See Mark Juergensmeyer, *The New Cold War: Religious Nationalism Confronts the Secular State* (Berkeley: University of California Press, 1993). I do not think, however, that this analysis could be applied to the socialist/communist ideologies, which have been proved unable to merge with nationalism without hopelessly compromising their basic foundations. Their destiny, at least in the West, is more likely to take them ever closer to joining forces, however grudgingly, with Millian liberalism.

31. See Bernard Lewis, *Islam and the West* (New York: Oxford University Press, 1993).

32. Leon T. Hadar, "What Green Peril?," in *Agenda* (1994): 171 (originally, this article was published in the spring 1993 issue of *Foreign Affairs*).

33. Judith Miller, "The Challenge of Radical Islam," in *Agenda* (1994): 176 (originally, this article was published in the spring 1993 issue of *Foreign Affairs*).

34. See Kenneth Minogue, "Ideology After the Collapse of Communism," in Aleksandras Shtromas, ed. *The End of "Isms"? Reflections on the Fate of Ideological Politics After Communism's Collapse* (Oxford: Blackwell, 1994), 12.

35. See O'Sullivan, "Political Integration," 43.

36. Immanuel Kant, "To Perpetual Peace: A Philosophical Sketch," in *Immanuel Kant, Perpetual Peace, and Other Essays on Politics, History and Morals*, trans. Ted Humphrey (Indianapolis, Ind.: Hackett, 1983), 115.

37. Kant, "To Perpetual Peace," 112.

38. *The Federalist Papers* by Alexander Hamilton, James Madison, and John Jay (New York: New American Library, 1961), 79 (the quotation is from Madison's no. 10).

39. Kant, "To Perpetual Peace," 116.

40. Andrei Sakharov, "Dvizhenie za prava cheloveka v SSSR I Vostochnoy Evrope—Tseli, Znachenie, Trudnosti" [The Movement for Human Rights in the USSR and Eastern Europe—Goals, Significance, Difficulties], in *Kontinent* (Paris), no. 19 (1979): 171.

41. Sakharov, "The Movement for Human Rights," 172.

42. Sakharov, "The Movement for Human Rights," 188.

III

POST-COMMUNIST TRANSITIONS

The last piece in the previous section surveyed the post-1991, post-Communist scene, in order to consider the fate of "ideology." "Ideology" of the Right and of the Left characterized much of the twentieth century. Shtromas chose to call it "the age of ideology." Would ideology continue to mark the twenty-first century? If yes, which ones? If not, what if anything would guide men's collective efforts? This section discusses economic and political reform in Russia and other post-Communist nations, as well as NATO's expanded role in constructing a viable new world order. It is informed by definite ideas about what ought to be the case. Classical liberal ideas about law, the free market and civil society, limited government, and a pluralistic democracy, are fundamental in Shtromas's view. So too is a deep respect for patriotism. The national identities of "free peoples," duly chastened and subordinated to universal norms of individual dignity and rights, should be the norm in the post-Communist world. His attachment to these ideals does not mean, of course, that he believes that they will automatically spring up "from under the rubble," as Solzhenitsyn has called it, of the collapsed ideocratic regimes. Far from it. In their light he realistically analyzed the post-Communist scene, mapping in fairly specific terms a viable path into a better future.

While fully informed about the full range of the former republics of the USSR, as well as Central and Eastern European nations, Shtromas rightly focuses on

Russia, the continental giant whose fate is all-important for regional and European stability. Almost everyone agrees that Russia needs a genuine free market economy, and in "The Transition to a Free Market System: The Hillsdale Plan and the Other Plans" (1994) Shtromas lays out what he considers the best route to this goal: "instantaneous and truly total privatization," "prices and wages freed," and a fully convertible currency. In its light he criticizes the actual course taken in Russia, as well as other proposed paths (the 1999 essay, "What Should Be the Next Stage in the Process of Russian Reform?" analyzes the sometimes disastrous Yeltsin-Gaidar-Chubais reforms).

What characterizes his thinking is the thought that the means must be tailored to the end: in order for a free market economy to occur, the economy must be freed from political ownership and control. Halfway measures will not even produce halfway results. The current incoherent policies have only aggravated and prolonged a bad situation and possess no potential for amelioration. Lest someone counter that such a line of thought, with all it entails, is too doctrinaire or harsh, Shtromas's analysis of the current oligarchic-kleptocratic system gives pause: if the status quo is as he describes, it is utterly unacceptable on moral and economic grounds. Shtromas's question then becomes imperative: what alternative path to the desired free market goal is both principled and viable? And for the person who may wonder about those left out in the abrupt transition he advocates, Shtromas seeks to reassure him: "social security" will be taken care of by means of "negative taxation" (a concept borrowed from Milton Friedman), which will provide a minimal standard of living and thorough job retraining.

Genuine economic reform, however, requires political reform. In Shtromas's view the former is "a means to the main end—the end of dismantling the Soviet totalitarian state, of evacuating political power from the realm of the thus recreated civil society, of the institution, as a result, of an authentic Rechtsstaat." Here, too, Shtromas has definite ideas about proper government and about the deeply corrupt character of post-Communist Russian governmental institutions and the cadres that fill them. More broadly, he sees something of an iron triangle involving soft-minded, halfhearted reformist governmental officials, a corrupt state bureaucracy in bed with monopolistic oligarchs, and a demoralized Russian citizenry that may prefer market reforms but is afraid of the risks of change, especially in the face of the current corruption. This harsh view is not unique to Shtromas; Solzhenitsyn, for example, has said as much. Fatal mistakes early on led to this morass failing to dismantle the Soviet-era "state bureaucracies"—new wine should not be put in old bottles—and attempting to induce the former Communist bureaucrats and fast-moving kleptocrats to genuine market behavior by transferring to them the commanding heights, and huge chunks of the economy. Shtromas refuses to call this "reform." Genuine political and economic reform still awaits Russia, and the longer they are postponed, the deeper and wider become the ills that confront post-Communist Russia. Above all one must replace the Soviet-type "master-state" with a Western-style "service-state—a state that is called to serve the needs of the civil society resurrected by that very same process of genuine privatization," i.e., one "dependent from and accountable to the public."

One often hears today about the Russian populace's hankering for Great Power status and about an irresponsible political class's stoking of these desires. Shtromas agrees with half of this view. "Today the imperial syndrome largely dictates Russia's state policies, in spite of the overwhelming indifference and largely explicit hostility by the citizenry to any neo-imperialist designs." How to handle this aggressive posture is a question, however, not only for responsible Russians, but also for Europeans and Americans. It is thus a necessary concern of NATO, the North Atlantic Treaty Organization. Russia looms large in Shtromas's counsels concerning the NATO Alliance, which since the end of the Cold War has struggled to redefine its mission and composition. In his view, Russia's genuine national interests are not threatened by an enlarged NATO with the demonstrated will to defend "the space between Germany and Russia proper." The inclusion of Poland, Hungary, and the Czech Republic in NATO are steps in the right direction, but still fall far short of what a true instrument of collective security should be. Shtromas's main counsel to Western NATO leaders is fairly direct: do not be cowed by Russian bluster. Continue your expansion on two tracks. In your new phase and identity as a "Euro-Atlantic collective-security" organization whose field of operations extends outside NATO's "own main core," by all means include and involve Russia. But your original mission—"the containment of the USSR"—abides. It should "staunchly remain [in transformed terms] the deterrence of Russia from relapsing into her traditional imperialist antics." This means that NATO "will have to extend its defensive shield, in the strictest terms of Article V guarantees, all the way to the present western borders of Russia." In Shtromas's view, responsible Russian politicians and pundits will find Western resolve a bracing aid in their efforts to chasten expansionist sentiment and to build a proper Russian "nation-state." Others might ask if containment is the appropriate response to a Russia that has officially renounced an ideological foreign policy and aspires to become a more or less "normal" player in international politics.

9

The Transition to a Free Market System: The Hillsdale Plan and the Other Plans

ALEKSANDRAS SHTROMAS

I. POST-COMMUNIST SOCIETIES: ACHIEVEMENTS AND PROBLEMS

The anticommunist revolutions in the USSR and Eastern and Central Europe, having started in 1989, were triumphantly concluded on August 21, 1991, with the collapse of communist rule in the Soviet Union and with the Soviet Union itself being formally dissolved in December of the same year. The fall of communism in the USSR and the subsequent dissolution of the Soviet state made the victory of the anticommunist revolutions in Eastern and Central Europe, the Baltic States, Moldova, the Transcaucasian nations and Russia itself secure and irreversible. The world has not only entered into the post-communist but the post-ideological era.

Post-Communism virtually brought to conclusion the twentieth century which, unleashed in 1914 by World War I, became the age of ideology—the age of active search for panaceas against the terrible ills of mankind (ills that have made possible the unprecedented tragedy of the war) in globally conceived universal ideologies such as communism and fascism; it was, accordingly, also the age of defense and struggle against aggressive undertakings of the various communist and fascist ideological regimes and of resistance to totalitarian

Reprinted from Richard M. Ebeling, ed., *Can Capitalism Cope? Free Market Reform in the Post-Communist World* (Hillsdale, Mich.: Hillsdale College Press, 1994), 81–117.

temptations these ideologies quite forcefully propelled around the world. If the end of World War II in 1945 saw the disappearance of the fascist ideological challenge from the world's stage, the failure of the communist-restorationist putsch in Moscow in August, 1991 did the same to Marxist-communism—to that ideological challenge that was the first to appear and the last to crumble. Into the next millennium the formerly Communist-ruled lands and their captive nations enter as genuinely free peoples engaged in an intense and freewheeling search for their organic cultural, social, and political identities as well as for their fairly defined places in the world, alongside, and in proper association with, other free nations.

That the nations of the former Soviet domain have become really free is eloquently proved by the fact that, having been liberated from Communist oppression, they promptly affirmed themselves as truly independent political entities and in no time successfully established themselves as fully sovereign and separate nation-states.

Political freedom is, however, not an unmitigated blessing. For it also implies the free nation's liberty to engage in conflict with other nations when the latter either deny it sovereign rights or contest its possession or claim of a territory that that nation considers legitimately belonging to it. Fortunately, there were no such conflicts involving Russia, which, to many people's surprise, quite willingly conceded its predominance over other nations of the former Soviet domain. But the Armenian-Azerbaijani dispute over Nagorno-Karabakh, the Georgian denial of sovereignty to Abkhazia and South Ossetia, and the rebellion of the Russian-speaking part of the population of Moldova's Transistria against Moldovan sovereignty over that region have created very acute and sometimes bloody conflicts that to this day remain unresolved and continue unabated. Sad as they may be, such conflicts are one of the clearest demonstrations of the respective peoples' genuine political liberty. It is only under the conditions of liberty that people may freely choose to engage in resolute struggle for what they believe are their vital interests and inalienable rights. And the more political liberty the twenty-first century sees, the more conflicts of this kind will probably proliferate. This is the natural and, therefore, unavoidable illness of growth and maturation of all social organisms, e.g., of nations.

The acquisition of political freedom by the post-Communist nations was also clearly expressed by their immediate transition from submissive meekness to suddenly uninhibited practice of freedom of speech; freedom of press; freedom of public manifestations; freedom of organizing various political parties and other public bodies; freedom of religion; freedom of movement within the country, of traveling abroad and of returning home; as well as of other basic freedoms and human rights that were absolutely denied them under Communist rule. Due to their unrestrained realization of all these newly acquired freedoms, the post-Communist nations have developed pluralistic political systems, which have provided them the opportunity of holding free and genuinely competitive democratic elections that most (though not yet all) of them have already taken advantage of more than once. This is to say that in the post-Communist lands the foundations of a liberal-democratic political order have been already quite firmly established. When, for example, in Georgia the democratically elected president Zviad Gamsakhurdia tried to abolish political pluralism by establishing a semi-fascist, one-party dictatorship, opposition forces initially suppressed by him somehow managed to come together and launch a successful counterattack. They ousted Gamsakhurdia from power, forcefully reasserted political pluralism, and resolutely restored in Georgia the fledgling foundations of a liberal-democratic political order.

Political freedom and the pluralistic, liberal democratic order, as the natural outgrowth of that freedom, were, however, proved to be, though absolutely necessary, insufficient prerequisites for assuring the transition from a totalitarian to a free social system in any of the post-Communist lands. Although the democratically established post-Communist governments of those lands have genuinely set themselves the task of privatizing the economy, instituting the free market, and fostering all other institutions necessary for the recreation of a civil society functioning under the rule of law, none has so far succeeded in substantially advancing, let alone fulfilling, that task.

The most easily observable and more or less clearly definable explanation of this peculiar impasse is institutional. Indeed, the democratically formed and radical reform-oriented post-Communist governments inherited and swallowed hook, line, and sinker the monstrous state apparatuses of the old Communist regimes that continue to function as if nothing has changed and that not only strongly resist all attempts by the new governments to reform, reduce, and substantially change their structural-functional identity but are also sabotaging the respective governments' efforts to use them as instruments of reforms aimed at creating the new free social and economic systems, or—which is one and the same thing—their efforts to transform the present social and economic systems into authentic civil societies.

Indeed, the post-Communist governments wrongly assumed that the collapse of Communist Party rule and their own ascendancy to supreme political authority marked the end of the victorious anti-totalitarian revolution while in fact it was just its very beginning. Instead of, in the first place, destroying the old state apparatuses and liberating social and economic processes from the restrictive confines the apparatuses of totalitarian rule impose upon these processes, they started presiding over these same apparatuses and some, out of dogmatic respect for the principles of the rule of law, even engaged in playing the game of law abiding continuity with the old Soviet-type order. By so doing they have practically shot themselves in the foot.

In a very communist tradition, these new anticommunist governments have entirely disregarded the fact that political forms and processes are inseparable from their substance and have wrongly assumed, therefore, that the political institutions they have inherited from the past will serve them as pliantly and obediently as they used to serve the Communist Party. And they probably would have done so, if the new governments were content to keep intact, preside over, and further strengthen the totalitarian system that the old communist state machinery so aptly embodied. But the new governments, by poising themselves to dismantle that system, have alienated the entrenched state apparatuses, which successfully sabotaged the governments' more radical moves and thus managed not only to ensure self-preservation but, through the state bureaucracies' envoys in the representative councils, also to force the governments, ostensibly for the sake of social cohesion and people's welfare, to proceed with the reforms in a slow, halfhearted manner and under their—the state bureaucracies'—total supervision and control. This is how the reformist post-Communist governments, by having put themselves into the position of the authority presiding over the conservative Soviet-type state apparatuses, have become prisoners of these apparatuses, which have virtually incapacitated them and stalled the reform processes initiated by them. It is exactly because of this that the projected reforms of the respective social-economic systems amounted to what the continental criminal lawyers call "attempts with faculty means"—not only did such irresolute, internally contradictory reforms fail to yield any substantial positive results but, as all half measures inevitably do, they significantly worsened the overall social and economic situation. Ironically, economically and in many other related respects of social life, this situation became even worse than it had been under superficially orderly and predictable "mature socialism."

II. THE "OTHER PLANS" OF TRANSITION TO THE FREE MARKET

This most obvious institutional explanation of the present crisis in post-Communist lands does not tell, however, the whole story. The reformist governments themselves, in addition to their conservative opponents in the state machinery and in the representative bodies inherited by those governments from the communist past, must be held responsible to a great degree for failing to ensure a radical dismantling of the communist-totalitarian legacy. The policies of reforms freely chosen by those governments were in themselves so irresolute and inconsistent that, even if fulfilled without any substantial hindrance on the part of their powerful opponents, they would hardly be able to bring about the desired transition to a free civil society functioning under modern liberal law.

Again, one could offer many explanations for the post-Communist governments' failure to elaborate policies of transition that would be adequate to the task they have set themselves to accomplish. Fear of massive bankruptcies and of ensuing mass unemployment which, presumably, would have followed a drastic transition to a free market system drained their courage to go straight for the introduction of such a system. The instinctive distrust of people (who, as the new rulers see it, being spoiled and demoralized by their socialist upbringing and experience, would hardly be able to work productively in a free enterprise environment, stealing instead everything put in that environment at their disposal and thus altogether destroying whatever has remained of the countries' productive facilities), pushed them not merely toward maintaining but even strengthening the state's supervision and control over the slowly but massively evolving (though mainly evolving beyond the pale of the still valid socialist laws) private economic activities.

For the same reasons, and in order to avoid trouble by too drastically injuring too many vested interests entrenched in the old statist economic system, their plans for privatization leave most enterprises in the state's hands for practically an indefinite period of time and also make sure that the state is firmly in charge of the privatization process itself. And this usually tends to ensure the status quo or, in other words, that the enterprises, even after privatization, basically remain in the hands of the same people who were in charge of them yesterday and remain so today.[1]

In Hungary the privatization of large state industries until July 30, 1993, when the government at last declared that mass privatization would start in early 1994, was not even in the government's plans. Instead, Hungary was speedily promoting new economic ventures based on attracting large sums of foreign investment. In this way the post-Communist government was trying to build a new modern economy almost from scratch. It reckoned that with the development of this new economy, the old state industrial enterprises would either adjust and get incorporated into it or, of course, the government permitting, they would be allowed to die their natural deaths. Apparently these expectations did not materialize and, as one sees from its July 30th Declaration, the Hungarian government was forced to have a change of heart on that issue and start seriously contemplating a special privatization program for its state industry.

In Poland all industrial state enterprises have been transformed into joint-stock companies. The stock, however, belongs to the state and is held by the Ministry for Privatization, which alone has the right to decide what enterprises are ready to be put on sale to private bidders, and then either sells the shares of these enterprises directly to such bidders or releases them onto the embryonic stock market. It is not surprising, therefore, that by 1993 over 80 percent of Poland's state enterprises were still in the state's full ownership, producing mainly loss and loot. In most of the remaining 20 percent the state still maintains a strong, sometimes even a controlling presence. The latest Polish government led by Hanna Suchocka has tried to speed up the process of privatization but her privatization bill was defeated in the *Sejm* (Parliament) as too radical and has had to be substantially revised and reduced. Nevertheless, the passage of this watered-down bill has been met by massive workers' strikes, which, for the time being have thwarted implementation. But even when these temporary obstacles

are eventually removed and the governments' privatization bill is finally realized, its implementation will put on the market only a relatively small
proportion of Polish state enterprises. The bulk of Polish heavy industry
will still remain the undivided property of the state, and no one can tell
how long this situation will last.

In former Czechoslovakia privatization has been divided into two separate
processes: one for small enterprises ("small privatization") and another for
large enterprises ("large privatization"). Small privatization is underway in
Czechoslovakia, spreading quickly and on the whole successfully. For the
large enterprises the process is, however, sluggish. The Czechs have invented
the voucher system of privatization, whereby citizens can acquire shares of privatized enterprises in exchange for vouchers issued to each of them on equal
terms by the government for a nominal fee. The distributionary sales of vouchers lasted until the spring of 1993 and on May 24, 1993, for the first time, shares
in about one thousand companies released for privatization in 1992 were
made available to the public in exchange for their vouchers. The process of
privatization, which has thus just started, promises to be quite protracted—
according to the government's plans, it should last for at least five years, but it
may last much longer if, for example, there are not enough bidders for buying
the shares of certain enterprises. It goes without saying that before the enterprises are sold, they remain state property; and the state is in charge of selling
them, too. This means that unprofitable enterprises are destined to remain in
the state's domain forever, unless the state deliberately chooses to kill them off
by stopping their subsidies and declaring them bankrupt, very much like it was
planned until recently in Hungary.

This rather moderate privatization plan elaborated by Czech leaders
seemed to their Slovak counterparts so unbearably radical that it became one
of the reasons for the subsequent split of Czechoslovakia. But, whatever the
differences between the respective politicians on that score may have been,
it is clear that in both the Czech Republic and Slovakia the large industrial enterprises will yet for a long time (and some, perhaps, even for good) remain
a part of the state-run (or socialist) economy.

The privatization plan elaborated for Russia by her Deputy Prime Minister
in charge of privatization, Anatoly Chubais, is supposed to be the most radical and prompt. Like the Czech plan, the Russian version also included
voucher distribution among the members of the public. But, according to
this plan, each enterprise released by the state for privatization, after it was
converted (also by the state) into a joint stockholding company, will have to
decide for itself in which way it wishes to be privatized. Officially approved
were three such ways or legal modes of privatization from which enterprises
have to choose one.

The first such mode consists of 25 percent of the shares being distributed
free of charge to the workers of the enterprise as nonvoting preference
stock, another 10 percent of the shares the workers would have to buy at a
30 percent discount and yet another 5 percent of the shares would be allo-

cated to the managers who would have to buy them for the full price of their 1991 book value. Altogether, the working collective would thus acquire 40 percent of the stock of which 15 percent will entitle their owners to participate in the enterprise's decision-making process by voting, i.e., 10 percent distributed among all employees, e.g., the managers, and 5 percent among the managers exclusively).

The second mode of privatization consists of the employees buying out up to 51 percent of the enterprise's shares (the controlling package) at the price 1.7 times higher than their 1991 book value. For the purchase of up to a half of these shares the employees could use their vouchers; for the rest they will have to pay cash. In order to adopt this mode of privatization it is required that not less than two-thirds of the workforce of the enterprise chose it in preference to the other two modes by secret ballot.

Finally, the third mode of privatization gives the employees 20 percent of the nonvoting preference shares free and leaves them the option of buying another 20 percent at the price 1.7 times higher than their 1991 book value.

In all three modes the remaining shares—it is either 60 (in the first and third modes of privatization) or 49 percent (in the second mode of privatization) of the entire stock—remain the property of the state and are supposed to be sold by the state to members of the general public in closed-bid auctions. Thirty-five percent (in privatization modes one and three) and at least 29 percent (in privatization mode two) of these remaining shares have to be sold for vouchers and the rest, for cash. Whatever remains unsold is retained by the state as the residue of its original property rights.

The Russian privatization plan clearly states that not all of the country's industry is going to be privatized. Defense industries, major producers of energy and natural resources, vital construction and transportation outlets, etc.—in other words, all the notorious commanding heights of the country's economy—are being explicitly excluded from the process of privatization and are to remain, as before, the undivided property of the state.

Is such a plan really radical and prompt? Unfortunately, it is not. Instead of changing the Soviet economic system by transferring in real terms the state's industrial enterprises to private ownership, this plan simply tries to legitimize the situation in which Russia's industrial enterprises actually find themselves today. Indeed, after the liquidation of the party apparatus and abolition of enforceable central planning, Russia's industrial enterprises already fell, in fact, under the effective control of their management, and partly also of their workforce, as in present conditions the latter is exercising on the management a much stronger pressure than does or is able to do the government. The only real change this kind of privatization is supposed to introduce consists in the transfer of full responsibility for the performance and the fate of the thus privatized enterprise from the government to the enterprise's management and workforce themselves. The government, in other words, seeks to renounce in this way its hitherto almost natural obligation to bail out an ineffective enterprise (granted, of course, it is not a part of the "commanding

heights" of the economy) either by direct subsidy or by showering on it practically free credit. This, by the way, explains why the "reactionaries" in the
economic bureaucracy so vehemently oppose this rather modest privatization plan and try, by hook or by crook, to sabotage its implementation—they
do not want to lose control over a large slice of state property and the numerous plush jobs that go with it.

I very much doubt, however, that under this privatization plan the government will really be able to shed its "bail out obligation" to the "second-
class" industrial enterprises in a truly effective manner, since under all the
three established modes of privatization the state is going to retain, at least
for the foreseeable future (and may be even permanently), substantial proportions of stock in all the thus privatized enterprises. And as long as the
state is going to remain in the position of an enterprise's substantial share-
holder, the government will not be able to absolve itself from the responsibility for that enterprise's survival and relative well-being. Hence, the fears of
the economic bureaucrats may be a bit exaggerated, reflecting more their instinctive dislike of any change that could even slightly diminish their standing or curtail their influence than a real threat to the survival of a number of
enterprises now resting comfortably under their leadership and control.

So much for the plan's radicalism. What about its promptness? According
to the plan, the enterprises, which are to be privatized in the ways described
above, have to be divided into annual sales-batches and put on sale one by
one within the year's privatization assignment until all of them, year after
year, are auctioned off. During how many years? The plan does not specify
the exact number of years, but one can rest assured that this process is going to be quite protracted and not necessarily successful; for the process, as
it is envisaged by this plan, gives no assurance whatsoever that, in the end,
the state is going to lose its ownership of substantial proportions of stock in
any of these thus privatized enterprises.

To sum it all up, privatization, as envisaged in Russia today, is in fact aimed
not so much at creating truly private enterprises as at legitimizing the leading positions in these enterprises of their present managers acting under the
pressure of their workforce and financial protection of the government. Under such a privatization scheme, one could hardly expect Russia's economic
system to change soon enough in any substantial way, a fact of which the
reform-minded Russian leaders were apparently very well aware themselves,
because soon after their privatization plan was adopted they started looking
for certain shortcuts in the transition to the free market, besides the privatization process.

In trying to introduce the market system prior to, and independently of, privatization and, at the same time, to stabilize the ruble, Russia's then acting
Prime Minister Yegor Gaidar decided to go for such a shortcut by decreeing effective January 1, 1992, a sudden "liberalization" of prices. The opposition,
skillfully masterminded by the Supreme Soviet Chairman Ruslan Khasbulatov,
thwarted this plan. With the collusion of the Central Bank, then operating un-

der the Supreme Soviet's exclusive control, the plan was soon (by the beginning of summer) undermined by runaway inflation, and in December of 1992 Khasbulatov engineered Gaider's removal from office.

It seems, however, that even without the opposition's foiling of Gaidar's plan, the latter had little chance of becoming truly successful. This was so not because the plan was too bold, as the opposition and also a number of Western analysts argued, but, on the contrary, because it was not bold and consistent enough. Some prices (e.g., those for fuel and energy, which inevitably reflected on prices of all manufactured goods) under this plan have not been fully "released," in the first place; and most enterprises, in order to remain afloat in the new price situation, had to continue to rely on state subsidies and artificially cheap credits. The latter logically followed from the former and both together doomed the reform to not achieving its goal before it was even put into practice. Yeltsin and Gaidar simply did not have the guts to present the people with drastic price increases on some staple consumer goods (e.g., on vodka) and were afraid of facing the social-political consequences of the inevitable reduction in the standard of living of people who were not gainfully employed in economically successful industrial, commercial, or financial enterprises, especially the numerous administrators and other political and economic bureaucrats. Nor were they ready to cope with the possibility of multiple bankruptcies and the level of unemployment that these bankruptcies could have caused. But they did not have any better ideas on how to introduce in a sufficiently swift manner a free market situation in Russia, and they therefore made a desperate move in this direction, as the Russians say, "na avos'"—on the off chance it might still work and create the necessary momentum for propelling Russia's economy into the free market. Predictably, it did not.

All these fears and hesitations with which the reformist governments of Russia and other post-Communist lands conceived their strategies for transition, the instinctive inclination of these governments to prefer a "public choice"–based, compromise-seeking policy over a policy based on a consistent and unhesitant pursuit of a straight and principled line directly leading to the institution of the free market, private ownership, and other attributes of an authentic civil society, have by themselves to a large degree determined the lack of progress in overcoming socialism's legacy in all of those countries. Their governments, in my view, simply do not know what exactly their correct strategies should be like; that is, they are not yet sure how much capitalism that strategy should strive for introducing and how much of statist socialism it should aim at retaining. And even when the respective government theoretically professes a commitment to a complete break with socialism and a belief in the necessity of instituting full-scale capitalism, it usually lacks the conviction that these goals are sufficiently popular and could in a democracy justify the cost that is entailed in the means that have to be applied in order to achieve them in an effective and resolute manner. Hence, the hesitations about what precise set of policies has to be chosen and followed through in order adequately to secure the best available results for the transition in the circumstances of that particular situation and time. This is basically why the transition policies that even the most radical post-Communist governments have so far chosen do not amount to anything approaching a consistent strategy but rather represent a mixed bag of accommodating compromises trying to provide "all things to all men."

Ironically, these hesitant, irresolutely well-meaning policies do not provide for a smooth or caring transition at all. On the contrary, the retention of socialist economic forms in a liberal political environment only exacerbates the destructive qualities of socialism, increasing the social dysfunctions and economic imbalances inherent in socialism to truly ruinous proportions. In a way, such policies, instead of diminishing and smoothing over the pains of transition, become in themselves the cause of some of the most damaging, crisis-generating developments in post-Communist societies. This, in addition to such policies generally conserves the old system, prolonging its rot and thus inadvertently creating yet more unnecessary obstacles to the very proceedings with the transition.

This irresolute ambiguity of the genuinely reformist post-Communist governments is to a great extent an exact reflection of the attitudes and orientations of the regular members of post-Communist societies, including their elites. In a socialist system everyone, without exception, was deprived of a recognized independent social position or standing. The regular member of a socialist society had neither private capital nor an individually determined social status. What an individual was worth, what influence he was able to exercise, entirely depended on the position he occupied in the totalitarian structure of the socialist state. It is true that a partocratic apparatchik's dependence for his elitist position on that particular state was absolute—in any other state he would have surely had no chance to remain a member of any elite at all— whereas a genuine professional would be able to continue to function in the same, or even in an advanced, elitist capacity under any system and in any state. Nevertheless, under socialism, even he, the genuine professional, was able to realize his potential (of course, to the extent to which such a realization was at all possible under totalitarian socialism) only by being attached to a position within the structure of that state; on his own, without that position, he, too, was a nobody.

For example, a qualified and talented engineer could be functional only when employed in a state enterprise; without a position in that enterprise all his professional qualifications would be wasted. True, in a post-Communist society, this engineer could switch to the fledgling private sector and start earning much more than he did when working for a state enterprise. But in post-Communist societies the private sector is so far functioning only in the very marginal areas of the economy and on a rather small scale, which is to say that, as a rule, it would be unable to offer our engineer an activity professionally as satisfying and fulfilling as is his job in the established state enterprise. Because of that, this engineer may prefer to stay with the state enterprise, even if lured by financial incentives to switch to the private sector.

How strongly would then our engineer be interested in his state enterprise's privatization? If he could become that enterprise's owner, he would have been very strongly interested in such a transition indeed. But instead he is sure he stands no chance of ownership, and not only because he does not have the money even to start contemplating such a possibility, but mainly because there are many people around who could, like him, aspire to ownership rights, and in the competition against such people he surely does not have a specific winning edge. He still could have had a strong interest in his state enterprise's privatization if he were sure that under new ownership it would survive and flourish and that the new owners would seek out, engage, and properly appreciate his talents and expertise. But he is not at all sure about it, while he knows that with the state at least the survival and continuous functioning of the enterprise, as well as his role within it, is going to be relatively secure. Furthermore, he also knows that in the post-Communist state his chances for promotion in that enterprise, as well as generally in the state sector, are much greater than they have ever been under the socialist system, where every partocratic analphabet had a built-in promotional advantage over him and where he was destined to serve under such an analphabet-boss all his life. It is now, in the era of post-Communism, that for the first time he can start aspiring to become a boss himself. Hence, there is not much incentive for our engineer to strive for the prompt privatization of his enterprise. In the new, post-Communist conditions he quite comfortably functions in a system based on state ownership and does not feel a particular urge to change it.

The conclusion that follows is that the governments of the post-Communist lands not only do not experience any strong public pressure boldly to go ahead with radical privatization plans, but that there is a certain intuitive reluctance on the part of quite large sections of the public to accept and follow such plans. What post-Communism has revealed is the complete leveling of societies that had the misfortune of going through the socialist experiment. The total state appeared to be the only institution keeping society together, providing it, for better or for worse, with a certain hierarchical structure, without which there remained nothing but entropy. One should not be, therefore, too surprised about people of various walks of life—"reactionary partocrats" and "progressive technocrats" alike—instinctively sticking, even after communism's collapse, to the total state, as the only available alternative to entropy or, which is one and the same, society's death.

The society's instinctive fear of losing the total socialist state as its only organizing device no doubt weakened immensely the government's resolve to do away with it and at the same time substantially strengthened the hand of the old state apparatus in its determination to sabotage and undermine the government's reformist drive. This is perhaps what constitutes in all post-Communist lands the root cause of the procrastination with, and halfheartedness of, the reforms theoretically undertaken with the view of transforming socialism into capitalism.

So, as we see, the hindrances to the institution of radical socioeconomic change in Russia and to a large extent also in other post-Communist lands are situated on three levels: the level of the surviving old institutions of the total socialist state (institutional resistance and sabotage); the level of the reformers' own ideas and plans for change (lack of vision and conviction, and, hence, of decisiveness in elaborating and pursuing an adequate and consistent strategy of change); and the level of the regular socialist man (continuing dependence on his place within the structure of the total state and, for the lack of the vision of a credibly acceptable alternative to that place, an instinctive reluctance to lose it). One should stress here the direct dependence of the third level on the second one; in other words, if the reformist leaders on the second level had come to embrace a convincingly clear vision of radical change and pursued that vision consistently as policy, the socialist everyman on the third level would have followed and supported such a policy of change not only without reservations but indeed joyfully and enthusiastically.

It follows that the present impasse in post-Communist transition is not at all a natural, let alone inevitable, phenomenon. The potential for making a decisive breakthrough to a radical policy of changing socialism into capitalism, and quite a strong one, is there and begs for its realization. Indeed, except for the seasoned and by now largely obsolete *nomenklatura apparatchiks*, no one in the entire post-Communist world wishes to go back to the old days of "mature socialism." In Russia alone, the combined data of the opinion polls, elections, and referenda shows that no more than 12–14 percent of the adult population are nostalgic about the communist past and that another 8–10 percent are bemoaning the loss of the empire (*derzhava*) and the USSR's superpower status (*sverkhderzhava*) without sympathizing with communism and the old regime at all. The rest, that is about 76–80 percent, are ready to embrace western-style capitalism in one form or another. And, of course, even a greater percentage of people value their newly acquired freedom very highly and are determined not to give it up, whatever it takes.[2] If they still continue, though to an ever decreasing degree, to stick to the remnants of the total state, it is because they see as yet no better alternative—the government has so far failed to provide such an alternative, and they are wise enough to ignore the calls of the political charlatans preaching restorationist ideas of the communist-fascist variety.

As a result, people in their daily lives start ignoring the government and lose interest in its ever vacillating policies. On an ever increasing scale, they use their newly born freedom for taking their fate into their own hands and do not mind pursuing their specific interests and goals by defying official policies, regulations, and even the law. What we are witnessing today all over Russia is massive unauthorized privatization of industrial, financial, and trade enterprises, together with land that by law still remains the exclusive property of the state. This is often called *nomenklatura privatization*, but it involves not only the *nomenklatura* but many more ordinary people, without whose cooperation and participation the *nomenklaturists* in present circumstances could hardly be as successful as they are in this quite massive drive for illicit privatization.

Parallel with such privatization, new, mainly unlicensed (or only partly licensed) business enterprises and initiatives of different kinds are proliferating in every Russian city, town, and even village. And, around these enterprises and initiatives, racketeering and similar private protection and extortion groups are building themselves up. Smuggling and money laundering activities are growing in scope as are the numbers of people involved and the corruption of public officials. A new socioeconomic system based on people's freewheeling venturing for personal gain is thus being spontaneously formed, and although this process is taking place mainly outside the framework of law, very soon the thus newly created social structures will start craving legal and political recognition. At this point the government will start experiencing true public pressure for proceeding with changes in a swift manner and then will have no choice but, at least in a "tailing" manner, to start institutionalizing the spontaneous public initiatives "from below," independently of whether it had any consistent ideas on how to go about this business or not.

Meanwhile, the processes described above are being naturally accompanied by the country's ever progressing political fragmentation. Local authorities, directly facing and being the first to deal with all these spontaneous social developments, act with regard to them as they find fit, not as the central government wants them to, and, when finding it necessary or merely opportune, publicly dissociate themselves from the central government by unilaterally declaring their particular region or territory a sovereign republic, a free city or whatever is in their view best for accomplishing such a dissociation. In Russia life is taking its natural course, but without the government's cooperation in legitimizing that course, it acquires a dangerously destructive and to a large measure a criminal character, plunging the country into an ever greater social and economic chaos within which the government becomes increasingly irrelevant. The transition to capitalism may be, of course, accomplished in this spontaneous, destructively chaotic way, too, but the amount of time such a transition will take and the price it is going to exact from more than one generation of Russians will be enormous. If only Yeltsin and his team had the correct ideas on how to start organizing the transition to capitalism from above, and also the guts for resolutely going ahead with the business of translating these ideas into real life, they could spare their people a lot of suffering and misery, and also relieve the rest of the world from the necessity of dealing with the globally destabilizing consequences that protracted suffering and misery in Russia will inevitably cause.

The real crisis in post-Communist lands is thus not political and even not economic; it is, in my view, first and foremost, a crisis of ideas—ideas on how to ensure the transition from monolithic socialism to pluralistic capitalism without inflicting excessive social damage. The economic and political crises in the post-Communist lands that we are witnessing today with such consternation are, in fact, mainly the direct result of that crisis of ideas. And these external crises will most likely continue unabated until either a set of consistent and sufficiently radical ideas on how resolutely to break with the socialist past is elaborated and then succinctly, with full conviction and commitment, translated into the respective governments' implementable strategies or until political fragmentation and complete breakdown of law and order spontaneously starts generating a new social and political system from below, with this process inevitably engendering the right ideas on the transition process for a successful government of the day to catch up with and follow as policy.

One should not, however, blame too strongly the post-Communist governments for not having found and formulated the right ideas for the transition. Such a transition is unprecedented in history and there is neither experience to base such ideas upon nor any preceding ideas to adapt to the new circumstances and then to follow. As the popular Russian humorist Mikhail Zhvanetsky once said, "It is easy to make fish soup out of an aquarium, but no one has yet found a way to make an aquarium out of fish soup."[3] Indeed, not only the post-Communist governments but no one in the entire world—East or West, North or South—could claim that he/she knows the right strategy for ensuring the transition from socialism to capitalism. This does not mean, however, that one should not try to think about such a strategy or refuse to come forward with new ideas on how best this unprecedented transition could be accomplished. After all, any human society, however perverse, is not exactly fish soup. It is still more of an aquarium where, by a due effort, living conditions could be significantly improved and even brought to normal standards. And if the main problem of such a "fish soup-like aquarium" is a crisis of ideas, there is probably no other way of solving this crisis but by constantly putting forward new ideas critical of and distinct from the previous ones.

III. THE HILLSDALE PLAN: ORIGINS

One among the many ideas on how to secure the transition to free market capitalism in post-Communist societies is the so-called Hillsdale plan. As one of the participants in the elaboration of this plan, I would not dare to claim that it is superior to other such plans or that it is substantially better than what the respective governments are trying to do in implementing their plans of privatization and marketization. What I would, however, venture to say is that our plan is markedly different from the other plans, either the ones discussed in academic literature or the ones put forward by political parties, their activists, and writers, as well as by the governments themselves, and as such it stands unique. I believe that by virtue of that uniqueness the Hillsdale plan deserves due attention and consideration. I also believe that since the ideas of our plan have never been tried and the results of trying to implement other ideas were so far pretty meager, the original Hillsdale plan with some amendments necessitated by the passage of time could still be used as a viable foundation for elaborating a practical strategy for the transition to capitalism in the former republics of the USSR, e.g., in some other post-Communist lands.

In its initial rough shape the Hillsdale plan evolved spontaneously three years ago, during the 1990 Ludwig von Mises lecture series. A delegation of prominent economists from Lithuania, a country that only a month before the event proclaimed its independence from the USSR, was invited to share with us their plans for economic reforms. The discussion of these plans continued in many informal sessions. They lasted late into the night every day for about a week and were very active, sometimes even heated. Among the most active participants projecting original ideas on how best to privatize the Lithuanian economy, on how to reform its finances and banking, on how to proceed with the land reform, and on other similar topics, were Hillsdale professors Charles Van Eaton, Gary Wolfram, and Richard Ebeling, as well as Univeristy of Georgia economist George Selgin and a number of other scholars participating in a special symposium of the Ludwig von Mises lecture series.

It was during these discussions that the Hillsdale plan was born. Suddenly, close to the end of the proceedings, it became clear to all participants that a quite consistent and interesting concept on how to make the transition to capitalism in Lithuania possible had evolved as a result of all these animated debates.

Our Lithuanian guests were also strongly impressed with these informal discussions. They invited George Roche, president of Hillsdale College, to visit Lithuania and inaugurate the newly founded Free Market Institute there. George Roche made two important speeches in Lithuania in which he encouraged his listeners to use the opportunity of a new beginning to boldly and unhesitantly establish an economic system truly free of government interference and encroachment, a system that would be able to demonstrate to the entire world the enormous advantages of a genuinely free market and the perniciousness of socialist planning and governmental regulation of the economy, which increasingly permeate the economic systems of the Western world. George Roche's speeches were translated into Lithuanian and published by a leading Lithuanian cultural periodical.[4] They received wide attention in the country and also served as the theoretical foundation for further developing the Hillsdale plan.

Later, in summer of 1990, at the invitation of one of the country's leading commercial banks, I visited Lithuania in order to present the Hillsdale plan to various academic, business, and political audiences, via radio, television, and lectures, as well as interviews and articles published in Lithuania's mass media. At the time of my visit to Lithuania, I had at my disposal, in addition to George Roche's Lithuanian speeches, a fundamental academic article on the problems of privatization of Lithuania's economy produced by Professor Gary Wolfram[5] and also the rich and novel ideas on the subject by another Hillsdale professor, Richard Ebeling, who was generous enough to share and discuss them with me on a regular, almost daily basis throughout 1990 and beyond. Roche's speeches, Wolfram's article and Ebeling's creative ideas have formed the foundations of the Hillsdale plan for which I considered myself a mere consenting spokesman.

In January 1991 Professor Ebeling and I traveled to Lithuania and Moscow, where we together continued to do what I was less ably doing alone when visiting Lithuania (and also Moscow and St. Petersburg) in the summer of 1990. On this occasion, we were able to address the parliaments of Lithuania and Russia and their various commissions and groups of deputies, trying to persuade them to adopt the Hillsdale plan as a guide for the privatization schemes they were discussing at the time. At the request of a group of members of the economic reform commission of the Russian parliament, I prepared a draft for Russia's privatization law; at the request of one of Russia's industrial giants, the chemical factory Azot, professors Ebeling and Van Eaton prepared a plan for that factory's privatization.

In the summer of 1991 Professor Ebeling and I went back to Lithuania and Moscow to participate in a number of important conferences and congresses. We also continued lecturing, publishing, and appearing on radio and television. I went on to continue that mission in Poland, Hungary, and in what was then still Czechoslovakia.

One article that we produced together was published in the Lithuanian magazine *Politika*.[6] Others we published separately. I was writing and publishing mainly in Russian and Lithuanian (but many of my writings were translated and quite widely published in Poland, Hungary, and Bulgaria, too),[7] that is for local consumption, while Professor Ebeling published his in English both in Lithuania and in this country for the attention of the professional economists and other interested academics here and there.[8]

Unfortunately, the practical results of our propaganda efforts were rather meager. Perhaps the ideas were too radical for most state officials or Soviet-educated academics to espouse and follow. But, I think, this obstacle could have been overcome if we had enough time and resources to do the job properly. I think, our campaign advocating the Hillsdale plan was too episodic and too weak to stand a chance of becoming a real success. We were only two people spending no more than a matter of days in countries where hundreds of other Western economists, academics, and officials from all kinds of influential institutions were preaching full-time in a massive and ubiquitous endeavor a message distinctly at odds with ours. It is no surprise that our voices were drowned out by that powerful and constant choir of Keynesian and Samuelsonian economic manipulators, especially because behind the voices of that choir the listeners were able to perceive lurking not only ideas but also big money. With our duo this was clearly not the case, and thus there was no big incentive to follow the message of our song.

IV. THE HILLSDALE PLAN: SUBSTANCE

Let me now briefly sum up the main ideas of the Hillsdale plan.

I think it would be fair to say that our concern with the privatization program was subordinated to what we regarded as the main task of the reform—the minimization of the state, the outright liquidation of all of its uniquely Soviet-type gigantic institutions dealing with planning, supplying, and managing the economy. Privatization was for us not so much an end itself as a means to the main end—the end of dismantling the Soviet totalitarian state, of evacuating political power from the realm of the thus recreated civil society, of the institution, as a result, of an authentic Rechtsstaat. This is what attracted me, a lawyer and a political scientist who does not know much about economics at all, to participate in the Hillsdale plan in the first place. And this is also, I think, why the Hillsdale plan was not very popular with the Lithuanian, Russian, and other countries' planners of economic reforms, all of whom, even those with scholarly identities, were inevitably state officials.

Our privatization plan was divided into two parts, the way privatization was later conducted in former Czechoslovakia. The smaller enterprises—such as small to medium retail stores, restaurants, launderettes, repair shops, handicrafts, other similar small to medium manufacturing outlets, etc.—had to be sold directly in auctions that would accept preliminary bids in sealed envelopes equal to or exceeding the state accorded value (in Russian called *balansovaya stoimost,*' the balance value) of the particular enterprise. The medium and large enterprises would have to be first converted into stockholding companies and then the ownership of the stock issued for each separate enterprise in the sum of that enterprise's state accorded (balance) value transferred from the state to the enterprise itself. The enterprise would thus receive the rights of "self-ownership" as a legal person and, after the transfer of these rights to it, would be reconstituted as an independent corporate entity led by a board of directors and supervised by a newly formed board of trustees.

In contrast to all other plans, the Hillsdale plan was one of instantaneous and truly total privatization. According to it, no industrial, agrarian, financial, or any other service enterprise remained in the state's hands. We only allowed, though quite grudgingly, for the Central Bank to be a part of the state's system, as well as the railways, electric energy supply networks, and some other communal and public services that could temporarily continue under the state's management.

It was also of crucial importance for the Hillsdale plan to make sure that the stock was transferred to the single enterprise and not to any concerns, trusts, productive unions (*ob'edinenie*) and other intermediary (between the enterprise and the state) bodies to which more than one single enterprise was subordinated. In our plan, such intermediary economic organizations were to be dissolved by the sheer process of share transfer to the single enterprise, and to no one above or outside of it. Later, when on the market, the enterprises could, for economic reasons, start forming trusts, concerns, and other similar unions again. But, it seemed to us, that in the beginning the method of according property rights exclusively to single enterprises was the only reliable way for breaking up monopolies, encouraging competition, and promoting self-sufficiency of smaller economic units.

According to our plan, the single enterprise, when accepting the stock into its ownership, had to sign to that effect a debtor's contract with the state in which the time for the enterprise's full repayment to the state of the nominal value of the stock received (usually, about three to five years) had to be stipulated. The enterprise's failure to repay this "foundation" debt to the state in the agreed time would make it insolvent with bankruptcy proceedings to follow. This is to say that in our plan the enterprise's survival depended on its ability to sell its stock on the stock exchange. The organization of stock exchanges and other institutions (such as investment companies) serving the capital market would be left to the enterprises and other private participants of transactions taking place in this market to deal with. The state had to be excluded from this process altogether.

This way of proceeding with the privatization of medium and large state enterprises, in our view, would have accomplished immediately, virtually in one single go and in its entirety, what one could call the "primary stage" of privatization—the stage at which all enterprises would be transformed into independent corporate entities, fully divorced from the state. In their new corporate capacity, the enterprises would enter (furthermore, form) the free market where, in order to survive and succeed, they would have to sell with profit their products and also—dependent of course on the success of these sales—to find for themselves their true owners, i.e., persons willing to buy their shares. It is in the thus established free market that what one could call "secondary privatization" starts taking place. In this secondary stage, the enterprises would either find for themselves real private owners, the stockholders, or, if they failed in that endeavor, go into liquidation. This process could take up to five or even more years and, in fact, it would never stop, as stock constantly changes hands and no enterprise operating on the free market could ever be entirely immune to bankruptcy.

Before the enterprise's stock was to be put on sale through stock exchanges and other public channels, the employees of that enterprise had to be given the right of buying its stock at the nominal price (that is without paying commission or other overheads, but not at artificial discount prices) directly from the enterprise. During the first six months of free sales of the enterprise's shares at the stock exchange and through other public channels, the right of buying them was to be accorded only to the respective country's nationals and enterprises. After this period of privileged buying, the stock had to be made available for purchasing to everyone equally, e.g., to foreign nationals and firms, too.

It follows from the above that the Hillsdale plan does not foresee either voucher privatization or any privileged distribution of stock among the enterprise's employees and managers. In the latter case, as was pointed out above, the enterprise's employees and managers are given the possibility of priority buying at the nominal price of as much stock as they like, directly from the enterprise. As for the vouchers, our proposal was quite different from the standard concepts of "voucher-privatization."

To be sure, we foresaw the issue of vouchers, too, but only for the limited sum of 40 percent of the difference between the state accorded summary value of all enterprises assigned for privatization and the total sum of savings held by the country's nationals in their bank accounts. We thought that on the whole people would be willing to invest into the successful enterprises' stocks more money than they had saved in their bank accounts. We also wanted to leave enough stock for firms and enterprises as well as for foreign investors to buy on the stock exchanges. The 60 percent difference between the summary value of all stock and the overall sum of peoples' savings catered in our calculations for all these purposes quite adequately. Vouchers issued for the remaining 40 percent of that sum had to go to the private individuals in order to enable and encourage them to buy more stock, but not in the way of their equal distribution among all citizens, as it is now done in Russia, the Czech Republic, and most recently in Bulgaria and elsewhere. There every citizen, even a newborn child, is accorded one voucher with equal nominal value, which, for example, in the Russian case is determined as ten thousand rubles in 1991 prices (the Russians calculated this amount as constituting in the overall sum of the vouchers issued percent of the total value of enterprises releasable for privatization). What we wanted to do was to combine the distribution of vouchers with the provision of social assistance to the most needy members of society, the ones, for example, whose income is below, or equal to, the officially established minimal standard of living. The overall sum attributed to issuing in vouchers would be thus divided by the number of people "in need of welfare" with each such individual receiving one voucher bearing the equal nominal value determined by the above calculations. In our plan, these vouchers had to be issued together with the transfer of stock to the enterprises, but they could be realized, that is exchanged for real stock, only in stock exchanges and through other public channels selling stock. This is to say that, being issued in the "primary stage" of privatization, vouchers could be used for acquiring stock only in its "secondary stage." (That would give enough time for establishing a market for vouchers, which later would be able naturally to expand to shares and other capital goods).

What I would like to stress here is the fact that by proceeding with privatization in this way not only is the market economy being created practically overnight, but also the state's economic apparatus is simultaneously rendered obsolete, with the economically relevant functions it used to perform (and still is performing) being without transfers or delays also privatized by the way of creating in the private sector stock and commodity exchanges, marketing and wholesale agencies, sales mediation bureaus and other similar service institutions.

The state's participation in the initial process of "primary privatization"—the transfer of stock to, conclusion of contracts with, and supervision of timely payments for the transferred stock, by the enterprises—is to be handled in Hillsdale plan's provisions exclusively by the Ministry of Finance and its local divisions, that is the state's fiscal authority and the only state institution that in the conditions of free market is, anyway, bound to grow and become more complex in its functions.

Simultaneously with such a total and instantaneous privatization—privatization accomplished in one go and throughout the whole economy—all prices and wages have had to be freed, too. Price controls, this last vestige of the state's direct management of the economy, must be rescinded once and for all, so that no loophole, allowing for even a partial or conditional restoration of economic management by the state, is left. And, of course, the state has to be also deprived of any authority to interfere into the process of free wages' settlements by the employers and employees.

Along and simultaneously with "primary" privatization and freeing of prices and wages, the local currency has to be made fully (not only internally) convertible, too, without any "justifiable" delays allowed to stand in the way of this financial reform. As long as the local currency is not fully convertible, the economy will refuse properly to serve the legal domestic markets, choosing instead the ones in which real, not phoney, money could be made and thus causing profound economic disruption. To ensure the stabilization of the local currency after it was made convertible, the Hillsdale plan proposed to attach it to a stable foreign currency, for example, to the U.S. dollar or the German mark (or to both simultaneously), according to that chosen foreign currency(ies) the status of legal tender, alongside with the local currency.

The money the state is to receive from enterprises for the stock that it transferred into their ownership has to be allocated, according to the Hillsdale plan, partly for social security compensations to those whose income falls below the established minimal standard of living, and partly for the personnel retraining needs. In the Hillsdale plan Milton Friedman's idea of negative taxation,[9] when slightly adjusted to the specific circumstances of the post-Communist situation, is considered to provide the best method for organizing social security payments to the needy.

Friedman links negative taxation—"a single comprehensive program of income supplements in cash"—to the positive income tax and specifically to the regulations providing for "personal allowances" establishing the amounts of nontaxable income. The peculiarities of the tax regulations in post-Communist lands, which would hardly change in substance before other, more profound economic changes took place, would make such a linkage absolutely impractical. Therefore, instead of linking negative taxation to positive income tax, we proposed to link it to the minimal standard of living. The latter, according to our plan, has to be calculated for every single day, very much like currency exchange rates, which are calculated daily, too. With such data at hand, there would be not much difficulty to determine whether a person's weekly or monthly income matched the minimal standard of living for exactly the same period of time for which it has been received. If it did not, the person in question would be entitled to receive from the state the difference in cash. This way of according negative tax is deemed by the plan temporary, lasting only until the transition had been settled and privatized enterprises had paid off their "foundation debt" to the state. But the negative tax itself is recommended as permanent. In time, with the taxation system brought into correspondence with the new economic conditions, it is to be separated from the minimal standard of living, linked, as the original proposal suggests, with the positive income tax, and used as the sole means of welfare provision by the state. The post-Communist states have a unique chance to escape the trap of the welfare state into which most of the Western states have already fallen, and this change lies in their consistent and permanent usage of negative taxation.

For the transition period, negative taxation provides, in our view, the best remedy for making the so-called shock therapy associated with it optimally therapeutic and minimally shocking. It also most effectively dispels the paralyzing horror stories about the unbearable price one has to pay for the radical transition from socialism to capitalism. The price, though not negligible, is, as we tried to demonstrate, quite a bearable one; it is, in any case, much less of a price than the really unbearable one of procrastination and indecision about radically dismantling the socialist system once and for all, which the post-Communist nations are currently so dearly paying.

One of the most numerous categories of the likely users of negative taxation will certainly be the trainees for new professions. There will be quite a lot of them, as in post-Communist countries a great many of the professions necessary for a modern society normally to function simply do not exist or are in extremely short supply. In post-Communist societies, to name but a few of such "missing professions," there are, for example, no real estate or travel agents, no probation officers or financial advisers, no credit providers or investment specialists, no salesmen or insurance brokers. In ridiculously short supply are bankers, lawyers, all kinds of contractors, even shop assistants; and those who perform these functions now, in order to be able to continue their professional activities in the emerging new, Western-type social and economic order are in great need of a very thorough retraining, too.

The original Hillsdale plan sketched out above could thus be briefly summarized in the following four points:

1. An instantaneous transfer on credit of the state's property rights over every single medium and large enterprise to that enterprise itself as to an independent corporate entity; direct and prompt sale by the state of its small to medium size enterprises to the highest bidder in auctions;
2. Simultaneous freeing of all prices and wages;
3. Simultaneous transformation of the local currency into a fully convertible currency;
4. Introduction of negative taxation.

The Hillsdale plan did not, however, end with this proposal, which basically concentrated on state property in industry, trade, finance, and other services but did not encompass the formally non-state "socialist cooperative" property, e.g., the property of the collective farms. We have outlined some basic proposals on these issues, too. Among the issues dealt with in other parts of the Hillsdale plan were: (1) the agrarian (land) and collective farms' reform; (2) the ways of attracting foreign capital investment; (3) the bank reform and monetary emission rights; (4) the incentives for formation of new private businesses; (5) the provision of legal foundations for regulating the functioning of a free market and private ownership based economy; and (6) the basic principles of taxation.

I am mentioning these six points only to give the reader a better idea of the scope of the Hillsdale plan. I am not going to deal with these points at any length or depth because of the considerations of time and space, but also because of their derivative nature. The six points mentioned above follow from the basic idea on how the main breakthrough to a market-based civil society in post-Communist lands should be accomplished. The chief purpose of this paper was to explain this basic idea first, and, on that basis, to initiate a further, and, perhaps, a more detailed discussion of the issues involved. The practical ways of dealing with privatization in post-Communist lands will be presenting the scholarly community with a lot of different debatable issues for yet some time to come, and I would like to see the ideas of the Hillsdale plan figuring in such debates prominently and developing further through exposure to continuous discussion, critical comments, and challenging counterproposals.

To be entirely frank, I still believe that the Hillsdale plan offers the best solution for the problems of transition from socialism to private property and market-based civil society; and, moreover, that all the other plans tried for accomplishing that transition in various post-Communist lands have not as yet made our plan obsolete. When the attempts at applying all the other plans are exhausted and new alternative plans are being sought by the local protagonists of the transition again, the Hillsdale plan will, I hope, stand ready for all those seriously considering a resolute rejection of the remnants of socialism and a committed, unhesitant pursuit of "capitalist construction" to use and make a reality.

NOTES

1. On the "other plans," see Janos Kornai, *The Road to a Free Economy: Shifting From a Socialist System* (New York: W.W. Norton, 1990); Janos Kornai, *The Socialist System: The Political Economy of Communism* (Princeton, N.J.: Princeton University Press, 1992); Kazimierz Z. Poznanski, ed., *Constructing Capitalism: The Reemergence of Civil Society and Liberal Economy in the Post-Communist World* (Boulder, Colo.: Westview Press, 1992); Michael Keren and Gur Offer, eds., *Trials of Transition: Reform in the Former Communist Bloc* (Boulder, Colo.: Westview Press, 1992); Bruno Delago, et al., *Privatization and Entrepreneurship in Post-Socialist Countries* (New York: St. Martin's Press, 1992); Shafiqul Islam and Michael Mandelbaum, *Making Mar-*

kets: Economic Transformation in Eastern Europe and the Post-Soviet States (New York: Council on Foreign Relations Press, 1993), and a few more similar collections.

2. This data on public opinion in Russia is based on my continuous comparative analysis of monthly opinion polls conducted by two authoritative poll-taking Russian institutions, The Russian Academy of Sciences' Institute of Public Opinion (CIOM, headed by the prominent Russian sociologist Yuriy Levada) and the Institute of the Sociology of Parlimentarism (headed by Nuzgar Betaneli) since the spring of 1991. I supplemented these with data provided by the results of the June 12, 1991 presidential election and the April 25, 1993 referendum, as well as with data of some relevant results of opinion polls conducted not on a regular basis but by special commission. One of them, jointly conducted by the Russian Academy of Sciences' Institute of Sociology and Virginia University in September 1992, deserves special attention. According to its results, only 12.6 percent declared their opposition to privatization, while 83 percent were not simply in favor of it but declared their firm support for the country's transition to full-blown capitalism. Among the latter group, interestingly, a substantial proportion were people bitterly critical of the Yeltsin regime. They apparently were the same people who in other sections of the poll accused Yeltsin of mismanaging the reforms and of thus permanently relegating Russia to backwardness and dependency on the developed Western world (for a summary of that poll's results, see: Vladimir Loyevetsky, "Obshchestvennoe mnenie—o delakh privatnykh" [Public Opinion—on Things Private], in *Moskovskie novosti* [Moscow News], No. 40, October 4, 1992).

3. I am indebted to Professor Martin Malia for drawing my attention to the Zhvanetsky story containing this expression.

4. See *Svyturys*, no. 4 (February 1991): 21ff.

5. At the time, Wolfram's article was available in the form of a conference paper. It was published as G. Wolfram, "Lithuania and Its Transition to a Market Economy: How to Begin," in Robert W. McGee, ed., *The Market Solution to Economic Development in Eastern Europe* (Lewiston, N.Y.: Edwin Mellen Press, 1992). Wolfram developed his Hillsdale plan–related ideas in later writings, too; see, for example, his "A Note on Converting the Ruble," in *The Freeman* 41, no. 1 (January 1991), and "Real Transition to a Market Economy," in *The Economist of Lithuania*, no. 2, 1992.

6. no. 22, 1991.

7. The most fundamental and comprehensive presentation of my ideas on the Hillsdale plan was published in Russian by the "thick" magazine *Grani* (*Facets*) 46, no. 161 (1991), as "Privatizatsiya" (Privatization); appended to the text of the article was also my draft of the "Law on Privatization," written at the request of, and submitted to, the Russian Parliament. All my other quite numerous publications on the subject were either derivatives or various versions of the text published in *Grani*.

8. Among Ebeling's numerous publications on the subject, I would single out his *Privatizing the Lithuanian Economy: Proposals and Possibilities* (a separate pamphlet, published by The Future of Freedom Foundation in Denver, Colorado, 1991) and "Economic Reform in Russia: The First Year," in *News and Views* 1, no. 2 (spring 1993). See also his "A Program for Privatization and Market Reform in Lithuania," in *The Economist of Lithuania* (fall 1991).

9. For a popular but pretty adequate explanation of the concept, see Milton Friedman and Rose Friedman, *Free to Choose* (London: Secker and Warburg, 1980), especially 120–26.

10

What Should Be the Next Stage in the Process of Russian Reform?

ALEKSANDRAS SHTROMAS

1. The Crash of August 17, 1998, from my perspective, was the second major explosive crisis of the Soviet political and economic system (the first one occurred in 1991). It is quite likely that the Russian authorities, spooked by the collapse, will try to persevere in their attempts to preserve the remaining rudiments of that system and even resuscitate them despite the fact that that they have spectacularly proven to be bankrupt and by all accounts should have been scrapped once and for all a long time ago. Should that be the case, a third—and, in all likelihood, final—major crisis of the remnants of the Soviet system will be all but inevitable. This, hopefully, will—by an enormous price again, however—bring the Soviet system in contemporary Russia to its well deserved end.

2. Amazingly, the August 17 Crash was not precipitated by the bankruptcy of the Russian economy as a whole. The crisis only struck its state-monopoly sector comprising major enterprises and companies that had been carried over intact from the Soviet era and managed to embed themselves in the post–Soviet Russian economy and power structure. But the semi-shadow and shadow enterprises were by and large not too

Reprinted from a paper submitted to the "Possev" Conference, Moscow, May 22–24, 1999. Translation from the Russian by Eugene Ostrovsky.

heavily affected by the Crash; on the contrary, in its immediate aftermath, they moved to the foreground and, to everyone's surprise, managed, somehow or other, to feed the country and ward off the famine
and wholesale misery that otherwise should have ineluctably followed a
crisis of such magnitude.

The relatively high level of proliferation of shadow business enterprises in the country was, first and foremost, the result of the dramatic
overall liberalization of political life and, also, of the enervation of the
state's punitive action against private entrepreneurship—processes that
took place since 1992. By no means could it be seen as the result of officially conducted economic reforms, which were mainly aimed at incorporating the Soviet socialist *nomenklatura* into what the official reformers imagined to be the "new Russian capitalism." I'll return to this
point in greater detail later on.

The shadow business sector we are talking about consists, by and
large, of medium and small companies that have long since forsworn the
Russian ruble and conduct their transactions in U.S. dollars, thereby ensuring their financial stability and avoiding confiscatory taxes by disclos-
ing to the government only that portion of their profits—of course, de-
nominated in rubles—that they themselves are willing to pay.

In this sense the August 17 Crash can be viewed as a convincing political triumph of freedom, democracy, and the market principles as well
as graphic proof that the socialist economic system is utterly nonviable
even if partially, though mainly formally, removed from the state's direct
control.

3. The Russian government is currently facing a dilemma: (a) either to try
   to nurture back to life the oligarchic economy and continue subsidizing
   mammoth money-losing enterprises, or (b) to nudge them toward their
   natural economic destiny, i.e., bankruptcy, and, subsequently, reorganization along truly free-market (i.e., capitalistic) lines. As mentioned in
   paragraph 1, any attempt to stick to the former policies will inevitably
   lead to a new, even more severe crush of these economic dinosaurs that
   survived the Soviet era and continue to be maintained on life support by
   government largesse, thus sweeping away with themselves the entire official economy of Russia. Only the latter policy option can provide for a
   relatively crisis-free development of the Russian economy, enabling it
   one day to attain normalcy and rise to its feet.

4. If this objective is to be attained, the primary requirement is for the government to try to coax the productive sector of the Russian economy out
   of the shadows and semi-shadows, above all by adopting a sensible tax
   code designed to encourage profitable business activities. Another requirement is to stabilize the ruble. At this point, I can see no other feasible way of achieving this objective than by instituting a currency board
   system under which each ruble printed by the government will have to
   be fully backed by the currency reserves of the country's central bank.

Currently, Russia has nowhere near the level of reserves required, but they can—and should—be built up with loans from international lending organizations. The currency board option would solve, at a stroke, the problem of weaning the Russian economy from dependence on the dollar and luring into the marketplace (including for investment purposes) the more than $40 billion that the wary Russians currently keep under their mattresses. And the third such substantial requirement is to create a favorable political environment so as to entice foreign moneybags to invest in the Russian economy, particularly through selling bankrupt Russian companies to prospective domestic and foreign investors at bargain-basement prices.

In other words, it's high time that the Russian government stop its long-lost war with the productive sector of the Russian free-enterprise economy and establish lasting peace with business on terms acceptable to the business interests that have managed to stay afloat—or, better yet, on terms dictated by the business sector to the powers that be. There is no other way! The state, which has lost this protracted war, can only survive if it totally and unconditionally capitulates to the victorious free enterprise sector.

5. I have indicated above (in paragraph 3) that the Russian government should push toward bankruptcy the oligarchic economy and all those enterprises that have been on life support, breathing only with the help of immense, unproductive government spending. In other words, all subsidies and other incentives paid out of the meager state treasury must be discontinued right away (we are not talking, of course, of real private bank loans or private investment designed to keep afloat companies that currently lose money but have the potential to turn things around).

The question is how to reorganize these still unproductive companies operating in the putatively private sector of the Russian economy once they are allowed to go under. The answer in a nutshell is "re-privatization." But in order to gain a proper insight into the meaning of this term, we must discuss at least the principal drawbacks of the privatization carried out in Russia over the 1992–1994 period.

6. Boris Yeltsin and his hand-picked team of anticommunist reformers (above all, Yegor Gaidar with his aides, Burbulis, et al.), who had spent their entire adult life memorizing and parroting Marxist bromides, apparently failed to assimilate a simple truth very clearly spelled out by none other than Karl Marx himself: a genuine social revolution cannot be successful unless it seeks to demolish the old state machinery; all the more so, if its leaders try to achieve their objectives by pressing that decrepit state machinery into the service of the revolution. The "Yeltsin revolutionaries," who came to power in the wake of the pathetic coup attempt in August 1991, began by destroying the power structure of the Communist Party. But that was the extent of their revolution; the new

rulers simply filled the vacuum left by the liquidation of the party's power apparatus, placing themselves in its stead at the head of the extant Soviet state, and making no attempt to change it (with the obvious exception of the "independent" Congress of People's Deputies and its creature, the Supreme Soviet, that turned themselves into hotbeds of resistance to reform and to all other attempts to change the status quo. Still, even that took some doing; for more than two years, the government tried to reach an understanding with the legislature on the basis of the very same Soviet constitutional system recognized as legitimate by both parties to the new Russian diarchy). Such a halfhearted approach to systemic reform accompanied by the government's strenuous efforts to preserve, whatever the cost, constitutional continuity from the Soviet past to the post-Soviet present, as expected, led nowhere, except confusion and gridlock.

Even after the "dispersal" of the Congress of People's Deputies in 1993, the Soviet state machinery, intact in all its essential features, refused to yield to, or at least refrain from sabotaging, the reformist strictures of the new leaders—the "Yeltsin revolutionaries from above." To the contrary, having used the new leaders to get rid of the remnants of the Communist Party supervision web with its secret police, economic police, planning and procurement bodies, and other controls, the state bureaucracy for the first time ever felt genuinely unfettered and omnipotent. Thus emboldened, the bureaucracy proceeded to block any innovation seriously threatening to undermine its newly acquired power. As a result, Yeltsin's "revolutionary government" became, in effect, hostage to the state machinery it nominally led. Meanwhile, having shed the "Communist Party shackles," the bureaucracy turned into an unaccountable structure operating like a criminal organization in the sense that it dropped all pretense of serving the state or the people and set about pursuing strictly the goals of self-preservation, self-perpetuation, and expansion, trying to strengthen its dominant position in society and, above all, preserve and expand the powers and privileges of its own power elites. Corruption that had been eating at the foundations of all government structures as far back as in the Brezhnev epoch, became now all-pervasive and all but officially sanctioned; pretty clearly, it is, at the very least, a poorly disguised dominant factor of political and social life in Yeltsin's Russia.

The openly Mafia-like bureaucracy and its reformist top leadership in government were rushing headlong to collision, and privatization was slated to become the field of battle. However, the privatization campaign, as planned by Anatoly Chubais, did not pursue aggressive goals; it was designed as a ploy to lure the economic bureaucracy into the capitalist "snare" and disarm it by transforming the old *nomenklatura* into a new class of large and medium capitalist property owners.

The trepidation before the powers that be, which is an inescapable, seemingly congenital condition of an average Soviet intellectual; his persistent and, as often as not, successful attempts to dupe the authorities and achieve his own objectives, which were not infrequently at variance with those pursued by the regime—in short, the specific mentality rooted in Soviet experience shaped the Chubais privatization campaign that the people aptly put down as a gigantic fraud using a Russian word that rhymes with "privatization." The reformers' plan was simplicity itself: they hoped that, having acquired legal ownership rights to the state property under their management, the former heads of chief directorates, chairmen of productive associations, heads of various ministries' departments, company bosses—in short, the class of people known as "red directors" together with their counterparts in agriculture, the so-called red landlords—would become dyed-in-the-wool capitalists, develop a market outlook on life, and create all the requisite trappings of a truly capitalist economy.

The plan was fatally flawed, however, if only because the state-controlled economy structurally remained unchanged and its old managers persisted in their old ways, although in their new role of owners they felt their oats and shed all inhibitions that had crimped their style when they were simply bureaucrats lording it over the fiefdoms entrusted to their tender care by the party. Thus, the hopes that "somehow everything will turn out all right" and "things will fall into place by themselves" were dashed again, as evidenced so graphically by the August 17 Crash.

7. Still, privatization had the potential of becoming a real field of battle where the old Soviet state machinery could be demolished once and for all and the old master-state transformed, through genuine privatization, into new service-state—a state that is called to serve the needs of the civil society resurrected by that same very process of genuine privatization.

I would venture to say that my privatization plan of 1990–1991 contained a set of guidelines of just such a privatization effort. Let me summarize its salient points for they might come in handy in any attempt at re-privatization and help to steer it clear of the kind of pitfalls in which the 1992–1994 privatization campaign got mired.

So, looking back on 1990, when the privatization issue was vigorously debated in the Soviet media, I decided to contribute my two cents' worth. I delivered an article on the subject to the Izvestia newspaper but it was turned down. Numerous attempts to have it printed in other periodicals were equally futile. Finally, I succeeded in prevailing upon *Literaturnaya Gazeta* to print my article, albeit in abridged form (see "Tri kita reformy," issue #6 [533?] of 2/13/91, p. 7). It drew the attention of a group of deputies of the Supreme Soviet of the Russian Federation who asked me to draft a bill "On the Privatization of State-Owned Enterprises." The full text of my article together with the draft bill was subsequently printed in *Grani* magazine (# 161, 1991, pp. 290–312).

In a nutshell, I suggested that privatization should be all-encompassing rather than selective, and carried out instantaneously rather than in a gradual, step-by-step manner. To this end, a law was to be passed acording to which the government had to transfer the ownership rights to all its enterprises to those same individual enterprises possessing the status of legal persons. In order that the transfer could be effected all at once, the government was to loan to each of the enterprises it owned a quantity of stock that it will be issuing in the amount equal to the enterprise's reevaluated book value. After a certain period of time as determined in each stock transfer contract (one to three years), the enterprises were to pay back to the government the full value of the stock from the funds raised in the free equity and capital markets set up by the enterprises themselves. Naturally, successful, competitive companies would realize significant profits from the trading of their stock and would have no trouble settling their accounts with the government within the predetermined time frame, while those that would prove incapable of attracting investors and thus unable to pay back their debt, would be forced into bankruptcy and, hence, lose their status as independent legal persons. Obviously, between these two extremes of "market destinies" there would be a gray area featuring companies that would manage to sell part of their stock, but not enough to pay back their debt on schedule. In such cases these "middle-ground" companies could have their debt restructured so as to give them more time to adapt to the new environment and find their sea legs in a market economy that has already taken off.

Such an approach to privatization, in my view, offered a number of important advantages. First of all, it would privatize the grassroots individual enterprises, i.e., the legal persons occupying the lowest rung of the Soviet economic hierarchy, rather than their administrative conglomerates—from the chief directorates of the former economic ministries to all manner of production associations, trusts, companies and other purely managerial structures comprising more than one grassroots enterprise. This would put an end immediately to all monopolies, including those that for some unfathomable reason are considered to be "natural" ones, and right away competition would become the guiding principle of the economy. In such an environment, elimination of all price and wage controls certainly would never become tantamount to "shock therapy" (much less "shock without therapy"). Furthermore, with the emergence of well-functioning capital and equity markets, the common people could purchase the stock of privatized companies and, instead of losing all their savings, reinvest them in economic units promising a good return on the investment in the future. In the same future, the market and its needs would determine which new companies, associations, and other "multiple-unit" business entities would spring up. The paramount task at the first stage of privatization was to deconstruct the Soviet economic system and it could only be accomplished through privatizing individual ground-level enterprises. And once the deconstruction phase was over, a new economic system could be constructed following the natural laws and trends underlying the operation of a market economy.

Another major task that the proposed privatization approach could accomplish was building a wall of separation between economics and politics, i.e., removing the government from the economic arena and thereby promoting the emergence of a genuinely civil society. Not only would the instantaneous privatization deprive the government of the right to control the economy and interfere with the managerial and commercial decision-making activities of economic entities, but the government would be totally excluded from the very process of privatization itself. The responsibility for privatization *per se*, i.e., the task of selling companies to their new, real owners, and for all its attendant procedures, would devolve upon the companies themselves, which, if they were to survive in a new environment, would have to lose no time in setting up the requisite equity markets and other mechanisms for trading their stock and reform their operations in such a way as to make themselves as attractive as possible to potential investors.

In other words, having been handed ownership rights, enterprises would have to take it upon themselves to sell their stock knowing full well that their future depends on the success or failure of that undertaking. Thus, individual enterprises would have to create collectively a capital market with all its structures, such as stock exchanges, investment firms, and the like. Having at last become masters of their own destiny, enterprises would be forced to start looking for their real owners in the marketplace, and the strong and viable ones would have no trouble finding them. Meanwhile the government would have absolutely nothing to do with this "secondary," or real, privatization.

Under the "secondary" privatization approach, the employees were to be given first crack at their company's stock on attractive terms before trading in it begins. During the first six months of trading, Russian physical and legal persons would have had an exclusive right to buy the stock of the privatized Russian enterprises, and only after that full access would have been granted to all comers, including foreign citizens and companies.

8. This "dual" excursion into the past, in my view, is important in that it should help determine some of the main principles and methods of the coming reprivatization. Thus, for instance, comprehensive privatization implies a transfer to private hands not only of the tools of production, but also its means, i.e., those natural resources (above all, land) without which no enterprise can exist and flourish as an independent entity. We are going to touch upon the issue of privatization of farmland (unfortunately, the prospects of reprivatization in agriculture at

this point in time are nonextant as farmland has never been truly privatized) somewhat later. As for the oil, gas, coal, timber, metal, and other industries engaged in the mining and processing of mineral and other natural resources, their reprivatization should be carried out by directly transferring the ownership rights to individual enterprises, thereby getting rid of the middleman, such as the former Soviet chief directorates, trusts, concerns, and associations, like Gazprom, Lukoil, Sibneft, Yukos and their ilk, that have undergone phony privatization and mutated into putatively private companies. Since the government maintains a sizable (and in many cases, controlling) interest in these pseudoprivate companies, it should be relatively easy to reprivatize them by breaking them up, as proposed above, even in those cases where companies of this kind would not be subject to liquidation under the letter of the bankruptcy laws. As these mammoth companies, which often enjoy monopoly power, are broken up, the new economic entities will have to compete with one another, and competitive pressures would pretty soon sort out the losers from the winners by solving the problems of prices, wages, profitability and thus, viability of each such enterprise.

9. Let me make it clear at the outset that I do not intend to propose any top-down structural reforms in agriculture. Merely recognizing farmland as subject to private ownership and anchoring its status as such, including the right to buy and sell land, in law should be enough to solve eventually all the main issues of agrarian reform. It is important that the members of today's successors of the erstwhile collective farms should hold real shares, including land, tools, and other elements of "collective" property, as full and unlimited private owners. In such a case, it will be up to the individual members of today's collective farms to decide their future. Some of them will undoubtedly try to sell their shares to the highest bidders among those who will be eager to continue as farmers and proceed to buy out their colleagues. Others might prefer a cooperative approach to farming and accordingly will pool their shares again (naturally, retaining the right to reclaim them at any time), but on a new contractual basis. Such cooperatives might adopt novel charters delineating the authority of the board, setting forth the procedure for electing board members, and describing the functions and level of compensation of full-time managers either chosen from among board members or hired from outside.

10. It goes without saying that forming joint-stock companies or setting up cooperatives are not the only routes of genuine privatization (or reprivatization). Just as in agriculture the government can and should nurture fully private farms, so in all other sectors of the economy enterprises can be sold, lock, stock, and barrel, to private persons (both physical and legal) without being preconverted into joint-stock companies. Unless individual components of the now defunct mammoth

"private structures" are giants in their own right (the Uralmash Machine-Building Plant or the ZIL Autoworks are cases in point), they can be simply auctioned off. All potential buyers would be required to submit sealed bids setting forth the specific terms and conditions on which they would agree to take over a given enterprise. A certain minimum price below which no bids would be accepted should be set. Such an approach means that not only the stock and other securities should circulate freely on the capital market, but also the enterprises themselves in their direct, immediate, and full physical embodiment. Furthermore, the government should encourage the privatization effort and through its policies create incentives for potential buyers. The government should also encourage the reorganization of the enterprises in the throes of privatization with a view to helping them adapt, as best they can, to the requirements of the marketplace.

Above all, the government should do its utmost to encourage private efforts to create new enterprises. It is important to note, however, that such encouragement should be confined to political help. The siren calls for the government to set up banks for the development of a "real sector of the economy" and other proposals advocating direct government financing of economic initiatives should be resolutely turned down. All measures of this sort are the work of the devil, as the saying goes, and can only distort the natural trends in the country's economic development.

At this point, it is logical to turn to the problems besetting Russia's system of banking and other lending institutions, which, if left festering, will surely undermine all reform efforts.

11. It is high time the Russian banks finally got around to doing what they are supposed to do, viz. serve their clients and grant all manner of loans. Having foreclosed on the property of a defaulting or insolvent debtor, the bank must sell it with all due dispatch and immediately convert the proceeds into new loans. Private banks must not engage in delivering financial services to the government either. The Central Bank and its local affiliates should be the only agencies receiving and distributing state funds under the budget. In its dealings with lower-level budget offices the Central Bank, obviously, should be given the right to open correspondent accounts at private banks; other than that, private financial institutions should be prevented from independently handling government monies, lending them, or using them for other purposes of their own. By the same token, state-owned banks (ideally there should be only one representative of the species—the Central Bank) should be deprived of the right to lend money to private economic entities or otherwise finance their activities. All these prohibitions are designed to put an end to the functional chaos that is the name of the game in the Russian banking sector today. First of all, the state bank (the Central Bank and its affiliates) must become the

state's real and sole banker and sever all direct ties to economic and other private entities and organizations, allowing them to be served exclusively by private banks. Secondly, private banks should be forbidden to own and control nonfinancial entities, including mass media. So long as banks are allowed to run TV channels, coal mines, oil fields, or smelting plants, there will be no normal banking system in Russia and the country will be deprived of the benefits of a well-oiled credit market.

Of the many thousands of private Russian banks only about 750 emerged relatively unscathed from the August 17 Crash. Most of the survivors were local banks with a primary focus on their charter responsibilities, i.e., financial activities. These institutions should be used as a cornerstone of a new credit-cum-banking system. In my view, the principal strategic objective should be getting major foreign banks involved, letting them transform the surviving Russian banks into more wide-ranging financial institutions operating on the basis of normal world standards. Foreign banks could also provide an uninterrupted inflow of capital for profitable investments and credits; more important still, they will be in a position to judge which Russian economic entities, whether in industry, agriculture, or services, deserve credit infusions as showing the most promise in terms of meeting the needs of the world market. In other words, foreign banks are the surest and most dependable source of foreign investment without which there is no way of putting the Russian economy back on track.

12. If the economy and economic processes in general are insulated from government influence, the budget appropriations to maintain the bureaucracy can be cut back by several orders of magnitude. Part of the savings thus realized could and should be spent on strengthening and developing the civil justice system. There is no dearth of highly trained civil law experts in Russia, but few of them are currently employed in the field of civil justice. A major raise and a boost in prestige for judges could be instrumental in attracting to the bench the cream of the country's crop of civil law experts. The judiciary should also be buttressed by a sufficiently powerful bailiff corps. If Russia is to attract massive foreign investments and entice major foreign banks to enter its market, her judiciary must become truly effective and authoritative.

Clearly, the Russian civil laws leave much to be desired. Suffice it to mention the Land Code that has been eternally stuck in limbo and the still pending right to buy and sell land. Neither is there a Trade Code. On the positive side of the ledger, some of the principal civil laws, including a new Civil Code, have been put into effect; they are quite adequate to institute order in the crucial areas of civil justice. It is not so much the lack of good laws as the glaring flaws in their application and implementation that are Russia's biggest problem. If it can be solved along the lines I have suggested herein, it could just prove to be the proverbial main link in the chain that would ultimately pull the Russian economy and society out of its morass and onto the normal path of development.

13. To cut public spending, it is not enough to put the bureaucracy on a diet. Additional savings can be realized from introducing an insurance-based health care system; increasing the retirement age; gradually doing away with free higher education; and reviving Nemtsov's reform of the utilities support payments (the latter reform, while withdrawing federal subsidies, in no way precludes the local authorities from subsidizing the utilities—as long as they do it from their own pocket. If this is how Moscow's Luzhkov or any other mayor deems advisable to spend his resources, nobody should stand in their way).

In other ways to smooth the transition from dependence on subsidies to self-sufficiency, I can recommend the principle of "negative taxation" proposed by Milton Friedman. It basically obligates the government to pay cash subsidies to its citizens to make up the difference between the subsistence minimum, tracked on a daily basis, and their actual daily income. The proceeds from the sale of enterprises in the course of reprivatization should be used, first and foremost, to fund the negative tax program. If, as seems quite likely, the reprivatization campaign initially fails to generate enough money for this purpose, the shortfall can be made good by means of a special sales tax surcharge. This kind of mechanism is particularly attractive by virtue of being non-egalitarian and providing financial support only to those who are truly incapable of earning a living. It is also the cheapest option that has no affect on prices (except to the extent that they will be slightly boosted by the special sales tax surcharge). Furthermore, this approach leaves the recipients free to choose how to spend their support payments; some people will go to the bakery to buy bread, others may blow their windfall on perfume. One final advantage of the negative tax program is that as the living standards rise, it will tend to diminish and ultimately vanish.

14. All the above ideas only make sense provided Russia chooses to stay on the path of normal economic development, which implies its increasing integration into the world economic system. One would think that there is no alternative. However, it is far from a no-brainer. There exists a strong nostalgia for the stagnation era associated with Brezhnev's name when the USSR existed as sort of a separate, "virtual" planet, functionally autonomous from the rest of the world and in no way dependent on it. That "virtual planet" operated on the basis of a seemingly normal exchange of goods and services, which somehow managed to provide people with low-paying jobs and permitted even the most backward industries to stay afloat. Of course, it was nothing if not an illusion; the Soviet economy was inexorably sliding downhill

until it found itself on the very edge of the abyss and the powers that be were forced to attempt, however timidly, a version of reform, which became known as *perestroika*.

This pressure for moving back to the closed Soviet world, to the "virtual planet" sealed off from the surrounding world, should not be viewed as evidence of a resurgence of communism or socialism. The truth is simple: having opened its doors to the world, the Russian economy (as well as those of Ukraine and Belorus) has failed to find its niche in the international marketplace—that competitive edge or more precisely the competitive advantage that ensures the survival in the global economy of even the most backward countries, such as Fiji or Jamaica. As in the Soviet times, Russia to this day remains the supplier to the world of its raw materials and some weapon systems. Ukraine and Belarus do not have even such an outdated comparative advantage in the global economy and by that are worse off than Russia. So the nostalgic sentiment has nothing to do with ideology and everything with a longing for the lost, relative sense of well-being—however meager and largely illusory. The "back to the past" trend is little more than a nostalgic dream about a world that no longer exists; that cannot be put together again; and that, even when it projected an image of strength and solidity, was rapidly degenerating into a self-destructive chimera. Suffice it to recall the pervasive shortages of just about everything and the fictitious nature of the official wages and salaries.

It is this desire to "move backward," rooted in nothing but pure illusions, which is behind the observed trend toward the reintegration of the former Soviet economies and states that has been elevated to the status of official policy in Belarus. The Russian government does not dare to challenge it openly and feigns interest in the integration game—at least for now. Ukraine, too, has been leaning more and more toward reintegration with Russia and Belarus. As a matter of fact, Ukraine is here a decisive factor; its example may sway the borderline economies of Romania and Slovakia and get them entangled in the nostalgic reintegrationist movement, too. As a result, there might reemerge a fairly large, neo-Soviet-style, closed economic space.

Needless to say, the reintegration of the former Soviet economic space cannot but lead the countries it entrains into a new blind alley and bankruptcy. Hence, it seems to me that Russia has no other option but to continue looking, as vigorously as possible, for a way to join the world economic system and use all the help it can get to find its comparative advantage in it. Once Russia succeeds, she will be able to pull to this same end its floundering Belarussian and Ukrainian partners in their so far futile integrationist endeavor to one or the other side.

At the risk of sounding presumptuous, I will take the liberty to submit that the above sets forth the only realistic, if admittedly difficult, option for Russia to join the world. Obviously, any theory is subject to revisions (sometimes, of major proportions) once it is put to the test of practical implementation. However, following preordained dogma is here not the issue; the issue is to determine the main vector for the forthcoming new stage of Russian reform, and such vectors are dictated by objective realities and the demands for real action to be taken to solve real problems.

11

To Expand Beyond Enlargement:

A Few Thoughts on Preserving NATO's Original Identity without Hindering Its Transformation into a Euro-Atlantic Collective Security System

ALEKSANDRAS SHTROMAS

After Poland, Hungary, and the Czech Republic have received official invitations to join the Alliance, NATO's enlargement has acquired an irreversible momentum. The millions of words written in debating the wisdom and utility of the enlargement policy have thus been rendered futile and cleared the grounds for a new turn in the debate of Europe's and NATO's future. Inevitably, this debate will have primarily to focus on the ambivalence of the thus conceived process of NATO's enlargement, on its clumsy and protracted character that by itself, instead of advancing European security, may undermine its very foundations, together with the Alliance's original effectiveness and clarity of purpose.

The real issue at stake is actually not NATO's enlargement as such but the will of the United States and its NATO allies to commit themselves to the real defense of the space between Germany and Russia proper that in 1989–1991 had been freed from Soviet dominion or, as the saying goes, the will to have one's soldiers die and risk the destruction of one's cities in defending remote places, be it Gniezno or Szeged, of which, in the immortal words of Neville Chamberlain, "we know nothing." The inclusion into the NATO Alliance of only the three countries mentioned above makes the presence of such a will

Reprinted from a paper presented to the Second Annual Association for the Study of Nationalities (ASN) Convention at Columbia University in New York City, April 24–27, 1997, pp. 1–15.

doubtful indeed, as these countries are geographically closest to NATO's own territory and do not even have a common border with Russia (except for the Polish–Russian border in the tiny Russian exclave of the Konigsberg/Kaliningrad region). Even if Russia wanted to attack these three countries, she would be unable to do so without first occupying Ukraine and militarily taking over Belarus—a formidable task that could not be accomplished suddenly or easily enough for NATO to be caught unawares. Fareed Zakaria recently reminded us that the prominent British historian A. J. P. Taylor had remarked that the 1925 Treaty of Locarno by which Britain and Italy promised to defend France and Belgium, "rested on the assumption that the promises made in it would never have to be made good—otherwise the British Government would not have made them." Zakaria then states that exactly the same situation repeats itself in the extension, by the way of membership, of NATO's security guarantees foreseen in article 5 of the treaty only to the countries that are not exposed to a direct threat and thus do not need them. "That is why," he concludes, "Deputy Secretary of State Strobe Talbott can assert that the movement closer to Russia's borders of the most powerful military alliance in the world does not actually threaten Russia. As Tweedledee says, "if it was so, it might be; and if it were so, it would be: but as it isn't, it ain't. That's logic."[1]

On the other hand, a limitless enlargement of NATO, however protracted, would no doubt weaken the Alliance, which in its present shape has a well organized and smoothly functioning infrastructure, adequate resources, and unmatched military potential. I find Edward Luttwak's formula: "Add Poland, and NATO is no more"[2] a bit extreme and overalarmist—it seems to me that adding the three designated countries to NATO will not significantly dilute its present strength but if all the formerly communist-ruled European states were to join NATO at the level of Hungary's or the Czech Republic's readiness to do so, the coherence and might of the Alliance may suffer greatly indeed.

This obvious ambivalence of NATO's enlargement is, in my view, rooted in the accidental origins of its adoption as American, and later NATO's as a whole, official policy. Since the "end of Cold War," NATO, almost instinctively, tried to solve its identity crisis not by the way of enlarging but by that of engaging Russia, together with all the former Soviet satellites and dependencies, into a cooperative relationship aimed at ensuring together the collective security in Europe. It was for this purpose that the Partnership for Peace (later referred to as PfP) had been created. Consequently, at the time of the initial planning for NATO's post–Cold War future the issue of keeping the former Soviet dependencies in Central and East Europe secure from a possible threat on the part of the "new Russia" was not even posited or considered as a problem that needed to be specifically addressed. It was assumed that Russia's and the other post-Communist states' joint and constructive involvement with NATO through PfP is to solve that problem automatically and without any further ado.

This assumption has never been shared, however, by most of the post-Communist states that continued to consider Russia as, at least potentially, an imminent threat to their newly acquired independence and freedom, and which therefore were resolutely determined to seek NATO's firm guarantees of their security against possible Russian aggression—the kind of security the PfP explicitly denied them. Actually, the PfP, in which they found themselves banded together with Russia and all other (with the notable exception of Tadjikistan) formerly Soviet ruled or dominated states, became for them in itself a source of frustration, as Russia, by her sheer size and strength, as well as preeminent significance in the eyes of NATO's core, inevitably acquired in it the position of the dominant actor. The countries of the former Soviet Bloc suddenly started to feel in this partnership as if they were back in the Warsaw Pact—deprived of NATO's article 5 security guarantees and coalescing around Russia, though this time not in the capacity of a declared foe of, but of an entity ostensibly attached to, NATO. It was at the April 1993 official opening of the U.S. Holocaust Museum—an occasion that the attending heads of East European states, especially Lech Walesa and Vàclav Havel, used for actively pressing the freshly elected President Clinton to get their respective countries accepted as full members of NATO (that is, to get article 5 security guarantees extended to them)—that the present policy of NATO's enlargement started taking shape. While the former President, George Bush, for better or worse, firmly withstood such pressures, president Bill Clinton willingly yielded to them, although he did so in a typically inconsistent Clinton fashion, that is without changing the main course of the previous administration's policy aiming in the first place at the establishment, in cooperation with Russia, of a Euro-Atlantic collective security system and, through it, "the new world order."

Hence getting Russia to acquiesce to the thus conceived NATO's enlargement plan became the main concern of the Clinton administration, ever since that plan was declared U.S. official policy in the president's October 13, 1993, speech at the summit meeting of the Visegrad Four in Prague. After many ups and downs in a protracted and sometimes dramatic negotiation process, the 1997 Helsinki Summit between Clinton and Yeltsin, followed in May by the signing of the Founding Act by all NATO's heads of state and Russia in Paris, have finally settled the issue of Russia's (very grudgingly conceded) reconciliation with a partially enlarged NATO in exchange for, among other things (such as the membership of the Paris Club and the transformation of G-7 into the "Summit of the Eight"), the creation of the Permanent Joint Council in which Russia was to acquire "a say" (though ostensibly "not a veto") in NATO's decision-making process. Then, and only then, did Madrid follow, formalizing the "first stage of NATO's enlargement" to the apparent satisfaction of both the Clinton and Yeltsin administrations but not to that of too many other parties involved or having a vital interest in this process.

Let me make clear that I do not find anything wrong in the United States and her NATO allies' attempts to tighten the cooperative links between

NATO and Russia. Nor, in contrast to Dr. Henry Kissinger,[3] do I abhor the idea of NATO becoming a Euro-Atlantic collective security system. On the contrary, I happen to believe that such an extension of NATO's role is in the present circumstances not merely commendable but vitally necessary. The assumption by NATO of this novel function would entail its commitment to act not only in defense of the Alliance's member-states, which are virtually not anymore under the threat of a direct attack from any quarters, but also in the capacity of a Euro-Atlantic peacekeeping and peace-building force outside NATO's own main core. It is for these, and only for these, peacekeeping and peace-building purposes outside of the area protected by NATO's own defensive shield that Russia should, in my view, be firmly enlisted as the Alliance's full-blooded partner via the organizational forms of her close and permanent association with it foreseen by the PfP's and the Founding Act's provisions. However, there is, I believe, no need whatsoever to accord to Russia any voice at all in NATO's inner arrangements or in the fulfillment of its obligations under the provisions of articles 4 and 5 of the treaty. This is to say that, at least to me, NATO's new identity as a collective security system should not in any way undermine or dilute its old identity of a clearly defined and coherent political-military alliance, whose primary aim had always been the containment of the USSR and, in the post-Soviet context, should, in my view, staunchly remain the deterrence of Russia from relapsing into her traditional imperialist antics. I am convinced that, if NATO is to continue to remain what it always used to be, these by now two identities of the Alliance should be kept entirely separate and by no means interfere with one another.

It is true that if NATO is to retain in the new post–Cold War situation its original identity of a proper political-military alliance, it will have to extend its defensive shield, in the strictest terms of article 5 guarantees, all the way to the present western borders of Russia. For without such an extension, without it covering Ukraine and the Baltic States in the first place, NATO's original determination to counter a possible Russian offensive beyond her western frontier could not be realistically sustained. In other words, in order for NATO to retain its original identity of an Alliance that had been unequivocally determined to counter any kind of a Soviet attack beyond the then East–West divide, it is absolutely necessary for it firmly to place today its defensive perimeter onto the present western frontier of Russia proper. The failure to do so would inevitably spell the end of the Alliance that, at its inception in 1949, NATO was made to be and has always been since.

The expansion of NATO's protective shield to the western frontier of Russia could have been, and still can be, achieved, it seems to me, without either compromising its new role as a collective security system (one that would fully include Russia) or even without venturing for a formal enlargement of the Alliance's membership. For the security guarantees provided by article 5 of the treaty may be extended to the states wishing to accept such guarantees also through bilateral treaty arrangements between these states and NATO proper, whether the latter is or is not going to be inclusive of Poland, Hungary, and the Czech Republic. These arrangements may vary from country to country. In the case of Ukraine, for example, NATO can become, in concordance with such a treaty, the (article 5) guarantor of Ukraine's neutral status, while in the case of the three Baltic States the arrangements may be of a full-fledged military alliance, unless the Baltic States, reassured by NATO's security guarantees, would, along with the Ukraine and Finland, opt for neutrality, too. There is no doubt that, perhaps with the exception of Lukashenka's Belarus, all states that border Russia on her western frontier would be most eager to accept article 5 security guarantees from NATO in any form NATO would be willing to offer them. It is, after all, for receiving such guarantees that these states seek NATO's membership in the first place, not for the mere prestige of being able to boast equal membership of the world's most powerful political-military entity. With such guarantees in place, the process of NATO's enlargement could acquire a normally steady course that would not be unduly hastened by the impatient urge of the countries applying for membership to have their security protected instantaneously. Indeed, with the borders of Ukraine, Poland, and the Baltic States thus rendered secure, all other countries in the territorial space between Germany and Russia proper would be automatically protected against any encroaching or directly expansionist move by Russia.

As a prerequisite for such an arrangement, NATO would be wise to demand that Ukraine and the Baltic States conclude with Russia firm and unequivocal nonaggression treaties pledging that no interventionist or any hostile act aimed against Russia or any part of her territory will ever take place from the territory(ies) of the cosignatory(ies) of such a treaty(ies) and, vice versa, that Russia, recognizing the established borders between herself and the treaties' co-signatories, is forever to refrain from applying force or the threat of force in her relationship with them. Negotiation, arbitration and adjudication procedures for the authoritative peaceful resolution of disagreements and disputes between Russia and her cosignatories in such non-aggression treaties should be clearly established by these treaties, too. In addition, the conclusion of some treaties on the enhancement of economic cooperation between Russia, Ukraine, Belarus, and the Baltic States should be strongly encouraged, e.g., of treaties on conditions of unhindered access of Russian merchant and fishing fleets to the port facilities in the Baltic and Black seas, as well as on the regime of free transit of goods in international commercial exchanges through the territories of all the signatories. The recently signed Russo–Ukrainian Treaty could serve as a model for the first step in developing such arrangements. With treaties of this kind in place, the official Russia would lose even the slightest justification for her capricious and totally irrational pretenses of being mortally scared by the possibility of an attack from NATO, or any of her western neighbors acting as its proxies. Whether it likes it or not, official Russia will have to acknowledge that all these treaties provide a perfectly reliable infrastructure for developing steady, peaceful, and cooperative relations between Russia and her western neighbors, as well as the rest of Europe and the whole western world.

Let me conclude the above arguments by saying that the Madrid invitation for the three designated countries to join NATO without the extension of article 5 security guarantees to the countries that border Russia on her western frontier and that thus most badly need them, smacks to me of no less than a new edition of the infamous Yalta deal, whereby the Russian "sphere of influence" is to be limited to the boundaries of the former Soviet Union, while Russia is to concede the right for the former Warsaw Treaty states to be basically free to act as they please, e.g., to join NATO whenever the latter will deem them fit to do so. So, let us call a spade a spade—what happened in Madrid was not the abolishment of divisions in Europe making the old continent one and indivisible sphere of cooperating democracies; it was a mere move of the dividing line between Russia and the West from the borders of the former Soviet Bloc to the frontiers of the former Soviet Union. As the Yalta agreement led to the Cold War, the Madrid deal, in a very similar fashion—by tempting Russia to assert more completely its dominion over the "sphere of influence" thus granted to her by the West—could lead to a new round of East–West confrontation, the disastrous impact of which on the security situation in Europe and the entire world could not be overestimated.

I fail to understand those political analysts and statesmen who seem to be convinced that, after the fall of Communism and the end of Soviet empire, Russia stopped representing a threat to her neighbors and thus to world peace. It is so damningly obvious that the Yeltsin administration since late 1992 did everything in its power to bully the former Soviet republics and even Poland back into submission to Russia's *diktat* that such views almost seem to come from a different world, entirely isolated from information about what is going on on this planet. And what is the whole Russian vehement opposition to NATO's enlargement about, if it is not about resisting the definitive loss of "natural" space for her eventual re-expansion? What other meaning could be attached to Russia's persistent opposition to NATO, to her whole treatment of the relationship with it as a zero-sum game? Could any professional political operator or analyst seriously believe that Russia may indeed feel in any way threatened by NATO, whether expanding or not; or that Russian policy-makers are really ignorant of the fact that NATO is a purely defensive alliance that threatens no one and that only those who themselves plan to trespass against NATO's defensive perimeter may justifiably feel threatened by it? And if this is the case, then there should remain no doubt about Russia's opposition to NATO's expansion being nurtured exclusively by Russia's own expansionist intentions and plans.

What surprises me even more is the apologetic attitude that the Western statesmen always display when negotiating NATO's enlargement with Russia —as if indeed they are trying to take away from Russia what is legitimately hers. Overwhelmed by an inexplicable guilt complex, they try in a meek voice of a mischievous child to explain their behavior to the Russians as innocuous, and by no means attempting to do anything that could bode ill to Russia's interest, as these are understood by the Russian leaders themselves. By adamantly refusing to admit the obvious, namely that the Alliance is expanding in order to restrain Russia, they find themselves drawn into bargaining with Russia about what in the end boils down to the division of "spheres of interest." When, for example, Yeltsin, in his typically nondiplomatic language, declared that the addition to NATO of any members of the CIS or of the former Soviet republics that are not currently members of CIS (that is of the three Baltic States) would force him drastically to reconsider the whole of the at present quite cooperative relationship between Russia and the West, his western interlocutors not only did not rebuke him, but took his threat very seriously and—in order to avoid the risk of "unnecessarily" complicating relations with Russia—accepted (though tacitly, of course) Yeltsin's demand practically without reservations, as, at least for the time being, a done deal. In his meeting with the Secretary of State, Madeleine Albright, on July 12–13, 1997, in St. Petersburg, Russian Foreign Minister Yevgenity Primakov again stressed that NATO should "not touch" the Baltic States because that area is of "special interest" to Russia and Russia is ready to issue to these states her unilateral guarantes of their sovereignty. Mrs. Albright responded to this with the usual platitude about NATO membership being in principle open to all "democratic market systems in Europe," but the same day, July 13, addressed the meeting of Baltic foreign ministers in the Lithuanian capital Vilnius telling them in no uncertain terms that the U.S.–Baltic Charter now in preparation for signature in September "will not be a security guarantee but a document enabling us to cooperate on the basis of common aims and qualities."[4]

At least in my book, this "concessionary" attitude to Russia is wrong in principle; moreover, it is counterproductive, because, instead of taming Russia's inherent imperial instincts, it forges them into a presentable policy line fully legitimized by the West. I will return below to some more discussion of this crucially important point. Here, I think, it should be enough just to say that by refusing radically to oppose official Russia's delusions of what constitutes the greatness of state power, by accepting from Russia, as a normal expression of her "specific" national interests, what by any usual standards could not be seen as anything other than a severe case of political pathology, the West acts against its own long-term interests, as well as against the best interests of Russia herself.

Most often, however, one hears arguments maintaining that Russia is now a democracy that, as such, has stopped being aggressive and that, because of this fact, there is no need anymore of deterring her from attempting forceful expansion. Those who say such things usually add to these statements a qualification: "as long as Yeltsin and the reformists stay in power." Then the proponents of these arguments proceed to reason that NATO's expansion to Russia's borders may somehow undermine Yeltsin's ability to retain the helmsmanship of the Russian state, apparently suggesting that the public, frustrated by his inability properly to protect Russia from the West's domination, will vote the present administration out of office and elect into government anti-westerners of the extreme communist and nationalist variety. Hence, according to their logic, it is preferable to bargain with Yeltsin than, by taking an intransigent stance, provoke his loss of power and thus make come true the worst fears about the renewal of East–West confrontation or, in other words, the initiation of the second edition of the Cold War.

This logic is to me totally faulty for many reasons, but mainly because nothing could be further removed from Russia's political reality than the arguments the proponents of this logic are using. All the opinion polls conducted during the last several years consistently suggest that the Russian electorate is least of all concerned about NATO and that less than 30 percent of the population considers the West generally, and NATO in particular, as forces representing an external threat to Russia. Asked in two of the latest representative country-wide opinion polls about NATO's enlargement, only 18.5 percent of those polled said they believe that it could result in a certain intensification of the military threat to Russia; another 10 percent were concerned that NATO's expansion could lead to Russia's further political isolation from Europe and the world; the rest either did not see anything wrong or ominous about it at all or did not have an opinion.[5] It is important to stress in this context that in an earlier representative country-wide opinion poll conducted by Russia's International Center of Sociological Research, 70.4 percent of the polled said that Lithuania's entry into NATO is Lithuania's own internal affair and should be of no concern to Russia, while 24.8 percent disagreed and the rest did not have on this issue an opinion.[6] Hence, if one bears in mind a process of democratic change of government by fair elections, NATO's expansion even on the scale of embracing the states formerly belonging to the USSR, could hardly cause the radical communist-nationalist accession to power of which so many western analysts are rightly afraid. If one, however, meant the change of government by a coup—a very likely possibility, but one never knows—it is absolutely certain that no NATO action could either provoke it or even be used as an excuse for having staged it. One could really rest assured that if a coup against Yeltsin were ever to take place, it would be mounted for reasons and goals that have nothing to do with NATO whatsoever.

Let us, however, look at the bottom of the problem and openly admit that as yet Russia is not a democracy in the western sense of this concept. True, during the last decade Russia became an open society with a free press and free elections, but this fact so far failed to translate itself into the transformation of Russia's Soviet-type master state into a servant-state dependent from and accountable to the public. At the same time, the reality of power of that master-state in the new conditions of relative freedom has greatly diminished at home, to say nothing about the crumbling in the wake of the demise of the "evil empire" of its international influence or about the very necessity to face the former fourteen republics of the USSR transformed from what used to be Russia's own backyard to what her officials now dismissively call the "near abroad." In this situation, the post-Soviet Russian state has, almost by instinct, put itself to the task of restoring by whatever means available to it its former power and prestige. Gradually, this task took priority over any other tasks that the Russian polity was initially set to accomplish in its transition from communism, which is to say that today again the imperial syndrome largely dictates Russia's state policies, in spite of the overwhelming indifference and largely explicit hostility by the citizenry to any neo-imperialist designs.

One could try to define the substance of the current Russian polity by using a variety of concepts borrowed from the arsenal of comparative political theory. To me, the closest such definition would be an elective oligarchy—according to Robert Dahl's well-known scale of identification of political regimes,[7] it would come closest to an odd combination of hegemonic political institutions trying to assert themselves over an increasingly polyarchic sociopolitical reality. Whatever theoretical definition one would, however, care to apply, the basic point behind any of them would be the plain fact that the current Russian polity, despite or in spite of all changes that affected it during the last decade, still remains the "clumsy, unintelligent monster called the traditional Russian state." According to the author of these words, Sergei Kovalev, who after Andrei Sakharov's death rightfully inherited the title of the living conscience of Russia, this traditional Russian state . . . "is inherently incapable of properly evaluating situations because it feeds off myths alone and in some sense is a myth itself. It cannot live without using force, because its essence is deified, impersonal power divorced from the power of society. The Russian state does not know how to resolve problems bloodlessly, for blood is its favorite food. Moreover, it does not really know how to resolve problems at all. It only knows how to create them."[8]

Hence, according to Kovalev and other like-minded true Russian democrats, for their country to turn into a fully trusted member of the international political community and to be accepted as such, first and foremost, by her immediate neighbors, Russia has finally to overcome the traditional "mythological" essence of her statehood by establishing full-blooded democratic rule. I would venture, in addition, that this task could only be achieved if, at last, Russia also managed to assume the identity of a proper nation-state, as opposed to that of an abstract geopolitical entity that does not know any national boundaries and therefore seeks imperially to extend itself to whatever borders its rulers deem to be consistent with their current external goals. And the accomplishment of this task would also have to start within the present Russian Federation which, by having accorded equal status of a federated unit to a Russian region and to a non-Russian republic (and in some cases even subordinating non-Russian national autonomies to Russian regions), has so far been unable equitably to sort out the relationship between the Russian nation and the non-Russian nations within the Russian union-state itself.

NATO's extension to the western Russian borders, far from compromising these tasks, would greatly—and, I would even say, decisively—assist Russia in their achievement. The Russian leadership and every significant section of Russia's present political elite, including even the Zyuganovites, is—the rhetoric to the contrary notwithstanding—vitally interested in a cooperative relationship with the West. They all are more than aware that if Russia is to have a standing chance to recover from the devastation of seventy-odd years long communist plague, this chance could only be realized with the West's assistance and through its goodwill. When Boris Yeltsin threatens fundamentally to reconsider Russia's relationship with the West in the case of Western noncompliance with some of his demands, he, of course, is simply bluffing (though, as shown above, not only Clinton and his coleaders in NATO are prone to take his bait but even some respectable academic analysts are susceptible to doing so, too). In fact, Yeltsin (or, for that matter, anyone else in his place) would have no choice but to adjust to any conceivable western "affront," as he has adjusted to the present enlargement of NATO, in spite of calling it at the same time the greatest mistake the United States has made since the beginning of Cold War and, moreover—a blunder that brought U.S.–Russian relations to the lowest point since the 1962 Cuban Missile Crisis (what a perfectly unmistakable Soviet confrontational logic!). This reality of official Russia's attitude to the West gives, by the way, a lie to the prolific arguments about NATO's inability and unwillingness to fight Russia for Riga or Kiev. As in the period of the Cold War NATO's deterrent effect was strong enough to prevent the outbreak of open fighting along the then East–West divide, so would it be equally, if not much more, effective now in preventing the fight flaring up on Russia's western borders. The situation may, however, become entirely different if Ukraine and the Baltic States were left for a substantial period of time in the by now notorious "gray zone."

Thus, with NATO's defensive shield extended to Russia's western frontier, Russia would, willy-nilly, have to accept the fact that there is no space anymore left for her imperial expansion beyond that frontier and, consequently, start seriously reconsidering the essence of Russia's statehood itself. Being put in this way into NATO's strict corset, Russia's traditionally-minded, statist-oriented political elites (e.g., Yeltsin and his associates) may even arrive at the conclusion that it is, after all, necessary for Russia to get into the gear of transforming herself into a proper nation-state and to begin building into the Russian state system genuinely democratic institutions. NATO's very proximity to Russia, having empirically proved that it contains neither danger nor threat, could thus in itself become a potent stimulus for Russia's democratic change.

The above was also to say that I consider the extension of NATO's protective shield to Russia's western frontier to be an act working not only in the security interests of the post-Communist states of Central and Eastern Europe, but also one that in the long run would strongly enhance vital national interests of Russia herself. There are many Russian politicians who are very much aware of the positive impact NATO's expansion may have on Russia and who do not shy away from publicly stating their position on that issue. Beside Sergei Kovalev, Galina Starovoitova, Konstantin Borovoy, Irina

Khakamada, Valeriy Borshchov, Lev Ponomarev, Anatoliy Shabad, to name but a few, took such a pro-NATO stance in an unhesitant and straightforward manner. Even the avowedly nationalistic general-turned-politician, Aleksandr Lebed, never fails to state that he does not see any danger accumulating for Russia because of NATO's eastward expansion. I know of many more prominent Russian political figures who fully share this view, too, but because of their proximity to the Yeltsin administration avoid expressing it publicly. Very typical in this respect is the case of Yeltsin's former Foreign Minister Andrey Kozyrev. As minister, he strictly followed Yeltsin's line, threatening, together with his boss, to bring about, in case of NATO's enlargement, the notorious Cold Peace that was supposed to become the modern substitute for Cold War; he also staunchly defended his government's actions in Chechnya and elsewhere in the world. Even in private discussions with his friend, the above quoted Sergei Kovalev, he would press on with the same officialdom supporting arguments.[9] Now, a mere deputy of the state Duma, Kozyrev is Russia's most outspoken partisan of NATO's enlargement. Stating so openly their views, the pro-NATO Russian politicians are obviously not afraid of provoking against themselves the wrath of their electors which, bearing in mind the data of public opinion polls cited above, is not at all surprising. This is to say that NATO's expansion, if consistently pursued and properly explained, could eventually win strong support among quite large sections of the Russian population, which would be able readily to find spokesmen and representatives among some prominent members of Russia's extant political elite.

Among many other available arguments in favor of NATO's "expansion beside enlargement," I would like to bring up, in conclusion, only one more. If NATO's article 5 security guarantees were extended to the Ukraine and the Baltic States, their nervousness about Russia and her potential imperial intentions would be effectively dissipated. Under NATO's protective umbrella, these states would happily abandon the many reservations that now prevent them from wholeheartedly engaging with Russia a variety of mutually beneficial joint ventures and quickly start developing between themselves and Russia a system of close cooperation based on mutual interests, respect, and trust. In due course, a reliable foundation for the establishment between Russia and her immediate western neighbors of not merely a cooperative but of a truly friendly relationship could thus be built up. And what could be a better guarantee of lasting peace in the area than such a voluntarily evolved friendly cooperation between neighbor-states? At present, however, within the context of the controversies about the extent and limits of NATO's enlargement, an opposite tendency—that of growing mutual suspicions, tensions, and recriminations—is gathering momentum.

Regional cooperation that the Baltic States, immediately after having become independent, started fostering among themselves and with other newly independent states on the former western rim of the Soviet Union is now getting increasingly aimed at the creation of a defensive alliance stretching all the way from the Baltic to the Black Sea. With Lukashenka's accession to power, this endeavor, insofar as the participation in it of Belarus was concerned, came, however, to naught and, for it to be rescued and proceeded with further, Poland had to be actively involved in the process of its gradual formation. In the fulfillment of this task Lithuania has taken upon itself the role of the prime mover. During 1996–1997, Poland and Lithuania have started creating a series of joint state institutions that together are supposed to bring about a close union of the two states. The first such institution to come into being was the Polish–Lithuanian Parliamentary Assembly in which forty legislators—twenty members delegated by the parliament of each participant state—took seats. The next to be instituted was the presidential council, and the joint Polish–Lithuanian military unit, the Litpolbat, followed suit. On July 16, 1997, the Lithuanian governmental delegation in Warsaw started negotiations with its Polish counterparts on realizing the agreement reached by the two prime-ministers, Wlodzimierz Cimoszewicz and Gediminas Vagnorius, in the beginning of 1997 about establishing a Polish–Lithuanian governmental council under the joint chairmanship of the two heads of governments. The head start for Poland's involvement into a wider, "Baltic–Black Sea," regional alliance was then given by the first meeting of the five presidents—those of the three Baltic States, Poland's Alexander Kwasniewski and the Ukraine's Leonid Kuchma—which took place in May 1997 in Estonia's capital, Tallinn. It was decided there that the participant countries should hold regular consultations, strengthen cooperation between themselves in all spheres of mutual interest, and call another summit meeting in September (one has to remember that by September the U.S.–Baltic Charter will be ready for signing), inviting to it also the president of Finland.

Since Poland is soon to become a full-fledged member of NATO and in this capacity, if attacked, would be able to bring to her defense the whole of the Alliance's military force, her participation in such regional arrangements, especially if they evolved into a real defensive alliance, may prove to be of enormous significance. After all, Yugoslavia formally has never been a member of NATO, but because of her military cooperation treaties with NATO members Greece and Turkey, she was treated as a de facto member protected by the article 5 guarantees. It may be that what Greece and Turkey did for Yugoslavia, Poland could do for the Ukraine and the Baltic States.

Be that as it may, in the present situation the Ukraine and the Baltic States are bound to do everything in their power to strengthen their military cooperation with the view of making themselves optimally able to withstand together whatever steps Russia may take against them. These efforts would, no doubt, displease Russia and make her take certain countermeasures aimed at undermining the cooperative efforts undertaken by her western neighbors. All these inevitably unpleasant developments could, however, be effectively avoided by taking the Ukraine and the Baltic States directly under NATO's protective umbrella.

This is my case for suggesting that NATO's first priority is to expand by way of extending, on the basis of bilateral arrangements, the Alliance's security guarantees under the provisions of article 5 of the treaty to any state to the west of Russia wishing to accept them, and that this expansion is to be put into motion separately from, and ahead of, the process of NATO's enlargement. I also suggest that both these initiatives—expansion and enlargement—are to proceed without seeking Russia's consent or acquiescence, as there is nothing in them that may injure or otherwise adversely affect Russia's legitimate interests. These legitimate interests, far from being ignored or neglected by NATO, are, on the contrary, to be put at the center of its attention—in the process of expanding and enlarging itself, NATO is to do everything in its power to firmly and unequivocally defend and promote Russia's legitimate interests in the areas coming under NATO's protection. The soothing manner in which NATO treats Russia today, by fortifying her ostensible contentions about the hostility of NATO's very move eastward, is in fact profoundly detrimental to Russia. Instead of helping Russia to evolve into a civilized and cooperative political entity, ready to get organically integrated with the western world, it actually freezes the artificial confrontational stage Russia has set up for the purpose of endlessly playing the zero-sum game between herself and the West. And in this sense such Western attitudes to Russia greatly obstruct her ability to move in the direction of getting thoroughly and irreversibly "Europeanized."

Finally, I suggest that in following the line of honoring and promoting Russia's legitimate interests, NATO is fully to include Russia in the Euro-Atlantic collective security system that it is currently building up. In this endeavor Russia is indeed to be treated as NATO's most important partner, that is in the manner prescribed by the provisions establishing the PfP and the Permanent Joint Council. By actively engaging Russia in cooperation within that functional framework, NATO would be opening to her yet another important channel for integration into Europe and the western world. One is not to mix, however, apples with oranges—Russia's major engagement into one aspect of NATO's activities does not at all entail her inclusion, or getting any kind of say in, the spheres related to the rest of NATO's functions, chiefly those concerned with security matters of its members and partners. Russia's ill conceived contentions about NATO being a threat to her interests could only be further boosted up by NATO's conceding to her demands to have a voice in these matters, too.

NOTES

1. See *The New York Times*, March 26, 1997.

2. See *The Los Angeles Times*, April 16, 1997.

3. See a number of his recent articles in various media outlets, i.e., "The Dilution of NATO," in *Washington Post*, June 8, 1997.

4. See RFE/RL *Newsline*, no. 72, parts 1 and 2, July 14, 1997.

5. See *Nezavisimoe Voennoe Obozrenie*, June 7–13, 1997, where the results of the two opinion polls conducted by Galop International and the Russian Public Opinion and Market Research Institute were analyzed.

6. See *BNS* (Baltic News Service) *Report*, "In Contrast with the Kremlin Leaders, the Russian Population Does Not Object to Lithuania's Membership of NATO," published by the foremost Lithuanian daily, *Lietuvos Rytas*, March 20, 1997.

7. See Robert Dahl, *Polyarchy: Participation and Opposition* (New Haven, Conn.: Yale University Press, 1971), especially 1–17, where the conceptual framework is laid out.

8. See Sergei Kovalev, "Russia After Chechnya," in *The New York Review of Books*, vol. 44, no. 12, July 17, 1997, p. 28.

9. For a witness account of a private conversation on this subject between Kozyrev and Kovalev, see Charles Gati, "Who's Right on Chechnya? A Conversation at the Kozyrevs'," in *The New York Times*, January 29, 1995.

IV

THE BALTIC PENDULUM

Shtromas was not the usual practitioner of Soviet studies, and his unconventional outlook was rooted in his own experience in Lithuania. He had witnessed firsthand the great political-ideological conflicts of the twentieth century played out on Baltic ground. The three next chapters are devoted to the Baltic States, and they are perhaps the best illustrations of the extraordinary insight that Shtromas often brought to Soviet studies.

In "The Soviet Method of Conquest of the Baltic States," Shtromas chides western policy-makers and scholars for misinterpreting Soviet expansion as that of a traditional great power. He explains the peculiar process of Sovietization among the Balts. First, the USSR obtained diplomatically formal guarantees or informal assurances of noninterference by other states. Next, it instigated a crisis in the targeted country in order to introduce military forces and to obtain political concessions. And finally, it assigned veteran party cadres to positions of power in order to secure Moscow's preeminence. Shtromas drives the lesson home. He compares the successful incorporation of the Baltic states with Soviet failure in Finland, where Stalin had to curb his ambition in the face of aroused indignation in the West and determined resistance from the Finns.

In "The Baltic States as Soviet Republics: Tensions and Contradictions," Shtromas takes up the internal dynamics of Sovietization. A "divide and conquer" strategy was employed, whereby social cleavages are exploited through the selective application of reward and coercion. Shtromas then shows the shallowness of such a foundation: resistance grew in dissidence; service degenerated into careerism; acceptance became little more than compliance. In "How Political are the Social Movements in the Baltics?" Shtromas describes the ways, during Gorbachev's tenure, that national identity ultimately prevailed over Soviet power. A configuration of forces infused the Baltic opposition movements: the anticommunist politics of dissidents, the within-system politics of conservationists, and the survivalist politics of native communists. In showing that it was a common foe that unified these loosely aligned forces, Shtromas impressively anticipates the contours of the multiparty systems that would soon characterize post-Communist politics in the Baltic states.

12

The Soviet Method of Conquest of the Baltic States: Lessons for the West

ALEKSANDRAS SHTROMAS

THE ROLE OF IDEOLOGY IN SOVIET CONQUEST

Most Western historians agree that the Baltic issue played an important role in shaping the alliances of World War II. In their view, it was Britain's reluctance to grant the Soviets a free hand in their dealings with the Baltic States that precipitated the breakdown of British–Soviet talks in the summer of 1939 and led Stalin to conclude the notorious Nonaggression Treaty with Germany, which in this respect was much more compliant with Soviet demands than Britain or France. "For all practical purposes," writes D. M. Crowe, Jr., "The Baltic question ended any hope for a strong British-Soviet front against Hitler."[1] D. Kirby also implies that the Nonaggression Treaty with Germany was concluded by the Soviet Union, in preference to a pact with Britain and France, because "the British and French negotiators showed little enthusiasm for the Soviet plan . . . but the Germans emphasized their readiness to adopt a benevolent attitude towards vital Soviet interests in the Baltic area."[2]

No one can deny that the Baltic issue played a certain role in Stalin's choice of sides in the growing conflict between Nazi Germany and the Allied

Reprinted from Aleksandras Shtromas, *The Soviet Method of Conquest of the Baltic States: Lessons for the West* (Washington, D.C.: Washington Institute for Values in Public Policy, 1986), 1–43.

Powers. However, one should not exaggerate it. There is very little doubt that in the aftermath of Munich and the fall of Czechoslovakia Stalin had already dismissed the possibility of an alliance with the Allied Powers against Hitler and took a firm course toward forging an alliance with the latter, which for him was now the surest way not only to stay out of war but, even more importantly, to precipitate the outbreak of war between the major anti-Soviet powers of the world (and what could be a happier event than such a war for any Soviet leader, let alone Stalin?). The negotiations with the British and French were therefore conducted by Stalin mainly in order to induce Hitler to raise the stakes (for example, concede to the USSR the Baltic states) for Stalin's agreement to conclude the pact with Germany, in preference to the one with Britain and France, but not in any serious way that could have really brought about an anti-Hitler coalition treaty between the Soviet Union and Britain and France.

In this respect, it is worthwhile to remember that Hitler was not entirely forthcoming in meeting all Stalin's demands concerning, if one uses D. Kirby's expression, "vital Soviet interests in the Baltic area." According to the Secret Additional Protocol to the Treaty of Nonaggression Between Germany and the USSR of August 23, 1939,[3] the "northern boundary of Lithuania shall represent the boundary of the spheres of influence of Germany and the USSR,"[4] which meant that Finland, Estonia, and Latvia were thus assigned to the Soviet Union, whereas Lithuania had to fall to the German "sphere of influence." Only after many deliberations was this agreement changed by the Secret Additional Protocol to the German Soviet Boundary and Friendship Treaty signed on September 28, 1939.[5] According to the protocol, the Soviet Union got hold also of Lithuania[6] in exchange for conceding to Germany the province of Lublin and some parts of the province of Warsaw in Poland, which had been assigned to the USSR by the earlier Soviet-German Secret Additional Protocol to the Nonaggression Treaty of August 23, 1939.

Some historians, especially the Lithuanian émigré ones, believe that since the Polish territories given by Stalin to Hitler for Lithuania were by no means of an equivalent value, Hitler agreed to that trade-off only because of Lithuania's blunt refusal of his demand to attack Poland simultaneously with Germany and to regain by so doing Lithuania's Polish-occupied (in 1920) capital Vilnius, together with substantial territory of the Vilnius region.[7] In their view, President Smetona's noncompliance with Germany's demands made Lithuania of not much use to Hitler, and he was happy to give it to Stalin for anything, thus punishing Lithuania for her anti-German attitude.

This, I believe, is another historical misconception of the events that took place during the preparation and outbreak of World War II. In fact, Hitler rejected every approach by Stalin about conceding Lithuania to the USSR after, as much as before, Lithuania's refusal to be a party to Germany's aggression against Poland. Hence, Lithuania's position made no difference in Hitler's attitude to its fate.

Only when on September 25, 1939, Stalin finally agreed to undersign the liquidation of the "independent Polish rump-state,"[8] did Hitler, in exchange, waive his claim to Lithuania, conceding it to Stalin for the Polish territories that now, together with the rest of ethnic Poland, had been permanently assigned to the German Reich. Thus, the exchange of Lithuania for the Polish territories, under these new circumstances, was for Hitler a tremendous gain that he certainly would not have allowed to pass by him even in the event of Lithuania's total compliance with every German demand. This means that Lithuania's fate was sealed by events and deals beyond its control, and there was nothing it could have done to change this fate.

These and other "partial" historical misconceptions are rooted in the Western overall misconception of the nature of ideological powers and their international behavior. By instinctively ascribing to those powers traditional imperialist motivations and dismissing the ideological ones as practically irrelevant facade, most Western historians usually end up missing the wood for the trees and thus getting most of their interpretations of the otherwise extremely well-researched and thoroughly collated facts entirely wrong. It is in a sense a dogmatic blindness. For most of these historians are virtual prisoners of their own pragmatic political philosophy, which requires them to assess all historical facts and circumstances under their scrutiny according to one narrow analytical framework of expedient power interests, and strictly prohibits any trespasses into different frames of reference. Hence, their interpretative horizon is by definition extremely limited. It does not stretch beyond territorial gains, security deals, economic advantages, strategic positions, and their likes. All facts have to be assessed exclusively against these criteria whether they fit them or not. There are simply no other relevant criteria and there should not be any.

Within that particular frame of reference the interpretation of the Nazi–Soviet Alliance is doomed to be limited to either that of Crowe's and Kirby's emphasizing the Soviet desire for territorial gain or to that of some others who without denying that desire stress the overriding importance for the USSR to go, in the face of a German threat, for the best security deal on offer. The originator of that latter interpretation was not a mere historian but Winston Churchill himself. In his broadcast of October 1, 1939, he explained that the USSR had to enter into the pact with Nazi Germany in order to be able to build up its line of defense against a potential German aggression, the future "eastern front," as far to the west as possible.[9] After the war, when he should have known better already, he repeated this thesis. In his *War Memoirs*, Churchill wrote:

> On the Soviet side it must be said that their vital need was to hold the deployment positions of the German armies as far to the west as possible, so as to give the Russians more time for assembling their forces from all parts of their immense empire. . . . They must be in occupation of the Baltic States and a large part of Poland by force or fraud before they were attacked. If their policy was cold-blooded, it was also at the moment realistic in a high degree.[10]

The consistent misinterpretation of the motives of Soviet behavior in 1939 by a man of Churchill's caliber and status should, however, not surprise us too much, for the statesmen learn about politics from no other sources than the books of historians whereas the historians get their inspirations from the speeches and deeds of leading statesmen. It is therefore only natural for both to think about the present in terms that firmly belong to the traditions of the long-gone past.

That Stalin, upon whom the decision about the outbreak of World War II ultimately rested, sought an alliance with Hitler for the specific purpose of unleashing that war is an idea so alien to the Western "mainstream" histori- ans and policy-makers that they find it very difficult to swallow. It simply does not make sense to them. From their pragmatically biased point of view, a power that is on the defensive and whose national security is threatened by a more powerful and dynamic neighbor simply cannot afford to entertain such grand and, no doubt, dangerous plans. It is therefore axiomatically ob- vious to them that war "was not the intention of Soviet policy" and that "the events of September 1 and September 3 could not be foreseen on August 23"[11]—obvious, in spite of the plain fact that on August 23, it was not simply foreseen but explicitly decided that the events of September 1 should actu- ally take place[12] and that it was hardly possible for anyone to overlook or ig- nore the possibility, or rather certainty, of the September 3 Anglo-French re- action to these events. After all, British and French guarantees were given to Poland in March 1939, not by any secret additional protocols, but publicly and in a binding manner.

The mainstream Western historians of World War II know these facts very well indeed but nevertheless continue to insist upon their view that if only the Western powers had been less "dilatory and half-hearted," more willing "to concede Stalin's exacting conditions, especially a free hand in the Baltic states,"[13] the Nazi–Soviet Pact would have never been concluded. Alas, the Western powers were not sufficiently forthcoming in meeting Soviet demands and in these circumstances "it is difficult to see what other course Soviet Rus- sia could have followed."[14] The attempts at exonerating Stalin and laying the full responsibility for his concluding the pact with Hitler at the doorstep of Britain and France were again authoritatively exacerbated by Churchill who, in tune with the leading Western historians of World War II, stated that the fact that the 1939 Nazi–Soviet agreement was made "marks the culminating fail- ure of British and French foreign policy and diplomacy over several years."[15]

The dogmatic blindness of Western pragmatists, be they scholars or politi- cians, is best exemplified by the above utterances. Stalin's acceptance of an alliance with Hitler is to them in itself sufficient evidence that Hitler had of- fered Stalin a better security deal than the Allied Powers and that it is the fault of the latter that they did not come up with something that would have out- matched Hitler's bid. But this is simply and blatantly untrue. If one can free himself of dogmatic assumptions and examine the facts on their own merit, one will inevitably arrive at the obvious conclusion that the anti-Hitler coalition with Britain and France was for the USSR an incomparably better security arrangement than anything that a Nazi–Soviet alliance could have offered. For whatever the deficiencies of the concrete terms of such a coalition were, it would have certainly kept Hitler out of Poland, far removed from the Soviet Union's frontiers, and this, together with French and British guarantees of the USSR's security against German aggression, would have made Hitler's attack against the Soviet Union, as well as World War II in general, virtually impossible.

Actually, Stalin was actively and genuinely striving for exactly such an arrangement when during the mid-1930s he used all means in his power to get the Allied Powers to agree to a collective security deal with the USSR. At that time he feared, and one must admit that this fear was not entirely unjustified, that the Allied Powers would do nothing to stop Hitler from attacking one East European country after another, which would enable him in the end to launch an attack against the USSR and eliminate it as a "fortress of communism." But as soon as this situation changed, as soon as in the Soviet view it became realistically probable that the growing conflict between the Allied Powers and Nazi Germany might result in a war between them (the likelihood of such a turn of events was already realized by the Soviets in the aftermath of Munich in late autumn 1938, when Hitler began to neglect and violate the agreements that he and the Allied Powers had signed there), the Soviet interest in "collective security" vanished without trace. Now the worldwide cause of communism was best served by the USSR encouraging Hitler's expansionism to an extent that would indeed provoke a full-scale war between Germany and the Allied Powers. And the USSR, without hesitation, embarked on that "war-provoking" course, a course that promised to pry wide open the gates for the expansion of communism into Europe. This was a unique—though in narrow terms of national security an extremely risky chance for a decisive advancement of communism, and the Communist rulers of the Soviet Union could not allow this chance to pass by them. All reasons, such as the USSR's national interest, that could deter them from taking up this chance were of minor importance and had to be rejected.

To be sure, the Soviets still continued to pretend that their interest in a "collective security" deal with the West remained unaltered. The pretence enabled them on the one hand to keep Hitler constantly anxious about the real intentions of the USSR and thus to exact from him the highest possible price for the conclusion of the German–Soviet pact. On the other hand it made it possible for the Soviets to instill in the Allied Powers a false sense of security that kept Britain and France unprepared for the war until it actually broke out. As we see, Stalin's ruse worked pretty well on both accounts. Neither Hitler nor the Allied Powers had a good enough grasp of Soviet politics rightly to guess what Stalin was really after, and they did unwittingly fall into the trap that he had so skilfully set for them.

When Alain Besançon said that the "failure to understand the Soviet régime is the principal cause of its successes,"[16] he no doubt meant, among other instances confirming that maxim, also the Soviet success of 1939, which enabled Stalin to unleash World War II and at the same time instantaneously to extend Communist rule to a few countries to the west of the Soviet Union's 1939 frontier.

However, in terms of protecting the USSR's national security, this was no success at all. In these terms it was rather a disaster. For by unleashing World War II Stalin made it possible for Hitler to visit that war later on the USSR, which in 1941 he really did, causing the Soviet Union so much damage that in physical and material terms this country became that war's main victim. But in terms of expanding and consolidating Communist rule in the world, Stalin's policy was indeed an unqualified success, and, as far as the Soviet rulers were concerned, this was the only success that really mattered. After all, for the sake of the success of the Communist cause in Russia, Stalin has killed scores of millions of Russian people, and in this and other respects inflicted on Russia much more damage than Hitler and his whole war machine ever did.

This is perhaps the most important lesson that we can and at last should learn from the Nazi–Soviet alliance and the USSR's role in causing World War II. This lesson clearly teaches us never to mistake the USSR for a normal nation-state that in its own, maybe over-rapacious and under-civilized, way pursues what it regards to be best for Russia's national interests. The Soviet Union, as Charles Bohlen once succinctly remarked, is not a country but a cause. Indeed, it is the cause determined by the globally-conceived communist ideology that the party clique in charge of the USSR will pursue under all circumstances and, if necessary, at the expense of Russia's national interests, including also those of her national security.

To be sure, the interest of advancing the Communist cause and the Soviet national interest are not always mutually exclusive; sometimes they may entirely coincide as they coincided in the mid-1930s, when, as was mentioned above, Stalin was genuinely striving for a collective security deal with the Allied Powers. After all, the might of the Soviet ruling clique depends on the might of the country and people this clique rules. But if these sets of interests clash, as they do in most cases, including that of the Nazi–Soviet alliance, then the ideological interests will invariably take precedence over the national ones.

This is the key to understanding Soviet policy and thus the key to avoiding not only the historical misconceptions of Soviet political behavior but, more importantly, the fatal mistakes in Western conduct of East–West relations, mistakes such as the Moscow negotiations of summer 1939, the Yalta and Potsdam agreements of 1945, and a whole range of others where similar attempts at accommodating the Soviet Union were undertaken under the false assumption of its being just another nation-state that, in its own, rather peculiar manner, is fully committed to the defense and advancement of its national interests. The Soviet Union always was and always will be, as long as it remains a communist state, first and foremost an ideological power whose rulers have at heart only one single interest, that of Communist domination, not only over Russia and its vicinities, but over the entire world. Even when on the defensive, even when directly attacked in 1941 by Hitler, the Soviet rulers, be they Lenin, Stalin, or Gorbachev, have done and will always do their utmost to achieve the ultimate goal of Communist world control. As for Russia's national interests, they will always be strictly subordinated by the Soviet rulers to this particular goal and seen as valid and worth defending only insofar as they faithfully serve this goal.

This is perhaps the most general lesson to be drawn from the Nazi–Soviet alliance, the one providing the widest framework for the correct interpretation of all aspects of Soviet politics without exception. The fate of the Baltic states, which we are about to start examining, contains some other lessons that may be less general but that provide more practical guidance on how the West has to deal with the Soviets in the day-to-day relationship of peaceful coexistence with them on the same planet.

INITIAL STAGES OF BALTIC CONQUEST

Even before the second (September 28) Secret Additional Protocol was signed (and thus the fate of Lithuania sealed), the Soviet Union had started to take energetic measures aimed at establishing its rule in the Baltic states. After having decided upon what the tactical master plan for their takeover should be, the Soviet Union had chosen Estonia as its first target. The escape of a Polish submarine from internment in the harbour of Estonia's capital, Tallinn, was used by the Soviet government as a pretext for starting the action. The submarine had escaped on September 18, 1939, and already on the following day Molotov summoned the Estonian Ambassador to Moscow informing him that, since the Estonian government was unable to protect its coastline and territorial waters, the Soviet Baltic Fleet was from then on to undertake this task.[17]

A week later, on September 25, 1939, Molotov presented the Estonian government with an ultimatum demanding the immediate conclusion of a Soviet–Estonian military alliance providing for the establishment of Soviet military bases on Estonian territory. If Estonia refused to comply, Molotov warned, the Soviet Union would have no choice but to use military force against her, which, to be sure, was massively (about 250,000 men equipped with artillery, tanks, and planes) concentrated from mid-September along the Soviet–Estonian border (on top of the naval blockade of the Estonian coastline). Molotov made clear also that in the present circumstances Estonia could not count on any aid either from Germany or from the Allied Powers and, when the Estonian government established that this was indeed the case, it agreed, though reluctantly, to sign the proposed treaty. The Soviet–Estonian Mutual Assistance Treaty was signed on September 28, 1939, and the same day, Soviet troops rushed into that country to occupy the positions assigned to them in the Treaty's Supplementary Protocol (according to it, the number of Soviet troops stationed in Estonia was 25,000).

After the pattern was thus established, Latvia's turn came. Here excuses or pretexts such as the escape of the Polish submarine from Tallinn, or the sinking of a Soviet ship by a submarine off the Estonian coast, another Soviet bullying device used during the Soviet–Estonian negotiations of September 26–28, 1939, about the conclusion of the treaty, were not necessary any more. The Latvian government was forced to conclude the same sort of treaty (signed October 5, 1939) simply by the Soviets' using the Estonian precedent as a sufficient argument (substantiated by the same threats of using sheer military force against Latvia in case of her noncompliance).

Lithuania's treatment was somewhat different. In the first place, on September 26, 1939, the USSR quite politely offered to Lithuania to take over its capital city Vilnius, which the Poles had captured from Lithuania in 1920 and that now, after Poland's defeat and its (fourth) partition between Germany and the USSR, was under Soviet occupation. This offer, which was entirely consistent with the first Secret Additional Protocol to the Soviet–German Nonaggression Treaty of August 23, 1939 (it was explicitly stated in it that "the interest of Lithuania in the Vilna area is recognized by each party"[18]), was too tempting for the Lithuanian government to reject, especially since no strings were attached to it. But the situation drastically changed after Germany conceded Lithuania to the USSR. On October 2, 1939 (that is, four days after the second Secret Additional Protocol was signed between Germany and the USSR to this effect) the Soviet government presented Lithuania with a demand to sign, in exchange for Vilnius, an "Estonian-type" treaty. In the beginning the Lithuanian government resisted quite fiercely. The Soviet offer was at first rejected without much discussion, but after October 5, 1939, when Latvia finally ceded to Soviet pressure, signing such a treaty with the USSR and, moreover, when the Red Army concentrated a massive force in the Vilnius area and now also in Latvia, ready for a military attack on Lithuania from the east and the north, the Lithuanian government found that it had no choice but also to yield, like Estonia and Latvia, to Soviet demands: On October 10, 1939, the Soviet–Lithuanian Mutual Assistance Treaty, the last in the series, was signed in the Kremlin; and in a few days Soviet troops had taken over the bases established on Lithuanian territory according to this treaty.

The second stage in the process of Sovietization of the Baltic states was, however, delayed for more than half a year because Finland, in contrast to its southern neighbors, did not bow to Soviet demands. After having exhausted their patience in trying during the period between October 7 and November 13, 1939, to persuade the intransigent Finns to give in by voluntarily following the example of other Baltic states, the Soviets decided to use military force against Finland. On November 30, 1939, after a heated exchange of memoranda and notes between the USSR and Finland, the Soviet Union launched a military attack against Finland, thus starting the infamous Winter War.

Surprisingly, Finland proved to be not an easy prey for the overwhelmingly superior Soviet forces. The Soviet advance was effectively stopped by the Finns for several months at the Mannerheim Line, and the Winter War became a protracted affair. The utmost concentration of Soviet military might against Finland, standing on its own, appeared to be necessary for the war to be at least half-won by the Soviet Union. And it was only half-won indeed. The Soviets failed to impose on Finland the "people's government" of Otto Kuusinen, which they had formed (the same day Finland was attacked) in Terioki, the first town they occupied on Finnish territory; and instead the Soviets were forced to agree to sign a peace treaty with the same "bourgeois" (usually called "white" by the Soviet media) Finnish government that they fought with the intention of destroying it.

According to this peace treaty signed on March 12, 1940, the Soviet Union gained a certain part of the eastern and southeastern (the Karelian isthmus) Finnish territory but no real foothold in Finland itself (except for the Hango Peninsula, which the USSR got from Finland on a thirty years' lease). The Soviet leaders had to be content with the conversion of the Karelian ASSR (originally a part of the RSFSR), to which the newly acquired Finnish eastern territories were added, into a new union-republic, the Karelian-Finnish SSR. This new union-republic was supposed to serve as the basis for the incorporation into the USSR of the rest of Finland at some time in the future, but somehow this future never materialized.[19]

There was nothing unusual or new in the 1939 Soviet behavior toward the Baltic states. As on all previous occasions when the Soviets were prepared to go or actually went to war, they ensured beforehand that the war they were about to wage was an entirely "safe war," that is, a war that would not expose their system of rule in the USSR to any risks and that they could not lose too badly. For the war to be thus safe it was not enough to wage it against a minor and weak nation; one had to make sure that no major power would come to the rescue or defense of this nation. And it was a consistent pattern of Soviet policy to ensure that the nation they were about to attack was going to stand against them alone. When, for example, the Soviets attacked Georgia in 1921, they had received in advance an assurance from the then British Prime Minister, David Lloyd George, that Britain, the only real military and political presence in that area of the Middle East, was not going to interfere with their conquest of that country. Now, similarly, before taking any aggressive action against the Baltic states, the Soviets made sure that Hitler would give them a free hand in that area.

The Soviets deemed Hitler's permission for them to take over the Baltic states an entirely sufficient guarantee of the safety of that enterprise, because in their view the Allied Powers were not in a position to interfere with Soviet plans in any substantial way. Britain and France were already at war with Germany and had no direct access to the Baltic area anyway. In this respect, however, at least insofar as Finland was concerned, the Soviets proved to be wrong. The reaction of the Allied Powers to Soviet unprovoked aggression against Finland was very strong, determined, and even practical. Britain and France immediately started organizing an expeditionary corps to be sent to Finland and they found for the corps a direct access route to the battle via their ally, Norway. According to Churchill, the French were to send 50,000 "volunteers" and 100 bombers and the British a proportionate force.[20] Unexpectedly, the United States reacted very strongly too. The Americans not only unequivocally condemned the Soviet aggression but extended their unrestrained support for Finland's "glorious battle for independence and freedom." To crown it all, the League of Nations solemnly expelled the Soviet Union for its aggression against Finland.

The Winter War the Soviets had waged against Finland was not sufficiently safe anymore, and characteristically the Soviets immediately backed down on their original plan of conquering Finland and imposing upon her a communist government of their own making. Now they were happy to sign a peace treaty with the "white" Finns and limit their complete military victory over them to a token victory in political terms.

The memories of 1939–1940 have most certainly deterred the Soviets from applying to Finland, after she had suffered at Soviet hands her second military defeat in 1945, the treatment that no other country in the eastern part of Europe has managed to escape. Although "Finlandized," Finland has remained a liberal democracy and has never been turned into a client state of the USSR.

Two major lessons are to be drawn from this experience: first, that the Soviets will never start a risky war and, hence, as long as the West remains strong and determined to fight against or otherwise effectively counter Soviet aggression, the USSR will have no choice but to adhere to the principles of peaceful coexistence with the West; and second, that no nation, however small and weak, should ever give in to Soviet blackmail and threats even when standing alone against that giant power. Estonia, Latvia, and Lithuania lost their independence because they were intimidated into complying with Soviet demands; Finland, on the contrary, won her right to remain free because she refused to comply and, when attacked for noncompliance, bravely put up a vigorous fight against the Soviet aggressor. It was this fight that earned Finland such a determined and massive support of the nations of the free world, which even the Soviets were unable to ignore.

That it pays off to take an intransigent stand against Soviet aggressive acts was proved not only by Finland's Mannerheim in 1939–1940, but also by Yugoslavia's Tito in 1948. It was also proved during the Soviet-imposed blockade of Berlin in 1948–1949, and the Cuban missile crisis in 1962, the two most outstanding among the rare instances where the United States took an intransigent stance toward Soviet aggressive moves. And who knows what the Soviet empire would be like today if Hungary's Imre Nagy in 1956 and Czechoslovakia's Alexander Dubcek in 1968 had been as intransigent and determined to resist the Soviets as were Mannerheim and Tito during their time of trial.

There is, however, yet another lesson for the Western Alliance to learn from this experience: Action against any Soviet aggression, in order to be successful, must be taken timely, that is, as soon as a legitimate government of a country is subverted by the Soviets with the view of installing instead a stooge government chosen and supported by them. It was rather foolish, at least from the Soviet point of view, for the West and the Third World to start protesting about Afghanistan only after the Soviet military force was introduced into that country in December 1979, when those nations had remained completely silent in April 1978, when the real Soviet takeover in Afghanistan took place. After Afghanistan had been so compliantly conceded to them by the rest of the world, the Soviets felt that it was entirely proper for them to bring in troops to consolidate their grip on power over that country. The Soviet-installed but internationally recognized puppet government of Afghanistan was perhaps interested in the Soviet military presence in the country more than the Soviet Union itself; after all it was this "legitimate" government that called upon the Soviet Union to bring its troops in. It knew that without the Soviets it would be unable to retain power and the positions of privilege that go with it.

The situation in Afghanistan might have been entirely different if the West had refused to recognize as legitimate the government of Taraki and subsequently that of Amin, and if they had consistently followed through all the consequences that go with nonrecognition. In that situation the Soviets would have thought twice before sending their troops to Afghanistan and most likely would not have dared to do so. And without their presence the Communist regime in Afghanistan would have probably crumbled very soon without a protracted civil war and all the hardship that ensued as its consequence. Amin would have then been remembered as the last Soviet-Communist plant in Afghanistan, and no one in the world would have known of somebody called Babrak Karmal.

THE MODUS OPERANDI OF A COMMUNIST TAKEOVER

Only after the Winter War was over could the Soviet Union afford to concentrate again on its delayed plan of Sovietization of the other three Baltic states. A press campaign against the Baltic states, accusing them of harboring pro-Allied sympathies and plotting with each other behind the Soviet back with the view of undermining their alliances with the USSR, was mounted by the Soviet Union first, but already in May 1940 the Soviet government started to take practical steps aimed at the "final solution" of the Baltic problem.

This time Lithuania was chosen as the first target of the renewed Soviet attack. On May 25, 1940, Molotov summoned the Lithuanian Ambassador to Moscow and handed him a note accusing the Lithuanian authorities of kidnapping Soviet soldiers from their military bases in Lithuania and qualifying these acts as "provocative toward the Soviet Union" and fraught with "serious consequences."[21] The Soviet government demanded from the Lithuanian government "to halt such provocation actions, to take the necessary steps immediately to search for the Soviet soldiers who had disappeared and to transfer them to the military authorities of the Soviet bases in Lithuania."[22] In the conclusion of this note the Lithuanian government was warned that in the case of its noncompliance with the Soviet demands the Soviet government would be forced "to take other measures,"[23] the content of which remained threateningly unexplained.

The Lithuanian government responded to this note immediately (on May 26, 1940), and in the most compliant way, but the Soviet government remained silent. Then, on May 28, 1940, the Lithuanian government sent another message to Moscow reporting in detail about the findings of the Special Commission appointed by it to investigate the charges made by the USSR against the Lithuanian government agencies and their officials. This response this time came in a roundabout way: On May 28, 1940, the Soviet government issued an official communiqué broadcast by Moscow radio and published in the Soviet press, but the Lithuanian government still did not receive a reply addressed directly to it. The Soviet communiqué of May 28 amounted to a formal indictment of the Lithuanian government; this time it was made directly responsible not only for kidnapping soldiers but also for shooting one of them, a certain Junior Commanding Officer Butaev.[24] This "dialogue of the deaf" created such great tension and became so ominous that the Lithuanian government decided to send its prime minister, Antanas Merkys, to Moscow, in order to clarify the issues at stake in personal communication with Molotov. This proved to be of no avail either. Molotov did not want to listen to any explanations and rejected out of hand as falsified the information gathered by the Special Investigation Commission. Of course, he knew much better what was happening in Lithuania than the country's devious prime minister thought; and he was determined to make his point by lecturing and instructing him, but by no means was he prepared to listen to what he had to say. Thus Merkys learned that his minister of interior, Kazys Skucas, and the director of the Department of State Security, Augustinas Povilaitis, were the instigators of all the activities directed against the Soviet garrisons; that he himself was trying to turn the Baltic entente into an anti-Soviet alliance, and many other similar things.[25]

In desperation, the Lithuanian government sent its foreign minister, Juozas Urbsys, to Moscow to help Merkys's mission to succeed; he carried a new governmental message to Molotov and, most importantly, a personal letter from the Lithuanian President, Antanas Smetona, to the chairman of the Presidium of the Supreme Soviet of the USSR, Mikhail Kalinin. Nothing could be more reconciliatory and, one could say, even submissive, than these documents,[26] but they also failed to impress the Soviet leaders, let alone to move them even an iota. After the last session of talks with Molotov on June 11, 1940, attended by both Merkys and Urbsys, Merkys returned to Kaunas leaving his foreign minister, Urbsys, to continue with the business in Moscow on his own. The next day (June 12, 1940), an official decree was published in Kaunas dismissing the Minister of the Interior, Kazys Skucas, and the director of the Department of State Security, Augustinas Povilaitis (both of them, at Soviet request, were turned over to Moscow a few days later, and disappeared forever). These were the Lithuanian government's last desperate and, one must say, preposterous attempts to please (and appease) Moscow, to try to regain its trust of Lithuania's goodwill and by that, possibly, to avert the Soviet Union's further moves directed at finally destroying Lithuania's most precious possession—its independence and freedom.

What the Lithuanian government was unable (and probably also unwilling) to realize was the simple fact that there was nothing in its power to change Moscow's course or distract it from pursuing the master plan of Lithuania's full Sovietization. Whatever the Lithuanian government did to comply with Moscow's demands, Moscow's task was to remain totally indifferent. The prime goal on the road of Lithuania's Sovietization was the destruction of the incumbent government of that country and, in order to achieve this goal in the smoothest possible way, Moscow had to insist on the "criminal" record of this government, independently of how consistent this was with the real facts or even of how submissive to Moscow this doomed government was prepared to be. Moscow simply needed its own men to rule Lithuania; only they were to be trusted by it with the function of delivering Lithuania to the USSR in the precise way that Moscow planned for this process to take place. The old "bourgeois" leaders of Lithuania were simply unfit to fulfill this role in cahoots with Moscow and had to be removed and replaced by those who were fit.

On June 14, 1940 (the day the Germans entered Paris), just before midnight, Molotov summoned Urbsys to the Kremlin and handed him the famous (or, rather, infamous) Soviet Ultimatum to Lithuania.

The ultimatum stated that the Soviet government considered as established the fact that by the "actions taken against the Soviet troops in Lithuania"—four such actions were listed in the ultimatum, all known from previous Soviet documents—"the Lithuanian authorities tried to make unbearable the presence of Soviet troops in Lithuania."[27] Moreover, totally inconsistent with the evidence presented (in addition to the four cases mentioned above, arrests of Lithuanian citizens connected with the Soviet troops stationed in Lithuania were involved), the Soviet government considered as also established the fact "that the Lithuanian Government is wantonly violating the Treaty of Mutual Assistance concluded with the Soviet Union, and is preparing aggression against the Soviet garrisons, established in accordance with this Treaty."[28]

The second part of the ultimatum accused the Lithuanian government of having brutally violated the treaty by transforming the Baltic entente into, as the Soviet government for unclear reasons considered established, a "military alliance . . . directed against the Soviet Union."[29] For some peculiar reasons the decisive evidence for proving the anti-Soviet nature of this alliance was supposed to be the fact that "in February 1940 there was established a printed organ of this military entente, *Revue Baltique*, published in English, French and German."[30] But all these frantic inconsistencies and blatant abuses of elementary logic fade away before the conclusive, the real ultimate part of this ultimatum, which deserves to be quoted in full:

> The Soviet Government considers it necessary and urgent:
>
> 1. That the Minister of Interior, Skucas, and, the Director of the Department of Security, Povilaitis, be immediately delivered to the judicial authorities and tried as directly guilty of acts of provocation committed against the garrisons of the Soviet Union in Lithuania.
> 2. That a Government be immediately formed in Lithuania capable of assuring and determined to assure the proper fulfillment of the Treaty of Mutual Assistance between the Soviet Union and Lithuania and to suppress firmly the enemies of this Treaty.
> 3. That a free entry into the territory of Lithuania be immediately assured for units of the army of the Soviet Union which will be stationed in the most important centers of Lithuania and which will be sufficiently numerous to assure the enforcement of the Treaty of Mutual Assistance between the Soviet Union and Lithuania and to put an end to acts of provocation directed against the garrisons of the Soviet Union in Lithuania.
>
> The Soviet Government will wait for the answer of the Lithuanian Government until 10 a.m. of June 15. The failure to respond at the established time will be considered as a refusal to carry out the above mentioned demands of the Soviet Union with the responsibility for all the consequences of such refusal falling on the Lithuanian Government.[31]

The Lithuanian government, after a full night of deliberations during which it had established that no country was prepared to come to Lithuania's defense, decided that it had no choice but to accept the Soviet ultimatum, in spite of its total groundlessness and blatant illegality. At 9 a.m. on June 15, 1940, Foreign Minister Urbsys (still in Moscow but taking part in the cabinet meeting by phone) handed to Molotov, on behalf of the Lithuanian government, a brief positive reply to all Soviet demands. At 10 a.m., large contingents of the Red Army started crossing the Soviet–Lithuanian frontier and the same day occupied all of Lithuania.

The Lithuanian government resigned immediately after reaching the decision on accepting the Soviet ultimatum (before 9 a.m.), and President Smetona appointed General Stasys Rastikis as new prime minister in charge of forming the new government. Urbsys reported this decision to Molotov together with the acceptance of the ultimatum, but to his shock and surprise was told by Molotov that the choice of Rastikis was unacceptable to the Soviet Union and that the president, before appointing anybody to the prime ministerial office, had to consult first the USSR's Deputy People's Commissar of Foreign Affairs, Vladimir Dekanozov, who was now on his way to Kaunas. That was too much for President Smetona to bear. He declared that under such circumstances he had decided to reverse his decision about accepting the ultimatum and urged the cabinet to follow him in doing so officially. The cabinet, however, declined the president's suggestion. In its view, it was now too late to reject the ultimatum, since the Soviet troops were already pouring into the country, and the Lithuanian army, following its previous orders to let them in without resistance, was totally incapable of stopping them now. Smetona did not insist. Instead, he decided to leave the country, to thus assure from abroad the continuity of the constitutional order and the organization of resistance to the Soviet *diktat*.

According to the Lithuanian Constitution (article 71), in the president's absence all his functions in their full scope were performed by the prime minister. Hence, Antanas Merkys, who had already resigned from the prime minister's post, found himself in the position not only of acting prime minister but also of the acting president of the country. President Smetona explicitly endorsed Merkys to hold these offices before leaving the country. It was now Merkys's job to find a prime minister suitable both to him and to the Soviets. Merkys immediately suggested a few candidates for the prime ministerial office, but Dekanozov found them all unacceptable. The deliberations between Merkys and Dekanozov took about two days, until on June 17, 1940, Justas Paleckis, a liberal journalist and a member of the Populist Party, emerged as a candidate whom Merkys agreed to appoint to, and Dekanozov deemed suitable for, the job. On June 17, Paleckis and the "people's government" he had formed officially took office with Paleckis being also elevated to the post of the acting president of the republic.[32]

Paleckis's government was at first not communist. It was rather based on the principle of a "popular front coalition." It consisted of several prominent intellectuals, progressive but not members of any party, as well as of members of different "democratic" parties, among them Populists and Social-Democrats. There were only two communists among the ministers in the initial list of Paleckis's cabinet—but, significantly enough, they received the portfolios of the minister of the interior and of the director of the Department of State Security, which in that time of radical change carried probably more weight than all the other portfolios put together.[33]

After having completed the occupation of Lithuania, the Soviet government took Latvia and Estonia to task. On June 16, 1940, the governments of both these countries were presented by Molotov with similar ultimatums. The difference consisted only in that the arguments proving the noncompliance of these governments with the Mutual Assistance Treaties between them and the USSR were reduced from two to only one point, that concerning the Baltic entente and the unfortunate magazine, *Revue Baltique*, which so ominously failed to produce a Russian edition. As for the ultimative parts of these ultimatums, they also were reduced from three to only two points, the ones concerning the change of the governments and the free entry of Soviet troops into the respective countries. The response to the Soviet ultimatums by the two governments who had witnessed what had just happened in Lithuania was the same as that of the Lithuanian government; the new governments formed at Soviet request also followed the same popular front pattern but there, in contrast to the action of Smetona, who left Lithuania, the legitimate presidents of Latvia (Karlis Ulmanis) and Estonia (Konstantin Päts) remained in their countries and for some time presided also over the new regimes.[34]

This created certain difficulties in the process of formation of the new Latvian and Estonian "people's governments." Both incumbent presidents initially bluntly refused to sanction them. In response, orchestrated "popular demonstrations" in front of the presidential palaces of Riga and Tallinn took place, demanding the installation of "people's governments" and threatening, in case of refusal, to break the "presidential sabotage" by violence (many of these demonstrators were Soviet civil and military personnel; in addition a special shipload of such demonstrators was brought from the USSR to Riga by the Soviet cruiser *Marat* on June 18, 1940). As a result, in Latvia an unsigned (either by Ulmanis, who as president had to sign such decrees, or by anyone else in his stead) "Announcement of the Secretariat of the President of the Republic," proclaiming that a new cabinet led by Augusts Kirchensteins had been formed, was published in the official government gazette on June 20.[35]

In Estonia, on June 21, the demonstrations had been transformed into a stage-managed "popular uprising" against Päts, who was thus brutally coerced by the Communists to approve the cabinet formed by Johannes Vares-Barbarus. Despite the duress, Päts endorsed this government only after having secured the concession that no Communist would be on the list of its members. This is how "people's governments" were formed and started to function in Latvia and Estonia by June 22, 1940.

In any real terms these governments were not totally dominated and guided in every step they took by the now purely nominal heads of states, but by the special high-ranking emissaries of the Soviet government appointed for each Baltic state—Vladimir Dekanozov for Lithuania, Andrey Vyshinsky for Latvia, and Andrey Zhdanov for Estonia—with the Soviet polpreds (ambassadors) to those countries acting as their deputies and other members of the Soviet embassies' staff as supporting personnel. Very soon hundreds of Soviet citizens started to arrive from the USSR, most of them with special assignments to take up directly leading positions in the party and government apparatuses of the Baltic states, first and foremost within their armies and police forces. Among them were Soviet Communists of Baltic extraction; for example, in Estonia almost all leading positions were occupied by "Russian Estonians" (called "Yestonians" by the natives) who even until the present day, though to a lesser extent, are dominating the power *apparat* of that Soviet republic.[36]

The measures taken by all three new governments were from now on pretty uniform. First of all, Communist political prisoners were released everywhere and subsequently Communist parties were formally legalized, whereas the formerly ruling parties and their support organizations were banned. In fact, by these measures a one-party communist system was fully established by the end of June, in spite of the fact that many individual non-Communists were still members of the governments of all three countries. Most of them later joined the Communist Party but some either resigned (like the Lithuanian "people's government's" non-party intellectual deputy prime minister, Professor V. Kreve Mickevicius) or simply fled abroad (like the Lithuanian "people's government's" liberal minister of finances, E. Galvanauskas). A rapid expansion of governmental offices took place at the same time with the newly created (as well as vacated) ministerial positions being filled by Communists. By the beginning of July, the Communists were in the majority in each country's cabinet, which made possible the speeding up of the purge of the former governmental officials and their replacement by Communists and their supporters, many of whom, as was noted above, were Soviet citizens directly imported from the USSR.

These purges culminated in the two waves of mass arrests (each such wave accounting for thousands of victims in each country) on July 11–12 and 18–19 (before and after elections to the "People's Diets"), whereby the actually or even potentially noncompliant political, cultural, and religious elites of the three nations were put out of circulation by imprisonment and/or deportation to the USSR.

The next step was the announcement of elections for People's Diets to be held on July 14, 1940, in all three Baltic states. Changes in the electoral laws were introduced by government decrees, which were illegal in both form and substance (the constitutions did not permit electoral law to be changed by decrees, and the changes introduced were contrary to the electoral provisions of the constitutions then still in force). The obvious intention of these laws was to stage a Soviet-style election with single-slate candidates of the "Working People's Leagues" being unanimously voted in without any competition whatsoever. The implementation of that electoral system was not at all easy. Abortive (and severely suppressed) attempts to organize and present alternative electoral slates were made in all three Baltic states, with the most dramatic developments taking place in Estonia, but all were to no avail. The elections took place as planned and the officially announced (but hardly credible) results gave the usual 90-plus percent of the votes cast to the sole official slates of the Working People's Leagues.

All three thus "elected" People's Diets met on July 21, 1940. The same day the proclaimed, unanimously, of course, and by acclamation, the conversion of their respective states into Soviet Socialist Republics. The next resolution unanimously adopted by them was an application addressed to the Supreme Soviet of the USSR for accepting the newly established SSRs as member-states of the Union of Soviet Socialist Republics. The assemblies concluded their two-day sessions by adopting laws on nationalization of land (to go together with an agricultural reform) and of industry and banks; they also elected delegates to go to Moscow to present to the next session of the USSR's Supreme Soviet the applications for membership in the USSR.

The Supreme Soviet of the USSR met on August 1, 1940. On August 3 it had decided to adopt Lithuania and, on August 5 and 6, Latvia and Estonia, respectively, as union republics of the USSR.

This is how by August 1940 the Soviet takeover of the three Baltic states was completed in all actual and formal terms. After the forty-six years that have elapsed since, the position of the Baltic states remains exactly the same—that of countries that, being occupied by and forcibly incorporated into the Soviet Union, have ceased to exist as sovereign national and political entities and have virtually disappeared from the world's political map.

The history of the Sovietization of the Baltic states exemplified the general modus operandi of a Communist takeover. It is rather typical in terms of the close cooperation and coordination of action between the Soviet-Party state and its foreign constituencies that, however small and insignificant, the Communist Party may be in any country of the world and, if properly boosted up by unequivocal Soviet support, it can become a formidably strong political force fully able to seize and even quite effectively exercise state power. It is the same pattern of close coordination of Soviet and indigenous Communist action that allowed the Soviet state in 1918–1921 to take possession so effectively of the Ukraine, Georgia, and some other states newly formed on the former territory of the Russian Empire, or of a number of East European states in the aftermath of World War II. Basically the same pattern of coordinated action allowed for the establishment and consolidation of Communist minority regimes in countries like Angola (1975), Ethiopa (1974–1977), Afghanistan (1978), and many others.

It is not at all necessary that in all such cases the initiative of the takeover had to come from the Soviet Union, as in the case of the Baltic states. In recent decades these initiatives very often came from the indigenous power-greedy Communist parties and groups that, however, before acting upon such initiatives, had to solicit and secure full Soviet support, not only for that action itself, but also for the regime that was to be established by that action. Without Soviet support most of these regimes, even if established, would not be viable in any more or less long-term view, which does not preclude the possibility of some of them becoming independent of the USSR after the time required for proper consolidation of their power within the country (as in the cases of Yugoslavia, China, and Albania).

This is another lesson to be drawn from the incorporation into the USSR of the Baltic states. If only the Western policy-makers had learned these lessons in good time, they would have been much better equipped to deal with the Soviet Union, both during World War II and in its aftermath; they could probably have avoided the blunders of Yalta and Potsdam and perhaps even secured independence and democratic institutions for many a nation of Eastern Europe now under Soviet control. It is still not too late to start learning these lessons, for the Soviet Union in its expansionist pursuits continues successfully to apply almost without modifications the same modus operandi that it used in 1939–1940 with regard to the Baltic states.

Of special significance is the lesson to be learned from the experience of formation in the Baltic states of indigenous Communist administrations. In all these Baltic states the Communist parties were miniscule, sectarian, and clandestine bodies that nobody took seriously as politically relevant, let alone significant, groups. Suffice it to say that, even according to official Soviet data by the time of Soviet occupation in June 1940, the strength of the Baltic Communist parties was: in Lithuania, 1500 members,[37] in Latvia, fewer than 1000 members,[38] and in Estonia, only 130 members.[39] There were at that time few active Communist supporters and associates outside the ranks of the parties' membership—a few hundreds or thousands at the most.[40] These more numerous "fellow travelers" were as unrepresentative of the Baltic working classes or of any of the main sections of the populations of the Baltic states as the Communists themselves; they mainly consisted of some members of the radical intelligentsia and national minorities. And yet these small numbers of "Soviet constituents" were entirely sufficient for constituting the new Soviet-type administrations and establishing effective Communist control over all public bodies and economic units functioning in the Baltic countries, including also Estonia with her mere 130 Communists. This would not be so surprising had the Communists taken control over all walks of life gradually. An established power, however repugnant, acquires some sort of legitimacy by the very fact of its ability to exercise authority effectively and thus attracts as many collaborators as it needs (and usually many more than it needs). But the Baltic Communists established an effective administration immediately by appointing to all key positions only their own members and fully-trusted supporters, with the personnel imported from the USSR occupying supervisory and in most cases, second-rate positions. This is to say that one should never dismiss the Communists and their fellow travelers as an irrelevant political force, however marginal and weak, under normal situations, they may seem to be. In certain situations and with Soviet assistance, even the smallest Communist bodies may easily put themselves in power and exercise that power effectively from the moment they get it.

One should not easily dismiss the Communists also because their real strength, as well as the depth of their penetration into different regular bodies of the existing societies, can never be assessed in a precise manner. As the Baltic experience has shown, many highly regarded public figures never suspected of Communist sympathies (indeed many of them known to the public as people with established anticommunist reputations) were in fact crypto-communists who had shown their true colors only after the Soviets took over. Only then did it become apparent that the Communists had successfully infiltrated the noncommunist political parties of the Baltic states across their whole spectrum from left to right, with some of the crypto-communists occupying in these parties highly influential positions. Most of these crypto-communists posed as members of the liberal and social-democratic parties, but some also belonged to parties of right-wing nationalist and even explicitly fascist orientation. A few crypto-communists were well established in the armed forces of the Baltic states and even in the counter-communist department of the secret police. But the majority of Communist fellow travelers were to be found among members of the cultural elite of the Baltic states that belonged to no party at all. A few prominent Baltic nonparty writers, poets, journalists, scientists, and even musicians turned into Soviet-type politicians and administrators literally overnight, and some of the less prominent ones followed suit.

Perhaps the crypto-communist phenomenon explains best how it became possible to form in the Baltic states communist governments without many (and, in the case of Estonia, any) members of the Communist Party participating in them. One can be sure that crypto-communism is as widespread throughout the entire noncommunist world today as it was in the Baltic states in 1939–1940, and one should always bear it in mind when assessing the reality of the threat of a Communist takeover in any noncommunist country of the world.

There is nothing much that one could or should do to prevent and/or eradicate crypto-communism. As long as communist ideology is able to attract adherents there will inevitably be crypto-communists too. It is a phenomenon one has to live with and be aware of in order not to become complacently dismissive about the communist threat and its real extent in every country in the world, however minimal the visible strength of communism in a particular country may seem to be. In this respect it is important to note that official prohibition and persecution of communism and Communists in the right-wing dictatorships are the best breeding ground for crypto-communism. The same is true for democracies that are intolerant of or discriminatory against Communists. Anticommunist hysteria and witch-hunts of the type associated with the name of the late Senator Joseph McCarthy are in this respect also most unhelpful. They only manage substantially to restrict political and intellectual freedom of the society as a whole, in most cases directly affecting totally innocent people; and thus, instead of combating communism, they help it to recruit new adherents among people who would otherwise have never been attracted either to communism or any other similar radical creed. And it goes without saying that under such conditions a substantial proportion of these recruits will be swelling the ranks of the crypto-communists. Historical experience has proved that the more democratic and tolerant of communism and Communists the society is, the fewer crypto-communists there are in it. There is simply no need or incentive for a person of communist convictions to hide his true colors when he is able to express them openly without any hindrance or personal damage. It is true, of course, that undercover Communist agents will be trying to infiltrate militarily and politically sensitive establishments under any circumstances. But this is an entirely different matter, which is in the domain of the effective organization of national security and has very little to do with politics proper. Politically the best deterrent against crypto-communism is liberal democracy, under which communism as an ideology and political orientation is tolerated equally with all other ideologies and political orientations, that is to say, within the limits of the law that equally applies to all physical and legal persons.

International Agreements and Soviet Opportunism

The case of the Baltic states vividly exemplifies the Soviet attitude toward obligations under international agreements and treaties as well as the international law in general.

By 1940 the Soviet Union was bound in its relationship with the Baltic states by a series of quite complex international agreements and treaties. The first such mutually binding documents were the peace treaties of 1919–1920 between the USSR and every Baltic state separately, which established peace and good neighborship as general principles of relationship between them. In 1929 Estonia, Latvia, Poland, and the Soviet Union signed a protocol (known as the Litvinov Protocol) whereby the signatories took upon themselves an additional obligation to obey in their mutual relations the norms established by the Briand–Kellog Pact of August 27, 1928, stressing that thereby they renounced war as an instrument of national policy and committed themselves to seek resolution of conflicts by peaceful means only. This commitment was further elaborated and made more concrete in the Nonaggression and Peaceful Conciliation Treaties concluded between the Soviet Union and all the Baltic states in 1926 and 1932. These treaties, whose validity was supposed to last until December 31, 1945, and which were never abrogated by any of the parties involved, provided for an undertaking by all the contracting parties (e.g., the USSR) to refrain from any act of aggression against the territorial independence and inviolability, or against the political integrity, of their counterparts, no matter whether such aggression was to be committed with or without a declaration of war. Most importantly, according to these treaties, any disputes between their signatories that could not be resolved through normal diplomatic channels were to be submitted for settlement and authoritative resolution to a Joint Conciliation Commission.

Finally, in 1933, the Soviet Union signed with a number of states, among them Estonia, Latvia, and Lithuania, the Convention Concerning the Definition of Aggression in which all the signatories solemnly declared that no political, military, economic, or other claim might serve as excuse or justification for invasion by armed force, even without declaration of war, upon the territory of another state. On top of these documents came the Mutual Assistance Treaties of 1939 discussed above, which, despite the provisions allowing for the stationing of Soviet troops on the territories of the Baltic states, were still basically consistent with all the above agreements and treaties, as they explicitly stressed the inalienability of the sovereign rights of the contracting parties and their commitment to the principle of nonintervention in one another's internal affairs.

However, gross breaches of the USSR's formal international obligations and commitments vis-à-vis the Baltic states had already started with the preparations for the conclusions of these Mutual Assistance Treaties of 1939. First, by taking on September 19, 1939, direct action against Estonia and thus unilaterally depriving her of sovereignty over her territorial waters, the Soviet Union committed by any definition a straight act of aggression against this country. Second, there is no doubt that the Soviet Union coerced the reluctant Baltic states to sign these treaties by threatening them in case of noncompliance with direct military action. That this threat, substantiated by massive concentration of Soviet troops on the Baltic frontiers, was serious and real was later demonstrated by the Soviet attack against Finland that followed her unequivocal refusal to sign the Soviet-proposed Mutual Assistance Treaty. All these Soviet acts were committed in direct violation of the peace treaties of 1919–1920, as well as the Litvinov Protocol of 1929 and the Conventions Concerning the Definition of Aggression of 1933.

If in 1939, however, the threat of direct aggression against the Baltic states was not expressed in any of the Soviet public statements or documents (except for the Soviet note on the takeover of the Estonian coastline, which actually was not a threat but a straightforward declaration of the Soviet Union's taking this unilateral action against Estonia), Molotov's note to Lithuania of May 25, 1940, already implicitly contained such a threat. Everything that happened afterward was not simply a violation but, one could say, a direct unilateral denial by the Soviet Union of the principles of international law in general and of her international obligations to the Baltic states in particular. The Soviet Union behaved toward the Baltic states as if she had never pledged to them to settle any disputes unsolvable by normal diplomatic channels, by submitting them to the Joint Conciliation Commission provided for in accordance with the Nonaggression and Conciliation Treaties between the USSR and the Baltic states of 1926 and 1932. A proposal to this effect was never even put forward by the Soviet Union for the sake of outward demonstration of her compliance with mutually agreed forms of procedure, although this was supposed to be the ultimate instrument of conflict (any conflict!) resolution between the Soviet Union and the Baltic states. Redress beyond this level required, first, a formal abrogation of all Soviet–Baltic treaties and agreements and, second, a declaration of war. Neither of those measures was taken by the Soviet Union.

Instead, contrary to all mutually agreed arrangements, the USSR arrogated to herself discretionary powers for dissolving (and creating) Baltic governments and for using her military forces in the capacity of a "treaty-enforcing agency" on the territory of foreign countries in the Baltic area. Because the Soviet Union had signed with the Baltic states the Agreement Concerning the Definition of Aggression, which stipulated that no political, military, economic, or other consideration could serve as excuse or justification of invasion by armed force upon the territory of another state, the USSR, by resorting to such measures, in fact, as B. J. Kaslas succinctly pointed out, "defined itself as an aggressor, such a presumption being irrefutable, *de juris* and *de jure*, with absolutely no evidence to the contrary being admissable."[41] Moreover, by presenting the Baltic states with the ultimatum of June 14 and 16, 1940, ostensibly aimed at strengthening and enforcing the Mutual Assistance Treaties of 1939, the USSR, in fact, broke those very treaties since under them she had undertaken a solemn obligation "never to infringe upon the sovereign rights of these states, with particular pertinence to their political structure and social and economic organization."[42]

The story of the incorporation of the Baltic states into the USSR clearly and most illuminatingly demonstrates the opportunistic nature of the Soviet Union's attitude to international law and her own international obligations. As long as there are forceful external restraints on the Soviet Union's international behavior, she will reluctantly honor them; as soon as the opportunity is offered to take another grab without exposing herself to any substantial risk (which, under conditions of an ongoing war between Germany and the Allied Powers, the Nazi–Soviet Secret Protocols practically excluded), the Soviet Union will be ready to breach any international obligations, any norms of international law, and go in this respect to any lengths in order to take full advantage of such a situation. This is as true of the Soviet Union today as it was at any other period of Soviet history. It was after all Lenin who said that the dictatorship of the proletariat is "rule based directly upon force and unrestrained by any laws."[43]

The nihilistic attitude of the Soviets toward international law and their international obligations under treaties with other countries also extended itself in 1939–1941 to their relations with Germany. As soon as they felt that they could breach some parts of the German–Soviet agreements without wrecking the whole relationship and being severely punished for that breach, the Soviets did not hesitate to go ahead with plans that were either inconsistent with or even directly contrary to the treaties and secret protocols concluded between Germany and the USSR. The best-known example of such opportunistic behavior on the Soviet Union's part was its occupation and incorporation into the USSR, in June 1940, of the Rumanian territory of Northern Bukovina. According to the Secret Additional Protocol to the German–Soviet Nonaggression Treaty of August 23, 1939, the Soviet Union was entitled to get from Rumania only the territory of Bessarabia, which formerly belonged to the Russian empire, but not that of Bukovina, which had never been under Russian rule and was supposed to remain within Rumania. Hitler was furious about the blatant Soviet violation of the German–Soviet agreement concerning Rumania, but there was nothing he could have effectively done about getting Bukovina back from the Soviets. Having gotten away with that violation, the Soviets were preparing to take further steps that were eventually to lead to Rumania's definitive inclusion into their "sphere of influence." This was too much for Hitler to bear. In response to Soviet unilateral moves in this direction, he undertook a decisive action that cut Soviet expansion short and finally put what remained of the Rumanian state into the German "sphere of influence."

Another example of a breach of the German–Soviet agreements consisted in Soviet occupation, together with the rest of Lithuania's territory in June

1940, of the so-called Lithuanian strip that, according to the Secret Additional Protocol to the German–Soviet Boundary and Friendship Treaty of September 28, 1939, was to remain free of Soviet troops and be eventually transferred to Germany.[44]

Above all, however, Germany was outraged about Soviet liberal interpretation of what it meant to include a country into the USSR's "sphere of influence." For the Germans this was not at all identical with the abolition of that country's independent statehood and its incorporation into the USSR. From their point of view, such an action, prior to being undertaken, required a specially negotiated agreement between the USSR and Germany, and since the Soviets took the "incorporative" actions with regard to the Baltic states without negotiating them first with Germany, these actions were treated by the Germans as direct Soviet transgressions of the agreements concluded. In almost exactly the same way a few years later, the Soviets breached the Yalta and Potsdam agreements that they concluded with Britain and the United States in 1945. This shows that even the major powers have to be very careful about negotiating and entering into any kind of international treaty or agreement with the USSR. As long as such a treaty or agreement is not properly verifiable and does not contain credible measures of deterring the Soviets from violating its provisions, any international agreement concluded with the USSR is hardly worth the paper it is written on.

THE UNRESOLVED BALTIC PROBLEM

When on June 22, 1941, Hitler attacked the Soviet Union and thus forced Stalin to forge an alliance with the Allied Powers, one of the most important issues at stake became the Allies' recognition of the USSR's 1941 borders (including the incorporation into the USSR of the Baltic states). This issue was quite bluntly raised by Stalin in the course of the first Soviet–British talks in Moscow, in December 1941. When Foreign Secretary Eden tried to stall the discussion (by referring to the Atlantic Charter and the necessity of consulting his government), Stalin firmly retorted that the question of the Baltic states was "absolutely axiomatic" and ought not to require any governmental decision.[45] In response, Eden admitted that the Soviet Union was recognized as possessing de facto sovereignty of the Baltic states, but did not go further than that. When reporting to Churchill on his talks in Moscow, Eden actually argued for full recognition of Soviet demands and even suggested that "it is in our interest too that they" (the Soviets) "should be in strong position in the Baltic."[46]

Churchill, however, sharply rejected Eden's arguments, although a few months later, when the negotiations of the British–Soviet political treaty were in a deadlocked position, he himself was ready to accede to Soviet demands in regard to the Baltic states.[47] Actually, the treaty was signed on May 26, 1942, without any such concessions on the British part being made at all. The

Soviets were prepared to forego the 1941 frontier question in exchange for the Anglo-American offer of a second front and the twenty-year term of the Soviet–British political treaty itself.

In later negotiations among Stalin, Churchill, and Roosevelt the Soviet frontiers issue did not figure very prominently. There were larger issues at stake. Actually, Stalin tried to raise the issue of the Baltic states and the 1941 frontiers again at the Yalta Conference, but when his proposals were rejected he did not insist on them, preferring to concentrate on the more critical Polish problem.[48] Hence, the Baltic issue in Soviet relations with their Western wartime allies remained formally unresolved, which meant that both Britain and the United States could continue to stick to their original, pre-1941 position of nonrecognition of the Soviet takeover of the Baltic states. But neither did they raise the Baltic issue with the Soviets on their own initiative, let alone protest the Soviet reoccupation and retention of the Baltic states as part of the USSR's territory in 1944–1945. In fact, they tacitly adopted the line that was suggested by President Roosevelt as early as March 1942:

> With regard to the Baltic states, Roosevelt admitted that, were the area to be reoccupied by a victorious Red Army, neither Britain nor the United States could or would do anything about this. Why, then, should Stalin worry? In other words, Roosevelt was quite happy to bow to the inevitable, but did not wish to compromise by prior agreement the principles for which his government was fighting.[49]

As D. Kirby has pointed out, "the conclusion of the twenty-year treaty saved Britain the embarrassment of publicly reneging on her pledge not to recognize territorial changes during the course of the war. . . . The British and American governments managed to avoid recognition of the Soviet incorporation of the three states and . . . are still burdened with their moral obligations."[50] Burdened or not, both Britain and the United States continue to recognize the Baltic states as, in a legal sense, sovereign political entities. The legations of the pre-1940 Baltic states are still functioning in Washington and London, and their members enjoy the status and privileges accorded to diplomatic personnel.

Peculiarly, Nazi Germany, in spite of having shifted the Baltic states to the "Soviet zone of influence," never granted *de jure* recognition of their annexation by the Soviet Union. As B. Meissner explained, this was due to the fact that because "of the German–Soviet war, an exchange of the already completed ratification documents of the German–Soviet Border Treaty of January 10, 1941, never took place." Meissner thus concludes that in the view of the Federal Republic of Germany, "the Baltic states have not forfeited their sovereign international rights" either.[51]

In fact, none of the free states, except for New Zealand,[52] have recognized the *Soviet coup de force* against the Baltic states as being legally valid and deserving *de jure* recognition. This is enough to vindicate the view that "the Baltic states continue to exist in international law owing to the refusal of the other states to recognize their incorporation into the Soviet Union."[53]

The legal aspects of the Baltic problem contain serious political implications. Since the present status of the Baltic states is lacking any legal basis and therefore must be conceived as illegitimate, null, and void, the Baltic states should be seen as having an indisputable right to their status as fully sovereign nation states *ad hoc*, that is, without any preliminary conditions (such as a referendum or decision of any authority in Moscow) attached to the restoration of their sovereignty.

This means that all nations for whom respect for the rule of law is one of the fundamental principles can never become reconciled with the Soviet rule over the Baltic states and are willy-nilly committed to campaigning for the due restitution of their independence from the Soviet Union. Moreover, the fate of the Baltic states serves (or at least should serve) as a useful reminder for these nations instructing them on how they have to deal with the Soviet Union, especially when negotiating with her any agreements or treaties. The lesson to be learned from the Baltic case, as B. Meissner has succinctly suggested, is that "the guarantees and treaty assurances against the threat of totalitarian powers make sense . . . only when they are made in conjunction with a clearly recognizable deterrent."[54]

Finally, sooner or later, the time must come when Russia itself will recognize the supremacy of the principle of rule of law in relations with her own citizens as well as with other nations. In preparation for this change, the legal aspects of the Baltic case should be made absolutely clear and in this form propagated as widely as possible throughout the world, as well as within the Soviet Union itself and the areas under its dominion. This would be an invaluable contribution to an easy and uncontroversial solution to the Baltic problem in the hopefully not too distant future, when the possibility of such a solution becomes politically viable again.

It is of crucial importance that the lessons of the Nazi–Soviet Alliance and of the plight of the Baltic states are properly learned by the West and its policymakers. They contain everything that is necessary for an adequate and realistic understanding of the danger the Soviet Union represents to the outside world. They also teach how to defend freedom against the Soviet threat most effectively. These lessons show that by lending more support to the cause of freedom for the Baltic states, one is providing better protection of freedom here in the West. Freedom as everyone knows is after all indivisible. By more actively helping the Balts to restore their freedom, we will certainly be able to help ourselves. The Balts, by fighting against Soviet tyranny for their freedom, have already put themselves on the frontline for the defense of ours.

NOTES

1. D. M. Crowe, Jr., "Great Britain and the Baltic States, 1938–1939," in V. S. Vardys and R. J. Misiunas, eds., *The Baltic States in Peace and War, 1917–1945* (University Park: Pennsylvania State University Press, 1978), 128.

2. D. Kirby, "The Baltic States, 1940–1950," in M. McCauley, ed., *Communist Power in Europe, 1944–1949* (London: Macmillan, 1977), 23.

3. For the full text of the treaty and the Soviet Additional Protocol see R. J. Sontag and J. S. Beddie, eds., *Nazi–Soviet Relations, 1939–1941* (Washington, D.C.: Department of State, 1948), 76–78 (in future references referred to as *Nazi–Soviet Relations*).

4. Sontag and Beddie, *Nazi–Soviet Relations,* 78.

5. Sontag and Beddie, *Nazi–Soviet Relations,* 166.

6. Not of all Lithuania. A strip of Lithuanian territory (in its southwestern part) had to be given to Germany "as soon as the Government of the USSR shall take special measures on Lithuanian territory to protect its interests" (Sontag and Beddie, *Nazi–Soviet Relations.*) The USSR, however, totally ignored this obligation and even directly broke its explicit pledge not to put Soviet military forces in this area when Lithuania would be occupied by them. This (together with other similar Soviet breaches of the Soviet–German agreements) outraged the Germans and created much animosity and tension in Soviet–German relations of the time. The issue of "the Lithuanian strip" dragged on for a considerably long time (for more than fifteen months) until finally the Germans (after having already approved the Barbarossa plan about attacking the USSR in 1941) decided "to give in" by accepting from the Soviet Union, in exchange for the strip, 7.5 million gold dollars. Another German–Soviet Secret Protocol was signed to that effect on January 10, 1941, (Sontag and Beddie, *Nazi–Soviet Relations,* 267–68) making sure that the whole sum was paid by the Soviets "within three months after the signing of this Protocol." This time the Soviets were happy to keep their word and paid the whole agreed amount to the Germans by April 11, 1941 (that is, two-and-a-half months before Germany attacked the USSR and took the strip together with the rest of Lithuania and many other Soviet territories).

For a detailed and illuminating account of this most cynical episode in the history of diplomacy see B. J. Kaslas, "The Lithuanian Strip in Soviet–German Secret Diplomacy, 1939–1941," in *The Journal of Baltic Studies* 4, no. 3 (fall 1973).

7. See, for example, B. Jonaitis, "Politiniai faktai ir mitai" [Political Facts and Myths] in *Naujienos* (*News,* a Lithuanian daily published in Chicago) of November 4, 5, 6–8, 1982; B. Raila, *Raibos agavos* [The Giant Agavas] (London: Nida Press, 1983), 235–36.

8. Sontag and Beddie, *Nazi–Soviet Relations,* 103.

9. The Soviet propaganda has repeatedly praised Churchill for his "profound understanding of Soviet policies and defensive needs." In the notorious "Historical Memorandum" (*Istoricheskaya spravka*) issued in 1948 by the Information Bureau of the USSR's Council of Ministers under the title "The Falsifiers of History," this speech of Churchill's was quoted once more with a comment introducing that quotation and stating that Churchill was the first among Western politicians who had "enough acumen for understanding the essence of Soviet policy [toward Germany] and for recognizing that the [Soviet] build–up of the 'eastern front' was right." (*see Fal'sifikatory istorii, Istoricheskaya spravka,* [Moscow: Gospolitizdat, 1948], 57–58.)

10. W. S. Churchill, *The Second World War,* book 1, *The Gathering Storm: From War to War (1919–1939),* 9th ed. (London: Cassell, 1967), 351.

11. A. J. P. Taylor, *The Origins of the Second World War* (London: Hamish Hamilton, 1961), 263.

12. No other meaning can be attached to the joint German–Soviet August 23, 1939, secret statement that in "the area belonging to the Polish state the spheres of influence of Germany and the USSR shall be bounded by the line of the rivers Narev, Vistula and San;" furthermore, that "the questions of . . . the maintenance of an independent Polish

state . . . can . . . be definitively determined in the course of further political develop-ments" and that the governments of Germany and the USSR "in any event will resolve this question by means of a friendly agreement." (The Secret Additional Protocol to the German–Soviet Nonaggression Treaty of August 23, 1939, quoted from Sontag and Beddie, *Nazi–Soviet Relations,* 78.)

13. B. H. Liddell Hart, *History of the Second World War* (London: Cassell, 1970), 12, 13.

14. Taylor, *The Origins of the Second World War,* 263.

15. Churchill, *The Second World War*, 351.

16. Alain Besançon, "The End of the Soviet Mirage," *Encounter* 57, no. 1 (July 1981): 90.

17. This information is based on official documents of the Estonian government, a collection of which was published in Stockholm in 1955 (in Estonian) and taken for this article from D. Kirby's "The Baltic States . . . " in McCauley, p. 24. For much of the following information, in addition to the sources mentioned above, the materials col-lected in *Third Interim Report of the Select Committee on Communist Aggression* (House of Representatives, Eighty-Third Congress, Second Session, under Authority of H. Res. 346 and H. Res. 438, Washington, D.C., Government Printing Office, 1954) were used; see especially pp. 220ff (in future references cited as *Third Interim Re-port*). A certified copy of the minutes of the negotiations between Estonia and the USSR signed by Karl Selter, Estonian Minister of Foreign Affairs, together with his statement on the negotiations, is held in the Archive of the Consulate General of Es-tonia in New York and the Hoover Library in Stanford, California.

18. Sontag and Beddie, *Nazi–Soviet Relations,* 78.

19. After the conclusion of the Soviet–Finnish Peace Treaty, the Kuusinen govern-ment was transformed into the government of the Karelian–Finnish SSR, waiting there for the day when it would be able to extend its authority to the whole of Fin-land. The Karelian–Finnish SSR, with Kuusinen as its president, existed until 1956, when the Soviet leaders, responding to the insistent demands of the Finnish govern-ment, decided to extend a friendly gesture to Finland by abolishing the Karelian–Finnish SSR and reconverting it back to the status of the Karelian ASSR within the Russian SFSR. Kuusinen was then recalled to Moscow and in 1957 started a new career as one of the Secretaries of the CPSU's CC and a full member of the So-viet Union's ruling Politburo (this promotion shows only too clearly that the Soviet leaders were holding Kuusinen, one of their peers, in the relatively minor position of chairman of the *presidium* of the Supreme Soviet of a union republic for sixteen years, only with the view of promoting him one day to the major post of president of the whole of Finland. There is hardly another way to interpret this fact.)

20. Churchill, *The Second World War*, 573.

21. See the full text of the note in *Third Interim Report*, 319.

22. *Third Interim Report*, 319.

23. *Third Interim Report*, 319.

24. For the full text of that communiqué, see *Third Interim Report*, 320–21. The ev-idence now available shows that all the Soviet charges against Lithuania were totally groundless and therefore it is clear why the Soviet Union was determined not to al-low their discussion in any reasonable form. In such a discussion all these charges would have fallen apart and the Soviet purpose was not to allow this to happen—the charges had to be upheld at any cost as the necessary vehicle to lead the process of Lithuania's Sovietization to its very end. A good analysis of the existing evidence on

Soviet charges against Lithuania is given by B. J. Kaslas in *The Baltic Nations: The Quest for Regional Integration and Political Liberty (Estonia, Latvia, Lithuania, Finland, Poland)* (Pittston, Pa.: Euramerica Press, 1976), 236–38.

25. A detailed account of the Merkys–Molotov talks in June 1940 is given by the then–member of the Lithuanian Cabinet, Stasys Audenas, in *Paskutinis Posedis (The Last Meeting)* (New York: Romuva, 1966); for another such account see P. Maciulis, *Trys Ultimatumai (Three Ultimatums)* (Brooklyn, N.Y.: Darbininkas, 1962). A brief summary of these accounts in English is given by B. J. Kaslas, in *The Baltic Nations*, 238–40.

26. For the full text of A. Smetona's letter to M. Kalinin, see *Third Interim Report*, p. 327.

27. *Third Interim Report*, 333.

28. *Third Interim Report*, 333.

29. *Third Interim Report*, 333. In fact, the so–called Baltic Entente, a treaty among Lithuania, Latvia, and Estonia providing for periodical consultations of the foreign ministers of the three countries, was concluded as long before as 1934, and had remained unaltered in either word or substance since.

30. Poor souls, if they had only known in February 1940 what were to be the repercussions of the merely trilingual scope of this magazine, they certainly would have added Russian as the fourth language in which it was published and thus possibly could have either prevented—at least in the case of Latvia and Estonia, whose governments were not accused of kidnapping and murdering Soviet Soldiers or arresting their own citizens in order to launch an aggression against the Soviet garrisons—the whole fatal incident with the Soviet Union altogether, or at least, would have forced the Soviets to find some new arguments to justify their claims.

31. *Third Interim Report*. The end of the last sentence (after the words, "of the Soviet Union") is not included in the text published in *Third Interim Report* and was added in the author's translation from the official Russian text published in *Vneshnyaya Politika SSSR, Shornik dokumentov*, vol. 4, Moscow, 1946, p. 511.

32. This was unconstitutional since Merkys had no authority to concede the post of acting president although, as such, he had the right to appoint as his prime minister any person of his own choosing. Because of that "people's government" under the "Acting President" Paleckis (as well as all acts issued by that government) was illegal from its inception, even if one discounts the fact that it was imposed on the country by a foreign power and thus was illegal for this very reason.

33. This is actually the whole trick about the Communist use of the "popular front" cover. Later it was successfully applied in Czechoslovakia, Hungary, and other countries that during the interim stage of popular front governments were skillfully manipulated by the Communists, who were controlling the countries' security services, into falling under their total rule, to the exclusion (and, in most cases, extermination) of all other political forces of those countries. This trick, which later became so common, was actually used by Stalin for the first time in Lithuania and then in other Baltic states with no one in the world, as it seems, learning anything from this experience.

34. Both Karlis Ulmanis and Konstantin Päts formally remained in office until the mock elections to the People's Diets in July 1940, after which they were forced to resign and subsequently were arrested, deported, and vanished without trace. However, the authenticity of Konstantin Päts's resignation came under suspicion after three of his messages written in captivity reached the West in 1977. In one of them he explicitly states, "I am here as President of the Republic of Estonia" (quoted from the

text published by A. Küng in his *A Dream of Freedom* [Cardiff: Boreas Publishing House, 1981], 246). This statement could not have been made by Päts if he had really resigned, as the Soviets claim.

35. See *Valdibas Vestnesis* (Latvian title of the official government gazette) of June 20, 1940. The absence under such an act of the required signature of President Ulmanis, and of a cosignatory, made this act legally invalid. Therefore, A. Kirchensteins's "people's government" was an illegal body from the moment of its inception as much as its Lithuanian counterpart.

36. For more details see J. Pennar, "Soviet Nationality Policy and the Estonian Communist Elite," in T. Parming and E. Järvesoo, eds., *A Case Study of a Soviet Republic: The Estonian SSR* (Boulder, Colo.: Westview Press, 1978), 105–27, especially 120 ff.

37. A. Snieckus, *Ataskaitinis pranesimas V–me LKP(b) suvziavime apie LKP(b) CK darba, 1941 m. vasario 5d* (*Report on the Work of the Central Committee of the LCP(b) to the 5th Congress of the LCP(b) on February 5, 1941*), (Kaunas: State Publishing House of the Lithuanian SSR, 1941), 57.

38. *Istoriya Kommunisticheskoy Partii Sovetskogo Soyuza* [The History of the Communist Party of the Soviet Union], vol. 5, book 1: (1938–1945) (Moscow: Politizdat, 1971), 93.

39. A. K. Pankseyegv, *Na osnove leninskykh organizatsionnykh printsipov* (On the Basis of Leninist Organizational Principles) (*Talinn: Eesti Raamet*, 1967), 81.

40. The official (and, no doubt, overblown) Soviet estimate for Lithuania of June 1940 is about 6,000 such Communist supporters and associates outside the ranks of the Communist Party itself (see *Mazoji Lietuviskoji Tarybine Enciklopedija* [The Short Lithuanian Encyclopedia], vol. 2 [Vilnius: Mintis, 1966], 390). Of these 1,000 were members of the League of Communist Youth.

41. Kaslas, in *The Baltic Nations*, 273.

42. Kaslas, in *The Baltic Nations*, 273.

43. V. I. Lenin, *Selected Works*, vol. II (London: Lawrence and Wishart, 1947), 365.

44. How the Soviets got away with this violation by paying the Germans 7.5 million golden dollars has been briefly described in note 6.

45. For the text of the December 1941 Soviet–British talks see Sir E. L. Woodward, *British Foreign Policy in the Second World War*, vol. 2 (London: HMSO, 1971), 226–33.

46. Eden to Churchill, 5 January 1942, in PRO, FO, No. 106/86/38. Quoted here from D. Kirby, "Morality or Expediency: The Baltic Question in British–Soviet Relations, 1941–1942," in Vardys and Misiunas, 163.

47. For the protocols of the British–Soviet May 1942 negotiations see: PRO, FO, No. 665/506/59; they are summed up in D. Kirby's contribution to Vardys and Misiunas, 168 ff.

48. See B. Meissner, "The Baltic Question in World Politics," in V. S. Vardys and R. J. Misiunas, 146.

49. As reported by Lord Halifax to Foreign Office on March 9, 1942 (PRO, FO, No. 1279/5/38) and summed up by D. Kirby in his contribution to Vardys and Misiunas, p. 166.

50. As reported by Lord Halifax to Foreign Office on March 9, 1942 and summed up by D. Kirby in his contribution to Vardys and Misiunas, 172.

51. B. Meissner, "The Baltic Question in World Politics," in Vardys and Misiunas, 147.

52. In 1974, Australia's and New Zealand's socialist governments granted *de jure* recognition of the incorporation of the three Baltic states into the Soviet Union. However, in December 1975, when Gough Whittlam's socialist government in Australia was defeated and Malcolm Frazer's conservative government took office, one of the first acts of this new government was the repeal of that act of recognition, in itself an unprecedented event in international legal history. Robert Maldoun's new conservative government of New Zealand, however, did not follow suit and the act of recognition is still valid there.

53. Kaslas, in *The Baltic Nations*, 276.

54. In Vardys and Misiunas, 148.

13

The Baltic States as Soviet Republics: Tensions and Contradictions

Aleksandras Shtromas

REPRESSION AND RESISTANCE, 1941-1945

The incorporation of the Baltic states into the USSR was met by their peoples with almost total dismay but very little, if any, outward resistance. The process was handled by the legitimate Baltic governments, which decided against "senseless" armed resistance and gave in to Soviet pressure allowing the Red Army "peacefully" to occupy their countries. The people were thus caught unawares and reluctantly submitted to Soviet rule.

The Soviets and the local Baltic communists knew, however, only too well how insignificant and marginal their support in the Baltic countries was and how strongly the nations of these countries were in principle committed to resisting them. Therefore they planned well in advance a series of repressive measures aimed at breaking any resistance to Soviet rule in the area. To this effect Order No. 001223 of the NKVD (the People's Commissariat of Internal Affairs) of the USSR, "On the Operative Accounting of the Anti-Soviet and Socially Alien Elements," was issued as early as October 11, 1939, that is, the day after the conclusion of the Pact of Mutual Assistance between the USSR and Lithuania (the last such pact in the

Reprinted from Graham Smith, ed., *The Baltic States: The National Self-Determination of Estonia, Latvia, and Lithuania* (London: Macmillan, 1994), 86–117.

series of three) and more than eight months before the Baltic states were in any real terms taken over by the Soviet Union.[1] The only purpose such an order could have had was preparation for purging the Baltic states from all those who had the potential for organizing and carrying out resistance to Soviet rule.

This indeed proved to be the case. Deportations from the Baltic states were ordered by the USSR's People's Commissar of State Security, Merkulov, on May 19, 1941,[2] and the notorious, strictly secret, and extremely detailed "Instructions Regarding the Manner of Conducting the Deportation of the Anti-Soviet Elements from Lithuania, Latvia, and Estonia" were issued by Merkulov's deputy, Serov, sometime between February and June 7, 1941.[3,4] The ordered deportations started in all three republics simultaneously, on the night of June 13–14, 1941. During the one week that was left before the outbreak of the war (June 22, 1941), 34,260 persons were deported from Lithuania, 15,081 from Latvia, and 10,205 from Estonia.[5] This massive purge marked the peak of the constant wave of repression that, albeit on a much smaller scale, had taken place in the Baltic states throughout the entire period of Soviet rule in 1940–1941. These repressions were directed against political, public, and religious figures of the independence period and, more selectively, against people suspected of resistance or oppositional activities, making anti-Soviet pronouncements, or simply refusing to cooperate with the Soviet regime. It is estimated that Soviet repression and evacuations to the USSR in 1940–1941 cost Lithuania 39,000, Latvia 35,000, and Estonia (where Soviet forces stayed the longest and some conscription into the Red Army was effected) 61,000 citizens[6] (these numbers do not include many thousands of people imprisoned by the Soviet authorities but neither killed nor deported before the Soviets retreated from the territories of the Baltic states).

It is interesting, though, to note that these ferocious repressions totally failed to achieve their goal. If anything, they were counterproductive. These measures demonstrated the brutality and deviousness of the Soviet regime to many unsuspecting and, in the beginning phase of Soviet rule, entirely neutral people. In so doing, the repression contributed to the growth of resistance in terms of both the numbers of resisters and the determination to resist. The massive and indiscriminate character of Soviet repression hit many innocent people, but failed, in fact, to destroy the bulk of the organized resistance forces, whose preparations for an armed insurrection continued unabated. Indeed, the day after the German attack on the USSR an armed insurrection of the Baltic peoples against Soviet rule broke out, and it was so well coordinated and organized, so massive and determined to win, that the retreating Soviet troops were unable to quench it.

Of course, the spirit of Baltic resistance to Soviet rule was greatly increased by the precarious international situation and the almost unanimous conviction of the Baltic peoples that the imminent war between Germany and the

USSR would spell a rapid end to Soviet rule in the area. This conviction was strengthened and substantiated by the fact that Baltic political émigrés in Germany successfully took on the task of organizing and coordinating the activities of resistance groups within their respective countries. Without explicit German approval and direct support, they certainly would not have been able even to start such activity. The Germans were indeed extremely helpful to these émigrés, providing them with everything they needed to achieve success (including arms supplies, logistics, and the means to transport supplies to the Soviet-controlled Baltic territories). The Germans were keen to ensure that, on the day of the attack against the Soviet Union, insurrection behind Soviet lines would flare as widely and powerfully as possible.

The full story of the organization of resistance and the insurrection against Soviet rule at the outbreak of the German–Soviet war in June 1941 is best documented in the Lithuanian case. The Lithuanian ambassador to Germany, Colonel Kazys Skirpa, who organized and led the resistance from Berlin, published a book of memoirs in which he included all the relevant documents about the organization of that resistance and insurrection. It clearly transpires from these documents that as early as July 1940 Skirpa was busy forming in Berlin the Lithuanian Activist Front (LAF), an anti-Soviet resistance organization uniting all noncommunist segments of the Lithuanian political spectrum. These activities of Skirpa and his associates were supervised and, in a way, guided by the German Foreign Office via its liaison man with the Lithuanians, Dr. P. Kleist. The LAF was formally inaugurated on November 17, 1940, and, when ready to start combat activities behind Soviet lines, was transferred to the supervision and guidance of the Abwehr Amt (Intelligence Office) of the OKW (High Command of the Armed Forces). The OKW's liaison man with the Lithuanians, Colonel-Lieutenant Dr. Graebe, replaced Dr. Kleist. Very soon four special Lithuanian posts were established within the Abwehr system on the German–Lithuanian (not Soviet) border for constant maintenance of links and supply lines between the LAF center in Berlin and its branches in the country. As Skirpa emphasized, these posts played a crucial role in assuring the success of resistance organization in general and of the insurrection of June 23, 1941, in particular.[7]

What was true for Lithuania must have been true also for Latvia and Estonia, although corroborating documents are less readily available. Undoubtedly German support played a significant role in the successful organization of resistance and insurrection in all three Baltic countries, although one should not overestimate this factor. For without the genuine determination of the masses of indigenous peoples to join the resistance forces, without the faithfulness to the cause of liberation that assured the survival of the widespread organizational network of the resistance movements despite some "successful" arrests and disclosures made by the Soviets, the whole enterprise, with or without German support, could not have got off the ground and, even if it had, the result would have been nothing but a great flop.

Only part of the organized resistance forces was directly connected to the coordinating and supply centers in Berlin. Some such forces sprang up and operated independently without ever establishing any links with these centers or, perhaps, without even suspecting their existence; for example, the Berlin-based LAF's local Lithuanian network in 1941 numbered about 36,000 members organized in combat units and ready to strike, whereas the total force of organized combatants who participated in the Lithuanian insurrection of June 1941 was about 100,000, that is, "about three times the size of the members of underground organizations under the leadership of LAF."[8] Hence, without denying the significance of German support in making the resistance movements in the Baltic organizationally and logistically viable, one has to conclude that the German role was secondary and supplementary in nature, unable to determine or even to affect significantly the emergence and scope of these movements.

Popular uprisings on a massive scale took place in all three Baltic republics in June 1941. The Lithuanian insurrection started on June 23, 1941, the day after the German invasion, and it took the insurgents the next three days to free the whole of Lithuania from Soviet rule. Some places in Lithuania were freed more than a week before the advancing German armies marched in. The Lithuanian Provisional Government installed in power by the insurrections on June 23 immediately declared the restoration of Lithuania's sovereignty and effectively took charge of the country's affairs. Indeed, when German troops occupied Lithuania they found a country that, to their surprise and to the displeasure of the Reich's leadership, was effectively ruled by a legitimate national government. It took the Nazi authorities six weeks to dismantle this government (it was dissolved on August 5, 1941) and to put Lithuania under the control of their own occupational administration. The Provisional Government (except for three of its members) refused to be a part of the Nazi-installed local administration.

The Latvian insurrection, in which about 60,000 resistance fighters took part, followed almost immediately. On June 26, 1941, an official Soviet broadcast from Riga was forced to admit the fact that "Latvia was in open revolt."[9] On 28 June, the insurgents expelled the Red Army from Riga and announced the formation of a Latvian government. Soviet forces, however, regained control of Riga the next day, and they crushed the Latvian government. Nevertheless, the Latvian armed struggle against the Soviets continued until the Germans took Riga on July 1, 1941.[10]

A similar uprising took place in Estonia, with about 50,000 participants. Here it was a more protracted and a less spectacular affair; most of the time the insurgents were involved in guerrilla-style warfare rather than in a direct frontline confrontation with the superior forces of the Red Army. The Estonian guerrillas, however, fared quite well in this warfare: in its course they killed 4,800 Red Army men and took 14,000 prisoners.[11] They themselves lost only 541 fighters on the battlefield.[12] On July 7, 1941, when the Germans crossed the Estonian border, they "found on their arrival the national flags flying everywhere"—an indication of how effective the Estonian guerrillas were.[13] Indeed, in major parts of southern Estonia, the guerrillas had replaced Soviet local administrations with Estonian ones days and even weeks before the arrival of the Germans. "Tartu was under full or partial Estonian control from 10–28 July." The Estonian capital of Tallinn, as well as the whole northern part of the country, was under much firmer Soviet military and administrative control, which partly explains why there was no attempt to create an Estonian government.[14] An Estonian National Council for coordination of the activities of resistance forces, however, with the last preoccupation prime minister, Jüri Uluots, at its head, was formed at the very start of hostilities.

These national insurrections made absolutely obvious the illegitimate, antipopular nature of Soviet rule over the Baltic states. Soviet claims that the establishment of their regime was in accordance with the "unanimous popular will," and the masquerades of elections and other gimmicks that were supposed to substantiate these claims were blatantly exposed as fakes within hours. In other words, the mass insurrections of June 1941 indicated an explicit and total rejection of the Soviet regime by the overwhelming majority of the Baltic populations. The genuine collective will of these nations—to restore their non-Soviet, pre-1940 sovereign statehoods—had thus been actively expressed. In 1941 this will, however, was brushed aside and trampled upon by the new masters, the Nazis, as brutally and unequivocally as by the Soviets in 1940 (and, where they managed, in 1941).

During the German–Soviet war the Baltic nations found themselves in the most peculiar and unenviable situation of being unable to pursue their national aspirations by siding with either of the warring parties; as R. Silde-Karklins succinctly pointed out, "they had to resist equally the imperialist plans of both, the Germans and Soviets, thereby running the risk of being ground between the two."[15] The task of resisting both was indeed formidable. On the one hand, the Baltic peoples were reluctant to be used by the Germans as cannon fodder and tried to sabotage all efforts to this end; but, on the other hand, they were tempted to exploit for their own national ends the acute need of Hitler's embattled Reich to recruit them to military service. The idea was to establish under German auspices (but, if necessary, even by defying the Germans) an independent military force that, after an eventual German retreat, could engage in a struggle against the advancing Soviets. By enlisting Western support for this struggle, it was hoped that such forces would prevent the USSR from reestablishing its rule over the Baltic states and that these states would thus be put back on the map.

The attempts to implement this plan can be illustrated by the example of events in Lithuania. After the dissolution of the Lithuanian Provisional Government, German attempts to mobilize the Lithuanians for either German military service or industrial work in the Reich were so effectively sabotaged that, as E. J. Harrison pointed out, by the end of 1943 the Lithuanians had successfully wrecked almost all plans directed at using them for serving German needs.[16] Indeed, the initial plan to recruit people for work in Germany was fulfilled only by 5 percent, and the later (March 1943) attempt at creating a Lithuanian national SS legion (which was supposed to be not less than 150,000 men strong) was a complete failure, which the ensuing severe German repressions against the Lithuanians were unable to correct.[17]

Faced with such massive passive resistance, the Germans decided to change gear and get what they wanted by applying "cooperative" tactics. They allowed the Lithuanians to form an independent Territorial Defense Force and promised that this force would be used only within the Baltic area (along the Narva-Vilnius line). The Germans also agreed to accept the appointment as commander of this force of the highly popular nationalist general, Povilas Plechavicius. The response to the appeal calling on Lithuanian youth to join this force, which General Plechavicius issued on February 16, 1944 (the day of Lithuanian independence), surpassed all expectation. In a few days, more than 30,000 volunteers signed up, and an even greater number had to be turned down. As soon as the force was formed and acquired a militarily viable shape, however, the Germans broke all their promises. They ordered the incorporation of this force into the SS and thus put it under direct German command.

This turn of events outraged Plechavicius, who bluntly refused to bow to these orders and issued his own, disbanding the force altogether. As a result, the Gestapo arrested the general together with the members of his staff, imprisoned them all in a concentration camp, and indiscriminately executed 100 soldiers from among the few the Germans had managed to capture before the force disbanded (the rest of the captured troops, 3,500 of them, were integrated into the German Luftwaffe and sent to service airports in western Germany). The main contingent of the force, more than thirty thousand men in full uniform and with all their weapons, successfully went into hiding, thus forming the bulk of the Lithuanian guerrilla army later known as the LLA (Lithuanian Freedom Army), which was to fight against the Soviets for more than eight years.

Similar developments took place in Estonia where, in February 1944, Uluots, the last pre-Soviet prime minister of the country, issued an appeal along the same lines as that of Plechavicius and got the same tremendous response. Even those Estonians who had previously fled to Finland to avoid German conscription voluntarily returned home (after a German pardon for their desertion was granted) to join the newly formed Estonian Territorial Defense Force, assigned to defend Estonia against the Soviet advance. In Latvia, events took a somewhat different turn (because of Germany's extended hold over Courland), but the results were approximately the same.

This is how all three Baltic nations acquired, during 1944–1945, a token military force that, however ill-equipped and weak by any other standards, was sufficient for mounting a protracted guerrilla war. It was hoped that by engaging in such a war the Baltic nations would be able to attract Western support for the cause of Baltic independence from the USSR and thus ultimately succeed in achieving independence.

RESISTANCE AND REPRESSION, 1944–1952

It has been estimated that the initial (1945) strength of these guerrilla armies was 30,000 fighters in Lithuania, 15,000 in Latvia, and between 10,000 and 15,000 in Estonia.[18] The number of active supporters, liaison men, and other "part-time" guerrillas in each case was several times as large. From 1945 onward, the number of guerrilla fighters was steadily rising. The original nuclei of the guerrilla armies were joined by forces that had been clandestinely organized to fight the Germans, and after the Germans' retreat continued to fight against the Soviets.[19] Later, great numbers started to flee to the forests to join the guerrilla forces. These individuals consisted of several categories, which Misiunas and Taagepera have divided as follows:

1. "willing and unwilling German collaborators and draftees";
2. "men avoiding Soviet draft and Red Army deserters";
3. the victims of "Soviet land distribution and other social restructuring measures";
4. actual and/or potential victims of "Soviet screening and deportation campaigns";
5. peasants fleeing from or threatened by the farm collectivization process (and the deportations connected with this process), which was activated in 1949;
6. other individuals "when they could no longer take the insecurity of civilian life."[20]

The absolute number of active guerrilla fighters never grew much over the initial numbers. As Misiunas and Taagepera convincingly explained, this was because "the average life span of a forest brotherhood career has been estimated to be two years due to casualties, disease, and return to civilian life." Hence, "over the 8 years of intensive guerrilla activity (1945–1952), about 100,000 people may have been involved in Lithuania. . . . The Latvian and Estonian forest brotherhood may have involved a total of about 40,000 and 30,000 respectively, at one time or another."[21] This assessment is directly substantiated by a statement made by the director of the LCP Central Committee's Institute of the History of the Party, Romas Sarmaitis. In an interview with American journalist George Weller, Sarmaitis stated that, during the eight years of guerrilla war in Lithuania, 20,000 guerrillas and a similar number of Soviet troops perished on the battlefield.[22]

The last great influx of civilians (peasants fleeing from collectivization and deportation) into the guerrilla forces occurred in 1949. That year the guerrilla movements reached their peak, but they started declining sharply soon afterward. In 1950 they were practically over as nationwide movements in both Estonia and Latvia.[23] By 1951–1952 only about 5,000 guerrillas operated in Lithuania and by the end of 1952, the Unified Command of the Lithuanian Freedom Army (LLA) issued the order to end the armed struggle and proclaimed self-demobilization of the army.[24] In this order, however, the LLA issued a call to all its members and to all Lithuanians to continue the struggle for freedom by peaceful means.

After eight years of incessant and desperate fighting, the guerrilla war in the Baltics thus came to an end; the Baltic nations entered a period of peaceful coexistence with their Soviet rulers.

There is no doubt that in the beginning the guerrillas had commanded almost total popular support. The overwhelming majorities of the Baltic nations were involved in guerrilla activities, carrying out certain duties on behalf of the guerrillas, assisting in hiding and feeding them, and helping them in varying ways. Thus, for most of the time during the guerrilla war, the Soviets in the Baltic area controlled firmly only the larger towns and roads, whereas the countryside belonged to the guerrillas almost entirely.

In their struggle against the guerrillas the Soviets used a variety of means, of which straightforward armed combat was the least prominent and successful. From time to time the Soviets "combed" the forests, but their main repressive emphasis was placed on the destruction of the civilian environment that was conducive to guerrilla activities. To this end, annual mass deportations of native Baltic people to Siberia were carried out between 1945 and 1951. Relatives of the guerrillas and families friendly to them, as well as members of the "dispossessed bourgeoisie of towns and villages," were the first affected.[25] The biggest mass deportation took place in 1949, when all the "kulaks" and other peasants "barring the way to the collectivization of agriculture" were affected.[26] Overall, during 1945–1951, not less than 600,000 natives (or about 9 percent of the total native population) were deported from the Baltic area to Siberia and similar inhospitable (or even uninhabitable) places of the USSR; about half of the deportees came from Lithuania.[27]

For any contact with the guerrillas a civilian was liable to face the charge of treason and sentencing to twenty-five years in the labor camps. Aiding guerrillas under duress or the threat of death was no excuse; a Soviet citizen was supposed to die rather than help the enemy. In September 1944 instructions were issued to the NKVD troops to shoot any suspect on the spot and to burn down any house, farm, or village suspected of harboring "bandits."[28] These instructions were carried out throughout the following years. These unprecedentedly harsh, indeed genocidal, measures, which initially boosted the guerrilla forces, resulted in the long run in their demise.

Parallel to the mass repressions, the Soviets made every effort to enlarge the base of their indigenous popular support. They managed to retain as champions of their cause the tiny groups that had supported them initially— among them a certain segment of the national intelligentsia that had been antiestablishment during the years of independence. It would perhaps be wrong to suggest, as many people do, that such prominent national figures as Petras Cvirka or Antanas Venclova (Lithuania), Vilis Lacis or Augusts Kirchensteins (Latvia), and Johannes Vares-Barbarus, Johannes Semper, and Artur and Eugen Kapps (Estonia), chose to support the Soviet regime so unequivocally merely out of opportunism or careerist motivations. At the beginning, their motives were most likely sincere and, indeed, idealistic. And later? Then it was in any case too late: perhaps temptingly comfortable to stay in, too frightening to quit, or both. Having been incorrigible romantics during the years of independence, these progressive intellectuals learned only too well how to be even more incorrigible pragmatists under the incomparably harsher conditions of Soviet reality.

The ability to rely on these people and to use them for the consolidation and representation of the Soviet regime, though an important asset, was far from sufficient to make the Soviet authorities secure in their running of the Baltic countries. Therefore, in order to secure a firmer grip on power in the area, the Soviets urgently needed to sway to their side much larger, truly grassroots segments of the Baltic population. Their interpretation of events in terms of class rather than national struggle was quite effective for this purpose. Indeed, some natives, especially among those whose position in traditional Baltic societies was at the lower end of the scale and whose prospects for upward mobility were extremely limited, let themselves be convinced by Soviet official propaganda that the ongoing struggle in their countries had nothing to do with national liberty, which was only being used as a cover by the former ruling classes, who sought the restoration of their lost privileges.

Of course, under the "second Russians" (the regime established after the Soviets returned to the Baltic at the end of the war) the ranks of Soviet supporters were joined, in the first place, by great numbers of conformists and careerists, people who would have supported any ruling power either out of respect for its sheer might or, as the Lithuanian poet Vincas Kudirka, once wrote, "for a nugget of gold, for a spoonful of tastier food." But there were also quite a few people who went over to the Soviet side because they were genuinely converted to its "truth." The fact that the Soviet regime generously offered to young and ambitious people of humble origins ample opportunities for promotion and thus for leading positions within their respective societies—something that most had not even dreamed of under pre-Soviet conditions—was perceived by some as nothing less than the embodiment of social justice. Hence, by taking such opportunities, individuals were under the impression that they had taken up a great cause—the cause of the construction of communism, of a truly just and affluent society. They were genuinely unable to discern that, in fact, they had fallen for an old trick that newly established dictatorial regimes have used throughout history to compensate for their lack of legitimacy—the trick of recruiting a fraction of the lowest classes in the population to form a new establishment, an uprooted "praetorian guard." Such a group is easily manipulated because of its complete dependence on the regime not only for positions of power and privilege but for sheer physical survival.

Many different methods for the recruitment of that praetorian guard (or, as the official propaganda put it, the winning of the "children of Baltic workers and working peasants for the service to their own working people's state") were employed in the Baltic area as soon as the Soviet regime was reestablished there during 1944–1945 by the advancing Red Army. Newly set up educational facilities figured most prominently among them. So-called *rabfaks* (accelerated full-time high school graduation courses that paid their students quite generous stipends) were established in major cities for the most zealous adherents. A wide network of evening high schools for working youths (where one could graduate from high school without inter-rupting work) was evolved for those who were ambitious enough to attend. The graduates of these educational establishments were given a great deal of preference in getting places in the universities and other institutions of higher learning, whose first task now was to breed "in-house specialists" re-gardless of their academic qualifications.

For deserving activities—those who joined the Soviet militia forces, agreed to serve in the "extermination battalions" (semi-military units of native people specially formed to fight against the guerrillas later renamed "people's de-fenders' squads"), otherwise expressed their unswerving willingness to serve the Soviet system—special "educational shortcuts" were arranged. These took the form of either different "academies" preparing barely literate people in a few months to serve as judges, procurators, security and militia officers, eco-nomic managers, and so on, or party schools for people specially selected to enter the key apparatuses of party and governmental administration.

Through such means the Soviet regime within a few years managed to build up its Baltic cohorts of faithful and dedicated native cadres. This process was more prominent in Lithuania and Latvia than in Estonia, where the "native cadres" were primarily "Yestonians," that is, people of Estonian origin living in Russia, where they had been assimilated. These "Yestonians" were imported into Estonia in 1940–1941 and 1944–1946 to occupy leading positions and to assure the country's smooth Sovietization. Such people were also imported into Latvia and Lithuania, but there, especially in Lithua-nia, they were more equally mixed with genuine natives.

The relative success of this policy of promoting indigenous people who de-cided to rise via Soviet offices "from filth to wealth," apart from assuring the regime the necessary numbers of native workers for its cause, also produced a genuine ideological split within the Baltic societies. What was formerly a straightforward confrontation between occupied Baltic nations and the occu-pying foreign power thus was extended into a genuine confrontation between a tangible minority (several thousand) of the Baltic population, who for ideal-istic or opportunistic reasons embraced communist ideology and goals, and the great majority of the people, who refused to accept the Soviet regime and remained faithful to the ideology and goals of national independence.

In this sense, one could say that the guerrilla war acquired the dimensions of a genuine civil war. Indeed, as long as the open battle between the regime and the guerrilla (or partisan) armies went on, it provided a connecting link and a rallying point for the active expression of genuinely popular views and goals. The whole spectrum of the contradictory political orientation of the Baltic nations was manifested in this battle. There was little doubt that only a small minority converted to the new masters; the overwhelming majority was still committed to resisting them.[29]

The mood of resistance, so overwhelming in the beginning, started to flounder as years went by. With no support, let alone help, from the West (which preferred to turn a blind eye to the Baltic struggle for freedom), more and more Baltic people started to perceive their lonely struggle against the huge Soviet state machine as not only futile but nationally suicidal. They became keen to end it by any means. Among such people were several leading figures of the resistance movement, for example, the Lithuanians Jonas Deksnys, Juozas Markulis, and Kostas Kubilinskas. Knowing that they would not be able to persuade their colleagues in the resistance leadership to stop the armed struggle, they went so far as to become secret agents of the KGB, actively helping it (mainly by providing vital intelligence) to destroy the resistance movement from within. As a result of their collaboration, many thousands of their former friends and colleagues, together with their families, were killed or imprisoned for long years in Soviet labor camps. But they remained unrepentant, saying that if that was the price for assuring the nation's physical survival, it was worth paying.[30]

Thus, after eight years of desperate armed struggle, the period of open resistance started to come to an end. It did not finally stop because of a decisive Soviet military victory against the resisters. After all, the Baltic guerrillas had been defeated many times before and many times new volunteers had come to restore their ranks. In the 1950s, however, largely for the reasons explained above, no more recruits were available to continue this hopeless struggle. The fact that at a certain point fresh forces for further open resistance did not emerge and that the whole open resistance movement was slowly dying out does not at all mean that the Baltic nations had internally surrendered to the Soviet regime or had decided to accept it wholeheartedly. Rather, they had realized that direct opposition to the occupation, under the continuing circumstances of East–West peaceful coexistence, was not simply doomed to fail but was fraught with consequences that could be literally fatal. Hence, the Baltic peoples ceased their war against the Soviet occupier not out of acquiescence but because of their newly and very painfully acquired realistic perception of their political situation in the world. It was neither the Soviets nor the Baltic nations but political realism that triumphed. And therefore the war was far from over. As the subsequent chapter shows, the Baltic nations simply delayed the final act of their struggle with the occupier until better times, knowing by then quite well that these better times could not be brought by their efforts alone.

COMPLIANCE AND PROTEST, 1952–1982

When armed resistance broke down and compliance became the order of the day, the voice for the ideals of national independence vanished together with the identifiable organizational framework of opposition to Soviet rule. These ideals, removed from the visible social surface to take refuge in an atomized shape within the inner consciousness of individual Balts, yielded the social scene to the monopolistic dominance of Soviet official ideology and values. As a result, the latter, though never "interiorized" by the vast majority of people, assumed the position of the only moral and ideological bond holding the Baltic societies together. Needless to say, this situation caused the profound alienation of most individual Balts from the official societies in which they had to live. The hope that in time this alienation would soften and finally be replaced by genuine integration proved futile; in fact, as time went by, it only deepened. Moreover, and this was the most striking development, over time the alienation acquired an absolute and universal dimension that it had never had before.

Indeed, the limited ideological support the Soviet regime had initially achieved in the Baltic countries and had maintained (even increased) during the time of terror was gradually but irretrievably lost after 1952, during the time of peaceful coexistence of the people and the regime. It is paradoxical but nevertheless true: the apparently total victory of Soviet communism over Baltic societies gradually brought an equally total rejection of it within the moral and political consciousness of the Baltic peoples.

The ideals and expectations that Baltic people with communist convictions (or, at least, aspirations) had attached to the new regime completely failed to materialize. There was now less freedom and more injustice; poverty, instead of disappearing, sharply increased and, because of the collectivization of agriculture, became clearly irredeemable for all except a handful of top communist bureaucrats. The rivers of blood that had flowed so amply accomplished only one task: the seating of the new elite, the old-time communist apparatchiks and their newly recruited "praetorian guards," in positions of power and privilege. The continuing denial of national and individual rights could no longer be justified by either war or class struggle. In this respect, the new circumstances had a particularly strong, sobering effect on erstwhile communist idealists, who saw in them the betrayal of everything they had believed in and hoped for. It was a shocking discovery that appeared with such blatant clarity that communist sympathizers found it impossible to ignore it.

Despite this realization by the new elite (or the "new class," as Milovan Djilas put it), almost all of its members decided to soldier on. The majority continued out of purely selfish and careerist motivations such as fear and greed; a few had mixed motives, including the determination to use their newly acquired positions of influence for the benefit of their countries and people. Some, probably the most naïve and idealistic, failed to adjust to reality as it was and, by entering into conflict with its rigorous demands, were crushed or dropped by the system.[31]

The "realistically minded" native apparatchiks who learned how to avoid risks and continued to serve the regime obediently were perhaps more bitter about the situation in which they found themselves than anyone else. After all, it was they who, in their day-to-day activities, constantly experienced the stifling power of Moscow's directing hand and the humiliation of being deprived of any independent will and reduced to the status of robots blindly implementing whatever arbitrary and repressive decisions were handed down. Whatever their motivations for continuing in the positions of the new elite, their ambitions were deeply frustrated and their inner discontent and disappointment were rather overwhelming. This is how the Soviet regime lost among the indigenous Balts its last genuine, ideologically motivated, support. By the mid-1950s, it had gone completely, and sheer opportunism took its place.

The "breakdown of ideology" inevitably produced certain clashes that at least partially came into the open. The first such manifestations took place in Estonia. They started in 1946 with the suicide of Johannes Vares-Barbarus, the chairman of the Estonian Soviet government (and, before that the head of the "people's" government). There is strong evidence suggesting that the cause of Vares's suicide was the blatant contrast between his expectations for Estonia's future, which motivated him to become one of the main architects of her Sovietization, and the reality of the Soviet Estonia over which he presided.[32] Many, if not all, indigenous Estonian Communists had similar feelings. They tried to preserve Estonia's nationhood by whatever modest means were in their power. Alerted to these attitudes by Vares's suicide, the Kremlin closely watched the Estonian Communist Party and in 1950 decided to launch a purge of its indigenous leadership and membership. A great number of leading Estonian Communists, including the first secretary of the Central Committee of the Estonian Communist Party, Nikolai Karotamm; the chairman of Estonia's Council of Ministers, Arnold Veimer; and the chairman of the *Presidium* of the Estonian Supreme Soviet, E. Päll were accused of bourgeois nationalism, narrow localism, ostentatious isolationism from the rest of the USSR, and immersion in narrowly conceived and essentially nonsocialist national traditionalism.[33] As a result, the leadership of the Estonian party, as well as the whole apparatus of Estonian administration were "Yestonianized" and Russified more than ever before. The first secretaryship was handed over to Johannes Käbin, another "Yestonian" who hardly even understood the Estonian language; his duty was to assure that no more "deviations" would occur in the future, and he did his best to fulfill that duty.

A similar crackdown took place in 1958–1959 in Latvia. The main culprit there was Eduards Berklavs, the vice-chairman of the Latvian Council of Ministers and former first secretary of Riga's party committee. Together with him, the chairman of the Latvian Trade Union Council, A. Pinskis; the first secretary of the Latvian Communist Youth League, A. Ruskulis; and scores of other leading Latvian Communists were purged—charged with "Latvian bourgeois-nationalist deviation."[34] The chairman of the *Presidium* of Latvia's Supreme Soviet, K. Ozolins, also lost his job in the purge. He was replaced by Janis Kalnberzins, who had been removed from the post of first secretary of the

CC of the Latvian Communist Party, which he had held from 1940 until the purge in 1959 (as the man with overall responsibility for the party he was found guilty by association). A Russian communist of Latvian origin, Arvids Pelse, became the first secretary of the CC of the Latvian Communist Party and vigorously pursued into the early 1960s the task of removing every indigenous Latvian from a position of higher responsibility (even Vilis Lacis, the veteran chairman of the Council of Ministers, who publicly dissociated himself from the "deviationists" and was active in denouncing them, was dismissed from his post). Nevertheless, a 1971 letter from seventeen Latvian old communists (who preferred to remain anonymous), addressed to several of the world's communist parties, not only openly defended Berklavs's line but went much further by vigorously denouncing Soviet policies in Latvia. The letter demanded that the "fraternal parties" take up with the CPSU the gross breaches of "Leninist national policy" perpetrated in Latvia. This letter manifested with all clarity that, although suppressed, the national ideals of the native Latvian Communist establishment were as much alive as ever.[35]

Matters in Lithuania were different in appearance but not in essence. There were no party purges in Lithuania and no accusations of dissent or deviation against any party members. This was largely due to the fact that, unlike his counterparts in Latvia and Estonia, the first secretary of the CC of the Lithuanian Communist Party, A. Snieckus, was an outstandingly strong, inveterate and autocratic leader who, without interruption from the end of 1926, had practically been in sole charge of the Lithuanian Communist Party and in full control of everybody in it. There was no question of anyone in the Lithuanian party speaking out or doing anything at all without Snieckus's prior consent. He had total authority over his companions and also managed to carry this authority in his relations with Stalin and the whole Kremlin leadership. Snieckus's ruthlessness and implacability were legendary. During the time of deportations and repressions he would not spare even his closest relatives, let alone anyone else. Stalin personally was extremely impressed with Snieckus's performance and even used to say that the two of them were then the only real communists left in the whole of the Soviet Union.[36] Mikhail Suslov, who in 1944 was dispatched from Moscow to Vilnius as chairman of the Lithuanian Bureau of the CC of the All-Union Communist Party and whose job was to supervise Lithuanian communists in their fight against the "class enemy" and to "help" them to build a socialist society, was not only full of admiration for Snieckus, but fell heavily under his influence. Snieckus carried this influence until his death in 1974, which explains how he was able to get away with so many things that would have spelled the end of a party career for anyone else.

In the end, however, the disappointment with Soviet reality affected the fanatical Snieckus as much as it did other indigenous Baltic communists. But he was too experienced a politician to deviate openly from Moscow's line; he knew how to succeed and survive where Karotamm or Berklavs had failed.

A Lithuanian samizdat author writing under the pseudonym of T. Zenklys, who had known Snieckus quite intimately for a number of years, testified in his obituary on Snieckus that during his last twenty or so years in power (from the late 1940s or early 1950s) Snieckus changed beyond recognition. "At the beginning, Moscow could not even dream of a more assiduous servant of its will in Lithuania," wrote Zenklys. But "increasingly from year to year, one could perceive in Snieckus's activity a national orientation, a defense of the specific interests of Lithuania, an effort first of all to see to the country's proper development, to the rise of its prosperity."[37] So we see that a spiritual evolution, leading to disillusionment with the Soviet order and an understanding that false gods had been served, affected even the most dedicated and Stalinist Baltic communists, to say nothing of the others. True, some remained convinced communists and Marxists, but they stopped identifying their beliefs with the "real socialism" of the Soviet regime.

By the first half of the 1950s there were no more indigenous Baltic people who continued to support the Soviet regime out of idealism or conviction. Nor did any of the indigenous Balts still believe in communism as represented and implemented by this regime. Hence, the enforced situation of total outward compliance had been complemented by an equally total inward dissent. It goes without saying that inward dissent tends to find some forms of expression in social action and thus partially reduces the totality of compliance. This, however, does not change the peculiar combination of basic compliance with total dissent that has been the characteristic feature of the relationship between the Baltic peoples and the sociopolitical system in which they lived. To understand how this combination worked practically, it is necessary to distinguish between the then Baltic peoples' *teleological* and *practical-pragmatic* political orientations.

The teleological political consciousness coincides with the people's positive vision of the desirable political future for themselves, their nations, and the world around them. It therefore also implies a certain plan for political change, without which these future-oriented goals would remain unachievable. As I have argued elsewhere, the teleological political consciousness of the Baltic peoples was cohesive, lent itself to a proper definition, and was universal in the sense that it was shared by every native Balt, including even the most active collaborators with the regime.[38] It could be defined by the following five-trait cluster:

1. Reestablishment within its ethnic boundaries, for each Baltic nation, of a free and truly independent nation-state;
2. Transformation of the present political, social, and economic order into one that would be: (a) consistent with national traditions; (b) committed to putting national interests first; and (c) able to provide sufficient room for individuals and their freely formed associations to exercise independent initiative, defend their legitimate interests, and otherwise realize

their potential in all spheres of life, first of all asserting their true national–cultural identity.

3. Establishment of direct, tight, and durable political, economic, cultural, and person-to-person links with the Western world, accompanied by the removal of all restrictions on foreign travel and aimed in the end at the integration of the Baltic states into the community of Western nations;

4. Restoration on the territory of each Baltic state of an ethnically, linguistically, and culturally compact—if not entirely homogenous—national society (this aim was considered to be the highest priority in all three Baltic republics but was more acute in Latvia and Estonia, where the Russians and other minorities constitute nearly one half and two-fifths of their respective populations; in Lithuania the non-Lithuanians made up only about 20 percent, of whom the immigrant Russians are less than half);

5. Promotion within the framework of a nationally compact society of complete religious and cultural freedom for all.

How was this teleological orientation translated into the pragmatic attitudes toward social reality that determined everyday political behavior characterized by basic compliance with Soviet rule? Compliance required all Baltic people to accept a certain degree of conformism, which varied from one person to another. One could draw a certain continuum between total conformism and total nonconformism, within which one could place the practical–pragmatic political orientation of the great majority of the Balts. Indeed, very few were total conformists who built their whole lives and careers on unquestioning subservience to the regime and thus completely sold out their natural teleological orientation for the sake of security, power, and comfort. The majority of Balts who invested their lives in rendering political service to the regime managed to combine conformism with what one could call the conservationist orientation, or simply *conservationism*. This orientation expressed itself in the use of official position to do whatever was deemed possible for the preservation of the nation's identity, integrity, and its natural and spiritual resources—as well as for the enhancement of its relative welfare. The degree to which this conservationist attitude expressed itself delineated the limits of one's compliance with the regime. In certain cases, conservationists trespassed the limits of official toleration and, sometimes inadvertently, found themselves in a position of activist dissent.

Outbursts of extrastructural activist dissent (opposing certain policies of the regime or demanding change) started in the Baltic as early as 1956 (four years after the end of armed resistance) and continued unabated.[39] It is in these outbursts that the genuine teleological political orientation of the Baltic nations clearly manifested itself. But, even more important, ever-increasing coincidence between the people's practical–pragmatic and teleological political orientations had been marked. In other words, during the years 1956–1982, a diminution of compliance with official ideological and political demands and a growing assertion of the people's national selves (through protests, demands, samizdat publications, and various other forms of independent activity) slowly but steadily developed in all the Baltic republics.

Overt dissident activities in the Baltic states during the last decades, especially since the late 1960s, are sufficiently well-documented in various publications.[40] What should be said, however, is that, spontaneous mass manifestations apart,[41] systematic protest activities that at first were sporadic and focused on specific issues (religious rights, creative freedom, and freedom of information)[42] gradually began to center on more general issues of national and individual rights. Dissent acquired a more regular organizational pattern in the form of various groups and committees, as well as periodical samizdat publiations.

In Lithuania, two such committees were formed in open defiance of the regime: the so-called Lithuanian Helsinki Group (1976), which was one of several such groups formed in the Soviet Union in that year, and the Committee for the Defense of the Rights of Catholics (1980). The Helsinki Group, in spite of having lost by 1982 through governmental repression (or death) most of its active members, recruited new ones and kept itself alive throughout the 1980s. From the beginning of 1983, the Committee for the Defense of the Rights of Catholics has been submitted to a repressive onslaught by the authorities, which culminated in the trials of its leaders, Father Alfonsas Svarinskas, in May 1983 (sentenced to seven years of internment and three years of internal exile for anti-Soviet propaganda) and Father Sigitas Tamkevicius, in December 1983 (sentenced, under the same indictment, to six years of internment and four years of internal exile). Nevertheless, the committee has survived and continued its activities. A significant boost for the continuation of these activities was the protest letter in defense of Svarinskas and Tamkevicius signed by the unprecedented number of 46,905 people from seventy-one parishes in May–June 1983. There were a few other organized dissident bodies in Lithuania that did not operate publicly and were known mainly because of their samizdat output. One of such "invisible" bodies was the Lithuanian Liberation League (LLL), which assumed the leading role in organizing mass protest activities during 1987–1988 (it was in response to these LLL activities that Lithuania's party-state authorities agreed to the organization on June 3, 1988, by "loyal intelligentsia," of the Sajudis movement).

In Latvia, three such groups came into existence in 1975: the Latvian Independence Movement, Latvia's Democratic Youth Committee, and Latvia's Christian Democratic Organization. By 1976 they started to coordinate their activities and issued joint statements addressed to the government of the Latvian SSR, the Australian prime minister (Malcolm Fraser), and others. Another, more activist body, the Organization for Latvia's Independence, organized throughout the 1970s and the 1980s various protest actions, petitions, and demands. In 1987–1988, this dissident body played a role analogous to that of Lithuania's LLL.

In Estonia, two such groups acquired prominence by 1972: the Estonian Democratic Movement and the Estonian National Front. In 1974 another group, Estonian Patriots, came into existence, and the Association of Concerned Estonians was formed in 1976 after the government crushed earlier oppositional bodies. In 1978 two new groups, the White Key Brotherhood and Maarjamaa, mostly concerned with problems of cultural freedom, were formed in addition to the ones mentioned above. All these groups took a lead in organizing the mass demonstrations of 1987–1988 and thus precipitated the creation of the officially accepted Estonian National Front in spring 1988.

Lithuania was richest for samizdat periodicals not only in the whole of the USSR but also in Eastern Europe. Apart from the *Chronicle of the Catholic Church*, which in 1982 celebrated the tenth anniversary of its uninterrupted appearance, at least twelve other unofficial periodicals circulated in this republic. *Ausra* (The Dawn), the secular samizdat periodical, has appeared regularly since 1975. Between 1976 and 1979 a wide variety of different religious and secular samizdat magazines sprang up. Among the religious ones, *Dievas ir Tevyne* (God and Fatherland) and *Rupintojelis* (Sorrowing Christ) are worth mentioning; among the secular, *Varpas* (The Bell), which appeared since 1977, upheld the Lithuanian liberal tradition; *Alma Mater* (1979) tackled the problems of higher education; *Pastoge* (The Shelter) and *Perspektyvos* (Perspectives) discussed literature, philosophy, and the arts; a few others, such as *Tiesos Kelias* (The Way of Truth) and *Laisves Sauklys* (The Clarion of Freedom), both started in 1976, had no special profile but represented the nationalist orientation of the Lithuanians by dealing with a variety of different subjects. Several of these periodicals were stopped by the authorities, who discovered and severely punished their editors. However, *Perspektyvos* and *Dievas ir Tey*ne reappeared after a short interval in 1981, and in the same year *Tautos Kelias* (The Nation's Way), an entirely new samizdat periodical publication, was started.

In Estonia the periodical *Eesti Democraat* (Estonian Democrat) has been published since 1971, and *Eesti Rahvuslik Hääl* (The Voice of the Estonian Nation) appeared soon afterward. What is interesting and specific about Estonia's samizdat periodicals was the fact that some of them were published in Russian; thus the *Estonian Democrat* was published in Russian translation and there was also a special Russian-language samizdat periodical, *Luch Svobody* (The Beam of Freedom). Another Estonian samizdat periodical, *Poolpäevaleht* (The Semi-Daily), was started in 1978, but it was crushed by the authorities a year later (only six issues were published and circulated).

In spite of the ferocious repressions that the authorities applied to break down organized Baltic dissent, it not only persisted but also developed new forms of organized activities. It is significant that by the end of the 1970s dissident groups in all three Baltic republics had started to coordinate their activities and launched joint ventures. For example, on August 23, 1979 (the 40th anniversary of the infamous Molotov–Ribbentrop Pact), a joint petition bearing forty-five signatures of representatives of all three Baltic republics was issued in Moscow. The petition demanded that the USSR and the two

German states declare null and void the Molotov–Ribbentrop Pact, which assigned the Baltic states to the Soviet Union. This document must be singled out not only because it was one of the first exercises in Baltic unity of action but also because it marked a totally new departure in Baltic dissident politics. For the first time since armed resistance to Soviet rule stopped, the demand for full restoration of the national independence of the three Baltic states was forcefully made in clear and unequivocal terms by people prepared to risk the full consequences of such an act.[43] In fact the Baltic dissidents of the late 1970s had thus taken up, in a unified manner, the banner of their predecessors, the guerrilla fighters, and had committed themselves to carry it on, this time, however, exclusively by means of peaceful struggle. Thus the resistance movement of the Baltic states, in terms of publicly proclaimed goals, in 1979 returned to its 1940 starting point, in spite of the fact that in 1952 it had seemingly been smashed irreversibly. 1979 was thus a departure point at which the Baltic dissident movements overtly committed themselves to the cause of the restoration of their respective nation-states' independence. What the world saw in 1987–1991 as a sudden upsurge in the Baltics of independence-seeking national movements, sprang in fact from that August 23, 1979 petition and gradually developed into a potentially massive popular movement that erupted onto the social surface as soon as glasnost finally ended in people the fear, the belief in the effective mercilessness of Soviet persecution. With that the mood of hopelessness about effective resistance to Soviet rule, about engaging into a fight for the hitherto thoroughly hidden goals constituting the Baltic nations' teleological political consciousness, was dispelled.

The growing cooperation of activist Baltic dissenters with the dissident movement in Russia was extremely significant, too. A unity of purpose was established, whereby the Balts joined the struggle of the Russians for the democratization of the Soviet Union, and democratically-minded Russians made the cause of Baltic independence a part of their own program for democratic change in the USSR as a whole. The most symbolic expression of this unity was the fact that the petition of August 23, 1979, signed by forty-five representatives of the Baltic republics and demanding the restoration of the sovereignty of the Baltic states, was amended by a petition of support for it signed by five representatives of Russian democratic dissent: Mal'va Landa, Viktor Nekipelov, Tatyana Velikanova, Andrei Sakharov, and Arina Ginzburg.

The history of the cooperation between Baltic and Russian dissenters goes, however, much further back. In July 1968, a document written and signed on behalf of "Numerous Members of the Estonian Technical Intelligentsia," entitled "To Hope or to Act" gave a sympathetic but critical assessment of Sakharov's *Thoughts on Progress, Coexistence, and Intellectual Freedom* and formulated a program for democratic change in the USSR as a whole, which was conceived by the authors of this document as the prerequisite for the attainment of the freedom of both Russia and Estonia.[44] A similar document, "Program of the Democrats of Russia, the Ukraine, and the Baltic Lands," was circulated by samizdat channels approximately at the same time.[45]

In Latvia in 1968, Ivan Yakhimovichs protested against the Moscow trial of Aleksander Ginzburg and Yuri Galanskov, as well as against other convictions and persecutions of Russian dissidents.[46] Together with Petro Grigorenko and others, Yakhimovichs was active in protest activities concerning the Soviet invasion of Czechoslovakia and other issues. In a statement on the eve of his arrest (March 25, 1969), Yakhimovichs made an appeal addressed to Bertrand Russell, Alexander Solzhenitsyn, Andrei Sakharov, Petro Grigorenko, Alexander Dubcek, and others, expressing his commitment to the struggle for freedom and human rights not only in Latvia but in Russia, the Ukraine, Czechoslovakia, Poland, and elsewhere.[47]

In their turn, Sakharov and other Russian dissidents from the late 1960s onward campaigned for the release of Baltic political prisoners and regularly expressed their solidarity with the cause of Baltic freedom. The publicity that the Baltic appeals and samizdat publications received in Western media was possible only because Moscow dissidents transmitted them to Western correspondents accredited in Moscow (one should note that the petition of August 23, 1979 was launched in Moscow and the Lithuanian Helsinki Group was formed there in 1976). Baltic émigré literature also found its ways into the Baltic republics via "transmission points" in Moscow. Moscow's *Chronicle of Current Events* was regularly reporting on events in the Baltic and published extracts from Baltic samizdat documents giving special prominence to the reports from the *Chronicle of the Lithuanian Catholic Church*. The trial of the leading Muscovite dissident, Sergey Kovalev, took place in December 1975 in Vilnius (Lithuania), and one of the charges against him was the dissemination of the *Chronicle of the Lithuanian Catholic Church* via the *Chronicle of Current Events* and other means.[48] Accusations of assisting to propagate the *Chronicle of the Lithuanian Catholic Church* were also raised by the KGB against another prominent Russian dissident, Andrei Tverdokhlebov.[49] The Lithuanian Helsinki Group established in 1976 worked in close cooperation with the analogous group in Moscow. Even closer links between Baltic and other Soviet dissidents were forged in the labor camps where they served their sentences together.[50]

Through all these channels Baltic dissent firmly established itself as a constituent part of the wider USSR's democratic movement and also convinced this movement to embrace the cause of Baltic independence and freedom. As the *Chronicle of the Lithuanian Catholic Church* stated, the work of Russian dissenters for Lithuania "compelled the Lithuanian Catholics to take another look at the Russian nation. Their sacrifice is necessary for all persecuted Soviet people, it is also necessary for the Lithuanian Catholics."[51]

During the 1970s to the late 1980s, Baltic activist dissent, although firmly entrenched and ever-present as an important element in Baltic social and political life, was practiced only by a tiny minority of the Baltic people. Significant were, however, not so much the numbers of Baltic dissidents as the impact they made on the Baltic societies. Under their influence conservationism became much bolder and daring and it gradually embraced almost all native Balts. This process of totalization of "intrastructural" dissent was apparently overlooked by the party and Soviet authorities. When in 1987–1988, the activist dissidents started to attract to their protest activities a truly mass following, the Soviet Baltic officialdoms decided to neutralize them by encouraging the loyal members of the cultural and scientific establishments to take the lead in anti-Stalinist and similar mass manifestations expressing real grievances of the people with regard to the regime. The Baltic partocrats thought that by so doing they would isolate the dissidents, relegate them back to nothingness without direct repression, and then, through their traditionally obedient intellectual underlings, maintain effective control over the mass exercise of the liberties permitted by glasnost. This plan, as the next chapter shows, failed to materialize. The National Fronts of Latvia and Estonia as well as the Lithuanian Sajudis, although initially created by outwardly loyal Soviet intellectuals, soon acquired their own momentum and by 1989 had started to challenge the ruling communist parties and the Soviet regime. History was thus to prove that dissent in the Baltic states was total indeed and that the difference between conservationist and activist dissent was not of substance but only of method.[52] When, because of glasnost, the difference in methods became irrelevant, nothing was left to draw a dividing line between the few activist dissidents and the rest of the people—they organically and naturally merged into one cohesive entity committed to shedding their artificial Soviet identity and wholeheartedly to embrace the cause of restoration of their national independence and freedom.

NOTES

1. The text of Order no. 002113, issued by the NKVD of the USSR on 11 October 1939, is not available. Our knowledge of this order springs from explicit references made to it (invoking both the number and the date) in the "follow-up" orders of the people's commissariats of internal affairs and state security of the Baltic republics. Full texts of these orders are available and were published in English translation in the *Third Interim Report of the Select Committee on Communist Aggression* (House of Representatives, Eighty-Third Congress, Second Session, under authority of H.R. 346 and H.R. 438) (Washington, D.C., 1954) (hereafter referred to as *Third Interim Report*). Among such orders the following ones should be mentioned: no. 0054 of 28 November 1940, "On the Negligence in Accounting of Anti-Soviet and Socially Alien Elements," issued by the Lithuanian SSR's People's Commissar of Internal Affairs, Guzevicius (pp. 470–72); and no. 023 of April 25, 1941, "On the Organization of the Operative Accounting in the County [*uezd*] Branches of the People's Commissariat of State Security" (pp. 495–97). The second of these refers twice to NKVD Order no. 001223. See also no. 0037 of May 23, 1941, "On Preparation for the Operation Ordered by the Directive No. 77 of May 19, 1941, of the People's Commissar of State Security of the USSR" (pp. 515–20). Both no. 0023 and no. 0037 were issued by the Lithuanian SSR's People's Commissar of State Security, Gladkov.

2. The "Merkulov Directive," no. 77 of May 19, 1941, is referred to in Order no. 0037 of May 23, 1941, issued by Gladkov as the basis for "the direction, preparation

and execution of the operation of purging the Lithuanian SSR from the hostile anti-Soviet and criminal and socially-dangerous element" (*Third Interim Report*, 515). The text of this directive is not available.

3. The text of the notorious "Serov Instructions," which does not bear either a number or a date of issue, is published in the *Third Interim Report* under a misleading heading: "1. Moscow Instructions on Deportations, Order no. 001223." In fact, the "Serov Instructions" and the NKVD's Order no. 001223 are two entirely separate documents. Not only are their subjects different (accounting of the people to be purged in Order no. 001223, and the execution of deportation in the "Serov Instructions"), but so are their issuing organs (Order no. 001223 is consistently referred to as a document issued by the People's Commissariat of Internal Affairs, the NKVD, whereas Serov signed his instructions in his capacity as deputy people's commissar of state security [of the NKGB].) The attribution of a date "between February and June 7, 1941" to the "Serov Instructions" is based on the fact that: (1) the NKGB was only created, by its separation from the NKVD, in February 1941 (hence, it could not have issued any documents earlier than that); and, (2) the original text of the document was stamped as received in the NKGB office of the city of Siauliai on June 7, 1941 (for a detailed elaboration on the subject of the dating of the "Serov Instructions," see Dr. Constantine R. Jurgela's 'Review of Bronis J. Kaslas, ed., *The USSR—German Aggression Against Lithuania'*, *Ukrainian Quarterly* 29, no. 4 [winter 1973]: 407–11, especially 409–11).

4. For these figures see "Pirmoji sovietine okupacija (1940–1941)" (The First Soviet Occupation, 1940–1941), in *Lietuviu Enciklopedija* (Lithuanian Encyclopedia), vol. 15 (Boston: Lithuanian Encyclopedia Press, 1968), 369 (on Lithuania); *Latvju Enciklopedija* (Latvian Encyclopedia) (Stockholm: Tris Zvaigznes, 1950), 477 (on Latvia); and E. Uustalu, "Events After 1940," in A. Rei, ed., *The Drama of the Baltic Peoples* (Stockholm: Kirjastus Vaba Eesti, 1970), 320 (on Estonia).

5. This estimate is convincingly elaborted in R. Misiunas and R. Taagepera, *The Baltic States: The Years of Dependence* (1940–1980) (London: C. Hurst, 1983), 41.

6. See K. Skirpa, *Sukilimas Lietuvos suverenumui atstatyti: Dokumentine apzvalga* (Uprising for the Restoration of Lithuania's Sovereignty: A Documentary Survey) (Washington, D.C.: Skirpa, 1973), 26–33, 37–8, 115–16. For an extensive study of these events in English, see A. M. Budreckis, *The Lithuanian National Revolt of 1941* (Boston: Lithuanian Encyclopedia Press, 1968). An account of the LAF's inauguration, together with the texts of the minutes of its inaugural meeting and the Inaugural Act itself, is given in Skirpa, *Sukilimas*, pp. 90–100.

7. Z. Ivinskis, "Lithuania During the War: Resistance Against the Soviet and the Nazi Occupants," in V. S. Vardys, ed., *Lithuania Under the Soviets: Portrait of a Nation, 1940–65* (New York: Praeger, 1965), 65, 67. The 100,000 is a conservative estimate; in most other sources the figure given is "at least 125,000 men" (see J. A. Swettenham, *The Tragedy of the Baltic States: A Report Compiled from Official Documents and Eyewitnesses' Stories* [London: Hollis and Carter, 1952], 143).

8. Swettenham, *Tragedy of the Baltic States*, 143.

9. See Misiunas and Taagepera, *The Baltic States: The Years of Dependence*, 47.

10. Swettenham, *Tragedy of the Baltic States*, 143.

11. See Misiunas and Taagepera, *The Baltic States: The Years of Dependence*, 47.

12. *The Baltic States, 1940–1972: Documentary Background and Survey of Developments* (Stockholm: Baltic Committee in Scandinavia, 1972), 55.

13. Misiunas and Taagepera, *The Baltic States: The Years of Dependence*, 47. According to them, only 5,000 fighters were active in northern Estonia, mainly in forests and in the countryside.

14. R. Silde-Karklins, "Formen des Widerstands im Baltikum, 1940–1968," in T. Ebert, ed., *Ziviler Widerstand: Fallstudien aus der Innenpolitischen Friedens— und Konfliktforschung* (Düsseldorf: Bertelsmann-Universitätsverl, 1970), 215.

15. E. J. Harrison, *Lithuania's Fight for Freedom* (New York: The Lithuanian American Information Center, 1945), 46. For a detailed and well-documented treatment of the German failure to use the Lithuanians for their ends, see A. Dallin, *German Rule in Russia, 1941–1945: A Study of Occupation Policies*, 2d rev. ed. (London: Macmillan, 1981), 182–98.

16. Z. Ivinskis, "Lithuania During the War," 75, 78–81.

17. The Lithuanian estimate, first given by V. S. Vardys ("The Partisan Movement in Postwar Lithuania," in Vardys, *Lithuania under the Soviets*, 85) on the basis of a thorough analysis of a number of documents, is shared by all other authors who write about this subject. On Latvia, see R. Silde-Karklins, "Formen des Widerstands," 216. The Estonian figure follows from the analysis given in Misiunas and Taagepera, *The Baltic States: The Years of Dependence*, p. 81.

18. For example, in Lithuania it was the Legion of Samogitia, which "was formed in 1942 for anti-German purposes" (T. Remeikis, *Opposition to Soviet Rule in Lithuania, 1945–1980* [Chicago: Institute of Lithuanian Studies Press, 1980], 60); in Latvia it was the army of General Kurelis, which from December 1944 operated in Courland against the Germans. For more details on Kurelis, see sources as different as the publication of the Baltic Committee in Stockholm, *The Baltic States, 1940–1972*, p. 68; and, from the Academy of Sciences of the Latvian SSR, *Istoriia Latvi-iskoi SSR* (History of the Latvian SSR), vol. 3, 1917–1950, ed. K. J. Strazdin (Riga, 1958), p. 581.

19. Misiunas and Taagepera, *The Baltic States: The Years of Dependence*, 82.

20. Misiunas and Taagepera, *The Baltic States: The Years of Dependence*, 83–84. The facts on life span are referred to Vardys, "The Partisan Movement," in Vardys, *Lithuania under the Soviets*.

21. *Chicago Daily News*, August 17, 1961. This is a conservative estimate for the guerrillas' death toll. The more generally accepted one, given by the guerrilla sources themselves, is 30,000 (Vardys, "The Partisan Movement," 86; and J. Pajaujis, *The Soviet Genocide in Lithuania* [New York: Manyland Books, 1980], 108). Some outside estimates deem even this figure too conservative. Since the exact battlefield death toll cannot be established, Misiunas and Taagepera (*The Baltic States: The Years of Dependence*, 84) reasonably suggest a compromise solution between 20,000 and 50,000. As for the Soviet casualties, there is overall agreement that they must have been much heavier than those of the guerrillas. The guerrilla sources claim that they killed not 20,000 but 80,000 Soviet troops on the battlefield (see Pajaujis, *Soviet Genocide*, 108).

22. On Estonia, see J. Pennar, "Soviet Nationality Policy and the Estonian Communist Elite," in T. Parming and E. Järvesoo, eds., *A Case Study of a Soviet Republic: The Estonian SSR* (Boulder, Colo.: Westview Press, 1978), 116. Nevertheless, fighting in Estonia continued well into 1953 when, according to the chairman of the Estonian KGB, Ado Pork, it was largely crushed (A. Port, "Na strazhe zavoevaniy Oktiabria," *Kommunist Estonii*, no. 12 [1967]: 11). Separate guerrillas continued to operate in Estonia even in the 1970s, as A. Küng reports, referring to information about the execution in

1976 of a guerrilla fighter, Kalev Arro, published in the Soviet Estonian Press (A. Küng, *A Dream of Freedom* [Cardiff, 1981], p. 202). On the decline of guerrilla resistance in Latvia, see J. Rutkis, ed., *Latvia: Country and People* (Stockholm: Latvian National Foundation, 1967), 260. The last known major battle between the guerrillas and Soviet forces in Latvia took place in February 1950 (Rutkis, *Latvia,* 275).

23. Misiunas and Taagepera, *The Baltic States: The Year of Dependence*, 90; and K. V. Tauras, *Guerrilla Warfare on the Amber Coast* (New York: Voyages Press, 1962), 95. The actual warfare in Lithuania did not stop even after 1952, since several large guerrilla units disregarded the order and continued to operate well into 1954. Thus one of the guerrilla leaders, A. Jonusas, when interrogated by the KGB, declared: "In December 1952 I was appointed commander of the 'Darius' region. Three units— *Pilis* (Castle), *Jura* (Sea), and *Gelezinis Vilkas* (Iron Wolf)—belonged to this region and were subordinated to me. I continued in this post until June 21, 1954, i.e., until the day of my arrest" (Lithuanian Academy of Sciences, *Archyviniai Dokumentai: IX Rinkinys* [Archival Documents: Ninth Collection], ed. Z. Vasiliauskas [Vilnius: Mintis, 1968], 116). It is also indicative that the "extermination battalions," formed to fight the guerrillas "on the spot" in 1944, were finally disbanded only in 1954. Separate Lithuanian guerrillas remained active in the 1960s and 1970s. In 1965, *Tiesa* (Truth), the LCP daily newspaper, solemnly announced that the last Lithuanian guerrilla, Antanas Kraujelis, had been discovered by security forces and was shot in the battle that ensued, but five years later, in 1971, another such "last guerrilla," Henrikas Kajotas, was found.

24. Each administrative-territorial unit was given a quota for the number of people to be deported from its territory. Then a special commission consisting of the leading party, KGB, and Soviet officials of this unit would prepare a list of people to be deported. Since the deportations were usually performed in one or, at the most, two consecutive days, people on the list could avoid deportation if on these days they happened to be absent from home. However, the quota had to be met regardless of circumstances, and it always was, by deporting an equal number of the neighbors of the absentees, people who originally were not on the list at all.

25. Conservative estimates suggest that in 1949 alone about 200,000 Baltic natives were deported to Siberia and Kazakhstan. Of the 200,000, 60,000 were from Estonia. This is carefully calculated in R. Taagepera, "Soviet Collectivization of Estonian Agriculture: The Deportation Phase," *Soviet Studies* 32, no. 3 (July 1980): 379–97, especially 393. In my view, Taagepera's data allow us to put the estimated number much higher, up to 70,000–75,000. T. Parming, in "Population Changes and Processes" (Parming and Järvesoo, *A Case Study of a Soviet Republic*, 27), actually puts it to "at least 80,000." Conservative estimates cite 50,000 from Latvia (calculated in G. King, *Economic Policies in Occupied Latvia* [Tacoma, Wash., 1965], p. 83). Again, a conclusion that a higher number, at least 60,000–65,000, was involved, seems to me more justified by the data used. Misiunas and Taagepera arrived at the conclusion that at the least 80,000 were deported from Lithuania in 1949 (*The Baltic States: The Years of Dependence*, p. 96). Other, less conservative, estimates arrive at a joint figure more than twice as high, namely 456,000 Baltic deportees (see Silde-Karklins, "Formen des Widerstands," 222). The truth must be, as it usually is, somewhere in the middle.

26. According to Remeikis (*Opposition to Soviet Rule*, 42), not less than 300,000 were deported from Lithuania during these six years. The estimates for Estonia and Latvia are 145,000 (Parming, "Population Changes and Processes," 27) and 144,000 (*The Baltic States, 1940–1972*, 82), respectively.

27. In testimony before the U.S. Congress (*Fourth Interim Report of the Select Committee on Communist Aggression*, House of Representatives, Eighty-Third Congress, Second Session [Washington, D.C., 1954], pp. 1368–74), a former Soviet border guard, Lt. Col. Grigori Stepanovich Burlitski, stated: "against these people firearms are to be used and they are to be killed without any further ado. No court is necessary for them. If these people happen to take refuge or run into a house or into a farm or into a village, then this particular house or farm or village is to be considered a bandit farm, a bandit house or a bandit village and those houses or farms or villages are to be destroyed by fire." The facts about guerrilla warfare in Afghanistan show that Soviet instructions on how to fight guerrillas remained more or less unchanged since 1944.

28. The growth of party membership was slow but steady. Although in Estonia only fifty-six new party members enrolled in 1944, hundreds followed suit in 1945, so that by January 1946, 1,900 members—or 27 percent of the total membership—were already indigenous Estonians (see Pennar, "Soviet Nationality Policy," 118; and Misiunas and Taagepera, *The Baltic States: The Years of Dependence*, 77). In Latvia, by January 1, 1946, about one-half of the 10,987 members of the party were ethnic Latvians, of whom about 3,000 or 4,000 were indigenous (see King, *Economic Policies*, 183). In Lithuania, by June 1946, there were 11,354 party members, of whom about a third were indigenous Lithuanians. Not less than 1,500 were admitted after the war (calculated on the basis of data provided in the *Mazoji Lietuviskoji Tarybine Enciklopedija* [The Short Lithuanian Soviet Encyclopedia], vol. w [Vilnius: Mintis 1968], 384–86). However, one can assume that the growth of the Communist Youth League was much more spectacular, since most of those who genuinely went over to the Soviet side were young people. Unfortunately, no precise statistical data are available on this, except that in Lithuania, in 1945, the Communist Youth League counted 3,800 members, of whom 1,600 belonged to the "extermination battalions" or "people's defenders" squads (their total number at the time is estimated at about 7,000, a figure that is indicative of genuine Soviet support in Lithuania, since membership of these squads was voluntary). It is also known that in 1946, 6,000 members of this organization actively participated in the USSR's Supreme Soviet election campaign, and that by 1950 it counted about 34,000 members, of whom not less than 20,000 are supposed to have been indigenous Lithuanians (see "Lietuvos Lenino Komunistine Jaunimo Sajunga" [Lithuanian Leninist Young Communist League], in *Mazoji Lietuviskoji Tarybine Enciklopedija*, vol. 2, p. 391). The steady growth in the number of Soviet supporters is also demonstrated by the fact that the number of people executed by the guerrillas for collaboration increased throughout 1945–1949; according to Soviet sources, 13,000 people were thus executed in Lithuania alone (see Misiunas and Taagepera, *The Baltic States: The Years of Dependence*, p. 86, n. 24). One should note that only natives were liable to stand trial by the guerrilla tribunals for collaboration. Newcomers—Russians et al.—were not touched. These figures are more or less precise in showing the real extent of genuine Soviet support in the Baltic. As stated before, this support can be measured in thousands of people, whereas the remaining millions either opposed the regime or supported those who opposed it.

29. J. Deksnys, who, after braving the Iron Curtain three times lost all hope of Western support or help, described his experience and feelings in a series of articles published in the Soviet Lithuanian tabloid, *Svyturys* (Lighthouse) ("*Iliuziju suduzimas*" [The Collapse of Illusions], *Svyturys*, no. 9 [May 1692]: 10–11; no. 10 [May 1962]: 10–12;

no. 11 [June 1962]: 16–17; and no. 12 [June 1962]: 10–11). Although there is no doubt that the series was heavily doctored by Soviet editors, an attentive reader can discern in the articles some useful and persuasive pieces of genuine information. On the activities of J. Markulis, see Pajaujis, *Soviet Genocide*, pp. 106–7. *Remeikis (Opposition to Soviet Rule*, p. 56n and p. 269n) is doubtful about the extent to which Markulis's treachery affected the partisan movement and assumes that in his role as one of its leaders Markulis was representative of genuine resistance thinking and action. This is advertently but not very convincingly denied by K. K. Girnius in his review article on Remeikis's book ("The Opposition Movement in Postwar Lithuania," *Journal of Baltic Studies* 12, no. 1 [spring 1982]: 66–73, especially 67–68). There are also eyewitness accounts of Markulis's pronouncements, in which he boasted about his treachery and presented it as an act of patriotic heroism. It seems that K. Kubilinskas, a talented poet, had the hardest lot in trying to reconcile himself with what he had done. He became an alcoholic and died in 1962, before his thirty-ninth birthday.

30. Cases of dissent among the native members of the apparat and the party were the earliest ones. Even later "extrastructural" and overtly dissident pronouncements and acts came first from those Balts who held genuinely communist views and criticized the policies of the regime from the standpoint of anti-Stalinist Marxism and communism. It was natural for the naïve and idealistic (i.e., those who considered the Soviet regime their own and wanted to adjust it to their idealistic vision rather than to adjust themselves to its oppressive practices) to voice their genuine opinions and protests publicly and in the most simple-minded and straightforward manner. Some of them, like Ivan Yakhimovichs in Latvia or Viktoras Sevrukas in Lithuania, directly founded their petitions and protests on the principles of communist ideology and morality. But it should be noted also that many of those dissidents who did not invoke Marxist-Leninist or communist principles explicitly started their lives as convinced believers in communism and genuine partisans of the Soviet regime and were actually driven into dissent upon finding their convictions inconsistent with the Soviet social and political reality. Such prominent Baltic dissenters as Jüri Kukk (an Estonian scientist and party member who perished in the Gulag in 1981; for a most perceptive study on Jüri Kukk and the Baltic dissent generally, see R. Taagepera, *Softening Without Liberalization in the Soviet Union: The Case of Jüri Kukk* [Lanham, Md.: University Press of America, 1984]). Lidija Doronina-Lasmanis and Maija Silmale (both Latvian cultural figures), Tomas Venclova and Jonas Jurasas (both Lithuanian cultural figures), and many others belong to this category.

These facts corroborate the thesis that the first and most outspoken Baltic dissidents were former communist idealists. People of the traditional nationalist orientation were much more cautious and realistic in their fearfulness of the Soviet regime and thoroughly avoided any open confrontations or disputes with it. Only much later (in the mid-1970s) did some of them—such as Viktoras Petkus and Balys Gajauskas (Lithuanians) and others—start to join the overt dissident ventures already well on the move.

31. See A. Küng, *A Dream of Freedom*, 167.

32. Although N. Karotamm came from Leningrad, it would be wrong to consider him a "Yestonian" since he left Estonia in the 1930s as a political refugee and, like many other refugees from different countries, resided in the USSR for several years as an emigré. The same, to a certain degree, applies to E. Päll, who lived in Russia for many years but whose roots were nevertheless in Estonia.

33. For more details on the so-called Berklavs Affair and the purge in general, see A. Berzins, *The Unpunished Crime* (New York: R. Speller, 1963), 182–84, 255–62.

34. For the English text of that very revealing letter, see *Congressional Record*, February 21, 1972, pp. E1426–30.

35. This story was told to me by a person who witnessed a few conversations between Stalin and Snieckus.

36. T. Zenklys, "Pasibaigusi Lietuvos gyvenimo epocha" (The End of an Epoch in Lithuania's Life), *Akiraciai* (The Horizons), no. 3 (57), 1974, p. 7. A shortened version of this extremely interesting article is available in Russian; see A. Shtromas, "Dve stat"I T. Zhenklisa" (Two Articles by T. Zenklys), *Kontinent*, no. 14 (1977): 229–41.

37. See A. Shtromas, "Baltic Problem and Peace Studies," *Journal of Baltic Studies* 9, no. 1 (spring 1978): 3–4. The thesis about the universality of the teleological political consciousness of the Baltic people is elaborated in some detail and corroborated by existing evidence in Shtromas, *Politine samone Lietuvoje* (Political Consciousness in Lithuania), (London: Nida, 1980), 50–53.

38. In November 1956, on All Saints Day, spontaneous mass demonstrations and meetings broke out in Kaunas and Vilnius (Lithuania). The demands were for "Freedom for Lithuania," "Solidarity with the heroic peoples of Hungary and Israel," "Russians out of Lithuania," and so on.

39. Major dissident activities in and documents from the Baltic were regularly reported in the *Chronicle of Current Events*, clandestinely published in Moscow since 1968 and available in English translation from the publications of Amnesty International. The United Baltic Appeal regularly published *UBA Information Services*, a news-release series in which such information was given wide coverage with full texts of major documents made available. The same applies to the ELTA (Lithuanian news agency in the USA) monthly *Bulletin*, the *Latvian Information Bulletin* (published by the Latvian Legation in Washington), *Estonian/Baltic Events* (published by R. Taagepera), and *Lituanus*. Good collections of Baltic dissident documents are included in P. Reddaway, ed., *Uncensored Russia: The Human Rights Movement in the Soviet Union* (London: Cape, 1972); *Documents from Estonia on the Violation of Human Rights* (Stockholm: Estonian Information Centre, 1977); V. S. Vardys, *The Catholic Church, Dissent, and Nationality in Soviet Lithuania* (New York: Columbia University Press, 1978); and Remeikis, *Opposition to Soviet Rule. The Chronicle of the Lithuanian Catholic Church* was regularly published in English by the Lithuanian Roman Catholic Priests League of America in New York.

40. Mass demonstrations, spontaneous protest meetings, and other similar events were regular in the Baltic republics after November 1956. Another mass manifestation that developed into a full-scale riot took place in Kaunas in 1960, during the festivities devoted to the twentieth anniversary of Lithuania's Sovietization. On that occasion militia forces started shooting on the demonstrators, killing and wounding several people, which outraged the crowds to such an extent that they attacked and smashed the forces of law and order present in the city. Two more such mass demonstrations that developed into riots took place in Lithuania. One, in May 1972, was the result of the self-immolation in the central square of the city of Kaunas "for the freedom of Lithuania" of a young student, Romas Kalanta; it was his funeral on May 18, 1972, that turned into a demonstration that literally took over the city and held it for almost two days, until the troops were sent in to disperse it. More than five hundred arrests were made. The other, in October 1977, developed from a soccer match played in Vilnius between the local team and a team from the Russian town of Smolensk. On all occasions the overriding slogans were "Freedom for Lithuania" and "Russians out of our country."

In Estonia a mass protest took place on April 20, 1972, in the capital city Tallinn. It started as a result of the televised hockey world championship. When the Czech team defeated the Soviet team, hundreds of people, mainly students, burst onto the streets shouting "we won." Mass youth manifestations took place in Tartu (Estonia) in 1976 and in Liepaja (Latvia) in 1977 over pop music events. The most significant Estonian youth demonstrations took place in Tallinn, Tartu, and some other places in October 1980 over the issue of increased time allocation to Russian lessons in Estonian schools. Subsequently, a letter from forty prominent Estonian intellectuals expressed their full solidarity with and support for the demonstrators, who were extremely brutally dealt with by the militia and army troops.

41. In Lithuania, protests against violations of the religious rights of the people and of the Catholic Church itself, accompanied by appropriate demands, were systematically launched from 1968 onward. They culminated in a petition signed by 17,054 Lithuanian Roman Catholics and called for an end to violations by Soviet authorities of the right of the people to exercise their freedom of conscience, guaranteed by the Soviet constitution. The petition demanded termination of the practice of gross civil discrimination against religious believers. In December 1971 it was sent to the UN and, via its offices, to Soviet leaders in Moscow (for the English text of this petition, see Vardys, *The Catholic Church*, 144–49). In 1972 the publication of *The Chronicle of the Lithuanian Catholic Church* had started; it reflected the course of the systematic, massive, and regular struggle of Lithuanian Catholics for their rights. In Latvia, similar mass developments took place, mainly insofar as the rights of the Baptists were concerned, but Latvian Catholics were actively involved in protest activities, too.

In Estonia, recorded protests about the lack of free access to information and of freedom for culture-creating activity go back to 1958 and are connected with the activities of the leading Estonian dissident, Mart Niklus. In Latvia, similar acts could be traced to the early 1960s, in connection with the 1961 trial of the prominent Latvian poet, Knuts Skujenieks (later, other cultural figures were also tried). In Lithuania, such cases were recorded only in the early 1970s, as, for example, the 1972 memorandum of Jonas Jurasas, the Chief Director of the State Theatre in Kaunas, who refused to comply with the dictates of the authorities and pledged to work only in accordance with his own conscience. Similarly, the poet and architect Mindaugas Tamonis refused to inspect and restore crumbling monuments to the Red Army on nationally and religiously significant Lithuanian sites.

42. For the full English text of this petition, see *UBA Information Service*, news release no. 330/331, November 11, 1979 (supplement). Most of the forty-five signatories were arrested, tried, and received heavy penalties. There were reports that 35,000 signatures in support of this petition were gathered in Lithuania alone.

43. For its text in Russian, see Radio Liberty, *Arkhiv samizdat*, no. 70.

44. The Herzen Foundation in Amsterdam published it in Russian in 1970 as a separate pamphlet, *Programma demokraticheskogo dvizheniia Sovetskogo Soyuza.*

45. See his letter, "The Duty of a Communist," addressed to M. Suslov, in A. Brumberg, ed., *In Quest of Justice: Protest and Dissent in the Soviet Union Today* (London, 1970), pp. 129–32.

46. "The Duty of a Communist," 359–60.

47. For details, see *Delo Kovaleva*, a documentary report published as a separate pamphlet in New York in 1976 by "Khronika-Press."

48. For the records of his interrogation by the KGB, see *Index on Censorship*, no. 3 (autumn 1975): 56–61; more details on his case are available in *Delo Tverdokhle-*

bova, a documentary report published as a separate pamphlet in New York in 1976 by "Khronika-Press."

49. For a more detailed review of the links between Lithuanian and Russian dissenters, see Vardys, *The Catholic Church*, 151–55. The various ties between Estonian and Russian dissenters are explored and perceptively assessed by Sergey Soldatov, himself an Estonian and a Russian dissident at one and the same time. See his "Estonskii uzel" (Estonian Knot), *Kontinent*, no. 32 (1982): 223–38.

50. No. 15, 1975; quoted from *The Chronicle of the Catholic Church in Lithuania*, vol. 2 (Chicago: Loyola University Press, 1975), 357.

51. This idea I expressed in a number of previous writings. See, for example, A. Shtromas, "Prospects for Restoring the Baltic States' Independence: A View on the Prerequisites and possibilities of Their Realization," in *Journal of Baltic Studies* 17, no. 3 (fall 1986).

14

How Political are the Social Movements in the Baltic Republics?

Aleksandras Shtromas

Before the 1980s one hardly spoke of any significant social movements in the Baltic republics. Political apathy, bordering on hopelessness, as far as the masses were concerned, and an emphasized apoliticism of the intelligentsia, whose members never tired of stressing that their only concerns are professional, cultural, maybe aesthetic, but not at all political—that was the social situation in the Baltic states most of the time under Soviet rule.

This overall image of apathy, complacency, and acquiescence was, however, not entirely correct. Underneath there were many things happening, as very few Balts indeed were total conformists and total loyalists of the Soviet regime. Most of them were, rather, "conservationists." That is a special term I use for people outwardly loyal to the Soviet system, working within that system, trying to comply with the rules of the system, but at the same time using whatever position in the system they have to preserve their nation's economic, cultural, and historical heritage. They were trying especially hard to safeguard their nation's economic well-being, ecological situation and, of course, spiritual identity and heritage, by promoting art, literature, and other activities, mainly under the slogan "national in form and socialist in content," but more and more national in form and less and less socialist in content, as

Reprinted from Aleksandras Shtromas, "How Political are the Social Movements in the Baltic Republics?," *Nationalities Papers* 18, no. 2 (fall 1990): 15–21.

far as the circumstances allowed it. These people wore the disguise of Soviet loyalism for the benefit and the advantage of their own nation; that was the attitude I call conservationism in the Baltic states and that was the attitude that was prevalent among most native Balts.

There were, of course, in the Baltic republics at all times (since 1956) the so-called dissident movements, but they were always seen as something very marginal, very atypical and nonrepresentative of the actual social situation in the Baltic states. This was, however, a wrong image. To me, the dissidents are a normal and regular outgrowth of the conservationist majority of the Balts. What really used to happen was that when the conservationist activities would overstep the boundary of tolerance by the authorities, then, naturally, the authorities would react either by dismissing such people from whatever position they held or by even expelling them to the West or arresting and sending them to prison camps in Siberia. Most of the prominent dissident names that we know about in the Baltic are the names of people who were thus expelled from the system and then, maybe having no other place in life, embarked on other projects, such as creating Helsinki groups, or writing samizdat publications. But, on the whole, the underground movement, those who published the *Chronicle of the Lithuanian Catholic Church* and the Estonian underground magazines on the cultural heritage of Estonia, remained anonymous. The same applies to people who published other numerous samizdat periodicals; some of them were identified and then sentenced for their clandestine activities, like the Lithuanian dissident Vytautas Skuodis, who was a professor of geography at the University of Vilnius. On the whole, though, the KGB was not very successful in detecting the real authors and editors of those publications. The dissidents, very atypical and marginal in their risky behavior, in their readiness to stick out their necks and live with the consequences for being truthful and faithful to their principles and authentic attitudes and views, still belong to the broadly defined ranks of the conservationists: conservationists who broke into the light as a result of the repressive actions of the authorities.

Dissident orientations and attitudes, always and without any break, permeated the Baltic societies as a whole. The division between dissidents and conservationists is thus a rather artificial one. Potentially the whole nation, with very few exceptions of those who sold themselves totally out to the powers that be, was a dissident nation and, as such, was looking for any opportunity publicly to manifest its authentic outlook and orientation. The social movements that emerged in the Baltic republics so visibly and so spectacularly in 1988, were thus ready to emerge at any time. These movements embodied attitudes that the whole nation shared, only had not dared to express; and, when it expressed these attitudes, it did so mainly in loyal, conservationist forms.

A sign that the nations in the Baltic were starting to move came in the second half of 1986. At that point in time, the previously dreaded dissidents (whom everybody tried to avoid as if they were lepers, or maybe in present terminology, AIDS carriers) started to make an impact on the behavior of the masses of the Baltic nations. In summer 1986, in Latvia, suddenly two new dissident groups emerged. Parenthetically, it is important to stress that the Soviet authorities in the 1980s really made sure that all the dissidents that somehow made an impact, or made a mark, should disappear, either to the West, or, as was the case for the majority, to the Gulag. Most of the earlier movements that were still active in the 1970s had been effectively suppressed by the KGB by the 1980s.

In the summer of 1986 we suddenly see in the Baltic states a revival of old and the formation of new dissident groups. That means that by the second half of 1986, Gorbachev's perestroika and glasnost started to be felt in the Baltic areas. All at once people realized that these policies were not just another trick of the Soviet authorities, and that there was some substance behind these policies.

Latvia presented in this respect the most spectacular example. Latvia was always behind Lithuania and Estonia in dissident expressions. Surprisingly Latvia was the first to impress the Balts by the activization of two new dissident movements. The two bodies were the Helsinki '86 group and a massive ecological movement that later took the name of the Environmental Protection Club.

These two groups emerged in 1986, but the breakthrough came in 1987 when large numbers of people started to respond very eagerly to the appeals by these groups, their collection of signatures under petitions, and their calls for attending rallies and demonstrations to raise issues like environmental protection and national freedom, national symbols, Latvian national language, etc. These groups became acutely relevant as scores of thousands of people responded to their calls. The first such truly significant response was the mass rally that took place on June 14, 1987, at the freedom monument in Riga. It was in this way that the Helsinki '86 group called people to commemorate on that date the victims of the 1941 mass deportations. Even more people joined the demonstration in Riga on August 23 to protest the 1939 signing of the Molotov–Ribbentrop Pact. Of course, harsh repressions followed. The leaders of the Helsinki '86 group were arrested; some other leading members of the group were expelled to the West. But the repressions this time did not produce the intended effect. People started joining the demonstrations and events launched by the dissidents in even greater numbers and with hardened determination.

The more the repression of the Helsinki '86 group increased, the more prominent the ecological movement became. It assembled rallies with thirty, forty thousand participants. Their demands included not only ecological issues but also the legalization of Christmas and Easter holidays, as well as of the flying of the Latvian flag, the singing of the Latvian national anthem, and the use of other national symbols. They did what Helsinki '86 was unable to achieve: under the pressure of mass protests in July 1987, the

Latvian government announced that the environment-damaging project of building a huge hydroelectric power station was canceled. It was very much like the cancellation of the project to reroute the Siberian river in Russia, when the Russian public sensed the first fruits of its victory over the government. That is what happened in Latvia in 1987. That event reverberated throughout the whole Baltic area, showing that one could indeed achieve something by a concerted and powerful action of the people.

The same kind of events, as in Latvia, took place in Estonia and Lithuania. In Lithuania surfaced a new group, the Lithuanian Liberty League (LLL), which sprang into action like Helsinki '86 did in Latvia.

The growth in popularity of overt dissenters demonstrated an increasing defiance of the Soviet authorities on the part of the usually cautious Balts. Glasnost spelled some impunity for dissidents and their followers, which dramatically changed the behavioral pattern of large sections of Baltic populations. In the face of the threat of the dissidents really becoming a leading force in the new powerful mass social movements, the authorities turned to the established intelligentsia, especially to those who belonged to the privileged and authoritative creative unions (the writers' union, the artists' union, the composers' union, etc.) in order to steal the movement from the dissidents and, through these unions, put it under the control of the party.

The authorities thus tried to go along with society, presenting their "trustees" as the leading figures of the nation and hoping to relegate in this way the dissidents back onto the margins of society where, in the party's view, they really belonged. The creative unions, hearing that the dissidents called a demonstration to commemorate a special event, such as a massacre by Stalin, announced a parallel commemoration for the same event under their own auspices. They published such announcements in the official press, while the dissidents lacked such possibilities. The respective turnouts, presumably expressing themselves in favor of the authorities, would then be well publicized. Usually only a third or at best a half of the number that showed up at the official event turned out for the parallel dissident event. The party authorities were very pleased with these results. They demonstrated that people were much more willing to join officially approved non-dissident events to express their feelings. The party authorities saw in that a confirmation of the success of their policies.

But what happened next as a result of all those events—the creation of popular fronts—was unanticipated by the authorities. First of all, such a front was formed in late April 1988 in Estonia, and later, on June 3, 1988, in Lithuania; by mid-August it had also been created in Latvia. In Latvia it was delayed for many reasons, not the least because Janis Peters, the chairman of the writers' union, strenuously tried to thwart all attempts to create movements not under his control. Actually a radical and increasingly popular Latvian National Independence Movement formed itself in June 1988 under the leadership of a very well-known figure, E. Berklavs, who at one time had been the deputy prime minister of Soviet Latvia, but because of his nationalist stance was removed from all leadership positions, thereby becoming a symbolic dissident figure for Latvians.

This is how, in all the three republics, powerful popular fronts emerged. In the beginning they were quite meek, all committed to perestroika, supportive of Gorbachev, and trying to keep a safe distance from the dissidents. Very soon, however, they discovered that this cautiousness did not garner popularity. Some people looked at them with suspicion. That radicalized the popular fronts very rapidly.

By the end of 1988, all the popular fronts had a) committed themselves to the independence program, and b) started to play the role of an umbrella body that would accommodate (and thus domesticate) all kinds of dissidents. If initially the fronts had tried to keep a distance from the dissidents, by the end of 1988 they welcomed all of them into their ranks. The result was that many leading dissidents felt somehow outmaneuvered by the officially established cultural figures who successfully started to usurp what had been the dissidents' own domain and exclusive prerogative. The dissidents who had suffered, who had been incarcerated in the Gulag, were pushed aside and only offered modest roles on the sidelines of the popular front movements. Soon enmities became very apparent in the popular fronts of all three republics. Consequently, the united social movement that had accumulated a lot of strength started to split. Many groups and organizations that in the beginning identified themselves with the popular fronts (e.g., Lithuanian Sajudis) started pitting themselves against them either directly or by preserving their identity outside the popular fronts and carefully watching over the fronts' actions. The Movement for National Independence of Latvia still retains this sort of semi-independent watchdog position. The Lithuanian Liberation League confronted Sajudis on its electoral tactics, and together with the Lithuanian Helsinki Group and other similar dissident bodies began to criticize Sajudis for either being an agent of the enemy, or for collaborating with the enemy and making the Communist authorities legitimate in Lithuania. A three-way split has now become very apparent: there is a minority dissident movement simultaneously opposing both the officialdom and the popular fronts; there is a pluralistic majority movement acting under the umbrella of the popular fronts; and there are the authorities-inspired "social movements," such as the inter-fronts in Latvia and Estonia, and the "Vienybe-Yedinstovo-Yednost" movement in Lithuania, uniting mainly Russian-speaking "immigrants" (as the Russian-speakers are now called in the Baltic) who are opposed to the "nationalization" of the republics.

Where does the Communist Party come into this? I want to mention at least two points. First, during 1988–1989, in Lithuania especially, a full-fledged multiparty political system emerged. The Lithuanian parties that existed before 1939, except for the Populist Party, have all been reestablished, as well as new parties, such as the Democratic Party of Lithuania (which could be seen as the successor of the Populist Party from before the war). In Estonia and Latvia, the party political structure is not that visible. There are the

Social-Democratic and Social-Christian parties in Estonia; but they are rather minimal bodies. The Social Democratic party in Latvia, which was always very strong, has undergone a rebirth and is now well established but, within the Popular Front, it does not really have a big impact. Something very special that does not exist in Lithuania but does exist in Latvia and Estonia, are the citizens' committees uniting the citizens of prewar Latvia and Estonia and their offspring. They form an increasingly powerful movement. Hence, a political pluralist structure is already underway in all the three Baltic republics, but in Lithuania a full-fledged multiparty system is in place. In that sense Lithuania is much more advanced than even Poland, Hungary, or any other country of the former Communist bloc.

My second point is about the communist parties themselves. Having lost the popular fronts movements that they themselves helped to create, and finding themselves in a vacuum, the Baltic communist parties started to try to catch up with these movements, steadily conceding to them more and more points and attempting to create an impression that they are a genuine part of their respective nations, not merely Moscow's stooges. Suddenly the obedient, rubber-stamping Baltic Supreme Soviets, elected in Brezhnev's time, started to pass radical laws. Of course, they did so because the Communist Party told them to do so. Only later did their Russian-speaking deputies start to express some dissent over radical legislation, such as the acts annulling the Diet's decision of 1940 about joining the Soviet Union and proclaiming the Baltic countries Soviet Socialist Republic. But before that, Russian-speaking deputies were the first to vote for all those independence-favoring measures, because that was the instruction they received from the party. Thereby the party hoped to say: "We are with the people, we are communists, but in the first place we are Lithuanians (or Latvians or Estonians). We are not stooges of Moscow anymore." In Lithuania, for example, to impress upon the people its credibility, the party went as far as to separate itself from the All-Union party. Moreover, in the summer of 1989 the Lithuanian Communist Party sent its representative to Gotland (Sweden) where all political forces of Lithuania and of the Lithuanian diaspora signed a joint declaration, saying that they are all committed to Lithuania's full and total independence. The chairman of the All-Lithuanian Liberation Committee (operating from the United States and dedicated to destroying Soviet rule in Lithuania) and the head of the ideological department of the Lithuanian Communist Party's Central Committee signed that joint declaration, along with the Lithuanian Liberation League and Sajudis.

On November 13, 1989, the Lithuanian Communist Party positively responded to the appeal of Sajudis to participate in a conference with the Christian-Democratic Party, the Social-Democratic Party, the Lithuanian Workers' Union, the Green Party, and with Sajudis in order to draft a joint program of political action. On November 14 these political bodies issued a joint communiqué that stated that all of them commit themselves to seek the abolition of article 6 of the constitution of the Lithuanian SSR, which decrees that the Communist Party is the leading force of society and the state, and that they all will seek together to draw the necessary legislative conclusions from the Molotov–Ribbentrop Pact of 1939 and thus legally restore Lithuania's independent statehood. That became the common agenda the Communist Party shared with all the others.

It is interesting that the most radical political groups housing many prominent dissidents were excluded from that meeting, namely, the Lithuanian Liberation League, the Lithuanian Nationalist Party (the successor to the ruling party of Lithuania of 1926–1940), the Lithuanian Humanism and Progress Party, the Lithuanian Helsinki Group, and the Lithuanian Christian Democratic Union. All parties that were excluded were those that, even if invited, would not sit around one table with the Communist Party while the others would.

While discussing a joint political platform with the opposition, the Lithuanian Communist Party simultaneously negotiated with the CPSU CC's Politburo on "the construction of Lithuania's secession." It seemed that the Gorbachev faction in the Soviet leadership was prepared to concede the "release" of the Baltic states to "the second circle of hell," that is to agree to their formal independence, in order to gain recognition of that new status of the Baltic states by the United States and thus to remove the obstacle of the West's nonrecognition of the Baltic states as member-states of the USSR in the development of East–West relations. Independence within the present Soviet system is a possibility, whereas freedom is not.

If the large social movements that are now operating in the Baltic states, such as the popular fronts (e.g., Lithuanian Sajudis), started as supporters of the party, as groups who organize movements to help the party implement its policies of perestroika and glasnost, they have now become visibly and distinctively independent political movements, competing for power with the party, actually dictating their will to the party, and making the party move to an agenda the party has not chosen. If the Baltic societies were totally apolitical before 1988, they are now almost 100 percent politicized. If in the forthcoming republican elections this situation will result in the defeat of the communist parties, the relationship between the Baltic states and the USSR may acquire a confrontational character. The USSR may agree to release from its formal grip a country that is effectively under Communist control. In such a situation independence from the USSR would not mean freedom from the USSR. But if the Communists lost control over the Baltic states, their release from the USSR would mean that they gained freedom from Soviet political control altogether. To that the USSR could hardly agree, at least as long as the USSR is itself controlled by the Communist Party.

V

THEORETICAL AND PRACTICAL CONSIDERATIONS ON REVOLUTION AND POLITICAL CHANGE

The two chapters in part V were written before Gorbachev fell in 1991 and Putin came to power in 2000. Yet they anticipate both developments. Shtromas argues that the collapse of Communist rule in Russia was inevitable, and would be hastened by reform, and that the first stage of a movement toward a "modern, stable, and legitimate" regime will probably involve a government rather authoritarian, "rational and nationally minded." One reads with the eerie sensation of following a seer. Still, the conclusions result not from visions but from a searching political–historical analysis: an account of the necessary stages in the process of modernization. This section presents Shtromas's culminating diagnosis of Soviet totalitarianism and his introductory explanation of the necessity of a liberal world order.

The Soviet "partocratic" state had to reform, according to Shtromas, but could not. It had to improve its technology and economy, and it was the possibility of an American antimissile defense that provoked the appointment of the reformer Gorbachev. But precisely a sphere for independent action and individual incentives would make platforms for dissidents and in effect disavow the Socialist creed. Soviet institutions need not be inevitably "conservative," as some western scholars had maintained, for there was a tension between unbending party men and innovative competent men. Nor could the Russian party aggregate interests or bend to allow toleration, as other scholars asserted and as Yugoslavia and Poland seemed to prove. Here western scholars right and left missed the special importance of ideology to the Soviet Union. Any communist regime is inevitably judged by whether it approaches both a classless society and the socialization of the means of production. Ideology matters, if only to legitimate the increasingly unbelieving rulers. But the Soviet version could not backslide, as if to tolerate a temporary expedient on the way to socialism. For, unlike the satellites, the USSR had officially established socialism. Besides, should reform lead to demands for political reform, no Red Army waited outside to enforce Communist rule, as the Soviet army had intervened in Hungary in 1956 and Czechoslovakia in 1968. It was inevitable, then, that Gorbachev's attempt at revamping management led to demands for greater openness (glasnost), and that the subsequent restructuring (perestroika) could be nothing more nor less than the "death march" of communism.

Shtromas has a special understanding of revolution. Real revolution is "great revolution" in a more or less Tocquevillian sense. It is the necessary historical development of liberal and democratic society, albeit a development proceeding by fits and starts. A totalitarian or "ideocratic" takeover by a Hitler or a Lenin is then a reactionary coup, not a revolution in Shtromas's sense. So too is any oligarchic or monarchic takeover. A revolution, strictly speaking, is then the great revolution toward modern freedom and justice, of which the Revolution of 1688, the American revolution, and the great French revolution, are typical starts. The other coups or takeovers must be seen as merely temporary interruptions—fits rather than starts—along the way. Shtromas distinguishes four stages of the profound liberal democratic revolution. The beginning requires an incompatibility, a "dysfunction," between the needs of modernizing society and the "traditional" polity that governs it. A political dialectic develops. Some popular dissatisfaction must be present, and a national crisis too. But the key to the first stage is the "second pivot," that is, the appearance of an opposing source of official power. Example: the workers' strike committee during the Polish attempt at revolution in 1980. Once the old state is thrown off, a chaotic and dangerous second stage ensues. It is in this special social–historical condition that Shtromas locates a Hobbesian "state of nature," and here too, the opportunity for a takeover by "the most single-minded" zealots. This is Shtromas's explanation of the Bolshevik and the Nazi revolutions. They are merely millenarian waylayers of a nevertheless inevitable democratic modernization. Russia, then, has only now completed the second stage, the arrival at a fuller state of social freedom. In the third stage we may expect oscillations between freedom and authoritarianism, oscillations gradually leading to reasonable and representative institutions. While there will be traditionalist covers, as with the Orleanist monarchy that followed the Jacobin turmoil in France, the book of the future will present more or less democratic orders on the one side and more or less authoritarian orders on the other. We may expect "a Napoleon without Jacobinism" on the road to the ultimate culmination of Russian development, a democratic republic.

One might wonder whether the great changes involved in "moderniza-tion" and liberalism are so inevitable, so much a part of a determined histor-ical and social process. If Hitler had struck more decisively at Dunkirk, a vic-tory by England and the democratic powers would have been far less certain. Besides, the origin of progress and liberalism was at least affected by the enlightened philosophers (Hobbes and Locke among others). The role in modern societies of intellectuals, and other non-state powers such as the rich and the poor, seems greater than suggested by the theory of social dysfunc-tion and the "second pivot." Polish Solidarity obtained political power with its popular demonstrations, as did the Hungarian writers' union, and in each case before being an alternative power in the state institutions. Be that as it may—and Alex Shtromas would certainly have some compelling reply—no reader can leave his political–historical diagnoses without awe at the display of vast knowledge and downright prescience.

15

How Revolutions Proceed

ALEKSANDRAS SHTROMAS

A. INTRODUCTORY REMARKS

When Lenin formulated his "fundamental law of revolution"—the law according to which "for a revolution to take place it is not enough for the exploited and oppressed masses to realize the impossibility of living in the old way, . . . it is essential that the exploiters should not be able to live and rule in the old way"[1]—he, in fact, only reaffirmed an old and much more fundamental truth, first stated by Plato, that "changes in any constitution originate, without exception, within the ruling class itself, and only when this class becomes the seat of disunion";[2] "while so long as they" (i.e., the ruling class) "are of one mind . . . the city cannot be changed."[3]

Indeed, all revolutions that have changed an established and consolidated political order (or a city, a constitution, a commonwealth) into a new one, were the result of disunion and ensuing confrontation between the elites. Spontaneous popular uprisings and revolts have never been able, on their own, to produce a revolutionary change, for the simple reason that

Reprinted extracts from "How the End of the Soviet System May Come About: Historical Precedents and Possible Scenarios," in Aleksandras Shtromas and Mortan A. Kaplan, eds., *The Soviet Union and the Challenge of the Future*, vol. 1, *The Soviet System: Stasis and Change* (New York: Paragon House, 1988), 201–7; 271–86; 299–300.

they do not, and cannot, carry with them a political alternative to the existing system of rule. Even if an uprising or revolt were to shatter the existing political institutions to the extent of causing a power vacuum, as, for example, the revolt of Petrograd workers in February 1917 did, a united elite would have rapidly filled it by restoring the shattered institutions and putting them back into the position of political control. If, however, the elite were split, its change-oriented part could take full advantage of the power vacuum produced by a popular revolt for filling it by institutions under its own control, and to the exclusion of those of the shattered sovereign state power. This is what actually happened in Petrograd in February–March 1917, when the liberal "Progressive bloc" took advantage of the power vacuum in the capital city, produced by a spontaneous workers' revolt, and through the State Duma in which it had an absolute majority, abolished the monarchy, formed the Provisional Government, and thus assumed political power in Russia.

Along the same lines have developed also all other "great revolutions" known to history.[4] Among them the Russian revolution of February–March 1917 was, perhaps, unique in the sense that in its process a popular revolt had played a certain role, however secondary and subordinated, whereas in any other such revolutions it did not. There were, for sure, no popular revolts to play any part during either the English Revolution of 1642 or the Great French Revolution of 1789. Such "negative" facts concerning the role of the "people's action" in making a revolution allowed Jean Baechler to arrive at the quite categorically stated conclusion that "the seizure of power by the people, whether the proletariat or the bourgeoisie, is a pure myth, unsupported by a single fact,"[5] and thus historically to confirm Vilfredo Paretto's theoretical contention that "the essence of all revolutions is a change of the ruling élite," or even more simply, "a change of élites."[6]

This does not mean that in a revolution the attitudes of the grassroots population do not matter at all. They do matter indeed, and a great deal so. As all theorists of revolution have quite unanimously acknowledged, a profound all-round dysfunction between the civil society and the polity or, as Chalmers Johnson has put it, "a disequilibrated and dyssynchronized social system" is a prerequisite for a revolutionary change.[7] Such a dysfunction implies that in the population at large the desire for political change has become more powerful than whatever has been left of the allegiance to the political status quo. It is the population's indifference to the fate of the old regime, sometimes amounting to direct hostility toward it, that provides the necessary conditions for making the change-oriented elite's bid for "reconstitution of the state" realistic; nobody then prevents it from combating the conservative ruling elite and the polity it commands. In other words, for the revolution to be successful, the "reciprocity of expectations between rulers and ruled"[8] must first be broken down, to the extent of the old regime's total loss of legitimacy in the eyes of the overwhelming majority of the people.

In that sense the change-oriented elite acts in a revolution as the legitimate representative of the population, as the champion of the population's aspirations for a better future and thus enjoys the population's implicit and, when stimulated, also explicit support. This support, however passive, is especially crucial in the aftermath of the revolution. Even if rendered in the form of failing to rally around the forces of restoration, it is usually sufficient to consolidate the victory of the revolution over the old regime.

There is no doubt whatsoever that the French Revolution of 1789, made by the representatives of the Third Estate in the Estates General, did enjoy such a kind of support from the overwhelming majority of Frenchmen. Only one rather backward group of peasants in western France, the so-called Chouans, actively opposed the revolution and joined forces with the royalists enabling them to wage in the Vendée a local civil war that for a few years represented a major threat to the new, not yet properly consolidated postrevolutionary order; but, since there appeared no larger social group to follow them in rallying round the royalist cause, their resistance was doomed to fail. In Russia, there were no signs of loyalty to the old czarist regime even on the scale of the Chouans. The February Revolution of 1917 that did away with the czar was greeted with unqualified joy and enthusiastically accepted by all larger sections of Russia's population without exception. It is in this sense that a revolution is a truly popular event. Although its champion is the change-oriented part of the elite, that elite acts in the name and on behalf of the people, and the people recognize it as such.

The kind of revolution for which Lenin formulated his "fundamental law" and for which to materialize the elite championing it has to enjoy sufficient popular support, can be directed only against an oppressive autocratic regime that either bars the way for introducing change or imposes changes that the people cannot accept and deeply resent. It was because of that property of every revolution that Marx qualified what he termed to be a bourgeois revolution by the word democratic. For Marx, every revolution deserving that name had to be democratic, even if it was only a bourgeois-democratic revolution. When predicting the inevitability of the proletarian socialist revolution, Marx always stressed that it will have to take place because bourgeois democracy effectively excludes the workers from participation in it and, as far as they are concerned, is no more than an oppressive dictatorship.[9] For Marx, the socialist revolution by raising the proletariat, "the nine-tenths of the population," "to the position of ruling class" becomes tantamount to nothing more than "winning the battle of democracy."[10] The faithful followers of Marx who, unlike Marx, had witnessed the active and fruitful involvement of the proletariat into "bourgeois democracy," split their ranks because one part of them (e.g., Eduard Bernstein) proclaimed that the idea of the proletarian revolution had, in such new circumstances, become obsolete, whereas the other part (e.g., Lenin) intransigently stuck to it in spite of all change. But even the latter ones (e.g., Lenin himself), when trying to justify the inevitability of the proletarian socialist revolution, had to associate the moment for it to come about with such times when the ruling bourgeoisie would have no choice but to abolish democracy altogether and start ruling by employing openly dictatorial and terroristic means.

It was, in fact, Alexis de Tocqueville who first established that only in conditions of autocratic or authoritarian minority rule (which he, in breach with the classical Aristotelian tradition, called aristocracy) is revolution an adequate, and in some cases even inevitable, vehicle of political change.[11] According to him, revolutionary change in a democracy is totally out of place and completely unnecessary; democracy, being the most dynamic system, at the same time "renders society more stationary than it has ever been."[12]

This is not to say, and de Tocqueville himself never said so, that democracy cannot be overthrown by subversive, conspiratorial, and/or violent means. Contemporary history is a witness to only too many successful conspiracies and plots against democracy which, after having been destroyed, was replaced by ruthless, and, in most cases, sectarian, dictatorship. This is especially true in the case of infant postrevolutionary democracies, such as the one born in Russia in March 1917 and overthrown by the Bolshevik coup d'état in October of that same year, or the one established in Germany in November 1918 and destroyed from within by the nazis in 1933–1935, or the one brought about in 1931 by the republican regime in Spain and devoured by the flames of the civil war that ensued five years later. All of them followed the regular, historically set pattern for postrevolutionary developments whereby one of the few totalitarian movements operating on the margins of the society's political spectrum hijacks the revolution and, riding high on its tide, establishes itself as the total dictatorial state. All revolutions went through such spells of "Millenarian dictatorships,"[13] and in this sense the "Millenarianisms" of Peisistratus in Athens of the sixth century B.C. and of the Jacobins in eighteenth-century France are phenomena of the same order as the Bolshevik and Nazi "Millenarianisms" of the twentieth century.

Not only such infant democracies but every unstable democracy—a democracy that is established either in a country still besieged by acute social antagonisms or even in one that, in spite of being socially quite cohesive, is actively subverted by foreign-sponsored political groups—is prone to collapsing and yielding power to one kind of dictatorship or another. It is the first instance, that of acute social antagonisms, that makes democratic institutions so fragile in Latin America, Turkey, or Pakistan; and the second, that of foreign-sponsored subversion, that has driven most countries of Central and Eastern Europe between the two world wars from democracy to dictatorship. Here I leave aside those obvious instances when democracies have been destroyed and oppressive dictatorships imposed in their stead by direct foreign intervention as was the case of most countries of Central and Eastern Europe in the aftermath of World War II.

Nevertheless, the political acts leading to a democracy being overthrown have never assumed the character or dimension of a revolution. They were always perpetrated as coups d'état, although not always necessarily did they take also the form of a coup de force (Hitler, for example, in 1935, entrenched himself in power by a coup d'état that was not at all a coup de force).

It was again Lenin who stressed that "revolution is impossible without a nationwide crisis."[14] For only a crisis of such dimensions exposes the rottenness of the old regime, its total inability to cope with the problems society faces, its full functional inadequacy as far as the discharging of the state's normal duties is concerned—in other words, the profound all-round dysfunction referred to above. And it is also only such a crisis that provides the change-oriented part of the elite with the right opportunity to step in with its counter-proposals and counter-policies, pressing the ruling elite either to accept and carry them out or, alternatively, to abdicate and be replaced by the counter-elite.

If the ruling elite, or at least some of its powerful elements that would be able to prevail, accepted the counter-proposals and counter-policies, co-opted their movers into the ruling elite and introduced together with them the systematic changes sought, the revolution would be carried out from above, in an orderly though quite drastic manner. This process, which Chalmers Johnson calls conservative change, is nevertheless revolutionary for it not only results in the "reconstitution of the state," but also, sooner or later, involves a complete change of the ruling elite. But what if the revolution were to be carried out in a situation where the ruling elite would prove to be non-caring or "intransigent"[15] and thus unwilling to go for change even when faced by a raging national crisis? In such a situation are there any ways of removing the existing ruling elite and putting the counter-elite in its place? History shows that there are many such ways. In this context, I would like first, however, to draw the attention to a certain general rule common to all revolutionary transitions. This is the rule of the "second pivot," and it was first formulated by a Soviet samizdat writer, F. Znakov.

B. THE "SECOND PIVOT"

According to Znakov, for a revolution to take place the division between the elites has to be expressed in an institutional form. No other form will suffice. This means that the counter-elite has to assume control of a certain public or state body either already in existence as an integral part of the official system or called into existence by that system for the special purpose of crisis management and resolution. In some cases, one could add, such an institution may be formed without official sanction but has later to be officially recognized and thus incorporated into the official system as in the case of "Solidarity" in the Poland of 1980.

Alternatively, an existing public or state body where members of both parts of the elite were doing business and discussing outstanding issues together, may at a certain point be split into two, with one of the parts coming under the control of the counter-elite and thus becoming its spearhead, not any more for mere demands and pressures, but for bringing about practical political change directly, independently, and with disregard for the proper order of subordination and procedure. Such a split would already divide the existing "one-pivotal" political system into two separate pivots of power and social integration engaging in a confrontation for the assumption of full power.

Revolution, Znakov maintains, is on only when such a split of "one into two" occurs and an open confrontation between the thus formed two pivots of power and social integration ensues. Again, alternatively, a public or state body fully integrated into the official political system, if it came under the full control of the counter-elite, may, at a certain point in time, be split off from the integral systemic pattern and used as the "second pivot," too. Znakov calls the split of "one" (political system) "into two" the "critical mass" that unleashes the chain reaction called revolution. He summed it up by saying that "the emergence of the second pivot" (*vtoroy sterzhen'*) . . . "of power and social integration . . . is the general law of a revolutionary process." Elaborating on it, he wrote: "The experience of history indicates that the most essential requisite of any revolution, and the main fact portending its outbreak, is the formation on the legal surface of society of an institution, independent of the existent system of power and capable of setting itself off against it. . . . After such a *second pivot* of society's organization comes into being, the course and the fate of the revolution depends on the correlation of forces representing the old system of power and that second pivot, as well as on what shape their confrontation is taking."[16]

Indeed, if we look at the revolutionary developments in seventeenth-century England, eighteenth-century France, and Russia of February (March) 1917, they will all confirm F. Znakov's "second pivot" theory, as would also other less famous revolutions, if they really were revolutions and not mere putsches, coups d'état, or spontaneous uprisings and insurrections. The characteristic feature of all these revolutionary developments is the split of the existing autocratic political system into "two pivots" with each of them trying to establish itself as the "sole pivot," which in the case of the "first pivot" means restoration of the old order, and, in the case of the "second pivot," the creation around it of a new political system into which the "first pivot," if it is not entirely abolished, could be assimilated as a body of secondary importance.

In seventeenth-century England, the Long Parliament emerged as the "second pivot" challenging the authority of the king, Charles I, who, by declaring war on Parliament in 1642, finally split the political system of the country into two warring "pivots." In eighteenth-century France, the role of the "second pivot" was assumed by the representatives of the Third Estate in the Estates General, when they, on June 17, 1789, with the support of some representatives of other estates, proclaimed themselves the National Assembly of France and on June 23, 1789, refused to obey the orders of the king, Louis XVI, to dissolve this newly and spontaneously created body—the "second pivot" of the Great French Revolution of 1789. I always wondered why the French celebrate the 14th of July, the historically meaningless event of the storm of the Bastille, which took place even after the National Assembly was proclaimed the National *Constituent* Assembly of France (9th of July), rather than the 17th of June, which really marked the beginning of the French Revolution.

In Russia of 1917, the "second pivot" was instituted by the Provisional Committee of the State Duma, which was formed on February 27 (March 12), 1917, by the deputies of that semi-parliamentarian body who thus decided formally to obey the czar's decree of February 25 (March 10), 1917, about the State Duma's dissolution but did not abdicate their responsibility before the country (mainly members of the "Progressive bloc" led by the centrist Kadet–Constitutional Democratic-Party with the representatives of the left and some right-wing parties joining in).

F. Znakov's "second pivot" theory unites all the elements of revolutionary political change described above. It emphasizes that revolution is a result of a confrontation of elites, shows that its success is dependent on at least passive mass support for political change and, accordingly, on the degree to which the "old regime" has lost its legitimacy; but, most importantly, it shows the general way in which dictatorial political systems, be they autocratic, or oligarchic, enter into a "nationwide crisis" and, subsequently, meet their end. The way is that of these systems being blown up from within and split into two, each organized around a separate pivot; it is in the ensuing battle between these "two pivots" for the restoration of a "one-pivotal" political system that the fate of the revolution is decided.

C. THE REGIME'S INNER COLLAPSE

Leaving aside other possible variations of the formation of the "second pivot" in Russia, the Soviet Union, let us concentrate on a possible path of the party itself trying (in desperation) in order to strengthen its grip on power, to engage some within-system reforms.

If the party accepted this approach, it would find itself in a situation similar to that of Louis XVI, king of France, during the fifteen years of his pre-revolutionary reign (1774–1789). When Louis XVI succeeded to the French throne, France was in a terrible economic condition, which the young king, differently from his predecessor and grandfather, Louis XV (who knew better and therefore, like Mr. Brezhnev, decided to live on without even trying to cure the country's ills), was determined to sort out by introducing some "within-system" reforms. One of his first royal acts was the appointment of the famous French economic thinker and local government reformer, Anne-Robert-Jacques Turgot, to the post of comptroller general (minister of finance and virtually prime minister), who was given the necessary powers to implement this task. In two years Turgot prepared, and in 1776 issued, his famous Six Edicts containing a whole program of reforms including the abolition of a number of dues and offices as well as the whole traditional institution of the *corvée*. Turgot's reforms were, however, in direct opposition to the plans of the king and the establishment. They wanted slight "within-system" changes and what Turgot proposed amounted to a "system-rejective" change. Asked by the king to moderate his plan, Turgot refused to do so, prophetically pointing out that anything less than what he was proposing would not only fail to solve France's problems but would also confuse and deteriorate the situation even more. The result was predictable. Turgot was dismissed and his Six Edicts abolished. It seems to me symptomatic that Soviet intelligentsia called Kosygin, after the party refused to go ahead with his 1965 economic reform, "*ublyudochnyi Tyurgo*" (the poor man's Turgot), because his reform program, far from being as bold as Turgot's, was also much lower in economic quality, and also because, differently from Turgot, Kosygin remained in office.

Turgot's dismissal did not mean, however, that the king had changed his mind and renounced the reformist path. On the contrary, after having dismissed Turgot, Louis XVI put another reformist, Jacques Necker, who seemed to be much less radical and much more amenable than Turgot, in charge of the country's finances. Necker's impeccable anti-Turgotist credentials—in 1775 he published a pamphlet directed against Turgot, which was especially critical of his policies of free trade in grain—also encouraged the king to make Necker his choice as Turgot's successor.

Although a moderate and a compromiser, Necker was the person who actually engineered the outbreak of the French Revolution (by the way, it was his dismissal on July 11, 1789 that provoked the storm of the Bastille on July 14). Turgot was right. Reforms lesser than those proposed by him (and such were the reforms that Necker was trying to implement) got France into even bigger trouble. Extraordinary measures were now needed, not gradual reforms. In 1787, the king summoned the Assembly of Notables, asking it to approve of such extraordinary measures and close ranks around him to save the country, but was faced with a plain refusal. Instead the Notables asked the king to recall Necker to solve the country's outstanding problems (in 1781 Necker had also been forced to resign, having been accused of financial mismanagement) which, after some hesitation, the king did in 1788. It was Necker who persuaded Louis XVI that there was now no way out of the financial crisis other than to call the Estates General, a representative institution that had not been assembled since 1614, to approve of the necessary extraordinary measures, and insisted on double representation therein of the Third Estate (without which, he rightly argued, the whole enterprise would be void of any meaning). The rest of that story is well known and was briefly referred to above—the "second pivot" was thus introduced and the French Revolution began.

I have recalled here that piece of French eighteenth-century history because it gives us a classical example of the fall of a system whose ruling stratum considered the system's preservation their highest commitment and dealt with every arising crisis not with a view to its genuine solution but only to the system's survival. As one sees from this example, if the system is so outdated that it has no room left for a "within-system" change, even the most rigid policies are unable to save it; at the end of the day it is bound to collapse economically and, subsequently, socially and politically too. One used to say about the Bourbons (though after the revolution; the saying originated in 1795) that they forgot nothing and learned nothing. This is even more true of the Soviet partocrats. Until recently they still tried to follow the "no move" line of the old Bourbon king, Louis XV. Now, at least the top leadership with Gorbachev at its helm, decided to change this procrastinating line to the reformist path that Louis XVI followed with Necker's help. Allegedly introduced to solve the acutest developmental problems the country faces, this path has, in fact, been chosen only for the sake of increasing the system's chances for survival. It remains to be seen whether the results of these attempts to save the unviable system at whatever cost, will not be like those that Louis XVI himself witnessed in 1789.

I am far from suggesting that the change in the Soviet Union could follow the 1789 French model of change exactly. It is difficult to imagine that the party would ever even consider calling any sort of a representative assembly of the type of the Estates General (or *Zemskiy Sobor*). It is rather more likely that the Soviet Turgots, Neckers, and Calonnes (another reformist comptroller general of France who held this office in 1783–1787; it was he who persuaded the king to call the Assembly of Notables in 1787 but, having failed to get the latter's approval for the measures he thought necessary to introduce, resigned in despair) would have no choice but to preside over the process of their own institution assuming the position of a "second pivot," thus splitting the Soviet political system in order to get things really moving.

In its vain but insistent pursuits of a "within-system" solution of the aggravating economic crisis (which is of a permanent nature in the Soviet Union), the party could, for instance, establish a new institution of economic management, endowing it with large autonomous emergency powers. This institution could even be constructed as a quasi-representative body, for instance, as a system of economic councils operating on all administrative levels—local, republican, and All-Union. The seats on these councils would probably be distributed between the economic managers as well as some workers (the Soviet third estate) on the one hand and the representatives of the party on the other, the latter intending to use the councils as a forum for reaching a new consensus, i.e., not one of stagnation but one of "within-system" change, with the civilian technocrats. A similar body, the Collective Farms Council (*Sovet Kolkhozov*), was already instituted by the party in 1969, to solve, on the basis of such a consensus, some of the most acute problems of Soviet agriculture,[17] but this arrangement did not work as the party expected it to and, shortly after its creation, this institution disappeared into oblivion (by 1973 there was no further mention of it). Hence, I am not referring here to idle fantasies but to something that, though abortive and shortlived, has already taken place in reality as a certain way of dealing with acute economic situations. On the other hand, the party could prefer to avoid creating any new bodies and try to use an institution of state economic management already existing within the system for the same purposes, for example, Gosplan, which is the most general and senior economic office in the whole system. The result would hardly be any different one way or another. As F. Znakov pointed out, "any institution, new or old, if endowed with sufficient autonomous powers, could (and most certainly would) after some time of frustrating attempts to get the party's approval for necessary reforms, turn into the 'second pivot,' splitting the Soviet political system and starting in the vast country of the Soviets the process of so much needed (and desired) change."[18]

Of course, for those in whose view interest groups in Soviet society are identical to the offices operating in it (and who therefore refuse to admit that each Soviet office is an arena of latent confrontation between partocrats and technocrats, in fact the real interest groups operating in the Soviet society on an overall scale) the suggestion that Gosplan might be the potential Soviet "second pivot" seems to be not simply nonsensical but "breathtaking."[19] Indeed, Gosplan is one of the most "reactionary" Soviet institutions and, if one considers the Soviet Union as a system whose only constituent elements are internally coherent offices, the idea that, of all such offices, Gosplan should be considered as a likely "second pivot," must sound odd to say the least. It is exactly this "institutional" approach that was demonstrated by Jerry Hough, who, when refuting the idea about Gosplan's "revolutionary" potential, wrote that "although all technocrats are not so conservative as Gosplan, my sense is that the top governmental *apparatus* is rather more resistant to change than the Central Committee *apparatus*" (emphasis added).[20]

Since I have once already replied to these arguments, I shall allow myself to repeat them here once more:

> I do not think that Hough was fair when he presented . . . the conflict between the partocratic and the technocratic strata in Soviet society as (being, in my view) "one between the Party apparatus and all the other apparatuses of authority and management in the USSR." For . . . this conflict is not related to structural divisions of power and management in the Soviet system, but is of a socially ubiquitous character. Its manifestations could be identified within any single office as well as within any field of "unstructured" social activities. To me, all the apparatuses of the USSR without exception—not only the Party apparatus itself but the Soviet apparatus, the army, the security forces, the trade unions; in short, every single structure right down to the Red Cross and Crescent Society—are still dominated by partocratic forces. On the other hand, technocratic forces not only are present in all the apparatuses—inclusive of the Party apparatus itself—but growing more prominent and are making their presence felt to a greater extent in all of them. That is why it should have been evident that . . . "the tens of thousands of engineers and agronomists with managerial experience who work in the Party apparatus," if progressive, are progressive not only when they work elsewhere, as Hough wants me to believe, but wherever their work is done, e.g., in the Party apparatus itself. . . .

I completely agree with Hough that, as an office, Gosplan is one of the most conservative structures in the power apparatus of the USSR, which is only natural since under different circumstances Gosplan would doubtless be the first office to be dismantled. In my view, office interests as such, however, are not of paramount importance. Without discounting them altogether, one should take into account the differing social and political interests of various strata within the Soviet establishment on a wider scale, as in all bureaucracies, e.g., inside Gosplan too. Looking from this perspective, one must at least theoretically admit that in the USSR every major office could become a field of intensive struggle for dominance between the technocrats and the partocrats, and thus could turn into a stronghold of the technocrats from which they could launch an attack against partocratic rule. In this respect, one should bear in mind that Gosplan is by its very nature an office whose gates are open wider for technocratic penetration than the gates of other offices of equal influence and importance, which, by the way, makes Znakov's point (about the possibility of Gosplan becoming the "second pivot") "more sensible than at first glance it seems to be."[21]

There is yet another possibility for the Soviet political system's split and thus for the "second pivot's" appearance in the Soviet Union. The one suggested above (creation of new institutions of economic management or endowment of old institutions, for example, Gosplan, with new powers) is distinguishable by a regular pattern of "transfusion of power" from one "pivotal" institution to another that thus becomes "pivotal" itself (a process developing within the framework of the French model of change). This other possibility, on the contrary, is related to a process of a much more sudden nature.

In 1956, when the party denounced Stalin and promised to introduce reforms, people from all walks of Soviet life were strongly stimulated to bring their criticism of the system's performance and proposals of change into the open. Meetings discussing the decisions of the 20th Congress of the party, debates on Vladimir Dudintsev's controversial novel, *Not by Bread Alone*, and other similar public events, began to turn into a genuine mass movement that, although too shortlived to acquire an organized pattern, made an impact of lasting nature on Soviet society by giving birth to the overt dissident movement. The 1956 history may repeat itself if the party stayed long enough on its newly adopted course of glasnost (openness) and continued to encourage the intelligentsia and the grassroots population to speak their critical mind publicly. There is no guarantee that glasnost could be reliably controlled by the party all the time, for in the long run the Soviet population, at present still very skeptical and extremely reluctant to stick its neck out, may, after all, take glasnost seriously, transgress the narrow limits set for it by the party today, and use this newly found freedom of expression for system rejective purposes. Such a turn of events is much more likely at present than in 1956, since during the last "lenient" three decades people's fear of the regime has greatly diminished, while their trust in the rulers' goodwill has totally evaporated. It is also very likely that certain institutions might become the centers of these debates. Some clubs and academic institutions in Moscow are already showing signs of assuming this role by regularly organizing controversial lectures and discussions, for the time being only on cultural and historical topics, which the party, wanting to keep the intelligentsia appeased by satisfying at least some of its cultural needs, reluctantly tolerates[22] (by the way, that is how the Petöfi Club in Budapest was started in the early days of 1956).

The party would probably seek to suppress such spontaneous manifestations by people, as it did in 1956–1957, and would insist on keeping the discussion of all controversial issues exclusively within the official framework of the media and institutions supposed to deal with these issues under the party's direct control. In most drastic or specially selected cases of such grassroots manifestations, the party would have to resort to "exemplary" repressions of some of the new overt dissidents which, in the troubled situation of an "opened-up" crisis, could bring the organizations to which these repressed people belong to their defense. An unexpected and uncontrolled controversy can thus start between these organizations and the party whereby the former, especially if supported by any of the discussion centers mentioned above, could assert itself as the "second pivot," thus splitting the system before any other office could assume this role in a more regular way. This is actually what happened in Hungary in 1956 when, by having rallied in defense of its members Tamas Aczel and Tibor Dery against the CC, the Writers' Union's primary party organization (in association with the Petöfi Club) assumed its independence from the party apparatus and started to challenge its policies.

Hence, the *Hungarian model of change* can be added to all the others as the one along whose lines the change in the Soviet Union might be incepted.

D. THE RELEVANCE OF THE "SECOND PIVOT"

Indeed, in the two sub-scenarios, developed along the lines of the French and Hungarian models of change, the centrality of the "second pivot" issue is quite explicit. The same, I think, though not as explicitly, is also quite obvious in the first two scenarios, to which the Spanish and Czechoslovakian models of change appeared to be the closest. There, the split of the party's Central Committee (or of any other highest decision-making body—the Politburo, the Secretariat, etc.) into two separate pivots, with the second pivot thus being formed on the basis of a part of a previously whole institution, was implicitly suggested as the prerequisite for starting the process of change.

More complicated is the question of the same general rule of the second pivot operating in the cases of the scenarios of change based on the Portuguese and Chilean models. The fact that the army stages a military coup does not necessarily mean that it thereby assumes the role of the second pivot. In Portugal in 1974, it did indeed assume such a role; as it did in the Spanish Civil War of 1936–1939, as well as on some other similar historical occasions when the army revolted against the system, of which it was supposed to be a subordinated element, by staging a coup aimed at fundamental changes of a *permanent* nature amounting to the replacement of one political system by another. On most occasions, however, the army, when staging a coup, does not challenge the system within which it functions at all. On the contrary, it tries to consolidate that system, making it more cohesive and better able to withstand any attempts directed toward its split and subsequent destruction. The change it introduces in these cases amounts to a reinforcement of the same system's sole pivot by *temporarily* altering the mode in which it operates and the composition of the personnel who are running it. In fact, by staging such a coup, the army is continuing to act as a constituent element of the old system and not as its second pivot at all.

Most of the military coups, so often taking place in Latin America, the coups that brought the military to power in Greece in 1967 or in Turkey in 1980 (as well as previous such coups in that country) or in many other places (Thailand, Pakistan, etc.) are of exactly such a "system-preserving" nature.

Of that same nature was also the so-called military coup in Poland staged on December 13, 1981, under the command of party Chief and Prime Minister, General Woiciech Jaruzelski. The whole substance of this coup was preservation of the crumbling system of partocratic supremacy. It was, in fact, organized not by the military but by the ruling party apparatus, which just used for that purpose its own military branch operated by the party's envoys to the army, such as Jaruzelski, Siwicki, Kiszczak, et al., i.e., by pure partocrats dressed up in Polish generals' uniforms. The military branch of the party apparatus, as the one least disintegrated and best equipped with means of suppression, was rushed onto the scene to fortify all the other parts of this apparatus that were about to fall apart, and to crush at the same time "Solidarity" and all other public outlets able to provide the Polish people with independent power and influence.

It is worthwhile to note that the main Polish military force—its conscript army, together with the professional military officers that are in charge of it—were safely locked up in their barracks during the whole duration of that "military" coup. The coup was in fact perpetrated by the special security and police forces (the so-called ZOMOs). The regular military force could not be trusted with the performance of such a task. Only later were some regular troops brought in to help the ZOMOs to enforce "martial law." But they were always attached to the ZOMOs in a supplementary capacity and were put under their strict command.

There is little doubt, too, that the whole "military" operation started on December 13, 1981, was carefully planned during the entire period of Jaruzelski's occupation of the highest offices in the country, if not before, and not only in Warsaw but also in Moscow, which explains the numerous trips the Soviet Marshal Kulikov, the Chief Commander of Warsaw Pact forces, was making to Warsaw during the last months before the "military" rule was imposed.

I greatly doubt the possibility of an authentic military coup being staged either in Poland or, for that matter, in any other Soviet dependency. For the Polish Army, as well as the armies of all other Soviet satellite states, are not self-sufficient entities, but elements of the united forces of the Warsaw Pact run by Soviet generals and their party supervisors. These Soviet functionaries are in fact the real supremos over the whole Polish military establishment, and over Jaruzelski himself.

Since the party and the army of the Soviet Union are in full control of the party and, to no lesser extent, of the Army of Poland, any genuine rebellion of the Polish Army would have to be directed in the first place against its superior foreign authority, not against the Polish people, who in this event would wholeheartedly support their army and join with it in this liberatory (though desperate and, most likely, self-destructive) venture.

I do not exclude that in the event of Soviet intervention in Poland such a rebellion of the Polish Army could still take place, but then it would be led by genuine military people (colonels rather than generals) against not only the foreign intruders, but in the first place against Jaruzelski and his "military" establishment themselves. One should not overlook, however, the difficulty of realizing such a plan. The main problem here is that each separate army unit (e.g., the Polish Army) within the united forces of the Warsaw Pact has at its disposal only three days' combat supply of ammunition, the rest being controlled and supplied exclusively by the Soviet commanders of the Warsaw Pact forces themselves.

Since the Soviet Union is politically and militarily independent of any outside force, the situation with a military coup there would inevitably assume an entirely different character. Even if the party apparatus itself did engineer there a "military" takeover, like they did in Poland, it would become extremely difficult for it to keep the thus elevated marshals and generals in proper check and effectively prevent the Chilean model of change from being set in motion. The same would be true also for Jaruzelsi, Siwicki, and Kiszczak if there were no supreme Soviet command over them. But the Soviet Jaruzelskis, Siwickis, and Kiszczaks, after having staged a successful coup, would have nobody above them, which makes for a qualitatively different situation indeed. This is to say that in Soviet conditions if the army rose to take independent political action, it would inevitably assume the role of the "second pivot."

Indeed, in both my "military coup" sub-scenarios (based on the Portuguese and Chilean models of change) the army was considered as the force actually splitting the system with a view to its fundamental change and thus putting itself into the position of the system's "second pivot." Hence, the rule of the "second pivot" was here fully observed, too, without implying any crude assumptions that the army, every time it seizes power, actually acts as the system's "second pivot."

The "second pivot" issue is even more complex in the Polish model of change. Here we were confronted with a spontaneous grassroots movement developing outside the official system and therefore with one that by its own effort should have been unable to either split this system and produce its "second pivot" or directly affect it in any other way. In the light of F. Znakov's theory, such a spontaneous grassroots movement, whatever its form—strikes, riots, or demonstrations—is in itself unable to become the vehicle of political change; it could serve only as an indication of the degree to which society is ready for such a change. Indeed, in F. Znakov's opinion, the quite popular romantic view of revolutions as spontaneous mass uprisings, barricade battles between the insurgents and the government's armed forces, etc., is totally erroneous and antihistorical. "After the *second pivot* of society's organization had emerged, the fate of the revolution would be decided in the confrontation of forces representing the old system of power and the second pivot"; before that, spontaneous confrontations between unorganized grassroots rebels and the government would be either no more than symptoms of some wider "change-inducing" issues or, at best, powerful outside impulses for the "second pivot" to form itself within the system and start initiating the real process of revolutionary change, e.g., by organizing the disenchanted masses for an active support of those changes.[23]

It follows from the above that the Polish model seems to be relevant in terms of change only insofar as it could initiate developments within the official system leading to its split into "two pivots" in accordance with the other previously considered scenarios of change. Indeed, the Central Committee (or the Politburo) could split into two pivots on the grounds of the differing views of its members as to how one should deal with rebellious grassroots manifestations or which policies one should adopt in order to prevent the occurrence of such manifestations in the future. In a similar way such manifestations could serve as a pretext or stimulus for the army or any other public body to challenge the authority of the party's leadership and thus become "second pivots" themselves.

Grassroots manifestations are therefore able to trigger latent tensions within the official system and could be used by certain forces there as a proper, and probably long-awaited, opportunity for making their decisive bid for power, but by and in themselves they do not represent an independent and self-sufficient model of change. If that is really the case, why should one then consider the Polish model as a basis for a separate scenario of change at all? Is it not more correct to regard it as merely one of the many possibilities for the initiation of any proper scenario? The answer to that is "no," simply because the Polish situation of 1980 differed from others as far as the striking workers in Gdansk's Lenin shipyard managed to develop a coherent organizational structure not simply on a local scale, but in the form of a United Strike Committee, which very soon established its authority on a national scale (one should note that the existence in Poland of a strong, and at that time yet unsuppressed, overt dissident movement was in this respect of decisive importance, especially insofar as the process of formation of the United Strike Committee's authoritative leadership was concerned).

This organizational structure, being at its inception an "outside body" to the system, was, of course, not yet a proper "second pivot," since it could neither have split the system nor have immediately acquired a recognized place within it, in order to be able to produce such a split. But as soon as it emerged *beside* the official system it became an important force to be seriously reckoned with by the Polish Communist government. Faced with an outside public body of such magnitude and strength, this government had only two choices: either to crush it as an unauthorized (and thus, in official terms, illegitimate) creation or to grant it official recognition, at least to a certain extent. The latter alternative for which, after some hesitation, the Polish authorities temporarily opted when they accepted this United Strike Committee as a valid partner for the negotiation of a settlement with the strikers, meant nothing else but the institutionalization of this committee within the official system. This committee, and later the "Solidarity" trade union, by being thus institutionalized shook the foundations of Polish communist totalitarianism and assumed in it automatically the role of the "second pivot."

There were no inner constraints preventing this newly-established and officially recognized public body from fully realizing its immense potential. Without the external constraint of possible Soviet intervention, the whole official totalitarian system in Poland would have been toppled by this "second pivot" immediately and irreversibly. But the presence of this external constraint, of which all the forces comprising the Polish "second pivot" were only too well aware (not least because of the Catholic Church and the dissident Workers' Defense Committee, KOR, constantly drawing the workers' attention to it), restrained operations of this second pivot to an extent that allowed the official system to survive, remain essentially unaffected, and then redress itself by the means of the "military" coup.[24]

At any rate, the Polish model is just one more way in which the "second pivot" can be formed in society, with all the implicit consequences (and in the Soviet Union's case, with no artificial constraints to prevent it from fully developing, these consequences, as far as the regime is concerned, can only be fatal). The only difference is that here the "second pivot" emerges not as a result of the system's split from inside but because of the system's attempt at incorporating an outside body, unmergeable with it; the split is thus produced in the system by the incorporation of that body into it.

In conclusion, one should note that a power crisis in Poland or in any other satellite country can produce a profound destabilizing effect on the Soviet Union itself. After all, the Soviet bloc is an integral empire and everything that happens on its outskirts is bound directly to affect the center. In other words, a part of the empire setting itself firmly against the center and the center, in response, setting itself against that part of the empire also produces a "two-pivotal" situation with all the possible consequences that this situation may entail.

Poland, where the crisis is far from being settled, is still the strongest contender to produce such a two-pivotal situation again and thus strongly challenge the stability of the Soviet system itself. For everybody, in Poland and elsewhere, has now understood that no change will be possible in Poland or any other part of the Soviet bloc until changes occur in Moscow. Hence, any more worthwhile undertaking in Poland or in any other Soviet dependency, should be precisely timed and have sufficient strength to make a real impact on stability in Moscow.

E. CONCLUDING REMARKS ON THE NEXT STEP IN RUSSIA'S POLITICAL HISTORY

The "second pivot" is an issue of crucial importance insofar as it is the only reliable indication of the beginning of political change either in the Soviet Union or in any other authoritarian system. With the "second pivot" theory, Soviet watchers are acquiring a reliable instrument for a proper assessment of the significance of different events in their relation to political change. This applies especially to Kremlinologists whose criteria of evaluation of changes are now so confused and grossly lacking in methodology. But what kind of political change should we expect in the Soviet Union if the "second pivot" finally appeared there and started functioning? What are, in other words, the possible alternatives to the present Soviet political system?

Having explored the possible ways of, and positively assessed the prospects for, political change in the Soviet Union, one must also consider its foreseeable consequences. Western scholars usually discuss this problem in the context of a simple opposition between dictatorship and democracy or hegemony and polyarchy.[25] In other words, for them, change becomes a real issue only insofar as a hegemonic order can be replaced by a polyarchic one (or vice versa), or at least insofar as one can envision such a replacement. No wonder these scholars assess chances for political change in the Soviet Union as extremely grim. Indeed, if one identifies political change in the Soviet Union with the establishment there of a Western liberal democracy, one is bound to come to pessimistic conclusions. After nearly seventy years of effective suppression of political freedom, all the requisites of political society in the USSR have been rooted out, and it will take some time for them to reappear in that country.

In this context, the arguments about the inevitable replacement of partocrats by technocrats in the position of power also lose all their impressiveness for a Western scholar. As Walter D. Connor pointed out, the professionalization (or technocratization) of the Soviet elite is not necessarily linked with political change because technocrats are not necessarily democrats.[26] "The technical intelligentsia has essential skills, but most of its members cannot be numbered among the dissidents."[27] The broad masses of Soviet people, according to Connor, are also not a serious factor of change because, as he points out, they "do not demand legality, representative institutions, freedom . . . The interest in freedom and the rule of law is not broad enough, is not sufficiently a 'mass' interest, to make its accommodation critical."[28] Both these points about the technocrats and the masses are perhaps true, but political change in the USSR does not necessarily imply the establishment of "legality, representative institutions, freedom." Political change in the Soviet Union is indeed unlikely to involve the establishment of democratic rule, but it is very likely to establish a *rational* and nationally-minded government as opposed to the present *irrational*, single-ideology-based, and clique-minded regime. In fact, while the new rational government that would emerge from political change in the USSR would have the full support of the technocrats, as well as of the overwhelming majority of people, it may also be authoritarian for a significant period of time.

But, as I have argued elsewhere, "authoritarianism is not totalitarianism, because authoritarian rule does not necessarily encompass in a rigid framework all spheres of human life and activity."[29] Any new political regime in the USSR, authoritarian or not, will not only be compatible with a pluralistic economic pattern and with considerable autonomy for the economic system *vis-à-vis* the state (i.e., with the re-emergence of an autonomous civil society) but, if it is to command the support of the technocrats, must be explicitly based on these principles. Such a regime, authoritarian or not, will do away with the sole official ideology (in a framework of national ideology, quite a few political, social, and religious ideologies can coexist) and thus provide conditions for the emergence of a pluralistic ideological pattern in social life. Ideological pluralism, in its turn, implies more freedom for creative work and for expression of different interests, including those now represented by civic, national, and partially religious dissent (partially, because any degree of ideological tolerance would automatically solve the problems of most religious groups). Under such a regime, the necessary preconditions for creating a democratic system of government could evolve in due course, too, but the establishment of a democracy (polyarchy) is indeed not the most immediate and realizable task in the struggle to bring about political change in the USSR. The most important task here consists of liquidating totalitarianism, and this is what political change in the USSR is going to mean in the first place.

The first post-Soviet government of Russia may be, in a way, similar to the Bonapartist regime in France after Napoléon's 1799 18th of Brumaire coup, but without its Jacobin flare (I am referring here to the authoritarian form of Bonapartism, which Napoléon successfully used for building up a modern administrative system for the French state and for introducing a body of codified law, marking the borderline between France's civil society and her polity, rather than to Napoléon's ideologically-motivated plans of conquering Europe and establishing "progressive" France as the leading power on the continent). This first post-Soviet government of Russia, whatever its character or ideology (although there is little doubt that it will be technocratic in character and nationalist in ideology) and whatever the mechanism of the formation of the "second pivot" by which it will be created, before doing anything else, will have to solve the following three main problems:

1. The first is that of separating the civil society from polity—that is to say, dismantling totalitarianism and creating a comprehensive legal system that would provide the necessary conditions for effective functioning of social and economic institutions not under the discretionary rule of the party-state but under the rule of law, i.e., in an autonomous and basically self-sufficient way. Some could call it the reinstitution of private enterprise and free market.
2. The second is that of sorting out the complex network of tense, hostile and, in some cases, directly antagonistic intra-national relations within the Soviet Union, as well as in Soviet-dominated Eastern Europe, in order to create some organic ground for peaceful cooperation between Russia and other nations involved. It seems to me that any post-Soviet government will try to reach a consensus with the non-Russian nations of the area by conceding to their respective demands of either sovereignty or genuine autonomy in exchange for firm guarantees on the part of those nations of the inviolability of Russian national interests within respective national territories.
3. The third problem is that of putting an end to more than sixty years of artificial, purely ideologically-motivated and, by no rational standards necessary, confrontation between the East and the West, and of establishing, in accordance with the national interests of all parties involved, a pattern of Russia's genuine cooperation with the Western world, above all with the other superpower—the United States. This problem will be of special importance and its settlement of paramount urgency as it will, among other things, create the pattern of international stability and cooperation between major powers of the world, without which it would be virtually impossible to achieve a reliable settlement of the second problem of settling intra-national relations within the present Soviet realm of rule, as well as of other international issues in which Russia has a vital interest (e.g., the Sino-Russian conflict), and also very difficult to accelerate adequately Russia's economic development.

With Russia busy settling the above issues, both the present Soviet realm and the entire world should become much safer and better to live in.

NOTES

1. "Left-Wing Communism—An Infantile Disorder" (1920), quoted from Robert C. Tucker, ed., *The Lenin Anthology* (New York: Norton, 1975), 602. Lenin repeated here the idea he had first formulated and elaborated at greater length in his longish article,

"The Downfall of the Second International" (summer 1915). There, however, he talks, in the same terms, about the symptoms of a revolutionary situation only, whereas in "Left-Wing Communism," he unequivocally declares the quoted formula to be "the fundamental law of revolution."

2. *The Republic*, 545d (quoted from J. Adam's edition of *The Republic of Plato*, vol. 2 [Cambridge: Cambridge University Press, 1902]).

3. *Plato, The Republic* (quoted from A. D. Lindsay's edition of *Plato, The Republic* [New York: Knopf, 1992]).

4. The term "great revolution" was used by many theorists and philosophers, inclusive of de Tocqueville and Marx, but was defined as "reconstitution of the state" by George S. Pettee with a special view of providing a taxonomical distinction between revolution proper and all other political change brought about by drastic and/or violent means (such as putsch, coup d'état, etc.). For further reference, see George S. Pettee, *The Process of Revolution* (New York: Harper & Brothers, 1938), 3ff.

5. *Revolution* (Oxford: Basil Blackwell, 1975), 102.

6. *Treatise on General Sociology*, §2054, but also §2057 and §2058.

7. *Revolutionary Change*, 2d ed. (London: Longman, 1983), 108.

8. This is Max Weber's shortest and most general definition of legitimacy (quoted from Max Rheinstein, ed., *Max Weber on Law in Economy and Society* [Cambridge, Mass.: Harvard University Press, 1954], 328).

9. This idea permeates the whole of Marx's work, especially *The Class Struggles in France* (1848–1850), *The Eighteenth Brumaire of Louis Bonaparte* (1852), and *Civil War in France* (1871).

10. *Manifesto of the Communist Party* (1848); quoted from Robert C. Tucker, ed., *The Marx-Engels Reader*, 2d ed. (New York: Norton, 1978), 490.

11. *Democracy in America* (1835–1840). Especially relevant here is the Simon & Shuster (New York, 1964) edition, 274.

12. *Democracy in America*.

13. The term "Millenarianism" to characterize such movements and their rule was introduced and elaborated by Chalmers Johnson in *Revolution and the Social System* (Stanford: Hoover Institution Press, 1964), especially 35–39.

14. "Left-Wing Communism," 602. Popular revolt may cause such a "nationwide crisis" and/or be an expression of it.

15. For Chalmers Johnson's discussion of different kinds of courses of action open to the ruling elite during "power deflation . . . from conservative change to its polar opposite, complete intransigence," see his *Revolutionary Change*, 96–100 (the above quotation is on 96).

16. F. Znakov, *Pamyatnaya zapiska* (Memorandum), in Radio Liberty's *Arkhiv Samizdata* (Samizdat Archives), no. 374 (1966): 21–22.

17. The decision to create this council was formally adopted by the 3rd All-Union Congress of Collective Farmers; see *Tretiy Vsesoyuznyi S'ezd Kolkhoznikov, 25–27 noyabrya 1969 goda. Stenograficheskiy Otchet* (The Third All-Union Congress of the Collective Farmers, 25–27 November 1969: Stenographic Report) (Moscow: Kolos, 1970), 270–72. The details of its organization (from the Union Council to the district councils) and functions are given in its rules published in *Sbornik Postanovleniy Soveta Ministrov SSSR* (Collection of Decisions of the Council of Ministers of the USSR), no. 12 (1971), Art. 90.

18. F. Znakov, *Pamyatnaya zapiska*, 23.

19. Jerry F. Hough, "Thinking About Thinking About Dissent," in *Studies in Comparative Communism* 12, nos. 2 & 3 (summer/autumn 1979): 271.

20. Hough, "Thinking About Thinking About Dissent."

21. A. Y. Shtromas, "Rejoinder," in *Studies in Comparative Communism* 12, nos. 2 and 3 (summer/autumn 1979): 275–76.

22. A recent example is Yuri Borisov's lecture, "Stalin: the Man and the Legend," at the State Institute of History and Archives in Moscow, which was followed by an extremely sharp debate. For a vivid report on this event, see Elfie Siegel, "Die Moskauer kommen zusammen um Stalin zu kritikieren" in *Frankfurter Rundschau*, March 31, 1987, 4.

23. F. Znakov, *Pamyatnaya zapiska*, 22.

24. Hence, Jadwyga Staniszkis's concept of the "self-limiting revolution." For my more detailed account and assessment of the Polish events of 1980–1981, see A. Shtromas, "Poland: What Next?," *Free Life* 2, no. 4 (winter 1981–1982): 14–25.

25. The terms "hegemony" and "polyarchy" were introduced and elaborated by Robert A. Dahl with the view of making the usage of the terms "democracy" and "dictatorship" more differentiated and precise. See his *Polyarchy: Participation and Opposition* (New Haven, Conn.: Yale University Press, 1971).

26. This point is argued at great length in a special section, "Present and Future," of his article, "Differentiation, Integration and Political Dissent in the USSR," in Rudolf L. Tökes, ed., *Dissent in the USSR: Politics, Ideology and People* (Baltimore, Md.: Johns Hopkins University Press, 1975), 152–56.

27. "Differentiation, Integration and Political Dissent in the USSR," 156.

28. "Differentiation, Integration and Political Dissent in the USSR," 155.

29. A. Shtromas, "Dissent and Political Change in the Soviet Union," in Erik P. Hoffmann and Robin F. Laird, eds., *The Soviet Polity in the Modern Era* (New York: Aldine Publishing, 1984), 740.

16

Political Change and Political Collapse

ALEKSANDRAS SHTROMAS

A. CONCEPT AND PROSPECTS

Political change is a very broad concept. It has become common to divide it into "within-system" and "system-rejective" categories.[1] I believe that the Soviet political system has no room for substantial "within-system" change. Its basic feature is the unlimited power of the highly-centralized party apparatus, which exercises absolute control over all socially relevant activities and developments in the country, be they economic or social, governmental or judicial, educational or informational, cultural or artistic. If the monopoly and totality of that "leading role of the party" were to be affected by any change, it would mean that the change was "system-rejective" (since the logic of the system is such that there is no way the party can exercise its power on a scale other than the absolute and total one). Only if the "leading role" of the party was to be strengthened or at least left intact may the appropriate change be listed as a "within-system" one. But in this case one would be dealing merely with administrative change rather than with political change in the fullest sense.

Reprinted extracts from Aleksandras Shtromas, *Political Change and Social Development: The Case of the Soviet Union* (Frankfurt: Peter Lang, 1981), 95–101; 132–37; 144; 147.

It would be wrong to divide the views of Soviet dissidents into those advocating "within-system" and those advocating "system-rejective" change, according either to what they say about the matter or according to the reaction of officialdom to such views. There is here an absolutely objective criterion: those who advocate a "socialist market economy," a system of strict "socialist legality," creative freedom, or any other kind of genuine autonomy of social function or of an organizational unit outside the total control of the party are objectively striving for a "system-rejective" change, although they might think (or pretend to think) that they are asking for a "within-system" change. The stagnant pattern of the Soviet regime during the last sixteen post-Khrushchevian years (and Khrushchev was ousted from his position in 1964 because the rest of the leadership regarded his involvement in constant reorganization as dangerous to the system) is the best proof of the narrow limits for "within-system" political change.[2]

As long ago as 1966, F. Znakov had convincingly shown that any kind of a radical plan for "within-system" reforms aimed at improving the system's economic and managerial performance is incompatible with the survival of the regime and that the post-Khrushchevian Soviet leadership was very well aware of it.[3] That is why, according to him, by 1966 both the "left radical" (as represented by Kosygin) and the "right radical" (as represented by Shelepin)[4] fractions of the Soviet leadership willingly submitted to the *Marais* (marsh) or centrist fraction (as represented by Brezhnev), advocating the policy of "no change," i.e., of mere preservation of the status quo.[5] "The 23rd Congress of the Party (1966–A. S.) was nothing else but the Congress of the victory of the Marais,"[6] which to F. Znakov meant a frank admission by the whole leadership of the fact that the system over which they collectively preside had almost completely exhausted its dynamic resources, lost the potential for significant "within-system" change, and is committed to live with whatever vices are inherent in it, with no cure for them even being sought. As F. Znakov concludes: "The Soviet 'super monopolistic' system is incurably sick and aneurism of the aorta, a disease in which any more or less drastic move of the patient causes his death, is its sickness."[7] Almost fifteen years later Ilya Dzhirkvelov, not a dissident but a high KGB official who, in 1979 defected to the West, echoed this diagnosis independently from F. Znakov: "If the Kremlin tightens up still further . . . something could well crack; but if it allows liberalization, that too will lead to an unpredictable explosion. . . . The one certainty . . . is that something must happen. We cannot go on as we are for much longer."[8] Thus the term "political change" is used here in the sense of "system-rejective" change. The very nature of the Soviet system, especially in the situation in which it finds itself today, does not allow for any other usage of this term insofar as it applies to the USSR.

All this might sound too extreme and exaggerated to be totally convincing. Indeed, why should a "system-rejective" change take place if the party simply allows autonomy for some sections of the civil society and so to speak excludes them from its direct control and supervision, remaining at the same time in full control of political power in the country? It is true, the party has never allowed it to happen and has been guarding the totality of its "leading role" over all walks of life without exception most zealously, even equating it with the preservation of socialism itself. But isn't this due to the Soviet leadership's paranoia and if this is the case, why should we, rational people, accept this paranoic attitude as a true reflection of reality? Shouldn't we rather assume that important "within-system" changes can be objectively carried out in the Soviet Union without endangering the party's power and at the same time making the economic and social system much more efficient and strong? There is even some evidence available to support such assumptions. As we know, in some Communist countries (Yugoslavia, Poland, East Germany) the private sector is left in existence and it neither challenges nor interferes with the Communist Party's leading role; in Hungary, market mechanisms are widely used within the state-run socialist economy without exposing the system to any dangerous threats. Why then is the Soviet Union so special or different? Why could it not follow suit and introduce reforms of the same kind without risking the survival of the whole system of authoritarian rule by the party?

There are two main reasons why the Soviet Union is a special case and cannot afford in terms of the system's survival what other lesser European Communist powers can. *Firstly*, the Soviet Union, as the first and the oldest Communist power in the world, had fully attained its totalitarian (socialist) goal by 1936, i.e., before other communist powers even came into existence. That makes it principally different from, for instance, East Germany or Poland (except for Poland's agriculture about which I will talk later), where the private sector was not reintroduced but has not *yet* been fully abolished and survives as the remnant of the capitalist past (as it was in the USSR of the 1920s). Therefore, for the Soviet Union, in contrast to these other Communist countries, the introduction of reforms rehabilitating the private sector or any kind of autonomous economic or social activities means a retreat from what has been achieved, not a toleration of the temporary incompleteness of the achievement, and this makes the whole difference.

There are, of course, retreats and retreats. In Poland the retreat of 1956 from collective to individual farming was presented not as a failure of the socialist agriculture itself but as a result of its premature introduction which, bearing in mind that collectivization in Poland was accomplished only a few years before 1956, was even plausible. That would not apply to the Soviet conditions where collective farms are by now almost forty years old and although still internally resented as much as forty years ago, are proudly acclaimed as the true socialist, and therefore most progressive, organization of agricultural production. In Soviet conditions, such a retreat would mean an implicit recognition of the failure of the socialist agricultural system itself, the repercussions of such recognition being of a fatal nature to the socialist system as a whole. Not only such "huge retreats," but also even the slightest retreat from "mature and developed socialism" would be regarded in the Soviet Union as tantamount to the admission of socialism's bankruptcy. That is exactly the boost that the "intrastructural" dissident forces need to come into action and is actually what they have been patiently awaiting for many years. For as soon as the regime recognizes the reforms of "mature socialism" desirable in principle and as soon as it moves even a step toward their implementation, the "intrastructural" dissidents will gain the official platform to insist on the further widening of these reforms and will use it to its full extent, exposing the regime to the threat of losing, in the end, the control over the course of events altogether (in an embryonic form, this situation was already manifested during the 1965 economic reform, which the authorities hastily revoked exactly because of the enormous increase of intrastructural dissent activities that it provoked). In this respect one should remember two things. Firstly, that any such reform is bound to create on the social surface an organizational pattern autonomous from the party, which can easily turn into a stronghold of intrastructural dissent initiating changes unplanned and undesired by the party (after so many years of total integration into the political system, it would be plainly impossible to completely isolate any part of the economy from the overall pattern of that system and thus to repeat the trick of NEP); and secondly, that the Soviet Union is the only communist country (except China) where intrastructural dissent is a self-sufficient force, having nothing to fear from any outside forces, which makes it potentially more powerful and influential, and hence more dangerous for the regime, than anywhere else. That is why in the Soviet Union any move in the direction of excluding from the total control of the party any section of civil society could (and most certainly would) be fatal for the survival of the system itself. A totalitarian structure does not tolerate exceptions or compromises: it is either total or totally disintegrates.

Secondly, the communist parties of Eastern Europe can allow for more flexibility in their respective countries and have more room for experimentation with economic and social reforms because they are strongly backed by an additional, "outside" factor of political stability represented by the Soviet Union itself with its overwhelming military power. Whatever the dissident forces in those countries would like to gain from these reforms (and on their own they would certainly be able to use these reforms for rejecting the system altogether), the Soviet Union will not allow them to proceed too far in this direction, as was shown by events in Hungary (1956) and Czechoslovakia (1968). That is why Hungary can afford to have certain economic freedom without risk to the party's supremacy, whereas the Soviet Union cannot. That is why the Soviet leadership did not mind allowing Czechoslovakia to go ahead with Otta Sik's economic reforms in the spring of 1968 (provided that they were not extended to other spheres), but did everything in its power to put down the expectations for similar developments in the Soviet economy, which at that time, thanks to Czechoslovakia's influence, had been strongly reboosted.

That is why Poland could have had its collective farm system dismantled in 1956 without affecting the basic foundations of the totalitarian system of the party's rule and also why, now in 1980, it can contemplate the introduction of some freedom for its workers to express their economic grievances—developments which, in the USSR, would be absolutely detrimental to the survival of that system. The overwhelming shadow of the Soviet Union over these countries is the best deterrent against all such developments getting out of hand and becoming a real threat to the party and its "leading role." It was only out of "respect" for this "shadow" that the striking Polish workers of 1980 agreed to recognize the inviolability of the leading role of the party while pressing for independent trade unions and being in the position to force the Polish (but not the Soviet) Communist leadership to accept all their demands. There is no such shadow, however, over the Soviet Union, which makes its totalitarian system more vulnerable than that of the others and forces its rulers to be as rigid and immobile as possible (i.e., as they really are).

I think, there is no doubt that if a situation, like that in Hungary of 1956; in Poland of 1956, 1968, and 1970 (let alone the one of 1980); in Czechoslovakia of 1968, etc., would occur in the Soviet Union, the Soviet totalitarian system would irreversibly collapse under its burden. In all the above countries, the totalitarian system in practice also collapsed but thanks to the Soviet Union's "fraternal help" was again resuscitated, like the Phoenix, and survives. Hence, the extreme cautiousness of the Soviet leaders and their unswerving intransigence in keeping the party apparatus in total control over all walks of life in the Soviet Union is not as paranoic as it might seem at first glance. It is actually entirely justified on most sober and rational grounds. This is, in a way, substantiated by the fact that the Soviet leaders are not alone in holding this attitude—the leaders of other ruling communist parties, who do not completely depend on the Soviet Union and have to count on their own resources for holding on to power, share it with them entirely. In many ways the latter are trying to preserve the absoluteness of their control over all walks of life in their respective countries even more eagerly and sometimes in more rigid forms than the CPSU itself. China, Albania, North Korea, and Romania are here the most obvious examples and Yugoslavia, due to very specific historic circumstances, represents the only "liberal" exception, although there the party remains as much in absolute control of everything and is as much insistent on preserving this position as is the CPSU and every other self-reliant communist party in power.

The "universality" of this phenomenon suggests that it really makes much more sense to assume that for the communist parties and their leaders, the obsession with the totality and absoluteness of their rule, far from being paranoiac or otherwise psychotic, is in fact the only rational way to keep the system assuring their ascendancy intact and to make it persistent for as long as possible. I am sure that these inveterate, extremely experienced and pragmatic politicians who rule the communist countries know exactly what they should be, and are, doing, and if they think that it is their political survival that is at stake in these issues, then so it must be. It seems that here again the real situation was neatly summed up by F. Znakov when he wrote: "It is self-evident . . . that the introduction of any measure incompatible with the supermonopolistic system of property[9] means for Russia the beginning of a social revolution."[10] And since we have already established that the whole history of the USSR was (and is) the history of the regime's continuous struggle against total dissent, it should be clear to us that the Soviet leadership's first and sole commitment is not to allow revolutionary (or in their terminology—counterrevolutionary) developments to take place in any shape or form—hence, stagnation, inflexibility, refusal to proceed with changes of any significance altogether.

Assumptions apart, the contention that any change affecting the totality of "the leading role of the party" amounts to a "system-rejective" change in general, can be substantiated by some positive evidence proving that it is not an exaggeration at all. As it was demonstrated by recent historical experience, as soon as in a critical situation an officially recognized public body becomes able to assume its independence from the main core of the party apparatus and starts challenging the latter's authority (with the main core of this apparatus, because of the critical situation, being unable to destroy and/or to bring this body back into the totalitarian fold immediately), the whole totalitarian system explodes and disintegrates (the formation on the social surface of an independent public body is alone sufficient to bring the critical situation about by simply exposing the latent critical issues). I am referring here, of course, to the unique historic experience of the few critical situations that, in certain communist countries, were brought out into the open, and in the first place to the most radical and explicit of them all—that of the 1956 Hungarian revolution, whose rapid development started with one party organization, that of the Writers' Union, asserting its independence from the party's Central Committee. The controversy developed over the latter's decision to expel the writers, Tomasz Axel and Tibor Dery, from the party, which the former rejected; the general confusion that reigned in Hungary in the aftermath of the 20th Congress of the CPSU and Rakosi's removal from office incapacitated the Hungarian party's Central Committee's ability to respond to the thus arisen "dual" situation in the usual repressive manner. The Central Committee under these circumstances failed even to disband the Writer's Union's primary party organization, which thus suddenly found itself in the position of a fully operational "within-system" body, independent from that system's main pivot, and challenging its authority by refusing to obey its decisions.

Another public body—the Petőfi Circle, a political propaganda and discussion club normally functioning within the Hungarian Communist Youth Organization—associated itself with the now independent Writers' Union's Party organization providing the platform necessary for free public discussion of all the outstanding issues of Hungarian society and politics. As soon as these comparatively modest public bodies established their "united" independence from the system, the whole power balance in Hungary drastically shifted. The nation immediately recognized in the thus positioned and functioning Petöfi Circle an institution representing and aggregating its genuine interests and demands and massively switched to its support, with large masses of people entirely ignoring their affiliations within the official system, into which they were until then coercively but firmly integrated. The Petöfi Circle suddenly found itself enjoying absolute authority with the people and thus wielding enormous power in the country, whereas the whole official totalitarian establishment, deserted by the nation, was rendered virtually powerless. Everyone knows what followed the Petöfi Circle's decision of October 22, 1956, demanding the abolition of a number of the most repressive decrees of the party as well as the introduction of other fundamental changes,[11] and the mass demonstration in Budapest on the October 23, 1956, in support of this decision: the total disintegration within a few days of the whole official system (the party itself ceased to exist) with a polyarchy quickly emerging to replace it. Without the Soviet tanks, whose intervention brutally crushed the consolidating polyarchy and forcefully restored the old system (though in a slightly modified form), the history of totalitarian communism in Hungary would have ended at that point forever.

It appears that there is nothing, except foreign intervention, that can stop the totalitarian communist system from disintegration once this process has set in. It is like a nuclear chain reaction that is virtually unstoppable after the critical mass has been reached. The "critical mass" necessary for that "reaction" to take place in a communist regime seems to be the occurrence of any break in the totality of the party's control, whereby at least one officially recognized public body, whatever its importance within the system, assumes its independence from the party and acquires the capability to make its own decisions, representing a challenge to the party's authority. Everything else follows from that as automatically as in a real nuclear chain reaction. Or as one Polish Catholic intellectual, commenting on the 1980 strikes in Poland, said: "It is like a thread. You pull one and the whole thing unravels."[12]

Therefore Janos Kadar was absolutely right when, in the June 27, 1957, report to the first All-Hungarian Conference of the newly-formed Hungarian Socialist Workers Party, after the suppression of the revolution (as mentioned above, the old Hungarian party of the Workers was dissolved during the revolution), he said: "The enemy . . . could organize the action against people's power only because he was able to take over certain *organizations* of the Party" (emphasis added).[13]

What he really intimated was the crucial importance for the system's very survival of keeping the totality of the party leadership's control over all walks of life intact. For as soon as any organization, even a constituent organization of the party itself, assumes independence from that total structure represented by the party's leadership, it will most certainly use it for initiating and supporting change undesirable for, or not planned by, the party. This by itself is capable of undermining the party leadership's overall authority (it is not any more in full and absolute control and has to bow to certain pressures from outside) but, with the inevitable shift of the support of the masses to such an autonomous organization (bearing in mind the profound popular resentment of totalitarian communism, this is the most natural thing that can happen in any communist country), the system as a whole becomes exposed to a real danger of being swept away altogether in the course of a few days or even hours.

B. HISTORIOSOPHICAL PREMISES AND CONSEQUENCES

It seems to me that all the misunderstandings and misrepresentations of the problem of political change in the Soviet Union spring from the failure to consider it in a wider historical (as well as theoretical) context—that of the stages in the development of the Russian revolution that started in February (March) 1917. One somehow tends to forget that the Soviet regime was originated in the course of the revolution by a revolutionary group with a view to fulfilling an extraordinary revolutionary task and that today this regime remains basically unchanged, e.g., in its practical structure and theoretical self-legitimization. The fallacy here is that, as a result, one treats the Soviet regime as a normal, traditionally legitimate political system, assessable purely on the grounds of its practical performance in aggregating the interests of different social groups and representing and serving their common interests. Putting the problem of political change in the Soviet Union into this frame of reference, one grossly distorts its very substance, whatever conclusions one reaches about the probability and imminence of the change itself.

In a traditionally legitimate political system, the problem of change posits itself as that of the system's ability to properly adjust to modern social developments and adequately cope with the challenges and demands with which modernity presents it. If that political system is not flexible enough and if it becomes increasingly rigid and unresponsive to society's new needs and expectations, it might start losing its traditional legitimacy very fast, exposing itself thereby to imminent change.[14] The approach to the problem of political change from the point of view of the political system's deteriorating legitimacy, when applied to the Soviet Union, makes no sense whatsoever. For in the Soviet Union, as well as in any other country governed by a regime originated as an instrument of revolutionary change, the problem is not one of the political system losing its legitimacy but one of that system's ability to establish itself as legitimate in the first place. Moreover, the whole point about the political system's adjustability to social reality is in this context also totally misleading. A regime like the Soviet one is not supposed to adjust to reality but, on the contrary, adjusts the reality to itself, according to its own specific ideological plan. It is on the basis of the result of the implementation of this plan (in the first place only projected and afterward already accomplished) that such a regime pleads for legitimacy and not on any pragmatically expedient managerial grounds at all.

Every such regime in its initial stage is based on the charismatic authority of an ideologically-minded leadership promising society to build upon the ruins of the ancien régime a "new order" that will be, if not immediately ideal, then at least will very soon entirely accommodate people's greatest aspirations. The issue at stake here is whether the new revolutionary political system could live up to these promises or not. Only if it could, would its "credited" charismatic legitimacy be transformed into a stable and actual one, acquiring in time a traditional character. If it could not, however, the initial "credited" charismatic legitimacy of this system would fade away very soon, even before having been solidly established. If this were the real outcome of that political experiment (and so far it has always been), it would in its own right spell the advent of a new political change. The regime, though entirely devoid of legitimacy, can survive for some time yet by its oppressive inertia but sooner or later it is bound to fall, giving way to a new political system that will represent a new stage in the civil society's postrevolutionary search for an adequate polity. Hence, the problem of political change for a revolutionary state posits itself not on the grounds of its adaptability to changing circumstances, as in the case of traditionally legitimate states, but on those of its ability to become traditionally legitimate by seeking to establish itself as an optimal alternative to the ancien régime, swept away by the "original" revolution.

Historical experience proves that the process of political change, once started by the overthrow of a traditional system that lost its original legitimacy, does not stop until a new political system, able to become fully legitimate, stable, and adequate to the society's needs, has been established in its place. The major point I try to prove here is to show that the Soviet political system has never been, and was never able to become, legitimate in the above sense of the word, which means that by its establishment the Russian revolution did not reach its goal and because of that still has to develop further, surpassing its Soviet stage. This has nothing to do with the Soviet system's growing inefficiency in terms of performance and the delivery of goods as such but with the failure of its basic ideological plan of which this inefficiency is only one of the many manifestations. It was precisely because of the failure of this plan that the Soviet system started in many respects to act as the czarist ancien régime had, including, in compliance with certain social demands, some attempts at adjusting to both tradition and modernity. This, however, does not justify the approach of assessing processes of change in the USSR as if they were identical to those going on in an ancien régime proper.

Before exploring the Soviet system in its historical revolutionary context in more detail, I would like to make a few additional remarks on the general problems relating to the theory and history of revolution. A revolution is the culmination of a profound dysfunction between a nation's civil society and its traditionally legitimate autocratic polity developing over a long period of time, in most cases because of the former's rapid modernization and the latter's failure (or organic inability) to adequately change in order to adjust and respond to this modernization (in Iran, this dysfunction arose in exactly the opposite way, i.e., by the polity imposing rapid modernization on civil society, which the latter was not ready to accept and against which it revolted; hence my qualifying remark about "most" instead of "all" cases). Via the mechanism of the formation of the "second pivot," described above, this dysfunction develops into a direct confrontation that starts off the revolutionary process, whose *first act* usually consists of sweeping away the ancien régime and thereby also undermining (using Hobbesian terminology) the very foundations of the Commonwealth itself. Although in the aftermath of the ancien régime's collapse, the "second pivot" usually establishes itself as the national political institution carrying supreme (although only provisional) authority and tries to consolidate a new political system around itself, its capability to effectively control the suddenly liberated varying forces of civil society is, in most cases, so limited that it is unable to prevent the nation from virtually relapsing into (again using Hobbesian terminology) the state of nature.

The aftermath of the first act of the revolution (the one that does away with the ancien régime) is therefore usually a period of almost unlimited liberty for the varying forces of civil society, especially those that are politically organized, to fully display their often irreconcilable views, goals, and ideals, e.g., by becoming involved in constant squabbles and clashes between themselves that are thus increasingly proliferating. The resulting unruly situation of a war of each against each (sorry about yet another reference to Hobbes) favors that political group that is most radical and single-minded in its vision and pursuit of change and therefore best at using the conditions of liberty for properly equipping itself (organizationally and otherwise) for the practical political achievement of its specific goals. The advantages of such a group enable it to emerge victorious over the others, seize the no-man's land of political power, and impose on the nation a strong and committed revolutionary dictatorship of its own making.

The introduction of this dictatorship represents the *second act* of the revolution. It marks the end of the period of postrevolutionary political chaos (though does not end it yet in real terms) by presenting the nation with a new, coherent, and forceful political system, which the group in charge seeks to perpetuate by all means in its power (hence civil wars, terror, etc.). This phenomenon, which in different forms and degrees, is characteristic of every revolution, could be termed the revolution's *Jacobin effect* because the Jacobin dictatorship established in France in 1792 is here the classical historical model.

In England, for instance, this Jacobin effect was displayed in 1648 when, after King Charles I's final defeat in the field, the radical elements of the army took over political power and purged the Long Parliament ("Pride's Purge"), leaving it to function with only the so-called Rump of about sixty of the most radical members. In England, however, the extreme manifestations of the Jacobin effect were not as extreme as in other countries and lasted for a relatively shorter period of time. After Oliver Cromwell had finally assumed the leadership of the first English republic, "Jacobinism," though still present and dominant until the end of his protectorate (1659), expressed itself in relatively moderate (Cromwell, himself a moderate, suppressed the extremists, e.g., by ejecting the Rump in 1653) and civilized forms.

This was not the case in either France under its properly Jacobin dictatorship of 1792–1794 (it actually lasted until 1799 but after the Thermidorian putsch of 1794 had been steadily decaying until overthrown by Napoléon's military coup in which, notably, a number of leading figures of the Jacobin regime actively participated) or in Russia where the Jacobin effect was materialized by the Bolsheviks and implemented in the still surviving Soviet regime that they had established.

The Jacobin effect, as an extreme voluntarist outburst of every revolution, has never been able to produce a political system adequate to what the civil society could accept as a viable alternative to the ancien régime and thus legitimate in a long-term view. None of the political systems produced in the past by the Jacobin effect were either long-lived or had a lasting impact on any nation's political culture. In the course of the revolutionary process, the Jacobin effect is transitory by its very nature and this could hardly be different in the case of the Bolshevik variant of Jacobinism in Russia, despite the fact that for a number of specific historical reasons Bolshevism has lasted longer than most of the other historical variants of Jacobinism.

After eventually having done away with the Jacobin effect and the political system produced by it (in ways similar to those by which the ancien régime was destroyed), civil society then enters into the *third stage (act)* of its revolutionary development. During this stage, a new political system is produced, which very often, in reaction to the Jacobin excesses, tends to restore some essential traits of the ancien régime and even lean on its traditional legitimacy (restoration of the Stuarts in England in 1660; restoration of the Bourbons in France in 1815, but also Napoleon's attempts to use modified forms of the ancien régime, like the monarchy, the nobility, the Emperor's court, etc., for what he deemed to be revolutionary purposes). This truthfully reflects people's acute nostalgia for the ancien régime's past as growing out of their profound disappointment with the Jacobin present, and for a certain period of time seems a perfectly acceptable political arrangement. In reality, however, the *restorationist effect* of the revolution very soon proves to be much less attractive than the nostalgic dreams about it. Disappointment grows again and the search for another political system, genuinely adequate to the civil society's modern needs, continues further through a series of ensuing political changes, starting with the removal of the political system produced by the restorationist effect and its replacement by a more radical regime. This might again be unsatisfactory, causing yet another political change, and so it can continue in a pendulum swinging manner, with its amplitude decreasing after each such change.

This period of political adjustment (and, hence, of political instability) lasts for some time (usually several decades), until the civil society through thus acquired experience of aspirations and disappointments forms a broadly-based political consensus that, when it is sufficiently mature, evolves a political system already acceptable to the whole of this society on a long-term basis and able to acquire genuine legitimacy based neither on promised (but unrealizable) new vistas nor on futile attempts at revival of the legitimizing legacy of the past, but on its own merits. With the establishment of such a political system the revolutionary period in the nation's life finally comes to an end. The main positive purpose of the revolution—the building up of a modern, stable, and legitimate political system, instead of the ancien régime irreversibly destroyed by the revolution's first act—is thus fulfilled and after a painful period of trial and error type experiments with different political arrangements, the nation at last overcomes the dysfunction between its civil society and polity, re-establishing itself as an adequately structured functional whole.

In England, this process of evolving an adequate polity and thus bringing the revolution to an end, went on until the Glorious Revolution of 1688; it was crowned in 1689 by the enthronement of William III and Mary II and the Parliament's enactment of the 1689 Bill of Rights. The English political system, thus established, acquired a permanent legitimate pattern and although modernized and altered in many respects by a number of "within-system" changes introduced during the last three centuries, continues to be basically the same in our time. In France, this process was much more complex and lasted for a substantially longer period. It passed through two republics, two empires, and one period of monarchist restoration until, in 1871, the French civil society was politically settled by the establishment of the Third Republic. The following periods of the French Fourth and Fifth (the present one) Republics have not changed any of the basic principles on which the Third Republic was built, introducing only modifications into this Republic's constitutional order.

Hence, there are several general traits characteristic of every revolution. To name but a few, namely:

1. Every revolution is a result of a deep dysfunction between the nation's civil society and its traditional autocratic polity failing to respond to the civil society's modern needs and thus losing its legitimacy;
2. Every revolution starts with the civil society overthrowing its ancien régime and subsequently finding itself in a virtual political vacuum;
3. Every revolution continues in the form of an endeavour to fill this vacuum, with the civil society "trying on" and changing different political systems (with the Jacobin and restorationist effects being their formative sources) until such time as a political system adequate to the civil society and its needs is at last evolved:
4. Every revolution ends with the establishment of such a socially adequate political system and finally consolidates its achievement by this new polity's acquisition of actual (as opposed to "credited") legitimacy.

It is therefore wrong to consider revolution as a single event simply doing away with the ancien régime. It is a complex process of replacing one political system, which has lost its legitimacy, by another, which has to acquire it and thus restore on a new basis the nation's functional wholeness, undermined at the start of the revolution because of the deep dysfunction between its civil society and polity. This revolutionary process occupies a significant period of time everywhere. In England, where it was shortest, it lasted forty-seven years (1642–1689); in France–eighty-six years (1789–1875); in Russia this process started in February (March), 1917 and, more than sixty-three years later, has not yet even come to the end of its Jacobin period, which began in October (November) 1917, only eight months after the start of the revolution itself, and from 1956 (the 20th Congress of the party) firmly entered into its last, "Thermidorian," stage.

Hence, the Russian revolution, which started in February (March) 1917, is as yet far from being accomplished. In fact, interrupted for such a long time by the stagnating Soviet-style communist dictatorship, it is now only in the very beginning of its development. The next political regime, which is about to replace the decaying Bolshevik Jacobinism will, according to the logic of all revolutionary processes, most certainly bear some restorationist features (although I do not envisage a straightforward restoration of a monarchic regime) and is hardly going to be the one with which the revolutionary process in Russia could be accomplished. For that some more political changes will probably be needed.

NOTES

1. See S. A. Kochanck, "Perspectives in the Study of Revolution and Social Change," *Comparative Politics* 5, no. 3 (April 1975): especially 313 ff.

2. For a detailed account of sociopolitical development (or, more precisely, non-developments) in the USSR after the fall of Khrushchev, see A. Brown and M. Kaser, eds., *The Soviet Union Since the Fall of Khrushchev* (London: Macmillan, 1975).

3. F. Znakov, "Pamyatnaya Zapiska," in *Radio Liberty Arkhiv Samizdata*, no. 374 (1966): especially 12–21.

4. F. Znakov uses here the distinction between right and left, which is common in the Soviet Union but exactly opposite to the usage of these terms in the West: the term "left" is applied here to the moderate liberal reformers and the term "right" to the neo-Stalinist hardliners, zealots of traditional Bolshevism.

5. Znakov, "Pamyatnaya Zapiska," 19–20.

6. Znakov, "Pamyatnaya Zapiska," 20.

7. Znakov, "Pamyatnaya Zapiska," 21.

8. Fifth of the series of articles based on interviews with Ilya Dzhirkvelov: "Radical changes needed to save Soviet Union from growing threat of economic catastrophe," *The Times*, May 29, 1980.

9. F. Znakov, following the Marxist methodology, divides the Soviet system into its economic base, which he calls the "supermonopolistic system of property," and

the superstructure corresponding to that base which in his view cannot be other than totalitarian.

10. Znakov, "Pamyatnaya Zapiska," 17.

11. The full text of that decision was published in the Hungarian newspaper *Szabad Ifjusag* on October 23, 1956; for extracts in English translation see F. Fejtö, *Behind the Rape of Hungary* (New York, 1957); T. Meray, *Thirteen Days That Shook the Kremlin* (New York: Praeger, 1959); J. Steel, ed., *Eastern Europe Since Stalin* (London: David & Charles, 1974).

12. As reported in *The Times*, September 12, 1980.

13. Quoted from *Vsevengerskaya Konferentsiya Vengerskoy Sotsialisticheskoy Rabochey Partii* (Budapesht, 27–29 iyunia 1957g.), Mosvow, Gospolitizdat, 1958, 58.

14. May I remind the reader that, according to Max Weber's classical definition, legitimacy means that there is a settled balance of reciprocity of expectations between rulers and ruled (*Max Weber on Law in Economy and Society* [Cambridge, Mass.: Harvard University Press, 1954], 328).

VI

LOOKING TOWARD
THE CHALLENGES FOR
THE NEXT CENTURY

Many urge a world of peace and freedom. Alex Shtromas thought seriously about what such a world is and how to get there. These final chapters enter provocatively into the "what." A free and peaceful world, Shtromas thought, must be a world of self-determining nations, which, with the "fission" and "fusion" required of the contemporary nation-state, will look very different from the West that we know. But the discussions concentrate upon the "how," the ways to peace in a world of free nations. Much responsibility lies with intellectuals. Shtromas took his own responsibility seriously and laid out a plan for his fellow intellectuals to be both researchers of peace and educators to peace.

The first of these chapters outlines an "international scholarly effort" to plan "the political organization of the world." The last outlines a "global education" that can "pave the way to true international harmony and perpetual peace." In between the reader obtains a picture of the international system needed, and of the republican unity, or collective identity, needed within each nation. These are striking plans. They are quite radical in character. A world of equal and self-determining national republics is to be linked by a "League of Peace," a league with teeth and not just parchment declarations. The league is to be empowered with codes of laws and rights, an international court, and—a military force more powerful than that of any and all states. This world body will even have authority to free many of the 1800 "stateless nations" of the world from the multinational or multicultural nation-states (less than 200 in number) of the contemporary world order. It is a sweeping project that involves breaking up many of the nation-states we know. But Shtromas supplies arguments. In these pages he confronts a number of skeptical critics, takes care to distinguish himself from predecessors such as Herbert Spencer and Ludwig von Mises, and traces the outline of his outline to Immanual Kant's *Perpetual Peace*.

The time is finally ripe, Shtromas argues, to realize Kant's great project. The obstacles put up by twentieth-century totalitarianism have fallen away. With the collapse of the Soviet Union, the most successful of this century's evil "ideocratic" twins, an artificially bipolar and divided world collapses as well. Meanwhile, modernization makes the world ever more homogeneous and requires a "global commonwealth" to deal with problems that are increasingly global. Shtromas dismisses the possibility of national solutions. He seems disillusioned by the experience of socialist planning. But he looks forward to global planning: his League of Peace can solve the problems evaded or suppressed by the contemporary system of nation-states. This league is to have an extraordinary jurisdiction. Its powers should include exclusive control of weapons of mass destruction, prevention of all armed conflicts, conservation and allocation of resources, arbitration of disputes among nations, and the establishment of a code of laws and a revised code of human rights, as well as a global court and a global military force. Most startling, perhaps, is the global authority's responsibility for "the fair distribution of national sovereignty." Justice demands "the right of all nations to self-determination" as well as other human rights. It is not fair, for example, that the Kosovo Albanians be held against their will by the Serbs (Shtromas wrote this before NATO's intervention in 1999). Shtromas prescribes international intervention to correct this and all other cases of nations held against their will.

The plan diverges most obviously from its Kantian original in the unequivocal right of each ethnic grouping to its own state should it desire it, and in the legislative, executive, and judicial powers granted to the global or semi-global authority. The first difference Shtromas acknowledges; the second, he qualifies somewhat. Membership in the league is voluntary, he allows, and a state may withdraw. Besides, even for members of the league only the decisions of global courts, alone of the global institutions, are to oblige unequivocally. Every state's own legislature and executive has right of approval over global laws and edicts. Whatever the qualifications, these assertions as to ethnic self-determination and supranational power are but two of the many points that exercise the critics to whom Shtromas replies in these pages. He always insisted that he did not intend world government—"the world cannot be governed"—and that the liberation of all repressed nations will lead to peace, not to aggravated enmity and wars. Perhaps the most searching interchange involves an objection that "greed" and the "desire for domination" will always lead some nations to imperial projects. Shtromas replies that modern republics, at least, do not war on one another; he acknowledges that his theory requires that all the world be republican. He also contends that greed for power is always a means to an end, not an end in itself, and the end is in the "realm of grand ideas." Even Hitler and Mussolini sought to impose a vision of world order. But might not putting down a liberal world order of equal rights seem a grand idea to superior glory-seekers, as it did to these two? One can see why education to liberal ideals is of such importance to Shtromas. He is in many ways more idealistic and optimistic than the idealistic and optimistic Kant. Unlike Kant, Shtromas does not rely much, if at all, on the perpetual threat of war to bring about the morals and behavior that make possible a league of perpetual peace.

The reader has the rare opportunity to see the contemporary project of a humane world provocatively explained and seriously defended. He himself can judge the sobriety and worth of Shtromas's plan for a pacified world of self-governing republican states, united by a commitment to perpetual peace.

17

The Strategy for Peace in a Changing World

ALEKSANDRAS SHTROMAS

I

There are two main trends in the world order, which lead to the conclusion that it is in the long term, unviable in its present state.

The first trend is expressed in the ubiquitous growth of nationalism. This growth indicates that the world, populated by at least 1,800 nations, simply cannot persist in the form of the 150 nation states,[1] which are the basic constituent elements of the present world order. The Hungarian Revolution of 1956, the attempt in 1967–1970 at creating the state of Biafra by splitting Nigeria on tribal (i.e., national) grounds, the actual splitting on national-territorial grounds of Pakistan and the emergence in 1972 of a new state of the Bengali nation, Bangladesh, are just the highlights of the worldwide process of reconstruction of the present system of states on genuinely ethnical lines which, now in more, now in less conspicuous forms, continues unabated.

In the development of the world order, the principle of plain sovereignty of state, which in present circumstances denies sovereignty for quite a number of nations, is thus being gradually replaced by the principle of fair distribution of

Reprinted with minor alterations from *Prospects for Peace in a Changing World Order* (London: ICF Publications, 1977), 1–11.

national sovereignty among all nations of the world. This principle is due to create a new constellation of states and thus a new basic structure for the world order.

The second trend is expressed in the growing necessity to deal with modern political, social, economic, technological, environmental, and other problems on a supranational and in many cases on a global level.

Various critical situations, which modern societies constantly face in their day-to-day life, usually reflect the inability of these societies to cope with certain classes of problems by themselves. Nevertheless, this is largely overlooked by too many who are still convinced that the solutions of all the main social problems have to be found within the framework of their own societies. Since problems facing modern societies are highly complicated, and in most cases clearly insoluble through normal measures within a national framework, radical measures are sought to put things right. But radical measures always tend to be simplistic; they usually have more to do with people's frustrated emotions than with the real social issues that they are supposed to tackle. This fully applies to socialist measures, such as nationalization, which are seen by many as being an absolute remedy for solving absolutely all social problems. Unfortunately they are not; and not only because they are too simplistic, but also and above all, because they are outdated.

Modern societies, unlike those of the nineteenth century, are not self-sufficient bodies any more, but inseparable parts of a world society that, though still in a most inadequate form of organization, is already in existence. In such a situation, radical changes in the structure and performances of one particular society represent the least relevant measures as far as the solution of the problems of that particular society is concerned. Moreover, such changes, if they put that society out of tune with the developments in world society, can only make its situation worse. A world society requires measures that provide for the solution of major social problems on a global scale. As for the appropriate measures taken on a national scale, they have at least to be in tune with what is going on globally. Because of that, neither nationalization; socialization (nor anything else of a simply "natio-", or "socio-" kind) are able to provide the right response to modern society's needs. Internationalization; globalization is able to do so.

The main difficulty in getting appropriate issues "internationalized" or "globalized" is the fact that, structurally, world society is basically still particularistic, i.e., it consists of globally uncoordinated states or systems of states (Marx would probably call this phenomenon a contradiction between the global nature of production and the particularistic form of its organization). In order to overcome this difficulty, the sociopolitical organization of world society (i.e., the world order) has to be brought into correspondence with the reality of its actual existence. This is the necessity forced upon the world by the objective results of its development and either such a correspondence must evolve, whatever the difficulties, or the existence of modern civilization or even of the human race itself, will be put in jeopardy.

The necessity for dealing with modern political, social, economic, and other problems on a supranational, and in many cases on a global level, is clearly, though perhaps spontaneously, reflected, inter alia, in the creation and the persistence of the United Nations Organization and its various agencies, and even more in the ubiquitous dissatisfaction with these international organizations—with their poor performances, with the limited scope of their ability to make an impact on the solution of the acute problems affecting mankind, etc. This dissatisfaction is, in its turn, reflected in the creation and development of more genuinely cooperative supranational institutions like EEC, COMECON, OAS etc., but these supranational institutions are merely regional, and therefore unable to cope with problems of global dimension. The oil crisis of 1973–1974 exemplifies this sufficiently well (if one looks at how it affected not only the EEC but also COMECON and the OAS, and how it led to the establishment of a constant pattern of relationship between these supranational bodies and OPEC, one clearly sees the insufficiency of the merely regional approach, and the vital necessity of having a global level of cooperation and coordination of national efforts; and this applies not only to the energy issue but to all sorts of other issues, too). What the world order really needs is an efficient supranational institution of global scope, or simply a global authority that would be able to deal appropriately with global problems.

Such a global authority would be of great advantage to all nations in coordinating their efforts in various fields of activities, and should also be able to assume some "naturally global" functions on the basis of its exclusive competence.

There are many obstacles hindering the establishment of global institutions with real authority for dealing with global issues but the genuine need of all societies to have such institutions is the irresistible driving force behind the development toward their establishment and toward the creation of a unifying pattern, making the world at least a governable unit.

Because of this, the process of change in the world order is not limited to the reconstruction of the existing system of states in accordance with the principle of the fair distribution of national sovereignty among all nations. This process of the differentiation of mankind is inseparable from another, no less important, process—the process of its integration. The world order thus emerging is going to consist not only of nation states as its basic elements, but, in addition to them, of supranational bodies of global authority as its most essential main elements, bringing the basic parts into a coordinated and, to a certain extent unified, pattern. Thus, the new, viable world order that is evolving and that is due to replace the present unviable one, is going to be based on the principle of fairly distributed national sovereignty, complemented by an entirely new principle of the sovereignty of mankind.

II

Both these trends in the development of the world order are fundamental and, if modern civilization is to survive at all the severe trials it has to undergo, they cannot be repressed. At the same time, however, the conditions in which mankind at present exists are hindering and perverting the natural development of the world order along these lines. It is not only, or even mainly, the notorious "egoism of states" and the inertia of the existing shape of states and state systems that are the obstacles in the way of such a development, but also and primarily the still mainly bipolar structure of the present world.

In a way, this bipolar structure manifests better than anything else the necessity of establishing a unifying pattern for world society. Leaving aside all the hypocrisy and wishful-thinking surrounding it, the East–West confrontation (the expression of the largely bipolar structure of the world), which is already several decades old and continues unabated, is basically nothing else but a struggle for the establishment of a universal world order able, inter alia, to evolve a global authority for dealing with global issues. The issue at stake in this struggle is not so much the universal world order itself, as the grounds, either polarchic or totalitarian—and these are incompatible—on which it is to be based. The situation created by this struggle is precarious. On the one hand it is artificially constraining the development of the universal world order and makes war, a war that is likely to bring the human race to extinction, seem the only viable way out of this state of artificial constraint. On the other hand, it exposes mankind to the threat of having a totalitarian world order imposed on it, which is an obvious perversion of the whole of world society's development. If mankind is to survive, a worldwide totalitarian system cannot; a totalitarian world order is a sham; it is a perversion of the very meaning of a universal world order, which would sooner or later be overcome. A genuine, organically-developed world order based, not on totalitarian imposition, but on consensus among free nations, should in the final end be established, whatever perversive trends appear on the way. But the whole problem is whether the human race will be able to survive if a totalitarian ordeal takes place on a global scale.

Totalitarianism is, in principle, unable to create a peaceful, cooperative, and in any sense genuine universal world order. First of all it does not solve problems but merely suppresses them, thus creating an even more aggravated situation in all fields of social life (The difficult problems the USSR and other countries of the so-called socialist camp face are living examples corroborating this point). Secondly, it will not be able to keep a universal world order on stable and lasting grounds; in time such a universal world order will inevitably collapse, with a "polycentric" totalitarian world, in which all the constituent parts constantly fight one another, taking its place (as George Orwell prophesied in *1984*, and as is already corroborated by the actual cases of splits and conflicts between China and the USSR, and the USSR and Yugoslavia). Finally, as a result of all these struggles, the worldwide totalitarian system will eventually collapse—but whether the human race will still be alive then is by no means certain. The threat of totalitarianism is thus not that of having an undesirable world order established on a long-term basis; in this respect totalitarianism is, in any case, unviable. Its real threat consists in the fact that it can bring the whole human race to extinction, or at least upset quite substantially the existence of a few generations of mankind.

The very fact of the bipolarity of the world's structure shows that the present system of states is unfit to serve as the basic material for the development of a genuine world order with a global authority as its unifying element. But even if the world got rid of its bipolar structure while the present system of states remained unchanged, it could still hardly produce on such a basis a reliable pattern of global unification. Quite a number of the existing states are simply unviable (artificial creations of the period of the Cold War or of the process of decolonization) or, even when viable to some degree, suffer very much from internal stresses (or are even conflict-torn) and because of that are extremely insecure. In almost all such cases one or a few states have a substantial stake in the internal conflicts of another state, which makes relations between such states tense, unreliable, and at all events incompatible with a pattern of genuine cooperation. One must recognize that the existence of such tense relations between separate states does not create the necessary conditions for the development of a global pattern of cooperation between all states without which it is hardly possible to establish an efficient and operational global authority based on a consensus among the nations of the world. Before such an authority could be practically envisaged, the substantial conflicts that exist between states have to be reliably solved and a pattern of stable cooperation among them has to be established. To achieve this without essential changes in the shape of a number of existing states and thus in the whole world system of states, is plainly impossible. Only when the right basic material for the build-up of a genuine world order is available, can its construction be reliably undertaken.

Of course, if the world gets rid of its bipolar structure the process leading to the appropriate reconstruction of the world system of states will become essentially easier. At present the conflicting super powers are involved in almost every local conflict on opposite sides, which either makes these conflicts insoluble in principle, or produces artificial solutions to them, reflecting not so much the genuine local interests involved as the correlation of forces of the super powers in that particular area or country. This situation will change substantially when the main powers of the world stop confronting each other and are able to direct their mutual efforts toward the achievement of reliable peace in all areas of the world, which even in terms of the purely national interests of these powers themselves, will be a great advantage.

Thus, the overcoming of the bipolar structure of the world and, more precisely, the disappearance of the totalitarian system in the USSR, should be seen as the main factor in the advancement of the organic development of a genuinely peaceful world order with a global authority working on behalf of, and in the common interests of, all the nations of the world.

III

Change in the state of the world order is not something that will occur all at once in a distant future. The world is in a permanent state of transition and changes in it are taking place every day. Since there are no situations or structures in present international life where the status quo can be considered reliably stable, one should be prepared to meet the most drastic changes that could take place anywhere, at any time.

The most dynamic element in this permanent process of change is not the world order as such, but its constituent elements—the present states and systems of states. There is, of course, plenty of wishful-thinking based on the assumption that the development of détente accompanied by the so-called process of "convergence" between capitalist and socialist societies (allegedly bringing them into one universal pattern of industrial society) will gradually remove the bipolar structure of the present world, replacing the relationship of confrontation between East and West, and thus between the two super powers, with a relationship of cooperation that, in turn, according to these same views, should be able to produce a universal world order already capable of providing solutions for all the most acute global problems facing mankind. The author of this present paper believes that the reality is completely different from these views. As long as the Soviet Union remains what it is today (or unless it achieves world dominion, a possibility that the author, for reasons partially explained above, is inclined to exclude from serious consideration), no essential change in the main structure of the world order can be envisaged. Change in the world order has up to now proceeded, is still proceeding and, for the time being, will continue to proceed on the level of separate states and state systems.

Under the circumstances of the already existing world society, changes of that kind should not be treated as merely local and isolated, since all of them affect to a certain (and in each particular case to a different) extent, the whole international system and contain implications felt all around the globe. But only when such a "partial" change affects the Soviet Union and its dependencies (or when, in the process of natural "peaceful competition" with the West, the Soviet Union loses its status as a super power) will the basic structure of the present world order be shattered and real prospects for the creation of a new universal world order emerge. This does not mean that through change in the Soviet Union a harmonious system of world order will emerge automatically from under the rubble; in the first instance, the situation in the world might become even more chaotic than before but this will be a "hopeful" chaos, a chaos from which a universal and harmonious world order can finally arise, whereas the present "orderly" situation in the world is, in these terms, hopeless to say the least.

The processes of change in a particular state (as well as in a system of states) are induced by the non-, under-, or misrepresentation in it of either the population at large, or of specific national and/or social groups. There are no states (and even more so, no state systems) in the present world where under- or misrepresentation of one sort or another is not institutionalized or otherwise practiced; in this respect the necessity for a change is affecting all modern societies to a certain extent.

A distinction should be made, however, between changes proceeding in polyarchic, open societies, and closed, hegemonic (or semi-hegemonic) ones; (both terms, "polyarchic" and "hegemonic," are borrowed by the present author from R. A. Dahl). In a polyarchic, open society, the forces of change, even if they act in violent or rebellious forms, are normally operating on, or near to, the social surface. They are, therefore, constantly apparent, clearly identifiable, and to a certain extent, measurable; the changes themselves are, because of that, predictable and proceed, by and large in an orderly manner. In other words, the process of constant, though at times very painful change, is the normal state of a polyarchic society that is flexible enough to adjust itself to even the most drastic change without breaking down politically or otherwise disintegrating; (the devolutionary trends in Britain, France, and some other countries, as well as attempts at the establishment of factories run by workers' collectives, or of workers' representation in the boardrooms of private and state firms all over the Western world, are illustrative of this point). In closed, hegemonic societies the trends toward change are usually highly latent; what one is able to see on the social surface, is a "monolithically" rigid structure fully under the control of an appropriate (and in most cases highly un- or misrepresentative) political leadership. Hegemonic societies are basically inflexible, lack enough room for "within system" political changes (this term is borrowed by the author from S. Kochanek), and therefore their capacity for survival in the case of a change in the pattern of representation is very low indeed. They usually break down suddenly, completely, and at the most unpredictable moments, creating a number of explosive situations in affected areas and thus in the closely interrelated world at large, which nobody is properly prepared to face up to (the events in Hungary, 1956; Battista's Cuba, 1959; Czechoslovakia, 1968; Portugal, 1974; etc., are illustrative of this point).

A distinction should also be made between changes in states and systems of states that proceed in the form of an open conflict accompanied by attempts at settlement, and those that proceed in the form of cumulative latent developments that burst out suddenly into open conflict. Change, in the form of open conflict, is taking place in such politically unsettled areas as the Middle East (including Cyprus) and Southern Africa, and in different pockets where an open struggle for national status is being pursued, such as Eritrea, former Spanish Sahara, or Iraqui Kurdistan. Change, in the form of cumulative latent developments, which either result in one sudden explosive change (as was the case in Nigeria, 1967; Pakistan, 1972) or appear "indicatively" in the open only from time to time (as in the cases of: acts of national resistance in Soviet Georgia in 1956 and 1975–1976, in Soviet Armenia in 1965, in Soviet Uzbekistan in 1971, in Soviet Lithuania in 1956, 1960, and 1972; "linguistic" conflicts in India and Belgium; outbursts of Croatian and other separatist movements in Yugoslavia; or of the Corsican or Breton autonomists in France; etc.) are characteristic not only of hegemonic societies but also of some heterogeneous societies of a non-hegemonic (semi-polarchic or even plainly polyarchic) kind, which, however, retain an uneven, outdated pattern of representation.

Although, as we have seen, the processes of change are ubiquitous and probably no society is completely immune from sudden change, the hegemonic states and some of the non-hegemonic states in heterogeneous societies are the most likely to explode suddenly at any given moment, producing drastic changes in the existing international system. In some cases such changes can destabilize the present world order to the extent of destroying its precarious, force-balanced structure and exposing the whole of mankind to new situations, systems, and conflicts whose development is most unpredictable (it is sufficient in this respect to imagine what would be the consequences and implications of a sudden breakdown of the USSR). That is why it is of primary importance to scrutinize deeply and constantly change-related developments, and the forces of change, in all hegemonic states and states in heterogeneous societies. The awareness of possible explosive changes within such states and systems of states should at least match, if not exceed, the awareness of the world about the changes taking place in polyarchic societies and in all situations of open conflict. Only if this is done can one expect to have a completely adequate attitude to the present world situation and to alternative developments implicit in it.

It seems to the present author that at least the following areas, now relatively (although superficially) peaceful, are fraught with potentially explosive change, which could have fatal consequences for the present world status quo:

1. The Black African continent (its political structure, inherited from colonial times, is ethnically unviable and in addition to that the majority of the states of that continent are based on the supremacy of one particular tribe over all the others).
2. The Indian subcontinent (the processes both of national and linguistic demarcation, both in India and Pakistan, affecting also parts of Burma, Sri Lanka, Iran, and Afghanistan, are still unaccomplished).
3. The Soviet Union and its dependencies.

4. Yugoslavia.
5. To some extent, and in specific ways, Latin America.

This means that the study of alternative situations and systems must be primarily concerned with these areas of the world.

IV

One must admit that the policies of the Western powers are highly inadequate for dealing with the changing world order. Rightly (though in a most general way) assuming that change might endanger peace and not knowing exactly what the nature of a particular change, its possible consequences and the dangers implied in it could be, the Western powers have always been afraid of change and still remain, therefore, strongly committed to the preservation of that very relatively peaceful status quo that is reigning in the present world (this also reflects the relative comfort of the Western societies in their present conditions). This commitment to the status quo is, for the Western powers, of such a high priority, that when their interest in its preservation is coincidentally shared, for whatever reason, by the Soviet Union, they are ready to work closely together with this "adversary power" without seeking any additional reasons for doing so (leaving aside the tacit endorsement given by the Western powers to the Soviet Union's military interferences undertaken to preserve the status quo in its own realm of rule, as the events of Hungary, 1956, and Czechoslovakia, 1968, have clearly shown, the joint effort of Britain and the USSR in helping Gowon's Nigeria to strangle Biafra, is one of the most striking examples of such mutual East–West cooperation).

The policy of preserving the status quo is not only immoral, it is also unviable from a very pragmatic point of view (by the way, it seems to the present author that a moral policy usually also turns out to be the most viable policy in purely pragmatic terms, at least when it is pursued on the basis of a knowledge of circumstances). To preserve the status quo permanently by endlessly sacrificing new Biafras, Hungarys, and Czechoslovakias to it, is plainly impossible. One is able to postpone change once, twice, but not forever. The moment will come when the change will be brought about, will be, so to speak, forced upon us, whether we want it or not. It will be difficult, virtually impossible for instance, to stop change in the USSR, which in its turn will produce a chain reaction of "unstoppable" changes in many other parts of the world; it is also difficult to imagine that change could be stopped, even by a concerted effort of the USSR and the West, if it takes place simultaneously in several countries, of Black Africa for instance, or even more so on a continental or a subcontinental level. Change in all the previously indicated areas (see sect. III) and even elsewhere, is inevitable; sooner or later it will occur independently of what we have to say about it, which means that the policy of the status quo is doomed to failure in advance. If the Western world is to retain an influence on world affairs and/or simply wants to survive, it has to drop its status quo–based policies and accept—the sooner the better—a policy of support for change, that is, of course, for that change that will be consistent with the principles of peace, freedom, justice, and democracy—principles on which the Western world is allegedly built.

Urgent measures are necessary in order to enable the Western world to accept such a policy and act in accordance with it. First of all, measures are needed that could substantially increase knowledge of the processes of change and of the forces striving for change in appropriate societies, particularly in those societies where the forces of change operate in latent forms, so that no new situation arising in any society (and in any part of the world) could be seen as an unexpected and/or inconceivable event, previous to its occurrence. In order to be adequately prepared to meet change one must first be aware of the possibilities of change and all its variations. This can be achieved only by a thorough study and constant scrutiny of each society and of each area of the world from the point of view of the trends making for change. Secondly, measures are required for ensuring proper modeling, on the basis of the knowledge acquired through such a thorough study and constant scrutiny, of various alternative situations and systems in particular areas (and thus in the world at large) which could emerge as a result of the process of change. Thirdly, measures must be taken leading to the elaboration of strategies for that change that would be desirable, and in accordance with which appropriate policies could be pursued and implemented.

Change, as was already mentioned, is, in most cases, developing in a situation of conflict, of a clash of interests. Thus it potentially threatens peace either on the local and regional or, sometimes, on the global level. Change, moreover, does not automatically promote freedom. In striving to achieve change, non-, under-, or misrepresented groups are tempted, in their frustration, to solve their respective problems in a totalitarian way, which very often seems to them the most radical, simple, and effective. However, historical experience shows that the totalitarian solution is always wrong and, in a long-term perspective, instead of solving problems, only creates new ones (although totalitarian solutions often manage to achieve certain extraordinary short-term ends in a quick and efficient manner, thus creating the illusion that they are capable of solving the most important problems of social existence).

Bearing in mind, therefore, that the very process of change is fraught with dangers to peace and freedom, the Western strategy for change must be that of promoting peace as the method, and freedom as the goal, of change in the world order. This will, hopefully, provide a viable Western alternative to the Soviet strategy for change, which advances violence as its method, and totalitarian rule as its goal. The Western policy of maintaining the status quo is, unfortunately, inadequate for providing such an alternative and gives the Soviets in this respect a very important advantage.

To promote freedom as the goal of change is not an easy task. Freedom does not automatically lead to harmony and peacefulness. On the contrary, it also liberates forces, which will advance the conflict of interests and aims and, therefore, many new trouble-spots and instabilities in the system of world order could be created through advancing freedom. For instance, the genuine conflicts between the many nations living under Soviet dominion, and also their grievances against some nations outside the Soviet Union, are completely suppressed by the Soviet regime and are, therefore, not of great international relevance at present. But, as soon as those nations are free, their respective conflicts will also be free to express themselves on the surface of international life. This will transform them into issues of major international concern or even of actual international conflict. One can easily foresee how complex, many-sided, and acute the conflict in relations among the many nations living in the Caucasian area of the USSR will become (with Russia, Turkey, Iran, and in some cases other countries, inevitably and deeply involved in them) as soon as the various nations are free to express and promote their genuine interests and goals. One can say the same, though probably to a lesser extent, about the German-Polish-Lithuanian-Belorussian-Ukrainian-Russian complex of relationships as well as about many other such complexes (for instance, the Rumanian-Hungarian-Czechoslovakian-Polish one, etc.).

The Western strategy for change has to take account of all the serious cleavages and potential conflicts that newly acquired freedom can bring to the surface of international life in so many parts of the changing world. Comprehensive programs for the resolution of these potential conflict situations, taking into account the interest of all parties involved and elaborating compromise solutions that would be acceptable to all those parties, have to be worked out in advance in order to enable the interested nations, and indeed the rest of the international community, to tackle them properly. This is, in part, already being done by the free representatives of oppressed nations (i.e., by their political emigres) but only an international scholarly effort can create something of a coordinated pattern of proposals for the type of change that will make freedom finally compatible with peace. The Western strategy for change should be based on such a coordinated pattern and thus become a real strategy for peace—peace not only as regards the means of change but also as regards its ends. There is no genuine peace without freedom, and there is no genuine freedom in a state of "peace" imposed by coercion, which only suppresses but does not eliminate genuine, deeply-rooted cleavages and conflicts.

A strategy for peace in its fullest sense, must be a strategy for peace in the conditions of freedom. Thus, in calling for the elaboration of a Western strategy for peace in a changing world one implicitly calls also for a Western strategy of freedom.

V

As should be clear from what has been said in the previous section, a concerted effort in research into appropriate problems must be undertaken if a viable Western strategy for peace in a changing world is to be elaborated. The main objective of such research will be the development of realistic alternative models for the political organization of the world. The modeling of alternative political situations and systems should proceed on three levels: global, regional, and the individual sate. All these three levels are to be treated as interrelated parts of an indivisible model of a global political system.

On the level of the individual state, the working out in advance of comprehensive peaceful programs for the resolution of both open and latent conflicts between different national and social groups within that state, forms the approach by which a viable model of an alternative political system for that state can evolve. The programs would take into account the interests and aspirations of all the parties involved or likely to be affected by these conflicts, and the guiding principles would be the broadening, evening out, and increase in accuracy of, the pattern of representation. In quite a number of cases, this might require a complete reconstruction of one or even several states, through splits, partial or total fusions, etc.

Worked out models of this kind will inevitably imply changes in neighboring states and thus in the appropriate regional political system as a whole. Thus, the second logical step in such research is the modeling of political situations and systems for whole regions, e.g., subcontinents, continents, intercontinental complexes, etc.

To work out comprehensive, peaceful models for particular states and regional systems of states is, in many cases, not a conceivable task at all. For instance, such running conflicts as those of the Middle East or of Southern Africa seem, under present circumstances, to be insoluble, except through a straightforward battle with the winners imposing their unilateral conditions on the losers; but it should not be forgotten that the intransigence of the conflicting parties in the above, as well as in many other cases, is to a great extent "inspired" by outside forces (and almost always by the super powers themselves) involved on both sides of the conflict and trying either to take advantage of the conflict situation itself, or of the possible victory of one of the conflicting parties. When forces on both sides of such a conflict are more or less equal (as is the case, for instance, in the Arab/Israeli conflict in the Middle East) the conflict acquires an air of permanency and comes to be considered as insoluble in principle. But in a different international context, for instance, in a context where the main world powers are genuinely cooperating for the sake of peace, or in a context where an operational global authority is already established, the same conflict could become not only manageable, but also soluble on a stable and even on a permanent basis. This means that the process of modeling appropriate national or regional alternative political situations and systems inevitably exceeds the boundaries, not only of the individual state, but also of a whole regional system of states and thus attains to an interregional i.e., global level.[2]

This is the "inductive" way in which the modeling of an alternative political situation and system on a global level inevitably begins. At the same time, the global modeling begun in this way is complemented by alternative models for different regions elaborated in their own right. Both then merge together into one pattern of "inductively" conducted research, aimed at elaborating an alternative model of the whole world order. But this is not the only way of conducting global political modeling. As was shown above (in sect. I) a lot of global problems exist in the context of contemporary world society that have to be solved in their own right, and the modeling of an alternative global political situation and system can be proceeded with independently, in terms of the need to solve these problems. That is how a "deductive" pattern of research aimed at elaborating an alternative model of the whole world order would be established, in addition to the "inductive" one. "Deductive" here implies that the models of the world order evolving from such research are to be tested and measured in terms of their consistency with the regional and national political systems and their development. This would involve the identification of obstacles hindering the organic development and implementation of appropriate world order models. Since these obstacles are located on regional and national levels, the research is led to focus on these levels. The purpose of global research on the regional and national level is to look for viable ways of overcoming these obstacles (alternative models for the appropriate regional and national systems being developed in their turn in order to bring them into correspondence with the elaborated world order model).

The research into alternatives has to be firmly based upon facts and circumstances established by research into the present political situation and systems. In these terms it is rather a "research into research" or an "extended research." Alternatives are not and should not be groundless inventions based on mere ethical assessments, or wishful or visionary thinking. The inadequacies of the present political situation and systems, the grievances, dissatisfactions, and frustrations, concerning these situations and systems, as well as the aspirations and activities, to bring change within them, are the objective expressions of the implicit alternatives, which then need only to be studied from this angle. There is plenty of research going on all over the world into present political situations and systems. The task is to systematize the data produced by this research and also, by identifying gaps and insufficiencies, to initiate new research projects with a view to completing investigations in order to provide a viable basis for research into alternatives.

NOTES

1. In fact less than 150, since some states belonging to bigger political units have only formal independence as is the case, for instance, with the Soviet bloc states in Eastern Europe.

2. One should, in this connection, remember the thesis of L. Wittgenstein about the contradiction insoluble in a system, 'n,' being not only soluble, but becoming a natural consistency in a broader system, "n + m."

18

The Future World Order
and the Right of Nations to
Self-Determination and Sovereignty

ALEKSANDRAS SHTROMAS

This chapter begins with a survey of the state of national sovereignty on the eve of the twenty-first century and a discussion of it in the context of the developing global system and the still ongoing East–West confrontation. Against this background, the prospects for the evolution of a universal world order system are considered, and the place, within the confines of such a system, for national sovereignty and, specifically, for exercising the right of nations to self-determination and sovereignty, is assessed. The article concludes by formulating the basic principles of international justice which, in the author's view, could provide a viable foundation for a just and peaceful world order. On the basis of these principles, today's major conflicts of national interests are evaluated and their tentative solutions suggested.

> "The future progress of the world is now possible only through a search for a mankind-wide consensus in moving towards a new world order."
>
> —M. Gorbachev[1]

Reprinted from the *International Journal on World Peace* 7, no. 1 (March 1990): 17–59, with a comment by Jan Knappert and a rejoinder by the author.

NATIONAL SOVEREIGNTY AND
THE TWENTIETH-CENTURY WORLD

In the contemporary "interdependent world," national sovereignty in its classical absolute meaning remains an entirely valid concept. This is so despite the otherwise logically persuasive reasoning to the contrary by integration and convergence theorists. To be sure, some of the formally sovereign nation-states do not possess actual sovereignty. These are, in the first place, those states that, being in fact fully dependent territories of other states, are dressed up by their foreign masters as formally sovereign entities. Among such only formally sovereign states, the East European and Outer Mongolian satellites of the Soviet Union should be mentioned in the first place. But, in 1989, not only these states, but even most of the union-republics of the USSR itself, started the process of reclaiming their actual sovereignty and so far are successful in this daring endeavor.

The states that are sovereign only formally should not be, however, confused with the states that are in possession of their national sovereignty, but whose governments for certain reasons chose to submit themselves to foreign tutelage and protection. For example, some clique-states whose dictatorial governments are unable to sustain themselves in power on their own usually choose to submit themselves to mightier foreign states that, for either ideological or pragmatic reasons (or, most often, a mixture of both), practically assume supreme authority over these states. Some communist clique-states—such as Cuba, Ethiopia, Angola, *et al.*—which have become Soviet client-states on their own accord, could be cited here as examples, and equally also various military and autocratic clique-states (popularly known as "our own bastards") whose dictatorial governments, posing as saviors of their nations from communist conspiracy, plead, in most cases successfully, with the United States for support and protection, and become, as a result, American client-states.

Unlike such odd cases, most of the "normal" modern nation-states, the major ones less and the minor ones more, are bound to limit their sovereignty, sometimes quite substantially, by the nature of goals they are setting themselves to achieve, and by the mere fact of their involvement in international economic and political structures. A typical Third World country that is setting itself the goal of rapid industrial development, in competing for foreign investment, is bound to offer the potential investors the most attractive terms and conditions; once established in such a country, the multinationals or other powerful investor-companies inevitably start wielding substantial influence on the state in which they operate, and the sheer possibility of their disinvestment forces the host-states to do the investors' bidding, whether they like it or not. Similar is the situation of the states which, when seeking outside credits or loans, have to accept the conditions attached to them. In the second half of the 1970s, the British Labor government, for example, in exchange for a substantial loan bailing Britain out of serious economic trouble, agreed to accept the creditor's International Monetary Fund's conditions, which included severe cuts on the government's public spending and other measures that went against the grain of the very principles to which the British Labor Party was firmly committed. Also, each international treaty or covenant is in substance a limitation by the participating nation-states of their absolute sovereignty on issues, and to the extent, determined in the respective treaties and covenants.

In all these cases, however, such self-limitation of sovereignty is voluntary. A truly sovereign state, if it is prepared to bear the economic and political consequences of such an act, can willfully break all its international commitments and resume full and absolute sovereignty at any moment. This is what Iran under Khomeini had done, and Albania under Enver Hoxja did even three times until her complete independence from any outside power was firmly established. Even Panama, which is usually regarded as a virtual semicolony of the United States, under General Noriega, blatantly defied the authority of that dominant power and managed to get away with it. To put an end to this defiance, the United States had to resort to direct military intervention in Panama. It follows from the above that, in "our interdependent world," sovereignty can still be used to its full absolute extent practically by every independent nation-state, however minor and seemingly dependent on outside powers and forces it may seem to be. Only a few nation-states, however, are prepared to use the potential of absolute sovereignty to its full extent. These are in the first place the ideocratic (communist or Islamic), "narcocratic" (as Panama under Noriega had been), and racially discriminating (in the first place, South Africa) states, which are not prepared to sacrifice for full-fledged participation in the present world order the ways in which they operate and, in defending them, have to make use of their unfettered sovereign rights. Most other states, those that intend to serve the pragmatically, not ideologically-dogmatically, defined interests of their respective societies, and which are also ready to comply with at least the minimal standards of internationally acceptable behavior, would willingly engage in all kinds of international joint activities and organizations that demand certain limitations of their sovereignty. These states, together with a number of international bodies in which they, or some sections of their societies independently of them, participate, constitute the foundation of the present world order.

THE PRESENT WORLD ORDER

One of the most adequate models for understanding the present relationship between national sovereignty and world order is provided by James Rosenau's adaptation theory.[2]

According to that theory, sovereign nation states in their self-perceived best interests adapt to the international environment, limiting respectively in the process of such adaptation their sovereignty. The process of global adaptation consists not only of nation-states coexisting with, and adapting to, each other and the international alliances and organizations that they themselves are creating. Rosenau stresses the growing role in world politics of independent non-state actors and supranational bodies, stating that at present "the universe of global politics has come to consist of two interactive worlds with the overlapping memberships, a multicentric world of diverse, relatively equal actors and a state-centric world in which national actors are primary."[3] He places special emphasis on the fact that the nation-states are gradually becoming embedded into the multicentric world of international institutions and increasingly act, not so much as sovereign entities, but as offshoots of these international institutions.

It is, no doubt, true, as Rosenau suggests, that, along with interstate alliances; the norms of international law regulating the behavior of, and relationship between, the states; and various International Governmental Organizations (IGOs)—on a global level the United Nations Organization and its various agencies, and, on regional levels, the European Economic Community (EEC) and its communist counterpart, the Council for Mutual Economic Assistance (COMECON), the Organization of American States and the Organization of African Unity, not to mention the North Atlantic Treaty and Warsaw Treaty Organizations—the present-day world order is to a large degree also shaped by, and includes, various international nongovernmental interest and pressure groups, financial and trade organizations, some other supranational public bodies (the INGOs—International Nongovernmental Organizations), and even authoritative individuals who act independently on the global stage (such people as, for example, Armand Hammer and Andrei Sakharov, Mother Theresa and Elie Wiesel). It is also true that all these actors on the international stage shape the present world order. What is, however, untrue is that the world order thus taking shape possesses the potential for organic development into a universal and coherent world order system.

Too many states, among them such powerful ones as the Soviet Union and China, not only refuse, but are also inherently unable, to become gradually embedded into a world order system that is formed by forces and factors that are not of their own deliberate making. These states, with their centrally planned economies and globally defined ideological goals, are in principle unassimilable and, therefore, participate in the world order only very partially and exclusively with the view to use the positions to which they are entitled in it to their own advantage. As long as these states retain their present systemic identity, they will inevitably remain in any wider world order context alien inclusions, not only prohibiting the world order's consolidation into a coherently unified system, but also trying to subvert it from within and submit to a singular order identical to their own. Because of that, on the level of global IGOs, the present world order represents no more than an institutionalized incarnation of East–West confrontation, and, on the level of INGOs, it shapes itself into a dangerous asymmetry between official and unofficial representation actively, and in many cases profitably, used by the USSR and other totalitarian powers for the purpose of subordinating the INGOs to their influence. When, in the nongovernmental international agencies and other INGO-type public bodies, truly independent (and in most cases genuinely oppositional to their governments) actors from the liberal democratic countries are confronted with professionally trained official representatives of the USSR (as well as of other totalitarian states), ostensibly posing as members of namesake non-state independent public bodies also opposing the policies of Western governments, the results of activities of the thus structured INGOs are bound to work in favor of anti-Western forces. This is not to say that genuinely independent and oppositional forces from communist lands do not participate in world politics. They indeed do participate in it and quite actively, too; but, being devoid of legal recognition in their respective states, they are never able to become a part of, and work on a regular basis with, any of the most influential INGOs. Their participation in world politics is thus reduced to playing episodic roles in the world media and to loose association with some inevitably minor international bodies that have no permanent representation on them of communist officialdoms. This, for now a rather crystal-clear situation, may probably become more confused with some prominent Soviet dissidents having recently acquired an official status of "people's deputies," Polish Solidarity being made part of the government in a coalition arrangement with the communists, and Vaclav Havel elected president of Czechoslovakia. For the time being, however, everything remains basically as it has ever been. As a result, Rosenau's two-tier world order resembles much more a global battlefield between the superpowers than a global system with the potential for becoming universally cooperative and harmonious. Even in the world of INGOs—with the USSR dominating, or allying itself to, the anti-Western forces operating outside the Soviet realm of rule and the dissidents of communist lands associating themselves with external antitotalitarian and pro-Western forces—confrontational bipolarity of East and West remains a predominant factor.

The assumption of "moral equivalence" of all states, East and West alike, is the major mistake of Rosenau and most other analysts of global politics. They simply ignore the ideocratic nature of the Soviet state, assuming (without even bothering to substantiate their assumption) that the USSR, on a par with the United States and other nonideocratic nation-states, is just another powerful actor in the "state-centric world in which national interests are primary." In this world, according to Rosenau, all actors equally have one and the same prime concern, which is to "cope with the security dilemma" and the same equal principal goal, which is to "preserve territoriality."[4]

The major and overriding goal of Soviet foreign policy, which from the inception of the Soviet state till present, has always been the establishment of a communist world order,[5] is thus fully dismissed without even being discussed.

This I find not simply wrong but perverting the whole perspective on the present world order and its problems. One has to agree here with Morton Kaplan, who says that the analysts who "see current Soviet policy merely as

Tsarist policy in new guise in response to permanent Russian national interests" mechanically project old concepts onto new circumstances and, as a result, fail "to incorporate the lessons of the twentieth century concerning national power."[6]

The objective necessity of establishing a world order system is today universally recognized. Moreover, most states loudly proclaim themselves
staunch champions of a cohesive world order system. They want, however,
not any world order system, but only the one that would be consistent with
the order established in their own particular states. The governments of
these states would never consider surrendering even a small part of their
sovereignty to any supranational system whose requirements contradict the
norms and standards on which their own national order is based.

The problem here is not limited to the most obvious cases of communism
and liberal democracy, both of which are seeking a world order based on
their respective, and mutually exclusive, principles. The Iranian ayatollahs
are also very keen on building a world order system, provided it is based on
their interpretation of Islamic principles, which are incompatible with both
communism and liberal democracy. One should not underestimate the seriousness of the late Ayatollah Khomeni's proposition to Gorbachev to
abandon his Marxism for Islam and join the ayatollah in the endeavor of creating an "antisecular" (meaning, in fact, anti-Western) Islamic World Order.
But, as long as an Islamic or a communist world order remains an impractical proposition, the communist or Islamic rulers of their respective states
will cling steadfastly to the principle of national sovereignty, using it as a
weapon for resisting the influences of hostile (giaourish or capitalist) principles spreading from abroad and, also, for advancing a congenial world order system.

Even the opposition to the EEC in liberal democracies of Western Europe
is inspired not so much by the EEC's opponents' unswerving commitment to
the legacy of unlimited national sovereignty as by their fear of the European
community's inimical influence on the established or envisaged domestic order of their particular state. The left-wingers in the British Labor Party opposed Britain's joining of the EEC because, in their view, membership in
such a "capitalist cartel" would practically preclude Britain's development
along socialist lines. Mrs. Thatcher, on the other hand, is reluctant to plunge
Britain into closer association with European institutions because of the socialist trends that, in her view, are increasingly permeating the European
Community and also some of its member-states. If she only could be sure
that the European community would not overrule or undermine her domestic reforms aimed at enhancing the "spirit of free enterprise" and promoting
"popular capitalism," her objections to Britain's deeper integration into Europe would, no doubt, be much less adamant.

The biggest trouble of the twentieth century is that the most powerful nation states, each followed by an array of allied and satellite-states, clash with
one another not so much because of irreconcilable national interests but

mainly because of conflicting visions of what a right world order system should be like. Hitler and Mussolini fought World War II not so much for what could be defined as Germany's or Italy's straight national interest as for a fascist "New (European and World) Order" that was equally unacceptable to the liberal democracies and communist USSR. Also, the post–World War II East–West confrontation, which continues to the present day, is by no means rooted in the conflict of national interests of any kind, as Russia has no territorial disputes with any Western power and is not involved with the West in any trade wars or other competitive economic pursuits; and, as far as influence zones are concerned, these were delineated by the postwar settlement to Russia's more than full satisfaction and have never been seriously challenged by the West since. The East–West confrontation is in substance not geopolitical (although it often expresses itself in geopolitical terms) but ideological, and it centers almost exclusively on global, that is, world order–related, issues: the USSR, seeking to establish a communist world order, congenial to itself, is committed to the revolutionary expansion of the Soviet-type communist system, whereas the West resists such attempts on the part of the USSR, aspiring—though without formulating this as its policy objective—for the replacement of the Soviet system in Russia by another system which, being more congenial to the West's own system, would stop threatening the basic security and stability of the West through engineering its communist transformation. To sum it up, one could say that, in the present East–West confrontation, the main issue at stake is not which nation is going to dominate the world, as only too many analysts would have it, but on what universal foundations—communist-totalitarian or liberal-pluralistic, and these are incompatible—the future world order is going to be based.

THE FUTURE WORLD ORDER: MULTIPLICITY OR UNIVERSALITY?

It is the contention of this paper that a communist-totalitarian world order cannot, and will not, be established. This is so, because a communist world order—which, according to Marx, must be unitary—is unable to institute or, if once instituted, to maintain a monocentric structure. Polycentrism in a world dominated by a single ideology can only be sustained by each center claiming to be the sole correct interpreter of that ideology and brandishing all other centers as heretically revisionist. As a result, the communist world order system will fall apart, degenerating into a world consisting of many feuding parts with each party trying to force its supremacy upon the others.

The impossibility of communist monocentrism has been already convincingly proved by the relatively short history of extant communist states. The powerful Soviet Union has been unable to control all the communist powers that were in the first place established and controlled by it. Moreover, after having split away from their founding "Soviet Mother," these powers either became extremely hostile to the Soviet Union—China and Albania are cases in point—or, as in the case of Yugoslavia, became the targets of Soviet hostility. If not for the powerful presence and containing influence of the West, the Soviet Union would have certainly attacked Yugoslavia in 1948 and China in 1969, with bloody wars ensuing as the result of these attacks. We have already witnessed a Vietnamese communist invasion and subsequent occupation of an equally communist Kampuchea, as well as a Chinese communist attack against an equally communist Vietnam. Just imagine what the situation would be if the whole world became communist and no restraining influence could be exercised on it from outside. The Orwellian scenario of *1984*, according to which the three totalitarian communist superpowers are in a constant state of war with one another, would be beyond doubt not mere fiction but historic reality. It is unlikely that wars between or among communist powers would be as sloppy as Orwell has envisaged them to be in his novel, and that they would proceed along the lines of recent war between Iraq and Iran. It is much more likely that these wars would be fought on a full nuclear scale, and this means that communist world control will most certainly spell the end of mankind. Communism is thus in principle incapable of providing the foundation for a coherent and lasting world order system.

But, furthermore, communism has by now practically lost even the capacity of being a viable contender for shaping the world order system. Today communism is everywhere in retreat and nearing its demise. The communist rulers themselves have finally realized that their dogmatic adherence to communist ideology ruined the countries they rule to such an extent that only drastic system-rejective changes introduced from above could save them from being brought down by the system's cracking under the pressure of forces that they cannot control. Indeed, the major independent communist powers—the Soviet Union, China, and Yugoslavia—seem to be almost in a race with one another for the promptest riddance of the last vestiges of communism in their respective lands. Sooner or later, Albania, now the last immutable communist state, is inevitably going to join this race, too. It is doubtful, however, that this race is going to proceed smoothly. Already today we can observe in each team too many runners heading in opposite directions. As the ruthless suppression of democratic opposition in China since June 1989 demonstrates, the forces of conservative communism are not likely to give up the system that endows them with limitless power and privileges without putting up a dogged resistance and trying to bring about serious restorationist upsets, which may dramatically increase international tension and provoke a final desperate attempt by conservative communists to put the world under communist control by sheer force. But even without such restorationist upsets, communist powers, notwithstanding their perestroikas, remain in substance what they have always been, and cannot help but pursue their traditional global policies aimed at the institution of the communist world order. In fact, many leading communists see perestroika as the necessary respite before these policies could be resumed with full vigor. This is to say that, although objectively communism is not anymore a serious contender for world domination and control, it still continues to play the traditional role of such a contender and retains the ability to inflict upon the world serious damage. Hence, the East–West confrontation is far from being over, in spite of the East having already lost it on all practical counts and trying at the moment to adjust to this fact.

Gorbachev's proposals about creating a new world order, made in his speech to the UN General Assembly in December 1988, are, as mentioned above, a mere plea of a weakened rival to, at the moment, an overwhelmingly stronger opponent for an armistice, during which the communist system could put itself together and prepare for a new attack. Gorbachev's projected world order is a multiple one (*mnogovariantnyi*), not universal. It boils down to the same old principle of peaceful coexistence between the socialist and capitalist systems that dominated Soviet international politics in the pre-Gorbachev period, only with more peacefulness added to it. The change, defined as "new thinking," is thus quantitative rather than qualitative. Its central idea is each nation's freedom of choice—but this time allegedly of genuine choice—between the already established and competing systems of capitalism and socialism. The full exclusion of the use of force in external matters and close East–West cooperation on global issues (such as disarmament, development, external debts, ecology, outer space, solution of regional conflicts, human rights, international system of adjudication, etc.) would assure, according to Gorbachev, not only the uninhibited exercise of this freedom of choice but, most importantly, the survival of mankind and the possibility for its further progressive development. As Gorbachev repetitively stresses, in the nuclear era the common interest of mankind in survival has to take precedence over all partial interests of classes and nations. Summing his "new world order" proposal up, Gorbachev declared: "It is a fact of fundamental significance that the formation of the peaceful period will take place under the circumstances of the existence and rivalry of various socio-economic and political systems. However, the substance of our international efforts, one of the key positions of new thinking, consists precisely in giving to this rivalry the quality of sensible competition in the conditions of respect for the freedom of choice and balance of interests."[7]

There are two points that make Gorbachev's "new world order" practically indistinguishable from the old one. First, it is his substitute of national freedom as such, which naturally includes the free choice of a system of government, by the ambivalent freedom of limited choice between the already extant systems. Such a choice may be dressed up as free but exercised in fact under duress or direct coercion, as all previous "free choices" of a communist system have invariably been. Secondly, it is Gorbachev's unswerving commitment to the continuation of the old rivalry between capitalism and communism. Freely admitting that in the Soviet Union the communist system faces bankruptcy, Gorbachev nevertheless somehow seems to believe that this "historic rivalry" is bound to end by the worldwide victory of communism. In a roundabout way, Gorbachev is thus admitting that his "multiple world order" is only a transitory device for avoiding world war and the ensuing nuclear holocaust, and that, in the end, the "multiple world order" will be inevitably transformed into a universally communist one. If that is not old wine in new bottles, then what is?

Differently from Gorbachev, most Western world order analysts (with the exception of the technological determinists for whom advances in science and communication technology will automatically sweep away all systemic differences and bring about a united world) quite naturally accept the "multiple world orders" model as permanent and constant. Some of them, who refuse to see in the communist system anything more than a specific national form of government, ignore the ideological dimension of the East–West conflict altogether and try to find the formula for a viable world order system in rationally defined measures that could mutually advance the national interests of the world's major powers.

Others, who recognize the ideological differences between the USSR and the West but believe that for Russia communism is as organic and lasting as liberal democracy is for the United States and Western Europe, seek a framework in which a permanent accommodation of both systems in one world order could take place (the position of these analysts is almost identical with the views on peaceful coexistence of successive Soviet leaders).

Is pragmatism—either in the form of advancing the compatibility of national interest (identically defined for both sides), as the first group suggests, or in the form of putting common interests before the conflicting ones, as the second group suggests—a sufficient universal foundation to unite into a coherent world order system states based on mutually exclusive ideologies, values, and goals? I doubt it. Can a "multiple world order" system held together by such sheer pragmatism be viable in the long run? Together with Gorbachev, I say no, it cannot. A "multiple world order" system is either going to be replaced by a truly universal one or will fall apart, quite probably destroying, together with that world order system, the world itself. An authentic world order system must be indeed universal, not multiple.

A universal world order system does not at all presuppose, however, ideological homogeneity. On the contrary, as Hedley Bull has convincingly proved, an ideologically homogeneous world order, if such a thing ever came into existence, would be the most oppressive, conflict-ridden, and explosive world order of all.[8]

We have already reviewed the lethal consequences that the establishment of an ideologically homogeneous communist world order system would bring about. Very similar consequences would be brought about by any other ideologically homogeneous world order system—theocratic, fascist, neo-Russoist, etc. There is no such thing as a universal ideology that could unite and satisfy all people. By nature and, hence, also socially and culturally, humanity is an ideologically heterogeneous entity and needs communal structures that could accommodate its inherent heterogeneity as fully as possible.

There is, however, one universal ideology that corresponds to human nature and provides the necessary foundations for communal structures properly accommodating humanity's heterogeneity. This is the ideology of human rights. Tolerance is the catch word of this ideology, which makes it unique in the sense that it works not to the exclusion of other ideologies, but for accommodation within a given society of all ideologies. Nations that have politically organized themselves in concordance with the principles of human rights are intrinsically pluralistic and, hence, immune to stifling uniformity that goes together with any other but the human rights kind of ideological homogeneity. When engaging in a relationship with one another, these nations naturally extend the principles on which they are themselves founded to the outside world and by doing so lay down the universal foundation on which a viable world order system can be reliably built. Maximal equal rights for all individuals and their freely formed associations—for all nationalities, religions, cultures, and races; government by consensus or, to quote Abraham Lincoln, "of the people, by the people, and for the people"—those are the basic ideas that they emanate and that so easily find their application on a global scale.

It follows from the above that a viable world order system cannot accept as its universal foundation either pragmatic "multiplicity" or ideological homogeneity. The only universal foundation that can suit its purposes is liberal democracy.

It was the great German philosopher, Immanuel Kant, who, in his 1795 essay, *Perpetual Peace*, had first formulated this idea. According to Kant, the first definitive article of perpetual peace, the one that lays the basic foundation for a viable world order, shall establish that the constitution of each state (entering a perpetually peaceful world order) has to be republican. Kant defines a republican constitution as one that, "first, . . . accords with the principles of the *freedom* of the members of a society (as men), second, . . . accords with the principles of the *dependence* of everyone on a single common legislation (as subjects), and, third, . . . accords with the law of the equality of them all (as citizens)."[9]

Only when all states will become republican, one should go to the next stage and conclude the second definitive article of perpetual peace, according to which a federation of free states (*foedus pacificum*) is to be instituted. Kant strongly stresses that this federation has to be "a federation of nations but it must not be a state consisting of nations."[10] Kant is thus against the world state. He rightly believes that a single world government is incompatible with the natural division of mankind into nations and, hence, with national freedom. What he is advocating is a federal union of equal republican nation-states that retain their own sovereignty and extend it further by acting together on issues of mutual concern, but beyond the reach of any one particular state. Kant's *foedus pacificum* is, in fact, a global common-wealth of free and democratic nations.

THE FUTURE WORLD ORDER: NATIONAL SOVEREIGNTY VERSUS THE SOVEREIGNTY OF MANKIND

Although Morton Kaplan urges the democratic countries of the world to start uniting into a global democratic community without delay,[11] a truly global world order system can hardly evolve before the world's second great superpower, the USSR, remains communist and imperial. Kaplan's global democratic community, under the circumstances of continuous East–West confrontation, may become a valuable asset strengthening the Western hand in this confrontation, but it could hardly directly contribute to the creation of a global commonwealth anything more substantial than that.

For starting to build a truly global commonwealth of free and democratic nations it is not necessary to wait for all the countries of the world establish-ing a republican or, what is one and the same thing, a liberal democratic sys-tem, but it is necessary to terminate the East–West confrontation and thus also the still persistent bipolar structure of global politics. In other words, for the global commonwealth to become a reality, it would be sufficient to have a free Russia ready to join in a commonwealth type arrangement with the United States, Western Europe, and other liberal democracies of the world. The global dimension of such a new commonwealth would not be under-mined even if, at the time of its creation, China and Albania still remained communist-totalitarian states, South Africa were as yet not fully disentangled from the fetters of its apartheid system, and Burma would not have gotten rid of its ruthless military dictatorship.

A global commonwealth of free and democratic nations should not un-dermine the principle of national sovereignty by assuming superior legisla-tive powers or by subordinating to itself through global bureaucracies any national political and administrative institutions.

A voluntary agreement of free and democratic nations about establishing a global commonwealth will nevertheless have to involve the delegation by the founding member-states to this commonwealth of supreme power in cer-tain areas and on certain issues. The whole arrangement about establishing a global commonwealth would have very little meaning if it would not en-dow the established global institutions with some sovereign rights over-riding the sovereign rights of the member-states. International security and protection of human rights are perhaps the most important areas in which national sovereignty would have to be curtailed and supreme authority sub-mitted to the global commonwealth.

Any viable world order system crowned by a global commonwealth, in or-der practically to ensure international security, would have to endow the newly established institutions of global authority with the following functions at least:

1. Exclusive control over all weapons of mass destruction.
2. Prevention of all armed conflicts with the ultimate right of military interference in order to stop armed struggle (both these functions imply the necessity for the global commonwealth to possess a military force superior to the combined military forces of several most powerful member-states).
3. International arbitration and, when necessary, adjudication to settle conflicts between member-states (this function implies the acceptance by all member-states of an elaborate World Code of Laws, according to which international conflicts are to be settled, and of a functioning system of global justice passing authoritative and enforceable judgments on such conflicts by applying that code of laws).
4. Supervision over the implementation or, if necessary, enforcement of the conflict-settling decisions made by organs of global justice.

Similarly, in the area of human rights, the global commonwealth would have to be endowed with supreme authority of supervision over the application of a universally adopted World Code on Human Rights (such a code in an embryonic form already exists in the form of the Universal Declaration of Human Rights and the two supplementary covenants, one on civil and political rights and the other on social, economic, and cultural rights), instituting for this purpose within its structure a special World Court on Human Rights to serve as the highest body of judicial authority in cases involving violations of the World Code of Human Rights.

As is the case with every other international treaty or covenant, states participating in a treaty-based global commonwealth will retain their right freely to terminate their association with it and thus to restore their full sovereignty whenever they choose to do so. Furthermore, the expulsion from the commonwealth (and thus restitution of full sovereignty) will be the ultimate sanction the commonwealth could apply to member-states refusing to obey the decisions of its judicial institutions.

The decisions of the world courts would also be the only ones that the states entering into the global commonwealth would have to undertake to obey unconditionally and that would thus be binding on them. All other decisions of global institutions, before being implemented in the domain controlled by a member-state, would have to receive an explicit agreement of that state. Concrete decisions of global institutions, such, for example, as those on building pollution control centers or establishing energy-testing sites on a member-state's territory, would require as a prerequisite a contract between the global institution making the decision and the member-state agreeing to have this decision implemented on its

territory. The decisions of global institutions establishing general normatives, in order to become laws applicable in the domain controlled by
member-states, would have to receive proper ratification by the respective
competent authorities of these states.

THE GLOBAL COMMONWEALTH AND THE RIGHT
OF NATIONS TO SELF-DETERMINATION AND SOVEREIGNTY

A global commonwealth, the universal foundation for which is provided by
liberal-democratic principles, and that therefore has to accord to all individuals and nations equal human rights, would present most modern states, not
only the ideocracies and autocracies, with some difficult problems.

The first such problem is related to the multinationalism and multiracism
of a great number of a great number of so-called nation-states. Such states
are either underrepresentative minority states, like South Africa and Ethiopia,
or misrepresentative majority states, like Russia, Turkey, Romania, Sri Lanka,
and Spain; or incoherently heterogeneous states like Belgium, India, Sudan,
Lebanon, and Afghanistan. Under any regime, these established states would
be reluctant to recognize the equal right of all their constituent nations to
self-determination and sovereignty and face, as a result, radical territorial restructuring or even disintegration.

It is true that liberal-democratic states are much better equipped to deal
with the problems of multinationalism than are their nondemocratic counterparts; and the more developed and entrenched the liberal democratic order in a state is, the easier it is to arrive in it at a mutually agreeable solution
of these problems. Belgium represents here, perhaps, a typical example. The
unceasing struggle between the Flemings and the Walloons was tearing the
Belgian state apart for many decades. The Flemings were fighting for a separate Flemish state, while the Walloons resisted them and some, in desperation, even strove to merge their part of Belgium with France.

In the conditions of a developed liberal-democratic order, various views
on Belgium's future were openly debated, tested in elections, and otherwise
probed and tossed with by political parties, linguistic and cultural societies,
and other similar bodies. As a result, both feuding parties realized that, because of the indivisibility of Brussels, a Flemish city with a Walloon majority,
Belgium's nations will have to stick together, retaining Belgium as their common state. Thanks again to the country's entrenched liberal and democratic
traditions and procedures, a new constitutional settlement providing for a
fairer coexistence of the two nations in one state has been devised. This settlement divided Belgium into three separate autonomous regions of Flan-
ders, Wallonia, and Brussels. In July 1989, the final stitches were put to the
transformation of Belgium into a full-fledged federal state consisting of the
two separate national territorial communities with the binational capital becoming a third autonomous zone existing alongside the two main federated

entities. It goes without saying that this settlement could not satisfy all Belgians, and that it indeed contains a number of flaws and shortcomings. But it doubtlessly represented a very significant step forward in the solution of Belgium's intranational problems, which liberal democracy will surely be able gradually to improve, correct, and develop further in order to achieve as wide a consensus as possible.

After being transformed into a liberal democracy, Spain has also positively responded to the demands and grievances of its non-Castilians. The non-Castilian provinces were granted a large degree of autonomy and self-government, which, not only Andalusians and Galicians, but also the acutely nationalistic Catalonians accepted for the time being as satisfying their basic, if not all, demands. The Catalonians may still foster aspirations of full independence from Spain, but at the moment they clearly decided to concentrate on the usage of their newly acquired autonomy for consolidating and organizing themselves as a nation within the Spanish state. The Basques follow in the Catalonians' footsteps. If, under Franco, many Basques supported the radical national resistance organization ETA and approved of its militancy, now, under the conditions of liberal democracy, ETA's underground guerrilla forces increasingly find themselves in an isolated position. The majority of Basques did not stop being separatist—in this sense, their position is identical to that of ETA's—but, believing that now their separatist goals could be advanced and ultimately achieved by nonviolent political means, they roundly reject ETA's terrorist activities and increasingly refuse to back its clandestine paramilitary organizations.

Democratic institutions and procedures also assured a peaceful solution within the Canadian state of the Quebec problem. De Gaulle's slogan, *Vive le Quebec libre,* has been realized by a series of reforms of the Canadian federal system and the introduction of bilingualism on the All-Union level. Quebec is now indeed practically free, although it remains a part of Canada.

In a global commonwealth, however, the relative satisfaction of stateless nations with their place and status within a larger nation-state may change. Entities like Quebec or Catalonia could opt for a direct association with the global commonwealth and prefer to drop their present state associations, which would prevent them from doing so. Liberal-democratic institutions of the member-states and the global commonwealth itself should be able to assure a positive solution even of such problems, despite the inertial commitment of every state, however liberal and democratic, to preserve its territorial integrity and to resist separatism of any kind.

The problem of multinationalism is much more complex and acute in non-democratic countries and in the countries that, like India or the Philippines, could be classified as liberal democracies, but that were transformed into modern states as historically formed regional entities rather than nations, and thus have never been, and are not, nation-states in the classically European sense of this word. The rapidly developing process of national differentiation, which has spread far beyond Europe and at present embraces the entire world, made, however, such a historically and culturally defined regional basis for the formation of a modern state outmoded. With progressing modernization (or, which is one and the same thing, westernization) of traditional societies in Asia, their old broad regional identities, based on either a common religion (India, Pakistan) or a dominant culture (China), are eroding quite fast, giving way to national identities that fortify in those states splintering tendencies and lead to their ultimate partition into a number of proper nation-states. In Black Africa, on the other hand, the traditional tribal entities are growing and consolidating into proper national entities, too, which spells the necessity of radical reorganization in a not too distant future of most Black African states, whose identity is now based mainly on their colonial legacy and thus lacks an organic societal basis. Although then unsuccessful, the attempts in 1966–1970 to create the Ibo nation-state, Biafra, and thus to split Nigeria on ethnic grounds, emit to this effect a powerful signal indeed.

The integrity of those multinational states that came into existence before the national identities of peoples living in them were either properly formed, or started playing a predominant role, is already now visibly threatened. The Tamil struggle for separation from the Singhalese-dominated state of Sri Lanka, and the Sikhs' striving for the establishment of their separate state in the Indian province of Punjab, are just two examples of the explosive tendencies within these states. The common Muslim identity of the peoples of Pakistan was unable to prevent the splitting away from the Urdus and other smaller nations living in the western part of the country of the Bengalis situated in the country's eastern part who, with India's help, managed to establish in 1972 their separate nation state, Bangladesh. There are signs that the Hindu Bengalis of India increasingly identify themselves with the Muslim Bangladesh, tossing with the idea of splitting away from India and uniting the whole Bengali nation across the religious barriers in one separate nation-state. India's ploy to weaken Pakistan is thus turning nowadays increasingly against India herself, threatening her territorial integrity.

There are stateless nations in Asia whose territory is occupied by several states and who fight against all these states for their national independence. The Kurds are one such nation. Over 20,000,000 of them occupy a compact territory that is divided between five separate states—Turkey, the Caucasian area of the Soviet Union, Syria, Iraq, and Iran. Another such nation is the Baluchis living in Iran, Pakistan, India's Punjab, the southern part of the Asian USSR, and Afghanistan. There are also the Pathans living on both sides of the border between Afghanistan and Pakistan and a number of other similarly situated stateless nations.

There are no true nation-states in the whole of Black Africa. Most Black African states, as mentioned above, are heirs of former colonial entities, with their borders artificially cutting across many homogeneous tribal areas. Ethiopia, Africa's traditionally independent state, has always been, and remains, an empire of the Amharas who (together with the southern Tigres, acculturated by the Amharas) are otherwise known as the Abyssinian nation, which comprises only about a quarter of Ethiopia's population. For the last several decades, under both the Emperor Haile Selassie and the present communist regime of Colonel Menghistu, Ethiopia has been ravaged by a war of independence that the Eritreans and the Northern Tigres are conducting against Addis-Adaba, the capital of the Amharan (or Abyssinian) Empire.

Acute national conflicts that were for decades simmering under the monolithic surface of the communist world are also now coming out into the open and becoming visible. They powerfully call into question the validity of the state unity of many a communist state, starting with the Soviet Union itself. Only under liberal democracy, the search for the solution of the national conflicts besieging the multinational communist states could be properly instituted. The communist system is ideologically and politically too inflexible even to begin such a search. It is indicative that the Soviet non-Russians are the champions of democratic reforms in the USSR. The bitter experience of continuous defeats in their direct struggle for separation from the USSR taught them the lesson that the most realistic and viable way for them to achieve national independence lies through democratization of the political regime in Moscow. If previously independence from the USSR seemed to them a prerequisite for their becoming liberal-democratic nations, now they predominantly consider democracy on the All-Union scale a prerequisite for their independence (the Baltic popular fronts justified their decision to fight in the 1989 election to the supreme body of authority of the occupying power, the All-Union Congress of People's Deputies, by the slogan: "Through democratization to sovereignty").

There are only about 180 sovereign states in the present-day world. It is doubtful that this number would drastically change at the time when the conditions for the creation of the global commonwealth will become ripe. Some artificially divided states, such as East and West Germany and North and South Korea, may have by then already been merged in single nation-states; some, today only nominally sovereign states (e.g., those of the Soviet Bloc), could have their actual sovereignty recovered; and a few new nation-states may be created as a result of national-liberation struggle or peaceful constitutional arrangements, making a stateless nation sovereign. This will not radically change, however, the basic fact that the state-centric world is populated by more than 1,600 stateless nations, most of which are in one way or another engaged in a national movement striving for either equal rights or authentic autonomy or outright sovereignty. This struggle is not likely to relent until its ultimate goal is achieved, unless meanwhile the struggling nation was annihilated by its alien rulers.

It goes without saying that, as long as national strifes and conflicts continue to abound, the global commonwealth will be hardly able properly to fulfill its task of creating and safeguarding a peaceful and just world order system. For such a world order system to emerge and consolidate, it is necessary not only to found it on universally accepted liberal-democratic principles, but also effectively to apply these principles for achieving fair distribution of national sovereignty among all territorial nations of the world. A fair distribution of national sovereignty could not be achieved, however, without the present states going through thorough processes of fission: the USSR, Yugoslavia, Nigeria, and most other "structurally" multinational states would be the prime objects of such fission; fusion (Germany and Korea are the most obvious cases for it); and reshufflement (such, for example, as would be necessary between Ethiopia and Somalia for solving the Ogaden problem; between the USSR and Iran to bring into existence an integral Azeri state; among the five states housing the Kurds in order to form a sovereign Kurdistan; and between Spain and France for the sake of establishing a free Basque state, to say nothing of most Black African states and many other states without a proper national identity throughout the world). It is in initiating and managing these extremely difficult processes that the global commonwealth, and especially its institutions of international justice, will have to assume prime responsibility.

It was again Immanuel Kant who convincingly demonstrated that only equal independence of every nation, big or small, from any other nation can provide an adequate foundation for a perpetually peaceful world order. Defining the independence of all nations as a preliminary condition for perpetual peace, Kant formulated it in the following maxim: "No nation, be it large or small, may be acquired by another nation by inheritance, exchange, purchase, or gift,"[12] let alone by conquest or coercion. A global commonwealth, built upon a universally accepted liberal democratic foundation, would be bound to make this Kantian idea its own, which is to say that the liberal-democratic right of every nation to self-determination and sovereignty will have to be included into the commonwealth's constitution as its principal element. Equally, the states entering the global commonwealth would have to pledge themselves to obey the moral and legal normatives that ensure for each nation a real possibility to become a separate state related to the global commonwealth either directly or through a voluntary association with other states, and which, consequently, deny each nation equally the right to include or contain within its sovereign realm another nation against its will. Only after these normatives are universally adopted and subsequently developed into a set of legal provisions incorporated into a World Code of Laws, could the global commonwealth begin effectively to preside over the process of restructuring the world's political map in concordance with the thus formulated first principles of international justice.

Under the circumstances of an established global commonwealth capable of guaranteeing effective military security to all nations and states, Israel would have to drop its objections to the establishment of a separate Palestinian state. The United Nations Security Council Resolution 242 could thus be at last practically implemented and a lasting, though in the beginning uneasy, peaceful settlement between Arabs and Jews in the Middle East begin to evolve.

The problem of granting national sovereignty to stateless nations, which, as a result of foreign rule, became minorities in their own lands is more complex. The general principle that the global commonwealth should adopt for such anomalous cases is recognition of the inalienable right of each nation to be in sovereign possession of its historic homeland and capital city, whatever the arithmetic correlations in the ethnic composition of that homeland's or city's population may be. In this respect, the indigenous Fijians, who lost the majority in Fiji to immigrant Indians (43 percent of Fiji's population are native Fijians, whereas 51 percent are immigrant Indians), were right in forcefully asserting their political supremacy in the country, although in order to do so they had to resort to a military coup.

The dispute between the Abkhazes and Georgians over sovereign rights in Abkhazia should be resolved in a similar fashion, that is, in favor of the Abkhazes, although they are a 17 percent minority in their own republic where the Georgians constitute 41 percent of the population (16.5 percent of Abkhazia's population are Russians, 15 percent are Armenians, and the rest belong to a few smaller ethnic minorities). The main reason for according the minority Abkhazes sovereign rights in Abkhazia is the fact that they do not have any other homeland but Abkhazia, whereas the Georgians, Russians, and Armenians living there have their own historic homelands outside Abkhazia. The same principle must also be applied to the Crimean Tatars, a people forcefully deported from their historic homeland in the Crimean peninsula, but aspiring to return and settle there as a minority nation that is, however, endowed with sovereign rights in the place that is their sole historic homeland. It is on similar grounds that the Jews rightfully reclaimed, and took, sovereignty over their historic homeland of Israel. In the Lithuanian–Polish dispute over Lithuania's capital city Vilnius, which Poland had occupied in 1920 under the pretext that Poles constituted there a compact majority, the Lithuanians were right and the Poles were wrong, for without Vilnius, the sole and only capital city that the Lithuanian nation has, Lithuania's statehood would lose its historical continuity and proper integrity, while for the Poles Vilnius is just another provincial town on the margins of the Polish state whose being within or outside Poland does not affect the fate of the Polish nation in any substantial way.

In some cases, the territory of the historic homeland of a nation that has become a minority there could be divided between the indigenous and immigrant nations to the satisfaction of both. The enormous territory of Kazakhstan, where the native Kazakhs comprise only 36 percent of the population, has a solid Kazakh majority only in the Gur'ev, Kzyl-Orda, Url'sk, and Chimkent provinces of the republic. These four provinces, together with Kazakhstan's capital city Alma-Ata, the Alma-Ata province, and the rest of the southeastern Kazakhstan, could be consolidated into a viable nucleus of the Kazakh nation-state's proper territory, whereas the territories of northern Kazakhstan, where there are very few Kazakhs and the Slavs (Russians, Ukrainians, and Dyelorusslans) fully predominate, could be joined with Russia. The scarcely populated areas of present central and southwestern Kazakhstan could be then justly—that is, in accordance with the ethnic composition of the local rural population—apportioned to either Kazakhstan or Russia.

In each case, when a new nation-state is created, there are bound to remain on its territory significant numbers of people belonging to other nations and ethnic groups. These groups should get not simply equal rights but be granted, additionally, an extensive array of specific rights ensuring their full national-cultural autonomy. The protection of equal rights of all nationalities comprising a nation-state, and of those nationalities' specific rights ensuring their full national-cultural autonomy, will be another important area for the global commonwealth to deal with. The standards and norms determining the commonwealth's activities in these areas should be unambiguously set by the World Code on Human Rights ratified by all member-states.

Precise legal standards should also be set for the global commonwealth to handle irredentist claims that foster enmity among many a nation. These standards should be based on the following principle: insofar as a nation is in possession of its own homeland and an established capital city within it, that nation can claim only such territories not presently in its possession in which that nation at the time of claiming constitutes a compact majority, and, conversely, no nation can refuse to cede sovereignty over provinces in which a different nation constitutes a compact majority. Purely historical claims to territory, except claims to historic homelands and capital cities by nations that lost them because of genocidal policies toward them of foreign rulers, should thus not be considered valid. In that respect, the Albanian claim to sovereignty over the presently Serbian province of Kosovo-Metohia, where the Albanians are the overwhelming majority, should be considered valid. The facts that at an early point in history Kosovo was the heartland of Serbia, and that 600 years ago the battle fought there, at Kosovo Polje, by the Serbs against the Ottoman Turks, decided the fate of Serbian statehood for many a century, should not be considered as justifying Serbian retention of sovereignty over Kosovo-Metohia. The two nations disputing sovereignty over Kosovo-Metohia have their established homelands outside that province and therefore their dispute over it should be resolved in favor of the nation that constitutes the majority of the disputed province's population, that is, in favor of Albanians. It goes, of course, without saying that Albania's sovereignty over Kosovo-Metohia should not adversely affect any civil, political, or cultural rights of the Serbian minority or prevent the Serbians from gathering, whenever they choose and in as great numbers as they wish, at Kosovo Polje to celebrate the anniversaries of their famous defeat there at the hands of the Ottoman Turks. Equally, if the Finns were to claim Leningrad (and historically they could do so even with regard to Moscow) or the Lithuanians claimed East Prussia, very few would have doubts about dismissing these claims outrightly in spite of their perfect historical justification. In the same way, the Hungarians have no valid claim to Transylvania, where the majority is Romanian, although historically Transylvania was an integral part of Hungary and at times even played the role of the pivotal heartland of that country. To be sure, the complaints about the harsh treatment by the Romanian state of the 2,000,000 strong Hungarian minority in Transylvania are fully justified. However, the gross violations on Romania's part of the Hungarians' human rights do not in any way invalidate Romania's sovereignty over Transylvania. These violations only called into question Ceausescu's government's overall ability to comply with international standards set for a state's treatment of its citizens and minority groups but could not justify claims for exemption of a territory containing a larger number of oppressed minorities from the sovereign authority of the Romanian nation-state. The anti-Ceausescu revolution in Romania was actually ignited by the Romanian authorities' brutal treatment of the Hungarians living in the Transylvania city of Timisoara. The fact that the ethnic Romanians in Bucharest rose against Ceausescu's regime in protest against the massacre of their Hungarian co-citizens of that city, and in defense of human rights of all Romanian citizens independently of their ethnic origins, bodes well for the elimination in post-Ceausescu Romania of the discrimination suffered by the Hungarian minority under Ceausescu.

In many respects the case of Northern Ireland is analogous to the Transylvanian case. The Protestant majority's identity there is firmly British and therefore any attempt to transfer sovereignty over Ulster from the UK to the Irish Republic would represent an intolerable violation of that majority's basic rights. The fact that this majority discriminates against the Catholic minority, and that the British government is not doing enough to remedy the situation, represents a case of minorities' human rights, but in no way can it affect the situation with regard to sovereignty, let alone justify its transfer. Even less problematic in this respect is British sovereignty over the Falkland Islands where the population is entirely British and thus the Argentinian claim to sovereignty over the Malvinas, however correct the Argentinian reading of history may be, has no validity whatsoever.

According to the same standards, Armenians have a fully justifiable claim to Nagorno-Karabakh (Artsak), where theirs is an 80 percent majority, but not to Nakhichevan, which, although historically an Armenian territory, too, is now mainly populated by the Azeris. The Armenians, because of that, do not even start claiming Nakhichevan, while the Azeris blatantly continue to cling to Nagorno-Karabakh, which neither historically nor demographically had ever been a part of Azerbaijan. The right in the Armenian-Azeri dispute is thus entirely on the Armenians' side. The Armenians would also be right to claim from Turkey the Ararat Valley, which is an indivisible part of the Armenian homeland containing the main spiritual center and supreme symbol of Armenia's nationhood, the holy Mountain of Ararat itself. Before 1921, when Lenin's Soviet Russian government ceded the Ararat Valley to Turkey, it was densely populated by Armenians; now it is scarcely populated at all, as if waiting to join Armenia again.

Contrary to beliefs of many students of world politics, the establishment on liberal-democratic principles of a global commonwealth does not necessarily either extinguish or even substantially erode the principle of national sovereignty, nor would it inevitably abolish the liberal-democratic right of all nations to self-determination and sovereignty. The idea of such a common-wealth is not to undermine but rather to amend and enhance national sovereignty by institutionalizing the sovereignty of mankind with the view of serving common interests of all nations and coordinating their mutual endeavors. The global institutions could be instrumental in providing for: fair and equal distribution of national sovereignty among the nations of the world, inviolable security of all member-states, just and peaceful solutions of international conflicts, and a better and more effective exploitation in the interests of all nations of mankind's common resources. The possibility for each nation to realize its full potential and exercise on equal grounds its right to self-determination and sovereignty would be enormously advanced by such a global arrangement.

COMMENT

To the Editor:

Dr. Shtromas's departure from Great Britain across the ocean was a great loss, and a gain for America. No sooner has he settled in his new country than he produces a new article on the future of the world as he sees it, in the interest of peace.

In general, I find myself in agreement with what Dr. Shtromas writes, but there are some aspects of the sociolinguistic situation that are relevant for our political solutions and so must be studied by all political scientists.

Shtromas begins by correctly distinguishing between real and "dressed up" sovereign states, citing Mongolia as an example of the latter. But then he writes: "in 1989, not only these states but even most of the union-republics of the USSR itself started the process of reclaiming their actual sovereignty and so far were quite successful in this daring endeavor." But were they? Could the author enlighten us with regard to his own native Lithuania? I have not yet heard that the Lithuanian ambassador to the Court of Saint James has arrived here in London, and that is always the true sign of sovereignty of a nation, new or old.

The Azerbaijanis have made themselves into a test case: they went farther than any other nation in clamoring for independence and, sure enough, Russian troops arrived and fired. It will be some time before true sovereignty comes.

Next, Shtromas discusses the states that voluntarily submitted to a "patron" state as "client" states, e.g., the "communist-clique states," such as Cuba, Angola, and Ethiopia. Their governments "submit" for "ideological or pragmatic reasons." Here, it might have been useful to underline that the true reasons were those governments' voracity for money, which probably dictated the ideology. It is for the same reasons that the Soviets now have to withdraw from those client-states. The money has been eaten. The clients, never loyal to any ideology, are looking elsewhere for funds. *Pecunia non olet.*

Otherwise, Shtromas has no doubts that it was money that forced governments to give up part of their sovereignty, witness his citing of the abject submission of Britain's Labour government to the IMF for the sake of money to pay for its dubious dissipation by 1979. It was the prelude to its fall, caused by its own reckless greed. Even Panama could not defy its source of money for long. Here, Shtromas introduces the term *narcocratic* for a state ruled by a government that is kept solvent by drug lords, perhaps inspired by Stan Andreski's (a Polish British sociologist) term *kleptocracy* for a government that sends international aid money to Switzerland. Among the defiant states that, Shtromas asserts, further racial discrimination is "in the first place South Africa," where, as everyone who is not blinded by dogma can see, the government has bent to pressure and is abolishing the last vestiges of discrimination. A truly racist government is that of the Sudan, where the blacks can be raided and legally sold as slaves, because Islamic law permits it. Other defiantly sovereign states are the ideocracies where Marxism or Islam encourages the governments to feel good because they are always right. Most other governments have yielded part of their sovereignty by treaty or otherwise.

In the next section Shtromas discusses bodies that can defy state governments, including individuals such as Armand Hammer (who ignored the British government's pleas for more safety in his oil rigs), Mother Teresa (who, by implication, told the Indian government that it is doing nothing for its poor and sick), and Andrei Sakharov (who dared to defy the world's strongest power: the Soviet government). Perhaps Shtromas should have made these points himself instead of letting me do so.

In the next section, Shtromas comes to his main subject, the new world order as he envisages it. He does not mention that what was said by the father of ideologies, Plato, is still true: only philosophers can be good rulers, since they have suppressed their greed (Plato, *The Republic*, edited by Desmond Lee, London: Penguin, 1974, p. 278).

It is true, as Shtromas says, that the really big states, China and the Soviet Union, are not assimilable into the new world order. They can do what they like, since they have nothing to fear. So, they would also subvert the new order. To that effect, they will have to be taken to pieces. For the time being, everything remains as it has always been. Those two big states have to strive for expansion or give up the dogma of their being absolutely ideologically right. In that context, I must disagree with Shtromas on the true reasons for which Hitler and Mussolini went to war. It was not their desire to export fascism and create a new world order on its basis, except insofar as fascism itself was no more than an expression of their own desire to dominate. Hitler was a dreamer, Mussolini a vain little Napoleon. They went to war with the illusion that they could conquer and hold immense empires as global emperors.

As long as there are such rulers on earth, there will be war. Stalin, Khrushchev, and Brezhnev went on enlarging the power of the Soviet Union. Castro and Deng Hsiao Ping are still busy doing the same for their own countries, in different ways. It is here that I disagree again with Shtromas where he writes, "in the present East–West confrontation, the main issue at stake is not which nation is going to dominate the world, but on what universal foundations—communist-totalitarian or liberal-pluralistic." I think it will depend on individual characters, as it always has in past empires.

I do agree, however, that communism, if it ever came to world power, would spell the end of the world, precisely because of its own military efficiency. I also agree that the present peacefulness is an armistice in which the Soviet Union can put itself together again after the economic strains of 1989. Gorbachev still seems to believe in the ultimate victory of communism; the "multiple" world order is a transient one for him.

Coming back to his ideal world order, Shtromas posits rightly that humanity is by nature inclined to diversity in culture and in the many forms of societies. The ideal state must show tolerance toward this variability. This tolerance is based on the equality of the citizens, which, in turn, is based on the most precious principle of them all: freedom.

In the next section, Shtromas sets out some aspects of his global commonwealth of nations, in which not all national governments would apply the principles of human rights to their citizens yet, e.g., Angola, Burma, etc. Can we force them?

Shtromas's ideals, when he comes to the middle of his paper, run away with him: "the global commonwealth should take full authority over . . . economic aid and development, protection . . . from famine." A Herculean task each of them, which will arouse fierce opposition in the "developing" states, which want to determine their own priorities for aid. It will also become ever more difficult to transport food to the ever increasing millions of "refugees from famine" (now estimated at 15,000,000, but more numerous in reality). Nor will individual states be told what to do with their energy, nuclear and other, or their communications. How will Shtromas regulate and manage demographic problems, e.g., "the rational use of manpower?" Will he ship the jobless to the job markets by the million? How will he tackle nations where crime seems to be endemic, such as Colombia or Sicily? Would he land police there? Seeing that a small state like Israel can ignore the UN troops whenever it wants to send its own troops to an area, will the big powers be deterred by such peacekeeping forces?

Nor can I agree that such functions of the global commonwealth would not interfere with the national sovereignty of member-states. That is precisely the problem we are facing in the EEC today. Already the so-called European Commission in Brussels is arrogating more power than it was ever meant to have, and it cannot be controlled by an elected body.

Shtromas himself acknowledges this problem when he posits global authority over "exclusive control over all weapons of mass destruction" (would Israel or Pakistan give up its atom bombs?), "prevention of all armed conflicts and . . . the right to stop armed struggle by military interference." Would Ethiopia or the Sudan agree with that, or Angola? Who will pay for the "military force superior to the combined military forces" of all other states? Or who will say that it is necessary to enforce "the conflict-settling decisions made by the organs of global justice?"

The British Commonwealth has never had troops at its disposal to, say, prevent armed conflict between India and Pakistan. Shtromas wants the global commonwealth to have "rights overriding the sovereign right of member states" to protect human rights. Would it have any effect in Lebanon? Would Ethiopia agree to have its human rights investigated? One human rights problem is already and increasingly insoluble, that of the so-called refugees who are simply illegal immigrants. They have to be sent back, for states like Hong Kong or even England are full to the brim. Yet, that forcible returning of refugees has created an outcry among the nations that do not have such problems themselves, but would not accept any more "refugees" if they arrived.

Shtromas claims that member-states, once they have joined the common-wealth, will be free to terminate their association. That is what the Southern (American) states thought in 1860, and it took five years of bloody civil war to make them realize that they were not sovereign states having voluntarily joined the Union. Nor could, say, the Ukraine secede from the USSR. The sovereign nations of today, such as Britain and France, are well aware of such a potential future and that explains the slow pace of the integration of the European community. One problem is the local ratification of laws passed by the union government regarding human rights, nuclear plants, etc.

In his next section, Shtromas comes to a problem that this writer has studied for years, that of the ethnic minorities. Shtromas takes as an example Belgium, where I have lived for many years. That is why I know that the Brussels Agglomeration does not, as Shtromas writes, have a Walloon majority. The facts are that most respondents have indicated "French" as their mother tongue on the census forms to which, they knew, their employers and house owners would have access, so that, if they filled in "Flemish," they would lose both their jobs and their accommodation. That is how Brussels became officially, but not factually, French-speaking. Walloon is something entirely different. In any case, Belgium is still a police state.

There is little hope for ethnic groups ever to gain statehood, as Shtromas admits. Nigeria reconquered Biafra, and China, Tibet, while Ethiopia and the Sudan are guilty of genocide in Eritrea and Nilotia, respectively, for the sake of the union. Only Bangladesh managed to secede, with military Indian help.

In his next section, Shtromas writes that there are no true nation-states in the whole of Black Africa. It is not clear whether he would accept Egypt and Morocco as nation-states, i.e., ethnic entities with a long history of statehood. In Black Africa, there are Burundi, Lesotho, Rwanda, Somalia, and Swaziland as states with an almost totally homogeneous population, although inversely not all the coethnics live in the same state, e.g., many Somalis live in Ogaden, an Ethiopian province. Botswana would also qualify as a nation-state, even though there are some groups within its boundaries other than Tswana-speakers.

In his paragraph on Ethiopia, Shtromas has been misled by the admittedly confusing ethnic names. He writes about the Northern and Southern Tigre and I would dearly like a footnote (footnotes are few and far between in this article). Northern Eritrea is inhabited by the speakers of Tigre, a Semitic language; they are Muslims. Northern Ethiopia is inhabited by a Christian people who speak Tigrinya, a related but quite distinct language. To make matters worse, this northern province of Ethiopia, south of the border with Eritrea, is called Tigray (rhymes with "my," but not with Tigre).

It is these latter, the Christian Tigrinya-speakers, who may have been dragooned into service with the Ethiopian army, although they do not exactly identify with the Amharic-speakers who live farther south; whether they together are what used to be called the Abyssinians is not certain. Nor is it clear what Professor Shtromas means by "reshufflement between Ethiopia and Somalia." Does he mean shuffling the Somalis across the border? Or does he mean redrawing the boarders, so that the Ogaden becomes part of Somalia? Not all of Ogaden is inhabited by Somalis, though. There are still some speakers of Oromo and other languages. The Muslim Somali are not kinder to the minorities (e.g., the Bantu) in their country than the Ethiopians are to them. The same is true for the Azerbaijanis on both sides of the Iranian–Soviet border, west of the Caspian. They behave quite ruthlessly toward the numerous "pockets" (a bad term, implying they should be removed) of Armenians. The Armenians are by far the oldest surviving race in Asia Minor, and one of the oldest Indo-European nations. Not only should Nagorny Karabakh be restored to the Armenian Republic, but all the land in between it and Armenia proper should be restored to the Armenians as well. The Russians favor the Azerbaijanis because they need their support against Iran; the Armenians will have to stay on the Russian side, surrounded as they are by an angry ocean of Turkic-speakers shouting, "Kill them!" If the 49 percent native Fijians are right in asserting their political supremacy in Fiji, then the Armenians should be given back their original Armenia, more than twice the size of the present Armenian Republic. Here, Dr. Shtromas applies the principle of a nation's original homeland, where they have no other. Right. By the same principle, the Turks should be removed from Cyprus, because they are only immigrants, but the Cypriots have no other country and have lived in Cyprus for 4,000 years. The Muslim Arabs should be removed from Lebanon, and the country should be restored to the Syriac Christians, who are the remainders of the original population of the country.

I know that none of this is realistic, because history does not apply justice but is, at best, the result of enforced compromises between the strongest parties. Yet, if one begins to reason on the basis of justice, one must apply the principle of the first inhabitants, not that of the majority, as Dr. Shtromas does in the case of the Albanians in Kosovo. If a squatter family settles in my house, it is still my house. The Romanians have by far the oldest rights to the old land of Romania, including Bessarabia (now called Moldavia) and Transylvania, because the Magyars, the Slavs, and even the Germans were later invaders. But, as Dr. Shtromas rightly notes, there is a time limit to which one can go back in claiming land once owned by one's ancestors. The Finns could claim Leningrad, and even Moscow, but I think they would settle for Karelia. I still think the Turks ought to return Constantinople to the Greeks as their ancient capital, precisely on the basis of Shtromas's historical principle. After all, the Turks could occupy it in 1922 only because George Curzon, then British foreign secretary, whose troops had occupied Istanbul in 1918, did nothing, since he was inept and lazy, and afraid to act.

I should like to see the list of Shtromas's 1,600 stateless nations; not all of them would make viable states if they were given independence, as anyone can see who looks around in the Third World. Hong Kong, however, does deserve independence, since it has proved itself to be a viable state. We hope that in a future commonwealth of nations, all minorities will be equal.

Jan Knappert

REJOINDER

To the Editor:

Dr. Jan Knappert honored me with an extensive, systematic, and thoughtful review of my paper for which I am very grateful to him. I am especially grateful for his very useful "footnotes" (most importantly, on the ethnic situation in Black Africa, but on other issues, too), providing the reader with some significant additional and not readily available facts pertinent to my discussion. On most of them, I stand corrected or amended.

Dr. Knappert may disagree with me on the nature of fascist ideocracies or on the driving motives behind the actions of ruling elites. My position on these issues has been made sufficiently clear in the paper and I stand by it. Which of us (if anyone) is right each reader will be able to decide for himself without additional explanation. I should perhaps say, however, that, to me, in ideocratic politics, greed for power or material possessions is always a means to an end, not an end in itself. The end always rests in the realm of grand idea, such as justice for one's people or to mankind as a whole. Lenin, Stalin, Hitler, and even the "vain little Napoleon" Mussolini, together with many of their truly idealistic associates, were people driven by that kind of grand idea and also, of course, by an all-devouring personal ambition to go down in history as the great personalities that have put these ideas into political practice. Hence, the impatience, the readiness to wage war, inflict terror, and commit any atrocities that, they thought, would allow them to see the realization of their utopian ends during their own lifetimes.

Knappert challenges my ideas on the possibility of establishing a global commonwealth on the basis of their realism. His questions: "Would Israel or Pakistan give up its atomic bombs?"; "Would Ethiopia or the Sudan . . . or Angola . . . agree to stop armed struggle?"; "Would Ethiopia agree to have its human rights investigated?"; or "Would international decisions on human rights have any effect in Lebanon?," imply a self-evident negative answer that is supposed to prove the utopianism of my propositions. May I assure Dr. Knappert that, under the present circumstances, my answers to these questions would be as negative as his own, and also remind him and the readers that the global commonwealth I am talking about could be built only after the prerequisites for its establishment, as these prerequisites were defined by Immanuel Kant in 1795, were finally realized. The main such prerequisite is each state's entering the global commonwealth (or, in Kant's own terms, *foedus pacificum*), republican (or, in more modern parlance, liberal-democratic) constitutional order. If Angola were a liberal democracy, there surely would be no need for the Popular Movement for the Liberation of Angola (MPLA) and the National Union for the Total Independence of Angola (UNITA) to struggle for power by waging war on each other as, after the 1990 general election, there is no need any longer to conduct by armed struggle the contest for power in Nicaragua. The same applies to Ethiopia, the Sudan, and other places torn by internal wars. Neither should any true liberal democracy be reluctant to allow an investigation of its human rights record, if such a need ever arose.

As for dependent nations, such as Tibet or Biafra mentioned by Knappert, their basic identity and full cultural and other collective human rights can be assured in a liberal democracy even without these nations breaking away from the original state in which they are minorities (by the way, as a result of democratization and federalization, an accommodation, however imperfect and temporary, of such diverse nations as the Ibos, Khausas, and Yorubas in one Nigerian state, has been achieved). But a true liberal democracy must also recognize the fundamental right of each nation to self-determination and, therefore, should not create any unsurmountable obstacles for a dependent nation's separation from the original state.

One could, of course, argue that the idea about liberal democracy becoming universally establishable, let alone established, is in itself utopian. I believe the recent developments in Latin America, South Korea, Eastern Europe, Mongolia, China, and many other non-Western lands give a lie to such a view, to the peculiarly Western condescending attitude toward the "lesser nations" that do not know any better and love to be ruled by ruthless dictators flattering their inferiority complex by petty imperialistic exercises and inflated aggressive-defensive postures. These developments also show that today the whole mankind has already firmly embarked on the road to liberal democracy, thereby transforming the vista of a liberal-democratic world order from an abstract possibility to a concrete probability.

But would Israel and Pakistan, liberal-democratic as they are, agree to give up their nuclear weapons and to submit themselves to a world-order system embodied in a global commonwealth? Yes, under certain conditions in which their national security would be firmly guaranteed, they certainly would. And what could be a better guarantee of their national security than a global commonwealth of which, along with them, the United States and the new democratic Russia were both members, equally committed to the principles of international justice and thus to the equal rights of nations to self-determination and sovereignty?

Knappert is right. In present circumstances my idea of a global commonwealth is absolutely utopian. At no point in my paper have I argued otherwise. On the contrary, throughout my paper I continuously stressed that, before a viable global commonwealth could emerge, all Kantian conditions for its establishment have to be fulfilled; among them, in the first place, the victory of liberal democracy in Russia (and China) without which the world-order system could not acquire its necessary universal foundation, defined by Kant as a republican constitutional order in all member states. But even this will not suffice for establishing a truly viable global commonwealth. For it to become a reality, liberal democracy, once universally established, must in due course assure that no nation continues to hold in bondage another nation and no state amalgamates in its structure any nation against its will. Only a world order in which such political realities will be implemented could be ripe for the establishment of a truly viable global commonwealth based on principles discussed in my paper. Could such a world order ever evolve? If it could not, then the idea of a truly viable global commonwealth, the Kantian *foedus pacificum*, would, indeed, remain forever no more than a utopia. But, if it could evolve, and all the signs indicate that it not only could, but by the end of the twentieth century most likely would evolve, then the Kantian *foedus pacificum* may become the naturally practical reality of the twenty-first century.

Unfortunately, Knappert left out of his otherwise very comprehensive review my discussion of the Kantian prerequisites for the creation of a truly viable global commonwealth and, because of that, most of his perfectly valid critical comments miss their point.

Aleksandras Shtromas

NOTES

1. M. Gorbachev, "Rech' M. S. Gorbacheva v Organizatsii Ob edinenykh Natsiy" (The Speech of M. S. Gorbachev in the United Nations Organization), *Izvestiya*, December 8, 1988, 1.

2. James Rosenau, *The Study of Political Adaptation* (New York: Nichols, 1981).

3. James Rosenau, "Patterned Chaos in Global Life: Structures and Process in the Two Worlds of World Politics," *International Political Science Review* (October 1988): 328.

4. Rosenau, "Patterned Chaos in Global Life," 337.

5. Gorbachev's "new thinking" on world politics has toned down but did not alter that overall goal, ostensibly putting it a step behind what he calls "the vital necessity of preserving world peace and furthering international cooperation in a world order framework" (Gorbachev, "The Speech of M. S. Gorbachev in the United Nations Organization").

6. Morton A. Kaplan, "Relations between East and West During a Regime Crisis and After Regime Change," in Aleksandras Shtromas and Morton A. Kaplan, eds., *The Soviet Union and the Challenge of the Future: Russia and the World*, vol. 4 (New York: Paragon House, 1989), 354.

7. Gorbachev, "The Speech of M. S. Gorbachev in the United Nations Organization," 2.

8. Hedley Bull, *The Anarchical Society: The Study of Order in World Politics* (London: Macmillan, 1977), 243–48.

9. Immanuel Kant, *Perpetual Peace and Other Essays* (Indianapolis: Hackett, 1983), 112.

10. Kant, *Perpetual Peace,* 115.

11. Kaplan, "Relations between East and West," 356–57.

12. Kaplan, "Relations between East and West," 108.

19

What Is Peace and How Could It Be Achieved?

Aleksandras Shtromas

WHAT IS PEACE?

Peace by its sheer logical nature is a negative concept. Its definition usually begins with the words "the absence of." It could be the absence of either war or conflict, violence or exploitation, as well as of any other similar and positively definable condition, but it is always "absence," not "presence."

The most widespread definition of peace is that of *absence of war*. It is, however, an ill-founded definition because it proceeds from the wrong assumption that peace and war are self-sufficient and mutually exclusive concepts, which they are not. In fact, as Jean Jacques Rousseau, William Penn, Immanuel Kant, Karl Marx, Herbert Spencer, Barthélemy De Ligt, and other major thinkers on the subject have strongly emphasized, historically peace was so far only a truce or cease-fire type interval between wars whose absence was yet never permanent and thus, in fact, nonexistent. Politically, both peace and war are thus referring not to the essence of a relationship between various political actors but merely to its form, to the sort of instruments employed by parties involved in such a relationship.

Reprinted from *International Journal on World Peace* 12, no. 1 (March 1995): 15–58, with a comment by Gordon L. Anderson and a rejoinder by the author.

Karl von Clausewitz, by defining war as the continuation of the same policy by different means, expressed it all in a nutshell. Actually, conquest, subjugation, and long-term enslavement of peoples can sometimes be achieved and perpetuated without ever resorting to a full-fledged armed conflict or, which is one and the same thing, war—peacefully so to speak (if peace is defined as merely the absence of war). This was, for example, the case with Austria's Anschluss by Hitler's Germany just before World War II or with the incorporation of the three Baltic states into Stalin's Soviet Union in the beginning of that war, as well as with innumerable other similar cases of recent and ancient history, all of which by any standards amount to a perversion of the very meaning of peace, though theoretically remain compatible with its definition as the absence of war.

Realizing that war and peace are concepts relative to one another and both dependent on the much wider concept of conflict, many peace-thinkers, and peace-dreamers too, thought that peace should be defined not simply as absence of war but as the *absence of conflict* altogether. What this definition postulates is the possibility of establishing at some point in the future a conflictless Utopia. But exactly because of its utopianism, because humans, being what they are, will always differ from each other in their views, opinions, interests, values, goals, and the like, and thus, if free, will inevitably engage in conflicts of various kinds, this definition is practically unviable. Such a definition is actually capable only of discrediting the whole idea of a peaceful world, and not only because of it being so unrealistic but, in the first place, because of being extremely dangerous. The very idea of a conflictless world is, alas, contrary to, and incompatible with, that of freedom and the preservation of inalienable human rights, which is freedom's main foundation. It is either the one or the other. *Tertium non datur*—the third option, as the Romans used to say, is not given. For the whole concept of human rights is centered around the liberty of people to pursue different goals, to hold different views, to establish for themselves different priorities (thus, also, different sets of interests), which usually are in competition with, and sometimes even in direct opposition to, one another. And there is obviously no substance in the liberty to differ and disagree if that liberty is not extended to people's ability to stand up and engage in struggle for the implementation of their different, and sometimes conflicting, views, goals, and interests.

The proponents of the theory defining peace as the absence of conflict bluntly refuse to recognize the existence of the unbridgeable discrepancy between imposed conflictlessness and freedom. They assume that conflicts of views, goals, and interests are expressions of sheer selfishness that deserve no better than ruthless suppression and unhesitant subordination to what this particular brand of theorists would deem, and prescribe as, the superordinate common interests of mankind. Hence, they strive for the institution by any means in their power of a world order that accords with their own vision of imposed conflictlessness, hoping that such an imposed order, even if at first coercive, will with the passage of time groom the people to accept it as the superior moral and political reality, the only one such reality worthy of truly conscious human beings. What these theorists fail to realize is that people will never willingly acquiesce to any variety of conflictlessness depriving them of both their individuality and natural collective identities, that although the people's real intentions and genuinely motivated actions could be temporarily suppressed by oppressive authority, their objectives, if not properly fulfilled, will in fact never be abandoned or forgotten but simply conserved and relegated, so to speak, to cold storage, and that, consequently, to enhance peace by denying the people their political freedom and basic human rights is a futile, furthermore, an absolutely impossible undertaking. Historical experience has invariably proved that thesis, most recently in the cases of the collapse of the USSR and Yugoslavia. In view of that experience, it should become apparent to everyone, including the advocates of the conflictless theory of peace, that any, even a relatively long-lasting, denial of freedom and human rights, far from automatically eradicating the causes of conflicts and organically inculcating the habit of the "peaceful" status quo, inevitably produces only more animosity, more bitterness, more determination to use violence in response to the violent suppression of peoples' genuine striving and thus, in the end, breeds more conflict, more unpeacefulness, more war. This is to say that conflicts subdued by denial of freedom and human rights are not resolved thereby; on the contrary, by being forcibly made latent, they are only grossly aggravated. In the long run they inevitably erupt and do so with vengeance, often provoking new civil and international wars and thus jeopardizing peace more than this would have been the case before their forceful suppression.

Hence, far from enhancing peace, imposition of conflictlessness is the surest way not to peace but to more conflict, more trouble, more real danger of an outbreak of an all-out war.

There is yet another school of thought defining peace as the *absence of violence*. Conflict is recognized here as not interfering with peace provided there is no violence used by the parties involved in the conflict and solutions for that conflict are sought exclusively by nonviolent (i.e., peaceful) means. It would be a fine definition indeed if people advocating it would be able to agree about what they mean by nonviolence. In some peace-research works the term violence is extended beyond all recognition by qualifications like "structural" (which includes in the concept of violence almost every coercive act of the state) or by violence's equation with any kind of real or imaginary injustice, such as, for example, the economic exploitation of the working classes, which leads to the conclusion that the abolition of capitalism and imperialism (even violently accomplished) should be regarded as a prerequisite for peace and nonviolence. Leaving aside the unacceptable political bias of these views, the very idea about the legitimacy of using violent means for achieving nonviolent ends or, using Rousseau's famous dictum, of "waging a war to end all wars," seems to be inconsistent on purely logical grounds.

The interpretation of the term "violence" is the key to providing the negative concept of peace with a positive content. And I believe that the best thing to do in this respect is to refrain from all sorts of extended interpretations and qualifications of this term altogether. One should just recognize violence for what it is. And, according to the dictionaries, "violence is exertion of any *physical force* so as to injure or abuse" (emphasis added) or, in other words, "*unlawful* exercise of physical force" (emphasis added). The maximal extension of this term that the dictionaries allow, is "*intimidation* by exhibition of the latter" (emphasis added)—no more than that. From that, one could proceed to thinking about the achievement of nonviolence and there is perhaps no better way to do that than critically, in the Kantian fashion, to follow the ideas of Thomas Hobbes.

Peace, when being defined in negative terms as the absence of violence or nonviolence in the straightforward terms given above, should then in positive terms mean the establishment of an effectively working system of authoritative conflict settlement and resolution, which could reliably efface the possibility (and in the final end the need itself) for resorting to the violent resolution of conflicts. In other words, peace as nonviolence requires putting an end to the state of nature among nations by the establishment of what Immanuel Kant defined as the *foedus pacificum* or the League of Peace. That is in fact how peace was conceived by the classical peace theory of Hugo Grotius and Charles Irénée Abbé de Saint Pierre and developed into a consistent and comprehensive project of a world order system by Immanuel Kant in *Perpetual Peace* (1795). Indeed, the necessity of establishing the League of Peace, as the only adequate condition guaranteeing a perpetually peaceful world order, was recognized not only by the classical but by the more modern peace theories, too. Claude-Henri de Saint-Simon, Auguste Comte, Pierre-Joseph Proudhon, Karl Marx, Herbert Spencer, Jean de Bloch, Norman Angell, as well as almost anyone else who tried to work in the field of peace theory, each on different terms and by different arguments, came to the same conclusion that peace acquires its adequate meaning only in the form of a global commonwealth which can truly become the League of Peace by way of subordinating itself to a single body of laws authoritatively regulating the behavior of its members with regard to both their own subjects and to one another as otherwise independent political entities.

In order to avoid any misunderstandings, it is necessary to stress that Kant's League of Peace has nothing to do with the idea of a world state. On the contrary, Kant explicitly, in no uncertain terms, opposes that idea saying that a world government—an institution superior in its sovereign rights to the national governments—is incompatible with peace among nations, which, thus deprived of their sovereignty will inevitably strive to regain it by all means in their power. According to him, the federation of free states forming the League of Peace (*foedus pacificum*) in accordance with the Second Definitive article 2 of Kant's proposed Treaty on Perpetual Peace, "would be a federation of *nations*, but it must not be a nation consisting of nations." "The latter," he explains, "would be contradictory, for in every nation there exists the relation of *ruler* (legislator) to *subject* (those who obey, the people); however, many nations in a single nation would constitute only a single nation, which contradicts our assumption (since we are . . . weighting the rights of *nations* in relation to one another, rather than fusing them into a single nation)."[1] What Kant really projects in his *foedus pacificum* is a multitude of fully sovereign nation-states voluntarily submitting themselves to a single body of laws in accordance with which conflicts and disputes between them could be properly either arbitrated or adjudicated and, as a result, authoritatively resolved. As we see, Kant strongly believes that a single world government is incompatible with the natural division of mankind into nations and, hence, with peace which could become perpetual only by the League and every nation-state within it meticulously observing and unconditionally honoring the inviolable principle of national independence and freedom. Kant's League of Peace is thus a voluntary federation of free nations that retain their own sovereign statehood, which they merely further extend and consolidate by acting together on issues of mutual concern but beyond the reach of any one particular nation-state's ability properly to handle, let alone reliably solve. Among such issues, the primary significance is accorded by Kant to authoritative implementation of mutually agreed principles of international justice and the provision, in accordance with these principles, of firm guarantees ensuring each nation's security as well as the equality of them all in their sovereign status and rights.

THE PREREQUISITES FOR PEACE

It goes without saying that the basic prerequisite for the establishment of such a global commonwealth is the ability of the participating states to agree on the basic principles of politics and justice on which it is to be founded. It was axiomatic for Kant that the establishment of the League of Peace can be a feasible task only to states that have adopted, and proved their ability stably to live under, a republican constitutional order. According to Kant, the first definitive article of his proposed Treaty on Perpetual Peace, the one that lays the basic foundation for the creation of a viable League of Peace, shall establish that the constitution of each state (founding or entering such a League) has to be republican. Kant defines a republican constitution as one that, "first, . . . accords with the principles of the *freedom* of the members of a society (as men), second, . . . accords with the principles of the *dependence* of everyone on a single common legislation (as subjects), and, third, . . . accords with the law of the *equality* of them all (as citizens)."[2] States that have accepted and live by the same basic principles of liberty and human rights encompassed into the republican order will have no difficulty, in Kant's view, to extend these principles to the supranational level and build the global commonwealth on their foundation, too, thus making it effectively into a League of Peace.

The idea that perpetual peace is the natural result of the republican con-stitutional order established by the member-states for themselves and ex-tended by their mutual consent to the global commonwealth has become since Kant a commonplace in liberal political theory. One of its strongest proponents was Herbert Spencer. According to Spencer, world society de-velops through two consecutive phases—the militant and industrial ones. In the militant phase force is the main instrument of societies' achievement and therefore war for such societies is not simply usual, not simply a nor-mal state of relations among competing political entities, but plays a truly dominant, moreover a determinant, role in their existence and develop-ment. In the industrial phase, however, war gradually loses its primary role, as it is not force anymore but economic production and exchange that be-comes the main instrument of industrial societies' achievement. Spencer recognizes of course that this process is not straightforward and that some industrial societies, his native England with its colonial wars in the first place, are strongly beholden to their militant past and only too often lapse into aggressive wars. Spencer calls such lapses "rebarbarization,"[3] but does not see it as a lasting, let alone permanent, phenomenon. "Social evolution throughout the future, like social evolution throughout the past," he writes, "must while producing step after step higher societies, leave outstanding many lower . . . but . . . in time to come, a federation of the highest nations, exercising supreme authority . . . , may, by forbidding wars between any of its constituent nations, put an end to the rebarbarization which is continu-ally undoing civilization." He then concludes by saying that "[w]hen this peace-maintaining federation has been formed, there may be effectual progress towards that equilibrium between constitution and condition—between inner faculties and outer requirements—implied by the final stage of human evolution."[4]

Ludwig von Mises, the great Austrian economist, follows in Spencer's foot-steps. For him, worldwide capitalism and liberalism provide the necessary and sufficient foundation for achieving perpetual peace. Writing thirty years after Spencer, von Mises, without denying the persistent ascendancy of "re-barbarization" (he calls it the expression of "transient atavistic impulses to-ward plunder and violence"), states that "by and large, one can say of the nations . . . that today inhabit central and western Europe and America that the mentality that Herbert Spencer called 'militaristic' has been displaced by that to which he gave the name 'industrial.'[5] But, he adds, the insurance of perpetual peace without any further lapses into "re-barbarization" demands "nothing less than the unqualified, unconditional acceptance of liberalism. Liberal thinking must permeate all nations, liberal principles must pervade all political institutions, if the prerequisites for peace are to be created and the causes of war eliminated. As long as nations cling to protective tariffs, im-migration barriers, compulsory education, interventionism, and *etatism*, new conflicts capable of breaking out any time into open warfare will continually arise to plague mankind."[6]

As for Kant and Spencer, so also for von Mises, the worldwide triumph of liberalism is inevitably going to result in the creation of a global commonwealth "that unites all nations on an equal basis." Von Mises believes that for such a global commonwealth to become the League of Peace, all the demands of the liberal mind would have to be met by its constitution. The liberal, von Mises continues, "sees the law of each nation as subordinate to international law and that is why he demands supranational tribunals and administrative authorities to assure peace among nations in the same way that the judicial and executive organs of each country are charged with the maintenance of peace within its own territory."[7] Even stronger than Spencer, let alone Kant, von Mises stresses the centrality for the successful establishment of a liberal world order—an order alone able to ensure perpetual peace—of the institution of private ownership of all means of production, exchange, and transportation, as well as of politically unrestricted free trade. When "the private ownership of the means of production prevails everywhere, an important motive for waging war has already been excluded," he writes, and further explains that this is so because in that situation "political institutions . . . render the transference of sovereignty over a territory from one government to another a matter of least possible significance, involving no advantage or disadvantage for anyone." This is reinforced by free trade that renders all state borders symbolic and makes all the political problems of possession and control obsolete. "A capitalist world organized on liberal principles," he concludes, "knows no separate 'economic zones.' In such a world, the whole of earth's surface forms a single economic territory."[8]

The fact that the liberal states, their continuous lapses into "rebarbarization" notwithstanding, do not wage wars against each other and tend not simply to cooperate but also create supranational bodies taking care of their common problems on a regular basis—the so-called IGOs and INGOs, the prototypes of the global commonwealth the theorists quoted above envisaged—has been also proved empirically.

According to the research on 357 wars that were fought during 1816–1982, conducted by J. David Singer and Melvin Small[9] and, separately, by Rudolph Rummel,[10] only two wars out of those 357 had democracies fighting one another. And even these two wars were highly untypical. One was the Roman Republic War of 1849 where the briefly democratic French Second Republic fought the newly established Roman Republic, helping the pope to re-establish his authority over the Roman State (which, in the view of the leaders of that Republic, was France's, as a Catholic nation's, duty). The second was the war ten Western democracies declared against another democracy, Finland, when the latter had allied itself with Nazi Germany to fight the war against the USSR in order to regain control of the territories the USSR forcefully took from Finland in 1940, after the conclusion of the Winter War initiated by the aggressive intervention of the USSR into Finland. Actually, the war on the part of the ten democracies against Finland was purely formal, in the sense that there was never a combat engagement between the armed forces of

these democracies and Finland, and because the declaration of war was necessitated by treaty obligations between these ten democracies and their ally
in the anti-Hitler coalition, the USSR, which is to say that this war had not
been provoked by any disagreements or hostilities between the ten democracies and Finland *per se*.

Although crucially important and absolutely necessary, liberal democracy
and capitalism can in themselves be sufficient to ensure perpetual peace only
if they include into their basic foundations yet another important prerequisite
of perpetual peace—the recognition and unwavering application of the right to
self-determination, which it would be wrong to take for granted. Liberal democracy as such does not automatically provide for the full implementation of
that right because it is first and foremost the rule of the majority, and the peoples seeking self-determination are usually minorities. As minorities, they may
enjoy in a liberal democracy, in addition to the equal rights of citizenship, certain special rights of religious, cultural, and even territorial autonomy, but, as a
rule, they are not entitled to secede from the state under whose sovereignty
they live. Of course, in a democracy, the minority peoples may air their grievances and even more or less freely (within the limits of law) advocate secession.
For that purpose, they may organize political parties and pressure groups; but,
being no more than minorities, they are hardly ever successful. The inertia of
statehood established on an integral territorial space, and the state's sovereignty
over that space protected by international law proclaiming the inviolability of
the state's borders, prevent the stateless peoples of the democratic states from
fully realizing their "inalienable" right to self-determination and sovereignty.

Because of that, it is on the whole doubtful whether multinational nation-
states could be fully liberal-democratic. The multinational state's dominant
nation, with regard to that same state's minority nation(s), inevitably constitutes itself as a constant and immutable ruling majority using the state's democratic institutions as an instrument of that particular majority's dictatorship.
For Aristotle, a democracy in which a majority rules in its own interests was
one of the most perverse political regimes. James Madison's primary occupation, when drafting the U.S. Constitution, was the prevention of formation
within the new American union-state of any constant majority. He clearly understood that the formation and consolidation of such a majority will mean
the end of liberty and the institution of the most dangerous and oppressive
tyranny—the tyranny of the majority.

In this sense, only the single nation is an entity naturally capable of establishing a true liberal-democratic order. Being an organically cohesive body of
people, it will strive to accommodate within its given unity as fully and as
comprehensively as possible the diversity of various group interests existing
within the nation and also the widest spectrum of ideas and programs aimed
at the best defense and enhancement of the national interest. In other words,
the Madisonian system of democratic rule exercised by majorities forming
themselves as flexible and changeable coalitions of various minorities is to its
full extent practically realizable only in a single-nation's state (which, no

doubt, the United States always has been and still remains). And, for the same reasons, only a single-nation's state can provide a maximum body of rights to its national minorities (differing from a nation, which is an ethnic group with a clear territorial identity, a national minority is an ethnic group that, having voluntarily chosen to be a part of another nation's state's citizenry and having been accepted into that citizenry, lives in that "other" nation's state without claiming any of that state's territory as its own). All this is to say that, by its very nature, the nation is a liberal-democratic entity, while even the institutionally most democratic multinational states are with regard to these states' minority nations oppressively dictatorial regimes. Of course there are exceptions that, as it is usually the case, only prove the rule formulated above. The nations of the UK, for example, stay together in one state because they have freely chosen to do so. The referenda conducted in Northern Ireland and Scotland (1979) on the issue of devolution from the UK have proved this to be an undeniable fact. Sometimes, people belonging to different nations develop in the course of history a supranational identity overriding their particular national identities, which allow them freely to form multinational states on the basis of such an overriding identity. The most telling example here is, of course, Switzerland. In other words, it is not at all necessary to get all nations as a matter of course into separate states, but it is absolutely imperative to grant all nations without exception the absolute and inalienable right to self-determination. It is by the way of using this right that every nation could freely decide for itself whether it wished to continue the historical tradition of staying in one state with the other nation(s) of that same state or would prefer to separate from its old state association and form for itself a new sovereign nation-state. This decision in a truly liberal democratic order should remain in the exclusive domain of the nation concerned and of no one else.

It was again Kant who before anyone else consistently argued for the right of all nations, big and small alike, to self-determination and equal sovereignty, seeing in it, along with the republican constitutional order, another most essential prerequisite for perpetual peace. According to the preliminary article 2 of his proposed Treaty on Perpetual Peace, such peace could not be achieved as long as there remains in the world a nation ruled by another nation without that former (ruled) nation's explicit consent. This idea was shared also by Spencer and von Mises, although the latter argued that the right to self-determination should be accorded not only to nations but to "inhabitants of every territory [who should be able freely] to decide on the state to which they wish to belong."[11]

THE KANTIAN *FOEDUS PACIFICUM* (LEAGUE OF PEACE). PURPOSES AND FUNCTIONS

The first task that the League of Peace should undertake is to outlaw the use of violence in international conflicts as well as in domestic disputes over autonomous and sovereign rights of peoples occupying a certain territorial entity within the single state's boundaries. This is not a simple task because it implies the right of the league to interfere into any armed struggle wherever it flared up, if necessary in a forceful manner, in order immediately to stop it; and, in order to be able to exercise that right effectively, the league should be in possession of an armed force superior to that of the warring parties, whoever those might be. When armed struggle is stopped, the league should be in the position to initiate under its auspices the process of direct negotiations between the parties to the conflict or, with their consent, provide for arbitration or adjudication of the issues that cause conflict between them.

It goes without saying that the process of settling such conflicts and disputes could never be properly effective and prompt without having in place an elaborate and consistent Code of World Laws voluntarily accepted as the supreme law by all the members of the league—a law, according to which such conflicts could be justly and authoritatively settled. The present international law unfortunately does not provide a sufficiently valid foundation for such a Code of World Laws, although, no doubt, most of its present provisions could be incorporated into that code as long as they are made consistent among themselves and with the guiding principles of the code, turning the latter into a noncontradictory legal document that could be effectively and unambiguously used by a proper court of law.[12]

International law of today recognizes, for example, the right of nations to self-determination and, at the same time, enshrines the principle of territorial integrity and the inviolability of borders of the sovereign states existing today. These two norms contradict one another, for the world, which is inhabited by about 1,800 nations, is divided into only about 190 states. The legal protection of the territorial integrity and inviolability of borders of these states practically excludes the right of the stateless nations living within them to use their right to self-determination fully, that is, to the extent of accomplishing secession from the extant state(s) under whose authority they happen to live. Hence, under present international law, the stateless nations are practically deprived of their right to self-determination, which renders that right, as far as these nations are concerned, purely declarative and formal, void of any real contents—a fact that was so eloquently exemplified by the reaction of the world community of sovereign states to the Russian military invasion into the Chechen republic, which had the audacity unilaterally to proclaim its independence from Russia. For the world's states—including the United States—this invasion was no more than a purely internal affair of the Russian state, and if there was any issue that could get the international community concerned in connection with that invasion, it was the violation of human rights that Russia may have been committing with regard to its own citizens in the course of the invasion. This was so, because Russia is under an international obligation to observe these rights, but, by virtue of the primacy of the principle of territorial integrity, whatever else happens within her territory is supposed to be a matter of exclusively internal concern for Russia's government.

In a Code of World Laws, such a contradiction would become unsustainable. The legal structure of that code presuming a strict internal consistency between its norms would demand that in the code a clear choice is made between according primacy either to the right of self-determination or to the right of the extant states to maintain their territorial integrity within the current borders. It goes without saying that in a World Code of Laws acceptable to a League of Peace, which is to be based on liberal-democratic/republican principles, the right to self-determination would have to take precedence over the right of the established state to maintain its territorial integrity, a position just opposite to the one that international law has practically taken today, without, however, making this position legally explicit.

Having established the right to self-determination as the prima facie case, the Code of World Laws will encounter yet another task—the task of elaborating legal norms regulating the resolution of territorial disputes between the nation-states—which the extant international law does not begin to solve at all, even in contradictory terms, as it does with regard to the right to self-determination. At present, international law accepts the historically and demographically based arguments for claiming sovereignty over a disputed territory as either equally valid or, again, as subordinated to the principle of territorial integrity of the extant states as it is shaped by the internationally recognized states' borders, that is, tends to accept the status quo as the legitimate reality, whatever the arguments to the contrary. In a World Code of Laws adopted by a liberal democratic/republican League of Peace, such a non-discriminatory attitude to the validity of arguments for making territorial claims could not be sustained.

The Code of World Laws will have to establish in an unambiguous fashion which claim—the demographic or the historical—has primacy over the other. It is quite apparent that, if the principle of self-determination is to be made consistent by that Code, the choice would inevitably have to go to the demographic factor as to the one providing the prima facie case and taking precedence over the historical factor. This was exactly the argument made by von Mises when he argued the necessity of according the right of self-determination to people of every territorial entity, not only to nations.

The Code of World Laws would have to introduce a reshaped attitude to international protection of human rights, too. At present, international law treats the rights of territorial peoples within the state under the overall umbrella of minority rights, that is on a par with the rights of groups associated by common cultural, linguistic, religious, and similar affinities, totally disregarding the territorial dimension of the problem of rights. What the Code of World Laws would have to do is to make a strict distinction between minority rights and the rights of territorial peoples to self-determination, including secession, as the right of that particular territory's majority.[13] Actually, the conflicts and disputes over rights of territorial self-determination and self-government, as all other cases about territorial issues, should be placed under one jurisdiction, whether such conflicts and disputes are between states or within-state, whereas the issues concerning individual human rights and the collective rights of the minorities should belong to an entirely different jurisdiction, specifically and exclusively concerned with personal rights, both individual and collective.

The League of Peace, along with the Code of World Laws, will have to adopt—of course, as in the previous cases, also by consensus of all its members—a universally valid Code of Human Rights. The foundations for this code are already laid down in the Universal Declaration of Human Rights adopted by the UN in 1948 and the two supplementary covenants of 1966— one On Civil and Political Rights and the other, On Social, Economic, and Cultural Rights. These documents, in the context of a League of Peace, should of course be made consistent, too, and not only within their own provisions but even more so with the basic principles of liberal democracy/republicanism by: a) strictly separating the issue of self-determination from this code and fully transferring that issue to the Code of World Laws; b) removing numerous restrictive clauses and stipulations from the present, often conditional and ambiguous, formulations of rights; c) substantially revising the Covenant On Social, Economic, and Cultural Rights in order to make it fully compatible with the principles of a liberal democratic world order and then transforming that covenant into a Statement of Intent, thus separating it from the Code of Human Rights altogether.

With the Code of World Laws in place, an Arbitration Committee and an International Court would have to be formed within the League of Peace to settle territorial conflicts and disputes, including the intrastate disputes over territorial peoples' self-determination and secession from the state under the authority of which they at present live. Under a different jurisdiction, that of the World Court on Human Rights, the League of Peace will act as the highest judicial institution, pronouncing judgments on disputes related to the rights of individuals and various minorities.

Once created, the global commonwealth will hardly be limited to acting solely as the League of Peace. There are some other issues that the peoples of the world could take care of more efficiently by acting together on a global level than either acting separately or not acting at all.

In the *first* place, the global commonwealth is likely to get the mandate for establishing its exclusive authority over issues and areas that are outside the domain of national sovereignty and that naturally belong to the sovereignty of mankind as a whole. The issues and areas that the international law treats at present as those of "equal opportunity" for all nations are, of course, the first to come under the full and exclusive sovereignty of mankind, embodied in the institutions of the global commonwealth. Among them are, for example, the world ocean and the international seabed with their resources; the outer space and the international territories, such as Antarctica.

Secondly, the global commonwealth may take full authority over the issues and areas that, at present, are inadequately handled by various weak international agencies, acting sometimes in concurrence, but more often in competition or even in confrontation with, the much more powerful nation-states pursuing their own particular self-interests. Among such issues and areas are economic aid and development, inclusive of the whole task of bridging the North–South divide; protection from, and relief in the cases of, famine, epidemics, natural calamities, and other disasters; assistance to, and resettlement of, the refugees, and so forth.

Thirdly, the global commonwealth will almost certainly be endowed with supreme authority, inclusive of coordination of efforts by nation-states and nongovernmental organizations, over such naturally global issues as the protection of the natural environment and solution of other problems related to human ecology; development, management, and regulation of safety standards in the fields of nuclear, laser, and solar energy; development and management of demographic problems (e.g., of rational use of manpower resources); international policing, especially in combating globally spread crimes (e.g., terrorism and drug trafficking); and coordination of, and supervision over, some globally vital areas of research, in the first place in the fields of genetics, cerebral biology, combat of killer diseases (cancer, AIDS, etc.), organ transplants, advanced energetics (inclusive of the development of new and alternative sources of energy), and information technology.

Fourthly, the global commonwealth would also have to establish a World Bank, emitting global currency (which should serve as a standard for national currencies) and concerned with prevention of or, if this failed, with providing remedies to actual financial crises.

None of the above functions would transform the global commonwealth into a world government because the performance of these functions does not take over any of the functions that the national governments can successfully or economically perform on their own. Nor does the performance of any of these functions require the subordination of national governments to the institutions of the global commonwealth or in any way interfere with the national sovereignty of the member-states. On the contrary, the execution of the global commonwealth of the sovereignty of mankind in the naturally global areas listed above should greatly assist the member-states in carrying out their sovereign authority to a much fuller extent and in an optimally effective manner.

The sovereign rights of member-states in the global commonwealth will be limited much more severely than in the cases mentioned above by the arrangements that were described previously and that would empower the commonwealth to act as the League of Peace. The member-states would lose in such an arrangement the right of going to war or using any other violent or coercive means against both other states and self-determination minded territorial peoples acting within the borders of the member-states themselves— a right that is considered to be the ultimate expression of the state's sovereignty and the surrendering of which is perceived as being tantamount to the surrender of national sovereignty itself. Even more severe infringement upon national sovereignty would be the member-states' duty to submit themselves to a supranational system of justice, not only in their relations with other states, but also in the ways they treat their own citizens. Further, the member-states would have to accept interference of a supranational military force into any armed struggle in which they may be engaged.

There is, however, nothing unprecedentedly novel in the states' self-limitation of their national sovereignty. By entering into mutually beneficial international treaties and covenants, states constantly limit their sovereign rights and, when such treaties and covenants are duly ratified by them, the provisions of these treaties and covenants acquire in the hierarchy of the states' laws a supreme status—even the provisions of the states' constitutional law have to be subordinated to the international laws ratified by them, with the former being brought into strict concordance with the latter.[14]

Analogous procedures would be applied to the arrangements instituting a global commonwealth. Before any of the universal world codes would become legally valid for the member-states, they would have to be ratified by those states and made a part of their national legal systems. The same goes for all the other provisions related to the institution of the global commonwealth, which could not be put in any other form but that of international treaties or covenants.

As is the case with every other international treaty or covenant, states participating in a treaty-based global commonwealth will retain their right freely to terminate their association with it and thus restore their full sovereignty whenever they choose to do so. Furthermore, the expulsion from the commonwealth (and thus restitution of full sovereignty) will be the ultimate sanction the commonwealth could apply to member-states refusing to obey the decisions of its judicial institutions.

The decisions of the world courts would also be the only ones that the states entering into the global commonwealth would have to undertake to obey unconditionally and that would thus be binding on them. All other decisions of global institutions, before being implemented in the domain controlled by a member-state, would have to receive an explicit agreement of that state. Concrete decisions of global institutions, such, for example, as those on building pollution control centers or establishing energy-testing sites on a member-state's territory, would require as a prerequisite a contract between the global institution making the decision and the member-state agreeing to have this decision implemented on its territory. The decisions of global institutions establishing general norms, in order to become laws applicable in the domain controlled by member states, would have to receive proper ratification by the respective competent authorities of these states, too.

The legislation passed by the global commonwealth, even if it is on issues over which the commonwealth has exclusive authority, should not be made directly and automatically applicable in the domains controlled by member-states, as this is at present the case in most of the extant federal states (e.g., the United States). Before any new norms of global legislation (for example, amendments to the universal codes of world laws) could be applied to a member-state, that member-state would have to pass these norms into laws itself first, thus making them—with appropriate corrections, exclusions, and amendments—its own law. The law would then have to be applied by the member-state or, within its jurisdiction, by the world courts, too, in the version in which it was passed by that particular state. This is to say that even in global commonwealth, supranational legislation and other kinds of legal and political decision-making affecting a member-state could become legally valid in that state only after they have become the laws or decisions of that member-state itself.

Such distribution of decision-making authority is probably the only way harmoniously to combine national sovereignty with the sovereignty of mankind. As long as the last word in legislation and decision-making generally belongs not to the global or any supranational but to national authority, national sovereignty, however self-limited by any supranational arrangements it may be, remains a valid and practical concept. It is rather indicative in this respect that the first radical step taken by the Baltic republics of the USSR to reassert their national sovereignty, without as yet formally breaking away from the Soviet Union completely, consisted in the passing by the respective supreme councils of these republics of constitutional amendments, according to which All-Union laws become valid in the republic only after they have been explicitly approved by the republican legislature, and in the form in which the republican legislator had passed them.

The viability of a global commonwealth based on such loose ties between its constituent parts, and with so much weight put on preservation within its boundaries of the traditionally divisive national sovereignty, depends mainly on the ability of the member-states of this commonwealth generally to agree about the basic principles and laws on which it is to be founded. To quote from an earlier work: "There are several conditions to be attached to the creation of a global commonwealth if it is to implement a genuinely peaceful world order: (a) the recognition of equal human rights for all individuals and nations of the world must be its basic principle; (b) a voluntary consensus of all nations, with no element of imposition or coercion within it, must be the source of its creation; (c) a negotiating procedure leading to a common agreement must be adopted for the elaboration of the Commonwealth's constitution and basic laws."[15]

Only if these conditions are fulfilled, can the states forming a global commonwealth see in it, not an impediment to, but an unqualified advantage for, successful pursuit and enhancement of their particular national interests. Even the clauses concerning the globalization of military security, which seem so substantially to limit the sovereign rights of the member-states in using their military power for the achievement of otherwise unobtainable national goals, would work out as a great advantage for the large majority of weaker nations, which would be thus, on the one hand, protected by the global commonwealth from attacks and assaults of stronger nations and, on the other, enabled to achieve their legitimate national goals by means of international arbitration or adjudication, exercised in accordance with generally agreed principles and rules of international justice.

All the above was to say that the ideas on the purposes and functions of a global commonwealth acting as the League of Peace presented in this essay were consciously designed so as to be fully consistent with the Kantian methodology in denying the thus conceived global commonwealth the potential of ever turning into a world government, and according the central place in the world system's edifice to the individual human being and the nation.

CONCLUDING REMARKS

The twentieth century, which was unleashed in 1914 by World War I, was the age of ideology, that is, an age of active search for panaceas against the terrible ills of mankind in globally conceived universal creeds, such as communism and fascism; it was, accordingly, also the age of defense and struggle against aggressive undertakings of the various communist and fascist movements and regimes, and of resistance to totalitarian temptations these movements and regimes quite forcefully propelled around the world. If the end of World War II in 1945 saw the disappearance from the world's stage of the fascist ideological challenge, the failure of the communist-restorationist putsch in Moscow in August 1991 did the same to Marxist communism, to that ideological challenge which was the first to appear and the last to crumble. Thus the anticommunist revolutions in the USSR and East and Central Europe, which started in 1989 and were triumphantly concluded with the collapse of communist rule in the Soviet Union, and with the Soviet Union itself being formally dissolved in December 1991, virtually brought the twentieth century to conclusion. The twenty-first century that then began is bound to be the age of nationalism—the age of liberation of territorial peoples who want to secede from the states they are at present incorporated into against their will.

Nationalism is not an ideology—it is an assertion of the natural collective identity of every people and of each individual within it. There is nothing ideological in seeking for one's nation an appropriate place within the global community of nations, although, since nationalisms very often clash, the nations that are parties to such clashes need to subscribe to certain universally acceptable democratic principles of international justice, which would provide the necessary foundation for presenting their particular claims as fair and based on universal right.

Since, in my view, the twenty-first century is going to be marked by much national unrest, rebellion, and warfare, it is now time for the community of free and democratic nations to initiate the work of introducing such norms of international law, which could be able to prevent all kinds of national warfare and provide for the settlement of national conflicts in accordance with that law. As I said above, every form of violence used in any international or intrastate dispute should be outlawed in the first place. The NATO military force could already now be dedicated to the authoritative enforcement of peace, wherever violence is going to erupt. The reaction of the international community, especially of the United States, to the Iraqi invasion of Kuwait should serve here as the appropriate mode. But what is going to be the next step after the use of violence in a conflict is forcefully terminated? Restoration of the *status quo ante,* as was the case in the Gulf War, will in most cases not suffice, as it would just freeze the conflict without eliminating its cause. So, then what? Protracted negotiations? Yes, of course, but such negotiations would be much more effective and productive, if they could be conducted in the form of arbitration and based on clearly formulated norms of international law; and if the points of that law were to come into dispute, authoritative adjudication would be in order.

Of course, with the passage of time, the problem of establishing a reliable and peaceful way for conflict resolution will most likely be instituted in a similar manner, even if the community of democratic nations will fail in timely fashion to undertake such an initiative. Peoples engaged in national conflicts, sick and tired of all the endless upheavals and constant bloodletting, will sooner or later—however grudgingly—have to come to an agreement by themselves on some universal principles of peaceful conflict resolution and thus finally establish a truly peaceful world order, that is, such a universal system that would be based on the recognition and resolute defense of inalienable human rights of both the individual and the nation, which, after all, is nothing but a collective personality, and by that also a uniquely individual entity. But why wait for these developments to take their natural, protracted, and costly course, if the buildup of the League of Peace could be initiated by the democratic nations of the world without any delays whatsoever? This is the question the leaders of NATO and the Organization for Security and Cooperation in Europe (OSCE)—organizations in which the United States has the decisive voice—should start addressing when elaborating their political strategies for the future.

COMMENT

Professor Shtromas has argued for a League of Peace based on sovereign nation-states rather than the existing territorial states. His article makes us aware of a major problem that needs correction before we can achieve world peace. This is that the existing territorial states that make up our

---

This comment by Gordon L. Anderson, Secretary General of the Professors World Peace Academy, is an adaptation of a paper presented at the National Conference on Peacemaking and Conflict Resolution at the Minneapolis Hilton and Tower, May 29, 1995, titled "The United Nations and the Problem of Sovereignty."

present world are not natural nor their borders sacrosanct. In fact, most of these borders were imposed by non-peaceful conquest. His solution is a mechanism for the creation of "nation-states" in which national groups can pursue their own genuine national interests. This comment will not question his concerns about the suppression of national minorities, which are rightfully voiced, and he deserves praise for his criticism of the status quo. However, the solution that creates "nation-states" at the expense of territorial states is problematic.

I will comment on this issue by discussing levels of "sovereignty" more generally and other issues of sovereignty that have confronted the United Nations of which we should be mindful. My conclusion will be that Professor Shtromas has accorded too much to the natural role of the state and that he, like many modern thinkers, views the state as performing more tasks than it should naturally perform. The modern state has been given, or assumed, many responsibilities for human well-being that are best left to individuals, families, and lower levels of society.

Professor Shtromas, by advocating a League of Peace, formulates a plan whereby states would voluntarily limit their sovereignty in international relations. If these same principles of voluntary association are applied within states, one must also limit the authority that a state has over its citizens. Shtromas recognizes this and argues that the state should abide by certain standards of conduct toward the human rights of individuals within those states. I agree with Professor Shtromas that if a state that does not punish murderers, rapists, or thieves within their territory or engages in such domestic violence on the state level, the UN (or League of Peace) should have the right to intervene on the basis of protecting the sovereignty of the citizens.

However, Professor Shtromas assumes that the state has the right in the first place to bestow these human rights. He does this because of his concept of a "nation-state" in which national groups organize a certain number of positive social activities for their members—and they are to do this with the administrative apparatus of the state. As such he is more a student of Kant, Hegel, and the policies of Kaiser Wilhelm, which led to the creation of the German national state, than he is of the American founding fathers who accorded ultimate sovereignty to the individual and accordingly limited the power of the state by minimizing its role in anything "ethnic," which in Shtromas's use of the term discussion can be translated "national."

The human desire for freedom and rights on the one hand and order and security on the other poses a dilemma to the establishment of any government or legal association. Law and order restrict the boundaries of human activity and creativity, but without law and order, human beings are prone to dominate, abuse, and manipulate other human beings for their own ends. The attempt to establish a United Nations that at once guarantees freedom and human rights to everyone on the one hand and world order and peace on the other is the globalization of this dilemma, which has only rarely been satisfactorily achieved at the level of the individual or family.

Professor Shtromas is right that a peaceful unity of the nations of the world will not come about unless all nations feel free to pursue legitimate national goals. In other words, each nation should have a dominion of sovereignty that it can claim as its own. However, peace within nations cannot come about unless each human being is free to pursue legitimate personal goals. Important as national sovereignty is, we should be more concerned about the sovereignty of individuals in a state than with the sovereignty of the nation itself. Individuals have a need for sovereignty over a sphere in which they can feel free to act, and they are the foundation upon which the nation is built.

State sovereignty must be restricted by an understanding of which goals are legitimate, and which goals are illegitimate. The American founding fathers defined the realm of legitimate activity of a sovereign in negative terms, i.e., those actions that do not inflict harm upon others. They viewed the formation of the American nation as a voluntary federation of participant states bound together for common purposes. Each citizen was considered a sovereign in the peaceful pursuit of happiness. The purpose of the federation was to guarantee the rights of each citizen by prohibiting domestic or outside forces from interfering in that pursuit. The League of Peace envisioned by Kant would be a voluntary forming together of sovereign nations, which for reasons of collective peace, and for mutual protection from more barbaric forces, would subscribe to a World Code of Laws.

Both the American founders and Immanuel Kant believed that their solutions were a reflection of a natural law given to us by the Creator of the universe, and as such were applicable to all people who had reached a high enough state of knowledge and moral development to comprehend them.

The United Nations, and the League of Nations that preceded it, are expressions of an imperfect attempt to create the perpetual peace that Kant envisioned. To some extent, the United Nations was to be an expansion of the principles of the United States to the world level. Neither the United States nor the United Nations has worked perfectly or peacefully, for in the end they are political compromises with the ideal. Sovereignty has never been truly given to all parties involved. The proper limits to sovereignty have never been fully agreed upon.

When the United Nations was founded after World War II, three major compromises with the ideal of perpetual peace were made:

- First, *a world power balance that did not represent the population of the world formed the basis for the security council.*
- Second, *existing territorial states which did not represent the population's voluntary identification with them were recognized.*
- Third, *financial assistance, technological assistance, and aid programs were to be funneled through the official representatives of recognized states, and not directly to the individual citizens or accountable corporations within those states.*

Professor Shtromas's article primarily addresses problem number two, but I think all three areas merit discussion. The reason I do so is that I believe it might be possible to transform the United Nations rather than to construct an entirely new League of Peace.

The first problem is *the structure of the UN Security Council.* Mohammed Jamali, a Tunisian signer of the UN, has argued against the idea of permanent membership in the Security Council (*International Journal on World Peace* 11, no. 3, September, 1994, pp. 5–13). The members who serve as permanent members were the major powers at the time of the founding of the UN, and were considered most able to provide global leadership and security. However, the world is in constant change. Fifty years after the UN founding, the world has changed dramatically. Jamali has suggested that the UN General Assembly elect the members of the Security Council every three years. This suggestion may have some merit if the problems surrounding legitimate national membership in the United Nations were solved. That is our second problem and must be solved before the first.

Dr. Clark Hosmer, a retired U.S. Air Force colonel, has suggested that the five nations' exclusive power to veto the other members of the security council is unfair to other members of the security council (*International Journal on World Peace* 11, no. 3, September, 1994, pp. 15–19). This arrangement inhibits the ability of the security council to take responsible action in the case that one of the five nations is recalcitrant. He suggests a system where the Security Council, as a body, could veto the actions of the General Assembly, like the executive can veto the legislative branch of government in the United States. Then, the General Assembly, in turn, could by a large majority override the Security Council's veto.

The second problem, which Professor Shtromas has addressed, is that the territorial states recognized by the United Nations represent *geographic boundaries which were drawn by conquering nations* "from above" and were not naturally organized "from below." "Nations," as distinct from territorial states, refer to cultural and/or ethnic identification rather than geography. Accordingly, he states that the world is inhabited by about 1,800 nations but divided into only about 190 states. The legal protection of territorial boundaries is a principle in conflict with the principle of self-determination of peoples and violates national sovereignty. Shtromas argues that UN priorities ought to be reversed. In other words, the UN should help guide the transformation of territorial boundaries to reflect the demographic concentration of nations.

While Shtromas has addressed a major defect in the present system of world order, his idea of setting up new geographic boundaries for every traditional nationality may be utopian and possibly quite oppressive. Modern migration has landed many national groups on the same soil in modern cities all over the world. Further, national groups are constantly undergoing change as they interact with others; so that one group inside one nation might more resemble its analog in another nation than other members of its own nation. Also, many individuals often want to change national identity without having to physically move their home, their family, or their business. It is unfair to sovereign individuals to either ask them to move to a nation-state more of their own liking, or rest content to live within a state reflecting the values of another national group.

The solution to the problem lies in the restriction on the power of territorial states so that state organization is decoupled from cultural identification. In other words, *I am suggesting the possibility of decoupling nation from state altogether.*

Major concerns of national groups have been related to the values that their children learn in public schools, state interference in family or religious activity, values promoted by the state as a whole, or tax structures and other policies that redistribute wealth and power from one group to another. These problems can be resolved by allowing national groups to establish their own schools, churches, and shrines on properties they own, and by forbidding the state to tax or subsidize one group more than another or perform any functions not voluntarily supported by all nations within the state. Conflict would greatly be reduced if the purposes of the territorial state were reduced to matters related to territory and security; defense against invasion of the territory; basic police services that protected individuals from murder, physical assault, and robbery; and obviously geographical services like the building and maintenance of roads.

The qualities that Shtromas and many others ascribe to "nation" are not necessarily territorial, but what many would call characteristics of "community." Community refers to the group with which one identifies and may take on the characteristics of a religious denomination, an ethnic group, neighborhood organization, or fraternal society.

When the United States was originally formed, the government established by the founders was extremely limited to the functions we would equate with "negative peace" or the absence of war and physical violence. Professor Shtromas defines peace similarly. Citizens would voluntarily organize themselves in ways consistent with their pursuit of happiness. They established schools, churches, and other institutions for the purpose of the education, maintenance, and welfare of those who belonged to the group.

To give national groups control of state power in republics freed from old empires is to ascribe a legitimacy to the state that it does not have in the first place. The same phenomenon has occurred in the United States during its "statist phase," which developed from 1860–1970, and was highly influenced by German thought. In this phase, members of various cultural, religious, and national backgrounds voluntarily gave over power for social welfare, education, and values to the dominant group, Anglo Saxon Protestants. The delegitimation of the federal state that has occurred since that time is a result of the state having assumed an unnatural role. The solution in the United States will not come from the new tribalism in state politics, but from the withdrawal of the state from responsibilities naturally given to sovereign individuals and communities ("nations"). It was a mistake for the United States to try to become a "nation-state."

An analogue of the "League of Peace," which has been well articulated by Professor Shtromas for international order, should be implemented within states as well. This structure was perhaps better reflected by the United States of 1835 encountered by Alexis de Tocqueville than by any territorial government or modern state that currently exists.

While I commend Professor Shtromas for advocating such a League of Peace on the international level, and agree that "territorial integrity" has been invoked to further the interests of some groups to the exclusion of others, I cannot rest content with a replacement of the modern state by a national state. It seems that neither option is valid. Rather, the minimal state, which honors the principle of subsidiarity, better affirms the sovereignty of individuals, families, and communities, and is the superior form of state organization.

A third problem for the present United Nations, which is in some ways a derivative of the first two and yet unique, is the problem of *providing development aid and technological assistance through designated state power channels*. In 1949, the United Nations developed Technical Assistance and Aid programs to assist the less developed and impoverished nations with resources from the developed nations. Because the right to national sovereignty and the "self-determination of peoples" was upheld as a sacred principle, it was determined that aid would go through the existing heads of existing governments. While the goal was to assist in the achievement of global equality, the process became one of near complete corruption. In some states, which originally supported the UN Declaration of Human Rights, the temptation to use financial and technological assistance to fortify one's own wealth and power was too great. The process corrupted many decent rulers, who set up Swiss bank accounts and used resources from First World countries to prop up their power at home. Secondly, the process made access to First World assistance so attractive that many ruthless people took power in revolutions of military coups in order to gain access to the riches intended for the poor.

In the late 1950s, Christian missionaries in many nations became highly critical of the process. Later, sociologists developed center-periphery theories that argued that the leaders in Third-World countries were puppets of the First World and were islands of the "center" within the periphery.

The basic problem was that neither true national sovereignty nor true individual sovereignty was recognized by the UN. Afraid to get involved in the internal affairs of existing states, the UN structure in effect operated on the principle "I am not my brother's keeper." Yet, individual conscience led many to recognize the gross injustice and violation of rights that increased in many states. However, many of the champions for human rights did not realize that the implementation of issues of sovereignty by the UN had caused some of this injustice to come about in the first place.

In the case of Latin America, the changeover from military dictatorships to democracies in the 1970s and 1980s was less a result of local demand for democracy than the inability of dictators to repay interest on international loans that they had diverted to Swiss bank accounts. Resigning with the spoils in their bank accounts, they proclaimed they were establishing free elections and democracy. However, it really served the dual purpose of maintaining the spoils of corrupt office and looking like they served the popular ideas of freedom and democracy at the same time. Today the people are left with the debt and the interest on it without having received the benefit of material assistance.

Development aid should not be transferred to "national groups" any more than it should have been transferred to the leaders of the territorial states during the past decades. It would set up incentives for oppression the same as the competition in Africa among tribes for state power. The United Nations and other world organizations must reform their policies on the method of the transfer of aid and technology. It should be given to private individuals and organizations that can be held accountable, rather than state governments or national groups that are amorphous and structurally irresponsible. Holders of state office are in constant flux and thus states cannot be held accountable. Assistance, especially financial loans, should be given to persons or entities that can be held legally accountable, and who have assets of their own that can be seized for lack of payment.

These three issues that I have mentioned do not, of course, exhaust a discussion of the UN or the issues raised by Professor Shtromas. However, unless both national and individual sovereignty are both better understood and addressed, we might create a League of Peace for international order and fail to produce the domestic social peace that people the world over long to achieve.

Gordon L. Anderson

REJOINDER

Since, in substance, I happen to agree with most of Dr. Gordon L. Anderson's ideas expressed in his comment on my article, it surprised me that he chose to criticize my views in a rather intransigent manner. Having given some thought to this paradox, I have come to the conclusion that Anderson's criticism is based not so much on the real differences in our approach to the problems under discussion, as on some profound misunderstandings on his part of what I had to say.

Misunderstanding number one is about the subject of my article itself. Anderson presumes that the article is devoted to the discussion of the rights of nations to sovereign statehood, while in fact this article is on the definition and prerequisites of world peace and the basic requirements for instituting and maintaining a peaceful world order. The right of nations to self-determination is treated in the article only as one, albeit not the sole or even not the main, prerequisite for peace. The main such prerequisite, in my view (as well as in the views of Immanuel Kant, Herbert Spencer, Ludwig von Mises, the three theorists whom I directly quote, basing my ideas on theirs, but also most other liberal thinkers), is the establishment in every state of a stable liberal-democratic/republican constitutional order, that is, of that minimal service-state where individual citizens are the true masters. It is indeed exactly the same modern state Anderson talks about, accusing me, without any foundation whatsoever, of holding an opposite view of the state—a view, according to which "the state has the right in the first place to bestow the human rights."

The above accusation constitutes misunderstanding number two. By no means could Anderson find, in either my present article or in the whole body of my written work, anything that would justify his statement about my concept of the state being one "of a nation-state in which national groups organize a certain number of positive social activities for their members and they are to do this with the administrative apparatus of the state." "As such," Anderson continues, "he [Shtromas] is more a student of Kant, Hegel, and the policies of Kaiser Wilhelm, which led to the creation of the German national state, than he is of the American founding fathers who accorded ultimate sovereignty to the individual and accordingly limited the power of the state by minimizing its role in anything 'ethnic,' which in Shtromas's use of the term [in the] discussion can be translated 'national.'"

To be sure, Kant's and Hegel's views on the state were in total opposition to one another and therefore cannot, without further elaboration, be lumped together: if Hegel had indeed provided the philosophical foundation for the enlightened Prussian statehood [Anderson's "policies of Kaiser Wilhelm"], Kant's vision of the state was liberal and served as one of the basic sources of inspiration to the American founding fathers, especially to James Madison.

I am also not entirely at ease with Anderson's notion of sovereignty, which he unequivocally accords to the individual, thus confusing sovereignty with the Lockeian concept of inalienable human rights, which the founding fathers laid in the foundation of the American Constitution. Sovereignty, as the supremacy (though not at all absoluteness) of power within society and independence from any outside power, is in liberal-democratic/republican systems (e.g., the United States) the attribute of the people (or the nation), i.e., the body of citizens acting as (and through) the state, not by any means an attribute of the individual who is subject to the laws passed by the state, although these laws cannot interfere with, let alone substantially limit or abolish, the inalienable rights of the individual).

I thought that it should be obvious to any reader of my piece that its red thread consists in trying to prove the point that peace can realistically and reliably be attained only among liberal-democratic/republican states that, like the American model Anderson so extensively uses, put the individual in the very center of the entire political edifice. To that effect I directly referred to Madison, not only to Kant, to say nothing about Hegel whom in this context

I do not mention at all. Hence, Anderson's suspicions and suppositions about my concept of the state being different from his or the vision of American founding fathers (which is not much different from Kant's) are wrong. I think Anderson attributed to me the erroneous view of the state, a view that I do not share, because of his misunderstanding of my usage of the terms "nation" and "national minority."

This misunderstanding, misunderstanding number three, has arisen, it seems to me, because Anderson apparently did not pay sufficient attention to my definition of the nation as an entity with a clear territorial identity given in counter-distinction to that of a national minority that lacks such an identity altogether. If he did, he hardly could have said that "[t]he qualities that Shtromas and many others ascribe to 'nation' are not necessarily territorial, but what many would call characteristics of 'community.'" "Community," he continues, "refers to the group with which one identifies and may take on the characteristics of a religious denomination, an ethnic group, neighborhood organization, or fraternal society."

Anderson not only attributes to me the views that are exclusively his own and contrary to mine, but also, whenever disputing my views on the nation, talks in fact about what to me are not nations at all, but mere national minorities. For example, accusing me of entertaining ideas on national self-determination that are "utopian and possibly quite oppressive," he refers to modern migration as the process that "has landed many national groups on the same soil in modern cities all over the world. Further," he adds, "national groups are constantly undergoing change as they interact with others; so that one group inside one nation might more resemble its analog in another nation than other members of its own nation." But migrants are individuals (even if they are large groups of individuals) who have freely chosen to leave their national homelands and settle in an alien land, thus exchanging their status of members of their respective territorial nations to that of national minorities in another nation's land or, as in the case of immigration to the United States, for assimilation into another nation. The fact that Anderson fails to distinguish between nations and national minorities is best exemplified by his statement that "'[n]ations,' as distinct from territorial states, refer to cultural and/or ethnic identification rather than geography."

In my perspective, however, it is not the nations but only national minorities that are identified by cultural and/or ethnic commonalities alone; the nation, in addition, has a clear "geographic" or territorial identity too. In my terms, without such an identity there is no nation and that is why within my frame of reference only nations, but not national minorities, are entitled to claim the right to self-determination. This right, I repeat, is, and should be, exclusive to territorial (geographically identifiable) nations that due to accidents of history fell, together with their territories, under the rule of another nation, and to this day remain a part of the integral territory of that other nation's state against their will. It is evident that most state-nations try their best to assimilate the stateless nations they rule into the main body of that state's titular nation.

The Castilians were quite successful in assimilating most nations of the Pyrenees and integrating them into one Spanish nation with a clear Castilian identity. But they did not manage to do this to the Portuguese who since 1640 asserted their separate identity by seceding from Spain and creating their own nation-state; neither were they successful in fully assimilating the Basques, the Catalans, and the Galicians who lived under Castilian rule in the state of Spain for the last half a millennium, and nevertheless did not lose their separate national identity or stop demanding that the right to self-determination and sovereignty be granted to them. The same goes for the Kurds in every state into which a part of their national territory is incorporated, but especially in Turkey, which, for centuries tried to assimilate them into the Turkish nation, euphemistically calling the Kurds "Mountain Turks," alas, to no avail. When I talk about 1,800 nations existing in this world, I mean nations in the above sense, that is, fully-fledged national-territorial entities, not mere national minorities of whom there are many more than 1,800 (parts of each of these 1,800 nations live as national minorities in the territories of other nations and plus there are many nationalities, such as the Gypsies, who do not have any territorial identity and everywhere exist only as national minorities).

The agenda of national minorities is entirely distinct from that of nations. What the minorities demand is not sovereignty but equality of citizenship and basic human rights with the members of the main state-nation as well as, in addition, some specific cultural and religious rights allowing them to retain, foster, and develop their separate identity—no less and no more— which shows that, by attributing to me the intention to grant culturally or ethnically defined minorities the right to self-determination and sovereignty, Anderson entirely misses the point.

Mr. Anderson also assumes that nations are external collectivist entities that impose themselves on the individuals, order them around at their whims and, by so doing, ignore the individuals' personal interests and rights. In this assumption he confuses the nation with authoritarian parties and/or governments that claim, in most cases fraudulently, to speak and act on the nation's behalf. In my understanding, however, nations are organic entities emanating from within society in the process of the individuals themselves freely determining their collective identities, which Ernest Renan so succinctly defined as the "every day referendum." It goes without saying that in this process the individuals are very extensively using their human freedoms and rights, and thus one could say that the nation is an entity produced by the free exercise of human rights by the individual. Therefore to restrict individuals in their free formation of nations or in their free participation in the nation's life and struggles for a better and freer lot is tantamount to a serious restriction, indeed gross violation, of individual human rights. At least in my usage of the term, the nation is not a body determined by certain objective criteria that then become mandatory for the individual to accept and unquestioningly submit himself to. The nation in my view is the creation of the free will of many individuals and exists only insofar as these individuals readily identify themselves as members of that particular nation and by that also with that nation itself. In this context it is necessary to say a few words about the United States, which Anderson refers to most frequently, making it in his argumentation the main positive example. To me the United States is in this world one of the very few mono-national states. It is inhabited by one nation, the Americans, who despite their different ethnic origins, came to the New World to join, and become one, with the Anglo-Americans who created that nation, gave it their identity and formed that nation's backbone. The fact that members of the American nation can hyphenate their identity by calling themselves Italian-Americans, Irish-Americans, Polish-Americans, African-Americans, Jewish-Americans, etc., does not change the fact that all Americans have a common national identity and constitute one integral American nation. The hyphenation shows only that, in addition to their main American identity, some of them are eager to identify themselves also as members of certain minorities which, among other things, clearly demonstrates that in a truly liberal-democratic/republican system, as the United States, the problem of discrimination of minorities is being successfully solved. In fact, by now the United States has no minority problem whatsoever. Figuratively speaking, it is the state of one nation, two subcultures, and one bottleneck, the subcultures being the so-called Native American Indians and the blacks (the two groups who were not immigrants but either lived there when the colonists arrived or were brought by the latter as slaves), and the bottleneck forming itself in some states overflowing with immigrants from Latin America who cannot be readily absorbed into the American society and therefore in a few places, such as California, New Mexico, Florida, or New York City, represents a temporary problem with regard to that society's identity. It needs to be emphasized, however, that all these problems are those of providing better, more conducive conditions for historically disadvantaged groups, such as the blacks and Native American Indians, to integrate into the American nation as equals, not of separatism or exclusiveness. Unfortunately, however, the United States is in this respect rather the exception than the rule, but an exception that points to the future of the world at large, if it is to become peaceful and civilized.

Having defined the Americans as a single nation, I am now turning to Anderson to ask a couple of pertinent questions. What does he mean when in the opening sentence of the comment he contrasts the existing "modern" or "territorial" state with the "sovereign nation-state"? What, in other words, is in his view the identity of the people who carry sovereignty in "modern," "territorial," liberal-democratic states? (I am not talking abut the states in which sovereignty lies in the hands of an autocratic ruler or a ruling clique, as is the case in many Arab states, Iran, Nigeria, Zaire, the remaining communist dictatorships, etc.) If it is not the nation, then what is it?

One could, of course, say that nationhood in modern democracies is conferred not by ethnic origin but by citizenship of a "territorial" state, which indeed is the case. Citizenship in this sense is a fine "supra-ethnic" concept, but only insofar as it is freely and willingly accepted by the citizens themselves.

There is, however, a problem with those citizens on whom their particular citizenship is imposed and who would prefer to drop it and, if free to do so, become citizens of either their own newly created nation-state or of another state by joining their territory with that of this other state (the latter in the case of artificially divided nations that would like to live as one nation in one state). Would the Chechens, for example, not renounce their present Russian citizenship and change it for the citizenship of their own state of Chechnya, if their attempt at so doing were not brutally suppressed by the Russian war machine? Did not the Lithuanians, Latvians, Estonians, Ukrainians, Georgians, Armenians, and other nations of the former Soviet republics joyfully rid themselves of their Soviet citizenship exchanging it for that of their own nation-states as soon as they were free to do so? This is actually a universal phenomenon common not only to nations freeing themselves from the yoke of oppressive regimes, but of many nations in the free world as well. Most Corsicans would, no doubt with the same joy, renounce their French citizenship as the Basques would their Spanish and the Sikhs their Indian ones.

Citizenship is therefore an instrument accommodating within the nationhood conferred by it those national minorities who, being of an ethnic origin different from that of the main state-nation, want to be rightful members of that nation's state without losing by the acquisition of such membership their identity as a separate minority. Thus, universal citizenship does not allow a democracy to turn into a blatant ethnocracy, but, by subjugating to itself the peoples who are not willing to carry it, it also becomes an instrument of national oppression even in free and democratic states. That is why I said in the article that liberal-democratic/republican constitutional order is in itself not sufficient to provide for stable peace. To achieve stable peace in this world, its constituent members, in addition to being liberal-democracies/republics, must also recognize the equal right of all nations to self-determination and sovereignty. As long as this right is not universally granted, there will be no peace in the world—the territorial stateless nations will fight for self-determination, whereas the respective governments dominated by the ruling state-nations will do everything in their power to assimilate or otherwise annihilate the stateless nations' separate identities. This is why I said in the article that true liberal democracy, some exceptional cases notwithstanding (e.g., UK, Canada), is best embodied in mono-nation states. I have to add that citizenship, besides including national minorities, may also be a multiethnic entity by definition, as it is the case in states whose identity is not that of a particular nation but one of a supranational but nevertheless organically compound entity. Such an identity is Switzerland's and Belgium's; should be, in my view, Bosnia's; and may become Prussia's, if a new Prussian state will eventually emerge from the present Kaliningrad province of Russia and some Prussian parts of Poland.

In view of what was stated above, I would now like to ask Anderson what he meant by saying that the solution to the problem he discusses with me in his comment "lies in the restriction on the power of territorial states so that state organization is decoupled from cultural identification," or, as he himself declares, suggesting, in other words, "the possibility of decoupling nation from state altogether." How does he suggest one does it? And with what body of people should then the state be "coupled"? Anderson does not answer these questions in any positive way, as "decoupling" is an entirely negative term that needs to be filled with positive content. I for one do not see how in present conditions the state can be anything but the nation-state, and would like to be enlightened on any possible alternatives to this "state of the state."

Finally, there is yet misunderstanding number four. It concerns the UN and its predecessor, the League of Nations. Anderson sees in them an imperfect attempt to create the Kantian League of Peace and assumes that it is my view, too. But it is not. The whole point of the Kantian league is that, in order to fulfill its purposes effectively, it has to consist of nations with established and consolidated liberal-democratic/republican regimes. Neither the UN is nor the League of Nations had been such a body. The UN is not so much the "united nations" as the "disunited governments" embracing entirely different views of the world (Weltanschauungs) and conflicting goals. To start forming a League of Peace, it is necessary to create first what Professor Morton A. Kaplan in the 1980s called the Demintern—a paraphrase to the Communist International, the Comintern—that is, a Union of the Democratic Nations of the World. By its composition NATO so far is perhaps the only international organization that could grow into such a Deminform and then gradually develop even into the League of Peace. However, being an exclusively defense-oriented alliance, NATO neither functions as a Deminform's prototype today nor contemplates developing in that direction. This is to say that, at least in my view, the Kantian League of Peace will have to become an entirely new venture, qualitatively different from any of the world bodies that have been in existence hitherto.

In conclusion, let me say again that I wholeheartedly agree with Anderson's ideas on the necessity of substantial reforms in the UN and the particular states that at present take upon themselves too much power over the individual and the private institutions of the civil society and should reassert the centrality of the individual and his human rights. But I am also convinced that all of his on the whole correct proposals, even if fully implemented, will hardly be able on their own to ensure perpetual peace. For that purpose to be achieved, it is necessary in my opinion to secure the victory for the liberal-democratic/republican constitutional order in each state as well as the universal recognition by these states of the prima facie status of the right of all nations to self-determination and equal sovereignty. Unless, of course, Anderson really knows something that this writer, because of his lack of imagination, fails to realize, namely a viable alternative to the nation-state, one that would effectively decouple the nation from the state. I look forward to hearing from him about it but meanwhile have to hold on to my original views expressed in both the article and this rejoinder.

Aleksandras Shtromas

NOTES

1. Immanuel Kant, "To Perpetual Peace: A Philosophical Sketch," in Immanuel Kant, *Perpetual Peace and Other Essays on Politics, History and Morals*, trans. Ted Humphrey (Indianapolis: Hackett, 1983), 115.

2. Kant, "To Perpetual Peace," 112.

3. See his "Facts and Comments" (1902), in Stanislaw Andreski, ed., *Herbert Spencer: Structure, Function and Evolution* (London: Nelson, 1972), 207 ff.

4. *Principles of Sociology*, vol. 3 (1896), quoted from Stanislaw Andreski, ed., *Herbert Spencer*, 212.

5. Ludwig von Mises, *Liberalism in the Classical Tradition* (1927), translated by Ralph Raico, 33rd ed. (Irving–on–Hudson, N.Y.: The Foundation for Economic Education and Cobden Press, 1985), 151.

6. Ludwig von Mises, *Liberalism in the Classical Tradition*, 150.

7. Ludwig von Mises, *Liberalism in the Classical Tradition*, 148.

8. Ludwig von Mises, *Liberalism in the Classical Tradition*, 112–13.

9. See J. David Singer and Melvin Small, *The Wages of War 1816–1965* (New York: Wiley, 1972); J. David Singer and Melvin Small, *Resort to Arms: International and Civil Wars, 1816–1980* (Beverly Hills, Calif.: Sage, 1982), especially table 4.2.

10. Rudolph J. Rummel, "On Fostering A Just Peace," *International Journal on World Peace* 1, no. 1 (autumn 1984): 4–15.

11. Ludwig von Mises, *Liberalism in the Classical Tradition*, 109.

12. A valiant and productive effort to codify the extant international law with amendments and revisions dictated by its codification and necessitated by the need of making this law enforceable has been undertaken by Grenville Clark and Louis B. Sohn in their famous *World Peace Through World Law*, first published in 1958. Their project, by the way, foresees the dismantlement of all national military forces and the creation of the single United Nations' military force. For an elaboration of this proposal, see the second edition of their book (Cambridge, Mass.: Harvard University Press, 1960), 5–6.

13. This argument has been made by the eminent international lawyer Antonio Cassesse (see his "Political Self–Determination—Old Concepts and New Developments," in A. Cassesse, ed., *UN Law/Fundamental Rights: Two Topics in International Law* [Alphen aan den Rijn, The Netherlands: Sijthoff and Noordhoff, 1979], 137 ff), and later developed into the concept of several classes or generations of rights by the Australian philosopher Eugene Kamenka (see his "Nationalism: Ambiguous Legacies and Contingent Futures," in Aleksandras Shtromas, ed., *The End of "Isms"? Reflections on the Fate of Ideological Politics After Communism's Collapse* [Oxford: Blackwell, 1994], 125–41).

14. Hans Kelsen, *Principles of International Law* (New York: Holt, Rinehart, and Winston, 1952).

15. Alexander Shtromas, "A Peaceful World: Ideal and Reality," in Jeanne Tchong Koei Li, ed., *In Search of a New World Order: The Need for New Initiatives* (Taipei, Taiwan: Pacific Cultural Foundation, 1980), 105.

20

Nations, States, and World Peace: Rejoinder

ALEKSANDRAS SHTROMAS

In the first place, I wish to thank all commentators for the high honor they accorded to me by taking the trouble to read my article and, furthermore, to devote their valuable time to writing a thoughtful response. Before engaging in a substantive discussion of the issues the commentators have raised, I would like, however, to disassociate myself from certain views some of them chose to ascribe to me and, then, went to great lengths to refute, wrongly claiming that these views were mine.

Professor Pierre L. Van den Berghe, for example, suggests that I am perpetuating "the Eurocentric canard . . . that 'liberal democracies' are fundamentally peaceful. . . . ," and, as evidence proving that it is indeed a "canard," cites examples of Western democracies' brutal conquest of "countless peoples all over the world" and the establishment in the thus conquered colonies of "Herrenvolk democracies" (I am consciously omitting Van den Berghe's first example of "stateless . . . societies . . . engaged in limited but incessant warfare with their neighbors," as to me stateless societies cannot be classified into liberal democracies or despotisms—categories that apply only to the states and by that, since most states were originally conceived as

Reprinted from the *International Journal on World Peace* 13, no. 1 (March 1996): 63–88, for the symposium to which this rejoinder was written, see the *International Journal on World Peace* 12, no. 4 (December 1995): 43–48.

kingships, to those states that have already reached quite a high stage of their development). At no time and nowhere have I said, however, that democracies are by nature fundamentally peaceful. All I said was that they do not wage war *against each other*, a fact that has been empirically proved (see my references in the main article) and convincingly elevated to a theoretical thesis in both the sources I quoted and in the more recent studies by Professor Bruce Russett and his colleagues.[1] I have also made absolutely clear, it seems to me, that not only am I fully aware of the historical facts Van den Berghe cites but also that, in my view, even in contemporary highly developed liberal democracies the phenomenon that Herbert Spencer called "rebarbarization" has not yet been fully eradicated. Actually, the fact that to this day even in some of the leading Western liberal democracies (e.g., France, Spain, etc.) "rebarbarization" is still very much in evidence underpins my whole reasoning about the necessity of recognizing, at last, the principle of self-determination as a prima facie right of nations. I believe that if there were any novel ideas in my article, the most important one among them was perhaps the idea according to which liberal democracy *alone* is *not* sufficient for ensuring world peace and that its insurance on a stable and permanent basis would require, *in addition*, the recognition of the right of nations to self-determination and sovereignty.

Professor Richard Ebeling, criticizing my stance on using the Universal Declaration of Human Rights (1948) and the adjacent covenants (1966) as the foundation for the *future* Code of Human Rights, similarly falsely assumes that I propose to accept these documents *in toto*, that is, inclusive of "the mirage of social justice" that was incorporated into the Covenant on Social, Economic, and Cultural Rights and that Friedrich von Hayek had so aptly and rightly criticized. If Ebeling would have read my article more attentively, he would have had to admit that his critical comments on that score are totally beside the point, as, in fact, I have never even considered proposing any such or similar measures. Fully agreeing with Hayek's criticism of this document, I have explicitly stated in my article that this covenant, in order to become compatible with the principles of liberal democracy, would have to be substantially revised and then transformed into a Statement of Intent, which would thus separate it from the Code of Human Rights, and deprived of any legally binding status altogether.[2] Ebeling somehow overlooked that, to me, not only this covenant but all these three documents are no more than a presently extant indicator of the tendency for the international law to develop in the future and that, in the context of the League of Peace, they all will have to be substantially revised in order to become consistent "not only with their own provisions but even more so with the basic principles of liberal democracy/republicanism."[3]

I have mentioned these two instances of unwarranted criticism to show that my libertarian-anarchist opponents apparently have the inclination to read into the texts offered for their reviewing a statist bias even when it is not there to be found. They apparently are in dire need of having at hand even a bogus statism, because then they know exactly what their reaction to a concept under their critical scrutiny should be and how to use the occasion of producing a commentary for propelling, once more, their own well treaded views and positions. As a matter of fact, I also consider myself as belonging to the libertarian tradition and am not inclined as to easily concede my libertarian identity to attempts at putting me, wrongly I believe, on the other side of the argument.

Ebeling also tries to put me at odds with Ludwig von Mises by stating that "Mises did not believe in the right of self-determination of nations." But all Mises said was that the right of self-determination "is not the right . . . of a delimited national group, but the right of the inhabitants of every territory to decide on the state to which they wish to belong." What he in fact meant by so saying was that no one else but the people themselves should make the decisions on defining who should exercise sovereign authority over the territorial space they inhabit. But is this not what *self*-determination is all about? Is "self-determination" of a delimited national group not presupposing that someone else, someone from without, has to introduce the criteria for that "delimitation"?

To emphasize this aspect of self-determination as strongly as possible in the aftermath of Versailles, at which the victorious allies led by David Lloyd George and Georges Clemenceau applied the Wilsonian principle of national self-determination by carving up the defeated empires into hosts of new nation-states in accordance with what *they deemed* to be "delimited national groups," was vitally important indeed. Having emphasized this aspect of *self*-determination loudly and clearly, Mises then stresses that in our time the free exercise of the right of self-determination "would have led to the formation of states composed of a single nationality . . . and to the dissolution of states composed of several nationalities." It thus turns out that, after all, Mises actually did believe in the right of nations to self-determination, and that between his and my understanding of this right there is no difference whatsoever, because for both of us self-determination is what it is only when people themselves freely decide how and by whom their respective territories should be ruled.

Actually, by making such a decision, the people self-determine themselves as a nation in the first place, and only subsequently do they draw from this act of self-determination as a nation appropriate political conclusions. Any other method of defining their national identity inevitably produces the effect of "delimited national groups," which Mises had so rightly criticized. And, consequently, Mises logically concluded that "[t]he formation of states comprising all the members of a nation group was the result of the exercise of the right to self-determination, not its purpose."[4] It is exactly what I am saying, too, but Ebeling prefers not to listen. Instead he attacks me for allegedly holding the opposite view, according to which the right to self-determination is an a priori given right of a "delimited national group"—a view that is as alien to me as it is to both Mises and Ebeling themselves (here I have to remind the readers once again that to me the nation is not simply an *ethnos*, as my opponents invariably assume it to be, but an *ethnos with a distinct territorial identity*).

As I have implicitly pointed out in the article under discussion and explicitly and unequivocally stated in other writings,[5] a nation to me is constituted only and exclusively by the process of free self-identification of every single individual with that nation and by the implicit acceptance of this individual into the nation's membership by other individuals who have self-identified themselves analogously. To paraphrase Joseph Ernest Renan, the nation is thus a territorial human community established and sustained by an everyday plebiscite.[6]

It follows from such a "fluid" concept of the nation that the collective rights of nations have no other substance than that which is formed by the extension into the public domain of the right of the individual to a free choice of his/her collective national and political identity exercised simultaneously by a relatively large number of people. In other words, national rights are a multitude's sum-expression of every member's of that multitude individual right to determine the scope and the identity of the state of which he wishes to be a citizen. To conclude, the right of nations to self-determination and sovereignty is thus firmly rooted in individual human rights and projected onto the sociopolitical surface as a natural extension of these rights either actually exercised or merely claimed by a multitude of people acting as individuals in a simultaneous manner.

Indeed, if an individual's right to his freely self-determined nationhood is ignored, let alone outrightly denied or suppressed, if the individual is thus forced into quiescence with a nationhood that he deems to be an alien imposition upon him, then that individual is being deprived of his primary right to personal liberty without which none of the other rights accorded to him in an abstract and limited, exclusively individualistic fashion, make any sense. They simply lose all substance, become totally spurious, entirely fictitious, and practically nonexistent. As a matter of course, all thus accorded individual rights, by binding the individual to a political entity that is alien to him, turn into a pointed denial to that individual of his basic liberty, his primary right to be what he really is or wants to become. For man, in Emile Durkheim's perceptive words, is *homo duplex* (dual man) consisting of two inseparable but distinct selves, the individualist and collectivist ones, both of which need equal recognition by, and conducive conditions for free expression within, his social environment. Furthermore, according to Durkheim, the individual can meaningfully satisfy his drive for free self-realization only when he can do so among, and for, the people his collectivist self organically identifies itself with.[7] To pretend otherwise, to try to reduce the human being to only one individualist self is to transgress against man's true, that dual, nature. It seems to me that it is exactly what Ebeling, together with Van den Berghe and Anderson, is trying to do.

Nor did I ever suggest that the creation of the sovereign nation-state for each single nation is what the right to self-determination is bound to produce as the result of its free exercise. In the article I have quite unequivocally stated that "it is not at all necessary to get all nations as a matter of course into separate states, but it is absolutely imperative to grant all nations without exception the absolute and inalienable right to self-determination. It is by the way of using this right that every nation could freely decide for itself whether it wishes to continue the historical tradition of staying in one state with the other nation(s) of that same state or would prefer to separate from its old state association and form for itself a new sovereign nation-state."[8]

Hence, the right of self-determination logically encompasses in my view also the right to the nation's free self-extinction. Ebeling's remark that " . . . if a group of individuals chose to belong to a nation-state dominated by another linguistic and cultural group because they viewed their own language and culture as 'backward,' and wanted to completely absorb the national characteristics of the larger group, they would have to be permitted to do so, even if their free choice meant the end of their own language and culture" therefore sounds to me as something pretty obvious and not worthy of a special emphasis, although for reasons known only to himself Ebeling presents this remark as the ultimate argument that in his opinion should totally undermine what he wrongly deems to be my whole concept of self-determination. Somehow Ebeling forgot not only what I said in the above quotation, but also that in the previous rejoinder (to Anderson's first comment) I have once more explicitly stated my position on this issue and, in addition, cited a few cases of nations who without much ado were successfully assimilated by other, "grander" nations and, one could say, have actually volunteered for such a thoroughly full assimilation.[9]

Let me now address some of the substantive issues contested by the commentators and state more clearly my position on them. I would group these issues under two broad titles: (1) The state and the nation; (2) The League of Peace and the Global Commonwealth.

THE STATE AND THE NATION

Van den Berghe's position with regard to the state is basically anarchist. According to him "[t]he state is the ultimate social parasite, a self-legitimating protection racket, a killing machine run by the few to steal from the many." In my view these characteristics could not be applied to the state as such but only to self-serving perverse regimes resulting in excessive states that try to take upon themselves the functions of ultimate social and economic management and control. Like Anderson and Ebeling, I believe that social and economic management and control should be left to "the private sector and private channels of financing and control, since . . . [the] welfarist, redistributive and interventionist policies [of the states] have merely tended to aggravate and intensify disagreements and disputes among the members of society" (quoted from Ebeling's comment where he, in turn, refers to Anderson's first comment). Moreover, in my view, if and when the state starts squeezing the private sector by taking these and other socioeconomic functions upon itself and thus monopolizing the channels for peoples socialization, it indeed becomes, quoting Emile Durkheim again, a "sociological monstrosity."[10]

This, however does not mean that every state is bound to be such a monstrously perverse institution. In contrast to Van den Berghe, I share the Aristotelian view that man is a political animal and that thus only within the state he becomes fully human. Man needs the state to establish bonds with other men on the basis of their commonly agreed upon principles of justice and to subordinate himself, together with his fellow men who share the same ideals of absolute justice, to the laws based on these principles of justice. It is in this way that man can start living a good life befitting him as a conscious spiritual creature and thus separate himself from the animal kingdom where life has no higher purpose than mere living and is thus devoted to no more than sheer physical survival.

Founded on competitive interaction of a multitude of people seeking to achieve their self-defined personal goals and uniting or dividing themselves in accordance with these goals, the human society is not unlike an ever continuous sport game that, in order to be played effectively, needs a consensual view of justice-based rules equally applicable to all players, as well as a system of supervision and enforcement of these rules executed by a referee who as a matter of course does not himself participate in the game and can therefore stay impartial with regard to the players. In society it is the state's function to promulgate such rules and, at the same time, to do the referee's job by enforcing them. For this purpose the state is endowed by society with supreme (sovereign) power that Max Weber, in contrast with social power which evolves in a mutually balancing act as a "constellation of interests," had defined as the power of domination (*Herrschaft*).[11] And, according to Weber again, the state remains a legitimate entity only as long as it is not trespassing the limits exclusively external to its sphere of authority, by encroaching into the social power game, and does not become—what, because of its inherent superiority of power, it is in such a case bound to become—the main, if not the sole, real player in that game itself. If and when the state, by thus encroaching upon society, starts losing its legitimacy, which Weber defines as a "settled balance of reciprocity of expectations between rulers and ruled,"[12] it sets itself on the course of self-destruction. Sooner or later the thus instituted illegitimate regime that turned the originally correct service-state into a perverse master-state is, in Weber's view, bound to be replaced by a new regime, one that, by having restored the correct service-type state, is able to start commanding legitimacy again.

I think that by this "Aristotelian-Weberian" reasoning one can quite precisely define the concept of the "good state," that is, the state that is limited to its original purpose of rule-making, rule-implementation, and rule-adjudication for a society otherwise freely, without any state interference, exercising its social activities in all the domains, spiritually and economically satisfying the needs of that particular society and of each of its individual members. Van den Berghe will certainly disagree with my "Aristotelianly" positive view of the state but, I am sure, other participants of the discussion would in principle subscribe to such a view without much hesitation.

It seems to me that the issue that divides my views from Anderson's and Ebeling's is not that of the state as such. Insofar as the state is not a master-state but a service institution satisfying the political and legal needs of a free society, it is, as I understand in their view too, the natural and permanent form of humanity's organization. What, I think, puts me apart from Anderson and Ebeling is, as I see it, their lack of appreciation of the fact that states do not arise randomly but are instituted by people who in the course of historical interaction evolved a common spiritual identity that was uniquely theirs and that separated them from others who in the process of that same historical interaction evolved a different spiritual identity that was also uniquely theirs. Such differences of identity formed different societies that, for the sake of retaining and protecting their uniqueness, instituted on the territories they occupied their respective states, jealously asserting and protecting the independence of these societies from each other. The issue of identity that is separating societies and states from one another is the least elaborated one in the general theory of the state and needs, perhaps, some preliminary explanation without which the differences of opinion on that score between me and my opponents may remain rather obscured.

The first states known in history were founded when several tribes previously unrelated to each other united for a common cause in opposition to other such tribes and, by that, have established for themselves a new common identity superseding the tribal ones. In order to translate their newly evolved common identity into sociopolitical reality, these tribal clusters built for themselves a center or a city where they have instituted their by now common government and whose name they began to use for their new self-identification. Having subordinated their previously freewheeling villages to that city and to the government established in it, they transformed these villages into a joint, integral territorial space that acquired definite borders and, within these borders, one supreme body of political authority placed in the city.

The numerous city-states of ancient Greece represent classical examples of the states' origins in general terms described above. Why did the numerous *phyles* (tribes) and *phratries* (kinship groups) of which the Greek nation at that time consisted not form a united Greek nation-state but instead consolidate into many separate city-states? Why did the Greeks not identify themselves as such, but exclusively as Spartans, Athenians, Corinthians, Thebans, etc., treating in each of these cities members of other cities as aliens or *meteks*?

The answer here is twofold. First, in the vicinity of Greece there were no other nations comparable by the level of their civilization to the Greeks. The tribes that lived around Greece could be easily dismissed as barbarian in counter-distinction with which the Greeks did not need, as yet, to consolidate themselves into a coherently united national force. Second, some of the Greek phratries got themselves involved in acute disputes and wars with each other over all sorts of practical problems, which caused these phratries to develop with the passage of time clashing value systems and concepts of justice. Other adjacent phratries, even if directly uninvolved in the particular conflict, had to take a stance on it in accordance with their own largely interest-dictated value systems and concepts of justice. In the long run, like-minded phratries formed among themselves natural associations resulting in their building of separate common cities as centers uniting them into separate consolidated societies, each functioning under one government and system of law, that is, in their becoming separate states, each with a particular identity that it was committed to protect by all means in its power. It was again Aristotle who said that only the state "reaches the level of self-sufficiency . . . and . . . exists for the sake of living well,"[13] or, which is one and the same, living in accordance with the value system and ideals of justice peculiar to the society that had established itself as a separate state in order to embody and protect from external assaults its thus asserted specific identity.

The political situation in Greece had drastically changed with the Persian invasion (492 B.C.). For the first time then the common Greek national identity had to take precedence over the particular, subnational identities of the various Greek city-states. Having in a concerted effort successfully defended their country from the Persians (by 499 B.C.), the Greeks were, however, unable to agree on the shape of their future political union which, because of Persia's continuing menacing presence, became an acute necessity. The mightiest city-states, Athens and Sparta, developed incompatible visions of the Greek union and entered into competition for acquiring within that bipolarly evolving union a dominant position. The result of this squabbling was the protracted Peloponnesian War (431–404 B.C.), which Athens lost but Sparta failed to take full advantage of its victory in effectively establishing the Greek nation-state under its dominion. Wars and squabbles among Greek city-states continued unabated until 338 B.C., when Athens fell to Philip II, king of Macedonia, and Greece finally became a nation-state ruled by the Macedonian kings.

Under the rule of Philip's son, Alexander III, "the Great," Greece defeated Persia on the latter's own soil and, as a result, created an extensive empire that incorporated the whole known civilized world of that time. Although the Greeks managed to impart to the various peoples fallen under their imperial rule a certain common supranational Hellenic identity, the degree to which that Hellenic identity had been imparted was not sufficient to subordinate their original identities to it. The Diadochi rivalries notwithstanding, this is one of the main reasons why very soon after Alexander's death the Greek empire fell apart. The Seleucids, the Ptolemies, and other Greek rulers of the parts of the former Greek empire, in order to keep themselves in power, had to adjust to the identities of the various peoples they ruled, later even sharing in their respective identities, alongside with retaining some basic elements of the Hellenic identity, too.

As we see, the state-sustained and state-promoted identity is not inflexible or permanent. It changes with the changing circumstances, and the state, being originally a reflection of the collective identity of a people inhabiting a certain territorial space over which that state's authority had been originally established, by expanding beyond that territory, is in some cases able to forge a common identity of the peoples incorporated into that state, but in most cases, is not. It worked with Greece, as Greeks were, after all, one nation. It did not work with the Greek empire that tried to forge a common Hellenic identity for a multitude of nations and entire civilizations but, by so doing, only managed to enrich and enhance the particular identities of the peoples incorporated into that empire. This is similar to what had happened to the later-day empires, too. The peoples of those empires were certainly enriched by learning the cultures and the more advanced ways of living of their imperial masters, only to get their indigenous identities enhanced and properly adjusted to the conditions of independent existence in the modern world. Overexpanded states usually fail to impart to all the various peoples taken over by them for rule a common identity that would be able to fully subordinate to itself the original identities of these peoples. Some of them get assimilated—a common statehood is indeed a great forger of new and expanded nations—but most manage to preserve their own identities causing in the long run the breakdown of the empires along the lines of those separate identities that the empires were unable to overcome. That this is indeed the case is duly reflected in the fact that no empire in human history had ever acquired a permanent existence and that by now all of them have either gone or find themselves on the brink of a final collapse.

The boundaries of territorial states were thus forming not in relation to some random factors or within mere natural geographical delimitations, as Anderson suggests they did or should do. These boundaries were originally drawn around the spaces of historical habitats of peoples sharing a common identity and determined to preserve and freely develop that identity among other peoples with different identities who, accordingly, drew borders around the spaces of their respective historical habitats and, by so doing, also made themselves state-peoples.

The identities drawing people into forming territorial states could be either subnational (ancient and medieval city-states, hosts of medieval principalities, some contemporary mideastern Arab kingdoms and emirates) or national, or, in certain circumstances—when, like in Switzerland, peoples of different nationalities established an identity that separated them from their main national bodies and the reasons for such separation voluntarily united them into a coherent political unit of their own making—supranational (among other organically supranational states, one should mention Britain, Belgium at its formation as state by the 1830 revolution against Protestant Dutch rule, Bosnia before the war initiated and conducted in 1992 by the communo-fascist forces of Serbia, potentially Eastern Prussia, and some others).

A supranational identity does not eliminate separate national identities. Swiss Germans remain German, and so are Swiss Frenchmen and Swiss Italians, but they do not identify themselves politically with their co-nationals in their respective main nation-states and consider "Swissness"—an identity based on their common attachment to individual rights and the principle of people's self-government that centuries ago drew them to escape from the oppressive rule of their respective "fatherland-states" into the freedom of the Alps where they were able to unite into a voluntarily established state of their own—to be the determinant factor for their self-identification. Within Switzerland, however, they jealously guard their separate national identities—all the twenty-two Swiss cantons are strictly uni-national entities and in case the uni-national substance of a canton is becoming compromised, it is divided into uninational half-cantons, as it was the case with the canton of Jura.

National identities, on the contrary, melt different *ethnoi* or nationalities into one nation with one overriding identity. There are very few nations in the world that could claim their origins to a single ethnic background. Most of Europe is made up of nations that are mixtures of indigenous local populations, their original Greek and Roman masters, the invading Germanic and/or Scandinavian tribes, Ottoman Turks, and the remnants of other early Asian or African invaders, such as the Moors, Mongols, Tartars, or the Huns. It is in this sense that Americans to me are a nation, not a supranational entity based just on common values and ideas, like the Swiss. Their origin as a nation is not at all different from the European nations, only the national mixture that merged into the Anglo-American national identity was of more recent origin (that is why we still have "hyphenated" Americans) and in its main European component consisted of descendants of already formed modern European nations that had the time to forget about their own mixed ethnic backgrounds.

The traditional subnational and supranational identities are exceptional creations of unique historical circumstances, with some of them, especially among the subnational ones, increasingly evolving into straight national identities. The main and the most typical identity in the contemporary world—the identity that became preeminent in the beginning of the modern era and that continues rapidly to spread today, along with the spread of modernization, throughout the globe, gradually assuming a universal dimension—is thus the national one, and that situation is likely to remain unchanged for the foreseeable future. It is mostly along the lines of separate national identities that old states split, merge, or reshuffle and new states form. Whether Nieli and Van den Berghe like it or not, the process of "unscrambling ethnic omelettes" takes place before our very own eyes every day and in all parts of the world, and all the appeals and prescriptions aimed at putting this process on hold remain largely unheeded. In practice it appears that such "unscrambling" is not as difficult, let alone impossible, as our two authors would have it. For within every multinational state that confers citizenship on the basis of *ius soli*—the principle of conferring citizenship that Van den Berghe so strongly, and rightly, prefers to its opposite, *ius sanguinis*, although, one should note, in most cases *ius soli* is just an extension of *ius sanguinis* and organically incorporates the latter as a primary entitlement to citizenship—the tension between citizenship and nationhood, insofar as it is caused by nations resenting their incorporation into other nations by the means of common citizenship, arises only between the state's main nation (the *Staatsvolk*, as Van den Berghe correctly calls it by its original German term) and its other (stateless) territorial nations, if and when the members of the latter overwhelmingly do not wish to share in the citizenship of a nation-state that they consider to be alien to them and, because of that, intend to become citizens of either their own states yet to be newly established or of other extant states.

Such kind of tension can never arise between the territorial nations, be they *Staatsvolks* or stateless, and national minorities which, as such—as people who have consciously chosen to live in a space that does not, and should not, belong to them—share, in fact, the national identity of the nation in whose state or stateless territorial entity they live. Not only do the national minorities not object to full citizenship rights of their respective nation-states being conferred to them (perhaps with the exception of those of their members who chose to identify themselves with a stateless nation within their state and thus share that nation's negative attitude to the citizenship of the *Staatsvolk* imposed upon them), they actually strive for full equality in all civic matters, not only in that of citizenship, within their respective *Staatsvolks*. Hence, in the case of the national minorities the tension between citizenship and nationhood arises only as a result of the minorities' discrimination by the *Staatsvolk*, of the latter's reluctance (by either exclusively adhering to the *ius sanguinis* principles of conferring citizenship or using other discriminatory policy devices) to grant the "alien minorities" full citizenship and other civic rights that would take care of their aspirations to be truly, not just formally, equal members of their host-nations without, at the same time, losing within that larger identity their specific, minoritarian national-cultural selves. In other words, what we are facing here is the problem of whether the nation should be determined as a civic territorial entity formed by the inhabitants' free self-identification with it (which would include in the nation also the members of ethnic and other minorities identifying themselves with that nation as its voluntary citizens) or should it be an entity a priori "delimited" by objective criteria, such as the person's ethnic origin, his/her belonging to a certain religious denomination, etc. (which would forcefully exclude ethnic and other minorities from the nations' civic scope regardless of the members of those minorities' willingness to identify themselves with that nation); that is, whether the nation-state should be a free association of willing citizens or an oppressive ethnocracy that in its extreme form could evolve into an unabashed racist dictatorship.

Since the national minorities are thus naturally excluded from the process of "unscrambling the ethnic omelette" (they indeed willingly remain, if allowed, scrambled in it), the whole process of that unscrambling becomes rather straightforward. There is actually nothing that is as inscrutably complex and thus practically insoluble about it as my opponents believe it to be.

It is in the context of these two totally different types of tension between citizenship and nationhood that it becomes so important to distinguish between nations and national minorities. The problem is, however, in my opponents' blunt refusal to admit the very reality of such a distinction and, because of that, in their arguing with me on the issue of the relationship between nations and states across the purposes of this whole debate. Van den Berghe, for example, explicitly and totally dismisses this difference, stating, in a rather nonchalant manner, that the distinction between nations (territorial entities) and national minorities (communal entities without a territorial identity within the state they settled) is not useful. However, the examples he cites as allegedly defying such a categorization of *ethnoi,* all fit very nicely into the two types of tension between citizenship and nationhood described above, which is what in this case really matters. His examples are also of purely taxonomic nature, which is to say that, as such, they provide no logical connection between themselves and the problem of either the theory or practice of the exercise by nations of their right to self-determination, which makes these examples in the context of our discussion hardly relevant at all. As for Ebeling and Anderson, all their suggestions and solutions are perfectly relevant to solving the problems of national minorities—and in this, that is, to the extent of tackling this problem alone, I fully concur with what they had to say on the subject—but they do not even start the discussion of the problem of the territorial stateless nations and the type of tension between citizenship and nationhood that takes place in their relationship with the *Staatsvolk.* All that both of them, together with Van den Berghe, say is that the state shall be denationalized or, using their own terminology, the state and the nation should be decoupled. What none of them suggest, however, is what other identity but the nation's could the modern state, thus decoupled, assume.

Subnational identities, if they were to organically develop into ones that have grown to become incompatible with that of the "mother-nation," would have to claim for themselves a new separate national identity, which, if such an incompatibility was in the prevailing view of the subnational entity in question real, would be an entirely legitimate claim indeed. It is not serious to talk today about new supranational identities of any specific regional or continental scope springing up either. The closest we have to such a novel identity is exemplified by the European Union, which, as everybody would, no doubt, agree, is far from even starting to evolve a supranational identity that could supersede that of the member-nations. Not surprisingly, the "best Europeans" today are the members of the stateless nations of Europe—the Belgian Flemings, the Basques, the Catalans, the Scottish, and Welsh nationalists. The European Union is for them an institution able to counterbalance their exclusive dependency from the nation-state they are citizens of but consider to be largely alien to them, and they also try to use that union as a vehicle for furthering the cause of asserting, and getting, the widest possible recognition of, their separate identities in the world at large.

The logic of the argument about decoupling nations from states, from the point of view of the considerations on the state's identity briefly outlined above, leads to one inescapable conclusion, namely that human society has already evolved, or is about to evolve, one common identity that renders, or is about to render, separate national identities either entirely obsolete or fully subordinated to humanity's global identity. If this were the case, the states into which humankind is to be divided could indeed be created by following natural geographic or rational economic and administrative delineations of the world's territory. Moreover, on the basis of such an argument one could make a plausible case for the establishment of one worldwide state with such geographically and/or rationally delineated territorial entities serving as that global state's basic administrative-territorial units. Van den Berghe's reasoning about the advantages of creating small, Luxembourg-type states would, under such circumstances, acquire a legitimate place, too, but not at present, when mankind's overarching global identity is a mere abstraction belonging to the sphere of pure wishful thinking that has no foundation whatsoever in the world's political reality that is, and so far promises to remain, fully determined and permeated by the various national identities into which mankind is divided.

Since the nineteenth century many analysts and researchers of world affairs have convincingly argued that functionally the nation state is becoming increasingly irrelevant and, in most instances, counterproductive. They have shown with facts in hand that all the important social and economic matters are actually being transacted and taken care of not anymore on the national but on either the subnational or the supranational or the global levels, and that the nation-states, by interfering in these transactions and setting the restrictive conditions under which their nationals could participate in them, only make themselves a nuisance and become an obstacle for people's free interaction, that sooner rather than later will have to be removed. Hence, they implanted and made rather trendy the view that the nation-state is soon destined to disappear from the world's stage and that it will have to cede its place to such new political units, which would be functionally rather than nationally relevant. In other words, these analysts, long before Anderson, Ebeling, and Van den Berghe, in fact predicted the forthcoming decoupling of nations and states and the evolvement of a new, functionally determined structure of the world's political order.

This view, which in the 1950s and 1960s became extremely popular, is primarily associated with the functionalist school in the field of study of international politics and with the name of the founder of that school Professor David Mitrany of the famous London School of Economics.[14] Another prominent member of this school, Professor John H. Herz, in a famous 1957 article forcefully argued that the demise of the nation-state is imminent and that the only solution to the problems mankind is facing in the modern era is global universalism based on mankind conceiving of itself as one unit.[15] However, the same John H. Herz, in a 1968 article, had to admit that his and his fellow-functionalists' views on that score were proved to be wrong.[16] "There are indicators . . . ," he wrote, "pointing in another direction: not to 'universalism' but to retrenchment; not to interdependence but to a new self-sufficiency . . . "[17] Herz attributed these indicators and their effects on the world's situation to the persistence of nations as entities into which mankind is organically and apparently immutably divided, despite the functional requirements for it to abandon national divisions and transcend to global universalism. In the result of his new inquiries into the problem of the world's political evolution, Herz unequivocally refuted his old convictions, unhesitatingly stating that in the modern world the nation, as the sole and only provider of people's coherent identity, is the body that legitimizes the state and thus the only form in which the state can sustain a stable and assured existence. In conclusion, Herz stated that the "function, then, of the future polity would still or again be that of providing group identity, protection and welfare; in short, the legitimate function of the nation. And this neo-territorial world of nations, in addition, might salvage one feature of humanity which seems ever more threatened by the ongoing rush of mankind into technological conformity of a synthetic planetary environment: diversity of life and culture, of traditions and civilizations."[18] So much for the feasibility and future prospects of decoupling nations and states, especially when the advocates of such decoupling do not even envisage an alternative identity for the thus decoupled states.

To Herz's arguments I could add only one point. Identity forms itself only in, and through, the relation to "otherness." Humanity as a whole cannot relate to any such "otherness" and, as long as it will not encounter other equally conscious and culturally evolving species, will be destined to develop different identities within itself. Nations are such obvious identities within mankind by which man recognizes himself in others, and as long as we are alone in the universe it is most likely to continue to stay this way. As Dr. Hayo Krombach of the London School of Economics put it, " . . . both, the self and the other, constitute in dialectic the socio-historical 'we,' the 'we' in interpersonal but also the 'we' in inter-national relations. . . . If we do not initiate the process of dialectical relation to others, the 'I'—be it a person or a nation—is quickly reduced to an empty or merely formal gesture. . . . Identity is not the isolated individual or nation. Whatever its reciprocally determined socio-historical, cultural, or political and economic content, identity is always and only relational and contextual identity."[19] All this is to say that so far there is no such identity that could organically sustain a world state or, to be more precise, any state that is not based on the identity of a nation, except for a few historically unique cases in which certain supranational identities were naturally formed and got themselves firmly entrenched.

There is hardly a better way to sum up the subject of nations and states than by quoting Pope John Paul II's 1995 speech to the United Nations. "A presupposition of a nation's right is certainly its right to exist: therefore no one—neither a State or another nation, nor an international organization—is ever justified in asserting that any individual nation is not worthy of existence. This fundamental right to existence does not necessarily call for sovereignty as a state, since various forms of juridical aggregation between different nations are possible. . . . There can be historical circumstances in which aggregations different from single state sovereignty can even prove advisable, but only on condition that this takes place in a climate of true freedom, guaranteed by the exercise of the self-determination of the peoples concerned. . . . Every nation therefore has also the right to shape its life according to its own traditions, excluding, of course, every abuse of basic human rights and in particular the oppression of minorities."[20]

THE LEAGUE OF PEACE AND THE GLOBAL COMMONWEALTH

Professor J. David Singer ends his comment by stating that the world must be governed. From what I said above it follows that I do not believe that either a world state or a world government is a sustainable or desirable institution. I do not think therefore that the world can be governed, although I firmly believe that it should be regulated by world law and coordinated in the performance of tasks that are global by their nature. On that issue I fully and unequivocally accept Kant's reasoning, although Ebeling, in contrast to Singer and in total misconception of my true position on that issue, criticizes me for trying to introduce under the guises of the League of Peace and Global Commonwealth nothing less than a world government having "allocational control and regulatory power over natural resources, information and communication networks or the training and distribution of 'manpower resources.'"

First, in no place, including my wildest dreams, did I suggest to endow the global commonwealth with any allocational controls or regulatory power over natural resources. If Ebeling read somewhere about any such propositions, it was certainly not in my article. Second, the gist of the whole idea about putting under the global commonwealth's authority the naturally global matters, such as the protection of the natural environment and solution of other problems of human ecology, safety standards in the fields of high-tech sources of energy, etc.; consists in withdrawing all these matters from the ineffective, often arbitrary and mostly counterproductive regulations and control by yet another layer of government. It seems to me that by globalizing safety standards, new Chernobyls could be much more effectively avoided and concerted efforts for finding new, safer, and better, ways for the disposal of nuclear waste and other dangerous materials would be much more productively initiated. The global commonwealth, having no coercive power of the state, could issue on such matters only recommendations based on professional expertise, which most likely would carry sufficient authority to be followed voluntarily—though, perhaps, with some assistance provided by the pressure of public opinion—by both the private sector and the states' institutions issuing and enforcing the laws and regulations under which the private sector is operating everywhere anyway. In other words, all the "globalizing" propositions were put forward by me exclusively, on the one hand, with the view of elevating rule-making on global issues to the global level, since only on that level it could be done adequately and effectively; and, on the other hand, for the sake of substantially restricting or altogether eliminating governmental interference into, and enhancing the freedom and scope of, private enterprise, world trade, and communication and information exchange.

If Ebeling did not get that, then, I must regretfully conclude, he did not read my article carefully enough. Consequently, all his rhetorical questions—like that on whether compensation for lost revenue will be paid to the country ordered by the global commonwealth not to sell some of its resources; or that on who shall punish the private land owners contravening decisions of the global commonwealth preventing them from using their land in a manner they find most profitable—sound absolutely hollow and out of context, as no word or sentence in my text justifies considering, let alone posing, any such questions. And also absolutely out of context here is Ebeling's taking on these issues not mine but Anderson's side, for there was no dispute between me and Anderson on the problems of the global commonwealth and its functions whatsoever; on the contrary, Anderson has explicitly expressed his solidarity with my views on that subject. As far, however, as my answers on the substance of Ebeling's rhetorical questions are concerned, they should be obvious to anyone familiar with my text, but for Ebeling's and, maybe, some other less attentive reader's benefit, I will repeat them: Yes, in my, and I believe also in Ebeling's, view, as a matter of course, no global commonwealth or any other supranational institution should have the right to interfere with any country's policy on handling its natural resources; and, as a matter of course, too, no authority should have the ability forcefully to deprive a private owner from the right of using his property in a way that he deems to be most profitable for him.

Both Singer and Ebeling think that the League of Peace may prove to be divisive and dangerous, if, as I suggested, it were to be formed now only by those nations that share common liberal-democratic/republican principles and values. Will it indeed? The world today is not as diverse as it used to be even a few years ago, to say nothing about the irreconcilably antagonistic nature of the world's diversity during the "high tide" period of the Cold War. Former communist states, although hesitantly and slowly, crawl toward liberal-democracy and try to integrate into the Western system. Even the remaining communist states, first of all the most powerful of them, China, try to adapt to the prevailing trends in the world economy and avoid direct confrontation with the West. Economic necessities force other "deviant states," in seeking pragmatic cooperation with the West, substantially to blunt their ideological intransigence and to tone down their anti-Western stance. Once established, the Western-only League of Peace, because of its sheer dominance in the world's economy and tremendous superiority in power over the rest of the world, will inevitably start attracting most of the other, thus far "inadmissible," countries, which, in order to earn the league's sympathy, protection, and favors, will try to adapt its standards and follow its example. What seems to be divisive may thus in fact become a catalyst of the world's integration and gradual unification.

Nor will the league necessarily have to intervene in the conflicts and troubles of nonmember states. For that purpose the UN is going to continue to be, as it is today, the main instrument. Hence, Ebeling's dilemma about the league members either "watching from behind their wall of common peace the remainder of the world periodically falling into cataclysms of conflict, cruelty and carnage" or assuming, with disastrous consequences, the role of the world's policeman, is ill founded. There are still many unresolved disputes and conflicts among the potential members of the league itself. The problem of Cyprus and other Greco-Turkish disputes, the controversy over Gibraltar between the UK and Spain, France's problems with Corsica and Spain's with the Catalans and Basques, to name but a few. The league would have to reach agreements on many underlying principles of conflict resolution before it would be able to do anything about settling these issues, and that is not going to be easy. But if and when these agreements are attained, they will in most quarters acquire the status of a standard to be followed, becoming a guiding light for many a nonleague country when trying to find a solution to similar conflicts and problems.

Talking about divisiveness, I must say, however, that generally, in terms of the methodology of dealing with the world's conflict-generating situations, I have nothing against it. To me divisiveness is not so much dangerous, as, in most cases, necessary, extremely useful, and even salutary. There is no doubt that the 1949 decision about creating NATO was divisive, but it was, in my view, a salutary decision. The 1938 Munich agreements, on the other hand, were of accommodating, nondivisive, nature but they were absolutely disastrous and, indeed, extremely dangerous. Hence, divisiveness, to me at least, is on its own not a sufficiently convincing argument to proclaim the formation of the League of Peace without delay dangerous or even premature.

In conclusion, I would like to express two positive remarks on Ebeling's contribution to the debate. The first concerns Ebeling's proposal about "the depoliticization, the privatization of foreign intervention." This proposal impressed me very much indeed. It was new to me and, at first consideration, seemed to open a fruitful avenue for actively seeking justice for the world. I concur with Ebeling's view that "[t]hose who see distress and hardship among peoples in other lands, and who desire to assist them, should not be restricted in forming associations and charities to pool their resources to supply such help. But neither should others who do not share that same concern, or who consider there to be other answers to solve those foreign problems, be compelled to provide assistance if they choose not to." I am only not too sure how practical in the world of states and their professional military forces such private initiatives may be. The example of the International Brigades in the Spanish Civil War shows that nothing practically relevant with regard to the correlation of forces fighting in that war could come out of that to a large extent truly private initiative without a relatively powerful state, the Soviet Union, standing behind it. On the other hand, the truly private volunteers fighting in the Nigerian Civil War on Biafra's side made no difference in the war whatsoever, although among them were a dozen or so professional pilots who were equipped through private fundraising with modern fighter-jets. Nevertheless, I think the idea is novel, creative, and worth further exploration and elaboration.

The second remark concerns Ebeling's optimism for the future, which I wholeheartedly share. Concluding his article, Ebeling wrote: "If in the next century countries begin to reject the remaining forms of political and economic collectivism which they now practice, a peaceful international order . . . will naturally and spontaneously emerge as governments restrict themselves to new forms of international 'rules of the game' consistent with individual liberty, private property, and the network of voluntary associations that form the structure of civil society. And if this occurs, we will have gone beyond artificial and inherently unworkable makeshifts like the League of Nations, the United Nations and alternative proposals for Leagues of Peace and global commonwealths." I only regret to say that if Ebeling equates the League of Nations and the United Nations, which indeed represented inherently unworkable makeshifts composed, in Van den Berghe's words, of "squabbling states," with the League of Peace and the global commonwealth projected in my article, it means that he either has as yet not thought his hoped-for international order through in a systematic and thorough manner and has to do some more thinking on these matters or that he was simply unwilling, when reading my article, to spend his time on going beyond the names of these institutions and finding out what were the real purpose and functions ascribed to them in my piece. What, I think, Ebeling indeed still fails to realize is that without global institutions uniting free and liberal-democratic nations in their quest for peace, international justice, and personal and national liberty, the international order envisaged by him would not be in the position of acquiring that structural consistency and completeness without which it could not be either properly materialized or stably sustained.

NOTES

1. See Zeev Maoz and Bruce Russett, "Normative and Structural Causes of Democratic Peace, 1946–1986," *American Political Science Review* 87, no. 3 (September 1993); Bruce Russett, et al., *Grasping the Democratic Peace: Principles of a Post–Cold War Order* (Princeton, N.J.: Princeton University Press, 1993); John R. Oneal, Frances H. Oneal, Zeev Maoz, and Bruce Russett, "The Liberal Peace: Interdependence, De-

mocracy and International Conflict, 1950–1985," *Journal of Peace Research* (February 1996).

2. See Aleksandras Shtromas, "What is Peace and How Could It Be Achieved?" *International Journal on World Peace* 12, no. 1 (March 1995): 31.

3. Shtromas, "What is Peace and How Could It Be Achieved?," 30.

4. All quotations from von Mises are taken from Ebeling's commentary where the source of quotation is indicated.

5. See, for example, my "Ideological Politics and the Contemporary World: Have We Seen the Last of 'Isms'?," in Aleksandras Shtromas, ed., *The End of "'Isms"? Reflections on the Fate of Ideological Politics after Communism's Collapse* (Oxford: Blackwell, 1994), 196 ff; and also Alexander Shtromas, "The Future World Order and the Right of Nations to Self-Determination and Sovereignty," *The International Journal on World Peace* 7, no. 1 (January–March 1990); Alexander Shtromas, "Religion and Ethnicity in World Order," *The International Journal on World Peace* 9, no. 2 (June 1992); et al.

6. For the rendering of Renan's Qu'est – ce qu'une nation?, see John Hutchinson and Anthony D. Smith, eds., *Nationalism* (Oxford: Oxford University Press, 1994), 17–18.

7. The idea of *homo duplex* was originally formulated by Durkheim in *Suicide* (1897) and later developed in *The Elementary Forms of the Religious Life* (1912). For a concise description of this idea directed, first and foremost, against the utilitarian concept of individual liberty, see Emile Durkheim's article published in *Scientia*, no. 15 (1914), "Le dualisme de la nature humaine et ses conditions sociales" ("The Dualism of Human Nature and Its Social Conditions"), published in Robert N. Bellah, ed., *Emile Durkheim on Morality and Society* (Chicago: University of Chicago Press, 1973), 149–13; for the expression *homo duplex*, see 152).

8. Shtromas, "What is Peace and How Could It Be Achieved?," 26.

9. Shtromas, "What is Peace and How Could It Be Achieved?," 52.

10. See Emile Durkheim, *The Division of Labor in Society* (New York: Macmillan, 1933), 27.

11. See E. Shils and M. Rheinstein, trans., *Max Weber on Law in Economy and Society* (Cambridge, Mass.: Harvard University Press, 1954), 328.

12. Shils and Rheinstein, *Max Weber on Law in Economy and Society*, 328.

13. Aristotle, *Politics*, trans. Carnes Lord (Chicago: University of Chicago Press, 1984), 36–37.

14. See, for example, his *A Working Peace System* (Chicago: Quadrangle Books, 1966).

15. John H. Herz, "The Rise and the Demise of the Territorial State," *World Politics*, vol. 9 (1957): 437 ff.

16. John H. Herz, "The Territorial State Revisited: Reflections on the Future of the Nation State," in *Polity* 1, no. 1 (fall 1968): 11–34.

17. Herz, "The Territorial State Revisited," 11–12.

18. Herz, "The Territorial State Revisited," 34.

19. Hayo Krombach, "The Dialectic of Identity: From Individual to Nation," in *The ASEN Bulletin*, no. 10 (winter 1995–1996), 44.

20. See the full text in *The New York Times*, October 7, 1995.

21

Competing Identities as Shapers of Personal Political Consciousness:
The "Collective Self" on the Eve of the Twenty-First Century

ALEKSANDRAS SHTROMAS

There are two main ways by which the concept of identity is treated and dealt with in scholarly discourse. The first, and the most widespread one, is indiscriminate and leveling. According to it, an individual's membership in, or association with, any collective human entity is an equal part of that individual's overall identity, and what he/she considers to be his/her ultimate identity is usually a result of clever indoctrination and manipulation of the individual's consciousness by the ruling establishments. It is thus the task of some truth-seeking ideologues to penetrate through the individuals' "false consciousness" and either "scientifically" to determine what really their ultimate identity is or simply liberate their "true consciousness" from the "social normatives" imposed upon them from outside, thus allowing people freely to assert their ultimate identity in the way they feel is best suited to their particular needs. The fallacy of the leading ideologies of the twentieth century, such as Marxism or Hitler's National Socialism, consisted exactly in their supposedly scientific, but in fact random, determination of people's ultimate identities, of which the people themselves were actually unaware—in the

Reprinted from a paper presented to the Colloquium on Identity and Territorial Autonomy in Plural Societies, sponsored on behalf of the Research Committee on Politics and Ethnicity (RC–14), International Political Science Association, by the University of Santiago de Compostela, Department of Political Science, Santiago de Compostela, Galicia, Spain, July 17–19, 1998, pp. 1–11.

case of Marxism this being a globally defined class identity and in the case of National Socialism, a racial identity expressed on a global scale by the multiple subordinated identities of racially pure Volks; and the fallacy of the contemporary postmodernist theory consists in its unhesitant rejection of the really extant hierarchical structures of people's identities, treating all of them equally as potential ultimate identities to be chosen from by the people in accordance with their individual priorities, be it class, gender, or race, sexual orientation, or ideological preference (it should be noted that the postmodernist nihilism with regard to the hierarchical structures of various identities of people as conceived by the people themselves has found its most salient expression in its advocacy of multiculturalism, a concept that is always based on an overarching ultimate identity into which minority cultures and religions are supposed to be organically incorporated).

The second way is based on the exploration of the reality of people's identities and their hierarchical structures with the view of discerning what people themselves determine as being their true ultimate identity and whether and how this ultimate identity corresponds with the ultimate identity established for them by the official "social normatives." It is in that way that this paper treats, and deals with, the problems of identity, trying to establish the sources of conflicts between various identities people bear and how these conflicts could be either prevented or solved without them provoking major explosive sociopolitical crises, which they so far very often do.

Any real, that is, genuinely felt by the individuals and shared by them, sociopolitical identity comes into being through the process of differentiation among people. In order to become "we," a group of people has to relate itself to another such group that it readily identifies as "they." In other words, the prerequisite for developing an identity (a sense of being a "we-group" genuinely assumed and shared by the individual members of that group) is either the formation from within or an encounter from without of at least two groups of humans; by relating to each other as "they" each develops a relatively clear concept of "we." It follows from this proposition that humanity so far is unable to become a meaningful identity that people could genuinely assume; such an overall human identity may meaningfully develop only after the human race encounters other sentient species. A simple encounter is by itself, however, also insufficient to forge, for the "we" and "they" firmly consolidated overall identities. For that to take place the "we" and "they" have to be mutually challenged for preeminence or domination. Encounters with barbarians and the Phoenician civilization were, for example, sufficient for the ancient Greeks to become aware of their overall Greek Identity but, because these encounters did not represent a real challenge to the Greeks, they in themselves did not change the ultimate city-state identities of the Greek people, which had evolved at a time when the Greeks were the only civilized people in the world known to them and because of that were unable to develop a meaningful overall Greek identity, in exactly the same way as we are now unable to develop a meaningful overall human identity. The situation did, however, drastically change when the Greeks were attacked by the Persians and had to unite in order to repel the Persian attack. It was at that time that the ultimate city-state identities of the Greeks started gradually to merge into an overall ultimate identity of being Greek first and Athenian, Spartan, or Corinthian second. That newly developed Greek national identity facilitated the task of Macedonia to create a united Greek nation-state, which Alexander III the Great soon transformed into a Greek world empire.

The above shows how ultimate identities are practically being formed both in historical reality and in people's individual consciousness. Ultimate identity is thus the one that establishes divisions of identity within the human race on a global scale. Practically speaking, it could be defined as a polity-forming identity. This is so, since each such ultimate identity seeks to preserve and enhance itself among (and, if necessary, against) other ultimate identities, through territorial delimitation and the establishment of sovereign authority over the thus delimited territorial space housing people adhering to a certain self-determined identity, separating them as a unique "we-group" from all the others defined as the "they-groups." In other words, an ultimate identity seeks to be embodied as the state—the only institution capable of providing people with self-sufficiency and thus enshrining and affirming their identity against all possible odds.

What then about other identities, those that do not serve as the basis for polity formation? They could either be abstract super-identities—identifiable by an outside observer but not present as means for meaningful self-identification in the consciousness of individuals forming the "we-groups" (beside the human identity, one could define as such super-identities also race and the so-called civilizational identities)—or the identities of the secondary type or sub-identities. There is no need to discuss in any detail the spuriousness of civilizational identity in terms of it being the basis for polity-formation. The so-called civilizational states, whenever they appeared on the world's stage, have always been imperial in their origin and, when left to their own devices, tended to split apart in concordance with some ultimate identities formed within the overall civilizational realm. The histories of China, Japan, and Korea or the Ottoman Empire, to say nothing of the Hellenistic Empire created by Alexander the Great or the Holy Roman Empire built by either Charlemagne or Otton I, are graphic demonstrations of this thesis, and the barrage of criticism provoked by Samuel Huntington's book on the clash of civilizations (this author was one among the many critics of this book, too) took care of this issue more than adequately.

More complex but similar is the situation with race, which, when it did provide a basis for a polity-forming identity, was mainly the substitute term for defining the indigenous people in contradistinction with the racially distinct nonindigenous colonial rulers. As soon as the indigenous people achieved for their administratively determined habitats the status of an independent polity, the symbolically overarching racial identity of the indigenous people immediately evaporated ceding the way to competing ultimate identities of Hausas, Ibos, and Yorubus in Nigeria; Kikuyus, Luos, and Kalenjins in Kenya (with the new overarching identities provided by the respective postcolonial states remaining shallow, shaky, and marginal); Vietnamese, Laotians, and Khmers (who established their separate polities) in Indo-China. As for the racially mixed societies, such as those of the United States, United Kingdom, France, or Malaysia, race forms in them a sub-identity that is either no different from other minority identities or, when it is different, the race is again a convenient term to describe the specific traits of that particular minority identity, not its racial identity per se.

Most of the generally acknowledged sub-identities, on the other hand, are not even full or proper identities at all. Biologically or societally (mainly by the division of labor in society) determined groups do not, in the view of this author, qualify for even being classified as proper sub-identities. For example, gender as such does not provide the person with an identity in any exact sense of this term, for both sexes, men and women, create together super-ordinate units, such as families, concubinates, and other similar partnerships without which the gender division loses its very meaning; and the real sub-identities within society are to be ascribed to these "gender-combining" units alone. For similar reasons, neither does age provide for the formation of any proper sub-identities. Class, stratum, or occupation generally do not provide a person with a proper identity either. Classes and strata usually combine in enterprises or other businesses and institutions (educational, cultural, scientific, media, etc.), which are distinguishable units within society and could in that sense qualify, individually or collectively, as bearers of a certain sub-identity. As interest groups, however, the feminists or gays, the pensioners and the youngsters, as well as the members of social classes, strata, occupational groups, etc., usually get organized and exercise pressure on public opinion and the authorities directly to make them all pay due attention to their particular needs and grievances. In this capacity, such groups, without necessarily representing a sub-identity, become, what one could call, policy-initiating or policy-forming groups. Policy initiating and/or forming groups are also the ones who do qualify as sub-identities. In addition to the ones briefly mentioned above, these are all kinds of minorities—national, religious, historical (in the United States, the African-Americans and the Native Americans form such historical groups that, for the purpose of convenience, can also be defined in racial terms), immigrant (some of these, for the same reasons, could also be defined in racial terms, for example, the Hispanics in the United States, the Turks in Germany or the Arabs in France), etc. None of these groups, sub-identities or not, except for stateless nations of whom we are going to talk later, have any problems with sharing with the main core of the people of the respective state the same ultimate identity either.

In terms of this paper, an identity is real only insofar as an individual human being willingly chooses it to define himself and his place in the world. In other words, real collective identities come about only as a multiplicity of acts of individual self-determination. This alone, as hinted above, is, however, not a sufficient factor in the formation of collective identities, for the acts of individual self-determination have to be also accepted as valid by the multitude of people who have chosen the same identity hitherto. In other words, it is not enough for a person to declare or even to profess his/her identity, it is also necessary that the group formed by that identity accepted this thus self-determined person as a legitimate member of the group in question. This situation produces in many a state substantial tensions and conflicts that could be defined as one of the aspects of the identity crisis in the contemporary world.

On the surface, as already mentioned above, people's ultimate identities are expressed by the states of which they are members. The state is, however, rather a modern institution. Before statehood came into being, people basically identified themselves by blood, that is by family connections that eventually grew to develop into extended tribes, which, when not nomadic, settled in villages. The creation of the state reflected the emergence of a higher order of people's identity. Even when related by blood and engaged in quite rigid structures of tribal hierarchies, human beings cannot avoid disputes over issues of basic ethical values and principles of justice, although such disputes were usually engendered by disagreements on practical issues, such as rights of using grazing lands, hunting or fishing privileges, the entitlements to getting a spouse, etc. Divisions over such issues would set apart some tribally interlinked groups that then would find allies in some distant villages among people that they did not know personally before but with whom they were able to develop a common identity based on the shared ethical values and principles of justice. What united these otherwise unrelated people was a common concept of good life, as Aristotle called it, and, in order to be able to live such good lives securely and independently, those people combined their territories, making them a single territorial unit. They then built for themselves a city that had to serve as the political center of that combined territorial space, which was thus transformed into the single city-state whose given name expressed the newly established common identity of the people living in that territorial space. The main purpose of the city-state was to embody in its laws and governing principles the particular concept of the good life the people of that city-state collectively embraced and to endow them with self-sufficiency necessary for their assured and undisturbed living of such a life. The classical case of state creation in ancient Greece thus fully corresponds with the principle of creating an ultimate collective identity by the multiplicity of individual self-determinations stated above. The city-states of ancient Greece have indeed coalesced in the process of their peoples' differentiation from one another by the way of expressing their unique (and thus differing from one another) spiritual identities on the basis of which they claimed for themselves, in order to embody and safely adhere to these identities, sovereign self-sufficiency.

Most states, however, emerged as a result of a conquest or the urgent need for the disparate tribes to unite in opposing the threat of a conquest by an

alien outside power. Typical for the latter case was the creation of the
Lithuanian Kingdom by the Grand Duke Mindaugas, trying to put together a
fighting coalition of local tribes and fledgling principalities to oppose the
Teutonic Knights' *Drang nach Osten* in the thirteenth century. The first Russian state, the Kievan Rus', was, on the contrary, created in the ninth century
by imposing on local Slavic tribes the rule of alien Varangian (Scandinavian)
princes and their troops. Alien invaders of various kinds created the Kingdom of England, which, for the last time, was conquered by yet another alien
people, the Normans, in 1066. Once created, even if that creation had been
accomplished in such an unnaturally perverse manner, the states in the person of their alien rulers did, however, their utmost to forge a common identity between their subjects and themselves, as without a common identity the
state of which they were the rulers could neither be preserved or entrenched. In many cases that identity-forging enterprise of the conquering
state power proved to be totally successful. Who in England ever remembers
that their country is formally still under foreign occupation accomplished in
1066 and never gotten rid of? In Russia the process of full mutual assimilation of the Varangian rulers and their Slavic subjects lasted about two hundred years but during the next two hundred years, before Kievan Rus' was
conquered by the Mongol-Tatars, the Russian state existed as quite a harmonious homogenous entity with a firmly established common Slavic identity
shared by the rulers and ruled alike that totally obscured, like in the case of
England, its alien origins. A great success story in forging a common French
identity was also the Kingdom of France that emerged as the result of Germanic Franks conquering the land of the Gauls and symbiotically assimilating with them.

This process of political symbiosis did not always, however, manage to
produce such neat results in achieving true homogeneity. Sometimes the old
identities of different peoples brought together by conquest or dynastic
intermarriages into one state obstinately persisted, despite the state's tireless
efforts to forge a common identity for its peoples. This usually was the case
when the state tried to impose the identity of a part of the state's population
on the rest of it, which had a different identity and was determined to resist
the political pressure to exchange it for an alien one. That is what happened
to the Spanish rulers who, since the fifteenth century, tried to impose a
Castillian identity on the various peoples living in the Pyrenean Peninsula
under their rule. In 1640 the Portuguese rebelled and seceded from Spain,
while the Basques, the Catalans, partly the Galliegos, and also the Andalusians still refuse to identify themselves as Spanish, that is to assume the
Castillian identity at the expense of their own one.

Spain represents a relatively mild case of a discrepancy between the identity of the state and the identities of the various peoples living under that
state's rule. Most of the extant states today are much more heterogeneous
than Spain and the peoples unwilling to share their state's identity are being
suppressed by the authorities in these states in a much harsher way than is the

case in democratic Spain. This—the conflict between the identity born by the state and indiscriminately imposed upon all its people and the identity of those people who have to bear that identity, too, but internally reject it as alien—constitutes the main crisis of identity in the contemporary world. It is a real and a very serious crisis, not like the one related to the allegedly clashing identities of special interest groups that is artificially conceived, tirelessly propagated, and practically instigated by the latter-day postmodernist scholars and their followers in the real world.

Most states in the contemporary world are claiming a certain national identity, although there are states whose identity is sub- or supranational. Every Arab state is a subnational entity whose identity is either dynastic (Saudi Arabia, Oman, Bahrain, Kuwait) or ideological (Syria, Iraq, Libya) or historically-traditional (Yemen, Egypt, Morocco). Subnational states are also the ones that divide on ideological grounds one state-nation into two states (North and South Koreas, China and Taiwan). The United Kingdom, Belgium, and Switzerland are supra-national states in the sense that different nations living in these states, in addition to their separate national identities, willingly share a supranational identity of the state itself. The English, Scottish, and Welsh nations are all identifying themselves as also British; the Walloons and the Flemings, as Belgians; and the four nations of Switzerland, as hyphenated Swiss. Not all supranational states are, however, as organically accommodating to their various nations as the above mentioned ones. Most of them are, in fact, not supranational but multinational states that try, without much success, to forge the many nations living in their realm into one nation with a single identity assumed and promoted by the state. India, Myanmar (Burma), and hosts of others are such supranational but in fact multinational states within which the identity of the state sharply clashes with the identities of many peoples who form these states. These multinational states are the main problem areas of the contemporary world, as it is in them that the crisis of identity in this world is taking the most acute forms.

In the course of history the identities of the states constantly changed. City-states consolidated into nation-states and nation-states grew into empires to be afterward again reduced to nation-states, but more often to supranational or multinational states. And in all these transitions the ability to forge and retain a common identity of the states' peoples played the determinant role. We could therefore predict with some assurance that explosive political instability in the world will continue as long as the identity of the extant states will not become fully coterminous with the identity of the peoples that inhabit them. Since the seventeenth century, European political developments have led to the creation in Europe of nation-states, that is, of states claiming to embody an identity of a single nation. This process continues unabated to the present day and is far from being completed. Large multinational states in Asia formed on the basis of broadly conceived civilizational identities are rapidly losing cohesion and show a clear tendency to disintegrate into a multitude of nation-states, too. On the other hand, the processes of urbanization in Africa are progressively consolidating the traditional tribal entities into full-fledged nations, challenging the stability of the postcolonial African states that poorly accommodate their political aspirations. All this is to say that we live in an era in which national identity has practically assumed on a universal scale the role of the ultimate identity of the world's peoples that in most cases does not adequately square with the extant identities of the world's multinational states.

The peoples who do not share their respective state's identity and who are trying instead to assert their own separate identity as the ultimate one, should be defined as nations without states or stateless nations. A nation is usually understood as an ethnic group or an *ethnos*, although very few nations could claim a single ethnic background. What they claim, however, is a single ethnic identity. There is no other nation that is more ethnically mixed than the Americans, but Americans of every ethnic background share the single Anglo-American ethnic identity, whatever the objections of the advocates of multiculturalism to that thesis may be. The English themselves are ethnically a very mixed bag, too, but the English nation is beyond anyone's doubt a single *ethnos* with a definite ethnic identity. An ethnic group or an *ethnos* consists therefore not so much of people sharing the same ethnic origins but, first and foremost, of people consciously identifying themselves as members of one particular *ethnos* built up to the exclusion of all other *ethnoi* (which does not preclude the possibility of some individuals' identification with more than only one *ethnos*), and recognizing one another as legitimate members of this *ethnos*. An ethnic identity is in itself, however, insufficient to make an ethnic group a nation. An ethnic group becomes a full-fledged nation only when, in addition to its members' identification with one another as conationals, it collectively identifies itself also with a certain territorial entity (a nation could thus be defined as a territorial ethnic group).

This is what makes the problems of stateless nations so different from those of national minorities, that is, such ethnic groups that have voluntarily chosen to be a part of another nation's state's citizenry and who live in that "other" nation's state without claiming any of that state's territory as its own (among national minorities, one could distinguish members of such nonterritorial nationalities as Roma Gypsies, as well as members of full-fledged nations whose territorial identity lies, however, outside the territory in which that particular contingent of the nation in question happens to live). These ethnic groups are readily accepting the state's identity as their own without necessarily compromising by so doing their specific ethnic identity, which they may practice within the confines of loyal membership of the state's civic nation. The problems of these minorities are twofold: first, they often suffer from discrimination practiced in regard to them even when formally they enjoy full rights of equal citizenship, which is also not always the case; second, they are often restricted, practically or even legally, in their ability to engage in activities aimed at retaining and enhancing their specific national–cultural identities. What these minorities are seeking is proper, nondiscriminatory accommodation within the other nation's state that accepted them as either residents or citizens, as well as legally and practically guaranteed possibilities to assert their specific identities and freely engage in lawful activities related to their exercise. In truly democratic states the problems of national minorities are usually solved without much ado, while, as a rule, the problems of stateless nations are not. For them to be solved in the way that could defuse the explosive consequences of the identity crisis that stateless nations bring about in the states in which they are situated, it is necessary to include into the list of basic human rights recognized and protected by liberal-democratic states the right of nations to self-determination and sovereignty. So far no state has done so.

All this is to say that the process of identity-creation and consolidation always has been and still remains the major source of political tensions and conflicts. Whereas, as already mentioned above, the reluctance to accept certain categories of people willing to become members of a "we-group" into that group creates difficult problems in regard to the situation and rights of minorities within a state, the imposition of the state's identity on peoples unwilling to share it—a practice proliferating throughout history and very much alive today—causes the birth and death of often unviable states, the very existence of which inevitably causes civil and interstate wars, rebellions, terrorism, and similar bloody and sometimes very protracted skirmishes.

22

Universal Values vs. Local Preferences and Guilt Complexes in Transition to Global Education

Aleksandras Shtromas

WHERE AND HOW THE PROBLEM ARISES

The problem in the title of my paper arises in the first place in the fields of education in humanities. Education in sciences and technology is by its very nature universal and global. The Newtonian laws of mechanics, Einstein's theory of relativity, the physical laws of Boyle-Mariotte and Joule-Lenz are everywhere the same, attributed to the same persons, and included in the educational process everywhere equally. Quantum theory, wherever it is discussed, cannot avoid references to Gottfried Wilhelm Leibnitz and Louis-Victor de Broglie, and it is impossible to establish the origins of nuclear energy without mentioning the pioneering work of the Cavendish Laboratory in Cambridge and of people such as Lord Ernest Rutherford and Pyotr L. Kapitsa. Some arts are approaching similar universal standards. Among them logic, mathematics, visual arts, and music should be mentioned in the first place.

A special case is literature. Great nations with rich literary traditions are here the first that tend to succumb to ethnocentrism. Anglo-Saxon countries, no doubt, are the champions of such literary ethnocentrism. Students

Reprinted from *Absolute Values and the Reassessment of the Contemporary World*, vol. 1 (New York: International Conference on the Unity of the Sciences [ICUS] Books, 1991), 363–78.

in Great Britain, Australia, or the United States who do not study German may leave school without ever having heard of Schiller, Goethe, or Heine, and Pushkin is associated for most of them with the name of their neighbors' dog rather than with that of mankind's greatest poet of whom, because he wrote in Russian, they have never heard at all. In terms of such literary ethnocentrism the Anglo-Saxons are closely followed by the French- and Spanish-speaking peoples. The Germans fare much better here with their curricula including a great deal of Anglo-Saxon and French classics as well as a few prominent Russian and Spanish authors. Smaller European nations are perhaps the best at trying to absorb in their education the entire world's literary tradition. They are closely followed in this endeavor by the Japanese and Koreans.

Education in literature, and even in music and visual arts, as well as in certain aspects of sciences too, encounters special problems under ideocratic regimes. It is not so much ethnocentrism as ideological intolerance and selectivity applied on a universal, that is, transnational, scale that is here the main issue. In Nazi Germany the so-called Jewish science, literature, and art were forbidden and thus, to name but a few, Mendelsohn Heine and Einstein became the "unmentionables." In both Nazi Germany and the USSR modern visual arts (e.g., abstract art) and music (e.g., serial music) were considered decadent and thus subversive—hence, together with their creators, they were excluded from the educational process. In the USSR at certain points in time, genetics and cybernetics were proclaimed "false bourgeois sciences" and prohibited. All literature even slightly critical of the official ideologies, let alone of the political systems and leaders, is banned in ideocratic regimes. Hence, sometimes the best contemporary foreign authors may be excluded from the educational process whereas some insignificant but "friendly" ones are introduced as the most important representatives of the literature of a particular nation. In the Soviet Union, for example, the communist English author James Aldridge, of whom very few people in England have ever heard, has been (and still is) portrayed as one of the most significant English novelists of this century. In summer 1988 the Soviet authorities decorated Aldridge for "an outstanding contribution to world literature" with one of the highest Soviet orders. George Orwell, on the contrary, when mentioned by the Soviet media before 1988 at all, was uniformly denounced as a reactionary literary charlatan. Only now, due to *glasnost'* and its present anti-Stalinist emphasis, *Animal Farm* has been made available to Russian readers for the first time and *1984* is promised to follow suit soon. Whether Aldous Huxley's *Brave New World* will also be published in the USSR remains, however, to be seen. The recent declaration (January 1989) of the new Soviet Chief Ideologist Vadim Medvedev states that works that renounce the idea of socialism and that are thus directed against the Leninist foundations of the Soviet state will continue to be banned in the Soviet Union. Although this statement was made by Medvedev in response to the growing demands of publishing in the USSR the works of Alexander Solzhenitsyn, it leaves no doubt about the very principle of ideological censorship of literature remaining intact in the USSR, despite *glasnost'*.

Similar examples could be quoted with regard to noncommunist or non-Nazi ideocracies, e.g., the theocratic Iran of the ayatollahs, the semi-theocratic Qadaffi regime in Libya or the Baathist regimes of Saddam Hussein in Iraq and Hafiz al-Assad in Syria. Under all ideocratic regimes even the study of the "acceptable" world's truly great classical literature is subordinated to preset dogmatic ideological interpretations. In such a guise it becomes so boring an indoctrinational enterprise that it either kills the students' interest in world culture altogether or awakens in some of them the quest for true culture but rarely achieves ideological indoctrination, which it is supposed to serve.

Censorship and indoctrination in many aspects of education quite prominently figure also in a number of states that, though authoritarian, are not exactly ideocratic. In South Africa 18,000 books have been banned. In Pakistan students are still not permitted to study Darwin. In Zaire, a Music Censorship Commission guards against any impulse to sneak in a forbidden thought in rhyme or rhythm. Egypt pursues a ban on Baha'i religion and the Egyptian educational system portrays it as an incarnation of evil itself. Similarly, in the education of many an Arab state, Israel, and thus the Jews as the nation of Israel, is demonized on an almost hysterical level: the students are taught that it is virtuous to kill Israelis, to inflict upon Israel any thinkable damage and that to seek the destruction of Israel is the sacred duty of every "conscious Arab." It goes without saying that the Israeli views and positions on contentious issues are banned; censorship does not allow them to appear either in the media or in school textbooks even for criticism and denunciation. Conversely, in Israel the educational system concentrates on presenting the plight of the Palestinians as mainly self- or Arab-inflicted and, despite censorship being much weaker than in any of the Arab states, practically does not allow the Israeli students an authentic Arab point of view blaming Israel—often not without justice—for the sufferings inflicted upon the Palestinian Arabs and the scorn with which it treats them.

WHAT IS THE PROBLEM'S SUBSTANCE

Bias, double standards, and other infringements of universal values figure most prominently in religious and historical education. We will leave alone here the education in these fields as construed by ideocratic regimes. They teach and preach only one creed to the exclusion and refutal of all the others and arrange history (by ignoring some facts, names, and events, willfully exaggerating or diminishing others, and inventing, if need be, events and facts that have never taken place) so that it fits their particular ideological preferences and prescriptions as perfectly as possible. That much, as far as teaching of history in the USSR is concerned, has now been admitted by the Soviet authorities themselves who, because of that, even decided to cancel history exams for students graduating from schools in 1988. It remains to be seen how objective is the new version of history that the Soviet authorities are supposed to approve this summer for the students to read during the next academic year. Judging by the current Soviet official pronouncements on historical matters, one could say with assurance that all the main ideological "sacred cows" of Soviet history will remain unrevised and the "sanctity" of the Bolshevik endeavor to transform Russia into the present Soviet socialist state is going to be vigorously reinforced. Nor are we going to delve here into the cases of indoctrination and censorship of religious and historical subjects taking place in theocracies and authoritarian regimes that are at war with a particular religion, philosophy, or nation. Their biases and preferences are rather obvious. What has, however, to be pointed out as strongly as possible is that even in the most liberal nation-states, educational standards suffer from the deeply entrenched tradition of religious and national self-righteousness. It is this self-righteousness that often clashes with universal humanitarian values. For from a self-righteous point of view the wars one's nation waged were always just, the enemies or competitors of that nation not simply wrong but very often entirely evil, and one's own nation's moral and cultural standards assumed to be if not entirely impeccable then in any case superior to those of the hostile or competing nations.

Universal standards, by occupying an increasingly prominent place in national mentalities of the more advanced Western nations, produce a clash with the entrenched tradition of self-righteousness with quite dramatic results—not only in education but in overall national self-awareness. One such result is the so-called national "self-hatred" that represents an inversion of self-righteousness and that is responsible for a lot of confusion in educational curricula and practice; another is guilt complexes related to some national deeds that are contrary to the universal humanitarian standards and that are therefore difficult to accommodate into an educational system based on the traditions of national and religious self-righteousness. In many instances such shameful historical episodes are either entirely ignored or hushed up by the extant educational curricula. There is, for example, a lot of confusion about the treatment of British colonial history in British education; or of the fate of American Indians in the U.S. education; and West German, Italian, and Japanese educational systems are still experiencing grave difficulties in coping with the problems related to the emergence in their countries of the fascist-type regimes and with the role these countries played in World War II. Hence, not only self-centeredness, self-congratulatory attitudes, and prejudices against other religions and nations, but also national "self-hatred" and guilt complexes are the derivatives of self-righteousness. Consequently, the main problem in historical and religious education is overcoming the tradition of self-righteousness in a way that would make national education compatible with universal humanitarian standards without, at the same time, inducing national guilt complexes and self-hatred.

HOW TO BEGIN TO OVERCOME ETHNOCENTRISM

Educational standards devised for overcoming ethnocentric self-righteousness should continue to be based on the extant principles that give priority to the study of the national language, literature, history, arts, geography, etc. Priority should also be given to the study of the students' own religion. As is already the case in many places now, the study of the national language should be extended to the study of classical and foreign languages (one of the foreign languages being studied on a par with the native one) and the study of national literature, history, arts, and geography to that of the literature, history, arts, and geography of the world at large. The emphasis on, and attention (e.g., the number of hours) devoted to "world studies" should be increased, with these studies acquiring a more systematic (i.e., less episodic) character.

More novel would be the proposition to introduce into educational curricula as an obligatory subject the study of the world's major religions other than one's own. That course should be taught either by the representatives of those "alien" religions or by nonreligious experts on the religions in question. By no means should the study of other religions be left in the hands of the clergymen representing the students' own religious faith. The problem of such "multifaceted" religious education is especially complex in the secularized educational systems (not only the USSR's but also the United States's) where students receive religious instruction not in school but, if at all, in their own denominational churches. It could be quite easily solved, however, by including the major religious texts, such as the Bible, the Koran, the Vedas and Upanishads, the Sutras, etc., into the curriculum of the course on world literature that should be made compulsory to all students. It is this solution that, in 1988, under the cloak of *glasnost'*, Soviet educationalists have started vigorously to advocate in specialist publications and in the mass media.

Every nation without exception has a historical, cultural, and ethical heritage of which it can be justifiably proud by any standards. At the same time, in every nation's history are some "dark episodes" of which as such it should be made aware by educational means without losing face or being denigrated. In the process of education students should also be taught about the negative or critical views on their nation's historical record propounded by the historians of other nations, both the supposedly hostile and the neutral ones. This approach to teaching must of course be reciprocal—indigenous explanations of the contentious "dark episodes" should be presented to students of all nations as well as to the indigenous students. For example, the Prussian militaristic tradition, negatively assessed by almost all non-German (and many German) historians, should be explained in the context of the

Golden Bull (1356) and the devastation caused by the Thirty Years War (1618–1648) in order to be properly assessed and understood. Every injustice has a plausible "good reason" in the eyes of the perpetrators of that injustice, and such reasons should be presented to the students, however spurious they may seem to be from the victim's or even an outsider's point of view. In the process of education students should learn to put themselves into the shoes of their nation's competitors and alleged enemies and thus try to gain a much more balanced and wide view of the subject of their study. The old Roman principle *audiatur et altera pars* (hear out the other party) must indeed become the first universal principle of historical education all over the world. Without the application of this principle, ethnocentric biases in education will never be overcome.

This is, however, only the first part of revising the process of education in history. The second and more important and fundamental part should consist of an objective evaluation of the historical record, which should be equally acceptable to all national educational systems, however conflicting with one another they may at present be.

WHAT VALUES ARE UNIVERSAL

The objective criteria for such universally acceptable evaluation were, in my view, adequately formulated by Immanuel Kant in his *Perpetual Peace* (1795), and I would suggest to use them as the main guide in our research on universally acceptable educational standards.

According to Kant, people are naturally divided by language and religion into separate entities. Each such separate human entity, or nation, is entitled to its own state and in fact is such a state, whether actually or as yet only potentially. Kant puts forward six preliminary conditions that in his view have to be fulfilled before perpetual peace among states could be established. The first two of these six conditions, which I deem to be most crucial to our purposes, are:

1. *Cessation of hostility between states* by a peace treaty providing for a mutually acceptable solution of all contentious problems, and in the first place those that caused hostility. In Kant's own terms, "No peace treaty can be accorded that status if at its conclusion there had remained a latent cause of a new war." If such a latent cause of a new war remained in the peace treaty, such a treaty would be no more than a mere cease-fire agreement. Kant is convinced that there are no such problems between states that could not be fully resolved by their mutual agreement, provided the states entering a peace treaty are guided by the universal moral values and principles elaborated by Kant's moral philosophy. Kant believes that sooner or later all states will have to accept these universal moral values. The only alternative to peace established on such terms will be the peace of mankind's common cemetery.

2. *Inviolable independence of every state, big or small.* "No state," Kant says, " . . . can be acquired by another state either by inheritance or exchange, purchase or gift," let alone by conquest or coercion. Thus for Kant, the cornerstone of a viably peaceful world order is the practical realization by every nation without exception of its primordial and inalienable right to establish and maintain an independent state. The incorporation of any actual or potential nation-state, in full or even partly, into another nation's state is a priori a gross injustice that is bound to foster enmity and war as long as that injustice is perpetrated. Kant concludes that for perpetual peace to materialize it is necessary for the extant states to agree that each nation should also be a state and that thus no nation state is entitled to include and/or contain within its borders another nation. Equal statehood for all nations is for Kant the primary universal moral value, the first principle upon which to safely base perpetual peace.

There is, however, much more to making perpetual peace a reality than just the universal recognition of this particular principle of national independence and equal statehood for all nations. In Kant's view, the first definitive article of perpetual peace among states has to establish that the civil order of each state should be *republican*. Kant defines the republican civil order as the one that is based, "firstly, on the principle of individual *liberty* of the members of society (as people); secondly, on the principles of *dependence* of all (as subjects) on single common legislation; and, thirdly, on the law of quality of all (as citizens)." Only republican states could agree on each nation's equal and inviolable right to independent statehood; only in republican states the decisions on war and peace would require an agreement of the people, and the people who have to carry the burdens of war are not likely to give their agreement to wage war easily. This view of Kant has been indeed vindicated by the latest historic experience. With one marginal exception (that of the so-called Roman Republic War of 1849 between democratic Rome and France), there were no wars between liberal democratic states either in the nineteenth or the twentieth centuries (for more details, see: J. David Singer and Melvin Small, *Resort to Arms: International and Civil Wars, 1816–1980* [Beverly Hills, Calif.: Sage, 1982], table 4.2; R. J. Rummel, "On Fostering a Just Peace," *International Journal on World Peace* 1, no. 1 [autumn 1984]: 4–15, especially 10 ff).

The first definitive article of perpetual peace, having provided for the universal establishment of a republican civil order, would create the necessary conditions for the conclusion of the second definitive article of perpetual peace, according to which a federation of free states is to be instituted and, consequently, a new basis for international law and its application created. This federation would have to be "a union of peoples but by no means a state of peoples." The state befits only one people and the coexistence of many peoples in one state would reduce them all to one people only, which would deny the fundamental right of each nation to equally independent statehood and thus also undermine the very foundations of the republican civil order.

For the federation of free states to remain stable, a third, and the last, definitive article of perpetual peace is necessary. According to that article, "the right of *world citizenship* should be limited by the conditions of universal *hospitality*," which means that foreigners are granted only the right of visiting a state without being treated by it as enemies but are not granted the automatic right of becoming that state's guests. The granting to a foreigner of the right to be another state's guest, as well as the rights of settlement and naturalization, will always have to remain an exclusive prerogative of the host states themselves. This clause on hospitality is aimed at effectively preventing any attempts at surreptitious colonization, forceful acculturation, and assimilation of one nation by another, and, thus, at securing the continuity of the federation in its original, stable, and peaceful shape.

It follows that for Kant the basic universal value on which perpetual peace could securely rest is the rule of law, ensuring maximal equal freedom to all individuals and all nations established on a global scale. The same basic universal value should be recognized as the underlying principle of a truly global education. The application of that value to the teaching of history of those ancient nations and city-states that have ceased to exist does not represent too much difficulty. Once applied to the uncontroversial historical past, that same value could then be extended to the evaluation and interpretation of the history of the existing nations and states.

Almost all nations in the course of their history have been both aggressors and victims of aggression, oppressors and victims of oppression. Both England and Russia, countries that later developed into huge colonial empires, were themselves colonized and ruled for centuries by the Vikings. In Britain that foreign rule was never formally terminated, but the Norman Vikings, having become the rulers of England, did not append the conquered country to their larger empire but made it the metropolis, a center from which they ruled other areas under their dominion (e.g., Normandy itself). Because of that, the Normans had to adjust to England, assimilate with it, and thus acquire there a status of legitimate national rulers. This in time they managed to achieve. Within about two centuries from the year 1066, the trauma of foreign rule had almost entirely dissipated indeed, and the English nation recovered its consciousness of being independent, which it has never lost since. The same adaptation of Viking rulers to the ruled nation took place within about 150 years (during the mid ninth to late tenth centuries) in the Russian Viking state of Kievan Rus, which is regarded by all historians as the first and fully authentic Russian nation-state. This state, however, was destroyed in the thirteenth century by the Tatar-Mongol invasion, as a result of which Russia, for about 300 years, was subjugated to a ferocious foreign colonial yoke, a traumatic experience from which Russia has never fully recovered.

Poland, which is usually perceived as a constant victim of Russo-German imperial designs, has always been in its own right an imperial nation that for long centuries oppressed and tried, with some success, to assimilate the

Ukrainians, Byelorussians, and even the non-Slavic "allied" Lithuanians. In the sixteenth and seventeenth centuries, Poland also attempted to incorporate Sweden under the Polish crown, but, alas, to no avail. In the beginning of the eighteenth century the Swedes definitively defeated Poland and practically brought about the destruction of the Polish-Lithuanian Commonwealth (*Rzeczpospolita Obojega Narodow*), of which the main beneficiary was Russia whom Poland in the sixteenth and seventeenth centuries also desperately tried to put under her control. After having lost the war against Russia (by the Nystat Treaty of 1721), the Swedes, unconditionally conceded, defeated Poland to Russia's "sphere of influence." The division of Poland followed shortly afterward and was completed by 1795.

According to Kantian standards, the Spanish have to recognize that the conquest of Mexico and Peru, their rule of the Netherlands, and attempts at conquering England in the sixteenth century represent shameful instances of Spanish history. Conversely, the English must admit that their treatment of Ireland throughout centuries belongs to the most abhorrent experiences recorded in human history. Generally speaking, by Kant, each nation's efforts at establishing independent statehood, resisting foreign assault and rule should be approved of, whereas all attempts by one nation at subjugating another nation to its rule, all instances of colonization and incorporation of a separate nation into a larger imperial or nation-state system should be condemned. This principle provides the most important, universal value-based guiding line for our understanding of the problems of the present world, where about 1,800 nations are divided into only about 180 states, some of which can hardly qualify as even full-fledged nation states (the borders of many extant states blatantly cut across natural ethnic boundaries; this is the case with a great number of new African and Asian states, which inherited the artificial borders of former Western colonial entities to which these states were the political successors, let alone the two German and two Korean states).

Kantian values underlying his plan of perpetual peace also call for the approval of all movements in history that have sought to undermine despotic regimes in order to advance the republican civil order. According to Kantian criteria, the Glorious Revolution of 1688, the American Revolution of 1776, the French Revolution of 1789, and the Russian Revolution of February 1917 have thus to be commended, as they were seeking to replace despotic rule by a republican regime; and, on the contrary, Pride's Purge, the Jacobin coup or the Bolshevik seizure of power should be condemned, as they sought to destroy the emergent republicanism and, when successful, introduced a new, and in most cases a much more ferocious, form of despotism. Foreign intervention by invitation and on behalf of the indigenous forces fighting for a republican civil order, such as General Lafayette's or Kosciuszko's troops' participation in the American war for independence, is also fully justified, as it corresponds to Kant's third definitive article concerning hospitality.

As mentioned above, Kant's concept of perpetual peace envisages the necessity of establishing a world federation of free states as opposed to the world state envisaged by the Marxist and some other concepts of mankind's future. The world federation of free states could also effectively be adopted as the universal value and goal on which global education should be based. Ensuring the freedom of every nation and its full independence in dealing with its internal problems, such a federation provides an ideal framework for effectively dealing with supranational, regional, and/or global issues. Kant emphasized that such a federal arrangement would submit all nations equally to the rule of international law and to the regime of arbitration and adjudication that would serve all of them as the firmest guarantee of peace and security. Global education could take up that Kantian point in order to dismantle with its help the very concept of an "enemy-nation," and to show that all conflicting issues between nations seeing each other at present as implacable enemies could be resolved amicably and on a permanent basis, provided all nations adhered to republicanist values and installed republican-type regimes.

Although in a nuclear age the guarantee of peace and security is, no doubt, the issue of primary and overriding importance, there are many other vitally important issues for mankind's survival that only a world federation of free states would be able effectively to tackle and solve. One of such issues, as Professor Klaus Schleicher tirelessly emphasizes in his pioneering works, is the protection of mankind's natural environment. Among other similar issues, one could name the rational use, distribution, and management of mankind's common resources: energy, world ocean, outer space, international territories (e.g., Antarctica); protection against famine, epidemic diseases, natural calamities, and other disasters; regulation of the growth of the world's population and organization of rational use of the planet's manpower resources; effective protection of universally recognized human rights; and some others.

Against the background of the ever-growing need for international, indeed global, cooperation on these issues, most international conflicts would look rather petty and demand urgent resolution for the sake of making such a cooperation not simply possible but truly effective. This is one of the most important points that global education has to put forward and constantly emphasize. Global education, if it is worth that name, has to stress the fundamental unity of mankind's tasks and purposes, advocate global cooperation on all vital issues that affect mankind's survival and well-being, and, by proposing practical solutions to international conflicts, put these conflicts in their right perspective as concerning issues that, compared with unifying factors, are of secondary importance and that, given the goodwill to adhere to Kantian universal values, are also perfectly soluble.

HOW GLOBAL EDUCATION COULD BE INTRODUCED

Educators who are committed to the development of global education, after having agreed on adopting the Kantian concept of perpetual peace as the basis for universal values on which global education should be based, could organize themselves into various national and international committees for revising the existing national curricula and textbooks. To proceed with their work fruitfully, such committees could adopt the methodology of repentance and self-limitation set out for nations as wholes by Alexander Solzhenitsyn in his essay "Repentance and Self-Limitation in the Life of Nations" written for the collection of articles, *From Under the Rubble* (1974), that he edited in Moscow and issued there as a samizdat publication, which was later reprinted in the West.

According to Solzhenitsyn, mankind can be saved only if nations radically change their basic orientation from self-glorification and self-justification, that is, from "blaming all the *others*—neighbors and the distant ones; geographic, economic, ideological competitors—and always justifying only oneselves," to "repentance and search for one's own mistakes and sins." Speaking about Russia, Solzhenitsyn maintains that every Russian is to a certain degree an accomplice of the horrible crimes of the Soviet regime that cost the Russian nation alone about 70 million lives and that it is therefore false to blame for these crimes simply "them," the regime, as if it were an abstract alien force, and to portray the Russian nation as a mere victim of that alien force. Repentance, not only in Russia, but everywhere else, has thus to start as an *internal* process affecting everyone with regard to what she or he did to other individuals and groups and then rise to *external* dimensions, concerning one's nation's sins against other nations. Such repentance should be totally uncompromising. "I think," Solzhenitsyn writes, "that if one is to be mistaken in one's repentance, it is better to make a mistake on the bigger side, to the benefit of others." And, he adds, "One has to assume beforehand that there are no such neighbors before whom we are innocent." Repentance to Solzhenitsyn is, however, not a purpose in itself but a means for "opening the path for a new relationship. A new relationship also among nations." For that new relationship to be achieved, the process of repentance has to be a mutual one and result in a mutual pardon.

It is in this way that globally-minded educationalists could initiate the revision of their respective national curricula and textbooks and then bring the revised versions together with those of other similarly revised national curricula and textbooks, trying to make them all not simply compatible but also universally acceptable. Globally-minded educationalists may thus become the pioneers, paving through education the way to true international harmony and perpetual peace.

There is, however, one specific but crucially important issue with which neither Kant nor Solzhenitsyn deal in an explicit and practical manner. This is the issue of how and on the basis of what principles territorial disputes between nations have to be settled. The basic value system that both these thinkers share should point in the direction of application of the following principle to the settlement of these issues: Insofar as a nation has its own homeland and an established capital city within it, that nation can claim only

such territories not in its possession in which that nation at present constitutes a compact majority. Purely historical claims to territory should thus not
be considered as valid. Hence, if the Finns were to claim Moscow and
Leningrad or the Lithuanians East Prussia, these claims should be dismissed
in spite of their perfect historical justification. On the contrary, the Jews as a
nation without a homeland had a justifiable claim to their historic homeland
in Palestine and the Lithuanians to their capital city Vilnius occupied in 1920
by Poland, under the pretext that Poles constituted there a compact majority. According to the same standards, one has to recognize that the Armenians have a justifiable claim to Nagorno-Karabakh but not to Nakhichevan,
which although historically an Armenian territory, is now populated mainly
by the Azerbaidzhanis. It is significant to note that the Armenians do not
even start to claim Nakhichevan, while the Azerbaidzhanis refuse to renounce their possession of Nagorno-Karabakh. Apparently Armenian education has been much closer to universal standards than the Azerbaidzhani
education, although both were developing for the last sixty-five years or so
within the uniform framework of the Soviet educational system.

Solzhenitsyn's concept of national self-limitation is wider than the nation's
mere commitment to keeping itself within its own ethnic boundaries and
thus to its withdrawal from all foreign parts, to non-expansionism and nonaggression. Solzhenitsyn preaches self-limitation also in terms of industrial
and technological expansion at the expense of the environmental balance.
He calls it *farsighted self-limitation*. In his view, there can be no limitless
progress on a planet with a limited surface and finite resources. This is yet
another fundamental universal value worthy of being seriously considered
by globally-minded educationalists. It goes without saying that such farsighted self-constraint could not be implemented without a globally-
achieved consensus on the development and distribution of available resources. It is both morally and realistically impossible to demand of the rich
and the poor nations that they equally renounce development without making the necessary provisions for a gradual improvement of living standards
and, at the same time, for the gradual leveling of living standards, across the
globe and among different social strata. Education for rational and cautious
use of our finite resources, for treating environmental protection as the primary issue in the developmental process, and for the enhancement of social
justice, should become, together with national and individual freedom, another cornerstone for the standards of a truly global education.

GLOBALISM AND ETHNOCENTRISM

One should beware of total counter-opposition between global and "ethnocentric" educational standards. Global educational standards based on universal humanitarian values may be successfully introduced only if they are
treated as an extension of, and elaboration upon, the national educational

standards. On the whole, globalism may be valid only insofar as it is able successfully to encompass and accommodate *all* separate nations with their diverse interests and cultural legacies into one entity (*e pluribus unum*). If globalism is to be introduced from above and in opposition to "ethnocentrism" (or nationalism), it will not only not work but, if insisted upon, would inevitably become oppressively counterproductive. Globally-based education can be successfully and fruitfully evolved only on the basis of education firmly entrenched in the traditional system of positive national values, such as love of, or pride in, one's nation; fond (though not necessarily uncritical) appreciation of its historical and cultural heritage; primary concern about one's nation's continuous well-being; and determination to keep that nation's separate identity intact and unsubordinated to any other national identity.

One of the methods that could be successfully used to advance global education is "interpenetration" of national curricula. As in schools where classical education is not yet totally extinct, students learn about Pericles, Mucius Scaevola, the Gracchi brothers, and other heroes of ancient history exemplifying the Greek and Roman traditions of civic virtue, all schools could introduce in their curricula the study of the heroes of extant foreign nations. It would be good to study in Austrian schools the lives and works of such Hungarian national heroes as Lajos Kossuth and Sander Petöfi, and in Spanish schools those of such Cuban, Filipino, and Dutch national heroes as, respectively, José Marti, José Rizal, and the stadtholder William of Orange. The lives and works of such national heroes should be studied not only in the schools of "opponent" nations but also in the schools of the neutral ones. The globally-minded educationalists could compile an international list of national heroes to be recommended for study in the schools throughout the world. This would certainly make a substantial contribution to mutual empathy among the nations of the world, to their better understanding of each other's problems, and thus to the promotion of globalism.

Only love for, and devotion to, one's own nation creates a proper understanding of, and empathy with, all fellow human beings that love their own nations and are devoted to them. Internationalism that demands the abrogation of national sentiments and loyalties, substituting for them the love of mankind as a whole, is in essence inhuman and leads to most dangerous ideological aberrations. It is on such internationalism that ideocracies of the theocratic, Marxist, or fascist nature are based. Only such internationalism is solid, humanitarian and valid, that organically evolves from nationalism and, consequently, from "exchanges of nationalisms." The task of the global educational standards is thus not the elimination of nationalism but the capitalization on the positive nationalist values in such a way that would prevent the degeneration of nationalism into either blind patriotism (devotion not to one's nation but to one's state—"my country, right or wrong") or jingoistic chauvinism (belief in one's nation's exclusivity and/or superiority over other nations).

One could justifiably argue that the ideas and proposals put forward in this paper are in the present circumstances rather utopian or, at least, politically unrealizable and thus impractical. Unrealizable at present they may be, but impractical they are not. For if a considerably large and influential group of international educators would set itself the task of elaborating, along the lines of these and similar ideas, model global curricula on the main controversial subjects (such as religion, history, and literature in the first place) taught in the schools, the fruits of their work could become the seed from which the tree of global education in the practical world would start growing.

Bibliography of
Aleksandras Shtromas

Prepared by David J. Bobb, Hillsdale College

Alexander Shtromas published books, chapter contributions to books, and articles in nine languages. This bibliography includes books, articles, and reviews written by Shtromas between 1963 and 1994. It does not include over forty articles published in the Soviet Union between 1952 and 1973.

The bibliography is organized under two broad categories: (1) books and monographs, and (2) articles. "Books and Monographs" includes full-length books written by Shtromas, shorter monographs written by Shtromas, books edited by Shtromas, along with his contributions to those edited volumes, and chapters written in books he did not edit. "Articles" includes scholarly articles published in refereed journals, and other articles published in general interest and cultural periodicals. Within each category the items published in English are listed first; items published in other languages are listed in the following order: Lithuanian, Russian, German, French, Hungarian, Polish, Czech, and Japanese. When the title of a publication is in a language other than English, the English translation of the title is included in parentheses. Items are listed within each subcategory starting with the most recent item.

On March 9, 2001, the Aleksandras Shtromas Library and Archives were established at Vytautas Magnus University in Kaunas, Lithuania, Shtromas's hometown.

I. BOOKS AND MONOGRAPHS

Books in English

Political Change and Social Development: The Case of the Soviet Union. Vol. 1, European Forum Series. New York: Peter Lang; 1st ed., 1981; 2d ed., 1990.

Monographs in English

The Jewish and Gentile Experience of the Holocaust: A Personal Perspective. Worcester, Mass.: Assumption College, 1989.
The Soviet Method of Conquest of the Baltic States: Lessons for the West. Washington, D.C.: Washington Institute for Values in Public Policy, 1986.
To Fight Communism: Why and How. New York: PWPA Publications, 1985.
Who Are the Soviet Dissidents? Bradford: University of Bradford, 1979.
The Strategy for Peace in a Changing World Order. London: ICF Publications, 1977.

Books in Lithuanian

Horizons of Freedom, assembled by Livtas Mockunass. Vilnius: ALK baltos lankos, 2001.
Political Consciousness in Soviet Lithuania. London: Nida Press, 1980.

Books in Russian

Criminal Law of Foreign Countries. Vol. 1, *Sources of Criminal Law* (1971); Vol. 2: *Crime, Culpability, Imputability* (1972); Vol. 3: *Unaccomplished Crime and Complicity* (1973). Moscow: University of Patrice Lumumba Press, 1971–1973.
Juvenile Delinquency in Capitalist Countries. Vol. 2, *Prevention.* Yuridicheskaya Literatura, 1970.

Monographs in Russian

Foreign Legislation on the Position of the Defendant in Preliminary Investigation of Crimes. Moscow: All-Union Institute of Soviet Legislation, 1970.
Foreign Legislation on Defence in Preliminary Investigation of Crimes. Moscow: All-Union Institute of Soviet Legislation, 1970.
Foreign Legislation on the Application of Scientific and Technical Means and Methods in Investigation of Crimes. Moscow: All-Union Institute of Soviet Legislation, 1968.
Preventive Legislation of Capitalist Countries. Moscow: All-Union Institute of Soviet Legislation, 1967.

Edited or Co-Edited Books in English, with Contributions, in English

Editor. *The End of "Isms"? Reflections on the Fate of Ideological Politics After Communism's Collapse.* Oxford: Blackwell, 1994. Contributed, "Ideological Politics and the Contemporary World: Have We Seen the Last of 'Isms'?"

Co-editor, with Morton A. Kaplan. *The Soviet Union and the Challenge of the Future.* 4 Vols. New York: Paragon House; London: Macmillan, 1988–1990.

The Soviet System: Stasis & Change. Vol 1. 1988. Contributed, "Introduction," with M. A. Kaplan, "On Totalitarianism and the Prospects for Institutionalized Revolution in the USSR and China—A Commentary on Sections 1 and 2," and "How the End of the Soviet System May Come About: Historical Precedents and Possible Scenarios."

Economics & Society. Vol. 2. 1989. Contributed, "Introduction" with M. A. Kaplan.

Ideology, Culture, and Nationality, Vol. 3. 1990. Contributed, "Introduction," with M. A. Kaplan, "Marxism-Leninism in Contemporary USSR," and "Multinationalism and the Soviet Future."

Russia and the World, Vol. 4. 1989. Contributed, "Introduction," with M. A. Kaplan "Post-Soviet Russia and the West: Prospects for East–West Reconciliation Viewed from a European Perspective—A Commentary on Chapter 6."

Co-Edited Books, in Russian

Co-editor, with R. Lantsman, et al., *Cybernetics and Forensic Sciences.* Vilnius: The Lithuanian Institute of Forensic Sciences, 1966.

Co-editor, with J. Nainys, S. Lauzhikas, et al. *Scientific Works of the Lithuanian Society of Forensic Scientists.* Vol. 2. Kaunas: Sviesa, 1965.

Co-editor, with A. Chepas. *Collection of Scientific Works of the Lithuanian Institute of Forensic Sciences.* Vol. 1. Vilnius: The Lithuanian Institute of Forensic Sciences, 1963.

Chapters in Books, in English

"The Baltic States as Soviet Republics: Tensions and Contradictions." In Graham Smith, ed. *The Baltic States: The National Self-Determination of Estonia, Latvia, and Lithuania.* New York: St. Martin's Press; London: Macmillan, 1994.

"Transition to a Free Market System: The Hillsdale Plan and the Other Plans." In Richard Ebeling, ed. *Can Capitalism Cope? Free Market Reform in the Post-Communist World, Champions of Freedom.* Vol. 21. The Ludwig von Mises Lecture Series. Hillsdale, Mich.: Hillsdale College Press, 1994.

"The Inevitable Collapse of Socialism." In Richard Ebeling, ed. *The Global Failure of Socialism, Champions of Freedom.* Vol. 19. The Ludwig von Mises Lecture Series. Hillsdale, Mich.: Hillsdale College Press, 1992.

"The Role of Europe in Creating a Peaceful World Order," and "The Rise and Decline of Europe from Limited Government to Unlimited Democracy: A Comment." In C. D. Gruender and E. Moutsopoulos, eds. *The Idea of Europe: Its Common Heritage and Future.* New York: PWPA Publications, 1992.

"The European Ethnic Conflicts and the Search for Their Solutions." In Frederick S. Pearson, ed. *Europe at the Crossroads: Integration, Disintegration, Implications for North America.* Detroit, Mich.: Wayne State University Press; Washington, D.C.: Freidrich Nauman Foundation Press, 1992.

"Russia on the Road to Political and Economic Freedom: A Commentary." In Richard Ebeling, ed. *Austrian Economics: Perspectives on the Past and Prospects on the Future, Champions of Freedom.* Vol. 17. The Ludwig von Mises Lecture Series. Hillsdale, Mich.: Hillsdale College Press, 1991.

"Universal Values vs. Local Preferences and Guilt Complexes in Transition to Global Education." In *Absolute Values and the Reassessment of the Contemporary World: Proceedings of the Seventeenth International Conference on the Unity of Sciences*. Vol. 1. New York: ICF Publications, 1991.

"The Foundations and Goals of Soviet Foreign Policy." In D. W. J. McForan and J. Knappert, eds. *Soviet Expansionism*. London: CAUSA-UK Publications, 1987.

"The Situation of the World and the Unification Movement." In Andrew Wilson, ed. *The Future of the World*. New York: ICF/ERF Publications, 1987.

"The Baltic States." In Robert Conquest, ed. *The Last Empire: Nationality and the Soviet Future*. Stanford, Calif.: Hoover Institution Press, 1986.

"On the Annexation of the Baltic States and the Personality of Baltic Communists." In Ingrida Kalnins, ed. *The Baltic Tribunal Against the Soviet Union*. Baltimore, Md.: Baltic World Conference Publications, 1985.

"Pacifism and the Contemporary International Situation," and "The Soviet Union and the Politics of Peace." In Peter van den Dungen, ed. *West European Pacifism and the Strategy for Peace*. London: Macmillan, 1985.

"Dissent and Political Change in the Soviet Union." In Erik P. Hoffmann and Robin F. Laird, eds. *The Soviet Polity in the Modern Era*. New York: Aldine Publishing, 1984.

"Official Soviet Ideology and the Lithuanian People." In Rimvydas Silbajoris, ed. *Mind Against the Wall: Essays on Lithuanian Culture Under Soviet Occupation*. Chicago: Institute of Lithuanian Studies Press, 1983.

"On the Proposal to End the Danger of War in Europe." In Morton A. Kaplan, ed. *Global Policy: Challenge of the 1980s*. Washington, D.C.: WIVPP Publications, 1983.

"Possibilities of Change From Within the Soviet Union." In M. Lewis, ed. *A World Without Communism: How to Achieve It and What It Will Mean*. Washington, D.C.: Council for the Defence of Freedom, 1982.

"The Issues of War and Peace: Public Opinion in the East." In *Realities of War in the 1980s*. Huy: University de Paix Publications, 1981.

"Peaceful World: Ideal and Reality." In Jeanne Tschong Koei-Li, ed. *In Search of a New World Order—The Need for New Initiatives*. Taipei: PCF Publications, 1981.

Chapters in Books, in Lithuanian

"Democracy in Inverted Commas and Without," "Response to the Editor's Questionnaire," and "On the Restoration of Lithuania's Independence." In G. Vitkus, ed. *Studying Political Science*. Kaunas, Lithuania: Sviesa, 1990.

"At the Source of Lithuanian Universalism." In Tomas Venclova, ed. *Lithuania and the World*. Chicago: ASL Publications, 1981.

Chapters in Books, in Russian

"The State of Russia's Reforms and Possible Ways for Their Continuation." In Boris Gubman, ed. *Russia and the West: A Dialogue of Cultures*. Tver: Tver University Press, 1994.

"In the World of Images and Ideas of Aleksandr Galich." In Nina Kreytner, ed. *The Enchantment of Good and Evil: The Life, Fate, and Creative Works of Aleksandr Galich*. Moscow: Progress Publishers, 1992.

Chapters in Books, in German

"Pacifism in the Ideological Struggle." In Armand Clesse and Waldemar Molinski, eds. *Protests for Peace, Worries About Security: The Peace Movements and the Future of West European Defence.* Munich: Universitas Verlag, 1984.

"The Propaganda Factor in East–West Relations." In L. Gabriel, G. Radnitzky, and E. Schopper, eds. *The I-Weapons: Information in the Power Game of Politics.* Munich: Herbig Verlag, 1982.

II. ARTICLES

Articles in English-Language Journals

"Unity in Diversity: How the Variety of Ethnic Values Could Be Accommodated in a Universal World Order." *Social Change,* no. 1 (spring 1994).

"Religion and Ethnicity in World Order." *The International Journal on World Peace* 9, no. 2 (June 1992).

"The Future World Order and the Right of Nations to Self-Determination and Sovereignty." *The International Journal on World Peace* 7, no. 1 (January/March 1990).

"How Political Are the Social Movements in the Baltic Republics?" *Nationalities Papers* 18, no. 2 (fall 1990).

"Soviet Occupation of the Baltic States: Political and Legal Aspects." *Science, Arts, and Lithuania,* no. 1 (fall 1990).

"How the Baltic Was Won." *The European Journal of International Affairs,* vol. H, no. 4 (spring 1989).

"On the Current Political Situation in Lithuania." *Occasional Papers on Baltic Political Action,* nos. 2/3 (September 1988).

"Sparing with Historical Truth: A Review Article on Soviet Publications on Lithuania." *Journal of Baltic Studies* 19, no. 2 (summer 1988).

"Dissent, Nationalism and the Soviet Future." *Studies in Comparative Communism* 20, nos. 3/4 (autumn/winter 1987).

"Prospects for Restoration of the Baltic States' Independence: A View on the Prerequisites and Possibilities for Their Realization." *Journal of Baltic Studies* 17, no. 3 (fall 1986).

"The Building of a Multi-National Soviet Socialist Federalism: Success and Failures." *Canadian Review of Studies in Nationalism* 13, no. 1 (spring 1986).

"The Incorporation of the Baltic States into the Soviet Union: Legal Aspects." *East European Quarterly* 19, no. 4 (January 1986).

"The Incorporation of the Baltic States into the Soviet Union: Political Aspects." *East European Quarterly* 19, no. 3 (September 1985).

"Soviet Criminal Law After Brezhnev." *The Soviet Union/L'Union Sovietique* 11, part 3 (1984; published as part of a symposium).

"To Fight Communism: Why and How?" *The International Journal on World Peace* 1, no. 1 (fall 1984).

"Political and Legal Aspects of the Soviet Occupation and Incorporation of the Baltic States." *Baltic Forum* 1, no. 1 (fall 1984).

"Language, Culture and Ethnic Entity in the Soviet Socialist System." *Plural Societies* 15, no. 3 (October 1984).

"Review of Soviet Law After Stalin." *The Russian Review* 40, no. 2 (April 1981).

"The Soviet Ideology and the Lithuanians." *Russia,* no. 3 (1981).

"East–West Detente and Western Support for Soviet Dissidents." *Proceedings of the Medical Association for Prevention of War* 3, part 4 (March 1980).

"Dissent and Political Change in the USSR." *Studies in Comparative Communism* 12, nos. 2–3 (summer/fall 1979).

"The Legal Position of Soviet Nationalities and Their Territorial Units According to the 1977 Constitution of the USSR." *The Russian Review* 37, no. 3 (July 1978).

"Baltic Problem and Peace Studies." *Journal of Baltic Studies* 9, no. 1 (spring 1978).

"Preservation and Promotion of Peace in a Changing World." *Proceedings of the Medical Association for Prevention of War* 3, part 2 (January 1978).

"Crime, Law and Penal Practice in the USSR." *Review of Socialist Law* 3, no. 3 (September 1977).

"The Relationship Between the Individual and the State in the Soviet Union." *Proceedings of the Medical Association for Prevention of War* 2, part 10 (November 1975).

Articles in German Scholarly Journals

"On the Current Situation in the USSR." *Ost Blick* (View Toward the East), vol. 3, nos. 9 and 10 (September and October 1987).

Articles in French Scholarly Journals

"How the Baltic States Became Soviet." *L'Alternative* (The Alternative), no. 12 (1984).

Articles in Polish Scholarly Journals

"Jewish and Non-Jewish Attitudes to the Holocaust," *Nauka dla Pokoju* (Science for Peace), vol. 1, no. 2/3 (1990).

Articles in Czech Scholarly Journals

"Hope Against Hope: Russian Politics in the Period of Transition and Prospects for the CIS." *Mezinarodni vztahy* (International Affairs), no. 3 (1993).

Articles in English-Language Periodicals

"The Jewish and Gentile Experience of the Holocaust." *The World and I*, vol. 7, no. 2 (February 1992).

"To Foreign Eyes." *Boston College Magazine,* vol. XLVM, no. 1 (winter 1989).

"Socialism in Transformation." *The World and I*, vol. 4, no. 1 (January 1989).

"The Nazi–Soviet Alliance and the Fate of the Baltic States." *The World and I*, vol. 2, no. 4 (April 1987).

"Making Sense of Stalin." *The World and I*, vol. 1, no. 8 (August 1986).

"Assessing the Results of the 27th Congress of the CPSU." *The World and I*, vol. 1, no. 4 (April 1986).

"How the Soviet System May End." *The World and I*, vol. 1, no. 1 (January 1986).

"Does Andropov Matter?" *Speak Up* 11, no. 1–2 (January/February 1984).

"Andropov in Retrospect." *Our Canada* 7, no. 2 (February 1984).

"Poland: What Next?" *Free Life* 2, no. 4 (winter 1981/1982).

"Marxist Ideology and Soviet Dissent." *Speak Up* 10, no. 8 (August 1983).

"Captive Nations and the Free World." *Speak Up* 6, no. 11 (November 1980).

"USSR's 1977 Constitution." *Speak Up* 6, nos. 5–6 (May/June 1980).

"Soviet Dissent: Content and Forms." *Speak Up* 5, no. 11–12 (November/December 1979) and vol. 6, no. 1 (January 1980).

"The Opposition in the Soviet Union." *Speak Up* 3, no. 11–12 (November/December 1977) and vol. 4, no. 1 (January 1978).

Articles in Lithuanian Periodicals

"Nations in the Post-Communist World Order." *Metmenys* (The Outline), no. 66 (1994).

"The Advantages and Drawbacks of the Lithuanian Constitution." *Amzius* (The Age), no. 4 (February 1994).

"How Does the Opposition Learn from the Government's Mistakes." *Amzius* (The Age), no. 6 (June 1993).

"The Relations Between the Nation and the Government in the Light of the May 23rd Referendum." *Akiraciai* (The Horizon), no. 7 (July 1992).

"The Fate of a Sceptic: Reflections on the Case of 'Comrade Juozas.'" *Akiraciai* (The Horizon), no. 2 (February 1992).

"Some Thoughts on Some Newest Lithuanian Laws." *Akiraciai* (The Horizon), no. 1 (January 1992).

"Lithuania-Europe's Hong Kong." (co-authored with Richard Ebeling), *Politika* (Politics), no. 22 (1991).

"The Difficult Path of Reforms in Lithuania." *Syyturys* (Lighthouse), no. 19 (October 1991).

"The Lost Party." *Syyturys* (Lighthouse), no. 17 (September 1991).

"In Struggle for Lithuania, Europe, Culture." *Syyturys* (Lighthouse), no. 5 (March 1991). "A Historical Chance to Destroy Socialism." *Gimtasis Krastas* (Native Land) (June 6–12, 1991).

"The Holocaust: The Experience of the Jews and of the Gentiles." *Krantai* (The Shores), no. 23/24 (November/December 1990).

"Poetry and Polity." *Krantai* (The Shores), no. 19/20 (July/August 1990).

"On Lithuania, the Specific Nature of Her Culture and Other Factors Shaping Her Independent Future." *Sietynas* (Constellations), no. 6 (1989).

"The Possibilities for the Restoration of Baltic States' Independence." *Naujoji Viltis* (New Hope), no. 21 (1988).

"Thoughts on Lithuania, the USSR, and the World Situation." Akiraciai (The Horizon), no. 5 (May 1984).

"Is the Soviet Union on the Verge of a Crisis?" *Teviskes* Ziburiai (The Lights of Homeland), no. 12 (March 1984).

"In Struggle for Lithuania, Europe, Culture: Some Thoughts on B. Raila's Work." Akiraciai (The Horizon), no. 2 (February 1984).

"The New Trends in Soviet Politics and Their Implications for the Future." *I Laisve* (Toward Freedom), no. 89 (1983).

"The Soviet Union after Brezhnev." Europos *Lietuvis* (The Lithuanian European Weekly), nos. 41–45 (October/November 1983).

"The Lessons of the 1905 Great Vilnius Parliament." Akiraciai (The Horizon), no. 2 (February 1981).

"Between Lenin and Pobedonostsev: A Polilogue." (co-authored with T. Venclova, K. Almenas, and V. Trumpa), *Metmenys* (The Outline), no. 39 (1980).

"Personal Responsibility and Totalitarian Society." *I Laisve* (Toward Freedom), no. 75/112 (1979).

"The Prospects for Change in the Soviet Union under Gorbachev." *Naujoji Viltis* (New Hope), no. 21 (1988).

Articles in Russian Periodicals

"The Last Word is Not the Bureaucracy's, But the People's." *Posev* (Sowing), no. 5 (September/October 1993).

"The Hillsdale Plan for Russian Economic Reform." *Grazhdanskaya Mysl'* (Civic Thought), no. 3 (September 1993).

"To Turn the Master-State into the Servant-State." *Grazhdanskaya Mysl'* (Civic Thought), no. 1 (July 1993).

"To Look to the Future with Assurance." *Posev* (Sowing), no. 2 (March/April 1994).

"Privatization." *Grani* (Facets), no. 161 (November 1991).

"An Attempt at a Prognosis." *Posev* (Sowing), no. 4/5 (September/October 1991).

"Privatization in the *USSR.*" *Demokraticheskaya* Rossya (Democratic Russia) (June 28, 1991).

"The Three Foundation Stones for a Reform." *Literaturnaya Gazeta* (The Literary Gazette) (February 13, 1991).

"On a Viable Economic Reform in Post-Communist Lands." *Soglasie* (Consensus) (December 31, 1990).

"The Ideas and Images of Alexander Galich." Novyi *Zhurnal* (New Review), no. 170 (March 1988).

"The Contradictions of Perestroyka." *Posev* (Sowing), no. 1 (January 1988).

"Democracy in Inverted Commas and Without." *Strana i Mir* (Our Country and the World), no. 12 (December 1984).

"The World of Alexander Galich." *Vremya I My* (Time and We), no. 45 (September 1979).

Articles in Hungarian Periodicals

"The Phenomenon of Xenophobia in Europe East and West: A Comparative Perspective." *Magyar Narancs* (Hungarian Orange) (March 1994).

"The Roots of the Communist and Extremist Nationalist Successes in Russian and East European Elections." *Magyar Narancs* (Hungarian Orange) (January 1994).

"The Limitations for Solution of Ethnic Grievances in Liberal Democratic States." *2000* (March 1991).

"Optimistic Tragedy." *Beszcld* (Behind the Bars) (March 16, 1991).

"The Nation, Its Arts, and Democracy." *Magyar Naplo* (Hungarian Letters), vol. 11, no. 39 (September 1990).

Articles in Polish Periodicals

"On the Baltic States." *Kontakt* (Contact), nos. 11 (55) and 12 (56) (1986); no. 3 (59) (1987).

Articles in Japanese Periodicals

"The First One Thousand Days of Gorbachev." *Chishiki* (Knowledge), no. 11 (November 1987).
"A Scenario for a Possible Demise of the Soviet Empire." *Chishiki* (Knowledge), no. 12 (December 1985).

Index

About the Author

Aleksandras Shtromas was born April 4, 1931, in Kaunas, Lithuania, and died June 12, 1999, in Hillsdale, Michigan. As a boy he experienced the Soviet and then the Nazi occupations of his native land; he and his sister, in hiding, were among the very few to survive the destruction of the Lithuanian Jews in which his father, mother, and most of his relatives perished. His father, prominent and cultivated, had been sympathetic to communism, and after the war the young Shtromas was adopted by Antanas Snie῾ckus, the extraordinary first secretary of the Lithuanian Communist Party. But the mature Shtromas changed from communist idealist in Lithuania and Moscow to dissident in Moscow and then, as an academic in England (1973) and later in the United States (1989), to prolific critic of Soviet totalitarianism and imperialism. His first jobs were in various legal institutes in Lithuania and the USSR. By 1966–1970, for example, he had become senior research fellow and acting head of the Division of Comparative Law in the All-Union Research Institute of Soviet Legislation in Moscow. Later, after his expulsion from the Soviet Union, he held teaching positions in peace studies and politics at the University of Salford, Bradford, England (1974–1989) and then in political science at Hillsdale College, Hillsdale, Michigan (1989–1999). He also held visiting appointments at the University of Chicago; the Hoover Institute on War, Revolution, and Peace; Assumption College; and Boston College. Shtromas wrote extensively in various languages, as the bibliography in this volume attests, including, in Russian, *Juvenile Delinquency in Capitalist Countries*, vol. 2: *Prevention* (1970), and, in Lithuanian, *Political Consciousness in Soviet Lithuania* (1980). Perhaps his best-known work in English is *Political Change and Social Development: The Case of the Soviet*

Union ([1981], 1990, 2d ed.), which is one of his many writings, rare among Sovietologists, that showed how collapse of communist belief would lead to the collapse of the Soviet monolith. Some of his most telling diagnoses of the Baltic countries and of the USSR appear in articles and chapters, such as those he selected for this his final volume.

About the Editors

Robert Faulkner is professor of political science at Boston College. He is author of *Francis Bacon and the Project of Progress* (Rowman & Littlefield, 1993), *Richard Hooker and the Politics of a Christian England* (1981), and *The Jurisprudence of John Marshall* (1968); and he is co-editor, with Paul Carrese, of John Marshall's *Life of George Washington* (2000). He has also written about Jefferson, Lincoln, Holmes, Bickel, and other American statesmen and intellectuals, as well as Aristotle, Machiavelli, and other political philosophers. His most recent topics have been Bacon's *New Organon*, Locke's republicanism and critique of religion, and the Enlightenment. He is presently completing a study of honorable ambition.

Daniel J. Mahoney has taught political science at Assumption College since 1986. He is author of *The Liberal Political Science of Raymond Aron* (1992), *De Gaulle: Statesmanship, Grandeur, and Modern Democracy* (1996), and *Aleksandr Solzhenitsyn: The Ascent from Ideology* (2001). He has also edited and introduced the writings of Raymond Aron, Pierre Manent, and Aurel Kolnai. His essays and reviews have appeared in such diverse journals as the *Public Interest*, the *National Interest*, *First Things*, *Perspectives on Political Science*, *Commentaire*, *Polity*, *Society*, and the *Weekly Standard*. He is presently working on a Solzhenitsyn reader in conjunction with Edward Ericson, and completing a study of the political thought of Bertrand de Jouvenel.